KU-504-518

This book is dedicated to Bruce and Bruce, as is the author.

MENTAL HEALTH, INCAPACITY AND THE LAW IN SCOTLAND

Hilary Patrick

Solicitor and Honorary Fellow, School of Law at
Edinburgh University

Contributions by:

Margaret Ross, Senior Lecturer School of Law,
University of Aberdeen and Vice Chair of the Mental Welfare
Commission for Scotland

Lynn Welsh, Head of Scottish Legal Affairs and
Irene Henery, Legal Assistant at the Disability Rights Commission

Tottel
publishing

Published by

Tottel Publishing Ltd   **Tottel Publishing Ltd**
Maxwelton House   **9-10 St Andrew Square**
41-43 Boltro Road   **Edinburgh**
Haywards Heath   **EH2 2AF**
West Sussex
RH16 1BJ

ISBN 13: 978-1-84592-062-3
ISBN 10: 1-84592-062-7
First published 1990 entitled *Mental Health, the Law
in Scotland* by LexisNexis Butterworths
© Tottel Publishing Ltd 2006
First published 2006 entitled *Mental Health, Incapacity and
the Law in Scotland*

British Library Cataloguing-in-Publication Data
A catalogue record for this book is available from the British Library

Typeset by Marie Armah-Kwantreng, Dublin, Ireland
Printed and bound in Great Britain by
M & A Thomson Litho Ltd., East Kilbride, Glasgow

FOREWORD

by the Right Hon Bruce Millan

In 1999 (pre Devolution) I was asked by Scottish Ministers to chair a committee to review the Mental Health (Scotland) Act 1984. The Committee included a wide range of individuals with experience and expertise in the field of mental health, Hilary Patrick one of them.

Hilary had earlier provided an annotated version of the 1984 Act which I found invaluable in navigating the intricacies of the law as it then existed. More generally, and during all of the Committee's work, Hilary made a significant and positive contribution to our deliberations and to the conclusions that we reached.

The Committee reported to the Scottish Executive in January 2001. We concluded that the 1984 Act, which was a consolidation measure, was out of date and suffered from a number of serious deficiencies. There had not in fact been a comprehensive reform of mental health law since 1960.

We recommended therefore that the 1984 Act should be repealed and replaced with a new Act of the Scottish Parliament. We also made a very large number of detailed recommendations. The Executive supported our proposals with few exceptions.

The result has been the Mental Health (Care and Treatment) Scotland Act 2003. The Act has been implemented in stages and has recently come fully into force.

The Committee's particular recommendation, which had been supported by very many of the representations we received, that the legislation should be based on principles written into the Act itself, has been followed.

The principles are essentially related to improving the rights of patients. Patients should, for example, have their wishes and feelings as to their treatment taken properly into account and be involved wherever possible in decisions on their treatment. They should have the necessary information and support to enable them to do so.

There should be no discrimination on the grounds of age or sex or any other consideration. Care should wherever possible be on an informal basis, provide the maximum benefit to the patient and involve the minimum restriction on his or her freedom. Carers' views, needs and circumstances should be taken into account.

The detailed provisions in the Act are designed to reflect these principles. Thus in the minority of cases (and it is a small minority) where compulsion cannot be avoided, the grounds for compulsion have been tightened and a new Mental Health Tribunal has been established as the forum for considering such cases, replacing the sheriff courts and making its decisions with more regard to the individual circumstances of the patient and what is proposed for him or her by way of a plan of care. Compulsion in the community (which still arouses controversy) is now an option in appropriate cases to minimise the disruption to a patient's life otherwise involved by admission to hospital. The patient is encouraged to participate in the proceedings.

Getting the law right is of course only a part of a bigger picture. Patients generally are more likely to be concerned with the availability and adequacy of services than with the detailed provisions of the law. There are inevitably resource constraints and mental health does not generate the high profile demand for extra resources that some other parts of the health sector can. It is very easy therefore for mental health to drop down the political agenda even when recognised by government as a priority.

Again the law itself cannot deal with all forms of discrimination and mental disorder is often poorly understood and stigmatised, not only in the less responsible parts of the press.

Positive signs are that the Scottish Executive has established an expert group to monitor the implementation of the new Act, has initiated a programme of research on mental health issues and has actively supported anti-stigma campaigns.

But those issues – and there are many more – are not just a matter for the Executive but for all those concerned with mental health.

Hilary Patrick is very well qualified to contribute to this necessary ongoing work, since she combines expertise in the law with a strong commitment to the rights and needs of those suffering from mental disorder.

This new book therefore does not only provide an account of the law, important as that is, especially in view of its inevitable complexity, but also sets the law in a wider and more comprehensive context. It is particularly timely, in view of the current changes in law and practice.

The book will be of interest, and an important point of reference, for all those involved professionally with mental health, in the health service, in social work, in voluntary organisations, as well of course as in the law. It is also designed to be accessible to, among others, patient groups, carers and patients' advocates.

It also deserves to attract a more general readership for, directly or indirectly, mental health concerns us all.

Bruce Millan
Glasgow
May 2006

PREFACE

This book is written for all those people in Scotland whose lives are affected by mental illness. It should also be helpful for people with dementia and their carers and for people with learning disabilities. Although the disabilities are different, some of the legal issues are similar, insofar as they relate to the way the law deals with people with varying degrees of mental capacity.

As well as covering health and community care law, it considers other areas where having a mental disability can affect a person's life, whether it be facing discrimination in employment or services, seeking access to housing or caring for children. As such, the book is more than just a guide to the Adults with Incapacity Act and the Mental Health (Care and Treatment) Act, important as these are.

The contents of the book are, therefore, wide ranging. Part 1 contains a short look at the social and health care background and examines the legal sources of mental health law in Scotland. Despite the passing of the Adults with Incapacity Act and the Mental Health (Care and Treatment) Act, mental health law comes from many sources; the common law, statutes, the European Union, and, crucially, human rights law. This Part outlines each, and assesses their impact. Chapter 2 looks at the main statutes. Chapter 3 looks at key organisations, and Chapter 4 considers ways in which the service user can be empowered in the process.

Most people facing mental health challenges seek medical treatment, and only a small minority will become subject to compulsory measures. For this reason Part 2 deals with issues of general medical law, such as capacity and consent to treatment, the right to insist on certain forms of treatment, confidentiality and planning for future incapacity. Part 3 deals with the impact of compulsory measures and Part 4 with the role of the new Mental Health Tribunal for Scotland.

Part 5 looks at decision-making for people who lack capacity to take medical, welfare or financial decisions, both under the Adults with Incapacity Act and also under the common law.

Care in hospital is appropriate for only a small number of people, and Part 6 looks at community care and people's rights to services. Part 7 looks at the protection of people at risk.

Part 8 (by Margaret Ross) considers the impact a mental disorder may have on a person's day to day life, whether it is making contracts, serving on a jury or seeking employment or housing. Part 9 (by Lynn Welsh and Irene Henery) considers protection against unlawful discrimination.

Parts 10 and 11 are slightly different. They consider the impact of the law on various different groups, including women, people from the minority ethnic communities, people with dementia or learning disabilities, refugees and asylum seekers, children and young people, and in Part 11, carers. These parts contain a mixture of new material and highlighting of those sections of the book which are particularly relevant for people in the relevant group.

The interaction of the mental health and criminal justice systems is extremely complex. Part 12 attempts to set out the rules as clearly as possible.

Part 13 looks at the bodies responsible for ensuring standards in health and social care and Part 14 is unusual in a law book, in that it attempts to give some guidance as to what happens when things go wrong. Legal action is rarely the answer, but a person may wish to put in a complaint or seek an official enquiry. On those rare occasions when legal action may be appropriate, chapter 51 looks at some of the areas of possibility.

One area the book does not attempt to cover is welfare rights and benefits. There are many excellent publications and much good information. Appendix 2 gives further information.

Very few readers will need (or want) to read this book from start to finish, but it is hoped it will provide a useful source of reference and provide sufficient signposts for further reading for those with a particular interest in an area. To keep the book within fairly manageable limits, where there is accessible information elsewhere, the book cross refers to this, and does not simply repeat it.

While I hope the book will be of use to lawyers, it is not aimed exclusively at them. Many other people have an interest in these matters. Doctors (including GPs), social workers (particularly mental health officers), independent advocates and welfare rights workers may all find something of interest. The book attempts to avoid legalistic language (although some of the legal provisions it describes are very complex) and I hope that it will be of use to users of services, families and carers.

Since 1990 I have worked almost exclusively on issues concerning mental health and the law in Scotland. It has been a fascinating time! The years have seen the development of progressive incapacity legislation, conceived by the Scottish Law Commission and fostered by the Alliance for the Promotion of the Incapable Adults Bill, of which I was pleased to be a steering group member.

Soon after that, the then Health Secretary established the Millan Committee under the chairmanship of the Rt Hon Bruce Millan, a former Secretary of State for Scotland. It was a great pleasure to be a member of that Committee and to work under the direction of an intelligent and skilful politician, who was able to combine genuine commitment to vulnerable people with realism and an understanding of the issues. Bruce Millan's clarity of mind (as well as his famous attention to detail) helped produce a result which was, I believe, humane, principled and progressive.

The Millan Committee's recommendations were largely taken up by the Scottish Executive and it was exciting and impressive to see how the Parliament held the Executive to account during the Committee stages of the Bill. With those two Acts of the Parliament we can now say that Scotland is amongst world leaders in mental health law.

Law on its own does not change people's lives. Far more important are people who care, responsive services, access to real jobs and public education to remove stigma. But progressive laws are one of the building blocks of reform. They create the framework in which services operate, they can impose legal obligations to provide services of a certain standard and if, as in the Scottish legislation, they are built around principles of respect and equality, they can be a powerful tool in the fight against stigma. This why I continue to work in this field.

I have met some inspirational people during this time: academics, researchers, civil servants (yes!), politicians (Scottish, naturally), workers in health and social care and so many impressive people across the voluntary sector in Scotland, to whose dedication, innovation and professionalism I pay tribute here. You know who you are! But none have made me cry, or catch my breath with admiration, like the family members, service users and carers who have shared their stories with me. The good humour, sympathy and mutual support I have seen has been truly life-enhancing.

One of the difficulties of this book has been in choice of language. The Mental Health (Care and Treatment) Act talks of 'mental disorder', which includes mental illness, learning disability and personality disorder. It refers to a person with a mental disorder as a 'patient', whether or not he or she is in fact a patient at that time. (The Adults with Incapacity Act talks of the person lacking capacity as the 'adult'.)

Many people tend to talk about 'people with mental health problems', rather than mental illness. Others do not like this phrase, which they feel portrays the person as a victim. Others refer to 'service users', even though the person may not at that time be using any services at all.

Radicals from down south refer to 'survivors', people who have survived the psychiatric system. One suggestion is to refer to people 'facing mental health challenges'. This term clearly expresses the courage and strength shown by so many people living with debilitating and life-threatening illness.

These discussions are not just a matter of political correctness. Coping with stigma, prejudice and discrimination is part and parcel of living with a mental disability, and the language we use can either reinforce that stigma or help confront it. This book tries to do this, but occasionally has to use the terms in the legislation for the sake of clarity.

Many people have helped this book come together. John Blackie, now Professor John Blackie of Strathclyde University Law School, was the co-author of its predecessor, *Mental health: a guide to the law in Scotland*. He retains a keen interest in the issues and would have wished to have been part of its successor. Unfortunately pressure of other commitments made this impossible, but I hope he will appreciate the way this book attempts to build on that earlier work .

I was extremely fortunate to have colleagues of the calibre of Margaret Ross, Lynn Welsh and Irene Henery. Margaret Ross combines work as a senior academic with an important role as Deputy Chairman of the Mental Welfare Commission. Her combination of legal expertise and practical humanity has made her contribution invaluable. Lynn Welsh and Irene Henery of the Disability Rights Commission in Scotland are committed to using the law to challenge discrimination and stigma, and Part 9 of this book reflects their commitment. All three have been a pleasure to work with.

The following people gave help, information or advice. Paula O'Connell and Karen Reid of Tottel Publishing were a pleasure to work with, and their professionalism and good humour are to be commended. Audrey Walker and her staff at the Signet Library provided a first rate research service. (Unfortunately this meant I did not spend as much time in their wonderful library as I would have wished.) Others include Sandra McDougall, Jan Killeen, Adrian Ward, Fiona Tyrell, Adrienne Sinclair Chalmers, Sandra McDonald and the very helpful enquiry line at the Office of the Public Guardian, Jane Rubens, Donald Lyons, Rhiann Hunter, Cheryl Minto, John Armstrong, Ronnie Franks, Eddie Follan, Ros Lyall, Karen Wood, Marjorie MacRae, David McClements, Jan Causon, Philip Shearer and the Edinburgh Carers' Council. I would like to thank Robert Richard the art tutor at Glasgow South Integrated Training for his help in selecting the striking painting for the front cover design and to George McIntosh, the talented artist of the piece.

The following people commented on specific parts of the book: Kate Fearnley, Gillian Wilson, Hunter Watson, Jim Thomson, Marion White, Eppie Sweeney, Richard Morran, Maureen Sturrock, Eddie Follan, Allison Alexander, Cheryl Minto, Jim Dyer, Keith Maloney, Sandra McDougall, Karen Wood, Marion Ulas and Sandra McDonald. I am very grateful to them. The errors remaining are, of course, the author's.

I am grateful to the Clark Foundation for Legal Education, which provided a grant to kick-start the production of this book.

Finally can I thank my family, and particularly Bruce, who has manfully put up with long 'discussions' about abstruse points of health law over the years. Ruth, Catherine and Robert have all suffered from this very demanding fourth child, and their resigned tolerance is appreciated.

The law is stated as at 1 May 2006.

Hilary Patrick
Edinburgh

CONTENTS

Contents

TABLE OF CASES

TABLE OF STATUTES

1

TABLE OF ORDERS, RULES AND REGULATIONS

TABLE OF EUROPEAN AND OTHER MATERIALS

GLOSSARY OF COMMONLY
USED TERMS

1984 Act   The Mental Health (Scotland) Act 1984, replaced by the Mental Health (Care and Treatment) Act.

Adult   (Under the Adults with Incapacity Act), a person unable to take a welfare, financial or medical decision because of mental disorder or inability to communicate. See Part 5.

Advance statement A way for a person to communicate his or her wishes about medical treatment, should the person become unable to take such decisions in the future. (Sometimes called a 'living will' if it deals with end of life decisions.) Advance statements have legal recognition under the Mental Health (Care and Treatment) Act. See chapter 10.

Appropriate adult The person who should support a person with a mental disorder who is interviewed by the police in connection with a crime. See 44.03.

Assessment order   A court order made during a criminal trial, transferring an accused person to a psychiatric hospital for assessment. See 45.11.

Approved medical practitioner An experienced psychiatrist approved for the purposes of the Mental Health (Care and Treatment) Act. See 44.03.

Code of Practice   As used in this book, the Mental Health (Care and Treatment) Act Code of Practice, unless there is specific reference to one of the Adults with Incapacity Act Codes.

Compulsory treatment order An order under the Mental Health (Care and Treatment) Act for detention in hospital or compulsory community measures for up to six months. See chapter 14. May be preceded by an **interim compulsory treatment order**. The equivalent in the criminal justice system is a compulsion order.

Continuing attorney	A person given a power of attorney in relation to financial matters. See chapter 26.
Court of Session	The court in Edinburgh which deals with some important matters and appeals under Adults with Incapacity Act and Mental Health (Care and Treatment) Act.
Designated medical practitioner	A doctor appointed by the Mental Welfare Commission to give second opinions for medical treatment. See 3.31.
Direct payment	A way of ensuring that a person needing community care services can buy them him or herself, with funds provided by the local authority. See chapter 27.
Granter	The person who grants a power of attorney. See Part 5.
Guardian	A person appointed by the sheriff under the Adults with Incapacity Act. The guardian has powers, as listed in the appointment, to take medical, welfare and/or financial decisions for an adult with incapacities. See Part 5.
Examination of facts	A hearing held by a criminal court when an accused person is unfit to plead. See 43.04.
Hospital direction	A criminal justice order, combining a prison sentence with detention in hospital. See 45.31.
Hospital managers	They are given special duties under the Mental Health (Care and Treatment) Act. Usually the term means the health board running the hospital. The trust delegates its duties to hospital staff, but remains legally liable for performing the duties. See 3.04.
Independent advocate	A person who can help a person express his or her wishes about care and treatment. See chapter 4.
Intervention order	A one-off order under the Adults with Incapacity Act. It can deal with medical, welfare or financial matters. See Part 5.

Mental disorder	As defined in the Mental Health (Care and Treatment) Act, it includes mental illness, learning disability and personality disorder.
Mental health officer	A specially trained and experienced social worker with a special role in legal proceedings under Mental Health (Care and Treatment) Act and the Adults with Incapacity Act.
Millan Committee	The Committee which reviewed the Mental Health (Scotland) Act 1984.
Named person	The person with special powers to represent the patient's interests in proceedings under the Adults with Incapacity Act and/or Mental Health (Care and Treatment) Act. See chapter 4.
New directions	The report of the Millan Committee.
Power of attorney	A document appointing a continuing or welfare attorney. See Part 5.
Public Guardian	The person responsible for keeping the registers and monitoring the operation of the Adults with Incapacity Act. See chapter 3.
Responsible medical officer	The psychiatrist responsible for the care of a person subject to a compulsory Mental Health (Care and Treatment) Act order.
Scottish Law Commission	The independent body which advises the Scottish Executive on law reform.
Sheriff principal	A senior sheriff.
Treatment order	A court order made during a criminal trial, transferring an accused person to hospital for treatment. See 45.20.
Tribunal	The Mental Health Tribunal for Scotland, which has taken over from the sheriff court all matters relating to compulsory measures under the Mental Health (Care and Treatment) Act. See Part 4.
Restricted patient	A patient who has come to hospital from the criminal justice system and is required to be subject to special restrictions. All significant decisions are made by the Scottish Ministers. See Part 12.

Transfer for treatment direction	A direction by Scottish Ministers transferring a person from prison to hospital because of his or her mental disorder. See 47.12.
Welfare attorney	A person appointed under a power of attorney to take welfare, and sometimes medical, decisions for another. See chapter 25.

PART 1
INTRODUCTION AND
BACKGROUND

Chapter 1

THE LAW IN CONTEXT

1.01 Mental health and incapacity law deals with complex issues of human rights and ethics. As part of medical ethics, the law seeks to balance individual autonomy and society's duty to protect people at risk. As social welfare law, it challenges the role of the state and helps the citizen seek redress. It scrutinises discrimination law to ensure that it provides proper protection to people facing mental health challenges. Human rights law underpins the structure, offering the imaginative lawyer the opportunity to challenge poor practice.

Mental health law matters. If robust and effective, it can improve individuals' lives. This book takes the approach that mental health law is about more than compulsory measures or incapacity. It is about protecting people at risk, about civil rights and responsibilities and supporting family relationships. It deals with social inclusion, access to jobs and education.

Nearly three quarters of Scots know of someone close to them who has had a diagnosis of mental illness at some time.[1] It is not surprising that this area of law has become increasingly important, as a growing number of users of services, advocates and carers grapple with the issues.

This chapter provides some background. It looks very briefly at mental health and social care in Scotland, and looks in more detail at the sources of the law forming the subject matter of this book.

For a comprehensive and sensitive overview of the issues for services, see the report published by Dr Sandra Grant prior to the implementation of the Mental Health (Care and Treatment) Act.

[1] Scottish Public Attitudes Survey on Mental Health, 2002.

MENTAL HEALTH CARE IN SCOTLAND

Health care

1.02 Mental healthcare is one of the priorities of the National Health Service in Scotland. There is a bewildering array of new initiatives.[1]

These reflect a growing openness about mental health issues and concern to reduce stigma and exclusion, as well as commitment to tackling specific issues.

The majority of people with mental health problems seek treatment voluntarily, through their GP. Only a very small proportion see a psychiatrist. Of those, an even smaller proportion (around one in 10) go to hospital. Just over one in 10 of those people go under compulsory mental health act powers.[2]

Most people with learning disabilities do not need to be in hospital unless they also have a mental illness.[3] A very small number of people need secure accommodation on a compulsory basis, usually because of persistent anti-social behaviour or sexual offences. Around 170 people in Scotland are living in hospital under compulsory provisions.[4] The Millan Committee, which reviewed mental health law in Scotland, recommended an expert review of the law relating to people with learning disabilities.[5]

There are around 70,000 people in Scotland living with dementia. In the later stages, many people need care in hospital, care homes or nursing homes.

[1]   See the Scottish Executive's mental health website.
[2]   Scottish Health Statistics.
[3]   See *The same as you? A review of services for people with learning disabilities*, Scottish Executive 2000.
[4]   J Russell and P Robertson, 'The use of Scottish mental health legislation for people with learning disabilities' (1999, unpublished research seen by the Millan Committee and the *Same as you* review).
[5]   *New directions*, recommendation 4.6.

Social care

1.03 Major changes in the way local authorities provide community care followed the National Health Service and Community Care Act 1990. Local authorities ceased being major providers of community care. Instead care managers were to assess client's needs and purchase packages of care using a variety of providers, including the private and voluntary sectors.

Major changes have been a growing understanding of the importance of carers, the introduction of direct payments, allowing people to purchase their own care, and the introduction, in Scotland, though not in England and Wales, of free personal and nursing care for people over 65.

The effectiveness of these measures depends on the resources available to meet need. Community care is not a cheap option. People living in the community often complain they do not receive the help and support they need.

Stigma and discrimination

1.04 It would be futile to deny the stigma and discrimination experienced by people living with mental health challenges and learning disabilities. This can range from discrimination in employment and services, poor coverage in the press, to physical and mental harassment.

Anti-discrimination law can help. We have seen how laws prohibiting race and sex discrimination can lead to a general improvement in underlying attitudes. Unfortunately the Disability Discrimination Act 1995 is a poor vehicle for effecting social change.[1]

Directives from the European Union require the United Kingdom to outlaw any discrimination on the grounds of disability (which includes mental illness and learning disability). Comprehensive legislation could help challenge inequalities and educate public opinion.

Anti-stigma campaigns are also needed. The striking *See me* campaign was launched in 2002. It has a national publicity programme and local and national anti-stigma action. It monitors the press and features individuals prepared to speak to the media about their experiences. See Appendix 2.

All public authorities and health boards have a duty to promote an anti-discrimination culture. See chapter 37. This may have more far-reaching effects than relying on the flawed Disability Discrimination Act.

[1] See Hilary Patrick, 'The Disability Discrimination Act: failing people with mental health problems?' June 2002, SCOLAG Journal, 101–4, and July 2002, 122–123.

SOURCES OF LAW AND THEIR IMPACT

1.05 This section looks at the legal background to mental health law in Scotland. The law comes from various sources. This book covers most of the issues in some detail. (It does not deal with welfare benefits, both because they change frequently and because there is much useful information already available. See Appendix 1.)

The complexity of the different rules means that this book is necessarily complex. This simply reflects the fact that a mental illness or learning disability may affect many areas of someone's life. It may involve restrictions and disqualifications, but it may also provide some rights and entitlements. Whether the law has the balance right is for the reader to judge.

Common law

1.06 The common law of Scotland is the underlying law of the country, as established over the years. It is as important as statute law, although it is more difficult to access, as it is not set out in Acts of Parliament. Some people describe this law as 'judge-made' law, but others say that judges do not make the law, but merely explain it.

The common law in Scotland has many sources. These include church law, old trade customs and usage, Roman law, and, rather unusually, certain important legal scholars (called the 'institutional writers') from as far back as the seventeenth century, whose works may even now be consulted and quoted to settle difficult questions.

The common law develops through a system of 'precedents'. In general, a case decided by a higher court is binding on a lower court, insofar as it describes the law. A decision of the Court of Session binds the sheriff courts and a decision of the House of Lords binds the Court of Session. There is much debate as to whether the House of Lords can bind itself!

Common law and mental health issues

1.07 The common law is the basis of a number of the topics dealt with in this book. For example, the rules about consent to medical treatment and whether someone has the mental ability to sign a contract, get married or make a will are all questions of common law. Medical negligence is also a matter of common law.

Uncertainty of common law

1.08 One of the problems with the common law is that Scotland is a small country and not many people take out the court cases needed to enable lawyers to establish what the law is. The courts often look at cases from other countries, particularly those with similar legal systems. In a complex case, a court may refer to judgments from England and Wales, Canada, Australia or New Zealand.

This means that sometimes there is no specific legal authority for a particular question. An example would be whether advance directives about medical treatment are binding under Scots law. See chapter 10.

In such circumstances, all a lawyer can do is attempt to predict what he or she thinks the courts would say. Any reader frustrated by occasional lack of certainty in this book should bear this in mind.

The common law is subject to Acts of Parliament, which can remedy deficiencies and pass new laws overruling previously established common law rules. The Adults with Incapacity (Scotland) Act is an example. It established a new legal regime for medical, welfare and financial decision-making, replacing earlier common law, some of which dated back to the Middle Ages.

With the increased importance of human rights law, common law is sometimes found wanting. For example, in the *Bournewood* case, (see 8.04) the Court of Human Rights in Strasbourg said that the common law of England and Wales did not provide adequate procedures and rights of appeal to authorise a patient's detention in hospital. For this reason, statutes and statutory instruments now set out many matters previously left to the common law. For example, the Mental Health (Care and Treatment) (Scotland) Act provides for regulations to deal with the security of people in hospital. This was previously a matter for the common law.

Statute law

1.09 Statute law is law passed by Parliament. This can be either the United Kingdom Parliament (for example the Disability Discrimination Act 1995) or, since 1998, the Scottish Parliament (for example the Adults with Incapacity (Scotland) Act 2000 and the Mental Health (Care and Treatment) (Scotland) Act 2003).

Matters such as health, childcare, education and social work are devolved to the Scottish Parliament.[1] This means that the Scottish Parliament can pass laws dealing with these matters. Other matters, such as welfare benefits, immigration and taxation, are 'reserved matters' and only the Westminster Parliament can deal with them.[2] (Issues concerning asylum seekers have highlighted problems with this system. The United Kingdom government's dispersal policy has meant some asylum seekers live in Scotland, but the Scottish Executive has no power to ensure they receive the standard of service they need.)

All statutes since 1998 are now available on the Office of Public Sector Information website. The website shows all Acts of the UK and Scottish Parliaments. For all Acts passed since 1999 there are also explanatory notes, which attempt to explain the legislation to non-lawyers. These are also available on the website.

Parliament can repeal or amend an Act of Parliament in a subsequent Act. Many statutes, such as the Social Work (Scotland) Act 1968, have been considerably amended. (There are already amendments to the Mental Health (Care and Treatment) Act.) A person studying a statute needs to ensure it is up-to-date. Unfortunately neither the statutes on the official website nor hard copies for purchase are up-to-date. The prospective purchaser should check at a law library or law publisher to see if a better version is available. A law library can advise if a particular section of an Act is up-to-date.

1   Scotland Act 1998, s 28.
2   SA 1998, s 29(1).

Statutory instruments

1.10 Statutory instruments are regulations made under the authority of an Act of Parliament. An Act can give Ministers power to prepare regulations.

Some regulations require the active approval of the Parliament, while others become law unless the Parliament votes against them. Once passed, the regulations become law in the same way as Acts of Parliament. Both the United Kingdom and Scottish Parliaments can pass subordinate legislation.

Statutory instruments generally deal with detailed matters which would be too time-consuming for the whole Parliament. There are many statutory instruments dealing with matters arising under the Adults with Incapacity Act and the Mental Health (Care and Treatment) Act, covering, for example, matters such as rules of procedure, transferring patients outside Scotland and supervision of guardians by local authorities.

An Act of Sederunt is like a statutory instrument. It sets out rules of the Court of Session, usually relating to court procedure.

All statutory instruments (including Acts of Sederunt) since 1987 are on the official website. Unfortunately there are very many of them, and searching can be difficult. With the name or number, the search is easier.

Sources that are more helpful are the Scottish Executive's Adults with Incapacity and Mental Health Law websites.

The footnotes to this book describe statutory instruments as 'SIs' and Scottish Statutory Instruments as 'SSIs'.

Law of European Union

1.11 As part of the European Union, the United Kingdom can be obliged to pass laws complying with European Union requirements.[1] If the government fails to comply with certain Directives from the European Union, the Directive may itself be regarded as part of Scots law.[2]

Most EU Directives relate to trading and economic matters, but the European Union has an interest in social policy. It issues Directives concerning, for example, welfare benefits, employment and discrimination. (For example, following an EU Directive,[3] the United Kingdom government must amend the Disability Discrimination Act to ensure that it offers better protection against discrimination on the grounds of disability.)

[1]   European Communities Act 1972, s 2(1).
[2]   *SpA S.A.C.E v Italian Ministry of Finance* [1970] ECR 1213.
[3]   Council Directive 2000/78/EC of 27 November 2000.

EUROPEAN CONVENTION ON HUMAN RIGHTS

1.12 Although the United Kingdom has no written constitution or Bill of Rights, its adoption of the fundamental rights set out in the European Convention on Human Rights (ECHR) goes some way towards addressing this gap.[1] The European Convention on Human Rights sets out various fundamental rights, such as freedom from detention, the right to family and private life and the right to a fair trial. It is now part of Scots law.[2]

This happens in three main ways. Firstly, whenever the Scottish Parliament passes new legislation, such as the Mental Health (Care and Treatment) Act, it has to be satisfied that the new law complies with the requirements of the European Convention on Human Rights.[3] Otherwise the legislation is not valid.

Secondly, when the courts interpret the law, they must decide whether it is in accordance with the European Convention on Human Rights.[4]

Thirdly, all public authorities in Scotland must act in a way which respects human rights.[5] Public authorities include health boards and hospitals, local authorities, the Mental Welfare Commission for Scotland, the courts and the Mental Health Tribunal for Scotland.

The adoption of the European Convention on Human Rights is a fundamental change in the way the courts interpret the law. Any new Act of Parliament, existing provision in a statute or rule of common law can be open to challenge if it is in breach of the European Convention on Human Rights. Such questions can come before the Scottish courts or, as a last resort, before the European Court of Human Rights in Strasbourg.

[1]   The Convention for the Protection of Human Rights and Fundamental Freedoms. Signed by the Council of Europe in Rome in November 1950.
[2]   Under the Human Rights Act 1998 and the Scotland Act 1998.
[3]   Scotland Act 1998, s 29(1)(d).
[4]   Human Rights Act 1998, ss 2–4.
[5]   HRA 1998, s 6.

Human rights and mental health

1.13 Some of the European Convention on Human Rights provisions are particularly relevant to mental health issues. Article 2 guarantees the right to life. The human rights court has said this imposes a duty on the state to protect people at risk of suicide.[1] This Article might also allow a challenge to discrimination in healthcare, such as the failure of a health board to make heart surgery available to someone with a learning disability.

Article 3 prohibits inhumane and degrading treatment or punishment. People have used this Article to challenge the use of restraint,[2] the giving of medication by force[3] and the use of seclusion in psychiatric hospitals.[4] Poor conditions in hospital or failure to provide medical treatment could, if sufficiently severe, amount to inhumane treatment.[5]

Article 5 prohibits detention other than in accordance with law. It permits the lawful detention of someone of 'unsound mind' and imposes requirements as to due process.[6] Article 6 stresses the importance of proper legal procedures.[7]

Article 8 guarantees respect for private and family life and correspondence. This very wide article could cover, for example, being able to challenge one's nearest relative,[8] access to records,[9] taking children into care and freeing a child for adoption.[10]

At the time of writing there have been surprisingly few cases in Scotland dealing with the human rights of people facing mental health challenges. By far the majority of cases before the Scottish courts have dealt with general matters relating to criminal law.[11]

There have been several important cases in England and Wales, and it would seem likely that we will see more cases in Scotland in the future.

See Appendix 1 for further reading.

1   *Keenan v UK* [2001] ECHR 242.
2   *Herczegfalvy v Austria* [1992] ECHR 58.
3   *R (on the application of Wilkinson) v Broadmoor Special Hospital Authority* [2001] EWCA Civ 1545. See 16.38.
4   *R v. Ashworth Hospital Authority ex parte Munjaz* [2005] UKHL 58.
5   See remarks of the Commission in *Tanko v Finland* (No 23634/94)(1994), unreported.
6   The key case is *Winterwerp v Netherlands*[1979] ECHR 4. See 11.35.
7   See *Matter v Slovakia* (Application no. 31534/96) (1999). Delay of 20 months in hearing case concerning applicant's mental capacity was unreasonable and a breach of his rights under Article 6(1).
8   *JT v UK* [2000] ECHR 133.
9   *Gaskin v UK* [1989] ECHR 13.
10   *Bronda v Italy* [1998] HRCD 641. *Kutzner v Germany* [2002] ECHR 160.
11   See Greenhill, Mullen, Murdoch, Craig and Miller, 'The use of human rights legislation in the Scottish courts', Scottish Executive Social Policy Research (2004).

Absolute and qualified rights

1.14 The right to freedom from inhumane and degrading treatment is an absolute right, but the other rights are qualified in varying ways.

Article 2 recognises self-defence as an exception to the right to life. Article 5 gives someone the right to liberty but permits the lawful detention of someone of 'unsound mind'.

Article 8 recognises that the right to respect for family life, correspondence and privacy can be restricted if permitted under domestic law and necessary in the interests of (among other things) public safety, crime prevention, health and safety or the protection of the rights and freedoms of others.

Interpreting ECHR

1.15 The human rights court recognises that it is for national states to make their own laws and interpret them according to conditions locally.

It allows governments some discretion to weigh up competing demands and priorities, subject to compliance with the overall requirements of the European Convention on Human Rights. The court calls this the 'margin of appreciation'. The result, to the layperson, is that the court's decisions may seem somewhat conservative.[1]

The court is very concerned to ensure that any restriction of a person's rights is in proportion to the risks posed. The court will consider whether the restriction is a reasonable response in the light of the circumstances in the particular case. It calls this 'proportionality',

Any restriction of rights must be lawful. This means that it should comply with Scottish law and legal procedures and with ECHR law. The law must be open, accessible and provide proper rights of appeal. The common law sometimes fails this test.

Generally Scottish law gives greater guarantees than are available under the European Convention on Human Rights, but human rights law gives an opportunity to test both law and practice against defined human rights standards.[2] People can challenge apparent injustices in a way not previously possible. We will see that one case, the so-called *Bournewood* case, is having a major impact on law and practice in Scotland. See 25.36.

[1] See, for example, *B v UK* No 6870/75, 32 DR (1981). 'Deplorable overcrowding' and 'less than satisfactory' sanitary arrangements at Broadmoor hospital were not inhumane and degrading treatment within Article 3 ECHR. Contrast *Napier v Scottish Ministers Court of Session* (IH) 26 April 2004. Court held that 'slopping-out' regime in Barlinnie prison was a breach of Article 3.

[2] See Robertson, 'Using human rights as a vehicle for cultural change at the state hospital' (2003) 19 Scottish Human Rights Journal.

Duties of the state

1.16 Human rights legislation mainly affects public bodies, but the state has a positive duty to ensure that private individuals do not breach human rights.

For example, the government of the Netherlands breached human rights law because Dutch law did not give adequate protection to a young woman with learning disabilities who had suffered abuse.[1] The government of Germany breached the human rights of a young woman who was unlawfully detained in a private psychiatric hospital.[2]

In the same way, the Scottish Executive owes a duty to ensure Scottish law and practice protects the human rights of people facing mental health challenges. Local authorities and hospitals must take action to protect people against abuse or other neglect of their rights.

1   *X and Y v The Netherlands* [1985] ECHR 4.
2   *Storck v Germany* [2005] ECHR 406.

UNITED NATIONS DECLARATIONS AND RESOLUTIONS

1.17 The United Nations has made several important declarations and resolutions about the rights of people living with mental health challenges or learning disabilities. These include the UN Declaration on Human Rights (1948), the UN Declaration on the Rights of Mentally Retarded Persons (1971) and the UN Declaration on the Rights of Disabled People (1975). In 1991, the UN General Assembly agreed a resolution on *The protection of persons with mental illness and the improvement of mental health care.*[1]

These documents are useful statements of intent and set standards by which to judge Scottish law, but they do not have legal force in Scotland.

1   Resolution 46/119.

CODES OF PRACTICE, GUIDANCE AND DIRECTIONS

1.18 All those involved with the mental health system will be aware of the large number of circulars, guidance notes and Codes of Practice. There is a three-volume code of practice for the Mental Health (Care and Treatment) Act. There are seven Codes of Practice under the Adults with Incapacity Act legislation. The Scottish Executive has issued many important circulars about the operation of community care in Scotland.

What legal status do these documents have? If a local authority does not comply with its duties under a code or guidance circular, would legal action be possible?

The answer depends to some extent on the precise legal status of the document. Some have a higher legal status than others. For example, several of the Codes of Practice under the Adults with Incapacity Act state that while there is no legal duty to comply with the Code, the Code is a statutory document and there may be legal consequences if the relevant body fails to comply with it.[1]

1   See, for example, the *Code of Practice for Local Authorities exercising functions under the Act*, Scottish Executive (2001), para 1.20.

Codes of Practice

1.19 Codes of Practice are of particular importance. The House of Lords has considered the legal status of the Mental Health Act Code of Practice in England and Wales.[1] A secure hospital's policy on seclusion (solitary confinement) differed substantially from guidance in the Code and a patient challenged this. The House of Lords said that a person to whom the Code is addressed must give 'cogent reasons' if he or she decides not to follow it. These reasons must be clear, logical and convincing.

People do not have discretion to depart from the Code as they see fit. The Code is a statutory document, laid before Parliament. Parliament expects people to follow it, unless they can show they have a convincing reason for not doing so.[2] If human rights are involved, a departure from the Code will be subject to particularly careful and intense scrutiny.[3]

The Department of Health now advises staff to record their reasons for any departure from the Code. The Mental Health Act Commission for England and Wales will treat unexplained departures from the Code as an indication of poor practice.[4]

The House of Lords' judgment does not bind the Scottish courts, but will be highly influential if a case comes to court. The Codes of Practice in Scotland have similar legal status to the English and Welsh codes.

Ministers have a statutory duty to draw up Codes of Practice giving guidance to people with duties under the legislation.[5] The Mental Health (Care and Treatment) Act specifically requires anyone carrying out his or her duties under the Act to have regard to the relevant provisions of the Code.[6] Ministers consulted widely before producing the various Codes and laid a copy of each Code before the Scottish Parliament.

This book assumes that compliance with the relevant Codes of Practice is more than just good practice. Anyone failing to do so without good reason may have to justify his or her action in the courts.

[1]   *R v Ashworth Hospital Authority ex parte Munjaz* [2005] UKHL 58.

[2]   See Lord Hope at para 69.

[3]   Lord Hope at para 74.

[4]   *Briefings on legal cases*, Department of Health, Gateway number: 5751.

[5]   Adults with Incapacity (Scotland) Act 2000, s 13. Mental Health (Care & Treatment) (Scotland) Act 2003, s 274(1).

[6]   Mental Health (Care & Treatment) (Scotland) Act 2003, s 274(4).

Scottish Executive guidance

1.20 Local authorities must perform their social work and community care duties under the 'general guidance' of the Scottish Ministers.[1] The Scottish Executive has produced a number of guidance circulars on the operation of the community care system. See Appendix 1. Some of the guidance is very clear. For example, two circulars require health boards and local social work authorities to introduce a care programme approach for people with a mental illness, including dementia.[2] For many years reports were that implementation of this approach was 'patchy'.

There may be grounds for legal action if a local authority does not follow Scottish Executive guidance, particularly if guidance is clear and unequivocal. At the very least, authorities should consider it.[3] If an authority fail to do so, someone injured by the failure may have a remedy by way of legal action or a complaint.

Some guidance circulars say they are not 'guidance' but merely 'practice guidance'. These might be less legally binding than guidance, but would be evidence of good practice in the event of a negligence claim. See 51.05.

For the effect of guidance on medical good practice, see 5.12.

[1]   Social Work (Scotland) Act 1968, s 5.
[2]   Circular SWSG 1/1992, repeated in Circular SWSG16/96.
[3]   See *R v North Yorkshire County Council ex parte Hargreaves*,The Times, 9 November 1994, *R v Islington London Borough Council, ex parte Rixon*, The Times, 17 April 1996.

Directions

1.21 One form of guidance that does have legal effect is a 'direction' from Scottish Ministers. Scottish Ministers have the legal power to issue directions to local authorities about the way they carry out their duties under the Social Work (Scotland) Act.[1] For example, the then Scottish Office issued directions to local authorities requiring them to offer a choice of accommodation to people moving to residential care homes.[2] These directions have the force of law.

[1]   Social Work (Scotland) Act 1968, s 51A.
[2]   The Social Work (Scotland) Act 1968 (Choice of Accommodation) Directions 1993.

Chapter 2

STATUTORY FRAMEWORK

2.01 This chapter looks at the major statutes forming the background to mental health and community care law in Scotland. As well as the Adults with Incapacity (Scotland) Act 2000 and the Mental Health (Care and Treatment) (Scotland) Act 2003, readers may need to become familiar with the Criminal Procedure (Scotland) Act 1995, which sets out the way in which the criminal courts can deal with people facing mental health challenges. The Social Work (Scotland) Act 1968, as amended, contains the legal framework for community care.

What follows is a brief introduction to the main pieces of relevant legislation, in the hope that this will assist readers' understanding when they study the more detailed provisions of these Acts.

ADULTS WITH INCAPACITY ACT

Background

Need for reform

2.02 The law needs procedures for substituted decision-making if a mental illness or learning disability mean someone is unable to take decisions in important areas of his or her life.

Before 2000 the law was complex, difficult to find and inconsistent. It came from a variety of sources, some dating back to the middle ages.[1] There were no underlying principles or philosophy. The law relied on an 'all or nothing' concept of incapacity. It did not recognise that someone might be capable of taking some decisions but not others. It could not offer solutions tailored to the person's needs.

In 1984 Adrian Ward published *Scots Law and the Mentally Handicapped*, followed in 1990 by *The Power to Act*. These highlighted anomalies in the law and called for reform.[2] Around the same time Scottish Action on Dementia started examining issues relating to dementia and the law.[3]

---

[1] Highlighted by the fact that most of those involved retained their Latin names. The financial guardian was the *curator bonis* (property manager). The

person who could take medical decisions was the *tutor-dative* (appointed representative). The temporary manager was the *negotiorum gestor* (business manager). The Mental Health (Scotland) Act 1984 introduced the welfare guardian. In theory, if someone's affairs were complex, all four people might have a role at some stage.

2   Both published by Enable Scotland.

3   See *Dementia: guardianship* (1987), *Dementia and the law: the challenge ahead* (1988) and an innovative study, *Mental health hearings for elderly people with dementia: a study of demand and feasibility* (Scottish Office Home and Health Department 1993) C Davison, M Gilhooly, J Killeen and D Hay.

Reform process

2.03 In 1991 the Scottish Law Commission, which advises the Scottish Executive on law reform, published a discussion paper, *Mentally disabled adults*.[1] It consulted widely, involving users of services and carers as well as the usual professional interests.

In 1995 it published its *Report on Incapable Adults*.[2] This report and the earlier discussion document are key sources of information about Scots law and mental incapacity prior to 2000.

The draft Bill attached to the Scottish Law Commission's report formed the basis of the Adults with Incapacity (Scotland) Act, which received Royal Assent in 2000. This followed consistent pressure from the Alliance for the Promotion of the Incapable Adults Bill, a coalition of over 70 professional, voluntary and user groups.

The Adults with Incapacity Act was the first major piece of legislation from the Scottish Parliament. It was a radical reform of the law affecting people unable to take medical, welfare or financial decisions. The Act came into effect in stages from April 2001, with the final part coming into effect in August 2004.

In 1997 the Scottish Law Commission published a further report, *Vulnerable adults*, following up issues arising from its earlier investigation concerning the protection of people at risk.[3] The Mental Health (Care and Treatment) Act took up several of these recommendations. In March 2006 the Scottish Executive introduced the Adult Support and Protection (Scotland) Bill to the Scottish Parliament. This aims to give further effect to the report's recommendations.

1   Scottish Law Commission Discussion Paper 94.

2   Scottish Law Commission Report 151.

3   Scottish Law Commission Report 158.

Outline of the Act

Parts 1 to 4: Principles and Institutions

2.04 Part 1 of the Act sets out the principles governing all interventions under the Act. It defines incapacity and gives people the right to appeal against a finding of incapacity.

Sheriffs deal with applications under the Act, with a right of appeal to the sheriff principal and, with his or her leave, to the Court of Session. The Public Guardian, who replaced the Accountant of Court, monitors financial matters under the Act and keeps the register of attorneys, guardians, etc.

Ministers must issue Codes of Practice supplementary to the Act. Local authorities and the Mental Welfare Commission must investigate people at risk.

Part 2: Attorneys

2.05 As well as strengthening and consolidating the law relating to financial attorneys (called 'continuing attorneys'), the Act creates a power of attorney for welfare and medical matters. This part of the Act came into effect in April 2001.

Part 3: Accounts and funds

2.06 This part removes a rule of banking law which had caused joint bank accounts to be 'frozen' if one of the account holders was unable to operate the account.

A new scheme allows a carer to access a bank account to meet regular financial obligations. This part of the Act came into effect in April 2001.

Part 4: Management of residents' finances

2.07 Approved hospitals, nursing and residential care homes can manage residents' finances, subject to safeguards. These provisions require comprehensive safeguards and implementation did not take place until August 2004.

Part 5: Medical matters

2.08 Part 5 deals with doctors' authority to treat people who cannot consent to treatment. It gives welfare attorneys and guardians the right

17

to be involved. It does not alter the common law duty of doctors in an emergency. It also covers consent to medical research.

The Scottish Law Commission recommended clarification of the law on advance directives ('living wills') and on withdrawing or withholding medical treatment. The Act does not deal with these matters.

This part of the Act came into effect in 2002.

Part 6: Intervention and guardianship orders

2.09 The Act introduces a new one-off 'intervention order'. This offers a flexible way to deal with single issues such as the need to sign a legal document or approve a welfare decision.

The Act creates a flexible form of financial and/or personal guardianship replacing the *curator bonis*, tutor-dative and Mental Health (Scotland) Act welfare guardian.

This part of the Act came into effect in 2002.

Part 7: Miscellaneous provisions

2.10 Among the important provisions are the limitation of liability for people acting in accordance with the principles of the Act and guardianship as a criminal justice option.

Principles

2.11 Including principles in legislation has been a feature of recent social welfare legislation, including the Children (Scotland) Act 1995 and the Mental Health (Care and Treatment) Act. The Adults with Incapacity Act principles are an important statement of the underlying philosophy of the Act.

Any intervention under the Act must benefit the adult. It must be the least restrictive option. Anyone intervening should consider the wishes and feelings of the adult, past and present and (if reasonably practical) those of his or her nearest relative, named person and primary carer. Anyone exercising powers under the Act should attempt to maximise the adult's skills.[1]

The principles are clear and unequivocal. Any intervention under the Adults with Incapacity Act, including any order made under the Act, must comply with the principles. Moreover, unlike, for example, the principles in the Mental Health (Care and Treatment) Act or the Children (Scotland) Act, the principles have 'teeth'.

A person acting under the Adults with Incapacity Act is not liable for a breach of duty of care if he or she has acted in good faith and in accordance with the principles. A person who has not acted in accordance with the principles, will not have the benefit of this limitation of liability.[2]

[1]   Adults with Incapacity (Scotland) Act 2000, s 1.
[2]   AWI(S)A 2000, s 82.

Sources of information

2.12 The Justice Department of the Scottish Executive maintains a very helpful website devoted to the Adults with Incapacity Act. This includes the full text of the Act, all regulations and the important Codes of Practice.

For detailed and comprehensive information, see *Adult Incapacity* by Adrian Ward.[1]

[1]   (W Green & Sons, Edinburgh, 2003).

MENTAL HEALTH (CARE AND TREATMENT) ACT

2.13 This Act received Royal Assent in April 2003. Like the 1984 Act, which it replaces, the 2003 Act deals with the use of compulsory measures in mental health care. It also contains important provisions for support and access to services for people who are not subject to compulsory measures.

The Act contains important provisions governing the role and duties of the Mental Welfare Commission, the establishment of the Mental Health Tribunal for Scotland, the duties of local authorities and health boards, access to advocacy, protection against sexual abuse and the right to appoint a 'named person'.

The Act also covers people who come to the mental health system through the criminal justice system.

Background

2.14 Calls for mental health law reform followed incapacity law reform. These reflected the growing strength of the user and carer movements. The development of community care, with more people receiving care in the community rather than as hospital inpatients, meant that the Mental Health (Scotland) Act 1984 was looking increasingly outdated.

Key bodies calling for change were the Scottish Association for Mental Health (SAMH), the Law Society of Scotland and the Mental Welfare Commission for Scotland. In 1995 SAMH, the Law Society and the Royal College of Psychiatrists' Scottish Division held a major conference, *Consensus for change?* which highlighted the demand for reform.

In 1999 the then Health Secretary, Sam Galbraith, established a committee to review mental health law in Scotland. Its chair, the Rt Hon Bruce Millan, was a former Secretary of State for Scotland. Its members included doctors, nurses, lawyers and health board managers, and crucially, users of services and carers.

The Millan Committee consulted widely to reach a consensus. Ideas of inclusion and empowerment influenced both the shape of the final report and the consultation process.

The committee's report, *New Directions,*[1] largely influenced the shape of the Mental Health (Care and Treatment) (Scotland) Act 2003. The Scottish Executive accepted many of the Millan Committee's recommendations.[2] The Mental Health (Care and Treatment Act came into effect in October 2005. The provisions relating to named persons and advance statements came into effect in October 2004. The right to appeal against excessive security came into effect in May 2006.

[1]   Scottish Executive 2001.

[2]   See *Renewing mental health law,* Scottish Executive (2001).

Impact of devolution

2.15 There is no doubt devolution has strengthened the process of reform of both incapacity and mental health law. The Scottish Parliament tackled its legislative tasks with energy and commitment.

Both Bills attracted cross-party support. The Parliamentary committees (the Justice and Home Affairs Committee and the Health and Community Care Committee) demonstrated their interest and commitment.

The Parliament has grown in confidence and the final shape of the mental health legislation benefited from its insistence on giving full effect to the Millan recommendations.

Reform in England and Wales

2.16 England and Wales have been slower to reform, and the process has been considerably more controversial.

The Mental Capacity Act received Royal Assent in 2005. This far-reaching reform has benefited from Scottish experience.

At the time of writing, the Department of Health appears to have shelved fundamental mental health law reform in favour of amendments to the 1983 Mental Health Act.[1]

---

[1] *Next steps for the Mental Health Bill,* Department of Health (March 2006).

Outline of the Act

Parts 1 to 4: Principles and Institutions

2.17 Part 1 of the Act sets out the general principles underlying the Act. Part 2 sets out the expanded powers and duties of the Mental Welfare Commission. This builds on the existing role of the Commission and gives the Commission powers to promote good practice and monitor the principles of the Act.

Part 3 establishes the Mental Health Tribunal for Scotland, which has taken over from the sheriff in proceedings for compulsory orders and appeals. The tribunal sits throughout the country, according to need. Each tribunal has a legal chair, a medical member (usually a senior psychiatrist) and a general member with experience in social care, including experience as a user of services or a carer.

Part 4 sets out the powers and duties of local authorities and health boards. Local authorities must provide support services and services to promote the social welfare of people in their areas. Health boards must provide appropriate inpatient facilities for children and young people and mothers with babies. Other health board and local authority duties are in Parts 15 and 17.

Parts 5 to 7: Compulsory measures

2.18 Parts 5 to 7 deal with detention under the civil procedure. The use of emergency detention should be less frequent in the future, due to the introduction of short-term detention direct from the community. The long-term compulsory treatment order can authorise either detention in hospital or compulsory powers in the community if appropriate.

Parts 8 to 13: Criminal justice system

2.19 The complex provisions of Parts 8 to 13 deal with people who become subject to the Act through criminal justice orders.

Part 8 makes changes to the types of orders available. The orders are set out in the Criminal Procedure (Scotland) Act 1995. Part 8 amends that Act.

Parts 9 to 13 mirror civil procedure, but there are complex rules about appeal rights for restricted patients.

Part 14: Healthcare assessment

2.20 Part 14 gives the service user and his or her named person and carer a formal right to request a healthcare assessment.

It makes changes to community care assessments when a mental health officer is considering a compulsory treatment order.

Part 15

2.21 Part 15 contains local authority duties to appoint mental health officers and health board duties to appoint responsible medical officers.

Part 16: Medical treatment

2.22 Part 16 sets out the rules relating to medical treatment of people subject to compulsory orders. There is a hierarchy of treatment safeguards, from treatments given under the direction of the responsible medical officer through to treatments requiring consent or a second opinion. Certain rare treatments require consent and second opinions. There are special safeguards for electro-convulsive therapy (ECT).

Part 17: Patient representation

2.23 Part 17 contains the rules allowing someone to appoint a 'named person' to act for him or her in legal matters under the Act. If a person does not appoint a named person, his or her primary carer is named person. If there is no carer, the nearest relative is named person. A person can make a declaration barring a certain person from acting as named person.

Part 17 gives everyone facing mental health challenges the right to access independent advocacy.

There is also a very important right to appeal against detention in conditions of excessive security. This will be particularly useful for people 'entrapped' in the State Hospital.

Part 18 to 21: Miscellaneous

2.24 Part 18 deals with miscellaneous, but very important matters. It covers Scottish Ministers' duty to prepare a Code of Practice, young patients' rights to education, relations between parents and children and research and information into the working of the Act.

The Act recognises advance statements in mental healthcare. Doctors and tribunals must take into account any advance statement a patient has made.

Important provisions regulating correspondence and other restrictions are in this Part, together with cross-border transfers, money for personal expenses and the informal patient's right to apply to the court if he or she considers he or she is unlawfully detained in hospital.

Part 19 incorporates many of the recommendations of the Scottish Law Commission's *Vulnerable Adults* report (see above) insofar as they relate to people facing mental health challenges. Local authorities must make enquiries where they consider someone may be at risk. The Act improves their powers to take action.

Part 20 contains complex provisions relating to people who abscond from care.

Part 21 deals with offences under the Act, including new sexual offences where there is exploitation or lack of true consent.

Part 22 deals with appeals.

Part 23 covers general matters and includes the important interpretation section.

Principles

2.25 One of the Millan Committee's most important recommendations was that the Act should set out a clear statement of the ethical principles underpinning mental health law. The Committee found broad agreement on these ethical principles and recommended they should be set out in the new Act.[1] The principles, influenced the final shape of the Millan Committee's recommendations.

The Committee recommended that anyone carrying out his or her functions under the Act should consider the impact of the principles. The principles would assist those operating the Act, help with problems of interpretation and could influence the development of good practice. The Mental Welfare Commission should monitor the operation of the principles. The principles should also influence the drafting of the Code of Practice.

¹   *New Directions*, recommendation 3.1. 23.13.

The Millan principles

2.26 The Millan principles were much more extensive than any previously incorporated in legislation. They were:

Non-discrimination—Whenever possible, people facing mental health challenges should retain the same rights and entitlements as those with other health needs.

Equality—People should exercise their powers under the Act without any direct or indirect discrimination on the grounds of physical disability, age, gender, sexual orientation, language, religion or national, ethnic or social origin.

Respect for diversity—Service users should receive care, treatment and support in a manner that accords respect for their individual qualities, abilities and diverse backgrounds and properly takes into account their age, gender, sexual orientation, ethnic group and social, cultural and religious background.

Reciprocity—Where society imposes an obligation on someone to comply with a programme of treatment of care, it should impose a parallel obligation on the health and social care authorities to provide safe and appropriate services, including ongoing care following discharge from compulsion.

Informal care—Wherever possible, services should provide mental health care, treatment and support without recourse to compulsion.

Participation—Service users should be fully involved, to the extent their individual capacity permits, in all aspects of their assessment, care, treatment and support. Staff should take into account the service user's past and present wishes, if they can establish these.

Service users should receive the information and support necessary to enable them to participate fully. Staff should provide information in the most accessible form for the individual service user.

Respect for carers—Those who provide care to service users on an informal basis should receive respect for their role and experience, receive appropriate information and advice, and have their views and needs taken into account.

Least restrictive alternative—Service users should receive care, treatment and support in the least invasive manner and environment compatible with safe and effective care, bearing in mind, if appropriate, the safety of others.

Benefit—Any intervention under the Act should be likely to produce for the service user a benefit that cannot reasonably be achieved other than by the intervention.

Child welfare—In any interventions imposed on a child under the Mental Health (Care and Treatment) Act, the welfare of the child should be paramount.[1]

[1]   *New Directions*, recommendation 3.3.

Principles in Mental Health (Care and Treatment) Act

2.27 The Scottish Executive broadly accepted the Millan principles,[1] but said legal reasons prevented it from incorporating them into the Mental Health (Care and Treatment) Act precisely as recommended by the Millan Committee.

It would be fair to say that the principles in the 2003 Act lack the clarity and force of the Adults with Incapacity Act principles. Despite this, the principles reflect the Millan intentions and apply whenever someone is exercising functions under the Act.[2] See 11.03 for more detail.

How well the principles will serve people in Scotland and how much they will influence practice remains to be seen. They represent a fundamental attempt to improve the way in which people subject to compulsory measures receive healthcare. They aim to ensure that staff consider people's views and encourage them to take part in the decision-making process.

[1]   *Renewing mental health law,* Scottish Executive (2001), para 2.3.
[2]   Mental Health (Care and Treatment) (Scotland) Act 2003, ss 1–3.

Further information

2.28 The Scottish Executive health department has a very helpful website dealing with the Mental Health (Care and Treatment) Act. This includes the full text of the Act and all the regulations, together with the Code of Practice, relevant forms and up-to-date information.

The Scottish Executive has worked with voluntary organisations to produce a number of guides on various topics, including some in Easy Read form.

CRIMINAL PROCEDURE (SCOTLAND) ACT

2.29 The Criminal Procedure (Scotland) Act 1995 has a complex relationship with the Mental Health (Care and Treatment) Act. The Criminal Procedure Act deals with the various orders the criminal courts can make when someone with a mental illness or learning disability comes before them. The Mental Health (Care and Treatment) Act has simplified and reformed procedures by amending this Act.[1]

Someone awaiting trial or a sentence can be moved to hospital if he or she needs this. The 2003 Act creates a short-term assessment order and the longer-term treatment order. A sentenced prisoner can also move to hospital.

When passing sentence, a court may send someone to hospital under a compulsion order rather than sending him or her to prison. It may make a hospital direction, which combines a prison sentence with a compulsion order. If it considers someone poses a risk to the public, the court may impose a restriction order. This means Scottish Ministers take all decisions about the person's discharge and absence from hospital.

For less serious crimes, the courts may divert someone from prosecution or may require someone to attend psychiatric services as a condition of his or her probation.

Once the person arrives in hospital, his or her care and treatment are matters for the Mental Health (Care and Treatment) Act.

[1]   Mental Health (Care and Treatment) (Scotland) Act 2003, Part 8.

SOCIAL WORK (SCOTLAND) ACT

2.30 The Adults with Incapacity Act does not deal with the provision of social care services. The Mental Health (Care and Treatment) Act imposes some duties on local authorities to provide services, but the framework for delivering social care is in the Social Work (Scotland) Act 1968.

This Act establishes local authorities' duties to provide social welfare services. Community care, direct payments and charging for social work services, such as day care and respite care, are in this Act. Similar duties to provide services for children and young people are in the Children (Scotland) Act 1995.

Since its passage in 1968, the Act has been substantially changed and modified. The NHS and Community Care Act 1990 introduced community care. The Community Care (Direct Payments) Act 1996 allowed services users to receive money to pay for care themselves. The Carers (Recognition and Services) Act 1995 introduced carer's assessments. The Community Care and Health (Scotland) Act 2002 strengthened these provisions.

As far as the author is aware, it is not possible to buy an updated copy of this Act. This makes it extremely difficult to access its provisions.[1]

[1]   An annotated and up-to-date version of part of the Act is included in the Community Care section of *W Green's Social Work Statutes* (W Green & Son, Edinburgh).

Chapter 3

KEY ORGANISATIONS

3.01 This chapter looks at some of the key organisations and individuals involved in operating mental health and incapacity law in Scotland. More detailed information is at the appropriate parts of the text.

SCOTTISH MINISTERS

3.02 The overall responsibility for mental health and social care is with Scottish Ministers, acting through the Scottish Executive Health Department.

Scottish Ministers have particular duties under the law. They must prepare Codes of Practice under the Adults with Incapacity Act and the Mental Health (Care and Treatment) Act, consult on these and lay them before Parliament. They must keep the Codes up-to-date and update them from time-to-time.[1]

Scottish Ministers are also responsible for drafting the various supplementary regulations, consulting on them and laying them before Parliament.

Scottish Ministers are responsible for the National Health Service in Scotland. They give guidance and set priorities.[2] Social care is generally the responsibility of local authorities, but they must act in accordance with general guidance from the Scottish Executive.[3] Scottish Ministers can give legally binding directions to local authorities.[4] They can hold an enquiry into a local authority's performance.[5] See 52.08.

Scottish Ministers have a particular role in relation to restricted patients, people who go to psychiatric hospitals from the criminal justice system. They must approve any periods of absence from the hospital and any transfers to a different hospital. See chapter 48.

The Scottish Executive commissions research on the working of the legislation. It can obtain information for research purposes from people with functions under the Mental Health (Care and Treatment) Act. This is subject to confidentiality rules.[6]

An important role of the Scottish Executive is information-giving. The Scottish Executive maintains important and informative websites on the

Adults with Incapacity Act and the Mental Health (Care and Treatment) Act. It has produced a number of helpful leaflets.

1   Adults with Incapacity (Scotland) Act 2000, s 13. Mental Health (Care and Treatment) (Scotland) Act 2003, s 274.
2   Under the National Health Service (Scotland) Act 1978, as amended.
3   Social Work (Scotland) Act 1968 (as amended by the National Health Service and Community Care Act 1990), s 5(1).
4   Social Work (Scotland) Act 1968 (amended as above), s 5(1A).
5   Social Work (Scotland) Act 1968 (amended as above), s 6A.
6   Mental Health (Care and Treatment) (Scotland) Act 2003, s 279.

HEALTH BOARDS

3.03 Health boards are responsible for the strategic planning of health services in their areas and provide health services on Scottish Ministers' behalf.[1]

Health boards have important duties under the Mental Health (Care and Treatment) Act.[2] They must provide appropriate services, such as services for children and young people and for mothers and babies.[3] They are responsible for ensuring the provision of advocacy services[4] and may have to justify their policies if people are held in conditions of excessive security.[5]

1   Under the Functions of Health Boards (Scotland) Order 1991 (SI 1991/570).
2   For a full list of their responsibilities, see Code of Practice, vol 1, chapter 4.
3   See 41.26.
4   See chapter 41.
5   See chapter 17.

As hospital managers

3.04 Health boards now run hospitals, with the demise of NHS trusts.[1] As hospital managers, they have certain duties under the Mental Health (Care and Treatment) Act. These include the duty to provide information,[2] to appoint responsible medical officers and to ensure appropriate procedures when someone becomes subject to compulsory measures.[3]

Hospital managers have a role in arranging any patients' transfers to other hospitals.[4] They delegate some of these duties to staff, but remain legally liable for ensuring that they are carried out.

The hospital managers of a private hospital are the owners of the hospital.[5]

1   National Health Service Reform (Scotland) Act 2004, s 1.
2   See chapter 17.
3   For example, if someone is detained under the emergency procedure, the hospital managers must ensure the relevant people are notified within the relevant timescales. Mental Health (Care and Treatment) (Scotland) Act 2003, s 38(3).
4   See chapter 19.
5   Mental Health (Care and Treatment) (Scotland) Act 2003, s 329.

State Hospitals Board

3.05 The State Hospitals Board for Scotland is the special health board which runs the State Hospital at Carstairs Junction. This hospital provides care and treatment for around 240 patients from throughout Scotland and from Northern Ireland who need to be detained under conditions of special security.

Scottish Ministers delegate the running of the State Hospital to the board.[1]

Some patients come to the State Hospital through the criminal justice system and others because they need the special care of the State Hospital. A person who is a patient in the State Hospital has all the rights of other patients subject to compulsory measures. A State Hospital patient has extra rights to appeal against transfer to the hospital and to appeal against remaining there when he or she no longer needs the special security of the hospital.

The Scottish Executive aims to supplement the high security of the State Hospital with a series of local medium secure units. This should help ensure that people do not remain in the State Hospital when they do not need high security care.

1   Mental Health (Care and Treatment) (Scotland) Act 2003, s 280.

LOCAL AUTHORITIES

3.06 Local authorities have a key role in providing community based services. These include community care services, services for children and young people, education and training. These duties are largely set out in the Social Work (Scotland) Act 1968 and the Children (Scotland) Act 1995.

Local authorities have key duties under the Adults with Incapacity Act and the Mental Health (Care and Treatment) Act and will have new duties to protect vulnerable people under the Adult Support and Protection (Scotland) Bill.

The Adults with Incapacity Act imposes general duties on local authorities. A local authority must:[1]

- Supervise welfare guardians in its area.
- Work with the Public Guardian and the Mental Welfare Commission on matters of common interest.
- Investigate complaints about welfare matters relating to welfare attorneys, guardians and people authorised under intervention orders.
- Investigate any circumstances where it is aware an adult's personal welfare may be at risk.
- Give welfare advice and information on request to guardians, welfare attorneys and people authorised under intervention orders.

The local authority may have to commence proceedings under the Adults with Incapacity Act for guardianship or a one-off intervention order if it considers this necessary. These duties are covered in detail in Part 5 of this book.

The Mental Health (Care and Treatment) Act obliges local authorities to provide support and welfare services for people living with mental health challenges and learning disabilities in addition to their duty to provide community care help. Local authorities provide the mental health officers who have a key role to play in any compulsory measures under the Act. See below.

[1]   Adults with Incapacity (Scotland) Act 2000, s 10.

MENTAL WELFARE COMMISSION

3.07 The Mental Welfare Commission for Scotland is an independent body with a major role in protecting the interests of people facing mental health challenges or incapacity. The Queen appoints the members, on the advice of Scottish Ministers.

The Commission has duties under the Adults with Incapacity Act and is responsible for monitoring the operation of the Mental Health (Care and Treatment) Act and promoting best practice in relation to the Act, as well as having an important role in protecting individuals, appointing second opinion doctors and reviewing the care of people subject to compulsory orders.

Both the Mental Health (Care and Treatment) Act and the Adults with Incapacity Act have strengthened and extended the Commission's powers.

Constitution

3.08 At the time of writing there are 22 Commissioners, of whom four are full-time. The Scottish Executive can make regulations specifying how many Commissioners there should be.[1] It has also made regulations governing Commission procedure.[2]

At least three of the Commissioners are medically qualified.[3] Regulations can prescribe other qualifications for other Commissioners.

Currently the Commission has a Social Work Commissioner and a Nursing Commissioner. They also have Commissioners with experience of using mental health and learning disability services and of caring for service users. There is now also an Advocacy Commissioner.

[1]   Mental Health (Care and Treatment) (Scotland) Act 2003, Sched 1, para 3(1)(a).
[2]   Mental Welfare Commission for Scotland (Procedure and Delegation of Functions) (No 2) Regulations 2005 (SSI 2005/442).
[3]   Mental Health (Care and Treatment) (Scotland) Act 2003, Sched 1, para 3(1)(b). For qualifications, see the Mental Welfare Commission for Scotland (Appointment of Medical Commissioners) Regulations 2005 (SSI 2005/261).

Protecting individuals

3.09 The Commission's primary focus has always been individual service users (whether or not they are subject to compulsory measures under the Act).

Its powers are much wider than those of the Mental Health Act Commission for England and Wales, which is primarily concerned with people subject to compulsion.

This role continues under the Mental Health (Care and Treatment) Act, although the Commission also has an important role in giving advice to a variety of bodies.

Visiting people

3.10 The Commission visits people subject to compulsory measures under the Mental Health (Care and Treatment) Act and people subject to guardianship and intervention orders under the Adults with Incapacity Act.[1] It should also visit people with welfare powers of attorney, once these have been registered and the Commission has received a copy.[2]

Unlike the 1984 Act, the Mental Health (Care and Treatment) Act does not specify how often such visits should take place. It allows the Commission to decide what is appropriate.

The Commission visits everyone subject to a compulsory treatment order within the first year of the order. If someone is living on a community-based compulsory treatment order, it will visit him or her within the first six months. It visits people on guardianship orders if it has concerns about their care.

[1]   Mental Health (Care and Treatment) (Scotland) Act 2003, s 13.

[2]   MH(CT)(S)A 2003, s 13(2)(e).

Visiting premises

3.11 As well as visiting people subject to compulsory measures, the Commission can visit any premises where people facing mental health challenges receive treatment or use services, including hospitals (public and private), care homes, secure accommodation, day services, prisons and young offenders' institutions.[1]

Such visits can be announced or unannounced[2] and the Commission may use the visit both to inspect the service and to meet people using it.[3] It may interview anyone using the service or any other appropriate person. Interviews may be in private. Anyone using the service may request a private interview with a representative of the Commission.[4]

The Commission visits every mental health and learning disability hospital service on an annual basis and some hospitals, such as the State Hospital, more frequently.

[1]   Mental Health (Care and Treatment) (Scotland) Act 2003, s 13(4).

[2]   MH(CT)(S)A 2003, s 13(6).

[3]   MH(CT)(S)A 2003, s 13(5).

[4]   MH(CT)(S)A 2003, s 14(1).

Medical examinations and inspecting records

3.12 Medical commissioners and medical members of staff can examine patients if necessary to enable the Commission to carry out its statutory duties.[1] Medical members of staff must be either Members or Fellows of the Royal College of Psychiatrists or have at least four years' experience of providing psychiatric services.[2]

Commissioners and Commission staff may inspect people's medical or other records.[3] They may be required to show their authority.[4]

1 Mental Health (Care and Treatment) (Scotland) Act 2003, s 15.
2 Mental Welfare Commission for Scotland (Authorised Persons) Regulations 2005 (SSI 2005/205).
3 MH(CT)(S)A 2003, s 16.
4 MH(CT)(S)A 2003, s 16(3).

Enquiries

3.13 The Mental Welfare Commission must carry out enquiries and may make recommendations in cases of ill-treatment, neglect and inadequate care.[1] The Commission will usually make informal enquiries or require a local authority or health provider to investigate, but it can carry out a formal inquiry either on its own initiative or on request.[2]

The Scottish Executive may ask the Commission to carry out investigations on its behalf. The Commission has carried out several important inquiries on behalf of Scottish Ministers.[3]

1 Mental Health (Care and Treatment) (Scotland) Act 2003, s 11.
2 MH(CT)(S)A 2003, s 12.
3 For example, in 2000 the Scottish Executive published the Commission's report of the inquiry into the care and treatment of Noel Ruddle. In March 2006 the Commission published its report into the care of Mr L and Mr M, which attracted some publicity. Details of other enquiries are on the Commission's website.

Nature of enquiries

3.14 A Commissioner generally chairs Commission enquiries. They are not usually formal enquiries with lawyers present. The Commission generally believes that it can obtain more information if it interviews the parties on a less formal basis.[1]

The Commission can hold formal enquiries if it thinks this appropriate. The enquiry is similar to a court of law, with evidence given under oath and the right to refuse to answer questions on the grounds of privilege or confidentiality.[2]

Even though its enquiries are generally informal, the Commission can insist on people attending to answer questions.[3] It is an offence to refuse to attend or to withhold evidence after being required to attend.[4]

[1]   See discussion in Commission's Annual Report 1995–6, page 13, following its enquiry into the care and treatment of Philip McFadden.
[2]   Mental Health (Care and Treatment) (Scotland) Act 2003, s 12.
[3]   MH(CT)(S)A 2003, s 12(3).
[4]   MH(CT)(S)A 2003, s 12(7).

Results of enquiries

3.15 The Commission publishes the results of its enquiries[1] and makes any necessary recommendations to health boards, local authorities, Scottish Ministers or other relevant bodies.[2]

These include the Public Guardian, the Care Commission, the person's mental health officer or responsible medical officer, a care home service, prison, young offenders' institution or any other appropriate person or body.[3]

In particular it can bring matters to the relevant organisation's attention to investigate if concerned that:

- Someone is unlawfully detained in hospital or there is some irregularity in the person's detention.
- Someone is being ill-treated, neglected or receiving inadequate care or treatment.
- Someone is living alone or without care and is unable to look after him or herself or his or her property or finances.
- A person's property is suffering loss or damage because of his or her mental disorder.[4]

Although the Commission cannot insist that organisations comply with its recommendations, it can issue good practice guidance based on its conclusions from an enquiry.[5] Failure to comply with such guidance could be subject to legal challenge.

[1]   Mental Health (Care and Treatment) (Scotland) Act 2003, s 10.
[2]   MH(CT)(S)A 2003, ss 7–9.
[3]   MH(CT)(S)A 2003, s 6(2).

4   MH(CT)(S)A 2003, s 8. The Commission has signed a memorandum of
     agreement with the Public Guardian, who has similar powers, about how
     they will exercise their powers. See the Commission's Annual Report 2001–2,
     para 4.2.1.
5   MH(CT)(S)A 2003, s 10(1).

Complaints

3.16 The Scottish Public Services Ombudsman (see chapter 50) has taken
over much of the Mental Welfare Commission's role in dealing with
complaints. The Mental Welfare Commission and the Ombudsman have
signed an agreement on how they will deal with complaints.[1]

1   Memorandum of agreement signed in September 2002.

Good practice advice

3.17 The Commission is responsible for promoting good practice in
relation to the Mental Health (Care and Treatment) Act, including the
principles of the Act.[1] It can publish guidance and information. It has
said that it will promote the principles of the Act and best practice
through research and its experience of monitoring the Act.

It intends to publish regular guidance on specific issues. It is setting
up a Principles Network to enable users of services and practitioners to
identify and promote the principles and best practice.[2]

1   Mental Health (Care and Treatment) (Scotland) Act 2003, s 5.
2   Mental Welfare Commission letter to chief executives of health boards and
     local authorities (October 2005).

Raising concerns

3.18 The Commission has wide powers to raise matters of general
concern with Scottish Ministers, local authorities, health boards, the Care
Commission and other bodies.[1] It has particular responsibility to Scottish
Ministers.[2]

It may also offer advice to a variety of bodies on request.[3] It may
publish such advice if the body concerned consents.[4]

1   Mental Health (Care and Treatment) (Scotland) Act 2003, s 7.
2   MH(CT)(S)A 2003, s 6.

3   MH(CT)(S)A 2003, s 9.
4   MH(CT)(S)A 2003, s 10(2).

Role in compulsory measures

3.19 The Commission is responsible for monitoring the operation of the Mental Health (Care and Treatment) Act.[1] It checks the paperwork and records of people who are being cared for or treated under mental health and incapacity law.

The Commission has wide powers in relation to the operation of the compulsory procedures of the Mental Health (Care and Treatment) Act. It receives notice of the use of compulsory measures and can discharge someone from compulsory measures if it considers this appropriate.

The Mental Welfare Commission does not intend to use its power to discharge people. It believes that the tribunal is the correct body to make decisions about compulsory measures. It will advise people to refer matters to the tribunal and it may itself refer a case to the tribunal.[2]

The Commission also has an important role in the consent to treatment rules for people subject to compulsory orders. It appoints second opinion doctors and can revoke treatment authorities if it does not consider they are appropriate.

More detail about these important duties is in Part 3 of this book.

1   Mental Health (Care and Treatment) (Scotland) Act 2003, s 5.
2   Mental Welfare Commission letter to chief executives of health boards and local authorities (October 2005).

Duties under Adults with Incapacity Act

3.20 Most of the Commission's duties are in the Mental Health (Care and Treatment) Act, but it also has duties under the Adults with Incapacity Act. These include investigating complaints about welfare attorneys or guardians and about people authorised under welfare intervention orders.

The local authority generally investigates these matters. The Commission becomes involved only if it is not satisfied with the local authority's investigation or if the local authority has failed to investigate.[1] If the Commission does investigate, it can take such steps as it thinks necessary to protect the adult's interests, including making an application to the sheriff.[2]

The Mental Health (Care and Treatment) Act requires the Mental Welfare Commission to visit people subject to welfare intervention orders or welfare guardianship and to welfare powers of attorney which have been registered.[3] The Commission should give information and advice to welfare guardians and attorneys and people authorised under welfare intervention orders. It should consult with the Public Guardian and any local authority on matters of common interest.[4]

Local authorities, welfare guardians and attorneys and people authorised under welfare intervention orders must make facilities available to enable the Mental Welfare Commission to carry out its functions.[5]

[1]   Adults with Incapacity (Scotland) Act 2000 (as amended by Mental Health (Care and Treatment) (Scotland) Act 2003 Sched 5), s 9(1)(d).
[2]   AWI(S)A, s 12.
[3]   Mental Health (Care and Treatment) (Scotland) Act 2003, s 13(2)(c).
[4]   AWI(S)A 2000, ss 9(1)(g) and (c).
[5]   AWI(S)A 2000, s 9(2).

Co-operation with the Commission

3.21 All relevant bodies must do what is necessary to help the Commission carry out its duties.[1] This includes Scottish Ministers, local authorities, health boards and special health boards, police forces, care services, prisons and young offenders' institutions, the Care Commission and the Scottish Public Services Ombudsman.

The list now includes people who provide services to health boards and local authorities.[2] Regulations may add other bodies.

The Public Guardian and local authorities must co-operate with the Mental Welfare Commission in carrying out their Adults with Incapacity Act functions.[3]

[1]   Mental Health (Care and Treatment) (Scotland) Act 2003, s 17.
[2]   Mental Welfare Commission for Scotland (Prescribed Persons) Regulations 2005 (SSI 2005/176).
[3]   Adults with Incapacity (Scotland) Act 2000, ss 6(1)(f) and 10(1)(b).

PUBLIC GUARDIAN

3.22 The Public Guardian, previously the Accountant of Court, does not have a role under the Mental Health (Care and Treatment) Act but has important duties under the Adults with Incapacity Act.

The Public Guardian supervises people with financial powers under the Adults with Incapacity Act and maintains the public register under the Act. The Public Guardian's Office is part of the Scottish Court Service. The Public Guardian's duties are:[1]

- To supervise financial guardians and people authorised under financial/property intervention orders.
- To maintain the Adults with Incapacity Act public register.
- To provide information and advice to people exercising financial functions under the Adults with Incapacity Act.
- To investigate complaints about people exercising financial functions under the Adults with Incapacity Act.
- To investigate if someone's property or financial affairs may be at risk. This might include taking such steps as the Public Guardian thinks necessary to protect the adult's interests, including making an application to the sheriff.[2]
- To consult with the Mental Welfare Commission and the local authority in relevant cases.

Further information is on the Public Guardian's website. This also contains helpful guidance leaflets and copies of the relevant forms.

The Public Guardian's office is extremely approachable and can be contacted by letter, phone or email.

[1] Adults with Incapacity (Scotland) Act 2000, s 6.
[2] AWI(S)A 2000, s 12.

MENTAL HEALTH TRIBUNAL

3.23 One of the major changes introduced by the Mental Health (Care and Treatment) Act is the creation of the Mental Health Tribunal for Scotland.[1]

Under the 1984 Act, the sheriff court dealt with all applications for detention and appeals against detention. The tribunal has taken over this role, which has been expanded by the Mental Health (Care and Treatment) Act.[2]

The tribunal service is independent of government[3] and the health service and has all the powers and privileges of a court.

The tribunal has not taken over proceedings under the Adults with Incapacity Act. These continue to go to the sheriff court.

[1] Mental Health (Care and Treatment) (Scotland) Act 2003, s 18.

2   For background, see *New directions*, chapter 9, *Renewing mental health law*, Scottish Executive (2001), paras 3.72–91, and Stage 1 Report of the Health and Community Care Committee of the Scottish Parliament, paras 65–75.

3   MH(CT)(S)A 2003, Sched 2, para 1(2). A member of the Scottish Parliament, Executive or administration cannot sit on the tribunal. Mental Health Tribunal for Scotland (Disqualification) Regulations 2004 (SSI 2004/154).

Constitution of tribunals

3.24 The tribunal system is headed by a President,[1] an experienced lawyer.[2] The first President is Mrs Eileen Davie. She is responsible for managing the system of individual tribunals throughout the country, and may convene tribunals. She can delegate certain functions to tribunal staff and/or panel members.[3]

Tribunals have three members, a legal, medical and a general member.[4] They hold their posts for five years but this can be extended or shortened.[5] A legal member convenes the panel. He or she must be a lawyer of at least seven years' standing.[6]

The medical member is a doctor, who must be either a member or fellow of the Royal College of Psychiatrists or have had at least four years' experience of providing psychiatric services.[7] The general member has either professional expertise in providing care services or experience as a user of services or carer.[8]

A panel of sheriffs is available to sit on the tribunal.[9] The President or a sheriff convenes any hearing involving a restricted patient.[10]

1   Mental Health (Care and Treatment) (Scotland) Act 2003, Sched 2, para 2.
2   Mental Health Tribunal for Scotland (Appointment of President) Regulations 2004 (SSI 2004/155).
3   Mental Health Tribunal for Scotland (Delegation of the President's Functions) Regulations 2004 (SSI 2004/373).
4   MH(CT)(S)A 2003, Sched 2, para 1.
5   MH(CT)(S)A 2003, Sched 2, para 4. Mental Health Tribunal for Scotland (Disciplinary Committee) Regulations 2004 (SSI 2004/402).
6   Mental Health Tribunal for Scotland (Appointment of Legal Members) Regulations 2004 (SSI 2004/286).
7   Mental Health tribunal for Scotland (Appointment of Medical Members) Regulations 2004 (SSI 2004/374).
8   Mental Health Tribunal for Scotland (Appointment of General Members) Regulations 2004 (SSI 2004/375).
9   MH(CT)(S)A 2003, Sched 2, para 2.
10 MH(CT)(S)A 2003, Sched 2, para 7(4).

Tribunal hearings

3.25 Tribunal hearings are convened as necessary and where necessary, including at the tribunal service's head office in Hamilton.

Hearings take place in a variety of health board and community based facilities. Health boards and local authorities must make accommodation available to the tribunal service on request.[1]

Tribunal hearings may be in hospitals. The fact that a hearing is in a hospital does not undermine the independence of the tribunal.

Legal aid is available for tribunal hearings, regardless of means. Patients and carers are encouraged to attend tribunal hearings and to give evidence.[2] One of the main criticisms of the sheriff court procedure was that so few people attended the hearings or gave evidence at them.

Decisions of the tribunal are by majority vote, with the convener having a casting vote.[3] The tribunal generally tells the parties of its decision soon after the hearing and must provide a written statement of its reasons.[4]

Part 4 deals with tribunal procedure in more detail.

[1] Mental Health (Care and Treatment) (Scotland) Act 2003, Sched 2, para 6(3).
[2] Research commissioned by the Millan Committee showed only 28% of people attended court. Of those only 18% gave evidence. *New directions*, Chapter 9, para 15.
[3] MH(CT)(S)A 2003, Sched 2, para 13(2).
[4] MH(CT)(S)A 2003 (as amended by the Mental Health (Care and Treatment) (Scotland) Act 2003 (Modification of Enactments) Order 2005 SSI 2005/465), Sched 2, para 13(4).

Tribunal powers

3.26 Tribunals have wide powers to deal with applications for orders, to hear appeals and to vary orders. They can question witnesses and to ask for further information. If a tribunal considers the care plans proposed for someone is inadequate, it can impose additional requirements if it gives the parties a chance to comment. See 14.21.

Monitoring and evaluation

3.27 The tribunal service aims to provide a responsive, accessible, independent and impartial service when making decisions on the compulsory care and treatment of people with mental health problems.

It must comply with the principles of the Mental Health (Care and Treatment) Act. As a public authority, it must comply with human rights law requirements and the public anti-discrimination and equality duties.

Overall supervision comes from the Council on Tribunals, which reviews the constitution and working of tribunals, and, from time to time reports on their constitution and working.[1]

The Council of Tribunals has a Scottish section, which was involved in approving the Mental Health Tribunal for Scotland's rules of procedure.[2] Council members visit tribunals to ensure they are operating within the Council's rules and that hearings meet the Council standards.[3]

The Council may prepare a special report on issues facing a tribunal. For example, in 2000 it published a report on Mental Health Review tribunals in England and Wales.

The Council does not deal with complaints about tribunals. The Scottish Public Services Ombudsman deals with complaints about administrative matters.[4]

The Scottish Executive intends to commission research into the operation of the tribunal system.[5] All tribunals should monitor their performance on at least an annual basis.[6] The tribunal service should provide induction and refresher training, including diversity training.[7]

[1] Tribunals and Inquiries Act 1992.

[2] See its Annual Report 2004–5.

[3] Council on Tribunals, *Framework of Standards* (2002).

[4] Scottish Public Services Ombudsman Act 2002 (as amended by Mental Health (Care and Treatment) (Scotland) Act 2003, Sched 4, para 13), Sched 3, para 4A. See chapter 50.

[5] See *Mental health law research: update and agenda 2005,* Scottish Executive, para 5.1.

[6] *Framework of standards* (above) standard 3(b).

[7] *Framework of standards*, standard 3(d).

DOCTORS

Approved medical practitioner

3.28 Certain functions under the Mental Health (Care and Treatment) Act are restricted to doctors who are approved medical practitioners.

Approved medical practitioners are doctors with qualifications, experience and training as set out in Directions from Scottish Ministers.[1] An approved medical practitioner must be a Member or Fellow of the Royal College of Psychiatrists or have at least four years' experience working in psychiatric services, and must have successfully completed an approved training course about the Mental Health (Care and Treatment) Act.[2] The Scottish Executive and Royal College of Psychiatrists have developed the course.

The doctor's health board must approve him or her as having special experience in the diagnosis and treatment of mental disorder.[3]

Each health board must keep a list of approved medical practitioners in its area.[4] The State Hospitals Board for Scotland maintains a separate list.

[1] Mental Health (Care and Treatment) (Scotland) Act 2003, s 22(1).

[2] Mental Health (Care and Treatment) (Scotland) Act 2003 (Qualifications, experience and training of approved medical practitioners) Direction 2005.

[3] MH(CT)(S)A 2003, s 22(2).

[4] MH(CT)(S)A 2003, s 22(3).

Responsible medical officer

3.29 Everyone subject to compulsory measures has a responsible medical officer.[1]

The responsible medical officer is a consultant psychiatrist on the staff of the hospital where the person is detained. When someone is subject to a community-based order, the responsible medical officer is on the staff of the hospital responsible for supervising the person in the community.

The responsible medical officer has a major role in decisions relating to compulsory measures and to the discharge and modification of any order to which the person is subject.

He or she is also responsible for operating the consent to treatment rules in Part 16 of the Mental Health (Care and Treatment) Act. For more details, see the relevant chapters in this book.

[1] Mental Health (Care and Treatment) (Scotland) Act 2003, s 230(1).

Appointment of responsible medical officer

3.30 The managers of the hospital where the person is detained (or which is specified in any order relating to the person) appoint the responsible medical officer.[1] The responsible medical officer must be an approved medical practitioner.

The hospital managers must appoint a responsible medical officer as soon as reasonably practical after an order is made or varied or a certificate granted.[2] (See Table 1.) This should normally be the day of the order or the next day, if the responsible medical officer is from a different hospital or service.[3]

If a patient already has a responsible medical officer, he or she can be the responsible medical officer under the new order.[4] This would generally be good practice.[5]

The managers may replace a responsible medical officer and may authorise another approved medical practitioner to be the responsible medical officer for a specific purpose or in particular circumstances, for example during a responsible medical officer's absence.[6] The Code of Practice stresses the importance of ensuring that appropriate arrangements are in place to cover periods of absence.[7]

When someone is transferred to another hospital, or is returned to hospital following an appeal against transfer, that hospital must appoint a responsible medical officer as soon as reasonably practical after the transfer or return.[8]

Similar duties apply when a detained patient comes from a hospital outside Scotland to a hospital in Scotland.[9]

[1]   Mental Health (Care and Treatment) (Scotland) Act 2003, s 230(4).

[2]   MH(CT)(S)A 2003, s 230(1).

[3]   Code of Practice, vol 1, para 9.03.

[4]   MH(CT)(S)A 2003, s 230(2).

[5]   Code of Practice, vol 1, para 9.04.

[6]   MI I(CT)(S)A 2003, s 230(3).

[7]   Code of Practice, vol 1, para 9.09.

[8]   MH(CT)(S)A 2003, ss 230(4)(e) and 230(4)(f).

[9]   Mental Health (Cross border transfer: patients subject to detention requirement or otherwise in hospital) (Scotland) Regulations 2005 (SSI 2005/467), art 29.

(Mental Health (Care and Treatment) (Scotland) Act 2003, ss 230(4) and 232 and SSI 2005/467) **Table 1—When health board/hospital managers must appoint responsible medical officer**
The health board/hospital managers must appoint a responsible medical officer following the:

The health board/hospital managers must appoint a responsible medical officer following the:

- Granting of emergency detention certificate.
- Granting of short-term detention certificate.
- Making of interim compulsory treatment order.
- Making of compulsory treatment order.
- Making of assessment order.
- Making of treatment order.
- Making of interim compulsion order.
- Making of compulsion order.
- Making of temporary compulsion order.
- Making of hospital direction.
- Making of transfer for treatment direction.
- Variation of compulsory treatment order.
- Variation of compulsion order.
- Transfer to another hospital.
- Return to original hospital.
- Cross-border transfer.

Designated medical practitioner

3.31 Part 16 of the Mental Health (Care and Treatment) Act provides for certain doctors to give second opinions about medical treatment under the Act. These doctors are called designated medical practitioners.[1]

The Mental Welfare Commission maintains a list of doctors with appropriate qualifications and experience to act as designated medical practitioners.[2] They are experienced consultant psychiatrists and receive training in their role from the Mental Welfare Commission. A number of them have experience in child psychiatry.[3]

Designated medical practitioners need not be approved medical practitioners.

¹   Mental Health (Care and Treatment) (Scotland) Act 2003, s 233.
²   MH(CT)(S)A 2003, s 233(1).
³   MH(CT)(S)A 2003, s 233(3).

NURSES

3.32 Nurses provide care in hospital, in residential care and in the community, as community psychiatric nurses. They have a major impact on the quality of care someone receives. All patients in hospital will have a key nurse and a nurse will often be the keyworker for someone receiving structured care under the care programme approach.

General duties

3.33 Nurses' legal and ethical duties do not come from the Adults with Incapacity Act or the Mental Health (Care and Treatment) Act but from the common law and their Code of Conduct.¹ This sets out nurses' duties about such matters as confidentiality and consent to treatment.

As employees of public authorities, nurses need to have some understanding of the relevance of human rights law to their work and should be aware of the new equality duties on public authorities, including the National Health Service, aimed at reducing discrimination on grounds of race, sex, age, sexual orientation and disability. See chapter 37.

¹   Nursing and Midwifery Council *Code of professional conduct: standards for performance, conduct and ethics* (2004).

Duties under Adults with Incapacity Act

3.34 A nurse working with people who may be unable to consent to treatment needs to become familiar with the Adults with Incapacity Act. If treating someone unable to consent to treatment, a nurse will need to satisfy him or herself that the treatment is lawful. (See chapter 8.)

Issues of restraint and other forms of restriction are largely matters for nurses. Chapter 9 looks at some of these issues. They raise major human rights concerns. Policies must be clear and accessible, with proper recording of incidents.

Nurses need to familiar with the principles of the Adults with Incapacity Act and aware that they may need to justify their practice with reference to the principles.

Duties under Mental Health (Care and Treatment) Act

3.35 Nurses have important duties under the Mental Health (Care and Treatment) Act. They are largely responsible for ensuring patients know their rights at various stages of the process and may need to link people to legal services and advocacy.

A nurse should familiarise him or herself with the Mental Health (Care and Treatment) Act principles and should examine his or her own and colleagues' practice in the light of the principles. The nurse may have particular responsibility for certain principles, such as ensuring the person's participation in the process and respect for diversity. A nurse will need to be able to justify any use of restraints and/or restrictions in light of the minimum necessary intervention principle.

If treating someone under the Mental Health (Care and Treatment) Act, a nurse will need to check the paperwork. A community psychiatric nurse treating a person subject to a community-based order may need to tell doctors if the person becomes unwilling to accept treatment or if he or she is not complying with the terms of the order.

If a voluntary patient tries to leave against medical advice, a nurse of the prescribed class can detain the person for up to two hours to enable a doctor to examine him or her with a view to short-term or emergency detention. See chapter 13.

A nurse needs to be familiar with his or her powers and duties under these provisions as well as the more general provisions of both Acts as they apply to a nurse's duties.

The Millan Committee said it should be the responsibility of NHS trusts (now health boards) to make sure nurses have a basic understanding of the Mental Health (Care and Treatment) Act.[1] The Mental Welfare Commission told the Committee that nurses did not always have an adequate understanding of the 1984 Act.

[1]   *New directions*, recommendation 7.18.

Millan Committee and role of nurses

3.36 Given the importance of community psychiatric nurses, the Millan Committee considered whether they should have a formal role in the compulsion procedure, perhaps giving a second opinion instead of the general practitioner.

Despite considerable support, the Committee did not recommend this change, but recommended that the Code of Practice should oblige GPs to discuss the possible use of compulsion with the community psychiatric nurse wherever possible.[1] The Code of Practice says that doctors should take account of information received from the 'multi-disciplinary team'.[2]

The Millan Committee also considered whether nurses should be able, with training, to become mental health officers.[3] Although the Committee accepted that nurses had many of the requisite skills, it believed mental health officers should continue to be independent of the health service and for this reason rejected the proposal.

[1]   *New directions* recommendation 7.17.

[2]   See, for example, vol 2, para 2.33.

[3]   *New directions*, paras 7.52–57.

Nurses and the tribunal

Giving evidence

3.37 A nurse may have to give evidence at the tribunal, as a key member of the care team. A nurse may wish to seek training to familiarise him or herself with this role.

A nurse who disagrees with the responsible medical officer and mental health officer that an order is necessary should discuss these views at the various multi-disciplinary meetings, so these views should not come as a surprise. A nurse owes a professional and legal duty to speak honestly at the tribunal, and cannot be criticised for so doing.

Acting as escort

3.38 A nurse may escort someone to a tribunal. The tribunal may ask for his or her views about the order sought. This raises several issues.

If the nurse is purely an escort, he or she may not have expected to answer questions. If he or she is not the nurse's key nurse, he or she should explain this to the tribunal. It is quite acceptable for the escort to explain to the tribunal that he or she does not know the patient well and is unable to offer a helpful contribution.

A nurse on escort duty must consider health and safety issues if he or she has to escort someone back to hospital having given information the person might find unacceptable. The nurse may wish to seek an extra escort.

Hospitals need to develop policies to deal with these issues. It may be that if a nurse is likely to give evidence he or she should not also act as escort, or perhaps it would always be preferable for the key nurse to act as escort, if possible.

As member of panel

3.39 Nurses are eligible to act as general members of the tribunal panel. Nearly 50 of the current general members are registered nurses. There has been a spirited discussion about some of the issues raised.[1]

[1]   Chris Turner, 'Seen to be Fair' (November) 2005 Journal of the Law Society of Scotland and the reply from Margaret Ross, 'Mental health tribunals: take another look' (March) 2006 Journal of the Law Society of Scotland.

MENTAL HEALTH OFFICERS

3.40 Mental health officers are social workers with particular qualifications and experience in mental health and incapacity matters. They have a crucial role in any compulsory measures under the Mental Health (Care and Treatment) Act.

They interview the person, advise the person about his or her rights, prepare applications for long-term orders and prepare social circumstances reports. Short-term detention requires the approval of the mental health officer. They also have functions under the Adults with Incapacity Act and the Criminal Procedure (Scotland) Act.

Training and qualifications

3.41 All mental health officers must be registered as qualified social workers, have a minimum of two years post-qualifying experience and have completed an approved course of mental health officer training.[1]

Mental health officers must be local authority employees, but do not need to be employed by the local authority which appoints them.[2]

If a mental health officer ceases to work for a local authority or fails to comply with the requirements about training or registration in directions from Scottish Ministers, any local authority employing him or her as a mental health officer must terminate the appointment.[3]

[1]   Mental Health (Care and Treatment) (Scotland) Act 2003, s 32(2)(b), Mental Health (Care and Treatment) (Scotland) Act 2003 (Requirements for appointment as mental health officers) Direction 2005.
[2]   MH(CT)(S)A 2003, s 32.
[3]   MH(CT)(S)A 2003, s 32(5).

Local authority provision

3.42 Local authorities must ensure that there are an adequate number of mental health officers in their area.[1] This includes ensuring an adequate out-of-hours service.[2] Lack of availability of mental health officers has traditionally been a problem.[3]

The Scottish Executive has produced national standards for mental health officer services.[4] All local authorities should disseminate information about how to access mental health officers.[5]

Local authorities are responsible for ongoing training, as set out in directions from Scottish Ministers.[6]

[1]   Mental Health (Care and Treatment) (Scotland) Act 2003, s 32.
[2]   Code of Practice, vol 1, para 9.16.
[3]   In her report *Towards implementation of the Mental Health (Care and Treatment) (Scotland) Act 2003*: *The National Mental Health Services Assessment*, Scottish Executive (March 2004), para 6.39, Dr Sandra Grant reported that there were insufficient mental health officers to fulfil the increased workload from the 2003 Act.
[4]   Scottish Executive 2005.
[5]   Standard 1.1.
[6]   MH(CT)(S)A 2003, s 32(4).

Appointment of mental health officers

3.43 Everyone subject to a compulsory order must have a mental health officer.[1] The local authority for the area where the person lives or lived before he or she went into hospital, appoints the mental health officer. If the person is from outside Scotland, the local authority for the area where the hospital is situated appoints the mental health officer.[2]

The local authority must allocate a mental health officer as soon as reasonably practical after the making of a compulsory order or the granting of a short-term detention certificate.[3] Similar duties apply when a detained patient comes from a hospital outside Scotland to a hospital in Scotland.[4] See table 2.

The Act does not require the local authority to appoint a mental health officer following the granting of an emergency detention certificate, but the Code of Practice says that if a mental health officer consented to the granting of an emergency certificate, he or she, or another mental health officer should remain involved. If a mental health officer was not involved, the local authority should allocate a mental health officer as soon as possible.[5]

As long as someone is subject to an order, he or she must have a mental health officer.[6] Local authorities should maintain appropriate lists to enable people quickly to identify their mental health officer.[7] The authority must put in place proper arrangements so that the patient, named person, carers, relatives and independent advocate can contact the mental health officer.[8]

The local authority may replace the mental health officer with another mental health officer or may authorise another mental health officer to act for a specific purpose or in particular circumstances.[9]

[1]   Mental Health (Care and Treatment) (Scotland) Act 2003, s 229.
[2]   MH(CT)(S)A 2003, s 229(3).
[3]   MH(CT)(S)A 2003, s 229(1).
[4]   Mental Health (Cross border transfer: patients subject to detention requirement or otherwise in hospital) (Scotland) Regulations 2005 (SSI 2005/467), art 28.
[5]   Code of Practice, vol 1, para 9.12.
[6]   MH(CT)(S)A 2003, s 229(1)(b).
[7]   Code of Practice, vol 1, para 9.14.
[8]   Code of Practice, vol 1, para 9.22.
[9]   MH(CT)(S)A 2003, s 229(2).

(Mental Health (Care and Treatment) (Scotland) Act 2003, s 232 and SSI 2005/467)
Table 2—When local authority should appoint mental health officer
The local authority must appoint a MHO following the:
•   Granting of short-term detention certificate.
•   Making of interim compulsory treatment order.
•   Making of compulsory treatment order.
•   Making of an assessment order.
•   Making of treatment order.
•   Making of interim compulsion order.
•   Making of compulsion order.
•   Making of hospital direction.
•   Making of transfer for treatment direction.
•   Cross-border transfer of patient to Scotland.

Chapter 4

SUPPORTING THE SERVICE USER

4.01 This chapter looks at measures in the Mental Health (Care and Treatment) Act to provide support to service users, through the named person and independent advocacy services.

NAMED PERSON

4.02 If a person is likely to become subject to compulsory measures, it is important someone else can be involved to protect his or her interests. Under the 1984 Act, this was the nearest relative, who was usually the person's spouse, a close relative or a carer.

It was not possible to remove an unsuitable nearest relative under the 1984 Act. This was in breach of the European Convention on Human Rights.[1] The Mental Health (Care and Treatment) Act allows a person to nominate his or her named person.[2]

If the person does not nominate someone, the primary carer is named person.[3] If there is no primary carer, the nearest relative is named person.[4]

Only people over the age of 16 can act as named person or appoint a named person. See 41.21 for the impact of the rules on children and young people.

See chapter 22 for the named person's role at the tribunal.

---

[1] See *JT v UK* (1998) Application No 26494/95 where the equivalent provision in the Mental Health Act 1983 for England and Wales was held in breach of the European Convention on Human Rights.

[2] Mental Health (Care and Treatment) (Scotland) Act 2003, s 250.

[3] MH(CT)(S)A 2003, s 251(1).

[4] MH(CT)(S)A 2003, s 251(5).

Appointing named person

4.03 Anyone over 16 who is competent to do so may nominate someone his or her named person.

It is advisable to ensure in advance that the person appointed is willing to act. A named person can refuse to accept the appointment, by notifying the appointer and the local authority. The person will have to appoint someone else.[1]

The appointer must sign the nomination form in front of a witness. The witness must confirm the person understands the effect of nominating a named person and has not been subject to any undue influence in signing the form.[2] There is no prescribed form for the nomination, but the Scottish Executive has prepared a guide with a suggested form.[3]

The following people may act as witnesses: registered clinical psychologists; doctors; registered occupational therapists; care service managers or employees; registered nurses; social workers and solicitors.[4]

[1]   Mental Health (Care and Treatment) (Scotland) Act 2003, s 250(6).
[2]   MH(CT)(S)A 2003, s 250(2).
[3]   *The New Mental Health Act: A Guide to Named Persons,* Scottish Executive (2004).
[4]   Mental Health (Patient Representation) (Prescribed Persons) (Scotland) (No. 2) Regulations 2004 (SSI 2004/430).

Effect of appointment

4.04 So long as he or she is able to do so, the appointer can cancel the appointment and may appoint someone else.[1] The Scottish Executive's guide contains a suggested form. One of the people listed above must witness the cancellation and confirm the person understands the cancellation and has not been put under undue pressure to cancel.

An appointment validly made remains valid even if the person making the appointment later becomes unable to nominate someone.[2]

[1]   Mental Health (Care and Treatment) (Scotland) Act 2003, s 250(4).
[2]   MH(CT)(S)A 2003, s 250(5).

Primary carer as named person

4.05 The primary carer is named person if the service user does not appoint anyone else.[1] If there is no primary carer and more than one carer, they may decide between themselves who should be named person.[2] If the primary carer is under the age of 16, he or she cannot act as named person. If there is another carer over 16, he or she is named person.[3]

The primary carer is the person who provides all or most of the care and support for the person. This does not include paid carers or carers working as volunteers for voluntary organisations.[4] For someone in hospital, the primary carer is the person who provided the care before he or she went into hospital.

If a carer does not want to act as named person, he or she may give notice to that effect to the cared-for person and to the local authority.[5] The nearest relative over the age of 16 will be named person.[6]

[1]   Mental Health (Care and Treatment) (Scotland) Act 2003, s 251.
[2]   MH(CT)(S)A 2003, s 251(3).
[3]   MH(CT)(S)A 2003, s 251(2).
[3]   MH(CT)(S)A 2003, s 329.
[4]   MH(CT)(S)A 2003, s 251(6).
[5]   MH(CT)(S)A 2003, s 251(5).

Nearest relative

4.06 The nearest relative is named person if the service user has not nominated a named person and has no carer or the carer is unwilling to act.[1]

The Mental Health (Care and Treatment) Act sets out a list of relatives in order of importance.[2] The person highest in the list is normally the nearest relative. The list is:

- Spouse or civil partner (unless they are permanently separated by agreement or court order, or one spouse or civil partner has deserted the other).[3]
- Partner, providing he or she has been living with the person for at least six months (or had been before the person went into a hospital or care home service).[4]
- Child, including stepchildren.
- Father or mother.
- Brother or sister.
- Grandparent.
- Grandchild.
- Uncle or aunt.
- Nephew or niece.
- Anyone who has been living with the person for at least five years, or had been when he or she went into hospital or care.[5]

If there are two people in the same position on the list, they may agree who should be nearest relative. Otherwise, brothers and sisters rank higher than half-brothers and sisters, and an older relative is preferred to a younger relative in the same category.[6]

Someone who is ordinarily resident abroad is not eligible (unless the service user is also ordinarily resident abroad),[7] and someone who is under 16 cannot be nearest relative.[8]

The nearest relative may decline to act, by giving notice to the service user and the local authority.[9]

[1]   Mental Health (Care and Treatment) (Scotland) Act 2003, s 251(5).
[2]   MH(CT)(S)A 2003, s 254.
[3]   MH(CT)(S)A 2003 (as amended by the Civil Partnership Act 2004), s 254(3).
[4]   MH(CT)(S)A 2003, (as amended by the Mental Health (Care and Treatment) (Scotland) Act 2003 (Modification of Enactments) Order 2005 (SSI 2005/465) and by the Civil Partnership Act 2004), s 254(7).
[5]   MH(CT)(S)A 2003 (as amended by SSI 2005/465), s 254(8).
[6]   MH(CT)(S)A 2003, s 254(4).
[7]   MH(CT)(S)A 2003, s 254(6).
[8]   MH(CT)(S)A 2003, s 254(6).
[9]   MH(CT)(S)A 2003, s 254(5).

Barring named person

4.07 Anyone wishing to change his or her named person can do so, provided he or she has the legal capacity to do so. A person can also take steps to ensure that someone he or she does not wish to be named person is not appointed.

Anyone over 16 may make a declaration that a certain person should not be his or her named person.[1] Even if that person is primary carer or nearest relative, he or she does not become named person. The declaration remains valid even if the person who made it later lacks the mental capacity to change it.[2]

The declaration must be in writing and witnessed by one of the people listed above. The Scottish Executive's guide contains a suggested form. The witness must certify that the person making the declaration understands its effect and was not subject to any undue pressure.[3] If the person changes his or her mind, he or she may cancel the declaration on the same basis.[4]

[1]   Mental Health (Care and Treatment) (Scotland) Act 2003, s 253(1).

2   MH(CT)(S)A 2003, s 253(3).
3   MH(CT)(S)A 2003, s 253(2).
4   MH(CT)(S)A 2003, s 253(4).

Role of tribunal

4.08 The tribunal can appoint a named person for someone who does not have one. It may remove a named person if satisfied it is not appropriate for the person to act and may appoint a new named person in his or her place.[1]

The following people may apply to the tribunal for an order:

- The service user.
- The responsible medical officer.
- If the service user is a child, the person with parental responsibilities in relation to him or her.
- If the person is in hospital, the managers of the hospital.
- A welfare attorney or guardian.
- Any relative of the person.
- Anyone else with an interest in the person's welfare.[2]

The tribunal can make such order as it thinks fit, but must have regard to the principles of the Act. If a service user does not wish to have a named person and appears able to represent his or her own interests and arrange legal representation, the tribunal should consider whether there is any benefit to the service user in appointing a named person.

Guidance from the Mental Welfare Commission says a person should not have a named person if it appears the person has the capacity to make this decision, understands its consequences, and has not been subject to any undue influence in making it.[3]

The Act does not prevent the tribunal from appointing as named person someone whom the service user has attempted to bar as named person.[4] See above. That would be very unusual. The tribunal must act in accordance with the principles of the Act. The principles stress the importance of respect for the service user's wishes and feelings. Since the role of the named person is to represent the service user's interests, it would be unusual to appoint someone in whom the person has no confidence.

1   Mental Health (Care and Treatment) (Scotland) Act, s 257(1).
2   MH(CT)(S)A 2003, s 256.

3   *Named Person—Guidance for practitioners,* Mental Welfare Commission (January 2006).
4   In a declaration under MH(CT)(S)A 2003, s 253(1). The declaration provisions are subject to the tribunal's power to appoint under s 257 of the Act.

Mental health officer's duties

4.09 If a mental health officer is carrying out any of his or her statutory duties and needs to know whether someone has a named person, he or she should try to ascertain the identity of the named person.[1]

If there is no named person or if the situation is not clear, the mental health officer must inform the tribunal and the Mental Welfare Commission.[2] The mental health officer may apply to the tribunal for an order appointing a suitable person as named person.[3]

A case in England looked at the extent of the enquiries a mental health officer (called an 'approved social worker' in England and Wales) should make. The court said the social worker should work in a commonsense way in a difficult situation when trying to establish the identity of the nearest relative.[4]

If the mental health officer considers a named person is inappropriate, he or she should apply to the tribunal for an order removing the person and/or appointing someone else.[5]

1   Mental Health (Care and Treatment) (Scotland) Act 2003, s 255(2).
2   MH(CT)(S)A 2003, s 255(5).
3   MH(CT)(S)A 2003, s 255(7).
4   *Re D (Mental patient: habeas corpus)* [2001] 1 FCR 218.
5   MH(CT)(S)A 2003, s 255(6).

Conflict of interest

4.10 No one should agree to act as named person if this could lead to a conflict of interest. The Code of Practice gives guidance.[1]

1   Code of Practice, vol 1, para 6.09.

Named person and Adults with Incapacity Act

4.11 People acting under the Adults with Incapacity Act have an obligation to consult the named person. For this reason, someone anticipating incapacity may wish to appoint a named person even it is unlikely that he or she will become subject to Mental Health (Care and Treatment) Act measures.

INDEPENDENT ADVOCACY

4.12 Advocacy is a way of helping people express their own wishes and needs and make their own decisions. Advocacy workers can help people speak up for themselves or can speak on behalf of them if necessary.

> 'Advocacy enables people to make informed choices about, and to remain in control of, their own care. It helps people have access to the information they need, to understand the options available to them, and to make their views and wishes known.'[1]

The Mental Health (Care and Treatment) Act defines advocacy services as services of support and representation which enable people to have as much control or influence over their care and welfare as appropriate.[2]

There are many different types of advocacy. Which type would best suit an individual should be a matter of choice. Most advocacy workers work with individual clients, but there are also collective advocacy projects, which work with groups. Patients' councils and user groups and forums are examples of collective advocacy.

Advocacy is important for people who are people in hospital and for people living in the community. Most parts of Scotland now have some form of individual advocacy for people with mental disorders and several have collective advocacy. For the role of advocacy where someone lacks the legal capacity to appoint an advocate, see 24.30.

Advocacy is important for people subject to compulsory measures, but it can also be valuable for informal patients. Some informal patients may feel under pressure to agree to care or treatment plans in order to avoid the use of compulsory measures.

For this reason the Millan Committee recommended that everyone should have the right to an advocacy worker, whether living at home, in hospital or in a community setting.[3]

[1]   *Independent Advocacy, A guide for commissioners,* Scottish Executive (2000).
[2]   Mental Health (Care and Treatment) (Scotland) Act 2003, s 259(4).
[3]   *New directions,* recommendation 14.1.

Legal right to advocacy

4.13 Improved access to advocacy is one of the most important reforms introduced by the Mental Health (Care and Treatment) Act. Everyone in

Scotland who has a mental illness, learning disability or personality disorder has the right of access to independent advocacy.[1] This includes people subject to compulsory measures and informal patients, and applies whether people are living in hospital or in the community.

Health boards and local authorities must co-operate to ensure that independent advocacy services are available in their area. They must ensure that people have the right to access independent advocacy services.[2] They must keep an up-to-date a list of independent advocacy organisations in their area.[3]

Advocacy projects are becoming established throughout Scotland. There are gaps in services for children and young people, older people, people with dementia, people with physical and sensory impairments and people from black and minority ethnic communities.[4]

[1]   Mental Health (Care and Treatment) (Scotland) Act 2003, s 259(1).
[2]   MH(CT)(S)A 2003, s 259(2).
[3]   Code of Practice, vol 1, para 6.100.
[4]   Dr Sandra Grant, Towards implementation of the Mental Health (Care and Treatment) (Scotland) Act 2003, Scottish Executive (2004), para 5.9.4.

Duties of State Hospital

4.14 The State Hospital has special duties to provide advocacy. Advocacy is particularly important for State Hospital patients, all of whom are subject to compulsory measures and 60 per cent of whom are subject to the special restrictions of the Criminal Procedure (Scotland) Act.

The State Hospital must ensure that independent advocacy services are available to people in the State Hospital.[1] It should cooperate with relevant health boards and local authorities.

In addition, advocacy must be available for people who are no longer in the State Hospital because their detention has been suspended or they have been conditionally discharged. The State Hospital should cooperate with relevant health boards and local authorities to ensure that advocacy is available.[2]

[1]   Mental Health (Care and Treatment) (Scotland) Act 2003, s 259(7).
[2]   MH(CT)(S)A 2003, s 259(8)–259(10).

Making advocacy available

4.15 Specific duties in the Mental Health (Care and Treatment) Act supplement the general right to advocacy.

When short-term detention procedure or a compulsory treatment order is under consideration, a mental health officer must advise the person that he or she has a right to advocacy and assist the person to access services.[1]

There are similar duties if a compulsory treatment order or compulsion order is extended and/or varied, or if the responsible medical officer notifies the mental health officer he or she intends to apply to extend and/or vary the order.[2]

If someone comes to a hospital from outside Scotland or may move to a hospital outside Scotland, the mental health officer must help him or her access advocacy.[3]

Whenever someone becomes subject to a civil or criminal order, the hospital managers should make sure the person receives information about independent advocacy and help in accessing it.[4]

[1]   Mental Health (Care and Treatment) (Scotland) Act 2003, ss 45(1) and 61(2).
[2]   MH(CT)(S)A 2003 (as amended by Mental Health (Care and Treatment) (Scotland) Act 2003 Modification Order 2004 (SSI 2004/533)), ss 85(2), 89(2), 94(4C), 151(2), 155(2) and 159(4C).
[3]   Mental Health (Cross border transfer: patients subject to detention requirement or otherwise in hospital) (Scotland) Regulations 2005 (SSI 2005/467), arts 6(2) and 35(2).
[4]   MH(CT)(S)A 2003, s 260(2).

Good practice

4.16 The Code of Practice gives advice about managers' duties to make information available and about how mental health officers and hospital staff should help people access advocacy.[1]

Hospital staff must respond to any reasonable request for information about advocacy.[2] Staff should generally assume a request is reasonable, unless there is some unusual circumstance suggesting otherwise. Staff should record the request in the person's records and note how they responded.[3]

General practitioners should also have information about advocacy services and should be able to direct people to sources of help and information.[4] A person receiving treatment from a GP is also entitled to advocacy.

[1]   Code of Practice, vol 1, paras 6.120–130.
[2]   MH(CT)(S)A 2003, s 260(3)(b).

3   Code of Practice, vol 1, para 6.137.
4   Code of Practice, vol 1, para 6.138.

Independence

4.17 Advocacy must be independent. An advocacy worker cannot work effectively if he or she has a conflict of interest. Advocacy services are not independent if any of the following provides them:

- A local authority or health board in the area where the advocy services are to be received.
- A member of a local authority or health board in the area where the person is to receive advocacy services.
- Someone who is providing medical treatment, care and support or social welfare services to the person receiving advocacy.
- The State Hospitals Board for Scotland or any member of the Board, in relation to people who are or have been detained in the State Hospital.[1]

1   Mental Health (Care and Treatment) (Scotland) Act 2003, s 259(5).

Issues for workers

Confidentiality

4.18 There can sometimes be problems with staff recognising the authority of the advocacy worker. This may be because of patient confidentiality or concern that an advocacy worker is not acting in someone's best interests.

The question of confidentiality cannot arise if the person gives written permission for an advocacy worker to see his or her medical or social work records. If the person asks an advocacy worker to attend a meeting with the doctor or social worker, he or she can be assumed to have waived confidentiality.

Access

4.19 The Code of Practice says that where someone has decided to use individual advocacy, an advocacy worker has the right to be asked to attend meetings and consultations about the person's treatment or care, where practicable. An advocacy worker should have access to the patient at any reasonable time, to provide support or representation.[1]

The Code says that independent advocacy workers should be free to correspond or communicate in any other way with the person on matters relating to the person's care and welfare. The advocacy worker should receive information to help him or her act as advocate.

In all cases, of course, this depends on the agreement of the person. An independent advocacy worker must be familiar with his or her own confidentiality duties and should only seek access to someone's records if the person has authorised this.[2] It may be that the person does not want such a full role for the advocacy worker, but just help for a particular issue.

1   Code of Practice, vol 1, para 6.101.

2   Code of Practice, vol 1, para 6.102–3.

Complaints

4.20 Staff may sometimes be concerned that an advocacy worker is not acting in the person's best interests. They can use the advocacy service's complaints procedure or contact the Mental Welfare Commission for advice.

Limits to role

4.21 An advocacy worker may help someone at the tribunal. See Part 4. An advocacy worker should not agree to act as a named person. The roles are not compatible.[1]

1   Code of Practice, vol 1, para 6.148.

Appointing advocacy worker

4.22 No legal formalities are required to appoint an advocacy worker. The advocacy project should give the person information about the worker's role and the project's complaints and confidentiality policies.

Standards

4.23 It is essential that advocacy is of a high standard, that advocacy workers receive proper training and that they understand their professional roles. Most advocacy projects will be responsible for monitoring the quality of advocacy they provide, and this will be a feature of their contracts with commissioners.

The Advocacy Safeguards Agency, the independent body set up by the Scottish Executive to help the development of advocacy and monitor the quality of advocacy, has now ceased to operate. At the time of writing, a successor looks unlikely.

The Scottish Executive plans to work with NHS Quality Improvement Scotland and the Scottish Health Council to ensure the quality of services. It will also work on developing principles and standards for advocacy and a guide for commissioners.

NHS Boards commissioning advocacy services must ensure that services are of good quality, have adequate complaints procedures and proper evaluation.[1]

As advocacy projects become better established, it seems likely that the Scottish Executive will need to consider the need for professional regulation of advocacy workers.

[1] Letter from Lewis Macdonald, Deputy Minister for Community Care to Malcolm Chisholm MSP 23.1.06, in response to query from one of Mr Chisholm's constituents.

PART 2
MEDICAL TREATMENT AND CARE

Chapter 5

PATIENTS' RIGHTS

5.01 This part of the book looks at the law relating to medical treatment in general. Part 3 looks at the special rules where compulsory measures are used. This chapter looks at choosing a general practitioner and at people's rights to medical treatment. It considers some issues relating to other therapies. It also looks at new rights under the Mental Health (Care and Treatment) Act to seek a healthcare assessment and examines the rules relating to access to medical records and medical confidentiality.

Health Rights Information Scotland produces helpful leaflets. These include leaflets on patients' rights in the National Health Service, confidentiality, access to records and making complaints.

GENERAL PRACTITIONERS

Obtaining a general practitioner

5.02 Most people seek and obtain medical help from their general practitioner (GP). The GP can decide whether to refer someone on for further treatment and may contact the local authority for community care help. See Part 6.

Each health board must arrange for the provision of GP services in its area.[1] The health board enters into contracts with individual GPs to provide services.[2]

Everyone has the right to choose his or her own GP. All GP practices should have leaflets explaining the services they provide, and a person can ask to meet the doctor before deciding whether to apply to become a patient.

A parent or guardian, including a foster carer, chooses a child's GP. Where a local authority looks after a child, it chooses the GP.[3]

When someone is unable to choose a doctor, the primary carer or anyone authorised under the Adults with Incapacity (Scotland) Act may select the GP.[4]

Someone who is away from home and staying in another place for less than three months can ask to register with a GP on a temporary basis. The same applies to someone with no permanent address.[5]

1 National Health Service (Scotland) Act 1978, (as amended by the Primary
   Medical Services (Scotland) Act 2004), s 2C.
2 The contract is in the National Health Service (General Medical Services
   Contracts) (Scotland) Regulations 2004 (SSI 2004/115), as amended by SSI
   2005/337 ('The GP contract Regulations').
3 GP contract Regulations, reg 4.
4 GP contract Regulations, reg 4.
5 GP contract Regulations, reg 16.

Problems

5.03 It is rare for a doctor to refuse to accept a new patient, other than if
his or her list is full. A doctor must have reasonable grounds for refusing
to accept someone, and these cannot be discriminatory or linked to the
applicant's race, gender, social class, age, religion, sexual orientation,
appearance, disability or medical condition.[1] The doctor must advise the
person why he or she has refused to accept him or her.[2]

The person may apply to another GP or may ask the health board to
find a GP. The health board must consider the person's wishes when
allocating a new GP.[3]

1 GP contract Regulations, reg 17.
2 GP contract Regulations, reg 17(3).
3 GP contract rRegulations, regs 33 and 34.

Changing general practitioner

5.04 It is possible to change GP at any time, simply by applying to a new
GP to become a patient. If the new GP accepts the person, the health
board notifies the original doctor that the person has left the practice.[1]

1 GP contract Regulations, reg 22.

Removal from list

5.05 A GP can remove a patient from his or her list only if he or she has
reasonable grounds which are not discriminatory, as outlined in 5.03
above.[1] The General Medical Council advises doctors that is not
acceptable to remove someone from the list just because of the financial
demands the person places on the practice or because the person has
made a formal complaint against the doctor.[2]

A GP notifies the health board that he or she wishes to remove the person and advises the person of the reasons. If a GP can reasonably say that there has been an irrevocable breakdown in the doctor-patient relationship and it is not appropriate to give a more specific reason, he or she may simply state that the relationship has broken down.[3]

A doctor will generally give someone a warning that he or she may wish to terminate the relationship, unless this is inappropriate or impractical.[4]

A doctor may remove a violent patient from his or her list with immediate effect.[5] If someone has been violent or has behaved in such a way as to cause anyone in the surgery to fear for his or her own safety, the GP should report the matter to the police or a procurator fiscal and may then notify the health board that he or she wishes to remove the person from the list.

In finding a new doctor in such circumstances, the health board must consider whether the doctor has facilities to deal with the person's needs.[6]

[1]   GP contract Regulations, reg 20.
[2]   *Good medical practice*, General Medical Council (May 2001), para 24. An irrational decision could be subject to judicial review and challenge under the European Convention of Human Rights. See I Kennedy and A Grubb, *Medical Law* (Butterworths 2000), p 87.
[3]   GP contract Regulations, reg 20(2).
[4]   GP contract Regulations, regs 20(3) and 20(4).
[5]   GP contract Regulations, reg 21.
[6]   GP contract Regulations, reg 34(d).

SECOND OPINIONS

5.06 Anyone unhappy with a doctor's diagnosis can ask for a second opinion, but cannot insist on this.

Guidance to doctors from the General Medical Council says that doctors should *'respect the right of patients to a second opinion'*,[1] but the decision to refer is for the clinical judgement of the doctor.

[1]   Good medical practice (2001), para 19.

RIGHT TO MEDICAL SERVICES

5.07 Everyone is entitled to have a GP and to ask to see a consultant. A patient has the right to accept or refuse any treatment (unless the compulsory powers in the Mental Health (Care and Treatment) Act 2003 are invoked), but cannot insist on receiving certain forms of treatment.

There are two reasons for this. Firstly, this would be interfering with the clinical judgement of the doctor. The second reason is scarcity of resources. The courts accept that resources within the National Health Service are not infinite. They take the view that it is for health boards to set priorities and the courts should not interfere with this.

For example, the new drugs available to treat schizophrenia are not always available. This may partly be because of the cost. Many people complain about the limited facilities for psychotherapy or psychological treatments on the National Health Service. There is a serious shortage of child and adolescent psychiatrists in Scotland. It is unlikely that legal action to compel the delivery of a specific treatment or service would succeed.

Legal duties of Scottish Ministers

5.08 The legal duty on the Scottish Executive to provide health services is in general terms. Scottish Ministers must ensure a comprehensive and integrated health service in Scotland, providing medical, nursing and rehabilitation services. There must be hospital beds to meet all reasonable needs, bearing in mind the needs of the population.[1]

Scottish Ministers delegate their functions to health boards,[2] which provide hospital, community and GP services. Health boards provide health services on behalf of Scottish Ministers.[3] These services must be provided free of charge.[4]

[1]   National Health Service (Scotland) Act 1978, s 1 and Pt III.
[2]   NHS(S)A 1978, s 2.
[3]   NHS(S)A 1978, Pt III.
[4]   NHS(S)A 1978, s 1(2).

The courts and right to treatment

5.09 The courts in England have said that the duty of the National Health Service is not to provide a service that meets every need of every patient but to allocate resources sensibly and reasonably. No one can insist on receiving certain treatments, even if these are available and could be life saving.[1]

If a health board acts unlawfully, for example, by failing to follow government guidance on the provision of treatment, it may have to reconsider its decision to refuse a certain treatment (see below). Similarly a blanket policy of refusing certain treatments could be open to challenge.

[1]   See *R v Secretary of State for Social Services ex parte Hincks* (1890) 1 BMLR 93(CA); also *R v Central Birmingham Health Authority ex parte Walker* (1987) 3 BMLR 32; and *R v Cambridge District Health Authority, ex parte B* [1995] 1 WLR 898, where a father unsuccessfully sought experimental treatment for cancer for child B.

5.10 The failure of the authorities to provide life-saving medical treatment might be challenged under the 'right to life' provisions of Article 2 of the European Convention on Human Rights.

This did not succeed in a case in South Africa, which has similar human rights legislation. The court said that 'courts are not the proper place to resolve the agonizing personal and medical problems that underlie these choices.'[1] (The judge in the child B case (above) used very similar words.)

Human rights law imposes a positive duty on the state to protect the life of its citizens. It recognises that this is subject to the constraints of priorities and resources and cannot be an absolute obligation of the state.[2] It also recognises that doctors may withdraw treatment if they regard this as futile and unlikely to benefit the person.[3]

The author is not aware of any cases where someone has successfully taken legal action to force a health authority to provide a particular type of treatment under the European Convention on Human Rights. A health board may, of course, change its mind following the threat of legal action.[4]

Doctors cannot withdraw artificial nutrition and hydration from a competent patient who wishes it continued.[5]

[1]   See *Soobramoney v Minister of Health, KwaZulu-Natal* (1997) 50 BMLR 224 (SA Constitutional Ct). (Sachs J at [58].)
[2]   See *Osman v UK* [1998] ECHR 101, at para 116. A health professional has a duty of care to look after his or her patients (see 51.05) but this does not mean that the patient can insist on the best or most expensive treatments.
[3]   *NHS Trust A v M* [2001] 1 All ER 801, withdrawal of treatment for a patient in a persistent vegetative state was not a breach of Article 2. Also *R (Burke) v General Medical Council (Official Solicitor and others intervening)* [2005] EWCA Civ 1003, an unsuccessful attempt to force the General Medical Council to

change its guidelines on withdrawal of medical treatment. The court dismissed the idea that a patient could demand that a doctor provide treatment which the doctor did not think was clinically appropriate.

4   See 'Nurse wins breast cancer drug row', BBC News (3rd October 2005).

5   *R (Burke) v General Medical Council* (above), at para 53.

European Union rules

5.11 Under European Union rules a person may go abroad to seek hospital treatment and receive reimbursement of the expenses if he or she would experience 'undue delay' in receiving the treatment in the United Kingdom.[1] The test cases have generally involved treatment for physical illnesses, but undue delays in providing psychiatric or psychological services, for example, could also face challenge.

The test of what is an unreasonable delay depends on the facts of the individual case, including the seriousness of the person's illness and the pain the person is suffering, not government targets or accepted waiting list times.[2]

Before seeking treatment abroad, a patient should ask the health board to authorise payment of the cost. Otherwise the person will need to satisfy the courts that the delays he or she faced in Scotland were unreasonable.

1   *B SM Geraets-Smits v Stichting Ziekenfonds VGZ, H T M Peerbooms v Stichting CZ Groep Zorgverzekeringen*, ECJ, C-157/99; and *Abdon Vanbraekel and Others v Alliance nationale des mutualités chrétiennes*, C-368/98.

2   The *Queen, (on the application of Yvonne Watts), v Bedford Primary Care Trust and the Secretary of State for Health*, ECJ, C-372/04 (May 2006).

Effect of guidance

5.12 There may be certain circumstances where a patient could challenge the refusal of a doctor or hospital to follow government guidance on treatments. The National Health Service in Scotland receives guidance from NHS Quality Improvement Scotland, which provides advice on clinical practice and sets clinical and non-clinical standards of care to improve performance.

Though the Scottish Intercollegiate Guidelines Network (SIGN), NHS Quality Improvement Scotland has produced new clinical standards for managing schizophrenia, dementia, bi-polar disorder, post-natal depression and alcohol dependence. These standards contain recommendations for effective practice, based on current evidence. SIGN guidelines aim to reduce variations in practice and ensure that effective care is delivered uniformly throughout Scotland. Individual National Health Service boards should implement the guidelines in their area.

There might be circumstances where a failure to take account of SIGN guidelines could be challenged in the courts.

In an important case in England, for example,[1] a patient took court action when the health authority refused to allow him treatment with a new drug for multiple sclerosis. The court ordered the authority to rethink their decision, because the authority had ignored government guidance requiring health authorities to introduce trials of the drug in their areas.

1   *R v North Derbyshire Health Authority ex parte Fisher* [1997] 8 Med LR 327 (QBD). See also *North West Lancashire HA v A, D and G* [1999] Lloyd's Rep Med 399 (CA) where a health authority had failed to evaluate transsexualism as an illness and its decision not to permit operations for transsexuals was seen as an unlawful 'fettering' of doctors' clinical judgement.

Complementary therapies and private health care

5.13 Some hospitals now provide complementary therapies, such as acupuncture, massage or homeopathy. Many people find these helpful. Some are now available on the National Health Service.[1]

No one can insist on receiving complementary healthcare from the National Health Service. In the absence of any clinical guidelines recommending the use of such therapies, it is very unlikely a Scottish court would compel a health provider to provide them.

Waiting lists on the National Health Service for 'talking treatments' such as counselling or psychological treatments are often very long and some people may consider seeking help privately.

Anyone seeking private help should attempt to find out in advance the cost of the treatment and should try to establish whether the practitioner is a member of a recognised professional body.

It is important to note that anyone can call him or herself a 'psychologist',[2] 'counsellor' or 'psychotherapist'. No qualifications are required. If a practitioner is not a member of a recognised body, there will be no comeback if a client has complaints about treatment.

Anyone seeking private therapy should ask the therapist to explain his or her qualifications and whether he or she is a member of any recognised body, such as the British Association for Counselling and

Psychotherapy. This runs an accreditation scheme and receives and considers complaints about individual therapists.

1   For further information, contact the Information Service at the Scottish Association for Mental Health.
2   At the time of writing, consultations are underway to add psychologists to the list of professions registered with the Health Professions Council.

HEALTHCARE ASSESSMENT

5.14 Sometimes users of services and carers complain that it is difficult to make their views heard. It can be difficult to get help when someone's condition is deteriorating.

The 1984 Act gave the nearest relative the right to apply for the compulsory detention of the person. This was one way of ensuring that the relevant authorities formally considered a person's needs, but it often caused family friction. The Millan Committee recommended its removal.[1]

The Mental Health (Care and Treatment) Act gives a person with a mental disorder and his or her named person and primary carer the right to request a formal assessment of the person's needs.[2] If any of these people have concerns about a person's treatment or lack of treatment, they can request an assessment and oblige the authorities to give a formal response to their concerns.

Health boards should ensure that users of services and their carers and named persons are aware of their rights to seek a healthcare assessment.[3]

1   *New Directions,* recommendation 7.2.
2   Mental Health (Care and Treatment) (Scotland) Act 2003, s 228.
3   Code of Practice, vol 1, para 7.10.

Right to assessment

5.15 Either the person him or herself, the primary carer or named person may request the health board to assess the person's needs.[1] The request must be in writing. The health board should also respond to an informal request from the carer or named person. The Code of Practice says that a health board should respond to a request from a person's advocate as if it were from the person him or herself.[2]

The letter should be addressed to the health board for the area where the person lives (or is in hospital) and should ask the health board to assess the person's needs for mental health services.[3]

The legislation does not provide a form for the request. It might be necessary to seek help from a Citizens Advice Bureau or advocacy project. There is no need to include any further detail, but it might be helpful to include some information about the needs of the person which the applicant feels are not being met. A suggested form is at Appendix 3. (Form 6.)

[1]   Mental Health (Care and Treatment) (Scotland) Act 2003, s 228(2).

[2]   Code of Practice, vol 1, para 7.08.

[3]   MH(CT)(S)A 2003, s 228(2).

Duties of health board

5.16 Health board staff should consult with other health and social care colleagues in considering how to respond to the request.[1]

Within 14 days of the request, the health board must advise the applicant whether it intends to carry out the assessment.[2] If it does not intend to do so, it should explain the reasons.[3]

The Act does not set a time limit for carrying out the assessment. This depends on the urgency of the case and other demands on the health board's resources.

Someone dissatisfied with a health board's response can seek advice from the Mental Welfare Commission. A formal complaint under the NHS complaints procedure might be necessary.

[1]   Code of Practice, vol 1, para 7.09.

[2]   Mental Health (Care and Treatment) (Scotland) Act 2003, s 228(3).

[3]   MH(CT)(S)A 2003, s 228(3)(b).

Duties of local authority

5.17 The person and his or her named person and/or primary carer can also formally request a community care assessment under the same procedure. See 27.06.

ACCESSING MENTAL HEALTH SERVICES

Problems with access

5.18 The Millan Committee heard evidence that it can be difficult to access mental health services. Services may not accept someone with a diagnosis of personality disorder or with problems from alcohol or substance misuse.[1] An early study in Ayrshire and Arran found that 46 per cent of those with this 'dual diagnosis' of mental disorder and substance misuse were initially refused help.[2]

The Mental Welfare Commission has highlighted some of the issues for people with addictions.[3] Unfortunately mental health services may not take people with substance abuse, but addiction services will not take people with serious mental health concerns, which might mean they are unable to comply with treatment plans.

The Commission recommends the development of specialist addiction services for people with mental disorders, and the Department of Health in England and Wales takes the same approach. There are some specialised dual diagnosis services in Scotland, but these are not available throughout the country.

[1]   *New Directions, paras* 4.89 and 4.120.

[2]   Scottish Executive Clinical Resources and Audit Group, Clinical Effectiveness Programmes Subgroup, Mental Health Scoping Group, Final Report, (March 2000), Appendix D, para 3.

[3]   Annual report 2001–2, pp 36–38.

Assessment of needs

5.19 A person with personality disorder or who misuses drugs or alcohol may experience many of the symptoms of mental disorder, including mood disorders, paranoia, or psychosis. The person may also be at risk of self-harm or suicide.

One way of formally asking mental health services to consider the person's needs is to ask for a healthcare assessment, in addition to a community care assessment, if the person has community care needs.

If services refuse help, anyone concerned can contact the Mental Welfare Commission for advice.

ACCESS TO MEDICAL RECORDS

5.20 Patients have the right to see their medical records, written or stored on computer, subject to certain exceptions. The rules apply to records kept by psychiatrists, general practitioners and other health professionals, such as clinical psychologists, nurses, and art therapists (if they are employed by the National Health Service).[1]

The Data Protection Act 1998 contains important principles relating to the way in which people must process information.[2] For example, people must deal with information fairly and in accordance with the law and must keep accurate and up-to-date records.[3] Health professionals and NHS managers must keep medical information confidential.[4]

[1]   The rules are complex and this section is a brief summary. For further information, see the Information Commissioner's website at www.dataprotection.gov.uk. A helpful leaflet for patients is available from Health Rights Information Scotland. For a useful discussion of some of the issues, see Cheryl Minto, 'Access to Health Records', (11) *The Point* (Scottish Association for Mental Health, summer 2003).
[2]   Data Protection Act 1998, Scheds 1–4.
[3]   DPA 1998, Sched 1.
[4]   DPA 1998, Sched 3, para 8.

Applying for access

5.21 People may ask their doctors or health professionals to show them the records for current treatment. For past records, a person must apply in writing, including by e-mail.[1] If someone does not know who to write to, the local health board can advise.

The record holder should give the information within 40 days. A fee may be payable to see information added earlier than this.[2] There may be a fee for copies. The information should generally be in a form or format the person can understand.[3]

[1]   Data Protection Act 1998, s 7(2)(a).
[2]   DPA 1998, s 7(2)(b).
[3]   DPA 1998, s 7(1)(c).

Who can apply

5.22 The person holding the records will accept an application if satisfied the person understands the nature of the application. A person may appoint someone else to apply on his or her behalf.

A child or young person in Scotland aged over 12 can apply to see his or her own health records.[1] Someone with parental rights and responsibilities in respect of the young person may also apply for access. These people will not be able to see records of consultations or examinations the child or young person would have regarded as confidential.[2]

When someone is unable to apply, a person with authority under the Adults with Incapacity Act, such as a welfare guardian or welfare attorney, may apply on the person's behalf. If there is no such person, it might be necessary to apply for an intervention order under the Adults with Incapacity Act to authorise access to the records. As with children and young people, the order will not authorise the person's representatives to see records of consultations regarded as confidential.[3]

When someone has died, his or her personal representative, executor or administrator and anyone with a claim for compensation because of the person's death may apply for access. A person can stop access even after his or her death and a note to that effect can be included in the records.[4] Confidential consultations are not disclosed even after death.[5]

1   Data Protection Act 1998, s 66.
2   Data Protection (Subject Access Modification) (Health) Order 2000, (SI 2000/ 413), ('the Access Modification Order'), para 5(3).
3   Access Modification Order, para 5(3).
4   Access to Health Records Act 1990, s 3(1).
5   AHRA 1990, s 5(3).

Refusing access

5.23 A person holding health records can withhold information if:

- Giving the information would be likely to cause serious harm to the patient's physical or mental health or that of someone else.[1]

  (If the person holding the records is a doctor, he or she decides whether to withhold the information. If not a doctor, the record holder should consult an appropriate health professional[2] before communicating any information.[3])

- A record discloses information relating to an identifiable third party, unless that person gives permission.[4] The person must not withhold consent unreasonably. This rule does not apply to health professionals named in health records.[5]

- The information is in a report to the court or children's panel in certain circumstances, such as child protection or adoption proceedings.[6]

The person holding the records need not tell the applicant that information is withheld. If there was not a good reason for withholding information, the person affected can make a complaint or contact the Information Commissioner for advice.

[1]   Access Modification Order, para 5(1).
[2]   Generally the doctor most recently dealing with this aspect of the patient's care. Access Modification Order, para 2.
[3]   Access Modification Order, para 6(1).
[4]   Data Protection Act 1998, s 7(4).
[5]   DPA 1998, s 7(4)(c).
[6]   Access Modification Order, para 4(2).

Amending records

5.24 If someone considers any information on his or her medical record is incorrect or misleading, the person can ask the record holder to correct or remove the information.

If the person holding the records refuses, the applicant can apply to the Information Commissioner. If the Commissioner disagrees, the person can apply to the court.[1]

There is no compensation for mental distress caused by inaccurate records, but if someone suffers physical or financial damage because a record is inaccurate, he or she can also claim compensation for mental distress.[2]

Compensation may also be available if personal information is lost, damaged, destroyed or given to someone else without proper authority.

[1]   Data Protection Act 1998, s 14.
[2]   DPA 1998, s 13.

Complaints

5.25 The National Health Service complaints procedure deals with complaints under the Data Protection Act. See chapter 50. The Information Commissioner can review the health service's decision. A person can also take legal action.

ACCESS TO MEDICAL REPORTS

5.26 The Access to Medical Reports Act 1988 gives patients the right to see any medical reports prepared by doctors acting for insurance companies or employers (either before employment or through an occupational health scheme).

Access to reports

5.27 If someone wishes to see his or her report, the doctor should deliver it to him or her.[1] The doctor may refuse to deliver the report, or part of it, if he or she considers this would be likely to cause serious harm to the person's physical or mental health.[2]

A doctor can also refuse to hand over information containing information about a third party or which would identify a third party who has given information about the person. This does not apply if the third party is a health professional who has been caring for the person or if the third party consents to disclosure of the information.[3]

[1]   Access to Medical Reports Act 1988, s 4(1).
[2]   AMRA 1988, s 7(1).
[3]   AMRA 1988, s 7(2).

Amending reports

5.28 A person can refuse to allow a doctor to deliver the report to the body which requested it[1] and can ask the doctor to amend any inaccuracies in the report.[2]

If someone believes a doctor has wrongly denied him or her access to medical reports, he or she may take court action.[3]

[1]   Access to Medical Reports Act 1988, s 3(1).
[2]   AMRA 1988, s 5.
[3]   AMRA 1988, s 8.

CONFIDENTIALITY

Source of rules

5.29 A patient is entitled to assume any consultations with a doctor or other medical staff are confidential. Generally they are, but the rules are complex.[1] The law comes from various sources:

- The common law.
- The Data Protection Act 1998. (This largely replaced the Access to Health Records Act 1990, which continues to deal with records of patients who have died. Each institution holding confidential information must appoint a 'data controller' to ensure compliance with the Act and its principles.)
- Article 8 of the European Convention on Human Rights, which provides for respect for an individual's family life and privacy.
- Codes of Practice from the General Medical Council,[2] the Nursing and Midwifery Council,[3] the Health Professions Council[4] and the National Health Service in Scotland.[5]
- Guidance from the Scottish Executive.[6]

The various sources are not necessarily consistent. There have been very few court cases in Scotland looking at the duty of confidentiality in any context. Much of the following relies on cases from England and Wales.

Different rules apply for children and young people and when someone has a mental incapacity. See below.

See 42.05 for sharing information with carers.

[1]   Health Rights Information Scotland has produced patients' leaflets on confidentiality and access to records ('The patients' leaflets').
[2]   *Confidentiality: Protecting and Providing Information*, April 2004. ('The GMC guidance'.)
[3]   *Code of Professional Conduct: standards for performance, conduct and ethics*, July 2004. ('The NMC guidance'.)
[4]   *Standards of conduct, performance and ethics: Your duties as a registrant*, 2003.
[5]   *NHS Code of Practice on protecting patient confidentiality*, Scottish Executive (2003). ('The NHS Code'.)
[6]   Each National Health Service organisation must appoint a 'Caldicott or information guardian' to oversee the rules. *Caldicott guardians in the NHS*, (1999) NHS Scotland MEL 19. The guardian oversees how staff use personal health information and ensures respect for patient confidentiality.

Duty of confidentiality

5.30 The basic rule is that a doctor or health professional must keep information about his or her patient confidential.[1] This duty survives even after the patient has died.[2] Information should not be passed to anyone else without the patient's consent or in other special circumstances.[3]

1   See *A-G v Guardian Newspapers (No 2)* [1990] 1 AC 109. *Lord Advocate v The Scotsman Publications Ltd*, 1989 SC (HL) 122.
2   Access to Health Records Act 1990, s 4(3).
3   *AB v CD* (1851) 14 D 177.

Where breach allowed

5.31 The basic duty of confidentiality is not absolute. Patient information may be disclosed:

- If the person consents.
- To other members of the health team and, with the person's consent, to others in the care team outside the National Health Service.
- To NHS managers for accounting and statistical purposes.
- In anonymous form for research programmes.
- If required by a court or in connection with legal proceedings.
- In the public interest.

Disclosure with person's consent

5.32 A person may agree to have information shared with his or her relative, carer, named person or advocate, or may indeed request this. Provided the health professional is sure that the person has the mental capacity to make such a request, he or she is entitled to share the information with anyone nominated by the person. If necessary, the health professional may require the person to confirm his or her consent in writing.

As well as this kind of *express* consent, the circumstances of the case may *imply* the person's consent. For example, if a person asks a carer or advocate to attend an interview or examination, he or she must intend that they will hear confidential information. If someone agrees to see a consultant, he or she is assumed to have agreed that a secretary may type a referral letter and the GP will give information to the consultant.

Disclosure to health team

5.33 A doctor or health professional may disclose information to other members of the health team and should tell the person about this.[1]

If someone objects to the sharing of information within the team,[2] the doctor or health professional should respect this unless this could risk serious harm or death to others,[3] but should explain the consequences to the person.

[1]   NHS Code, para 5.4.
[2]   Patients' leaflet: *What are my rights?*
[3]   GMC guidance, para 10.

Disclosure to other agencies and carers

5.34 The doctor should obtain the patient's express consent to any sharing of information outside the health team, such as to local authority social work or education departments. It is not possible to imply such consent. It may be necessary occasionally to dispense with consent in the public interest, for example if child protection issues are involved.[1]

It may also be necessary to disclose information to carers, paid and unpaid, to ensure that they are able to care. Such information should be shared on a 'need to know' basis. One of the principles of the Mental Health (Care and Treatment) Act 2003 recognises the importance of providing such information to the carer of the person as he or she might need.[2]

If, for example, a doctor or mental health officer is considering discharging someone, it might be important to tell the carer about the possible side effects of medication or other risk factors, if the person being discharged is not able to monitor these matters him or herself. If the person does not consent to the sharing of such information, those treating him or her may have to consider whether the care options are feasible.

[1]   See below.
[2]   Mental Health (Care and Treatment) (Scotland) Act 2003, s 1(5).

Disclosure within NHS

5.35 Doctors may be required to give information to the National Health Service for the purposes of claiming payment[1] or for audit purposes. All doctors have a duty to participate in clinical audit. Generally such information is anonymous. It may not be possible for a doctor to treat a person who refuses to agree to this.[2]

[1]   This is an example of implied consent to disclosure. A patient must agree that the doctor has to receive payment for his or her work. See *Duncan v Medical Practitioners' Committee* [1986] 1 NZLR 513. (A New Zealand case.)
[2]   GMC guidance, para 14.

Disclosure for research purposes

5.36 No one can become part of a research project without express approval,[1] but information and statistics may be used for public health and research purposes. Such research might relate to the prevalence of a condition in a particular area, for example, or an analysis of the risk factors relating to a certain condition. Such information should be anonymous.[2]

Information which identifies someone should not be disclosed without his or her consent.[3]

[1] See 7.22.
[2] See *R v Department of Health, ex parte Source Informatics Ltd* (1999) 52 BMLR 65 (CA). The Court of Appeal in England held it was not a breach of confidence to hand over information which had been 'acceptably anonymised'.
[3] GMC guidance, para 16.

Disclosures required by law

5.37 The law may require disclosure. A doctor or health professional must disclose information if a judge or sheriff orders this during legal proceedings.

There are other circumstances where a health professional is required by law to divulge information given to him or her in confidence, such as notification of certain communicable diseases. The doctor should tell the person, but consent is not necessary.

A health professional should not disclose personal information to a solicitor, police officer or officer of a court without the person's express consent[1] but in exceptional circumstances he or she may pass on information in the public interest (see below).

[1] GMC Guidance, para 20.

Disclosure in public interest

5.38 There may occasionally be circumstances where it is appropriate for a doctor or health professional to breach patient confidentiality in the public interest. The professional involved, and ultimately the courts, must make a judgement balancing the person's rights to confidentiality with the wider public interest.[1]

Health professionals may breach patient confidentiality to prevent a serious risk to the health or safety of the patient or someone else, to prevent a serious crime being committed or to assist in the investigation of a serious crime.[2]

Any health professional who breaches confidentiality must be prepared to justify this, if necessary to a court. The General Medical Council says the test should be that the benefits to the individual or society of the disclosure outweigh the benefits to the individual and society of keeping the information confidential.[3]

The health professional should try to inform the person and obtain his or her consent to disclosure, if practicable. If the risk is serious, lack of consent is not necessarily crucial.

[1] See *W v Egdell* [1990] 1 All ER 835. W was a restricted patient living in a secure psychiatric hospital in England. Dr E examined him in connection with an appeal against detention. He believed W posed a more serious threat to the public than his doctors realised. W withdrew his appeal, and his doctors did not see Dr E's report. Dr E sent his report to the hospital and the Secretary of State. W sued for breach of confidentiality. The Court of Appeal dismissed his claim. W posed a serious risk to the public. There was a public interest in ensuring that those who cared for him were in full possession of the facts. Even though Dr E obtained the information on a confidential basis, he was entitled to inform the authorities.

[2] See, for example, NHS Code, para 7.5.

[3] GMC guidance, para 22.

Duty of care and confidentiality

5.39 A doctor or health professional might be under a duty to breach confidentiality to protect someone who might be at risk. This could be risk to the person him or herself or risk to others. The law recognises that in certain circumstances the health professional's duty of care to the patient or third person is greater than the duty to respect confidentiality.

The NHS Code of Practice is clear that health professionals have a duty to act to protect people who may be particularly vulnerable. The Code says that if a child or vulnerable adult may be in need of protection or at risk of death or serious harm, professionals should notify the relevant authorities.[1] Any doctor who fails to disclose information where someone may be a victim of neglect or abuse must be prepared to justify this.[2]

There is also clear guidance from the National Health Service in Scotland regarding children and young people at risk. A health professional should establish whether someone has children living in the home and if a professional is concerned about their welfare, he or she must pass on that information. This duty overrides any duty of confidentiality.[3]

In a case in the United States, the courts held a hospital liable when it discharged someone who had told his therapist of his violent intentions towards a woman, whom he later killed. The court said that because of the real risk of danger the person posed, the therapist would have been entitled to reveal this information to the woman, even though he obtained the information in confidence.[4]

[1] NHS Code, para 7.5.
[2] GMC guidance, para 29.
[3] *Sharing information about children at risk of abuse or neglect A guide to good practice,* NHS Scotland. (The local authority has a duty to try to keep families together and to provide services to help the child. See 31.23.)
[4] *Tarasoff v Regents of the University of California* (1976) 131 Cal Rptr 14 (Cal Sup Ct). Perhaps equally interesting is why the doctor discharged him from hospital if he remained a risk to others.

Impact of human rights law

5.40 Human rights law recognises the need to balance respect for confidentiality and the need to protect people who may be at risk.

Article 8 of the European Convention on Human Rights gives a right to privacy. The Article allows interference with that right in the interests of, among other things, the prevention of crime and the protection of the health, rights and freedoms of others.[1] Any such interference must be in accordance with the law and necessary in a democratic society.[2] This means that the steps taken must be proportionate to the risks involved.

Articles 2 and 3 of the European Convention on Human Rights impose positive obligations on the state to act to protect its citizens from the risk of death, assault or other inhumane treatments.[3] If the authorities knew or ought to have known of a real and immediate risk to the life or safety of an identified individual, they should take such measures as they can to avoid that risk.[4] Those measures could include liaising with the relevant bodies and sharing information as appropriate.[5]

Human rights law recognises that professionals must balance the risks and disadvantages of various courses of action. This is very similar to the approach of the General Medical Council and other professional bodies.

1   See *Andersson (Anne-Marie) v Sweden* (1998) 25 EHRR 722, where a psychiatrist contacted child protection authorities against the wishes of his client. The court held the breach of confidentiality was in the child's interests. It was necessary and proportionate, given the risks. Also *TV v Finland* 1994 Application No 21780/93), it was acceptable for prison staff to share information about a prisoner's HIV status. They needed to know this for their own and others' safety.

2   European Convention on Human Rights, Art 8(1). See also *Z v Finland* (1997) 25 EHRR 371 (EctHR), disclosure for the purposes of criminal proceedings justified, and *MS v Sweden* (1997) 45 BMLR 133, disclosure in connection with welfare benefits claim justified.

3   See *X and Y v The Netherlands* [1985] ECHR 4.

4   *Osman v the United Kingdom* [1998] ECHR 101, para 116, risk to life, and *E and others v the United Kingdom* [2002] ECHR 769, para 100, protection against sexual abuse.

5   *E v UK* (above) at para 98.

Adults lacking capacity

5.41 The law recognises that health professionals owe a duty of confidentiality even if someone lacks the capacity to enter into a confidential relationship with them. For example, it would not be appropriate for a doctor to pass on details to the press.[1] It will be appropriate to disclose information only if there are compelling reasons for breaching confidentiality, such as the person's health or welfare.

When someone is unable to consent to treatment, it may be appropriate to discuss relevant issues with family and carers. The Adults with Incapacity Act requires doctors treating someone to have regard to the views of the named person, nearest relative and carers, provided this is reasonable in the circumstances.[2] There may be someone with legal authority to access health information, such as a welfare attorney or guardian.

If someone lacks capacity but is unwilling to have information shared, the doctor should generally try to persuade him or her to involve others. If the person refuses, the doctor may reveal information to others if this is in the person's best interests. The doctor should tell the person, and it may be appropriate to involve a carer or independent advocate.[3]

1   *Re C (a minor) (wardships: medical treatment) (No 2)* [1989] 2 All ER 791 (CA), it
    was not appropriate to disclose details of the treatment of a severely
    handicapped baby.
2   Adults with Incapacity (Scotland) Act 2000, s 1(4).
3   GMC guidance, para 28.

Children and young people

5.42 A child or young person's right to confidentiality depends on the
young person's maturity and ability to take medical decisions.

While a child is growing up, the parents (or people with parental
responsibilities) will need sufficient information to enable them to take
medical decisions on the child's behalf. As the child becomes older, he or
she may wish to consult doctors on a confidential basis. Doctors usually
respect this.

The issues are particularly relevant and difficult where a young
person has a mental illness or learning disability. A young person may
wish to seek help without involving parents. The doctor may consider
the young person is at risk and feel the need to tell the parents.

There are no easy legal or moral answers to these questions, which
remain questions of judgement for the doctor concerned. In the section
below the law and guidance is set out, but it can only form a framework
for decision making in particular circumstances.

There are some useful booklets for children and young people.[1]

1   The Scottish Child Law Centre has a general booklet on confidentiality.
    Healthy Respect, an Edinburgh and Lothian body, has a confidentiality
    leaflet dealing with sexual health but with more general relevance.

Child able to consent to treatment

5.43 If a child is able to consent to treatment,[1] he or she is also likely to be
able to request a health professional to keep medical information
confidential. The doctor will generally respect this, unless there are
issues of risk (see above). If the child's mental health could be putting
him or her at risk, a health professional may wish to discuss the options
with carers.

A doctor should not breach confidentiality unless he or she considers
this is in the best interests of the child.[2]

Some commentators consider that such a breach of confidence should be limited to circumstances where a young person's life is threatened or he or she faces a 'demonstrable risk of serious harm'.[3]

This would be consistent with the guidance from the General Medical Council, which says that confidence can be breached in the public interest if the person, or a third person, is at risk of death or serious harm.[4]

[1]   Within the meaning of the Age of Legal Capacity (Scotland) Act 1991. See chapter 41.
[2]   *Re C (a minor) (evidence: confidential information)* (1991) 7 BMLR 138 CA.
[3]   I Kennedy and A Grubb, *Medical Law* (Butterworths 2000), p 1079 (relying on *Re W (A Minor) (Medical treatment)* [1992] 4 All ER 627).
[4]   GMC guidance, para 27.

Child unable to consent to treatment

5.44 Some children are unable, because of lack of maturity, to consent to medical treatment or to enter into a confidential relationship with doctors. The child's parents, or the person with parental responsibilities, decide about medical treatment. The parent needs such information as necessary to help him or her make such decisions.

A young person who is unable to consent to medical treatment because of a mental disorder may request a doctor to keep the consultation confidential. The General Medical Council advises that the doctor should try to persuade the young person to allow an appropriate person to be involved.

If the young person refuses, the doctor may disclose relevant information to an appropriate person, if he or she considers it essential to do so in the young person's medical interests. The doctor should inform the young person and, if appropriate, should consider involving an independent advocate or carer.[1]

[1]   GMC guidance, para 28.

Where parents are carers

5.45 If a child is at risk, perhaps of suicide or of abuse, and living at home, a doctor or social worker may have to consider whether parents need any information in order to help them care. A parent or guardian is entitled to information in so far, but only in so far, as he or she needs this to perform his or her parental responsibilities.[1]

Most codes of practice recognise that professionals can share information on a 'need to know' basis. Some families and carers claim that this does not extend to informal carers. Health professionals often refuse their need for information on grounds of patient confidentiality.

[1]   Children (Scotland) 1995, ss 1–6.

Advice for professionals

5.46 Decisions about breaching confidentiality are ultimately a question of judgment for the healthcare professional involved. Guidance from a professional body, such as the General Medical Council or the Nursing or Midwifery Council may be necessary. A confidential discussion with the Mental Welfare Commission may also be helpful.[1]

The Data Protection Officer (or Information Guardian of a National Health Service body) may also be able to help.

[1]   See useful practical advice in its Annual Report 2004–5, para 3.6.

Chapter 6

CARE IN HOSPITAL

6.01 This section looks at care in hospital. It is mainly for voluntary patients (sometimes called 'informal' patients). The section on discharge planning is relevant for all patients, including those subject to orders.

Some patients' rights are elsewhere in this book. The right to an advocate is at 4.13. The right to special facilities for mothers and babies is at 37.17. Para 41.26 looks at the need to provide appropriate facilities for young people admitted to psychiatric hospitals

Chapter 37 looks at hospitals' duties to try to meet any special needs of their patients.

PROTECTIONS FOR INFORMAL PATIENTS

6.02 A person entering a psychiatric hospital as a voluntary patient has the same rights and is subject to the same limitations as a patient receiving treatment for a physical disorder. Staff should tell the person about his or her rights in hospital when he or she arrives and will usually give the person a patients' handbook.

The major difference between treatment for physical disorders and mental disorders is that if a voluntary patient decides to leave hospital or refuses treatment, a doctor may use compulsory measures under the Mental Health (Care and Treatment) Act if the person meets the statutory tests for intervention.

This inevitably changes the nature of the doctor/patient relationship. Some people told the Millan Committee they had experienced undue pressure to remain in hospital or to accept treatment. Others may remain in hospital because of the fear of compulsory measures. Some people told the Committee that staff 'threatened' them with compulsory measures to persuade them to stay. Others said they had not realises they were free to go.[1]

The Mental Health (Care and Treatment) Act aims to try to reduce these problems as much as possible, through advocacy and a right to appeal against unlawful detention.

---

[1]   *New directions, para* 12.15–18.

Independent advocacy

6.03 The Millan Committee believed that an independent advocacy worker could be helpful in this situation.[1] An advocacy worker can help someone negotiate with the doctors and ensure that doctors understand and consider the person's views and wishes.

Greater rights to advocacy in the Mental Health (Care and Treatment) Act (see chapter 4) may help people understand their rights and the legal options open to them.

[1]   *New directions,* para 12.19.

Good practice

6.04 If someone does not wish to be in hospital and staff cannot persuade him or her to stay, they should not put the person under undue pressure. The person has more rights if he or she is subject to a Mental Health (Care and Treatment) Act order. Someone subject to compulsory measures can appeal against the order and there are formal reviews of medical treatment. These safeguards are not available to informal patients.

Staff sometimes try to avoid use of compulsory measures to reduce the stigma for the patient. This has to be balanced against the patient's needs for safeguards.

Another concern is that a person subject to compulsory measures is less able to negotiate treatment options with doctors than an informal patient. The Mental Health (Care and Treatment) recognises this. Even if the person is subject to an order, the Act requires respect for the person's wishes and feelings.[1] Doctors have to be able to justify treatment decisions in the light of this principle.

[1]   Mental Health (Care and Treatment) (Scotland) Act 2003, s 1(3)(a).

APPEAL AGAINST UNLAWFUL DETENTION

Background

6.05 The Mental Health (Care and Treatment) Act contains new protections against unlawful detention in hospital. These apply to anyone who considers a hospital is unlawfully detaining him or her.

There are various situations where a person may consider he or she is detained in hospital. Family, friends or health professionals may persuade the person to go to hospital. People may tell the person that if he or she does not go voluntarily, staff will use the compulsory powers of the Mental Health (Care and Treatment) Act. The person's consent to go to hospital may be more illusory than real.

Someone may be admitted to hospital in an emergency and too ill to agree whether to stay or leave. (As in the *Bournewood* case: see 8.04.) A person may be admitted under Adults with Incapacity (Act) provisions. This Act does not allow detention for any longer than is necessary.

While in hospital, a person's movements may be restricted and his or her freedom to come and go limited. A voluntary patient may be cared for on a locked ward in a situation amounting to detention.[1] Staff may tell the person that if he or she attempts to leave, they will use compulsory powers. The person may be able to argue the hospital is detaining him or her within the meaning of the European Convention on Human Rights.

[1]   See discussion in Annual Report of Mental Welfare Commission 1998–9, pp 18–21. The Commission recommends that hospitals review their policies on locked wards and make information available to patients. This will be particularly important in the light of the statutory protection now available to patients.

Appeal rights

6.06 Article 5 of the European Convention on Human Rights says that anyone detained for psychiatric treatment must have a right to appeal against the detention. (See 11.38.) The Mental Health (Care and Treatment) Act now provides that right of appeal.

A person who considers he or she is unlawfully detained can ask the tribunal to review his or her situation. If the tribunal is satisfied that an informal patient in a psychiatric hospital is unlawfully detained, it may make an order requiring the managers of the hospital to stop the unlawful detention.[1] This applies to National Health Service hospitals, independent health care services and the State Hospital (although it is not the practice to admit voluntary patients to the State Hospital).[2]

The hospital must comply with the tribunal's finding. (This does not mean that the person will necessarily leave hospital, as staff may use compulsory measures under the Mental Health (Care and Treatment) Act, but at least the person will have the rights of review and appeal which he or she did not have as an informal patient.)

Any of the following people may refer the matter to the tribunal: the patient, named person, a welfare guardian or attorney, the parent (or person with parental responsibilities) of a child patient, a mental health officer, any other person with an interest in the welfare of the patient (such as an advocate, nurse or carer) and the Mental Welfare Commission.[3]

For tribunal procedure, see Part 4. The tribunal does not provide forms for the application. A suggested form is at Appendix 3, form 3.

[1]   Mental Health (Care and Treatment) (Scotland) Act 2003, s 291.
[2]   MH(CT)(S)A 2003, s 329.
[3]   MH(CT)(S)A 2003, s 291(4).

CHANGING HOSPITAL

6.07 If someone in hospital wishes to move to a different hospital, he or she should discuss this with healthcare staff.

When a patient is from outside Scotland, a doctor may decide to return the person to the country from which he or she came. The doctor should consult the patient, who can appeal to the tribunal. See chapter 19.

VISITS

6.08 It is up to the hospital to decide what visits are appropriate. Most hospitals have regular visiting hours, but a visitor who does not find these convenient should ask if he or she can visit at a different time.

Occasionally staff may recommend that a patient does not receive visits. Potential visitors may ask to discuss this with staff. Hospitals are entitled to refuse access to any visitor, for example, if they are concerned about anti-social behaviour or believe a visitor is bringing illegal drugs/alcohol onto the ward. A visitor can ask the hospital to review the decision to exclude him or her.

Different rules apply to some patients subject to compulsory measures under the Mental Health (Care and Treatment) Act. See chapter 18.

MONEY IN HOSPITAL

6.09 Some people in hospital may qualify for welfare benefits, such as help from the Social Fund or a crisis loan. Others will not. For example, a crisis loan is not available to detained patients. If someone admitted to a psychiatric hospital has no money for occasional personal expenses, the hospital can make payments to him or her.[1] The hospital administers the scheme on behalf of central government.[2]

This can be an important provision where someone is away from home or otherwise unable to access money. Not all hospitals appear to be aware of this scheme.[10] It applies to National Health Service hospitals, including the State Hospital, which has established a fund for patients who would otherwise be without resources. Other hospitals need to do the same.

1   Mental Health (Care and Treatment) Act 2003, s 288.
2   MH(CT)(S)A 2003, s 288(4).
3   The author has had dealings with one hospital which denied all knowledge of the scheme.

PROTECTING POSSESSIONS

6.10 Whenever someone is admitted to a general or psychiatric hospital, the local authority must do what is reasonable to protect his or her possessions if no one else can do this.[1]

This duty extends to personal possessions, including pets. The local authority can enter the person's home, remove any possessions and put them in storage.[2] The local authority may recover its costs from the person. It does not have a duty to ensure the person's home is secure.

A mental health officer can offer advice.

1   National Assistance Act 1948 (as amended by the Local Government etc. (Scotland) Act 1994), s 48.
2   NAA 1948, s 48(2).

DISCHARGE FROM HOSPITAL

Discharge planning

6.11 Discharge planning for patients leaving acute psychiatric care is often inadequate.[1] Yet there is evidence that this is when people are most at risk.[2]

When someone on a Mental Health (Care and Treatment) Act order leaves hospital, those involved must consider his or her continuing care needs.[3]

1   See Simons, Petch and Richard, 'Don't they call it seamless care? A study of acute psychiatric discharge' Scottish Executive Social Research (26/2002).
2   See Stark, Hall, O'Brien and Smith, 'Suicide after discharge from psychiatric hospitals in Scotland' (1995) BMJ 311:1368–1369.
3   Mental Health (Care and Treatment) (Scotland) Act 2003, s 1(6).

Care programme approach

6.12 The care programme approach aims to ensure that people with long-term and complex mental health needs receive on-going care and supervision.

People with 'severe and enduring' mental illness (including dementia) who also have complex health and social care needs should have their on-going needs considered under the care programme approach.

All local authorities and health boards should have established the care programme approach in their areas.[1] A hospital should not discharge a person subject to the care programme approach until the health board has formally notified the local authority of their intentions, and the local authority has arranged to assess the person's needs for social care support and accommodation. Scottish Executive guidance requires the assessment to be a single shared assessment involving all relevant agencies.[2]

A hospital should not discharge the person until a suitable package of health, social care and accommodation is available in the community. The local authority must provide adequate funds for such care.

[1] See *Community Care: Care Programme Approach For People With Severe And Enduring Mental Illness Including Dementia*, Scottish Office Circular No 16/1996.

[2] *Guidance on single shared assessment of community care needs*, Scottish Executive Health Department circular CCD 8/2001 Annex, p 15, para 21.

Care for older people

6.13 The Scottish Executive has produced special guidance about discharging frail elderly patients.

A hospital should not discharge a patient unless it is satisfied the person will have adequate care in the community.[1] All hospitals should have discharge protocols to ensure that they consider people's needs before they leave hospital.[2]

[1] *Community care needs of frail elderly people*, Social Work Services Group circular SWSG 10/98.

[2] *Framework for the production of joint hospital discharge protocols*, Scottish Executive Health Department circular CCD 9/2003.

Continuing care

6.14 Because National Health Service care is free and most social and residential care is subject to charges, there is pressure on the NHS to ensure that people leave hospital as quickly as possible. Central government guidance spells out where the responsibility of the NHS lies.

The guidance says that the National Health Service should remain responsible for people who need 'continuing care'. This could be because of the complexity of a person's medical needs or the unpredictability of his or her illness.

A consultant should always take the decision to discharge a patient. The consultant should discuss the person's care needs with the local authority, relatives and carers.

Appeal against discharge

6.15 If a patient, carer or relative believes a patient should remain under the care of the National Health Service, any of them may appeal against discharge.

A doctor from another health board area can be involved if the patient is unhappy with the outcome of the review.[1] The hospital should give advice about how to appeal, including advice on independent advocacy. Advocacy services should be available to patients with mental disorders.[2] The patient, his or her carer, relative or advocate may make the appeal.

The appeal is to the Director of Public Health and should be made within 10 days of the notice of discharge. The patient remains in hospital while the appeal is outstanding. The person can make a further appeal to an independent consultant from another health board.

The use of the appeal system does not stop a patient from making a complaint if he or she remains unhappy about a decision to discharge him or her from hospital.

Cases have also gone to court[3] and to the health ombudsman (now the Public Services Ombudsman).[4]

[1] *NHS responsibility for continuing care,* NHS (MEL) 1996 22, reproduced in Scottish Executive Health Department circular CCD 8/2003 *Choice of accommodation: discharge from hospital.*

[2] Mental Health (Care and Treatment) (Scotland) Act 2003, s 259.

[3] See, for example *R v North and East Devon Health Authority, ex parte Coughlan* [2001] QB 213.

4 In February 2003, the Health Ombudsman reported four cases where he held that local authorities in England and Wales had incorrectly refused continuing NHS care to elderly disabled patients. He ordered the health authorities to pay compensation to the families of the patients (all of whom had since died).

Choice of accommodation

6.16 A person leaving hospital for residential care or supported accommodation arranged by the local authority has a choice of accommodation.[1] Guidance from the Scottish Executive explains the duties of local authorities and the National Health Service.[2]

1 Social Work (Scotland) Act 1968 (Choice of accommodation) Directions 1993.
2 *Choice of accommodation: discharge from hospital*, Scottish Executive Health Department circular CCD8/2003.

Chapter 7

CONSENT TO TREATMENT

7.01 This chapter looks at people's rights to accept and refuse medical treatment.[1] A person can accept or refuse treatment if he or she has the legal capacity to do so. This chapter looks at capacity. The following chapter looks at legal mechanisms introduced by Adults with Incapacity Act when someone lacks capacity.

This chapter does not cover issues relating to children and young people and medical consent. They are covered in chapter 41.

[1] For an interesting and readable discussion of some of the issues see Margaret Brazier, *Medicine, patients and the law* (Penguin Books 2003), chap 4. Although based on English law, many of the issues are similar.

CAPACITY TO CONSENT

7.02 It is a fundamental principle of the law that a competent person aged over 16 has the right to accept or refuse any treatment recommended by his or her doctors.[1] This remains the case even where the person will die without the treatment.[2] The person does not have to explain the reasons for his or her decision and may decide on rational or irrational grounds.[3] A doctor must respect a patient's decision even if he or she does not approve of it.

A patient's consent gives a doctor authority to act and the doctor will not be liable or require any further authority if he or she acts in accordance with it.[4]

A doctor who treats a capable patient against his or her wishes commits an assault. This could give rise to a claim for damages or even, theoretically, to a criminal prosecution.[5] It could also constitute 'inhuman and degrading treatment' under Article 3 of the European Convention on Human Rights.

[1] See the House of Lords judgment in *Re F (a mental patient: sterilisation)* (1990) 2 AC 1, the Scottish case of *Law Hospital National Health Service Trust v Lord Advocate*, 1996 SLT 848; and the important English case of *Re C (adult: refusal of medical treatment)* [1994] 1 WLR 290.

2   *Re T (adult: refusal of treatment)* [1992] 4 All ER 649 (CA). See also *B v A NHS Trust* [2002] 2 All ER 449, where a woman who was paralysed asked the court for permission to have her ventilator turned off. The court said the case should not have been necessary. She was mentally competent and entitled to refuse treatment.

3   *Sidaway v Board of Governors of the Bethlem Royal Hospital* [1985] 1 All ER 643 (HL), Lord Templeman.

4   *Law Hospital National Health Service Trust v Lord Advocate*, 1996 SLT 848.

5   *Airedale National Health Service Trust v Bland* [1993] 1 All ER 821 at 881–2.

Establishing consent

7.03 Consent may be express (where someone agrees to treatment verbally or signs a consent form) or implied (for example, if a person rolls up his or her sleeve for an injection).

Consent does not have to be in writing, but hospitals usually require written consent for surgical and other major procedures.

Importance of capacity

7.04 The crucial question is whether a patient has the capacity to consent to or refuse a particular treatment.

When someone has capacity, doctors must respect his or her decisions. If the person refuses consent, the doctor cannot treat him or her (unless the doctor considers there are grounds for using the Mental Health (Care and Treatment) Act). Even then, if the person has legal capacity and refuses treatment for a physical disorder, the doctor cannot give such treatment.

When a person lacks capacity, the doctor cannot rely on the person's consent, even if the person appears to give it. The doctor may use the Adults with Incapacity Act to authorise treatment or may consider whether the Mental Health (Care and Treatment) Act is appropriate.

Assessing capacity

7.05 In many cases it will be clear whether a person can consent to treatment. A doctor is entitled to assume someone is capable, unless he or she is aware of some reason why it is not possible to rely on the presumption.[1]

It is very important to stress that a diagnosis of mental disorder does not automatically mean someone is unable to take medical decisions.[2] Most people retain capacity to take medical decisions.

Some people, with fluctuating conditions, may be unable to take medical decisions at some times. (See below.) Some people can take some decisions and not others, and some people, with severe, progressive disabilities, may be unable to take any decisions.

A person may lose capacity temporarily, due to unconsciousness, panic,[3] pain[4] or the effects of legal or illegal drugs.

A doctor assessing someone's capacity must weigh up whether the person is able to take a particular decision at a particular time.[5] There is no 'all or nothing' test of incapacity.

1   *Lindsay v Watson* (1843) 5D 1194.
2   See Adults with Incapacity (Scotland) Act: *Code of Practice for persons authorised to carry out medical treatment or research under Part 5 of the Act*, Scottish Executive (2002) ('The Part 5 Code of Practice'), para 2.41.
3   As of the woman with 'needle phobia' who refused consent to an anaesthetic in childbirth. The court overruled her refusal because her fear had taken over and she was not capable of taking the decision. *Re L (an adult: non-consensual treatment)* [1997] 1 FCR 609.
4   An argument used too frequently in England in the 1990s to overrule the wishes of mothers in childbirth.
5   Adults with Incapacity (Scotland) Act 2000, s 47(1).

Role of doctor

7.06 Whether a person has capacity to consent to medical treatment is a legal question, which is ultimately a matter for the courts.[1] The courts rely on medical evidence.

The decision about capacity is not necessarily a highly technical one, requiring input from specialist psychiatrists or psychologists. General practitioners should be able to assess capacity as part of their general medical training.[2] In a complex case, a report from a consultant psychiatrist or clinical psychologist may be necessary.

There is some discussion on good practice in the Adults with Incapacity Act Code of Practice.[3] There is guidance on the Scottish Executive's Adults with Incapacity website.[4] The Mental Welfare Commission is developing a very useful guide.[5] Some doctors use a tool developed by American psychiatrists: the MacArthur Competence Assessment Tool.[6]

1   For example, under s 14 Adults with Incapacity (Scotland) Act 2000, any person in respect of whom a doctor has issued a certificate of incapacity may appeal that finding to the sheriff court.
2   See *Medical treatment for adults with incapacity: guidance on ethical & medico-legal issues in Scotland* (2nd edn, British Medical Association, October 2002). Available at www.bma.org.uk.
3   Part 5 Code of Practice, paras 2.40–2.47.
4   *Guidelines on the Assessment of Capacity,* Highland Council and Highland Health Board (January 2006).
5   *Consent to treatment: Mental health and the law: A guide for mental health practitioners,* Mental Welfare Commission draft document (April 2006).
6   P Grisso and PS Appelbaum, *Assessing competence to consent to treatment: A guide for physicians and other health professionals* (New York, Oxford University Press, 1998).

Factors in assessing capacity

7.07 Most of the case law comes from England and Wales. There is no reason to think the law in Scotland would be different. Guidance from the British Medical Association appears to rely heavily on English and Welsh cases.[1]

The Adults with Incapacity Act deals with the effects of incapacity. A person may be incapable of taking a decision if a mental disorder means he or she is incapable of acting, making or communicating the decision, or cannot understand or remember a decision.[2] The Adults with Incapacity Act does not deal with assessing capacity. We have to look to the common law.

The Mental Capacity Act 2005 for England and Wales gives a more detailed description, largely based on the common law. A person is treated as unable to make a decision if he or she is unable to understand the information relevant to the decision, to remember the information, to use or weigh the information to make the decision, or to communicate his or her decision (by talking, using sign language or any other means).

The Mental Capacity Act says it is sufficient if someone can understand an explanation given in an appropriate way (using simple language, visual aids or any other means of communication). The person must be able to understand the reasonably foreseeable consequences of deciding one way or another and what happens if he or she fails to make a decision.[3]

This definition provides a useful template for analysing the elements of medical decision-making.

1   *Medical Treatment for Adults with Incapacity: Guidance on Ethical & Medico-Legal Issues in Scotland,* British Medical Association (above).
2   Adults with Incapacity (Scotland) Act 2000, s 1(6).
3   Mental Capacity Act 2005, s 3.

Ability to understand treatment

7.08 A person is able to understand treatment if he or she can understand the nature, purpose and likely effects of the treatment and the risks associated with not having the treatment.[1]

The Adults with Incapacity Code of Practice says this means the person should be able to understand the nature of what is being asked and why, understand that the information is of personal relevance to him or her, understand the alternatives, understand that he or she can refuse, and understand the consequences of refusal.[2]

Some commentators have suggested that the test should be the person's *ability* to understand the treatment, not whether he or she does, in fact, understand it. Otherwise a doctor who is poor at explanations might find that he or she has a disproportionate number of incapable patients.[3]

The person needs to understand only the broad purpose and effects of the treatment, and the risks of not having the treatment.[4] To set too high a threshold of understanding would deprive too many people of autonomy.

A person may be able to understand certain routine procedures but not able to weigh up the risks and potential benefits of complex surgery or procedures, for example. The Adults with Incapacity Act principles suggest that staff should assist the person to make as many medical decisions as he or she can, even if more complex matters are decided elsewhere.

The courts have required a higher degree of understanding to refuse medical advice, particularly when someone's life is at risk.[5]

1   See *Re MB (an adult: medical treatment)* (1997) 38 BMLR 175 CA.
2   Part 5 Code of Practice, para 1.6.
3   In borderline cases, the doctor may assess actual knowledge, so this distinction may not be important in practice. See discussion in I Kennedy and A Grubb, *Medical Law* (3rd edn, Butterworths, 2000), pp 615–7.
4   *Sidaway v Board of Governors of the Bethlem Royal Hospital* [1984] QB 493.
5   *Re T (adult: refusal of medical treatment)* (1992) 9 BMLR 46.

Memory of decision

7.09 The Adults with Incapacity Act says a person may be unable to take a decision if he or she is unable to remember the decision. The Mental Capacity Act says that if someone can remember something only for a short period, that should not mean he or she is unable to take the decision.

Poor short-term memory does not necessarily mean that someone is unable to make a decision, although it may mean that a person cannot retain the information long enough to make a decision.

People working with people with dementia sometimes use consistency of decision-making as a tool for assessing capacity. The person may not remember the question, but if he or she always gives the same answer, it is reasonable to respect this.[1]

[1]   See Ward, *Adult Incapacity*, para 4.27.

Ability to weigh up information

7.10 A mental disorder may mean someone is unable to weigh up the information he or she receives. This may be from intellectual impairment, but it could also be the effects of a mental illness such as anorexia nervosa.

Sometimes a patient will not believe what the doctors tell him or her.[1] Sometimes the person might be able to understand what the doctor says but the illness might cause him or her to twist or distort information or ignore those parts which do not suit him or her.[2]

Such a person could not be said truly to be able to 'weigh up the information' about the proposed treatment.

[1]   *Re KB (adult) (mental patient: medical treatment)* (1994) BMLR 144. See also *Tameside and Glossop Acute Services Trust v CH* [1996] 1 FLR 762. The patient had a diagnosis of paranoid schizophrenia. She believed that doctors were trying to harm her. Her reasons were the result of distorted thinking because of her mental disorder. The court decided she did not have capacity.

[2]   See, for example, *Re C (A minor) (detention for medical treatment)* [1997] 2 FLR 180 (Fam Div).

Making a free choice

7.11 The law recognises that mental disorders may affect more than intellectual functioning. A competency test should reflect more than just the ability to understand and retain information and weigh up the risks.

Issues have particularly arisen when people with eating disorders have refused treatment. The person may understand the information from doctors, but may not truly be able to take the decision.

A doctor may use the Mental Health (Care and Treatment) Act to treat someone with anorexia who refuses treatment,[1] but sometimes doctors are reluctant to do so. This has given the courts an opportunity to consider the legal and ethical basis for overruling patients' decisions.

One of the ways in which the law has attempted to deal with these issues is to say that a person with a condition such as anorexia may not be able to make a true choice.

> '...It is a feature of anorexia nervosa that it is capable of destroying the ability to make an informed choice. It creates a compulsion to refuse treatment or only to accept treatment which is likely to be ineffective. This attitude is part and parcel of the disease and the more advanced the illness, the more compelling it may become.'[2]

In this case, the young woman was clearly able to understand what the doctors were telling her, but the court said she was not competent to decide about the treatment. She was not a free agent because of the effects of her illness.

The courts took a similar decision in another case, concerning a young woman with a personality disorder. The court said doctors should treat her despite her express refusal.[3] The judge said that:

> '[s]he could not be said to be capable of aiming a true choice as to whether or not to eat....she was crying inside for help but unable to break out of the routine of punishing herself.'

An obsessive-compulsive disorder or depression may make it difficult for someone to make a free choice. This test could also be relevant where a person is unduly suggestible, either because of a mental illness or learning disability or, for example, because of pain or stress.[4]

[1]   *South West Hertfordshire Health Authority v KB* [1994] 2 FCR 1051.
[2]   Lord Donaldson in *Re W (a minor) (medical treatment)* [1992] 4 All ER 627.
[3]   *B v Croydon Health Authority* (1992) 22 BMLR 13 (CA).
[4]   As in *Re T* above.

Inability to communicate decision

7.12 A patient may be unable to communicate a decision because of a mental disorder or because of a physical disorder, such as a stroke. The law may regard the person as incapable of taking the decision.

The Adults with Incapacity Act says a person is not incapable if he or she can communicate with help. Help could be from, for example, interpretation services, independent advocacy, technological devices[1] or involving a speech or language therapist or a psychologist.[2] See maximising capacity at 24.16.

1   Adults with Incapacity (Scotland) Act 2000, s 1(6).
2   Part 5 Code of Practice, para 1.7.

The test in practice

7.13 One of the most important cases examining medical decision-making was that of C, a patient in a special hospital in England.[1]

C had a diagnosis of schizophrenia and required surgery to amputate a gangrenous leg. The doctors believed that if he did not have the surgery he would die. C rejected the treatment.

The court held that, although C's general capacity was impaired by his schizophrenia, he was able to make a decision about treatment. He understood the nature, purpose and effects of the proposed treatment and was able to retain this information. He believed it, 'in his own way' and was able to weigh up the information to make a true choice.

1   *Re C (adult: refusal of treatment)* [1994] 1 All ER 810 (Fam Div).

Irrational decisions

7.14 C's decision appeared irrational. It seemed to disregard the medical evidence. This did not mean it was invalid. A competent patient may refuse treatment for reasons which are 'rational, irrational, unknown or even non-existent'.[1]

If the person is competent, the doctors cannot challenge his or her decision because they do not agree with it,[2] even if the outcome will be the death of the person or of her unborn child.[3]

An irrational decision may be *evidence* of a mental disorder. This may lead to an assessment that the person lacks capacity.

1   *Sidaway v Board of Governors of the Bethlem Royal Hospital* [1985] 1 All ER 643 (HL), Lord Templeman. *Re T (adult: refusal of treatment)* [1992] 4 All ER 649 at 652–3.
2   See, for example, *St George's Healthcare National Health Service Trust v S* (1998) 44 BMLR 160, where no-one, even apparently the woman herself, could understand why she was refusing treatment which could put both her own

and her unborn child's life at risk. The court held that there was no evidence that Ms S had any mental disorder and that the hospital must respect her refusal.

3   *Re MB (an adult: medical treatment)* (1997) 38 BMLR 175 (CA).

Fluctuating conditions

7.15 Particular difficulties arise if a person's health fluctuates, with periods of capacity and periods of apparent incapacity. When the person is able to take treatment decisions, these should be respected.

The situation is more complex if, when the person is free from symptoms, he or she denies that he or she has an illness. One of the leading authorities suggests that such a person does not understand the true situation and may not be competent to take a decision.[1]

While a person who lacks 'insight' into his or her condition may not be competent to take decisions, this is not the case if someone knows he or she has an illness but refuses treatment.

If the person is competent, a doctor should respect his or her wishes, even if he or she disagrees with the outcome. A person may have many reasons for refusing treatment, such as dislike of the side effects. In any event, as we have seen, a competent patient does not have to explain his or her reasons to the doctors.

1   See Kennedy and Grubb, *Medical Law* (3rd edn, Butterworths, 2000), p 634. This approach was adopted toward the young patient in *Re R (A minor) (Wardship: consent to treatment)* [1992] Fam 11, R had lucid intervals but when well denied her history of psychotic episodes and suicide attempts. The court said that she was not competent to take her own medical decisions.

INFORMATION TO PATIENTS

7.16 It is often said that consent will not be valid unless it is 'informed consent'. This concept is not, strictly, correct. If the patient receives information in broad terms about the proposed treatment his or her consent, inadequate information will not invalidate consent.[1]

The doctor owes a duty of care to his or her patients. Giving adequate information is part of that duty of care. Breach of the duty may give rise to a claim in negligence.[2] See chapter 51 for negligence.

1   *Chatterton v Gerson* [1981] QB 432; *Hills v Potter* [1983] 3 All ER 716; *Sidaway v Royal Bethlem Hospital* [1984] 1 All ER 1081. The judge in the House of Lords said only fraud or misrepresentation as to the nature of the treatment would invalidate consent.

2   See *Goorkani v Tayside Health Board*, 1991 SLT 94. A doctor who did not warn a patient of the risk of infertility had failed in his duty of care to the patient and the health board had to pay damages.

The 'reasonable doctor' test

7.17 The courts have had to deal with complex questions concerning the amount of information a doctor should give.

For many years the courts took a somewhat paternalistic view, following a 1985 House of Lords case.[1] The court said the amount of information a doctor should give a person in any particular circumstance was a question for the clinical judgement of the doctor at the time. This was sometimes called the 'reasonable doctor' test.

> 'Whenever the occasion arises for the doctor to tell the person the results of the doctor's diagnosis, the possible methods of treatment and the advantages and disadvantages of the recommended treatment, the doctor must decide in the light of his [or her] training and experience and in the light of his [or her] knowledge of the person what should be said and how it should be said.'[2]

If the doctor's action was in accordance with the standards generally recognised in the profession, there would be no breach of care.[3]

1   *Sidaway v Board of Governors of the Bethlem Royal Hospital* [1985] AC 871, Mrs S's doctor failed to tell her that a proposed operation carried a one to two per cent risk of damage to her spine. Mrs S was injured, but the House of Lords said that the doctor had acted in accordance with established medical practice and the hospital should not be liable.
2   Lord Templeman in *Sidaway* (above).
3   *Sidaway* was followed in Scotland in *Moyes v Lothian Health Board* [1990] 1 Med LR 463 (Court of Session (Outer House)).

The 'reasonable patient' test

7.18 In a later case, the House of Lords reconsidered the standard of medical negligence.[1] Medical standards, even if agreed by the majority of the profession, must be reasonable, responsible and defensible logically.

Following this judgement, the Court of Appeal in England said in an important case[2] that 'if there is a significant risk which would affect the judgement of a reasonable person, then in the normal course it is the responsibility of the doctor to inform the person of that significant risk.'[3]

This judgement stresses that it is the function of the courts to satisfy themselves that a doctor has given adequate information. It is not sufficient for the courts to rely on the expert evidence of doctors as to what is good practice in the profession.

This does not detract from the fact that in any individual case, it will still be up to the doctor to make a judgement about what information he or she should give. The doctor's decision will depend on the circumstances of the case, the receptiveness of the person and the doctor's analysis of the risks and benefits of treatment and of possible side effects.

It seems that the law is moving nearer to what some commentators call the 'reasonable patient' test. A health professional should give the information a reasonable patient would require. This reflects current concerns to respect patients' rights and autonomy.

1   *Bolitho v City and Hackney Health Authority* [1997] 4 All ER 771.
2   *Pearce v United Bristol Healthcare National Health Service Trust* (1998) 48 BMLR 118 (CA). See also *Chester v Afshar* [2002] 3 All ER 552 CA. A doctor failed to warn the claimant of the small risk of paralysis. Her claim succeeded even though she could not show that she would not have had the operation if she had known.
3   Lord Woolf.

Guidance to the profession

7.19 The General Medical Council has produced guidance for doctors on the information to give to patients. The current guidance says information may include:

- Details of the diagnosis, the outcome and the likely outcome if the condition is not treated.

- Uncertainties about the diagnosis, including options for further investigation prior to treatment.

- Options for treating or managing the condition, including the option not to treat.

- The purpose of a proposed investigation or treatment; details of the procedures or therapies involved, including treatment such as pain relief; how the person should prepare for the procedure; and details of what the person might experience during or after the procedure including common and serious side effects.

- Explanations of the likely benefits and the probabilities of success; and discussion of any serious or frequently occurring risks, and of any lifestyle changes which may be caused by, or needed by, the treatment.

- Advice if a treatment is experimental.
- How and when staff will monitor or re-assess the person's condition and any side effects.
- The name of the doctor with overall responsibility for the treatment and, if appropriate, the names of the senior members of his or her team.
- If doctors in training or students will be involved.
- A reminder that the patient can change his or her mind about a decision at any time and can seek a second opinion.
- If applicable, details of costs or charges the person may have to meet.[1]

The guidance recognises that it may not be possible to give such full information to every person at every time.[2] Someone is acutely ill, for example, may be unable to take in the information. A doctor should attempt to give the appropriate information when the person is able to understand.[3]

[1] *Seeking patients' consent: the ethical considerations,* General Medical Council (November 1998), ('The GMC ethical guidance'), para 5.
[2] GMC ethical guidance (above), para 4.
[3] GMC ethical guidance, para 13.

Information about side effects

7.20 Patients often complain that doctors do not tell them about possible side effects of the very powerful drugs they may require.

The General Medical Council advises doctors to tell people about 'common and serious side effects' and 'any serious or frequently occurring risks' associated with the treatment.[1]

[1] GMC ethical guidance, para 5.

Withholding information

7.21 Occasionally a doctor may refrain from telling a patient about possible side effects of medication or other treatments because he or she believes the information may distress the person. The person may have little choice about the treatment if he or she is subject to an order under the Mental Health (Care and Treatment) Act, and the doctor may feel it unhelpful to give him or her this information.

The House of Lords has said that a doctor may withhold information, including information about material risks associated with the treatment, if he or she believes that to pass on the information would be harmful to the person's mental or physical health.[1] The General Medical Council accepts this.[2] The doctor must have a good reason for this belief and must be able to justify the decision.

People should generally receive information about the purpose of treatment and any likely side effects. The fact that someone is subject to a compulsory order does not reduce his or her right to information.

The Mental Health (Care and Treatment) Act Code of Practice is clear that people subject to compulsory orders should receive information about the aims and effects of treatment.[3] Clinical Standards (see chapter 49) reinforce this. The standards for schizophrenia stress that people taking anti-psychotic drugs should have information about the effects of the drugs and of side effects, both when the drug is first prescribed and if it is discontinued.[4]

[1]   Lord Scarman in *Sidaway* (above).
[2]   GMC ethical guidance, para 10.
[3]   Code of Practice, vol 1, para 10.02.
[4]   Standard 8.4.

CONSENT TO RESEARCH

7.22 There are ethical guidelines governing the authorisation of research programmes in the National Health Service in Scotland. These are also international agreements, such as the Helsinki Declaration[1] and legislation from Europe.[2]

All National Health Service research requires the approval of local ethics committees. These independent committees check that research proposals comply with recognised ethical standards.[3]

The general rule is that no one may be involved in a research programme without his or her consent. The Adults with Incapacity Act authorises research in certain circumstances. See chapter 8.

[1]   Declaration of Helsinki of the World Medical Association 1964 (as amended).
[2]   Such as EC Directive 2001/20, concerning good clinical practice in the conduct of clinical trials on medicinal products for human use.
[3]   See Scottish Office circular National Health Service MEL 1992(GEN) 3.

Obtaining consent

7.23 If a health professional wishes to involve someone in a research project (other than research involving statistics and health patterns), he or she should seek the person's consent. The health professional should give the person as much information about the research programme as possible.

The General Medical Council advises that it is particularly important to take care when requesting the consent of a person who may be vulnerable because of a disorder or infirmity.[1] It might be helpful to obtain the services of an advocacy worker.

[1] GMC ethical guidance, above, para 37.

Chapter 8

PATIENTS UNABLE TO CONSENT

8.01 We saw in chapter 7 that doctors' authority to treat patients usually comes from the patients' consent. This chapter looks at doctors' authority to treat people unable to consent.

The common law allows a doctor to treat a patient in an emergency. The Adults with Incapacity Act contains a range of provisions allowing treatment in other circumstances.

The final part of this chapter looks at withdrawal of medical treatment and medical research where the person is unable to consent.

This chapter deals with adults. For children and young people, see chapter 41.

For the relationship between incapacity law and the Mental Health (Care and Treatment) Act, see chapter 24.

TREATMENT IN EMERGENCIES

Common law

8.02 In an emergency a patient may be unable to consent to treatment because he or she is unconscious, in pain or because of the effect of drink or drugs. The doctor has a common law power under the law of 'necessity' to treat the person,[1] unless he or she knows of any reason why this common law authority should not apply, such as a valid advance refusal.[2]

A doctor can do what is reasonably required in the person's best interests until the person is able to take treatment decisions.[3] Treatment is in someone's best interests if it is immediately required to save the person's life or to improve or stop deterioration in his or her mental or physical health.[4]

The common law authorises treatment only if someone is unable to give consent. If a person can consent and refuses, a doctor must respect the refusal, unless use of the Mental Health (Care and Treatment) Act is appropriate.

The Adults with Incapacity Act and the Mental Health (Care and Treatment) Act also deal with emergency treatment.

1   *Re F (mental patient: sterilisation)* [1990] 4 BMLR 1 (HL), the leading case relating to treatment under English law, but generally taken to reflect the law in Scotland prior to the Adults with Incapacity Act. See Scottish Law Commission, 'Report on Incapable Adults' (1995) SLC 151, para 1.10.

2   The author is not aware of any Scottish cases dealing with the effects of advance refusals in such circumstances. In the Canadian case of *Malette v Shulman* (1988) 63 OR (2D) 243, doctors who treated an unconscious Jehovah's Witness against clear wishes in a written advance statement were held to have assaulted her. There have been concerns in England about the legal authority for treating people who have attempted suicide. In England and Wales doctors may give emergency treatment if there is any doubt as to the person's intentions or capacity when he or she attempted suicide. If the doctor believes an advance directive is valid, he or she should respect it. *Reference guide to consent for examination or treatment*, Department of Health (2001), chap 1, paras 19–20. Available at www.doh.gov.uk/consent. See also *HE v A Hospital NHS Trust* [2003] EWHC 1017 (Fam), [2003] 2. Where life is at stake the evidence must be scrutinised with special care.

3   *Re F* (above), Lord Goff.

4   *Re F* (above), Lord Brandon.

Adults with Incapacity Act

8.03 The Adults with Incapacity Act does not replace the existing law, but supplements it.[1] It does not remove doctors' common law powers to treat someone in an emergency.

Under the Adults with Incapacity Act, certain treatments require special safeguards, such as a second medical opinion or approval of the court. See below. Doctors may give these treatments in an emergency to save someone's life or prevent serious deterioration in a person's medical condition.[2] A doctor giving such treatment must notify the Mental Welfare Commission within seven days.[3]

The Adults with Incapacity Code of Practice gives advice on emergency treatment. It recommends that a doctor use the general authority under the Act (see below) in every case where it is reasonable and practical to do so.

Only if there is too little time to complete the certificates should a doctor rely on common law powers.[4] Once the emergency is over, a doctor should use Adults with Incapacity Act procedures if the patient remains unable to consent.

1   Adults with Incapacity (Scotland) Act 2000, s 47(2).

2   In practice, the only likely treatment is electro-convulsive therapy, which is sometimes required as an emergency and life-saving treatment.

3   Adults with Incapacity (Specified Medical Treatments) (Scotland) Regulations 2002 (SSI 2002/275), (as amended by the Adults with Incapacity (Specified Medical Treatments) (Scotland) Amendment Regulations 2002 (SSI 2002/302)) ('The specified treatments regulations'), reg 5(2).

4   Part 5 Code of Practice, paras 2.4 to 2.6.

Impact of 'Bournewood' case

8.04 This is particularly important after the decision of the European Court of Human Rights in the *Bournewood* case.[1]

An autistic man who was unable to take medical treatment decisions was admitted to hospital in England and kept there without clear legal authority. The court held he was unlawfully deprived of his liberty within Article 5 of the European Convention on Human Rights, even though he did not attempt to leave and appeared 'compliant' with the regime in hospital. (See 9.15 for further discussion of this case.)

Human rights law requires that detention must comply with a procedure established by law. The person detained must have a right of appeal. The law of necessity includes neither.

If a doctor admits someone to hospital without his or her consent and the person is deprived of his or her liberty, as in *Bournewood*, the doctor should obtain proper authority under the Adults with Incapacity Act as quickly as possible. Failure to do so could be a breach of the person's human rights.[2]

1   *HL v UK* [2004] ECtHR 471.

2   The doctor can use the general authority under s 47 of the Act. (See below.)

Mental Health (Care and Treatment) Act

8.05 A doctor can treat a person subject to an order under the Mental Health (Care and Treatment) Act without consent if this is urgently necessary.[1] It is preferable for the doctor to use the Mental Health (Care and Treatment) Act rather than common law powers.[2]

1   Mental Health (Care and Treatment) (Scotland) Act 2003, s 243. (See para 16.28).

2   *B v Forsey* 1998 SLT 572, HL.

TREATMENT UNDER ADULTS WITH INCAPACITY ACT

8.06 The Adults with Incapacity Act contains a hierarchy of measures for the medical treatment of people who are unable to consent. For more detail about the background and procedures, see Part 5 of this book. The Adults with Incapacity Act calls a person unable to take a medical decision an 'adult'. This section does the same.

Principles of Act

8.07 Anyone exercising healthcare functions under the Adults with Incapacity Act must bear in mind the principles of the Act.[1] The principles require a person intervening under the Act to ensure that:

- The action will benefit the adult and there is no reasonable alternative.
- The use of Adults with Incapacity Act powers is the least restrictive option available, consistent with the purpose of the intervention. (For example, a certificate of incapacity should cover only the period the incapacity is likely to last).[2]
- The intervener has taken into account the wishes and feelings, past and present, of the adult as far as it is possible to ascertain them. Interpretation aids, interpreters or signers and/or independent advocacy services may be necessary.
- The intervener has considered the views of the adult's nearest relative, named person, primary carer, and any guardian or attorney.
- Insofar as an adult is able to participate in medical decisions, the intervener has encouraged him or her to do so.

[1] Adults with Incapacity (Scotland) Act 2000 (as amended by the Mental Health (Care and Treatment) (Scotland) Act 2003), s 1.

[2] See Part 5 Code of Practice, para 2.26.2.

General authority to treat

8.08 A doctor or other specified health professional has a general authority to treat someone unable to consent to treatment, provided the doctor or health professional issues the appropriate certificate of incapacity.

If a doctor or health professional considers that someone lacks the capacity to consent to the medical treatment proposed, he or she should issue a certificate in the prescribed form.[1] The form is on the Scottish Executive's Adults with Incapacity website. The certificate can last for up to three years provided the certificate complies with conditions in Regulations.[2]

The other health professionals who can sign certificates are dentists, opticians and registered nurses. Regulations may add to this list.[3]

If an adult's condition or circumstances change after the making of the certificate, the health professional can cancel the certificate and/or issue a new certificate as appropriate.[4]

The certificate authorises the health professional to give whatever medical treatment is reasonable in the circumstances to safeguard or promote the adult's physical or mental health.[5] This covers nurses and other people who carry out the treatment.[6]

The certificate can cover a specific treatment, such as an operation, or a range of treatments as set out in a treatment plan. If someone has a range of predictable healthcare needs, a treatment plan avoids the need for excessive certification.[7]

Any treatments not included in the treatment plan will require a new certificate.

[1]   Adults with Incapacity (Scotland) Act 2000, s 47(1).
[2]   AWI(S)A 2000, as amended, s 47(5).
[3]   AWI(S)A 2000, (as amended by the Smoking, Health and Social Care (Scotland) Act 2005), s 471A. The changes came into effect on 19.12.05.
[4]   AWI(S)A 2000, s 47(6).
[5]   AWI(S)A 2000, s 47(2).
[6]   AWI(S)A 2000, s 47(3).
[7]   For guidance, see Part 5 Code of Practice, paras 2.19–2.26.

Exclusions from general authority

8.09 Certain matters are excluded from the general treatment authority.

Use of force or detention

8.10 The general treatment authority does not authorise a healthcare professional to use force or detention, unless this is immediately necessary and only for as long as necessary in the circumstances.[1] The use of force should be the minimum necessary in the circumstances.[2]

If staff consider someone may need to be restrained or detained more than infrequently, an order under the Mental Health (Care and Treatment) Act or Adults with Incapacity Act may be appropriate.

The Mental Welfare Commission says that staff should seek an order if someone in a locked ward persistently tries to leave.[3] Others would argue that keeping anyone on a locked ward constitutes detention, whether or not he or she tries to leave.[4]

For more discussion about force and restraint, see chapter 9.

[1]   Adults with Incapacity (Scotland) Act 2000, s 47(7)(a).
[2]   Part 5 Code of Practice, para 2.55. This reflects the principles of the Act.
[3]   See *Rights Risks and Limits to Freedom*, (November 2002), the Commission's guide to the use of physical restraints and other limits to freedom. A new edition is in preparation.
[4]   See *Bournewood* above.

Involuntary admission to psychiatric hospital

8.11 The general treatment authority does not allow a health professional to admit someone to hospital for psychiatric treatment against his or her will.[1] Use of the Mental Health (Care and Treatment) Act may be appropriate.

Where a person unable to consent does not appear to resist or object to being admitted to hospital, a doctor can use the general authority. There is no need to obtain any further authorisation. An order is unnecessary and could be in breach of the principle of minimum necessary intervention.

If someone admitted to psychiatric hospital under the Adults with Incapacity Act later objects to or resists treatment, the doctor should use Mental Health (Care and Treatment) Act procedures rather than the Adults with Incapacity Act.[2]

[1]   Adults with Incapacity (Scotland) Act 2000, s 47(7)(b).
[2]   Part 5 Code of Practice, vol 2, para 7.28.

Treatments under Mental Health (Care and Treatment) Act

8.12 If an adult unable to take treatment decisions is subject to compulsory measures under the Mental Health (Care and Treatment) Act, a doctor cannot rely on the general authority to treat his or her mental disorder.[1]

The Adults with Incapacity Act may be relevant if someone subject to an order needs treatment for a physical disorder and is incapable of consenting to such treatment.[2]

1   The Mental Health (Care and Treatment) (Scotland) Act 2003 contains detailed procedures for authorising the treatment of people subject to compulsion who are incapable of taking treatment decisions. See chapter 16. It repealed s 48(1) of the Adults with Incapacity (Scotland) Act 2000.
2   Lack of capacity should not be assumed. See *Re C*, discussed at 7.13.

Where court proceedings

8.13 The general authority does not authorise treatment contrary to a court ruling.[1]

If someone starts legal proceedings concerning medical treatment, doctors should give only life-saving treatment or other treatment needed to prevent a serious deterioration in the adult's condition[2] (unless there is a court order prohibiting even this treatment).[3]

Similarly, if a doctor or health professional is aware of an application for a guardianship or intervention order with medical powers, he or she should give only such life-saving treatment or treatment to prevent serious deterioration.[4]

1   Adults with Incapacity (Scotland) Act 2000, s 47(7).
2   AWI(S)A 2000, s 47(9). The Code of Practice advises that it may be necessary to give routine treatments to prevent a serious deterioration. (Part 5 Code of Practice, para 2.64.)
3   AWI(S)A 2000, s 49(3).
4   AWI(S)A 2000, s 49. (Unless a court order prohibits such treatment. AWI(S)A 2000, s 49(3).)

Treatments subject to special safeguards

8.14 See below. These treatments cannot be given under the general treatment authority.

Where person with decision making powers

8.15 A doctor or healthcare professional cannot rely on the general authority if he or she is aware that there is a welfare attorney/guardian with medical powers or an intervention order relating to medical decisions. See chapter 25.

Treatments requiring special safeguards

8.16 Certain treatments require the approval of a second opinion doctor, appointed by the Mental Welfare Commission. Others require the approval of the Court of Session.

Treatments requiring second opinion

8.17 The doctor must obtain a second opinion from a Mental Welfare Commission appointed doctor before an adult can receive drug treatment for reducing sex drive or electro-convulsive therapy (ECT).

A second opinion is also necessary before an adult, unable to consent to the treatment, can have an abortion[1] or receive any medical treatment likely to lead to sterilisation, even if this is medically necessary.

The doctor giving the second opinion must be satisfied the adult is unable to consent to the treatment and that the treatment is likely to safeguard or promote the adult's physical or mental health.[2] He or she should bear in mind all the principles of the Act, including the past and present wishes of the adult and the views of any other person with an interest.[3]

For special safeguards if the treatment is for young people aged between 16 and 18, see chapter 4.

The second opinion doctor's certificate can last for up to one year.[4] If the health professional wishes to continue treatment after expiry of the certificate, he or she must seek a new certificate.

Despite considerable concerns about inappropriate use of some medications, long-term drug treatment for mental disorder for adults unable to consent to such treatment does not require special safeguards. The Code of Practice advises doctors to review the need for such treatment at the time the doctor renews the certificate of incapacity.[5] See discussion at 38.09.

[1]   The Abortion Act 1967 also applies.
[2]   Specified treatments regulations, reg 2(3).
[3]   Adults with Incapacity (Scotland) Act 2000, s 1(4).
[4]   Specified treatments regulations, para 7(2).
[5]   Part 5 Code of Practice, supplement issued June 2002, para 18.

Treatments requiring Court of Session approval

8.18 Certain serious or irreversible treatments require the approval of the Court of Session.[1] These are sterilisation (other than medically necessary sterilisation), surgical implantation of hormones to reduce sex drive[2] and (under the Mental Health (Care and Treatment) Act) neurosurgery for mental disorder and deep brain stimulation.[3]

The Court of Session must bear in mind the principles of the Act. The Court cannot give its approval unless it is satisfied that the treatment will safeguard or promote the physical or mental health of the adult and that the adult does not oppose or resist it.[4] The Court of Session must allow anyone with an interest in the adult's welfare to make representations.[5]

Similar rules apply under the Mental Health (Care and Treatment) Act for neurosurgery and deep brain stimulation treatments. See chapter 16. The Court of Session will need to consider the principles of that Act.

[1]   Adults with Incapacity (Scotland) Act 2000, s 48(2).
[2]   Specified treatments regulations, reg 3.
[3]   Mental Health (Care and Treatment) (Scotland) Act 2003, s 236. Mental Health (Medical treatment subject to safeguards) (Section 234) (Scotland) Regulations 2005 (SSI 2005/291).
[4]   Specified treatments regulations, reg 3. For discussion of what this means, see Ward, *Adult Incapacity,* paras 14.49–50.
[5]   Specified treatments regulations, para 3(2).

Where adult resists or objects

8.19 The Adults with Incapacity Act authorises doctors to give medical treatment to someone unable to consent to treatment even if the person objects to or resists the treatment.

If the adult requires treatment for a mental disorder, a doctor should consider whether the Mental Health (Care and Treatment) Act might be appropriate.

If someone objects to or resists treatment for a physical disorder, it may be appropriate to consider welfare guardianship, an intervention order or to seek instructions from a sheriff. (See 24.20.)

Where medical decision-maker

8.20 We will see in Part 5 that someone unable to take medical or other decisions may have a welfare attorney with power to take such decisions. A guardianship or intervention order may authorise someone to take medical decisions.

Anyone with concerns about the medical treatment of someone unable to take medical decisions can apply for an intervention or guardianship order. An order will ensure that healthcare staff consider the person's views.

This section looks at how health professionals must consult people authorised to take medical decisions. This section calls these people 'medical decision-makers'.

Limits on powers

8.21 A medical decision-maker may have been appointed by the adult him or herself before the adult lost capacity, or may be appointed by the court. It might be assumed that someone so appointed would be able to accept or refuse treatment for the adult, in the same way that a competent adult can take his or her own medical decisions.

Unfortunately the Scottish Law Commission and the Scottish Parliament were not prepared to give medical decision-makers this authority. The final say (unless there is an appeal to the court) remains with the doctors.

While this does not seem logically defensible, there is no evidence it is causing problems in practice. The Mental Welfare Commission has reported no attempts to challenge doctors' decisions since this part of the Adults with Incapacity Act came into effect.[1]

[1]   See Mental Welfare Commission Annual Report 2004–5, p 28.

Where medical decision-maker appointed

8.22 If a health professional knows an adult has a medical decision-maker, he or she should attempt to obtain the medical decision-maker's consent to the proposed procedure, if this is reasonable and practicable. If the medical decision-maker agrees to the procedure, the doctor may treat the adult or authorise others to do so in accordance with the general treatment authority. A health professional failing to obtain this consent cannot rely on the general treatment authority.[1]

Healthcare professionals should try to establish whether an adult has a medical decision-maker.[2] A decision-maker should advise healthcare professionals of his or her appointment.[3]

Whether it is reasonable and practicable to consult the medical decision-maker depends on the circumstances of the case. If an adult needs treatment urgently and the medical decision-maker is not available in person or on the phone, it might be reasonable to dispense with consent. If a doctor is considering a serious operation in the future, there should be time to contact the medical decision-maker.[4]

1   Adults with Incapacity (Scotland) Act 2000, s 50(2).
2   Part 5 Code of Practice, paras 2.69–70.
3   Code of Practice for people authorised under intervention orders and guardians Scottish Executive (2002), para 3.59.
4   Part 5 Code of Practice, paras 2.70–71.

Where medical-decision maker agrees

8.23 If the medical decision-maker agrees, the doctor or health professional can give the proposed treatment. Anyone with an interest (including the adult) may challenge the treatment decision in the Court of Session.[1]

1   Adults with Incapacity (Scotland) Act 2000, s 50(3).

Where medical-decision maker disagrees

8.24 If a medical decision-maker does not consent to the treatment proposed, the doctor or healthcare professional may accept his or her decision.

If, having considered the principles of the Act, the health professional wishes to proceed with the treatment, he or she must obtain a second opinion from a healthcare professional nominated by the Mental Welfare Commission. The Mental Welfare Commission has compiled a list of healthcare professionals in different specialisms for this purpose.[1]

The nominated healthcare professional will consult the medical decision-maker, and, if reasonable and practicable, someone authorised by him or her, such as an independent doctor.

If the nominated healthcare professional certifies that the treatment is appropriate (bearing in mind the principles of the Act), the adult may receive the treatment even though the medical decision-maker continues to oppose it.[2]

The medical decision-maker and any other person with an interest (including the adult) may appeal to the Court of Session. If the nominated doctor does not approve the treatment, the adult's doctor or anyone with an interest may appeal to the Court of Session.[3]

1   Adults with Incapacity (Scotland) Act 2000, s 50. This list is different from the list of 'designated medical practitioners' the Mental Welfare Commission keeps under s 233 of the 2003 Act. The treatments authorised under the Adults with Incapacity Act could relate to mental or physical health and the Mental Welfare Commission's specialists have a wide range of expertise.

2   AWI(S)A 2000, s 50(5).

3   AWI(S)A 2000, s 50(6).

Appeals about medical treatment

8.25 Anyone with an interest (including the adult him or herself) can appeal to the sheriff against a finding of incapacity.[1]

In addition, an adult or anyone with an interest in his or her welfare can appeal to the sheriff against a treatment decision, and, with the leave of the sheriff, to the Court of Session. In case of dispute where a decision involves a medical decision-maker, the appeal is to the Court of Session.[2]

When a Court of Session case is pending, a doctor can give only such treatment as is necessary to save the adult's life or prevent serious deterioration in his or her condition[3] (unless there is an interdict prohibiting even this treatment).[4] The general treatment authority is suspended.

1   Adults with Incapacity (Scotland) Act 2000, s 14.

2   AWI(S)A 2000, s 52.

3   It would be unfortunate if routine treatments which are not under dispute could not continue while the more serious matter is being resolved. The Code of Practice suggests healthcare professionals seek directions from the court. (Part 5 Code of Practice, para 2.64.)

4   AWI(S)A 2000, ss 50(7) and 50(8).

COVERT MEDICATION

8.26 At the time of writing, the Scottish Parliament is considering a petition seeking safeguards against vulnerable adults receiving covert medication.[1] This is the practice where staff put medicines in food or drinks so that the person does not know he or she is receiving the medication.

A person with legal capacity must never receive medication covertly. This would be an assault, a civil wrong. This does not mean it never happens.[2]

Where someone is unable to consent to treatment, and is likely to resist or object to the treatment, it may be appropriate for a doctor or healthcare professional to give medication covertly in exceptional circumstances.

The British Medical Association recognises that it may sometimes be appropriate to give medicines covertly where this is authorised by law, and as an alternative to giving the treatment by force.[3]

The Mental Welfare Commission has also issued guidance. This says covert medication should be considered only in exceptional circumstances.[4] Any decision to give covert medication requires the authorisation of the doctor who prescribed the treatment. This is a requirement of the Medicines Act.[5] The Mental Welfare Commission is consulting further on good practice.[6]

There is also guidance from the Royal College of Psychiatrists[7] and the Nursing and Midwifery Council.[8] Scottish National Care Standards say that even if the law allows treatment without the person's consent, the person should receive covert medication only if he or she has refused treatment and his or her health is at risk. Any use of covert medication should be recorded.[9]

All the guidance stresses that there must be a clear medical need for the treatment and that the measures must be necessary to avoid significant mental or physical harm to the person. The decision to give covert medication should be discussed within the team and with carers and significant others and recorded. Medication should not be given covertly for the convenience of staff.

The Royal College of Psychiatrists says such treatment can be justified only when there is no likelihood that the person will be able to take treatment decisions. It is not suitable for someone with a mental illness such as schizophrenia.

Giving medicines in a different form may alter its effects and may mean that the use of the medication is unlicenced.[10] A doctor should seek advice from a pharmacist before approving the covert administration of medication. Staff should make regular efforts to persuade the person to accept the medication and staff should regularly review a decision to give covert medication.

[1]   Public Petition PE 867 May 2006.
[2]   A Macdonald and others, 'De facto imprisonment and covert medication use in general nursing homes for older people in South East England' in *Ageing, Clinical and Experimental Research* (2004), 16, 326–330. The research showed that a number of nursing home residents with mild or no cognitive impairment were being given medication surreptitiously. See also A Treloar, B Beats and M Philpot, 'A pill in the sandwich: covert medication in food and drink' (2000) Journal of the Royal Society of Medicine, 93 (8): 408–411. Twenty-four out of 34 residential, nursing, and inpatient units surveyed in

South East England sometimes administered drugs covertly in food and drinks.

3   *Medical ethics today,* British Medical Association (2004).
4   *Rights, risks and limits to freedom,* Mental Welfare Commission (2002), para 8.9.
5   Medicines Act 1968, s 58(2)(b).
6   Letter from Mental Welfare Commission, 7 April 2006.
7   'College Statement on Covert Administration of Medicines' (2004) Psychiatric Bulletin 28: 385–386.
8   *Position statement on the covert administration of medicines* (August 2005).
9   National care standards, care homes for people with mental health problems (March 2005), standard 15.13.
10   Richard Griffith, 'Tablet crushing and the law' (2003) 271 Pharmaceutical Journal.

WITHDRAWING TREATMENT

8.27 The Adults with Incapacity Act does not deal with withdrawing or withholding treatment from someone unable to participate in a treatment decision, but may be relevant when such matters are being considered.[1]

The Scottish Law Commission recommended that the law should clearly state that a doctor can withdraw or withhold treatment if in the doctor's opinion such treatment is unlikely to benefit a person unable to take treatment decisions.[2] The Scottish Executive did not feel the time was right to cover this matter in legislation. It believed the law should develop according to changes in practice and medical ethics.

1   For discussion of the issues, see *Withholding and Withdrawing Life-prolonging Treatments: Good Practice in Decision-making,* General Medical Council (August 2002). (Challenged in *Burke,* below.) A comprehensive guide to good practice is in *Withholding and withdrawing life-prolonging medical treatment: guidance for decision-making* (2nd edn, British Medical Association, 2001).
2   *Report on Incapable Adults,* recommendation 76.

Impact of principles

8.28 The Adults with Incapacity Act imposes no duty on a doctor or health professional to give treatment he or she considers futile or not in an adult's interests.

The first principle of the Adults with Incapacity Act is that no one should intervene under the Act unless he or she is satisfied the intervention will benefit the adult.[1] In establishing benefit the doctor must take into account the views and feelings, past and present, of the adult and the views of relevant others.

A doctor does not have to give treatment which will not benefit the adult. The Code of Practice says there is no 'duty to provide futile treatment or treatment where the burden to the person outweighs the clinical benefit'.[2]

In the leading case in Scotland, concerning the withdrawal of medical treatment from a woman in a persistent vegetative state, the Court of Session said that the common law position was the same.[3] Lord Clyde said that:

> 'it is not part of the duty of the doctors ... to continue a treatment which serves no purpose beyond the artificial prolongation of existence. They would be in no breach of their general duty of care to her to discontinue such treatment in such circumstances...'.[4]

The court said that the question depended on the individual facts of the case and the best interests of the patient, bearing in mind the views of her family and carers.

[1]   Adults with Incapacity (Scotland) Act 2000, s 1(2).
[2]   Part 5 Code of Practice, para 2.62.
[3]   *Law Hospital NHS Trust v Lord Advocate*, 1996 SLT 848.
[4]   At para 861E.

English and human rights cases

8.29 An important case in England has clarified these issues.[1] The Court of Appeal said that decisions about withdrawing and withholding life-saving medical treatment depend on the individual circumstances of the case.

If a competent person requests doctors to continue artificial nutrition and hydration, a doctor should respect this, and should respect any refusal of treatment.

When someone is unable to take a decision and has never indicated whether he or she would wish to be kept alive in such circumstances, doctors must decide what is in the person's best interests. (Or in Scotland, what would benefit the person.) There is a very strong presumption in favour of prolonging life. If life-prolonging treatment is providing some benefit, it should continue.

If prolonging someone's life involves an extreme degree of pain, discomfort or indignity, the doctors may not be obliged to keep the person alive. There may be no duty to keep someone in a persistent vegetative state alive. All depends on the circumstances. It is not possible to attempt to define what is in the best interests of a person by a single test, applicable in all circumstances.

1   *R (Burke) v General Medical Council (Official Solicitor and others intervening)* [2005] EWCA Civ 1003.

Resolving difficult cases

8.30 From time to time difficult medical cases will have to go to court. The appropriate court is the Court of Session in Edinburgh. This has a supervisory role for children and for people with incapacities who are unable to protect their own interests.

The powers stem from the powers of the Crown as 'parent of the country'. In the same way that a parent decides about medical treatment for a child, the Crown had the final authority in questions relating to children and people with incapacities. The Court of Session in Edinburgh now operates these powers.[1]

The Adults with Incapacity Act did not remove the supervisory role of the Court of Session. Sensitive decisions about medical treatment under that Act still go to the Court of Session.

For this reason commentators seem agreed that, where there are disagreements about matters such as the withdrawal of life-saving treatment, and it is not possible to resolve these by negotiation, the appropriate court is the Court of Session.[2]

Failure to involve the court where appropriate may be a breach of the adult's or carer's human rights.[3]

1   Under the Exchequer Court (Scotland) Act 1856.
2   See Adrian Ward, *Adult Incapacity,* para 14.26. Sarah Elliston, 'Medical treatment' in *Butterworths Scottish Older Client Law Service* (Tottel Publishing), Division E, para 561.
3   *Glass v UK* [2004] ECtHR 103, but see comments of Court of Appeal at *Burke* (above).

Authority for research

8.31 Generally, no one can be involved in medical research unless he or she agrees (see chapter 7), but the General Medical Council recognises that there may be situations where it is appropriate to carry out research even where someone is unable to consent.[1] Research into the causes of the person's disability or into new treatments may be in the adult's interests or in the interests of others with similar incapacities.

The Adults with Incapacity Act permits research into the causes, diagnosis, treatment or care of the adult's incapacity or condition[2] only if it is not possible to carry out such research on someone who would be capable of consenting.[3] These rules apply to surgical, medical, nursing, dental or psychological research.

1   *Research: The Role and Responsibilities of Doctors,* General Medical Council (February 2002), para 48.
2   Adults with Incapacity (Scotland) Act 2000, s 50(2).
3   AWI(S)A 2000, s 50(1).

Authorising research

8.32 An independent Ethics Committee must approve the research. The researchers must also obtain the consent of a welfare guardian or attorney with relevant powers or of the nearest relative.[1]

The Ethics Committee must be satisfied that:

- The research is likely to provide a real and direct benefit to the adult, or if not, is likely to make a significant contribution to the understanding of the person's incapacity and provide a real and direct benefit to others with the same incapacity.[2]
- The adult does not seem unwilling to participate.
- The research involves no risk, or only a minimal risk, and no discomfort, or only minimal discomfort.[3]

The Ethics Committee may impose conditions on its approval.[4]

1   Adults with Incapacity (Scotland) Act 2000, s 50(3).
2   AWI(S)A 2000, s 50(4).
3   AWI(S)A 2000, s 50(3).
4   AWI(S)A 2000, s 50(5).

The Ethics Committee

8.33 The Ethics Committee has up to 18 members. If possible, at least one member should have experience of treating adults with incapacities.[1] There are three lay members. Local ethics committees cannot approve research where the participants may be unable to consent.

Before approving any research, the Committee must weigh up, among other things, the risks and inconveniences of the research as against the possible benefit for any adults involved, both during the research and in the future.[2]

The Committee must act in accordance with the principles of the Act.

1   The Adults with Incapacity (Ethics Committee) (Scotland) Regulations 2002 (SSI 2002/190). ('The Ethics Committee regulations'.)
2   Ethics Committee regulations, reg 6.

Chapter 9

RESTRAINT, FORCE AND DETENTION

9.01 This chapter looks at what the law has to say about the use of force, restraint and detention. There may be occasions where staff consider they need to restrain a person or to use force to give certain care or treatment. They need to ensure they are aware of the legal and ethical framework.

The Mental Welfare Commission has produced a code of practice for staff working in hospitals and residential care homes for people with dementia and learning disabilities.[1] This includes a section looking at the legal basis of the use of restraint. The following section is adapted from that document, with the permission of the Mental Welfare Commission.

This chapter uses the term 'restraint' to cover the use (or threatened use) of force to prevent a person doing something or to ensure that someone does something which he or she resists.[2]

The information in this chapter is relevant where people are in hospital and in care homes, day care services and in community settings, including people cared for by informal unpaid carers.

[1]   *Rights, risks and limits to freedom*, Mental Welfare Commission (2002). (New edition expected 2006.)
[2]   This definition is used in the Mental Capacity Act 2005. See, for example, s 6(4).

RESTRAINT AND THE LAW

9.02 The law relating to the use of restraint is largely the common law. See chapter 1. Certain powers may be available under the Adults with Incapacity Act and implied under the Mental Health (Care and Treatment) Act. There are also regulations under the Regulation of Care (Scotland) Act 2001 concerning the use of restraint by care providers. The law is subject to human rights requirements. See below.

The law starts from the premise that it is wrong to restrain the actions of another person without lawful excuse. Under the common law any unlawful restraint is an assault. In certain circumstances it could give rise to criminal liability. Unless a person can justify the use of restraint, he or she could be liable to a civil action for damages or could face a criminal prosecution.

Where restraint justified

Self defence

9.03 The common law recognises that someone may use force or restraint if there is reason to believe another person is about to cause him or her harm.

No more than the minimum necessary force can be used. If the person acts in bad faith or uses more force than is reasonably necessary, his or her action is outside the law.

Necessity

9.04 The common law also allows someone to restrain another person if this is necessary to prevent immediate harm to others or serious damage to property, or to stop someone from committing a crime. This could include stopping someone harming him or herself.

The level of restraint must be reasonable, and the restraint should continue only for as long as is necessary to bring the situation under control. (Any further restraint to punish the person is not justified.)

What is a reasonable or unreasonable length of time depends on the particular circumstances of each case.

In a Scottish case before the House of Lords, the court said the use of such powers in hospital should only be where someone 'is a manifest danger either to himself or to others'. The use of restraint by a private individual should be 'temporary' until the person can be 'handed over to the proper authority'. A doctor or nurse should use the Mental Health (Care and Treatment) Act and not common law powers if restraint could amount to detention.[1]

[1]   *B v Forsey*, 1988 SLT 572, HL.

Duty of care

9.05 If a learning disability, mental illness or personality disorder puts someone at risk, carers may have a legal duty to restrain the person in his or her own interests. Where an individual takes on a caring role, he or she owes a 'duty of care' to the cared-for person. This means that the carer must do what is reasonable to protect the person from reasonably foreseeable harm.

If a person's actions could put other vulnerable people at risk, staff have a duty of care to restrain him or her to protect other people. Hospital managers have health and safety duties to ensure the protection of their staff.[1] As public authorities, they have human rights duties to protect other patients against abuse. See 1.16.

In cases predating the Human Rights Act, the courts in Scotland accepted that nurses have a duty to use reasonable force to 'control' a mentally vulnerable patient, for the person's protection or to protect other patients. The force they use should be the minimum necessary and should not go beyond what is normal or permissible good practice.[2]

[1]   See an analysis of some of the English cases in Andrew Parsons, 'Violent patients: does staff safety trump patient care?' Solicitors Journal, 24 February 2006.
[2]   *Skinner v Robertson*, 1980 SLT (Sh Ct) 43. *Norman v Smith*, 1983 SCCR 100.

Consent

9.06 A person may consent to restraint because he or she understands that he or she is at risk. The consent is valid only if the person is mentally competent to take the decision. It is not valid if the person is put under undue pressure to consent or if the restraint is excessive, cruel, unnatural or unnecessary in the circumstances.

In some cases consent may be *implied*. It may be possible to rely on implied consent if the person has the legal capacity to object, is free to leave and accepts the restraint. Any undue pressure would remove the presumption of implied consent.

No one can consent to the use of restraint on behalf of another person, unless he or she has specific powers to take such a decision under the Adults with Incapacity Act. (See below.)

Safeguards

Restraint must be justified

9.07 Anyone using restraint has to be able to justify it, in a court of law if necessary. On the face of it, restraint is illegal. It is for the person using it to justify both the use of restraint and the way in which he or she used it. This is a requirement of the common law and the European Convention on Human Rights.

If restraint is excessive, unnecessary, degrading or unnatural, the courts are likely to regard it as an assault as well as a breach of human rights. Those involved could face criminal prosecution.

Care standards

9.08 The managers of care services owe a duty of care to residents or patients to ensure that staff operate any restraint properly. This involves having a policy about the use of restraint and the recording of incidents, spelling out in the person's care plan how restraint might be appropriate and ensuring that staff called upon to restrain someone have proper training and qualifications.

Regulations made under the Regulation of Care (Scotland) Act 2001 deal with care providers' use of restraint.[1] These Regulations apply to care home and day care services, but not National Health Service hospitals. The Regulations say clients must be treated with dignity and respect.[2] Restraint is appropriate only in exceptional circumstances, if it is the only practicable means of securing the welfare of the client or of other clients.

Staff must record any use of restraint in the client's personal file. The person providing the care service must keep a record of each occasion on which restraint/control is used, giving details of the form of restraint/ control, the reason it was necessary and the name of the person authorising it.[3]

The National Care Standards similarly state that staff must explain, justify and record any limits on a person's independence in his or her care plan and review the plan regularly.[4] Restraint should be used only as a last resort.[5]

[1] The Regulation of Care (Requirements as to Care Services) (Scotland) Regulations 2002 (SSI 2002/114).
[2] SSI 2002/114, reg 4.
[3] Regulation 19(3).
[4] *National Care Standards: Care homes for people with mental health problems*, Scottish Executive (December 2001) (revised March 2005), care standards 6.2, 17.
[5] Care standard 9.8.

Standards in National Health Service

9.09 Standards in the NHS are matters of 'clinical governance', the responsibility of the health board and hospital management. All hospitals and community health facilities in Scotland should have policies on the use of restraint, covering its use, training of staff, reporting, etc.[1] Research by the Mental Welfare Commission several years ago highlighted some instances where proper policies were not in place.[2] The Commission has also highlighted several areas of concern in practice.[3]

There is detailed good practice guidance for staff in England and Wales,[4] but there does not appear to be anything similar for Scotland.[5] The Mental Welfare Commission has said that advisory standards would help ensure greater consistency in the quality and use of restraint throughout Scotland.[6]

[1]   NHS Scotland, *Managing health at work partnership network guidelines,* Scottish Executive (2004), guideline 6.
[2]   Annual Report of Mental Welfare Commission 1995–6, para 5.1.
[3]   Annual Report of Mental Welfare Commission 2003–4, para 3.5.
[4]   National Institute for Clinical Excellence, *The short-term management of disturbed/violent behaviour in in-patient psychiatric settings and emergency departments* (February 2005).
[5]   The latest guidelines from the Scottish Executive are in *Safe care: consideration of the recommendations from the inquiry (England) into the death of David Bennett,* Scottish Executive Health Department (17 December 2004).
[6]   Annual Report, 2003–4 (above).

Professional standards and guidance

9.10 Most people working in care homes and hospitals are subject to professional standards. Professional standards may cover the use of restraint. Professionals will need to ensure that they can justify any decision to use restraint in the light of their professional and ethical standards.

The Millan Committee recommended that the Mental Welfare Commission give further guidance on the use of restraint in hospitals. The Mental Welfare Commission should also monitor good practice.[1]

[1]   *New directions,* recommendation 12.3.

Limits to common law

9.11 If someone is likely to need restraint on a regular basis as part of a care package, those involved should consider the use of a guardianship order under the Adults with Incapacity Act or a compulsory order under the Mental Health (Care and Treatment) Act. The person should have the rights of appeal to the courts or the Mental Health Tribunal and recourse to Mental Welfare Commission available under those Acts.

The Scottish Law Commission recommended that anyone exercising extensive informal controls over an adult's life on a regular basis should seek an Adults with Incapacity Act order.[1] Regular use of restraint would constitute exercising extensive controls.

If restraint could amount to a deprivation of liberty within human rights law, an order is essential. See below.

[1]   *Report on incapable adults*, para 2.53.

Reporting of incidents

9.12 Any injury caused during the use of restraint should be the subject of a critical incident review locally and should be reported to the Mental Welfare Commission. See chapter 52. Health boards are obliged to report incidents, and a growing number of local authority and voluntary and independent advisers now do so. The Mental Welfare Commission has established a protocol with the Care Commission for reporting incidents.

Each year the Mental Welfare Commission reports a number of injuries caused during the use of restraint. In the ten years to date, it has reported one death.[1] The Mental Welfare Commission investigates any such incidents.

[1]   Mental Welfare Commission Annual Report 2001–2.

Criminal offences

9.13 Both the Adults with Incapacity Act and the Mental Health (Care and Treatment) Act make it a criminal offence for someone carrying out functions under either Act to ill treat or neglect the person.[1]

The Mental Health (Care and Treatment) Act applies wherever someone is caring for a person with a mental illness, learning disability or personality disorder, whether or not the person is subject to an order under the Mental Health (Care and Treatment) Act.

Clearly the improper use of restraint could be ill treatment or neglect.

[1]   Adults with Incapacity (Scotland) Act 2000, s 8. Mental Health (Care and Treatment) (Scotland) Act 2003, s 315.

Human rights safeguards

9.14 Human rights law is likely to become increasingly important in considering matters such as the appropriate use of restraint. This is a matter for the Scottish courts as well as the Court of Human Rights in Strasbourg. See chapter 1.

Article 3 of the European Convention on Human Rights prohibits inhumane and degrading treatment. Poor practice on restraint could fall within this category. If treatment is inhumane and degrading, it is not a defence that it is necessary for the person's protection.

The use of restraint could also be challenged under Article 8, respect for private life. Article 8 permits interference with someone's autonomy if this is lawful and necessary for public safety, the protection of health or the protection of others. Any of these might be a justification for the use of restraint. The person should be told why he or she is being restrained, if possible.

A less known Article of the European Convention on Human Rights gives a right to liberty of movement within a country's boundaries.[1] Restraint could constitute a breach of this right. A person's freedom of movement may be restricted if this in accordance with the law and necessary in the interests of public safety, for the prevention of crime or for the protection of rights and freedoms of others. Restraint would generally be justified on one of those grounds.

Article 8 and protocol 4 allow interference with human rights provided the interference is 'lawful'. The common law can satisfy this requirement, but it must be consistent, clear and accessible.[2] Clear policies, ideally backed up by guidance in relevant Codes of Practice, provide such clarity and consistency. If a public authority has no such policy, this could be open to challenge on human rights grounds. See 9.29 below.

A very important human rights requirement is that any restriction of someone's liberty should be in proportion to the risk posed. Even where restraint is justified, it will be unlawful if the methods used are excessive or if it continues for longer than necessary.

---

[1]   European Convention on Human Rights, Fourth protocol, Art 2.

[2]   See *HL v UK* [2004] ECtHR 471 at para 116. (The *'Bournewood'* case.)

Restraint and detention

9.15 Under Article 5 of the European Convention on Human Rights, restraint constituting 'detention' does not satisfy human rights requirements unless there is legal authority for the detention. Such authority could be under the Mental Health (Care and Treatment) Act or the Adults with Incapacity Act. Reliance on common law powers is unlikely to satisfy the European Convention on Human Rights requirements of due process. See *Bournewood* case above.

The difference between restraint and detention is a matter of degree. There is no difference in the nature or substance of the controls. The law says restraint is a restriction on someone's liberty and detention is deprivation of liberty. Regular and consistent restraint may amount to detention.

Whether someone has been deprived of his or her liberty depends on the specific situation of the individual concerned. The court takes account of a range of factors such as:

- The degree and intensity of the controls over the person's movements.
- For how long these controls are likely to be necessary.
- The intentions of those controlling the person. If the intention is to stop him or her from leaving, there may be a deprivation of liberty even if the person does not attempt to leave or staff persuade him or her not to leave.
- How the controls are used. Physical restraints can amount to detention, as can the use of sedation and observation.
- What access to the outside world the person is likely to have, including access to family and carers.
- Whether the person is likely to attempt to leave. If someone attempts to leave and staff stop him or her, this is likely to be a deprivation of liberty. It is more complex if the person does not attempt to leave or makes an 'uninformed' attempt to leave, perhaps of not understanding where he or she is or where the door leads.
- Whether the cumulative effect of restrictions could amount to detention.[1]

Legal advice may be necessary as to whether arrangements amount to detention. The Mental Welfare Commission may also be able to give advice. Guidance from the Scottish Executive is expected.[2]

Arrangements that involve restraint to a certain degree but aim to give someone the maximum freedom consistent with any limitations because of the person's disability may not constitute a deprivation of liberty. They may be seen as respecting the person's right to life and health.[3] The courts in England have said that restrictions primarily for the benefit of the person, as opposed to protecting the public, might not be deprivations of liberty.[4]

It cannot be assumed that institutional care will always be more restrictive than care in someone's own home. The test is always to look at the individual circumstances of the case. In some cases quite severe restrictions in a person's own home may still give him or her a better quality of life.[5]

[1]   *HL v UK* [2004] ECtHR 471 at para 89.

[2]   *Adults with Incapacity (Scotland) Act 2000: Draft Guidance for Local Authorities on when to invoke the Act,* Scottish Executive (May 2006).

[3]   In commenting the Department of Health consultation on the *Bournewood* judgement, the Royal College of Psychiatrists said that a 'balance needs to be stuck between those articles concerned with the right to liberty, freedom and personal autonomy of a person, on the one hand, and the right to life and therefore access to health care, as and when appropriate, on the other. We do not see these as opposing rights but rather that good health (and access to treatment for mental or physical illnesses) is part of ensuring these other freedoms.'

[4]   *R (Secretary of State for the Home Department) v Mental Health Review Tribunal* [2002] EWCA Civ 1868; *R (G) v Mental Health Review Tribunal* [2004] EWHC 2193. Relying on decisions in *HM v Switzerland* [2002] ECtHR 157 and *Nielson v Denmark* [1988] EHRR 175, where apparent detention was a responsible measure by the competent authorities/person in the applicant's interests. There was no detention in such circumstances.

[5]   See R Robinson and L Scott-Moncrief, 'Making Sense of *Bournewood'* (2005) 5 Journal of Mental Health Law, pp 17–25.

RESTRAINT AND ADULTS WITH INCAPACITY

9.16 This section looks at how the Adults with Incapacity Act affects the law relating to force, restraint and detention.

We have seen that a person exercising informal controls over someone's life on a regular basis should consider whether it is appropriate to apply for a Part 6 order. In reaching a decision, the carer should consider the principles of the Act.

Importance of principles

9.17 The Adults with Incapacity Act principles are an important safeguard in considering the appropriate use of restraint. A court giving a guardian powers to restrain an adult must consider (among other things) whether the restraint will benefit the adult and whether it is the least restrictive alternative.

Anyone using his or her authority under the Act to restrain someone must consider the principles. This means considering whether a less restrictive alternative would suffice and whether there is an alternative, such as changes in the regime.

Medical treatment

9.18 If someone is incapable of taking medical decisions, the doctor or health professional treating him or her will have a general authority to do what is reasonable to safeguard or promote the adult's mental or physical health if he or she signs the necessary certificate of incapacity.

The health professional cannot use force or detention unless this is immediately necessary and only for so long as necessary.[1] This should be a temporary measure.[2] If ongoing restraint or detention is appropriate, the person should consider seeking an order under Part 6 of the Adults with Incapacity Act or the Mental Health (Care and Treatment) Act.[3]

A health professional with general authority under the Adults with Incapacity Act can give medical treatment to an adult unable to consent to treatment even if the adult objects to or resists the treatment. If the adult is likely to object on an ongoing basis, the health professional should consider an Adults with Incapacity Act or Mental Health (Care and Treatment) Act order and may wish to seek instructions from a sheriff. See 24.20.

[1] Adults with Incapacity (Scotland) Act 2000, s 47(7).

[2] See *Report on Incapable Adults*, Scottish Law Commission, para 5.31.

[3] The Part 5 Code of Practice mentions the possibility of Mental Health (Care and Treatment) Act orders, but not guardianship orders in this situation (para 2.55). A local authority has duties to apply for an order if needed to protect the adult's interests. Adults with Incapacity (Scotland) Act 2000, s 57(2).

Restraint and guardians

9.19 It is perhaps unfortunate that the Adults with Incapacity Act is not clear how far it is appropriate for a welfare guardian to use force, restraint or detention if the adult does not comply with the guardian's instructions. This contrasts with the Mental Capacity Act for England and Wales, which clearly limits the circumstances in which a guardian (called a 'deputy') can use force or restraint.[1]

A doctor acting under the general authority cannot use force or detention, but there is no such limitation on guardians. Instead the Adults with Incapacity Act gives a guardian specific powers if the adult does not comply with his or her instructions.

The guardian can arrange for the return of the adult to the place where he or she is required to live and can seek a court order requiring the adult to comply with the guardian's decisions.[2] If the adult does not return, a police officer may return him or her. The police officer may use 'reasonable force' to do so.[3]

It is interesting to contrast the very detailed powers given to the police with the absence of any similar powers to guardians. It could be argued that if Parliament had intended to give guardians the power to detain or restrain it should have spelt this out.

The Part 6 Code of Practice does not envisage the use of force or detention by guardians. It says that on occasions a guardian may have to 'insist' on having his or her way, but it links the use of compulsion to the enforcement procedures in the Act.[4] Alternatively, it suggests, a guardian may wish to seek directions from the sheriff.

It may be that the law should draw a distinction between local authority guardians and personal guardians for these purposes. A personal guardian who is a carer may be able to rely on common law powers and duties to restrain the adult. The law is less happy with statutory bodies relying on common law powers, particularly when a statutory code is available.[5]

---

[1]   Mental Incapacity Act 2005, s 20. The Act permits restraint only if the adult is unable to take a decision, the restraint is necessary to prevent harm to the adult (not harm to others) and the restraint is a proportionate response.

[2]   Adults with Incapacity (Scotland) Act 2000, s 70.

[3]   AWI(S)A 2000, s 70(5).

[4]   Paras 5.49, 5.70–71, 5.85–86.

[5]   *B v Forsey* (above) and *HL v UK* (above).

Applying for power to restrain

9.20 The sheriff has very wide power to make orders dealing with 'all aspects' of the welfare of the adult.[1] It may be that this includes power to authorise the use of restraint, if the sheriff considers this is necessary in accordance with the principles of the Act.

It would be good practice for any prospective guardian envisaging the use of restraint, force or detention to refer to this specifically in the guardianship application. Such significant limitations on the adult's civil liberties should be explicit, not implied in a general grant of powers to take all welfare decisions.

The Mental Welfare Commission reports that some orders include the power to restrain and/or detain an adult in the interests of his or her health and safety.[2]

Where the chief officer of the local authority is guardian, he or she will want to ensure that the restraint policy in the place where the adult is to live is acceptable and properly monitored. The guardian remains liable for the proper performance of his or her functions. A guardian could be liable of criminal neglect if people acting on his or her behalf are negligent or poorly trained.

[1] Adults with Incapacity (Scotland) Act 2000, s 64(1)(c).

[2] See Mental Welfare Commission Annual Report 2004–5, p 60. The courts have given local authority guardians powers to restrain adults in the interests of their health or safety, to accompany adults whenever they leave the house and to restrict the people with whom adults have contact. The Mental Welfare Commission describes these powers as 'robust'.

Attorneys

9.21 The Act does not give welfare attorneys any power to exercise force or restraint. The power of attorney document could specifically authorise the attorney to exercise such restraint as the person might need, in accordance with the principles of the Act. If the document does not give such powers, the attorney will need to rely on his or her common law powers and duties (see above).

If a power of attorney contains the power to approve where an adult should live, this could include the power to decide the adult should live in a place which may restrict his or her liberty, if appropriate under the principles of the Act.

RESTRAINT AND MENTAL HEALTH (CARE AND TREATMENT) ACT

9.22 There is very little in the Mental Health (Care and Treatment) Act or its Code of Practice dealing with the use of force and restraint. There is even less, so far as the author is aware, about time out or seclusion. See below.

If a patient challenges the use of such procedures, the hospital will need to be able to demonstrate that it has the legal authority to act and that its action is an appropriate response in the individual circumstances of the case. It will also need to show that staff have acted in accordance with the principles of the Mental Health (Care and Treatment) Act and, in particular, the principle of minimum necessary intervention.

The Mental Health (Care and Treatment) Act authorises the use of compulsory measures where a person's mental disorder makes him or her a risk to others and the person's ability to take treatment decisions is significantly impaired. A person may be detained in hospital or required to live in a specified place in the community. The person may be required to accept medical treatment even if he or she does not consent to the treatment.

The law says that the statutory powers in the Mental Health (Care and Treatment) Act include any related powers necessary to operate the powers given in the statute.[1]

[1]   Bennion, *Statutory Interpretation* (4th edn, Butterworths LexisNexis), section 174. See *Bodden v Commissioner of Police of the Metropolis* [1990] 2 QB 397.

In hospital

9.23 Although the Act does not state this explicitly, if someone is detained in hospital, staff have authority to restrain the person if he or she attempts to leave the ward or the hospital without the consent of the responsible medical officer. The person cannot leave the hospital without the authority of the responsible medical officer.[1]

A person subject to compulsory measures under the Mental Health (Care and Treatment) Act will generally be subject to an order requiring him or her to accept medical treatment under Part 16 of the Act. Medical treatment is widely defined. It includes nursing and care.[2] Nursing could include restraining someone to prevent risk to self or others, if necessary and in accordance with the principles of the Act.

The Act authorises the giving of medical treatment where the person does not consent. The Act does not say that staff may use force or restraint to give such treatment if the person resists, but this is a necessary consequence. The Act prohibits the use of force to treat a person in the community.[3] The implication is that someone in hospital can receive treatment by force in certain circumstances.

The Code of Practice deals with the use of force, but only in the context of urgent treatment. Staff using force to give urgent treatment should have received training in its use and should include details about any use of force in their report to the Mental Welfare Commission.[4]

Draft guidance from the Mental Welfare Commission deals with the use of restraint under the Mental Health (Care and Treatment) Act. The guidance says that force should be used only if it is necessary and the result cannot be achieved in any other way. The use of force should comply with the principles of the Act. Force is appropriate only if the person persistently resists treatment. It is best practice to wait and try again later, unless the situation is urgent.[5]

[1] See, for example, Mental Health (Care and Treatment) (Scotland) Act 2003, s 127. Only the responsible medical officer can suspend the terms of a compulsory treatment order to allow the person to leave.

[2] Mental Health (Care and Treatment) (Scotland) Act 2003, s 329.

[3] See, for example, s 241(4).

[4] Code of Practice, vol 1, para 10.87.

[5] *Consent to treatment: Mental health and the law: A guide for mental health practitioners.* Mental Welfare Commission draft document April 2006.

In community-based settings

9.24 Staff supervising someone living on a community-based compulsory treatment order should not use force or restraint to keep the person there, if the person attempts to leave. A community-based compulsory treatment order does not detain the person in the community facility, but requires him or her to live in the place specified in the order.

If the person leaves, he or she is in breach of the order. The person may be brought back to the place where he or she is to live, or taken to hospital. This does not mean that there is a power to detain or restrain the person in the community. People living in the community cannot receive medical treatment by force. See above. This means that they cannot receive nursing care such as restraint.

Where a hospital-based order is suspended and a patient is kept in the charge of a nurse or other person, it would seem likely that the person in charge can restrain a patient attempting to leave. The person remains subject to the control of the responsible medical officer and the person in charge, even though the order is suspended.

Additional safeguards

9.25 The fact that a person is subject to compulsory measures under the Mental Health (Care and Treatment) Act does not remove the need for monitoring and recording of the use of restraint. All the safeguards above apply.

The principles of the Act, and in particular the principle of minimum necessary intervention, mean that any restraint should be justifiable in the circumstances and the minimum necessary to deal with the situation.

A nurse or other health professional unable to show he or she has acted in accordance with good practice and with reference to the principles of the Act might have difficulty in justifying his or her action to a court.

A person whose liberty is restricted in this way could appeal to the tribunal under section 291 of the Mental Health (Care and Treatment) Act. See 6.05. The tribunal could decide that, although the person is an informal patient, he or she is unlawfully detained.

Good practice guidance

9.26 There is little in the extensive Mental Health (Care and Treatment) Act Code of Practice about the use of force or restraint.

The Code of Practice recommends that staff advise informal patients of their rights when they are admitted to hospital. This should include information about any restrictions on movement staff may prescribe. The Code concludes that inappropriate use of restraint or limitations to an informal patient's liberty might constitute ill-treatment or wilful neglect.[1]

[1]   Code of Practice, vol 1, paras 8.05-07.

SECLUSION AND TIME OUT

9.27 Seclusion (solitary confinement) is 'at a very low level' in Scottish psychiatric hospitals.[1] Another more common practice is 'time out', removal of a patient from a facility for a short period. The Code of Practice gave guidance on good practice for the 1984 Act,[2] but as far as the author is aware, the matter is not covered in the lengthy Code for the 2003 Act. This is unfortunate.

A judgement of the House of Lords in an English case may influence practice and policy in Scotland. A patient in Ashworth hospital took action to challenge the hospital's seclusion policy, which differed substantially from that in the Mental Health Act Code of Practice.

Although the patient accepted that it was appropriate to use seclusion in his case, he argued that seclusion breached his rights under Articles 3 and 8 of the European Convention on Human Rights and was not a 'lawful' interference with his liberty as required by Article 8. The House of Lords (by a majority of 3 to 2) dismissed his appeal.[3]

1   Annual Report of Mental Welfare Commission 1998–9, p 31.
2   Mental Health (Scotland) Act 1984 Code of Practice, Scottish Home and Health Department (1989), para 4.8.
3   *R v Ashworth Hospital Authority ex parte* Munjaz [2005] UKHL 58.

House of Lords judgement

9.28 The English and Welsh Code of Practice says that the only purpose of seclusion should be to contain severely disturbed behaviour likely to cause harm to others. Seclusion should be a last resort and used for the shortest possible time. It should not be a punishment or threat, part of a treatment programme, or used because of shortage of staff. It should not be used where there is any risk of suicide or self-harm.[1] All hospitals must have clear written guidelines on the use of seclusion and there must be regular medical reviews.

Ashworth hospital, a high security hospital, had a written policy which departed from the Code in substantial ways. The policy envisaged situations where a patient would be secluded for longer than seven days. Reviews were not as regular as those envisaged by the Code. The hospital argued that the Code did not deal with the special requirements of its patients.

The House of Lords held that the proper use of seclusion as set out in the Ashworth policy did not constitute inhumane and degrading treatment under Article 3 of the European Convention on Human Rights. The hospital had a duty to ensure that its policy did not breach Mr M's human rights. The policy contained sufficient safeguards, such as regular monitoring, rights of appeal and regular review. It was an appropriate response to the risks posed.

The policy was not a breach of Article 5, either. Mr M was properly detained in the hospital. Article 5 is not concerned with someone's treatment or the conditions of his or her detention.[2]

The seclusion breached Mr M's rights to family and private life under Article 8, but the court was satisfied this was lawful and necessary to prevent crime and reduce the risk to other people.

1   Para 19.16.

2   *Ashingdane v United Kingdom* (1985) 7 EHRR 528, 543, para 44. See also *Bollan v United Kingdom* (application no 42117/98) (unreported), 4 May 2000, p 9. Disciplinary steps imposed on a prisoner in Cornton Vale prison were modifications of the conditions of her detention and outside the scope of Art 5(1).

Need for clear policy

9.29 The House of Lords accepted that a seclusion policy can be 'lawful' without being based on statute law. It can be based on the common law or another source. To comply with the European Convention on Human Rights, the law must be transparent, accessible, predictable and consistent.[1] This is necessary to protect patients against the abuse of power and arbitrary conduct. The Ashworth policy provided this transparency.

Hospitals and care homes in Scotland may feel that they can justify the use of seclusion because of their common law duty of care to other patients and to staff who work in the hospital. The House of Lords recognised this.

To comply with human rights requirements and satisfy the criterion of foreseeability, policies must be accessible and formulated with precision.[2] The House of Lords pointed out that in *Bournewood* the European Court of Human Rights had criticised the common law's lack of any clear procedural rules.[3]

If hospitals or care homes use seclusion and time out, they need clear and accessible policies to comply with human rights requirements. Guidance from the Scottish Executive in the Code of Practice or statutory direction would reinforce the lawful basis of such policies.

These considerations are also relevant to the use of restraint. Clear guidance in statutory Codes of Practice would provide appropriate human rights safeguards.

1   Lord Hope at paras 91–2 and 98.

2   *Sunday Times v United Kingdom* (1979) 2 EHRR 245, para 87.

3   Lord Scott at para 123.

Chapter 10

PREPARING FOR FUTURE INCAPACITY

10.01 This chapter looks at how a person can ensure doctors consider his or her wishes and feelings should he or she become unable to take medical decisions in the future. It considers advance statements in all areas of medicine, special rules under the Mental Health (Care and Treatment) Act, appointing a welfare attorney and the role of the named person.

ADVANCE STATEMENTS

10.02 An advance statement sets out a person's wishes about future health care should the person become incapable of taking treatment decisions in the future. A person with legal capacity can accept and refuse any treatment. See chapter 7. An advance statement is an attempt to ensure that doctors respect a person's wishes in the future, should the person be unable to take such decisions because of illness or infirmity.

A person may make an advance statement in any area of medicine. They can be particularly important in mental health care. The Mental Health (Care and Treatment) Act gives recognition to advance statements where someone is subject to a compulsory order.

Many people will not see the need to make an advance statement. Someone facing illness discusses future treatment options with his or her doctor as a matter of course, and the doctor considers the person's views when deciding what treatment to recommend.

Some people are prepared to rely on the decisions of their doctor should they become incapable of taking medical decisions. Others may wish for the greater certainty an advance statement can provide. An advance statement gives a formal procedure for ensuring that the person's input is taken seriously and the person is a partner in care.

Types of statement

10.03 Perhaps the most common form of advance statement is an advance refusal of treatment (see below), but there are other forms.

Consent to future treatment

10.04 A person can sign an advance statement consenting to future treatment, such as treatment for a physical or mental condition likely to recur. If the doctor is satisfied such a statement is valid, he or she will consider its terms if the person receives treatment under the Adults with Incapacity Act or Mental Health (Care and Treatment) Act. Both Acts require doctors to consider the person's wishes and feelings, past and present.

A doctor is unlikely to rely on advance consent if someone resists treatment when unable to take treatment decisions, and will generally use the Mental Health (Care and Treatment) Act or Adults with Incapacity Act procedures. However, such a statement can be useful to a doctor considering whether and how to act in a certain situation.[1]

[1]   For an example of the positive results such a statement can provide, see the case of Mrs A, Annual Report of the Mental Welfare Commission 2000–1, p 37.

Requiring certain treatments

10.05 An advance statement could state that if a person is ill, he or she would prefer to receive certain treatments.

A doctor must consider these views, but is not obliged to give any specific treatment. The doctor's decision depends on the person's clinical needs and the cost and availability of the treatment. See chapter 5.

Statement of wishes and feelings

10.06 Some people prepare statements of wishes, feelings and values instead of making advance statements. A statement of wishes and feelings sets out in general terms the person's attitudes to such matters as life-prolonging treatments and future care.

These statements do not attempt to anticipate the types of decisions which may be necessary, and they do not bind doctors or other healthcare professionals. This gives extra flexibility according to the circumstances.

These statements can assist decision-making when someone becomes unable to take treatment decisions. The principles of the Adults with Incapacity Act and Mental Health (Care and Treatment) Act mean that anyone intervening under those Acts must consider them.

There is no particular form for such a statement. It could detail the person's general values, beliefs and concerns and/or express the person's views about certain treatments.[1]

1   For an example, see Ward, *Adult Incapacity*, Appendix 5, Pt 5.

Advance refusals

Common law

10.07 We saw in chapter 7 that every competent adult is free to refuse medical treatment, even if to do so could result in death or serious injury. A person may refuse treatment for a physical illness and treatment for mental disorder, although if he or she refuses treatment for mental disorder, Mental Health (Care and Treatment) Act measures may be used.

An advance refusal is the next stage. A person who is competent to take decisions about treatment should also be able to refuse consent to future treatment. Such advance refusals are often called 'living wills'. These are often concerned with end-of-life decisions.

The English courts have recognised the validity of advance refusals of treatment.[1] We saw above how C, a man diagnosed with schizophrenia, successfully obtained a court order preventing the doctors from amputating his gangrenous leg even though his life was at risk. The court said that his decision would remain valid if he later became unable to take medical decisions.[2]

The General Medical Council and British Medical Association both recognise the validity of advance statements.[3] The doctor must be satisfied that the person was legally competent when he or she made the statement, that the advance statement applies to the circumstances and that there is no reason to believe that the person has changed his or her mind.

Particular care is necessary if an advance statement refuses life-saving treatment.[4] (See 8.02 for emergency treatment and advance statements.)

The Mental Capacity Act 2005 for England and Wales gives statutory recognition to advance refusals of treatment.[5]

1   See *Re T (Adult: refusal of treatment)* [1992] 4 All ER 649, where the courts considered a refusal by a Jehovah's Witness of a blood transfusion.
2   *Re C (Adult: Refusal of Medical Treatment)* [1994] 1 WLR 290.

3   *Seeking patients' consent: the ethical considerations,* General Medical Council (November 1998), para 22. *Advance statements about medical treatment,* British Medical Association (2000).
4   *HE v A Hospital NHS Trust* [2003] EWHC 1017.
5   Mental Capacity Act 2005, ss 24–26.

Advance refusals in Scotland

10.08 Many commentators believe that the courts in Scotland would recognise the validity of a valid advance refusal of treatment.[1] The House of Lords, whose judgements are very influential in Scotland, recognises their validity.[2]

The Scottish Law Commission recommended that the Adults with Incapacity Act should clarify the law.[3] The Scottish Executive was not willing to include such a matter in legislation at that time. It believed the courts should continue to develop the law in light of changes in medical practice and ethics.

The Scottish Parliament did not intend the Adults with Incapacity Act to alter the common law on advance refusals.[4] Insofar as they were valid prior to that Act, they should remain valid.

1   Including the Scottish Law Commission (*Report on Incapable Adults* 1995, para 5.46).
2   *Airedale NHS Trust v Bland* [1993] AC 789 HL at paras 860 and 866.
3   *Report on Incapable Adults,* Recommendation 68.
4   See comments of the Deputy Minister for Justice, Mr Jim Wallace, on the passing of the 2000 Act. 'The provision [in section 1 of the Bill] does not..... have a bearing on the legal status afforded to an advance statement or living will that was made by an adult when they had the capacity to do so.' Scottish Parliament, Official Report, vol 3, No 14 Column 1382.

Adults with Incapacity Act

10.09 Although the Adults with Incapacity Act does not deal specifically with advance statements, the principles of the Act mean that an advance statement has considerable force. A doctor is bound to consider an advance statement as evidence of the person's wishes and feelings.

A doctor can intervene under the Adults with Incapacity Act only if the intervention will provide a benefit. There is an argument that an intervention may not 'benefit' the person if he or she has clearly stated that he or she does not wish it.

Benefit is more than 'best interests' and not simply a matter of the substituted judgement of the doctor. It was deliberately intended to include a greater reliance on the wishes and feelings of the adult.[1]

An advance refusal cannot oblige a doctor to act unethically or against his or her conscience, but a doctor would need to seek legal advice before overruling what appears to be a valid advance refusal applicable to the circumstances. It may be appropriate to refer the matter to the courts.

[1]   *Report on Incapable Adults*, para 2.50. The definition of 'best interests' in the Mental Capacity Act in England and Wales includes a reference to respect for the wishes of the adult. (Mental Capacity Act 2005, s 4(6).)

Making an advance statement

10.10 An advance statement can be in writing, in a letter to a doctor or in a formal document signed and witnessed. A doctor may record the person's wishes following discussions with the person and keep this with the person's medical notes. If the matter is important to the person, he or she will want to record it in writing.

The statement must be clear and unequivocal. A friend or adviser can read it over. It must cover the situation in question. If the refusal of treatment is intended to apply even if the result is the person's death, the advance statement should make this clear.

The person signing the advance statement must have the legal capacity to do so. The test is similar to the test for taking medical decisions, but, in addition, the person must understand the impact of the document he or she is signing.

If there is evidence that anyone (including hospital staff) put someone under pressure to sign an advance statement, it will not be valid.[1]

An advance statement cannot refuse basic hygiene, pain relief or feeding, or compel doctors to do anything illegal or unethical.

An advance statement refusing treatment applies only while someone is incapable of taking treatment decisions. If the person retains capacity, the advance statement is not relevant.

A person can change or cancel an advance statement at any time, so long as he or she is legally able to do so.

[1]   See *Re T (adult: refusal of medical treatments)* (1992) 9 BMLR 46.

Implications of statement

10.11 Making an advance statement refusing treatment is a very serious matter. The person needs to be sure he or she understands the full implications. Ideally, the person should discuss the content with a doctor or nursing staff.

Advance statements in psychiatry

10.12 A person can make an advance statement refusing psychiatric treatment.[1] All the rules above apply. A doctor should respect such an advance refusal, but if the person is at risk and the other grounds for compulsion apply, the doctor may consider the use of compulsory measures under the Mental Health (Care and Treatment) Act. This may mean that the person's treatment decisions are overruled.

Before the implementation of the Mental Health (Care and Treatment) Act, an advance refusal of psychiatric care had no legal force if someone was detained under the Mental Health (Scotland) Act. Detention under the 1984 Act was not a matter of capacity. Someone capable of refusing treatment could be detained. For this reason even a competent advance refusal was not legally binding. This remains the case in England and Wales.

The Mental Health (Care and Treatment) Act has reformed the law, as part of its commitment to the principle of respect for patients' wishes. Where someone is subject to compulsory measures under the Mental Health (Care and Treatment) (Scotland) Act, anyone intervening under the Act must take into account any valid advance statement the person has made and not withdrawn.[2] This applies to the tribunal, a doctor treating the person and a doctor giving a second opinion.

Anyone taking action conflicting with the terms of an advance statement must report this to the Mental Welfare Commission.[3] The Mental Welfare Commission will monitor the operation of these provisions.[4]

---

[1]   For a discussion of some of the issues, see JM Atkinson, HC Garner, H Patrick and S Stuart, 'Issues in the development of advance directives in mental health care' (2003) 12 Journal of Mental Health 463–474 and 'The development of potential models of advance directives in mental health care' (2003) 12 Journal of Mental Health 575–584.

[2]   Mental Health (Care and Treatment) (Scotland) Act 2003, s 276. The advance statement comes into effect if the person's ability to take medical decisions is significantly impaired. (MH(CT)(S)A 2003, s 276(1).) This is one of the

grounds for intervention under the Mental Health (Care and Treatment) Act. See chapter 11.

3   Mental Health (Care and Treatment) (Scotland) Act 2003, s 276(8).
4   Mental Welfare Commission Monitoring Priorities 2005–6.

Making psychiatric advance statement

10.13 An advance statement may cover mental health treatments the person wishes and does not wish to have. It may also cover matters other than treatment, such as whom to contact about care of dependants or pets, should the person become ill. The person may keep this with the advance statement but it does not form part of it.

The Scottish Executive has prepared a useful guide.[1] This includes a draft form of advance statement. There is no need to use the suggested form, but it complies with the legal requirements. The person should check whether a witness will charge a fee for witnessing.

Further guidance to professionals is in the Mental Health Act Code of Practice.[2]

1   *The new Mental Health Act: A guide to advance statements,* Scottish Executive (2004).
2   Vol 1, paras 6.44–89.

Validity

10.14 An advance statement is valid under the Mental Health (Care and Treatment) Act if:

- The person making it had the capacity to make it.
- It is in writing and signed by the person making it.
- The witness is one of the following: a registered chartered clinical psychologist, a doctor, an occupational therapist, a staff member or manager of a care service,[1] a registered nurse, a social worker or a solicitor;[2] and
- The witness certifies in writing that, in his or her opinion, the person making the statement had the capacity to make it.[3]

1   As defined in the Regulation of Care (Scotland) Act 2001.
2   Mental Health (Advance Statements) (Prescribed Class of Persons) (Scotland) (No. 2) Regulations 2004 (SSI 2004/429), reg 2.
3   Mental Health (Care and Treatment) (Scotland) Act 2003, s 276(2).

Advising relevant people

10.15 The Code of Practice advises giving a copy of the advance statement to the general practitioner and the responsible medical officer and/or mental health officer if appropriate, and asking them to file it in with the person's medical records. A community psychiatric nurse might also hold a copy.

The person signing may wish to tell his or her named person and carer and the hospital managers, if he or she is in hospital.[1]

If the person withdraws the advance statement, he or she should notify these people.

[1]   Code of Practice, vol 1, para 6.78.

Withdrawing statement

10.16 A person may withdraw an advance statement at any time provided he or she has the capacity to do so. The person must sign a withdrawal form and get this witnessed.[1]

[1]   Mental Health (Care and Treatment) (Scotland) Act 2003, s 276(3).

Crisis cards

10.17 Crisis cards are a form of advance statement. They are usually small, credit card sized cards and are generally issued by a group or organisation.

The person carries the card at all times. It includes the name of another person to be contacted in case of a mental health emergency. That person knows about the person's wishes about medical treatment, including the content of any advance statement and where that document is stored.

The person noted on the crisis card may be able to speak to the doctors on the person's behalf. He or she can monitor the decision-making about the person's care and treatment. For example, the person noted on the card will check that doctors consider any advance statement and if a doctor does not follow the wishes expressed in the advance statement, will check that the responsible medical officer notifies the relevant people.

The crisis card may spell out the person's views and wishes about medical treatment. If the person is regarded as incapable of taking medical decisions, the doctor should take the terms of the crisis card into account when treating the person under the Adults with Incapacity Act.

A crisis card does not comply with Mental Health (Care and Treatment) Act advance statement requirements unless it is witnessed and certified as above.

If someone with a crisis card draws up an advance statement, he or she should draw attention to the existence of the crisis card and make sure that the crisis card and advance statement do not contain contradictory provisions.

MedicAlert

10.18 One way of ensuring that an advance statement is available in an emergency is to register it with the Medic Alert Foundation (a registered charity). The person then wears a bracelet or necklet with details accessible from a 24-hour phone line. This ensures that the person's health wishes are known. For the address, see Appendix 2.

APPOINTING WELFARE ATTORNEY

10.19 As an alternative (or in addition) to signing an advance statement, some people may sign a welfare power of attorney. This authorises another person to take medical and other welfare decisions if the person is unable to act.

The advantage is that the attorney can take a decision in the light of the circumstances at the time. The attorney will bear in mind his or her knowledge of the person's wishes and feelings. The disadvantage is that the attorney's powers are limited. An attorney will not be involved in treatment decisions if the person is subject to a Mental Health (Care and Treatment) Act order.

APPOINTING NAMED PERSON

10.20 The Mental Health (Care and Treatment) Act allows someone to appoint a named person to act for him or her in connection with any compulsory measures under the Act.

The Mental Health (Care and Treatment) Act has reformed the Adults with Incapacity Act. Any person carrying out an intervention under the Adults with Incapacity Act must now consult the named person.[1]

For this reason, someone anticipating incapacity may wish to nominate a named person even if compulsory measures under the Mental Health (Care and Treatment) Act are unlikely. This could be particularly important where someone is not happy with the person who is his or her nearest relative. The person can link appointing a named person with an application to the sheriff to limit the powers of the nearest relative. See 24.28.

[1] Adults with Incapacity (Scotland) Act 2000, (as amended by the Mental Health (Care and Treatment) (Scotland) Act 2003 (Modification of Enactments) Order 2005 (SSI 2005/465)), s 1(4).

PART 3
THE USE OF COMPULSION

Chapter 11

COMPULSORY MEASURES

11.01 This chapter introduces the compulsory orders under the Mental Health (Care and Treatment) Act and considers some general issues. The Mental Health (Care and Treatment) Act provides for the following orders:

- Short-term detention direct from the community for up to 28 days.
- Emergency detention, for up to 72 hours.
- A nurse may detain someone in hospital for up to two hours to enable a doctor to examine him or her with a view to the use of short-term or emergency detention.
- The compulsory treatment order lasts for up to six months. It can be renewed for a further six months and then from year to year. The order can authorise either detention in hospital or, if the tribunal is satisfied this is appropriate, care and treatment in the community.
- The tribunal can make an interim compulsory treatment order lasting for up to 28 days. It can make further interim orders, provided the total duration does not exceed 56 days.

These orders are sometimes called 'civil' orders, to distinguish them from the criminal justice orders discussed in Part 12.

ETHICAL BASIS FOR COMPULSION

11.02 The use of compulsory measures is an extremely serious matter, as the person effectively loses the right to take medical decisions. Mental health law is unique in allowing doctors to overrule a competent patient's refusal of treatment.

It is possible to justify using compulsory measures on various grounds, such as risk (to the person or others) and the duty of society to offer help and protection to vulnerable members.[1] On the other hand, compulsory measures are a fundamental attack on the person's autonomy. There must be a clear ethical justification for their use.

The Millan Committee discussed these questions at some length.[2] There was universal agreement among the people the Committee consulted that compulsory measures remain necessary for some people at some times. It was necessary to balance the person's right to autonomy against society's duty to care for and protect people at risk.

The Committee recommended that mental health law should spell out the ethical basis for using compulsory powers. The Mental Health (Care and Treatment) Act does this in two ways. It spells out clearly the situations where compulsion can be used. It includes on the face of the Act a statement of the principles underlying the Act.

[1] For an interesting discussion of some of the issues, see JK Mason and GT Laurie, *Mason and McCall Smith's Law and medical ethics* (7th edn, Oxford University Press 2005), chap 20.

[2] See *New Directions*, paras 2.1–24 and chap 3.

Principles of Act

11.03 The Mental Health (Care and Treatment) Act principles largely mirror the Millan recommendations. (See 2.26 for Millan principles.)

The principles set out the ethical basis for compulsory intervention and the values underpinning it.

The Act requires everyone discharging a function under the Act to have regard to the principles.[1] This includes anyone using or contemplating the use of compulsory measures, such as a doctor, mental health officer or the mental health tribunal.

[1] Mental Health (Care and Treatment) (Scotland) Act 2003, ss 1–3.

Participation

11.04 A person exercising functions under the Act must have regard to the person's wishes and feelings, past and present.[1] Generally the first person to ask is the person him or herself, but it is also necessary to consider the views in an advance statement. It may be necessary to consider evidence from the person's family, friends or independent advocate about the person's past or present views.

Appropriate means to establish the person's wishes include communication aids, interpreters, signers and independent advocacy services.[2] If staff are unable to meet someone's needs for interpretation services, they should record this.[3]

Everyone exercising functions under the Act should consider how to enable the person to participate as fully as possible, and should bear in mind the need to give the person information and support. Information should be in a form the person is most likely to be able to understand.[4]

1   Mental Health (Care and Treatment) (Scotland) Act 2003, s 1(3)(a).
2   MH(CT)(S) A 2003, s 1(8).
3   Code of Practice, vol 1, para 1.03.
4   MH(CT)(S) A 2003, ss 1(3),1(10).

Respect for carers and others

11.05 People acting under the Mental Health (Care and Treatment) Act must consider the views of the named person, any carer and any welfare guardian/attorney,[1] provided it is reasonable and practicable to do so.[2]

They should, as far as reasonable and practicable, consider the needs of any carer of which they are aware and the importance of giving the carer the information he or she might need to help care for the person.[3] (This does not apply to making decisions about medical treatment.)

The Code of Practice recognises that in an emergency, time to consult and provide information may be limited.[4] It also advises people to bear in mind medical confidentiality.[5] (See chapter 5).

1   Mental Health (Care and Treatment) (Scotland) Act 2003, s 1(3)(b).
2   MH(CT)(S)A 2003, s 1(9).
3   MH(CT)(S)A 2003, s 1(5).
4   Code of Practice, vol 1, para 1.04.
5   Code of Practice, vol 1, para 1.05.

Least restrictive alternative

11.06 Anyone acting under the Mental Health (Care and Treatment) Act should bear in mind the range of options available.[1] People should carry out their duties under the Act in the least restrictive manner necessary in the circumstances, bearing in mind the other principles, the needs of any carer, the duty of reciprocity (below) and any other considerations.[2]

1   Mental Health (Care and Treatment) (Scotland) Act 2003, s 1(3)(e).
2   MH(CT)(S) A 2003, s 1(4).

Benefit and child welfare

11.07 Anyone carrying out duties under the Act should consider how to provide the maximum benefit to the person.[1]

For patients aged under 18, the child welfare principle applies.[2] Anyone carrying out duties under the Act should do so in the way that will best secure the child's welfare.

1   Mental Health (Care and Treatment) (Scotland) Act 2003, s 1(3)(f).
2   MH(CT)(S)A 2003, s 2(4).

Non-discrimination and respect for diversity

11.08 No one should operate Mental Health (Care and Treatment) Act powers in a discriminatory way. Staff should show respect for patients' cultural sensitivities.

Everyone with duties under the Act should consider how to ensure the patient's treatment is no worse than what someone who is not a patient would receive in a similar situation, unless this is justified in the circumstances.[1]

Staff must take into account the person's abilities, background and characteristics, including his or her age, sex, sexual orientation, religious persuasion and cultural and ethnic background.[2]

The principles also highlight the need to tackle discrimination. The relevant people should encourage 'equal opportunities' and observance of the equal opportunity requirements.

'Equal opportunities' means the prevention of discrimination on grounds of sex, marital status, race, disability, age, sexual orientation, language, social origin or other personal attributes, including beliefs or opinions, such as religious beliefs or political opinions.[3] This principle applies to Scottish Ministers, the Mental Welfare Commission, local authorities, hospital managers, mental health officers, responsible medical officers and other doctors and nurses.[4]

Health boards have similar equality duties. See chapter 37.

1   Mental Health (Care and Treatment) (Scotland) Act 2003, s 1(3)(g).
2   MH(CT)(S)A 2003, s 1(3)(h).
3   As set out in Scotland Act 1998, Sched 5, Part II, s L2.
4   MH(CT)(S)A 2003, (as amended by National Health Service Reform (Scotland) Act 2004, Sched 2), s 3.

Reciprocity

11.09 The final principle is of crucial importance. If someone has been or is subject to an order under the Mental Health (Care and Treatment) Act, people acting under the Act must have regard to the importance of providing appropriate services to him or her, including continuing care when the person is no longer subject to the order.[1]

1   Mental Health (Care and Treatment) (Scotland) Act 2003, s 1(6).

When principles do not apply

11.10 Certain people are not formally subject to the principles, because their relationship with the person does not come from the Mental Health (Care and Treatment) Act.

The principles do not apply to the person subject to the order, his or her named person, a primary carer, people working for independent advocacy services, the person's solicitor, a curator *ad litem* appointed by the tribunal or to welfare guardians/attorneys.[1]

1   Mental Health (Care and Treatment) (Scotland) Act 2003, s 1(7).

Impact of principles

11.11 The principles are relevant whenever someone is acting under the Mental Health (Care and Treatment) Act. Their use may help people subject to compulsory orders to feel that, so far as possible, people have considered their views and heard their concerns.

Sometimes there may be conflict between the various principles. The most common situation, where compulsory measures are under consideration, is where there is conflict between someone's unwillingness to receive treatment and care and the evidence that this could benefit the person. The doctors, mental health officer and (in some cases) the tribunal must weigh up the importance of respecting the person's autonomy and wishes in the light of the possible risks to the person and potential benefits of treatment.

The principles cannot be applied mechanically. Balancing the importance of the different principles and applying them to individual circumstances is a question of judgement. Adrian Ward has said, in connection with the Adults with Incapacity Act, that 'reference to the principles will usually assist—often decisively—in resolving points of difficulty in the application of the Act's provisions to particular circumstances, or of interpretation'.[1] The Mental Health (Care and

Treatment) Act principles may provide a similar yardstick for interpretation.

1   Ward, *Adult Incapacity,* para 4.2.

WHEN COMPULSORY MEASURES APPLICABLE

11.12 Compulsory measures under the Mental Health (Care and Treatment) Act are available only in certain clearly defined situations. The tests are broadly the same for all orders.

The Mental Health (Care and Treatment) Act grounds are more explicit than those in the 1984 Act. The basis of the 1984 Act test was essentially that compulsion was 'appropriate' and 'necessary'. This left too much discretion to the doctors and did not explain the basis on which a doctor would make his or her decision.

The Mental Health (Care and Treatment) Act contains the new concept of 'significantly impaired decision-making'. It is not possible to use compulsory measures unless the person's ability to take decisions in relation to care and treatment is in some way impaired because of his or her mental disorder.

The grounds for using compulsory powers are that:[1]

- The person has a 'mental disorder'.
- (For long-term orders), medical treatment that would benefit the person is available for him or her. ('Treatability'.)
- Without the treatment there will be a significant risk to the person's health, safety or welfare or to the safety of other people. ('Risk'.)
- Because of the mental disorder, the person's ability to take decisions about the treatment is significantly impaired. ('Significantly impaired decision-making'.)
- The order is 'necessary'.

1   See, for example, Mental Health (Care and Treatment) (Scotland) Act 2003, s 64(5).

Mental disorder

11.13 'Mental disorder' means mental illness, personality disorder or learning disability.[1] The Mental Health (Care and Treatment) Act does not define these terms. The law says they mean what a reasonable person would take them to mean.[2] In case of dispute, this would probably be what a reasonable doctor, rather than a layperson, would regard as mental illness.[3]

The Millan Committee considered whether to define these conditions more tightly, perhaps in accordance with the diagnostic manuals used by the medical profession.[4] It found no suggestion that doctors were using the broad definition in the 1984 Act inappropriately.[5] A broad definition avoids the risk of becoming outdated in the future.

Problems arise at the borders of the definition. A layperson might think, for example, that someone who self-harms should fall within the definition. A doctor might not, if he or she cannot identify a recognisable mental illness or personality disorder.[6]

It is not clear whether psychiatrists in Scotland would regard attention deficit disorder and social and behavioural problems in childhood as mental disorders.[7] For Mental Health (Care and Treatment) Act purposes, this is important not because compulsory measures might be appropriate but because if they are mental disorders, the person would gain access to rights such as independent advocacy. Services in Scotland would usually offer medical help for attention deficit disorder and social or educational care for behavioural problems.

The wide definition of 'mental disorder' does not mean that someone diagnosed with a 'mental disorder' becomes subject to compulsory measures. The other criteria in the Act must apply.

1   Mental Health (Care and Treatment) (Scotland) Act 2003, s 328.

2   *W v L* [1974] QB 711.

3   See *R v Mental Health Act Commission ex parte W*, The Times, 27 May 1988. See discussion in Francis Bennion, *Statutory Interpretation* (4th edn, Butterworths LexisNexis, 2002), para 363.

4   There are two manuals, the World Health Organisation's *International Classification of Diseases* (10th edn, (ICD-10)) and the American Psychiatric Association's *Diagnostic and Statistical Manual* (4th edn (DSM-IV)). Both list many mental disorders that psychiatrists in this country would not regard as matters for mental health legislation.

5   See *New directions*, chap 4 for discussion of some of the arguments.

6   See *Towards implementation of the Mental Health (Care and Treatment) (Scotland) Act 2003*, Scottish Executive (March 2004). Dr Sandra Grant reported the concerns of prison staff at Cornton Vale prison about the lack of national agreement about whether it was appropriate to use Mental Health (Care and Treatment) Act measures for women involved in serious self-harm, (para 4.5.35.)

7   DSM-IV lists both as mental disorders.

Mental illness

11.14 Mental illness includes psychotic disorders, (such as schizophrenia), obsessive-compulsive disorders, anorexia nervosa[1] and disorders of *mood*, (affective disorders) such as depression and bipolar disorder. It also includes organic disorders such as dementia and brain injury caused by alcohol use and delirious reactions to physical illnesses.

It should also include temporary conditions, such as drug-induced psychosis. The Mental Health (Care and Treatment) Act refers to mental illness, whatever its cause or symptoms. Mental illness caused by drug use falls within this definition. Compulsory measures might be appropriate. This does not mean that the person has a long-term mental disorder and entitlement to mental health services. See chapter 28.

Psychiatric diagnosis is not fixed. An individual may move from a diagnosis of schizophrenia, to bipolar disorder and then to personality disorder. Some psychiatrists and psychologists are beginning to question the value of diagnostic labelling. They are more interested in looking at the person's symptoms and considering how to treat them.

[1]   *South West Hertfordshire Health Authority v KB* [1994] 2 FCR 1051.

Personality disorder

11.15 Personality disorder is a problematic diagnosis. Some people refuse to accept the term, which they regard as deeply stigmatising. However most psychiatrists do regard personality disorder as a mental disorder and one for which, at least in its less severe forms, treatment is available.

Personality disorder differs from mental illness, in that it is something intrinsic to the person's personality, perhaps something he or she was born with. It covers a wide range of conditions, from borderline personality disorder, where the symptoms may seem very similar to mental illness, to anti-social personality disorder, often indicated by criminal behaviour and lack of remorse.

The Millan Committee heard that mental health services sometimes use a diagnosis of personality disorder to exclude people from help.[1] The Committee believed the law should be clear that people with personality disorder are eligible for help from mental health services and other rights, such as access to independent advocacy and support services. It recommended continuing personality disorder as a separate category within 'mental disorder'.[2]

It will remain rare to use compulsory measures where someone's sole diagnosis is personality disorder, as generally the other criteria for compulsory measures, such as significantly impaired decision-making and treatability, would not apply.

At the same time as the Millan Committee was reporting, the MacLean Committee was considering options for serious, violent and sexual offenders, including people with personality disorders. Its report is a useful survey of current thinking. The Committee concluded it was unduly pessimistic to say that treatment for disorders such as anti-social personality disorder did not work, but treatment does not need a health setting and is unlikely to work if given compulsorily.[3] Under current policy, if someone's disorder leads him or her to commit anti-social behaviour, the criminal justice system rather than the health system will deal with him or her.

[1]   See discussion in *New directions*, paras 4.84–93.
[2]   Recommendation 4.11.
[3]   *Report of the Committee on Serious Violent and Sexual Offenders*, Scottish Executive (2000), paras 10.26–34. The Millan Committee heard similar evidence. *New directions*, para 26.17. See *R v Secretary of State for Scotland*, 1999 SLT 279.

Learning disability

11.16 The term learning disability replaces 'mental handicap' used in the 1984 Act. Again, the Act does not define the term. It means what a reasonable psychiatrist would regard as a learning disability. The diagnostic manuals for psychiatrists contain definitions. These generally refer to intelligence and social and behavioural functioning.

Many people believe that it is inappropriate for learning disability to be included within a mental health act. A learning disability is not an illness and it is rare to use compulsory measures unless someone also has a mental illness or personality disorder.

A number of people with learning disabilities are detained under mental health legislation.[1] This number appears to be increasing. The Mental Welfare Commission carried out an audit in September 2004 and identified 229 people detained because of learning disability. There has been an increase in the use of compulsory measures generally, but the increase is greater in the case of people with learning disabilities, who are proportionately more likely to be subject to long-term orders and almost twice as likely to be subject to restriction orders imposed by the criminal justice system.

The Mental Welfare Commission was particularly concerned to note that a number of people with learning disabilities were cared for in high security environments which they did not appear to need. It hoped that the tribunals will give rigorous scrutiny to proposed care plans for people with learning disabilities, to ensure a more careful assessment of whether people need detention in hospital.[2]

A person with a learning disability may have care and support needs and might benefit from other provisions in the Mental Health (Care and Treatment) Act, such as access to independent advocacy. A person may need help with financial, medical and welfare decisions. Learning disability is within the Adults with Incapacity Act. Guardianship under the Adults with Incapacity Act can provide social support to enable someone to continue to live in the community.

The Millan Committee recommended an expert review of the law about the place of learning disability within mental health law.[3] The Scottish Executive accepted this recommendation. Learning disability is currently included in the Mental Health (Care and Treatment) Act, but this is to be a temporary measure.[4]

[1]   Robertson, Russell and Browm, 'The use of the Scottish mental health legislation for people with a learning disability' (1999) identified 178 people with a diagnosis of learning disability detained under the 1984 Act.

[2]   Annual Report of Mental Welfare Commission 2004–5, para 3.2.

[3]   *New directions* recommendation 4.6.

[4]   *Renewing Mental Health Law,* Scottish Executive Policy Statement (2001), chap 2, para 14.

Exclusions from the definition

11.17 The Mental Health (Care and Treatment) Act specifically excludes certain matters from the definition of 'mental disorder', as recommended by the Millan Committee.[1]

These are sexual orientation and conduct; dependence on/misuse of drugs or alcohol; harassment or alarming or distressing behaviour and acting in an imprudent way.[2] It is different if the conduct is *evidence* of a mental disorder.[3]

While misuse of drugs or alcohol is not of itself a ground for compulsion, it may cause mental illness, such as a drug-induced psychosis or Korsakoff's syndrome, caused by excessive alcohol use. Someone who has a mental illness caused in this way, whether temporary or permanent, may need psychiatric treatment, possibly under the Mental Health (Care and Treatment) Act.

The Mental Welfare Commission has reported that mental health services are sometimes unwilling to treat people whose mental illness is drug induced, (see 5.18) but there is no doubt they have the legal power to do so, and to do so compulsorily if necessary.

1   *New directions*, recommendation 4.13.

2   Mental Health (Care and Treatment) (Scotland) Act 2003, s 328(2).

3   See *W v Secretary of State for Scotland*, 1998 SLT 841. W was detained in the State Hospital. He claimed this was because he was a paedophile, and that the 1984 Act did not allow detention on the grounds of sexual deviancy. The court said that he was detained because of his mental disorder. His sexual deviancy was a symptom of his mental disorder. His appeal was dismissed.

Significantly impaired decision-making

Background

11.18 The Millan Committee was concerned to establish the ethical basis on which society takes compulsory powers to treat someone with a mental disorder. Many people giving evidence to the Committee argued that mental health law was discriminatory. Why should someone be entitled to refuse treatment for cancer or a blood transfusion, whatever the risks, but not refuse treatment for schizophrenia?

They argued that the law should respect competent refusals of treatment in both cases. The law should intervene only if someone was unable to take a competent decision. Incapacity law, which provides a framework for decision-making, should replace mental health law. This would be a non-discriminatory and fair approach.[1]

The Millan Committee accepted the force of these arguments but was concerned that in practice, linking compulsion to incapacity might lead to hard results.[2] Some people might not receive treatment from which they could benefit. A person retaining legal capacity could refuse treatment, even if the effects of, for example, depression or anorexia, had affected his or her judgement.

The Millan Committee attempted to produce a formula that recognised the ethical basis of the capacity test but linked it to a common sense and pragmatic approach. It recommended that it should not be possible to use compulsory measures if someone's judgement was unaffected by mental disorder. If mental disorder had distorted the person's judgement, he or she should receive the benefit of medical treatment and support.

This test, it is suggested, is perhaps less legalistic than the incapacity test. The Millan Committee recognised that mental illness or a learning disability can affect more than just someone's mental abilities, with which the capacity test is mainly concerned. It may affect the person's feelings, his or her emotions, judgement, and his or her ability to make a true choice. The significantly impaired decision-making test might be closer to the decisions psychiatrists actually make on the ground. It might also be less stigmatising than an incapacity test.

The Scottish Executive accepted the Millan Committee's recommendation, replacing 'impaired judgement' with significantly impaired decision-making.[3]

[1]   For an eloquent statement of the arguments, see Professor M Gunn, 'Reforms of the Mental Health Act 1983: the relevance of capacity to make decisions' (2000) 2 Journal of Mental Health Law 39–44.
[2]   See discussion in *New directions*, pp 54–58.
[3]   See *Renewing Mental Health Law*, Scottish Executive Policy Statement (2001), chap 3, paras 6 and 7.

Nature of the test

11.19 The distinction between significantly impaired decision-making and lack of capacity is subtle, but important. 'Significantly impaired decision-making', unlike incapacity, is not a legal term of art. Again, the Mental Health (Care and Treatment) Act does not define the term. It is up doctors and mental health officers to take a view, and the tribunal considering an order must consider the evidence.

Whether someone has significantly impaired decision-making is a similar question to whether he or she is 'incapable' of taking decisions within the Adults with Incapacity Act. A doctor may wish to consider whether the person can believe, understand or retain information about his or her condition or possible treatments[1] or whether he or she is able to make a 'true choice'.

Some people are clearly unable to take treatment decisions. A person may believe the doctors are trying to poison him or her or may not believe that he or she is ill. Someone who is anorexic may not believe that his or her life is at risk. Depression may so disable a person that he or she is unable to take any decision at all. These people would probably be regarded as incapable of taking treatment decisions.

Other cases may be more difficult. A person who has depression may refuse treatment or pose a risk to him or herself. The person may understand that he or she is ill and appreciate that the doctors are trying to help but may refuse treatment because he or she wishes to die or believes he or she is unworthy of help. It is not clear whether such a person lacks legal capacity, but clearly, the person's ability to take medical decisions is significantly impaired because of the depression. Compulsory measures could be appropriate.

The fact that someone has significantly impaired decision-making and is subject to compulsory measures does not mean that the person is unable to take treatment decisions in the future. The impairment of decision-making relates to decisions about medical treatment in general. The person may be able to make decisions about some treatments and not others. Draft guidance from the Mental Welfare Commission advises doctors assess the person's capacity to consent to each individual treatment.[2]

Significantly impaired decision-making is a more flexible concept than incapacity. The case law relating to capacity and incapacity is relevant, but not conclusive. If a doctor believes that a mental disorder is distorting someone's ability to make decisions about treatment to a significant extent, bearing in mind both the risks and the possible benefits of treatment, he or she can seek compulsory measures.

[1] Code of Practice, vol 2, para 1.22.
[2] *Consent to treatment: Mental health and the law: A guide for mental health practitioners,* Mental Welfare Commission draft (April 2006).

When decision-making not impaired

11.20 Impaired decision-making is not simply disagreeing with the doctors.[1] For example, someone who knows that he or she is ill, understands and believes the treatment options but who wishes, for example, to attempt to reduce the use of medication because of the side effects, does not have significantly impaired decision-making.

Even if the doctors disagree with the person's choice, they cannot argue that the mental disorder has impaired the person's ability to take medical decisions. If doctors are right and the person's condition deteriorates, he or she may come within the definition at a later stage.

These issues could apply even if someone wishes to take his or her own life. While the presumption should always be in favour of the preservation of life, there may be a situation where the doctors believe that the person's decision is rational and not affected by mental disorder. In that case they cannot use compulsory powers.

In the same way they cannot use compulsory powers to treat someone for a physical illness even though the result may be the person's death.

1   *New directions*, para 5.43. Code of Practice, vol 2, para 1.27.

Impact of the rules

11.21 It remains to be seen how this test works in practice. It has been generally welcomed as a practical solution to these complex issues. Giving evidence to the Joint Committee of the Houses of Parliament on the draft mental health bill for England and Wales, Dr Tony Zigmond, Honorary Vice-President of the Royal College of Psychiatrists, said:

> 'The notion that there is a particular cut off point one side of which somebody lacks capacity, the other side they retain capacity, is of itself wrong … One of the acknowledged difficulties with the current definition of "incapacity" is that it relies almost entirely on someone's ability to think, what we call cognitive ability, and we recognise that in the field of mental health, of course, emotions play a large part, and so at a very practical clinical level we think that the notion of impaired decision-making by reason of mental disorder would be much easier for people to understand and relate to patients with mental health problems and, of course, it would keep us in line with the provisions in Scotland.'[1]

The Joint Committee recommended that the Bill for England and Wales should follow the Scottish example and include an impaired decision-making criterion.[2]

1   Joint Committee on the Draft Mental Health Bill—First Report (March 2005), para 153.
2   Joint Committee report, para 156.

Risk

11.22 A person can become subject to compulsory measures under the Mental Health (Care and Treatment) Act only if there is a significant risk to his or her health, safety or welfare or to the safety of others. Any one of these grounds would suffice. One or more may be relevant. An example of risk to a person's welfare would be excessive spending or risks caused by lack of inhibition in someone with hypomania.[1]

The decision as to what is a significant risk is a matter for the clinical judgement of the doctors and other health and social care professionals.[2] It may be tested by the tribunal on appeal or during an application for a compulsory treatment order.

1   *New directions*, para 5.53.
2   *New directions*, para 5.57.

Level of risk

11.23 There is sometimes uncertainty amongst doctors and others as to the degree of severity of illness required to justify the use of compulsory measures. Some doctors appear to believe that if someone is not immediately suicidal or 'dangerous' it is not appropriate to use compulsory measures.

Whilst the facts of each situation may vary, the Mental Welfare Commission has given general advice. In its 1994–5 Annual Report it said that:

> '[s 17(1)] does not mean that there must be an immediate threat to life and limb … severity of symptoms or severity of distress may be sufficient to justify admission, especially if the alternative is likely to be a worsening of an already distressing situation and effective treatment or care is available in hospital.'[1]

In 2000–1, the Commission repeated this advice and said that:

> 'For a patient whose illness has recurred, early intervention with compulsory admission … may be appropriate, providing that there is sufficient evidence to predict that his or her health would seriously deteriorate without hospital treatment and the other provisions [of the 1984 Act] are met.'[2]

These comments were made in relation to the 1984 Act, which did not refer to 'significant' risk, but the Millan Committee expected the test in the Mental Health (Care and Treatment) Act to be broadly similar in effect.[3]

There does not appear to be any further guidance in the Code of Practice, but if the Mental Welfare Commission's advice still holds, this means that the statutory grounds can apply even if there is no immediate, life-threatening risk.

1   Page 25.
2   Annual Report of Mental Welfare Commission 2000–1, para 3.3, p 52.
3   *New directions*, para 5.53.

Risk assessments

11.24 Both the tribunal making orders or hearing appeals and a doctor signing a certificate have to make decisions about risk. The tribunal cannot make an order unless it is satisfied about the risk.[1] A doctor must not make an order unless the degree of risk exists.[2]

It appears generally accepted that risk assessment in psychiatry is poor[3] but there is evidence that it is improving.[4] Following the report of the MacLean Committee, the Scottish Executive set up the Risk Management Authority, which will develop tools of risk assessment. These tools are for people working with serious violent or sexual offenders, but they are likely to have a wider impact on practice.

The MacLean Committee discussed the various tools of risk assessment and concluded that relying on the clinical judgement of one professional was rarely sufficient.[5] A more structured approach, using information from actuarial studies and academic literature as well as multi-disciplinary input is likely to produce better results.[6]

It may be that tribunals will eventually require these tools. In the meantime, both tribunals and solicitors representing people at hearings should be prepared to test the evidence of risk rigorously. The tribunal may wish to hear evidence about possible risk from a range of professionals.[7]

[1]   See, for example, Mental Health (Care and Treatment) (Scotland) Act 2003, s 64(5).
[2]   See, for example, MH(CT)(S) A 2003, s 44(4).
[3]   The Royal College of Psychiatrists, in evidence to the Joint Committee on the Draft Mental Health Bill for England and Wales, said the techniques were highly inaccurate and unreliable. Joint Committee First Report, para 125.
[4]   Professor Tony Maden in evidence to the Committee, above.
[5]   *Report of the Committee on Serious Violent and Sexual Offenders,* Scottish Executive (2000), paras 2.18–37.
[6]   For a detailed explanation of risk assessment techniques, see Michelle Davidson, 'Risk' in JJ McManus and Dr L Thomson, *Mental health and Scots law in practice* (W Green & Sons, 2005), chap 5.
[7]   *New directions,* para 5.57.

Treatability

11.25 The tribunal will not grant a compulsory treatment order unless it is satisfied that medical treatment is available for the person and is likely to prevent the person's mental disorder worsening or to reduce any of its symptoms or effects.[1] This reflects the principle of *benefit*. It is not appropriate to make an order if the person is not likely to benefit from it.

Medical treatment is treatment for the mental disorder.[2] It is not just medicines or hospital care. It also includes nursing, care, psychological interventions, 'habilitation' (which includes education and training in work, social and independent living skills) and rehabilitation.

If any such treatment could benefit the person, there could be a compulsory order, provided, of course, that the other criteria for making an order are satisfied.

[1]   Mental Health (Care and Treatment) (Scotland) Act 2003, s 64(5).
[2]   MH(CT)(S)A 2003, s 329.

Necessity

11.26 An order cannot be made unless it is 'necessary'. An order is not 'necessary' if the person agrees to the proposed treatment.[1] It is not appropriate to apply for an order if someone agrees to admission to hospital and/or medical treatment on an informal or voluntary basis.[2] It may not be necessary to make an order if the person could be treated under the Adults with Incapacity Act.

[1]   Speaking on this section of the Bill, The Deputy Minister for Health, Mary Mulligan, said:

   'We cannot envisage circumstances in which a tribunal would decide that an order is necessary, as the bill requires, if the care and treatment can be provided with the person's agreement.' Scottish Parliament, Health and Community Care Committee, Official Report Meeting No 3, 2003, Column 3650.

[2]   Code of Practice, vol 2, para 1.21.

SAFEGUARDS FOR PATIENTS

Principles

11.27 Even though someone may be subject to compulsory measures, those treating him or her should show respect for his or her wishes and feelings, past and present. The person should be encouraged to participate in decision-making. His or her carer and named person should also be involved.

Advance statements

11.28 Those treating the person should have particular regard to any advance statement the person has made. If they overrule the statement, they will have to give notice to, among other people, the Mental Welfare Commission. See chapter 16. The Mental Welfare Commission has said it will monitor this carefully and may make further investigations if an advance statement is overruled.

Mental health officer involvement

11.29 Mental health officers are social workers who are independent of health services. See chapter 3. Whenever compulsory measures are proposed, doctors should seek a mental health officer's opinion, (although this may not be practical when a doctor is considering emergency detention, see chapter 13).

Short-term detention cannot take place without a mental health officer's approval. The tribunal can grant a compulsory treatment order even if a mental health officer does not agree to the order, but it must hear the mental health officer's views and take them into account.

The mental health officer consults with the patient, named person and carers and can offer a wider view of the person's social circumstances than that available to the doctors. Mental health officers act in accordance with the principles of the Act and they provide a safeguard against doctors acting inappropriately.

Information

11.30 The person and his or her named person should receive information about his or her rights throughout the process. If the person's first language is not English or he or she has difficulty communicating, special measures are required to ensure the person knows his or her rights and can participate in the process. See chapter 17.

Independent advocacy

11.31 Everyone with a mental disorder in Scotland has a right of access to independent advocacy,[1] and this can be particularly important when compulsory measures are being used.

When interviewing someone during the process of applications for short-term detention or a compulsory treatment order, the mental health officer must inform the person of his or her right to advocacy and take steps to ensure that the person has access to independent advocacy services.[2]

1   Mental Health (Care and Treatment) (Scotland) Act 2003, s 259.
2   MH(CT)(S) A 2003, ss 45(1) and 65(2).

Named person

11.32 The person can appoint someone to receive information about any compulsion proceedings. The named person can instruct legal representation if necessary. If someone does not appoint a named person, the primary carer is named person and if there is no carer, the nearest relative. See chapter 4.

Mental Welfare Commission and tribunal

11.33 Anyone subject to compulsory measures can contact the Mental Welfare Commission and can apply to the Mental Health Tribunal for the cancellation of the measures, except where the person is subject to an emergency certificate. Other people can take action on the person's behalf.

There is a further appeal on legal grounds to the sheriff principal and from him or her to the Court of Session. Chapter 15 deals with appeals.

HUMAN RIGHTS SAFEGUARDS

11.34 Mental health act law and practice must comply with the European Convention on Human Rights (ECHR).

In most cases the Mental Health (Care and Treatment) Act meets, and exceeds, ECHR standards, but if, for example, there are delays or non-compliance with the Act's requirements, this could be challenged. In this way the European Convention on Human Rights provides an additional safeguard for service users.

Article 5 of the ECHR provides that 'everyone has the right to liberty and security'. This is subject to certain exceptions. Article 5 permits the 'detention of....... people of unsound mind' if it is 'lawful' and 'in accordance with a procedure prescribed by law'. See chapter 9 for discussion about what constitutes 'detention'.

Detention must be lawful

11.35 This means any detention must comply with the law (either statute or the common law) and with the legal requirements of the European Convention on Human Rights. The leading case of *Winterwerp v Netherlands*[1] said that lawful detention on the grounds of 'unsound mind' requires:

- Reliable (and recent)[2] evidence of mental disorder. There should be a medical examination of the person before the detention takes place, unless there is an emergency.[3]

  (Mental disorder includes mental illness, learning disability or personality disorder. As with the Mental Health (Care and Treatment) Act, the term is flexible, as psychiatric practice changes. A person is not of unsound mind simply because his or her views or behaviour deviate from the norms of the society where he or she lives.[4])

- The mental disorder must be of a kind or degree which justifies detention, for example, because of the risks to the person or others.

- The continued presence of mental disorder throughout the detention. There must be a review of the detention at reasonable intervals, because the reasons initially making the detention appropriate may have ceased to exist.[5]

  (This does not mean that a person who no longer has a mental disorder must be discharged immediately, as it may be necessary to arrange aftercare for him or her. Where it took four years to make arrangements for someone who no longer had a mental disorder, this was a breach of Article 5(1), even though it was authorised under the Mental Health Act 1983.[6] In another case, intervals of 15 months and two years were not regarded as reasonable, particularly in the light of the patient's numerous requests for discharge.[7])

  Regular review is part of the Mental Health (Care and Treatment) Act, but there is no provision for regular review by the sheriff of Adults with Incapacity Act guardianship, even though this could deprive the adult of his or her liberty.

---

[1]   *Winterwerp v The Netherlands* [1979] ECtHR 4, at para 45.
[2]   *Zyzko v Poland* (36426/97), in decision as to admissibility of proceedings, 2001.
[3]   *X v UK* (A 46 (1981)).
[4]   *Winterwerp* (above), para 37.

5   *Winterwerp* (above), para 55.
6   *Johnson v the United Kingdom* [1997] ECtHR 88.
7   *Herczegfalvy v Austria* (A 244 (1992)).

Procedure authorised by law

11.36 The Mental Health (Care and Treatment) Act and the Adults with Incapacity Act provide lawful procedures for human rights purposes.

The *'Bournewood'* case said that the law of necessity (which doctors sometimes use in an emergency) lacks procedural safeguards, such as admission procedures, time limits, representation, and rights of appeal and review, to protect against arbitrary detention.[1]

Following this case it is not possible to rely on the law of necessity law to authorise long-term arrangements which deprive a person of his or her liberty, whether in hospital or in the community.

1   *HL v UK* [2004] ECtHR 471.

Reasons for detention

11.37 The person must be told why he or she has been detained, so that he or she can decide whether to exercise the rights of appeal under Article 5(4).[1]

1   See *Van der Leer v Netherlands* (A 170-A (1990)) paras 27–28. Article 5(2) refers only to giving information to people who have been arrested. The case makes clear it also applies to people who have been otherwise detained.

Right of appeal

11.38 A person detained or arrested must have 'speedy access' to a court to appeal against the detention.[1] A 'court' includes a tribunal, such as the Mental Health Tribunal for Scotland.

The appeal does not have to be a complete re-examination of the facts of the case, but must allow a proper consideration of whether the person continues to suffer from a mental disorder justifying detention.[2] If someone cannot exercise his or her right of access to the court, human rights requirements are satisfied if the person's named person or nearest relative can arrange legal representation for the person.[3]

What is 'speedy access to the court' is a question of fact.[4] Clearly if there is evidence of a change in the person's condition, a speedy review is necessary.[5] Where the law provides automatic review,[6] any proceedings must be heard in accordance with the time limits in the national law.[7]

The English courts have held that delays in hearings of the Mental Health Review Tribunal were a breach of human rights[8] and awarded (nominal) damages.[9]

1   European Convention on Human Rights, Art 5(4).
2   In *HL v UK* (above) the court held that a remedy such as judicial review was not an adequate right of appeal under Art 5(4). See paras 137–140.
3   Lady Hale in *MH v. Secretary of State for the Department of Health and others* [2005] UKHL 60 at para 27.
4   See *E v Norway* [1994] 17 EHHR 567, where an eight week delay too long. *Rutten v The Netherlands* [2001] ECtHR 482 where two months 17 days too long.
5   *M v FRG* No 10272/83 DR 104 (1984).
6   As, for example in the Mental Health (Care and Treatment) (Scotland) Act 2003, ss 101 and 165).
7   *Keus v Netherlands* (A 185-C) para 24 (1990).
8   *R (on the application of KB, MK, JR, GM, LB, PD and TB) v the Mental Health Review Tribunal and the Secretary of State for Health* [2002] EWHC 639 (Admin).
9   *R (on the application of KB) v South London and South West Region Mental Health Review Tribunal (Damages)* [2003] 2 All E.R. 209.

Procedural guarantees

11.39 To comply with Article 5(4), the proceedings do not have to have the same guarantees as under Article 6(1) (right to a fair trial), but the person must have access to a court and the opportunity to be heard either in person or, where necessary, through a representative.

The European Court of Human Rights has said that mental disorder may mean it is necessary to restrict or modify a person's access to a court, but the person must remain able to access the court. In fact, extra procedural safeguards may be necessary to protect the interests of people who are not fully capable of acting for themselves.[1] (For example, the Scottish rules oblige the tribunal to consider how to maximise the person's participation in the hearing if he or she is unable to attend. See chapter 23.)

The House of Lords has said extra procedural safeguards do not mean that there must be an automatic right of appeal if someone is unable to initiate proceedings him or herself. Others may be able to ensure adequate review.[2]

1   *Winterwerp* (11.35 above) at para 60.
2   See decision of the House of Lords in the English case *R (on the application of MH) v Secretary of State for Health* [2005] UKHL 60. The House of Lords held that while Art 5(4) requires a right of speedy access to the court, it does not envisage that in every case there will be reference to a court.

Legal representation

11.40 Human rights law states that there may need to be special procedural safeguards to ensure a person has a fair hearing under Article 5(4). All the special circumstances of the case must be taken into account. The case law does not state that legal representation is necessary in every case involving someone with a mental disorder, but the courts have generally said legal representation was necessary.

In *Megyeri*,[1] the European Court of Human Rights said that where someone is detained in hospital following criminal proceedings, he or she should have legal representation in any hearing relating to the continuation, suspension or termination of the detention in hospital, unless there are special circumstances. The court said it was compelled to reach this conclusion because of the importance of the issues of personal liberty and the fact that the person may have had diminished mental capacity.

In another case before the European Court of Human Rights, the patient had a legal training. His mental disorder prevented him from conducting court proceedings satisfactorily. The court said he should have had a lawyer.[2]

The Mental Health Tribunal rules say that a person may appear at the tribunal in person or through a lawyer.[3] The tribunal must interpret the rules in accordance with human rights requirements. If a patient represents him or herself, the tribunal must ensure that the hearing is fair. The presence of an independent advocate will help, but is not equivalent to legal representation.

Human rights law has a rule of 'equality of arms'. Each party to proceedings must have a reasonable opportunity of presenting his or her case to the court or tribunal under conditions which do not place the person at a substantial disadvantage to his or her opponent.[4] Allowing someone to represent him or herself in a mental health hearing could breach this principle.

1   *Megyeri v Germany* [1992] ECtHR 49, para 23.The court discussed the need for legal representation in terms of the person's right to challenge detention in

hospital, not to defend the criminal proceedings. See also *Woukam Moudefo v France* (A 141-B (1988)). The 'fundamental legal guarantees' of Art 5(4) require the provision of legal assistance, including representation, if this is necessary to make an application effective.

2   *Pereira v Portugal* [2002] ECtHR 161. See also *Bouamar v Belgium* [1988] ECtHR 1, para 60. Where a young person was being detained, informal proceedings were appropriate, but he should have had access to a lawyer.

3   Mental Health Tribunal for Scotland (Practice and Procedure) (No. 2) Rules 2005 (SSI 2005/519), r 54(3).

4   *Kaufman v Belgium* (No 10938/84), 50 DR at 115.

CROSS BORDER ISSUES

11.41 There can be complex legal problems if a person subject to compulsory measures under the Mental Health (Care and Treatment) Act needs help or protection abroad or even in another part of the United Kingdom. There are regulations dealing with hospital transfers in such situations. See chapter 19.

The Hague Convention on the International Protection of Adults could be relevant if a vulnerable person from the UK needs help in France, Germany or the Netherlands. The Hague Convention is relevant wherever a person or his or her property may be at risk because the person is unable to protect his or her own interests. See 24.32.

PRACTICAL MATTERS

Understanding timescales

11.42 The Code of Practice gives guidance on the various timescales in the Act.[1] In summary, the rules are as follows:

- If the Act specifies that something lasts for a number of **hours**, these should be counted in hours from the time of signing the certificate, etc. (For example, the nurse's holding power lasts for two hours from the commencement of the detention.[2])

- Where the Act specifies a number of **days or weeks**, these are counted from the beginning of the first day of the period. For example, the 28 day short-term detention begins at the beginning of the day (ie midnight) on which the doctor or other health professional issues the certificate.

  To calculate the length of short-term detention, add 27 to the starting date. (Not 28. The first day is day 1, not day 0). If necessary, deduct the number of days in the starting month. The detention ends at midnight on the resultant day.[3]

The person must be moved to hospital by midnight on day 3, counting the day on which the certificate was signed as day 1.[4]

- The same provisions apply where the time periods are **months or years**. The period is counted back from the beginning of the day on which the order was made. For example, a compulsory treatment order made on 28 January expires at midnight on 28 July. All references to days, weeks or months are to calendar days, weeks, months as appropriate.

- Where the Act refers to **'working' days**, these are days other than Saturday, Sunday or bank holidays.[5]

1   See introduction to Vol 1, paras 24–29.
2   Mental Health (Care and Treatment) (Scotland) Act 2003, s 299(2).
3   The author is grateful to Dr Jim Dyer for this suggestion.
4   MH(CT)(S)A 2003, s 44(5).
5   See, for example, MH(CT)(S)A 2003, s 47(8).

Forms

11.43 The Mental Health (Care and Treatment) Act has some prescribed forms, and many more forms have been approved by the Scottish Executive, the Mental Welfare Commission and the Mental Health Tribunal for Scotland. All are available on the Scottish Executive's mental health law website.

Forms may be submitted electronically.

Chapter 12

SHORT-TERM DETENTION

12.01 Most cases of detention are for a short period only. In 2004–5, just over 4,000 people were detained on emergency orders made under the 1984 Act. Around a third were discharged from detention when the emergency order expired. Just under a quarter proceeded to long-term detention.[1]

Short-term detention is authorised by one approved psychiatrist, who should seek the consent of a mental health officer.

Short-term detention is generally preferable to emergency detention, because of the greater safeguards it offers.[2] For this reason the Millan Committee recommended that the majority of admissions from the community should be by way of short-term detention procedure.[3] A doctor should use the emergency procedure only if he or she believes the short-term detention procedure would involve unacceptable delay.[4]

A person subject to a short-term detention order may appeal against detention.

[1]   Annual Report of Mental Welfare Commission 2004–5.
[2]   Code of Practice, vol 2, paras 7.24–26.
[3]   *New directions*, recommendation 8.24.
[4]   Mental Health (Care and Treatment) (Scotland) Act 2003, s 36(5). See below.

AUTHORISING DETENTION

Duties of approved medical practitioner

12.02 An approved medical practitioner (a psychiatrist approved by his or her health board) must examine the person.

If the approved medical practitioner considers it likely that the grounds for short-term detention apply to the person, he or she may sign a short-term detention certificate.[1] (The recommended form is on the Scottish Executive's mental health law website.) The doctor must sign the certificate within three days of the medical examination.[2]

The approved medical practitioner must consult a mental health officer and obtain his or her consent to the detention.[3] If the mental health officer does not consent, it would not generally be acceptable to approach another mental health officer.[4]

The approved medical practitioner should also consult the named person,[5] (if practicable).[6] The Code of Practice stresses the importance of taking the patient's views and wishes into account and of attempting to contact carers.[7]

1   Mental Health (Care and Treatment) (Scotland) Act 2003, s 44(9).
2   MH(CT)(S)A 2003, s 44(1).
3   MH(CT)(S)A 2003, s 44(3).
4   Code of Practice, vol 2, para 2.30.
5   MH(CT)(S)A 2003, s 44(10).
6   MH(CT)(S)A 2003, s 44(11).
7   See Code of Practice, vol 2, paras 2.26 and 2.33.

Grounds for detention

12.03 The approved medical practitioner can grant a short-term detention certificate if he or she believes it is likely that:

- The person has a mental disorder.
- Because of the mental disorder, the person's ability to make decisions about medical treatment is significantly impaired.
- The person needs detention in hospital to enable doctors to assess his or her need for medical treatment or to receive such treatment.
- If the person is not so detained, there would be a significant risk to his or her health, safety or welfare or to the safety of another person; and
- The granting of the certificate is necessary.[1]

For further discussion of these grounds, see chapter 11. The approved medical practitioner must certify why he or she believes these conditions are met.[2]

1   Mental Health (Care and Treatment) (Scotland) Act 2003, s 45(4).
2   MH(CT)(S)A 2003, s 44(9).

Conflict of interest

12.04 The approved medical practitioner cannot sign the form if he or she has any conflict of interest.[1] The rules are set out in Regulations.[2] There is a conflict of interest if the doctor is the person's relative[3] or works for or provides services to an independent health care service where the person will be detained.[4]

The doctor can act even where there is a conflict of interest, if delay would involve serious risk to the health, safety or welfare of the person or to the safety of other people.[5] The doctor should record in the person's notes why it was appropriate to act despite the conflict.[6]

There may be other circumstances where a doctor might consider he or she has a conflict of interest. An example might be if the person is the doctor's friend, colleague or civil partner. The doctor should consider whether it is appropriate to act.[7]

[1]   Mental Health (Care and Treatment) (Scotland) Act 2003, s 44(3).
[2]   Mental Health (Conflict of Interest) (Scotland) (No 2) Regulations 2005 (SSI 2005/380). ('The conflict of interest regulations'.)
[3]   That is, the child, grandchild, parent, grandparent, wife, husband, sister, brother, daughter-in-law, son-in-law, mother-in-law, father-in-law, sister-in-law, brother-in-law, co-habitee of the person, or the child, grandchild, parent, grandparent, sister or brother of a co-habitee of the person. Children include stepchildren.
[4]   Conflict of interest regulations, reg 2.
[5]   Conflict of interest regulations, reg 3.
[6]   Code of Practice, vol 2, para 2.16.
[7]   Code of Practice, vol 2, para 2.17.

Where person refuses examination

12.05 If the person refuses to allow the approved medical practitioner to examine him or her, the approved medical practitioner may have to consider emergency detention.[1]

[1]   Code of Practice, vol 2, para 2.27.

Where short-term detention not permitted

12.06 Short-term detention is not permissible if immediately before[1] the approved medical practitioner carried out the medical examination, the person was detained in hospital under:

- A previous short-term detention certificate;
- An extension of a short-term detention certificate;
- An extension of short-term detention under section 68 of the Act;

- An extension of a compulsory treatment order under section 114(2) of the Act; or
- An extension of an interim compulsory treatment order under section 115(2) of the Act.[2]

Short-term detention is possible if a person is subject to an emergency order.

[1]   A case under the 1984 Act considered similar wording. A person remained in hospital for 24 hours after her short-term detention had expired. She understood that she was free to leave. The court held that her subsequent detention under s 24 of that Act did not fall 'immediately after' the first. *R v Lothian Health Board (No 2)* (OH) 1993 SLT 1021.
[2]   Mental Health (Care and Treatment) (Scotland) Act 2003, s 44(2).

EFFECT OF DETENTION CERTIFICATE

Notifying hospital

12.07 The approved medical practitioner should ensure that the managers of the hospital receive a copy of the certificate before the person is admitted.[1] If the person is already in hospital, the approved medical practitioner must give a copy of the certificate to the managers as soon as possible after he or she has signed it.[2]

[1]   Mental Health (Care and Treatment) (Scotland) Act 2003, s 44(6).
[2]   MH(CT)(S)A 2003, s 44(7).

Transfer of person

Planning transfer

12.08 The short-term detention certificate authorises the person's removal to hospital, if he or she is not already in hospital. This must take place within three days of the issue of the certificate.[1]

(All the bodies likely to be involved in transferring people to hospital should draw up a psychiatric emergency plan to ensure that transfers are as smooth and safe as possible.[2] This includes hospitals, police, ambulance staff, local authorities and others. Users and carers should be involved in drawing up these plans.)

The person should go to hospital as quickly as possible after the approved medical practitioner signs the certificate. Even in an emergency, holding the person in a police car, police van or police cell for lengthy periods should be avoided, unless there are exceptional circumstances involving physical risk.[3]

1   Mental Health (Care and Treatment) (Scotland) Act 2003, s 44(5).
2   Code of Practice, vol 2, para 7.58.
3   Code of Practice, vol 2, para 7.54.

Involving the police

12.09 It may occasionally be appropriate to seek police involvement. The Code of Practice gives good practice guidance to attempt to reduce the stress on the person and carers.[1]

The police have statutory powers to be involved if someone subject to a short-term detention certificate absconds from the place where he or she is held while waiting to go to hospital.[2] A police officer may take the person into custody and take him or her to the hospital named in the certificate.[3] The principles of the Act require that any police involvement should take place in the least restrictive manner possible.

The police may be involved if it is not possible to gain entry to the place where the person is living. It may be necessary to go to court to seek a warrant authorising entry. The warrant can authorise a police officer to enter the premises, even if locked. See 20.13, 30.07.

The police may also be involved if there is concern about a possible breach of the peace. This might be necessary if those involved consider the person is likely to resist attempts to take him or her to hospital.

1   Code of Practice, vol 2, paras 7.56–7.
2   Mental Health (Care and Treatment) (Scotland) Act 2003, s 302. There is no specific mention of police involvement if someone absconds while being moved to hospital. The person moving the person may re-take him or her, but it is less clear that the person can involve the police under s 302 of the Act.
3   MH(CT)(S)A 2003, s 303.

Medical treatment

12.10 A person subject to short-term detention is subject to the rules on the giving of medical treatment contained in Part 16 of the Act.[1] This means that in certain circumstances a person may receive medical treatment to which he or she does not consent.

The doctors must take into account the terms of any advance statement the person has made. For details see chapter 16.

¹   Mental Health (Care and Treatment) (Scotland) Act 2003, s 44(5)(c).

Length of detention

12.11 The certificate authorises the person's detention in hospital for up to 28 days from the date of the certificate (if the person was already in hospital) or from the date of admission to hospital under the certificate.[1]

The person may leave hospital before the 28 days are up if the responsible medical officer cancels (revokes) the certificate.[2]

¹   Mental Health (Care and Treatment) (Scotland) Act 2003, s 44(5).
²   MH(CT)(S)A 2003, s 49(2). (See below.)

DUTIES OF HOSPITAL MANAGERS

Appointment of responsible medical officer

12.12 As soon as possible after the granting of the certificate, the hospital managers should appoint an approved medical practitioner to be the person's responsible medical officer.[1]

If the person already has a responsible medical officer, he or she may continue to act.[2]

¹   Mental Health (Care and Treatment) (Scotland) Act 2003, s 230(1).
²   MH(CT)(S)A 2003, s 230(2).

People to be notified

12.13 As soon as possible after the granting of the short-term detention certificate, the hospital managers must notify the person subject to the certificate, his or her named person and any welfare guardian or attorney.[1]

Within seven days of the granting of the certificate, the hospital managers should send a copy to the tribunal and the Mental Welfare Commission.[2]

¹   Mental Health (Care and Treatment) (Scotland) Act 2003, s 46(2).
²   MH(CT)(S)A 2003, s 46 (3).

Information

12.14 The hospital managers must take all reasonable steps to ensure that the person understands the effect of the order, and any rights of appeal he or she may have.

This includes information about the role of the responsible medical officer, the Mental Welfare Commission and the tribunal. The person should receive information about how to make appeals and obtain legal assistance.[1]

Where someone has communication needs or his or her first language is not English, the hospital managers must make special arrangements for an interpreter.[2]

For further details, see chapter 17.

[1]   Mental Health (Care and Treatment) (Scotland) Act 2003, ss 260(2)-(5).
[2]   MH(CT)(S)A 2003, s 261.

DUTIES OF MENTAL HEALTH OFFICER

Contacting patient

12.15 The mental health officer should interview the person subject to the certificate as soon as possible and should attempt to find out the name and address of his or her named person.

The mental health officer should advise the person about his or her right to advocacy and help the person make use of advocacy services.[1]

A mental health officer unable to interview someone or to identify a named person should record his or her attempts to do so. He or she should send a copy of the record to the approved medical practitioner not more than seven days after the doctor contacted him or her.[2] A form is available on the Scottish Executive's mental health law website.

[1]   Mental Health (Care and Treatment) (Scotland) Act 2003, s 45(1).
[2]   MH(CT)(S)A 2003, s 45(2).

Social circumstances report

12.16 Within 21 days of the granting of a short-term detention certificate, the mental health officer must prepare a social circumstances report and send a copy to the responsible medical officer and to the Mental Welfare Commission.[1]

The Scottish Executive's mental health law website has a form for the report. Good practice guidance is in the Code of Practice.[2]

If the mental health officer considers such a report would serve little or no practical purpose, he or she need not prepare one.[3] The mental health officer must write to the responsible medical officer and the Commission explaining his or her reasons.[4]

1   Mental Health (Care and Treatment) (Scotland) Act 2003, s 231(1).
2   Vol 1, chap 11.
3   MH(CT)(S)A 2003, s 231(2). For example, where there has been a recent report and no significant change in the person's circumstances. Code of Practice, vol 1, para 11.13.
4   MH(CT)(S)A 2003, s 231(2).

Preparing report

12.17 The social circumstances report should ensure that full information about the person's background and social circumstances is available to the responsible medical officer and the Mental Welfare Commission.

The report should include as much detail as possible and give details of the person's home background and the amount of support, if any, there is. More detail is set out in regulations.[1]

The mental health officer should make all reasonable efforts to interview the person. It would generally be unacceptable to omit this.[2] He or she should also interview relevant relatives and/or the primary carer, where appropriate. If the mental health officer interviews such people despite the patient's objections, he or she should inform the patient.[3]

The person subject to the certificate may ask for his or her named person or advocate to be present when the mental health officer carries out the interview.[4]

1   Mental Health (Social Circumstances Reports) (Scotland) Regulations 2005 (SSI 2005/310).
2   Code of Practice, vol 1, para 11.07.
3   Code of Practice, vol 1, paras 11.08, 11.09.
4   Code of Practice, vol 1, para 11.11.

APPEALS AND REVIEWS

Application to tribunal

12.18 Either the person subject to the certificate or his or her named person may ask the tribunal to cancel the short-term detention certificate.[1]

There is no prescribed form. All that is required is a simple letter addressed to the tribunal asking it to set aside the short-term detention certificate. Appendix 3 has a suggested form. (Form 1).

If the tribunal is not satisfied that any of the grounds for short-term detention are established, it must cancel the certificate.[2] The tribunal will consider whether the grounds for detention apply. Does the person have a mental disorder? Is his or her ability to make medical decisions significantly impaired? Is there a significant risk to self or others? Is detention necessary? It is for the mental health officer and responsible medical officer to satisfy the tribunal that the grounds apply, not for the patient to prove that they do not.[3]

Appeal against the tribunal's decision is available only on a point of law.[4] See chapter 15.

For tribunal procedure, see Part 4.

[1]   Mental Health (Care and Treatment) (Scotland) Act 2003, s 50(1).
[2]   MH(CT)(S)A 2003, s 50(4).
[3]   See *R (H) v MHRT North & East London Region* (2001) EWCA Civ 415; *L v Scottish Ministers* (IH) Court of Session, 17 January 2002; *Hutchison Reid v UK* [2003] ECtHR 94.
[4]   MH(CT)(S)A 2003, s 320.

Role of Mental Welfare Commission

12.19 The Mental Welfare Commission has the power to review the detention. The Commission can cancel the certificate if it considers any of the grounds for short-term detention are not established.[1] If the Commission cancels the certificate it must, as soon as possible, notify the person, his or her named person, any attorney or guardian, the hospital where the person is detained, the mental health officer and the tribunal.[2]

The Mental Welfare Commission has said that it does not intend to use this power. It believes that the tribunal should make decisions about detention. The Commission will take steps to ensure that patients can ask the tribunal to consider their case. It may refer a patient to the tribunal, perhaps if the person is unable to do this him or herself.[3]

[1]   Mental Health (Care and Treatment) (Scotland) Act 2003, s 51.

[2]   MH(CT)(S)A 2003, s 52.

[3]   Mental Welfare Commission letter to chief executives of health boards and local authorities (October 2005).

Role of responsible medical officer

12.20 The responsible medical officer must keep the person's condition under consideration and should from time to time consider whether the detention is necessary.[1]

If the grounds for admission no longer apply or the order is no longer necessary, the responsible medical officer should cancel the certificate.[2] The responsible medical officer should bear in mind the principles of the Act when considering whether to discharge the person.[3]

The Code of Practice says that the responsible medical officer should keep the person's condition under continual review and should carry out a review with input from the multi-disciplinary team at least once a week.[4]

If the responsible medical officer cancels the detention certificate, he or she should give written notice as soon as possible to the person subject to the certificate, the named person, any guardian or welfare attorney and the mental health officer.[5] He or she should also notify them orally.[6]

The responsible medical officer should notify the tribunal and the Commission within seven days of the revocation.[7] A form for cancelling the certificate is available on the Scottish Executive's mental health law website.

[1]   Mental Health (Care and Treatment) (Scotland) Act 2003, s 49(1).

[2]   MH(CT)(S)A 2003, s 49(2).

[3]   See chapter 11.

[4]   Code of Practice, vol 2, para 2.70.

[5]   MH(CT)(S)A 2003, s 49(3).

[6]   Code of Practice, vol 2, para 2.69.

[7]   MH(CT)(S)A 2003, s 49(4).

EXPIRY OF CERTIFICATE

Possible outcomes

12.21 On the expiry of the certificate, the person may leave the hospital. He or she may agree to remain in hospital as a voluntary patient. The responsible medical officer may recommend an application for a compulsory treatment order. (See below.)

If the person's condition unexpectedly deteriorates towards the end of his or her stay in hospital, the doctor may extend the detention and apply for a compulsory treatment order (see below).

The person cannot be detained for a further 28 days under the short-term detention procedure. Nor can a doctor grant an emergency detention certificate immediately after the expiry of the 28-day detention.[1]

[1] Mental Health (Care and Treatment) (Scotland) Act 2003, s 36(2). For what is meant by 'immediately' see 12.06.

Application for compulsory treatment order

12.22 If the responsible medical officer considers a patient needs to remain subject to compulsory measures, he or she should ask the mental health officer to make an application to the tribunal for a compulsory treatment order.

If the mental health officer makes an application, the authority to detain the person (and treat him or her in accordance with Part 16) continues for up to five working days from the end of the short-term certificate.[1]

The tribunal must hear the case within that period and may grant a compulsory treatment order or an interim compulsory treatment order.[2]

The tribunal service has had some difficulties in arranging hearings within the prescribed times. Its failure to do so has been challenged by way of judicial review.[3]

[1] Mental Health (Care and Treatment) (Scotland) Act 2003, s 68.
[2] Mental Health Tribunal for Scotland (Practice and Procedure) Rules 2005 (SSI 2005/420), r 8.
[3] See judgement of Lady Smith in *Petition for Judicial Review of John Smith, Mental Health Officer for Fife Council*, [2006] CSOH 44.

Impact of compulsory treatment order

12.23 A compulsory treatment order or an interim compulsory treatment order automatically cancels the short-term detention certificate.[1]

If the tribunal does not make an order, the responsible medical officer cannot make a new short-term or emergency order.

[1]   Mental Health (Care and Treatment) (Scotland) Act 2003, s 70.

Where application refused

12.24 If the tribunal refuses to make a compulsory treatment order, the Code of Practice says the responsible medical officer should immediately cancel the short-term detention certificate or extension certificate.[1] The author suggests the situation is somewhat more complex.

The responsible medical officer should consider the impact of the tribunal's decision carefully. It may be that he or she considers the short-term detention should continue for its few remaining days until there are suitable discharge arrangements.

The fact that the tribunal was not satisfied that it was appropriate to make a long-term order does not mean, of itself, that the short-term order was not valid and should not complete its course. There is a significant difference between the use of compulsory measures for up to 28 days and their long-term use.

Short-term detention might have been justified, but the tribunal might consider that, following treatment, informal measures would be appropriate. In such a case, the responsible medical officer may decide to allow the short-term detention to complete its course.

In other situations, there might be a stronger argument for discharge. If, for example, the tribunal is not satisfied that the person has a mental disorder or that medical treatment can help him or her, the grounds for short-term detention would be questionable.

Where the tribunal allows an appeal against short-term detention,[2] the responsible medical officer must, of course, immediately comply with the tribunal's decision.

[1]   Code of Practice, vol 2, para 7.86.
[2]   Tribunal rules of procedure (SSI 2005/519), r 52(5).

Limitations on new applications

12.25 If the tribunal refuses the application, can the mental health officer re-apply to a new tribunal? A mental health tribunal is a court. The law of contempt of court applies. No one can knowingly act to subvert the decision of the tribunal.[1]

This question has come before the courts in England and Wales. The House of Lords, in connection with somewhat different wording in the Mental Health Act 1983, said that there will be situations where the person's responsible medical officer may not agree with the tribunal's decision. The doctor should reconsider his or her opinion in the light of the tribunal decision but if he or she continues to consider an order necessary, he or she owes a professional duty to the patient and the public to keep to that view.[2]

The House of Lords said that it is generally not appropriate for an approved social worker (mental health officer) to make a new application for a long-term order within days of a tribunal decision refusing an order. An application is appropriate only if there is some change in the patient's circumstances, for example if the person's health deteriorates, if new evidence becomes known or if the person agrees to take medication at the tribunal and later refuses.[3]

If the circumstances have changed and the mental health officer makes a new application, he or she should advise the patient why he or she is seeking to reverse the earlier tribunal decision.[4]

1 *Pickering v Liverpool Daily Post and Echo Newspapers plc* [1991] 2 AC 370, referred to by Lord Bingham in *R v East London and the City Mental Health NHS Trust and another ex parte von Brandenburg* [2003] UKHL 58, at para 8.
2 Lord Bingham in *von Brandenburg* (above) at para 9(4).
3 Lord Bingham in *von Brandenburg* (above) at para 10.
4 *Von Brandenburg* (above) at para 12.

EXTENSION OF DETENTION

12.26 Normally if someone is likely to require further compulsory measures after the expiry of the 28-day period, the mental health officer should attempt to apply for a compulsory treatment order in good time during that period.

Sometimes a person's health may deteriorate unexpectedly towards the end of the detention. There may be no time to make an application for a compulsory treatment order before the expiry of the 28 days.

In a case under the 1984 Act, a person's health unexpectedly deteriorated towards the end of the 28 days. The doctors further detained him, relying on common law powers to protect people at risk. The House of Lords held that the doctors had acted illegally, despite the fact that the patient was seriously at risk.[1]

Parliament subsequently amended the 1984 Act,[2] and the Mental Health (Care and Treatment) Act keeps these provisions. It provides that if someone's condition deteriorates towards the end of a short-term detention, a doctor may extend the detention and apply for a compulsory treatment order. This procedure should be necessary only in exceptional circumstances.[3]

[1]   *B v F*, 1988 SLT 572, HL.
[2]   Mental Health (Detention) (Scotland) Act 1991.
[3]   Code of Practice, vol 2, para 2.82.

Granting extension

12.27 Any approved medical practitioner can grant an extension certificate.[1] Generally this should be the responsible medical officer.[2] The doctor should examine the person and issue the certificate within 24 hours of the examination.[3] The form of certificate is on the Scottish Executive's mental health law website.

The doctor can issue a certificate extending the detention if:

- The person's mental health has changed and, as a result, the doctor considers an application for a compulsory treatment order is necessary.[4]
- The grounds for making a short-term certificate still apply to the person.[5]
- There has been no application for a compulsory treatment order and it is not reasonably practical to make one before the 28-day detention expires.[6]
- The doctor has consulted a mental health officer[7] and he or she agrees to the extension.[8] The doctor need not consult a mental health officer if this is not practicable.[9]
- The doctor has no conflict of interest.[10]

[1]   Mental Health (Care and Treatment) (Scotland) Act 2003, s 47(1).
[2]   Code of Practice, vol 2, para 2.84.
[3]   MH(CT)(S)A 2003, s 47(1).
[4]   MH(CT)(S)A 2003, s 47(2).

5   See above.
6   MH(CT)(S)A 2003, s 47(3).
7   Ideally the person's mental health officer. Code of Practice, vol 2, para 2.86.
8   MH(CT)(S)A 2003, s 47(3)(c).
9   MH(CT)(S)A 2003, s 47(6).
10   MH(CT)(S)A 2003, s 47(2). See 12.04 above.

Effect of certificate

12.28 The certificate extends the authority for the detention and medical treatment of the patient for three days after the end of the 28-day detention.[1] Saturdays, Sundays and bank holidays are not counted in calculating the three days.[2]

When the mental health officer makes the application for a compulsory treatment order, the authority to detain the person continues for a further five days, as explained above.[3]

1   Mental Health (Care and Treatment) (Scotland) Act 2003, s 47(4).
2   MH(CT)(S)A 2003, ss 47(7) and (8).
3   MH(CT)(S)A 2003, s 68.

People to be notified

12.29 Within 24 hours of granting the extension certificate, the approved medical practitioner must give the certificate to the hospital managers.

He or she must also give notice to the person subject to the certificate, his or her named person, any guardian or welfare attorney, the mental health officer, the tribunal and the Commission.

The notice should state why the doctor granted the certificate and whether the mental health officer agreed. If not, it should explain why it was impracticable to consult the mental health officer.[1]

Although the legislation does not appear to impose a duty on the hospital to notify the person of his/her rights (see 12.14) this would seem to be a matter of good practice.

1   Mental Health (Care and Treatment) (Scotland) Act 2003, s 48(1).

Appeal against extension

12.30 The person can apply to the tribunal to cancel the extension.[1] Appendix 3, form 2 offers a suggested form.

The person can also contact the Mental Welfare Commission, which can cancel the extension.[2] It must notify all relevant parties if it does so.[3] The Commission is more likely to refer the matter to the tribunal if concerned. See above.

If the tribunal cancels short-term detention, the cancellation applies also to any extension of the detention.[4]

[1]   Mental Health (Care and Treatment) (Scotland) Act 2003, s 50(1).

[2]   MH(CT)(S)A 2003, s 51.

[3]   MH(CT)(S)A 2003, s 52.

[4]   MH(CT)(S)A 2003, s 50(5).

SUSPENSION OF DETENTION

12.31 Someone subject to a short-term detention certificate may leave hospital, either for a specific event, such as a hospital appointment or family event, or for a period, as part of the person's rehabilitation.

The person's responsible medical officer must authorise any such absence from the hospital.[1] He or she does this by suspending the terms of the certificate for a defined period.

The responsible medical officer should consult with the care team before authorising any such absence from the hospital.[2]

[1]   Mental Health (Care and Treatment) (Scotland) Act 2003, s 53.

[2]   Code of Practice, vol 2, para 2.99.

Suspending terms of order

12.32 The responsible medical officer issues a certificate suspending the terms of the short-term detention. The form is on the Scottish Executive's mental health law website. The form requires the responsible medical officer to deliver the certificate to the hospital managers.

The responsible medical officer may attach conditions to the suspension certificate, either in the interests of the person or for the protection of others.[1]

These conditions could include authorising supervision in the community, specifying where the person should stay or requiring him or her to grant access to a doctor, nurse or social worker on request.

The responsible medical officer should ensure that members of the person's care team are aware of the terms of the suspension.[2]

1   Mental Health (Care and Treatment) (Scotland) Act 2003, s 53(3).
2   Code of Practice, vol 2, para 2.98.

Responsibility for patient

12.33 The responsible medical officer remains responsible for the person's care. The person's family, carers, and all members of the care team should understand how to contact the responsible medical officer if they have concerns.[1]

1   Code of Practice, vol 2, para 2.102.

Cancelling suspension

12.34 The responsible medical officer may cancel any suspension certificate at any time, if he or she thinks this necessary in the interests of the person or for the protection of others.[1]

As soon as possible after cancelling the suspension, the responsible medical officer must give notice to the patient, his or her named person, the mental health officer, anyone supervising the person and the Mental Welfare Commission.[2]

1   Mental Health (Care and Treatment) (Scotland) Act 2003, s 54(2).
2   MH(CT)(S)A 2003, s 54(3).

TRANSFERRING HOSPITAL

12.35 While the Mental Health (Care and Treatment) Act contains provisions for the transfer of a person subject to a compulsory treatment order to a different hospital,[1] there is no similar power to transfer a person subject to short-term detention.

If at the time of the detention it becomes clear that another hospital would be more suitable, the person may be sent to that hospital rather than the hospital named in the order.[2]

1   Mental Health (Care and Treatment) (Scotland) Act 2003, s 124.
2   MH(CT)(S)A 2003, s 44(5)(a).

Chapter 13

EMERGENCY DETENTION

13.01 In an emergency there may not be time to arrange for a psychiatrist to examine a person. In these circumstances, emergency admission may be necessary.

A person subject to an emergency detention cannot appeal to the tribunal or ask the Mental Welfare Commission to review the detention. This means doctors should use emergency detention only in genuine emergencies.

The Millan Committee found that emergency detention was the preferred method of admission in around 96 per cent of cases under the 1984 Act, although this was not the intention of that Act. It was concerned about this possible breach of human rights.[1] The Mental Health (Care and Treatment) Act and the Code of Practice are clear that short-term detention is the preferred option, because of the safeguards it contains.[2]

If possible, the doctor should attempt to contact a mental health officer and obtain his or her consent to the admission. Some doctors' failure to do this was a recurrent problem under the 1984 Act.

[1]   *New directions*, paras 8.65–74.
[2]   Code of Practice, vol 2, para 7.24.

AUTHORISING DETENTION

Duties of doctor

13.02 The doctor should examine the person. In certain circumstances only a limited examination may be possible. It may be necessary for the doctor to obtain a warrant to gain access to premises.[1] The Code of Practice gives further guidance.[2]

If the doctor considers the grounds for emergency admission apply, he or she can sign a certificate authorising the detention.[3]

Any registered doctor can sign the emergency detention certificate. He or she does not need special psychiatric qualifications. The doctor may be the person's general practitioner or a doctor at an accident or emergency clinic.

As well as attempting to contact a mental health officer (see below), the doctor should, if possible, involve carers and the named person, if the person has one.[4]

Generally the doctor should sign the certificate on the day he or she examines the person. If the doctor examines the person after 8pm or does not finish the examination by 8pm, he or she can grant the certificate the next day. The doctor has four hours from the end of the examination.[5]

[1]   Under Mental Health (Care and Treatment) (Scotland) Act 2003, s 35. See Part 7.
[2]   Code of Practice, vol 2, paras 7.30–32.
[3]   MH(CT)(S)A 2003, s 36(1). The recommended form is on the Scottish Executive's mental health law website. The doctor can submit the form electronically.
[4]   In accordance with the principles of the Act. Code of Practice, vol 2, para 7.46.
[5]   MH(CT)(S)A 2003, s 36(12).

Where person in hospital

13.03 A doctor can grant an emergency detention certificate where someone is already in hospital.

Where a voluntary patient decides to leave the hospital against medical advice, a doctor may issue an emergency detention certificate. If someone attempts to leave before a doctor can grant the certificate, a nurse may detain him or her and seek a doctor (see below).

Staff can encourage a person to stay, but should not put people wishing to discharge themselves under undue pressure. A person is effectively 'detained' if he or she stays unwillingly in order to avoid compulsory measures.[1]

[1]   See guidance in Code of Practice, vol 2, paras 7.17–19.

Grounds for detention

13.04 A doctor may sign an emergency detention certificate if he or she believes it is likely that a person has a mental disorder and because of this, the person's ability to make decisions about medical treatment is significantly impaired.[1]

In addition, the doctor must be satisfied that:

- It is urgently necessary to detain the person in hospital to assess what medical treatment he or she needs;
- If the person was not detained, there would be a significant risk to his or health, safety or welfare or to the safety of any other person; and
- The delays involved in starting the short-term detention procedure would be undesirable.[2]

For further discussion of these grounds, see chapter 11.

The form of certificate requires the doctor to explain his or her reasons for granting the certificate.[3] The doctor must be satisfied that the proposed action is in accordance with the principles of the Act.[4]

1   Mental Health (Care and Treatment) (Scotland) Act 2003, s 36(3)(b).
2   MH(CT)(S)A 2003, s 36(3)(c).
3   MH(CT)(S)A 2003, s 37.
4   MH(CT)(S)A 2003, ss 1–3.

Contacting mental health officer

13.05 Because there is no appeal against emergency detention, the mental health officer has a particularly important role in safeguarding patients' interests. The doctor signing the certificate must consult with a mental health officer and obtain his or her consent to the detention, if practicable.[1]

If the mental health officer refuses consent, the person cannot be detained. This applies even if another doctor or a psychiatric specialist, such as a community psychiatric nurse, recommends the detention, or if the police have been involved.

Since 1984 the Mental Welfare Commission has consistently reported that a significant proportion of doctors have failed to attempt to contact a mental health officer and to give adequate reasons for so doing.[2] It sought legal advice and was advised that a doctor's failure to give an adequate explanation rendered emergency detention under the 1984 Act void.[3]

The Code of Practice says a doctor should make all reasonable efforts to contact a mental health officer before granting a certificate.[4] It is only in exceptional circumstances that this is not possible, such as where there is immediate, serious or life-threatening danger to the person or others, where no mental health officer is available or where the patient is likely to try to leave after the medical examination.[5] Initial monitoring of emergency detentions under the Mental Health (Care and Treatment) Act appears encouraging.[6]

All local authorities should have an out-of-hours phone number for contacting mental health officers. The Mental Health (Care and Treatment) Act says that local authorities must ensure that they have an adequate number of mental health officers to fulfil their duties under the Act.[7]

Contacting a mental health officer should not involve undue delay. While the mental health officer should generally visit the person, in exceptional circumstances he or she may give consent over the telephone.[8]

Generally the mental health officer should interview the person, but if this is not possible, either because a person refuses or is too upset to be interviewed, the mental health officer can consent without an interview if he or she has sufficient information about the circumstances.[9]

1   Mental Health (Care and Treatment) (Scotland) Act 2003, ss 36(3) and (6).
2   See, for example, Annual Report 2004–5, para 3.1.3.
3   See Annual Report of Mental Welfare Commission 2002–3, para 3.1.4.
4   Code of Practice, vol 2, para 7.35.
5   Code of Practice, vol 2, para 7.37.
6   The Mental Welfare Commission's Emergency detention monitoring report (April 2006) indicated mental health officer consent in 66% of cases considered, and adequate reasons for failure to obtain consent in all but a handful of cases.
7   MH(CT)(S)A 2003, s 32(1). This is also a requirement of the National Standards for mental health services published by the Scottish Executive in 2005.
8   Code of Practice, vol 2, para 7.43.
9   Annual Report of Mental Welfare Commission 2001–2, para 2.9.

Conflict of interest

13.06 The doctor cannot sign the form if he or she has any conflict of interest.[1] Regulations may specify the circumstances where there is or is not taken to be a conflict of interest.[2]

At the time of writing, there are no regulations dealing with conflict of interest for emergency detentions, although there are regulations dealing with conflict in other situations. Doctors' professional codes of conduct deal with when it is appropriate to treat family, friends or colleagues.[2]

1   Mental Health (Care and Treatment) (Scotland) Act 2003, s 36(3).
2   MH(CT)(S)A 2003, s 36(9).
3   See *Good medical practice* from the General Medical Council and advice from the Ethics Committee of the British Medical Association.

Where emergency detention not permitted

13.07 The doctor cannot sign an emergency detention certificate if the person was detained in hospital immediately before[1] the medical examination under:

- Another emergency detention certificate;
- An extension of a short-term detention certificate;
- An extension of short-term detention under section 68 of the Act;
- An extension of a compulsory treatment order under section 114(2) of the Act; or
- An extension of an interim CTO under section 115(2) of the Act.[2]

A person subject to a compulsory treatment order who is living in the community can be subject to emergency detention. The compulsory treatment order does not operate for the period of the emergency detention, but any powers of compulsory medical treatment remain.[3]

1   For discussion of 'immediately before' see 12.04.
2   Mental Health (Care and Treatment) (Scotland) Act 2003, s 36(2).
3   MH(CT)(S)A 2003, s 43.

EFFECT OF DETENTION CERTIFICATE

Transfer to hospital

13.08 The certificate authorises the person's removal to the hospital named in the certificate, or his or her detention in the hospital if he or she is already there. Para 12.08 (short-term detention) deals with the move to hospital in more detail.

The Code of Practice gives guidance on good practice for the transfer and the admission of a person to hospital following an emergency certificate.[1] A health professional should generally accompany the person, and ward staff should explain procedures to the person on admission.

The doctor must ensure that the hospital managers receive the emergency detention certificate before the person is admitted.[2] When someone is already in hospital, the managers must receive the certificate as soon as possible after the doctor signs it.[3]

The authority to take the person to hospital lasts for 72 hours from the time of the grant of the certificate.[4] The person may go to a hospital other than that named in the certificate if necessary.[5]

[1]   Code of Practice, vol 2, paras 7.49–62.
[2]   Mental Health (Care and Treatment) (Scotland) Act 2003, s 36(7).
[3]   MH(CT)(S)A 2003, s 36(11).
[4]   MH(CT)(S)A 2003, s 36(8).
[5]   MH(CT)(S)A 2003, s 36(8)(a).

Length of detention

13.09 The person may be detained in the hospital for up to 72 hours from admission. For a patient already in hospital, the time is 72 hours from the granting of the certificate.[1]

The emergency detention may end before the 72 hours have elapsed. The person may agree to stay in hospital informally and the doctor can cancel the certificate.

The doctor may discharge the person before the 72 hours are up, or the person may move onto a short-term detention before the 72 hours have expired.

[1]   Mental Health (Care and Treatment) (Scotland) Act 2003, s 36(8).

Medical treatment

13.10 The emergency detention certificate does not authorise a doctor to give medical treatment under Part 16 of the Mental Health (Care and Treatment) Act. If, during the currency of the certificate, a doctor wishes to treat the person, he or she should consider making a short-term detention certificate.

A doctor can treat a patient who consents or if the doctor considers it appropriate to sign a certificate under the Adults with Incapacity Act. See chapter 8.

In an emergency, a doctor can give treatment if he or she regards this as justified under the urgent treatment provisions of the Act. See chapter 16. The doctor must take into account any advance statement the person has made.

A doctor must report details of any treatment under the urgent treatment provisions, to the Mental Welfare Commission, giving the reasons for the treatment.[1]

1   Mental Health (Care and Treatment) (Scotland) Act 2003, s 243(6).

DUTIES OF HOSPITAL MANAGERS

Appointment of responsible medical officer

13.11 As soon as possible after the granting of the certificate, the hospital managers should appoint an approved medical practitioner to be the person's responsible medical officer.[1] If the person already has a responsible medical officer, that doctor may remain as responsible medical officer.[2]

1   Mental Health (Care and Treatment) (Scotland) Act 2003, s 230(1).
2   MH(CT)(S)A 2003, s 230(2).

People to be notified

13.12 Within 12 hours of receiving the emergency detention certificate, the hospital managers should notify:

- The nearest relative, if the person lives with the nearest relative.
- If the nearest relative does not live with the person, someone who lives with the person.
- The named person, if the managers know who this is.
- The Mental Welfare Commission.

Within seven days of receiving the emergency certificate, the hospital managers should also notify these people of the contents of the doctor's report.

If the doctor did not seek the consent of a mental health officer, the hospital managers must notify the local authority for the area where the person lives or, if they do not know where the person lives, where the hospital is situated.[1]

1   Mental Health (Care and Treatment) (Scotland) Act 2003, s 38(3).

Information

13.13 The hospital managers must take all reasonable steps to ensure that the person understands the effect of the certificate. This includes information about the role of the responsible medical officer, the Mental Welfare Commission and the tribunal.[1]

If someone has communication needs, or his or her first language is not English, the hospital managers must make special arrangements for an interpreter.[2]

For further details, see chapter 17.

[1]   Mental Health (Care and Treatment) (Scotland) Act 2003, ss 260(2)-(5).
[2]   MH(CT)(S)A 2003, s 261.

IMPACT OF CERTIFICATE

Duties of mental health officer

13.14 The Code of Practice envisages that the mental health officer will be involved in the person's transfer to hospital and will take steps to ensure that the person understands his or her rights.[1]

The mental health officer should do what is necessary to promote the person's interests. In particular, he or she should consider whether the person might benefit from independent advocacy services and contact them, if necessary, on the person's behalf.

[1]   Code of Practice, vol 2, para 7.68.

Review of detention

13.15 As soon as possible after the detention begins, the hospital managers must arrange for an approved medical practitioner to examine the person.[1] If possible this should be the person's responsible medical officer.[2]

If the approved medical practitioner is not satisfied that the grounds for emergency detention apply and that it is necessary for the person to be detained in hospital, he or she should cancel the certificate.[3]

If the approved medical practitioner cancels the certificate, he or she must notify the person and the hospital managers, as soon as possible after doing so.[4] The managers notify the relevant people.[5] A form for cancelling the certificate is available on the Scottish Executive's mental health law website.

When someone needs to stay in hospital for at least a short time and does not agree to do so, the doctor may start the procedure for short-term detention. If the responsible medical officer thinks a short-term order is likely, he or she should contact a mental health officer with a view to issuing a certificate as soon as possible.[6]

1   Mental Health (Care and Treatment) (Scotland) Act 2003, s 38(2).

2   Code of Practice, vol 2, para 7.77.

3   MH(CT)(S)A 2003, s 39.

4   MH(CT)(S)A 2003, s 40(1).

5   MH(CT)(S)A 2003, s 40(2).

6   Code of Practice, vol 2, para 7.72.

Safeguards

13.16 Because of the short timescales, there is no right to appeal against the granting of an emergency detention certificate.

The European Convention on Human Rights says that a person should be able to go to court to test the validity of any detention.[1] The European Court of Human Rights has recognised that appeal may not be practical in an emergency.[2]

If emergency detention under the Mental Health (Care and Treatment) Act becomes the normal route for compulsory admissions, as under the 1984 Act, this could be open to challenge under the European Convention on Human Rights.

Anyone concerned that a person has been wrongly detained under the emergency procedure can contact the Mental Welfare Commission. The Commission cannot discharge someone from emergency detention orders, but it can carry out an investigation after the event.

Monitoring the use of emergency orders is one of the Commission's priorities for 2005–6. It expects the number of emergency orders to decrease. It is publishing monthly information on its website from January 2006.[3]

1   Art 5.

2   See *Winterwerp v Netherlands* ECtHR (Series A No 33).

3   Monitoring priorities for 2005/6. On Commission's website.

Suspension of detention

13.17 A person subject to emergency detention may leave the hospital if the responsible medical officer authorises this.[1] The responsible medical officer can suspend the certificate for the appropriate period. The rules are the same as the rules for suspension from short-term detention.[2]

The responsible medical officer may cancel a suspension certificate if he or she considers this is necessary in the interests of the person or for the protection of others.[3] Again, the procedure is as for short-term detention.

[1]   Mental Health (Care and Treatment) (Scotland) Act 2003, s 41.
[2]   See 12.31.
[3]   MH(CT)(S)A 2003, s 42.

Expiry of certificate

13.18 When the emergency detention certificate expires, the person may leave the hospital or may agree to remain in hospital as a voluntary patient.

The person may be further detained under the short-term detention procedure. (This may happen before the expiry of the 72 hours.) If the doctor issues a short-term detention certificate, this automatically cancels the emergency detention.[1]

Alternatively the doctor may recommend an application for a compulsory treatment order. See below.

The person cannot be further detained under the emergency procedure immediately after[2] the expiry of the 72 hours.[3]

[1]   Mental Health (Care and Treatment) (Scotland) Act 2003, s 55.
[2]   See 12.06.
[3]   MH(CT)(S)A 2003, s 36(2)(a).

NURSE'S HOLDING POWER

13.19 A voluntary patient may decide to leave hospital unexpectedly. He or she may be at risk, but there may be no doctor available to examine him or her. If an approved nurse believes someone is at risk, he or she may detain the person in hospital for up to two hours to enable a doctor to examine him or her.

An approved nurse is a registered mental health or learning disabilities nurse.[1]

1   Mental Health (Class of Nurse) (Scotland) Regulations 2005 (SSI 2005/446).

Who rules apply to

13.20 The rules apply to any patient receiving psychiatric treatment in any hospital.[1]

They do not apply if someone is already detained under the Mental Health (Care and Treatment) Act or the Criminal Procedure (Scotland) Act.

They can apply to someone receiving treatment under a probation order, as an in-patient or outpatient.[2]

1   Mental Health (Care and Treatment) (Scotland) Act 2003, s 299(1).

2   MH(CT)(S)A 2003, s 299(1)(a).

Grounds for detention

13.21 The nurse may detain someone attempting to leave the hospital if no doctor is immediately available to examine the person and the nurse thinks it likely that:

- The person has a mental disorder;
- It is necessary for the person's health, safety or welfare or the safety of others that the person is immediately stopped from leaving the hospital; and
- A doctor needs to examine the person to establish with a view to an emergency or short-term detention certificate.[1]

The nurse must also bear in mind the principles of the Act. The Code of Practice gives some guidance.[2] It may be possible to persuade the person to stay in hospital until a doctor arrives.

1   Mental Health (Care and Treatment) (Scotland) Act 2003, s 299.

2   Code of Practice, vol 1, para 15.73.

Length of detention

13.22 The nurse can detain the person for up to two hours. If no doctor arrives within the first hour of the detention, the detention can continue until one hour after the doctor arrives.[1]

If a doctor does not see the person within the two-hour period, it would not be appropriate to detain the person for another two hours.[2]

[1]   Mental Health (Care and Treatment) (Scotland) Act 2003, s 299(4).
[2]   Code of Practice, vol 1, para 15.71.

Medical examination

13.23 An approved medical practitioner, a junior psychiatrist or another doctor who is not a psychiatrist may examine the person. The latter might be appropriate if the person is being held in a general hospital.

The doctor may decide no further compulsory measures are necessary or may grant an emergency detention certificate or short-term detention certificate.

People to be informed

13.24 The nurse should attempt to communicate as clearly as is possible to the person that he or she is detaining the person and why.[1]

As soon as possible after the detention, the nurse should take all reasonable steps to notify a mental health officer.[2] The mental health officer may then be able to approve a short-term detention, if the doctor considers this necessary.

The nurse must deliver a written report to the hospital managers as soon as possible, stating the time the holding period began and why the nurse believed it was appropriate to detain the person.[3] A form is available on the Scottish Executive's mental health law website.[4]

The hospital managers must send a copy of the report to the Mental Welfare Commission within 14 days of the date on which they receive it.[5]

[1]   Code of Practice, vol 1, para 15.73.
[2]   Mental Health (Care and Treatment) (Scotland) Act 2003, s 299(5).
[3]   MH(CT)(S)A 2003, ss 299(5) and (6).
[4]   Form NUR1. The nurse can complete the form electronically.
[5]   MH(CT)(S)A 2003, s 299(8).

Chapter 14

COMPULSORY TREATMENT ORDERS

BACKGROUND AND SCOPE

Outline of procedure

14.01 The mental health officer makes an application for a compulsory treatment order to the mental health tribunal. There is a formal hearing, where the mental health officer makes the case for the order. All relevant people can attend the hearing and put their case.

Two medical reports are necessary, one from an approved medical practitioner. The mental health officer submits a proposed care plan to the tribunal. The proposed care plan sets out the person's needs and how services hope to meet them.

A compulsory treatment order lasts for up to six months, and may be renewed.

Where orders appropriate

14.02 A compulsory treatment order is not appropriate if a person agrees to the care and treatment the doctors propose. If someone does not agree and the Mental Health (Care and Treatment) Act grounds apply, the doctors may request a mental health officer to apply for a long-term order.

This could apply to a voluntary patient, someone detained under short-term or emergency detention or someone receiving treatment under the provisions of the Adults with Incapacity Act. The person may be in hospital or living in the community. In most cases the person is already subject to short-term detention.

Community based orders

14.03 A major change from the 1984 Act is that a compulsory treatment order can authorise the use of compulsory measures either in hospital or in the community. This is one of the most controversial aspects of the new Act.

The Millan Committee recommended such orders as a less restrictive option for some people. If a person can receive safe and effective care without being detained in hospital, it is wrong to detain him or her in hospital.[1]

The Millan Committee recommended that orders be tailor-made to the needs of the person. The tribunal should grant only those powers it believes are necessary for that individual.

The Mental Health (Care and Treatment) Act adopts this approach, providing for a flexible form of compulsory treatment order, which can involve detention in hospital or a community alternative, where appropriate.

[1]   See discussion in *New Directions*, chap 6.

Concerns about community orders

14.04 Some organisations are concerned doctors will make too much use of the new order and that effective community services are not available. There is also concern that, once on an order, it will be hard to come off it. There are, however, certain safeguards:

- A person cannot become subject to a compulsory treatment order unless the statutory grounds for compulsion apply. See below. The vast majority of informal patients do not need compulsory measures, and this will continue to be the case.

- Community-based powers are appropriate only where they would provide a safe and viable alternative to compulsory hospitalisation. The doctors recommending them and the tribunal must be satisfied there is no less restrictive alternative.[1]

- The tribunal should not grant a community-based order if community services are inadequate to support it. The tribunal scrutinises applications and should reject those which do not offer a viable care plan. When the tribunal considers certain aspects of the care plan are essential, it can specify them as 'recorded matters'. See below. If a patient does not receive a service which is a recorded matter, the case comes back to the tribunal.

- The new, more rigorous tests for assessing whether a person should be made subject to compulsory measures (see chapter 11) may mean that fewer, rather than more, people become subject to compulsory measures.

- The person can appeal against the order and can request the Mental Welfare Commission to review the order. If any of the grounds for the order no longer apply, the tribunal will discharge the order.
- The Mental Welfare Commission is taking a particular interest in community-based compulsory treatment orders. It visits every person on a compulsory treatment order within the first year of the order. It intends initially to visit people on community-based orders within the first six months.[2]

The Code of Practice gives guidance to doctors and the tribunal.[3]

[1]   Code of Practice, vol 2, para 3.30.
[2]   *Monitoring priorities for 2005/6.* See Commission's website.
[3]   Code of Practice, vol 2, para 3.30.

MEDICAL REPORTS

Medical examination

14.05 Two doctors must examine the person. One of the doctors must be an approved medical practitioner. If the person already has a responsible medical officer, he or she should be one of the doctors.[1]

The other doctor should generally be the person's general practitioner,[2] but if it is not practical for him or her to examine the person, another approved medical practitioner may examine the person.[3] The second doctor should be independent of the first.[4] He or she should, if possible, have prior knowledge of the person.[5]

The doctors should examine the person separately[6] unless the person consents to both doctors examining him or her at the same time.[7] When someone is unable to consent to the examination, the doctors may ask his or her named person, guardian or welfare attorney for permission to examine the person at the same time.[8]

The doctors must examine the person within five days of each other.[9]

The Code of Practice gives guidance to doctors.[10] The doctor should consider both how the person appears on the day of the examination, and his or her past symptoms and history. The doctor will wish to seek input from the mental health officer and from carers or other people who may provide care in the future.

214

An independent advocate, carer or relative can be present if the doctor is happy this will not interfere with his or her assessment. If someone refuses to consent to the examination, the approved medical practitioner may have to consider short-term detention to allow a proper examination.

1   Code of Practice, vol 2, para 3.11.
2   Code of Practice, as above. The author understands that the Scottish General Practitioners Committee has agreed good practice with the Scottish Executive. A general practitioner can charge a fee for issuing a report, but not when he or she issues an emergency detention certificate, which is paid for under the GP contract. The tribunal service does not generally expect GPs to attend the tribunal hearing.
3   Mental Health (Care and Treatment) (Scotland) Act 2003, ss 58(2) and 58(4).
4   See Conflict of Interest Regulations, below.
5   Code of Practice, vol 2, para 3.12.
6   MH(CT)(S)A 2003, s 58(2).
7   MH(CT)(S)A 2003, s 58(6).
8   MH(CT)(S)A 2003, s 58(6).
9   MH(CT)(S)A 2003, s 58(3).
10   Code of Practice, vol 2, paras 3.19–22.

Content of medical reports

14.06 The form of medical report is on the Scottish Executive's mental health law website. The report should:

- State what type of mental disorder(s) the person has, whether mental illness, personality disorder or learning disability. (The doctors must agree on at least one form of mental disorder. If so, it does not matter if one doctor says the person also has another type of mental disorder.)
- Describe the person's symptoms and the way the disorder affects him or her.
- Confirm that the doctor is satisfied that all of the grounds for a compulsory treatment order apply and state why.
- List the measures the doctor recommends the compulsory treatment order should contain. Both reports must state the same measures.
- Include any other information the doctor considers relevant.[1]

The report from the approved medical practitioner must state whether the doctor considers the person should receive notice of the application.

The doctor should recommend withholding notice only if he or she believes giving notice would be likely to cause significant harm to the person or anyone else.[2]

This would only be in exceptional circumstances. The Code of Practice says that the doctor should discuss this with the mental health officer and other members of the care team.[3]

The approved medical practitioner should also state whether he or she believes the person is capable of arranging legal representation.[4]

[1]   Mental Health (Care and Treatment) (Scotland) Act 2003, ss 57(4) and (5).
[2]   MH(CT)(S)A 2003, s 57(6).
[3]   Code of Practice, vol 2, paras 3.35–6.
[4]   MH(CT)(S)A 2003, s 57(6)(c).

Grounds for order

14.07 Each medical report must confirm that the doctor is satisfied that:

- The person has a mental disorder.
- Medical treatment is available for the person, and is likely to prevent the mental disorder getting worse or alleviate some of its symptoms or effects.
- If the person does not receive such treatment there will be a significant risk to his or her health, safety or welfare or to the safety of any other person.
- Because of the mental disorder, the person's ability to make decisions about medical treatment is significantly impaired; and
- It is necessary to make a compulsory treatment order,[1] (usually because the person will not agree to treatment voluntarily).[2]

For further discussion of these grounds, see chapter 11.

[1]   Mental Health (Care and Treatment) (Scotland) Act 2003, s 57(3).
[2]   Code of Practice, vol 2, para 3.24.

Conflict of interest

14.08 Each doctor examining the person must be sure he or she does not have any conflict of interest.[1] The rules are set out in regulations.[2]

- There is a conflict of interest if either doctor is a relative[3] of the person, or if the doctors are related to each other.

- If the person is likely to be detained in a private hospital, neither of the doctors should work for or provide services to that hospital.
- Only one of the doctors may work full time in a National Health Service hospital where the person may be detained. The other doctor can work only a small part of his or her time in the same hospital.[4]
- If delay would involve serious risk to the health, safety or welfare of the person or to the safety of someone else, both doctors can come from the same National Health Service or private hospital. If one of the doctors is a consultant, the other must not work directly with him or her or under his or her supervision.[5]

There may be other circumstances where a doctor might consider he or she has a conflict of interest, such as where he or she is a friend, colleague or civil partner of the person. The Conflict of Interest Regulations do not overrule the doctor's professional judgement to consider whether it is appropriate to act.

[1]   Mental Health (Care and Treatment) (Scotland) Act 2003, s 58(5).
[2]   Mental Health (Conflict of Interest) (Scotland) (No. 2) Regulations 2005 (SSI 2005/380) ('The Conflict of Interest Regulations'.)
[3]   This includes a child, grandchild, parent, grandparent, wife, husband, sister, brother, daughter-in-law, son-in-law, mother-in-law, father-in-law, sister-in-law, brother-in-law, co-habitee of the person or the child, grandchild, parent, grandparent, sister or brother of a cohabitee of the person. Children include stepchildren.
[4]   Conflict of Interest Regulations, reg 4.
[5]   Conflict of Interest Regulations, reg 5.

DUTIES OF MENTAL HEALTH OFFICER

Information giving

14.09 If both of the reports comply with the requirements above, the mental health officer must apply for an order.[1]

As soon as possible after becoming aware that he or she will be making an application, the mental health officer must take all reasonably practical steps to identify the named person.[2] He or she must then give written notice to the patient, the named person and the Mental Welfare Commission.[3]

The mental health officer does not have to notify the patient if one of the medical reports recommends against this. If the mental health officer disagrees with the doctor's opinion, he or she may notify the patient.[4] The mental health officer should record his or her reasons for disagreeing with the doctor.[5]

In a case in England, the court said that it was not practical for the approved social worker to notify the nearest relative if the person had told the social worker she did not want this person involved. The social worker should consider whether doing so would lead to a breach of the patient's rights under Article 8 of the European Convention of Human Rights (respect for private and family life).[6] A mental health officer in this situation in Scotland would presumably advise the person to appoint a named person or a different named person (if the person was able to do so).

1   Mental Health (Care and Treatment) (Scotland) Act 2003, s 57(1).

2   MH(CT)(S)A 2003, s 59.

3   MH(CT)(S)A 2003, s 60(1).

4   MH(CT)(S)A 2003, s 60(2).

5   Code of Practice, vol 2, para 3.49.

6   *R (on the application of E) v Bristol City Council* [2005] EWHC 74 (Admin).

Interviewing patient

14.10 The mental health officer should interview the person and advise him or her about the application if the person has not received notice of the application. The mental health officer should explain the person's rights and what advocacy services are available, and assist the person to make use of independent advocacy services.[1]

If it is not practicable for the mental health officer to interview someone, he or she need not do so.[2] This would only be in exceptional circumstances. The mental health officer should speak to the named person, carers and relatives instead.[3]

More detail on how the mental health officer should carry out these duties is in the Code of Practice.[4]

1   Mental Health (Care and Treatment) (Scotland) Act 2003, s 61(2).

2   MH(CT)(S)A 2003, s 61(3).

3   Code of Practice, vol 2, para 3.56.

4   Vol 2, paras 3.40–58.

Mental health officer report

14.11 The mental health officer must prepare a report for the tribunal. The form is on the Scottish Executive's mental health law website. The report should state the patient's name and address and, if available, those of his or her named person and primary carer. It should include details of:

- The person's relevant personal circumstances.
- The steps the mental health officer has taken to interview the person and inform the person of his or her rights.
- The steps the mental health officer has taken to advise the person about advocacy services and to assist him or her to make use of advocacy services.
- If the mental health officer was not able to interview the person, why not.
- The mental health officer's views on the medical reports.[1]
- Any advance statement the person has made.
- Any other relevant information.[2]

[1]   If the mental health officer disagrees with the application, he or she should state what alternatives he or she proposes and should discuss this with medical colleagues. See 14.15 below.
[2]   Mental Health (Care and Treatment) (Scotland) Act 2003, s 61(4).

Assessment of community care needs

14.12 When a mental health officer considers someone has community care needs, he or she can formally ask colleagues in community care to carry out an assessment of needs under the Social Work (Scotland) Act 1968.[1] See Part 5 for community care.

For children and young people, the mental health officer may request colleagues in children's services to carry out an assessment under the Children (Scotland) Act 1995.[2] See chapter 41 for children's services.

The Code of Practice gives useful guidance to practitioners.[3] Local authorities must ensure that funding is available if a mental health officer is likely to seek a community-based order.[4]

[1]   Mental Health (Care and Treatment) (Scotland) Act 2003, s 227.
[2]   MH(CT)(S)A 2003, s 227(2).
[3]   Code of Practice, vol 1, paras 7.03–7
[4]   Code of Practice, vol 1, at para 7.06.

Proposed care plan

14.13 The mental health officer must prepare a proposed care plan to accompany the application. The proposed care plan sets out the person's needs for care and how the planned treatment will meet these needs.

The plan should follow discussion and agreement between the mental health officer and those who will be providing care for the person in hospital or the community. Before drawing up the proposed care plan, the mental health officer must consult with:

- The doctors who provided the medical reports.
- Anyone else who might provide medical treatment for the person's mental disorder under the order. (This could include community mental health services or a general practitioner).
- Anyone else who may provide community care services, children's services or any other services to the person under the order.
- Anyone else who may provide any other services to the person under the order. (This should include informal carers); and
- Anyone else whom the mental health officer considers appropriate.[1] Bearing in mind the principles of the Act, this would clearly include the patient, his or her named person and any attorney or guardian.

Apart from the doctors who provided the medical reports, the mental health officer need not consult the people listed if this is impractical.[2] It is hard to see how the mental health officer could prepare the proposed care plan without consulting the people who are to implement it.

The Code of Practice is clear that all relevant people and agencies should contribute to the preparation of the proposed care plan. If, for example, psychological interventions are proposed, the mental health officer must consult a psychologist. It is also vital that the mental health officer considers the views of the person and his or her carers.[3]

[1]   Mental Health (Care and Treatment) (Scotland) Act 2003, s 62(3).
[2]   MH(CT)(S)A 2003, s 62(7).
[3]   Code of Practice, vol 2, paras 3.70 and 3.73.

Content of plan

14.14 The form for the proposed care plan is available on the mental health law website. It should set out:

- The type of mental disorder the person has.

- The person's medical needs as identified in the medical reports.
- If relevant, the person's need for community care services or other services, such as childrens services.
- The medical treatment proposed to meet the person's medical needs.
- The social work or other local authority services proposed to meet the person's care needs.
- Any other treatment, care or services proposed.
- The compulsory powers sought.
- If the medical reports recommend the person's detention in hospital, the name and address of the hospital.
- If the application is for a community order, details of the measures requested.
- Services the mental health officer wishes to be recorded matters. See 14.22.
- The name and address of the hospital which will appoint the responsible medical officer if the tribunal makes a community-based order; and
- The aims of the care and treatment package set out in the proposed care plan, (including the aims of the compulsory measures sought).[1]

The Code of Practice gives guidance about applying for community-based measures, which it says are likely in only a limited range of circumstances. Each case must be judged on its merits, but community-based compulsory measures might be appropriate if they would provide a safe and viable alternative to compulsory hospitalisation; if the person has previously relapsed whilst not taking medication in the community and has put him or herself and/or other people at risk; and all other means of negotiation with the person have been tried and have failed.[2]

[1]   Mental Health (Care and Treatment) (Scotland) Act 2003, s 62(5).
[2]   Code of Practice, vol 2, para 3.30.

Application for order

14.15 The mental health officer must make the application within 14 days of the second medical examination.[1]

Provided both medical reports comply with the legal requirements, the mental health officer must make the application, even if he or she does not believe it is necessary. If this is the case, the mental health officer should discuss concerns with the doctors.[2]

The form of application is on the Scottish Executive's mental health law website. Together with the application, the mental health officer will submit the two medical reports, his or her report and the proposed care plan.[3]

[1]   Mental Health (Care and Treatment) (Scotland) Act 2003, s 57(7).

[2]   Code of Practice, vol 2, para 3.63.

[3]   MH(CT)(S)A 2003, s 63(3).

THE ROLE OF THE TRIBUNAL

14.16 This section looks at the ways in which the tribunal deals with the application. Chapter 22 deals in more detail with representation before the tribunal and chapter 23 looks at tribunal procedure.

All relevant people can make representations at the hearing and can submit evidence, such as a report from an independent psychiatrist. The patient and/or the named person may wish to seek legal advice.

Time limit for hearing

14.17 When someone is subject to a short-term detention certificate or an extension of short-term detention, the tribunal must deal with the application within five business days of the expiry of the detention.[1] The short-term detention continues for five days after the making of the application.[2]

The tribunal holds a first hearing within the five-day period. At that hearing, the tribunal either grants an interim compulsory treatment order or a full compulsory treatment order or refuses the application. If it grants an interim compulsory treatment order, it will fix a further hearing.[3]

All the relevant parties must have a chance to make representations and produce evidence at the first hearing.

[1]   Mental Health (Care and Treatment) (Scotland) Act 2003, s 69.

[2]   MH(CT)(S)A 2003, s 68.

[3]   Mental Health Tribunal for Scotland (Practice and Procedure) (No. 2) Rules 2005 (SSI 2005/519), r 8.

Decision of tribunal

14.18 Before the hearing, the tribunal members study the application, the proposed care plan and the reports. At the hearing they hear from the parties and the witnesses. The tribunal must bear in mind the principles of the Act when reaching its decision.

If the tribunal is satisfied that the grounds for a compulsory treatment order apply, it may make a compulsory treatment order.[1] If not satisfied, it must refuse the application.

Scottish Ministers may make regulations requiring the tribunal to satisfy itself about other matters before making a community-based order.[2] Ministers must consult on such regulations.[3] There are no such regulations at the time of writing and the Scottish Executive has no current plans for regulations.[4]

[1]   Mental Health (Care and Treatment) (Scotland) Act 2003, s 64(4).
[2]   MH(CT)(S)A 2003, s 64(5)(f).
[3]   MH(CT)(S)A 2003, s 64(9).
[4]   Code of Practice, vol 2, para 3.84.

Advance statements

14.19 The tribunal must have regard to any advance statement the person has made. It should consider whether the person's ability to make decisions about medical treatment is significantly impaired and whether the advance statement is valid.

If so, it should consider whether there has been any change of circumstances since the date of the advance statement which might have caused the person to alter the advance statement and whether the advance statement deals with matters on which it may make a decision.

If the tribunal authorises any measures which conflict with the person's wishes as set out in a valid advance statement, it must record the circumstances and the reasons why it overruled the advance statement. It must give notice to the patient, named person, any welfare attorney or guardian and the Mental Welfare Commission.[1]

It should also ensure that copy of its determination is placed with the person's medical records.[2]

[1]   Mental Health (Care and Treatment) (Scotland) Act 2003, s 276(7). The form of compulsory treatment order on the mental health law website contains provision for this.
[2]   MH(CT)(S)A 2003, s 276(8).

Terms of order

14.20 A compulsory treatment order will authorise various measures in respect of the person for six months from the date of the order.[1] The form of order is on the mental health law website.

The tribunal should bear in mind the Act's principle of least restrictive alternative, and grant only those measures it believes are necessary. The measures it can grant are:

- The detention of the person in hospital.

- Giving medical treatment to the person in accordance with Part 16 of the Act.

- Requiring the person to attend a hospital or clinic to receive medical treatment, (as detailed in the order or as directed by the person's responsible medical officer.)

- Requiring the person to attend to receive local authority community care services, children's services or other services, (as set out in the order or as determined by the responsible medical officer).

- Requiring the person to live at an address specified in the order.[2]

- Requiring the person to obtain the mental health officer's approval to any change of address.

- Requiring the person to notify the mental health officer before he or she changes address.

- Requiring the person to allow visits by the mental health officer, the responsible medical officer and anyone else providing services who is authorised by the responsible medical officer to visit.[3]

The order should specify the type of mental disorder the person has. It should name the hospital where the person is to be detained, or, if the order is to be community-based, the hospital which will appoint the person's responsible medical officer.[4]

---

[1]   Mental Health (Care and Treatment) (Scotland) Act 2003, s 64(4).

[2]   The Code of Practice says this would be unusual, vol 2, para 3.30.

[3]   MH(CT)(S)A 2003, s 66(1).

[4]   MH(CT)(S)A 2003, s 64(4)(a).

Variation of measures

14.21 The compulsory treatment order may not include all the measures that the mental health officer requested. The tribunal may impose other measures, in addition to or instead of those requested in the application.[1]

Before imposing new measures, the tribunal must give notice to all relevant parties of its proposals and give them a chance to make representations and produce evidence.[2]

The tribunal might make an interim compulsory treatment order while considering what further order it may make.[3]

If all relevant parties are present at the hearing, it is not necessary to give them notice.

[1] Mental Health (Care and Treatment) (Scotland) Act 2003, s 64(6).
[2] MH(CT)(S)A 2003, s 64(7).
[3] See below.

Recorded matters

14.22 In addition to authorising various measures, the order can specify certain recorded matters.[1] These are treatments, care or services the tribunal considers essential to the person's care.[2] The tribunal may list medical treatment, community care services, children's services and any other care, service or treatment as a recorded matter.

If the person does not receive a service which is a recorded matter, the responsible medical officer must report this to the tribunal. The Mental Welfare Commission may also refer any matter to the tribunal.[3] (See 15.26.)

Recorded matters are particularly important where people are subject to community-based orders. The tribunal will want to be satisfied that people receive adequate services in the community.

However they could also be important for people detained in hospital. If, for example, the tribunal considers a person should receive psychological treatments, it might specify this as a recorded matter, to ensure that it can review the case if the person does not receive such treatment. There are often long waiting lists for so-called 'talking treatments'.

[1] Mental Health (Care and Treatment) (Scotland) Act 2003, s 64(4)(a).
[2] Code of Practice, vol 2, para 3.91.
[3] MH(CT)(S)A 2003, ss 96 and 98.

Interim orders

Grounds for order

14.23 Instead of authorising a full compulsory treatment order, the tribunal may grant an interim order, for a period not exceeding 28 days.[1] The tribunal can make more than one interim order, but they cannot exceed 56 days in total.[2] Any party may apply for an interim order.

There are various circumstances when an interim compulsory treatment order might be appropriate:

- To enable the tribunal to hear further evidence.

- Where the tribunal is not satisfied that the proposed care plan is adequate and needs to see a revised care plan before it comes to a final determination.

- Where the tribunal is considering granting different measures from those applied for and must notify the relevant parties of its intentions.[3]

The tribunal can make an interim order only where it is satisfied that the medical grounds for the order apply.[4] These are the same as the grounds for a compulsory treatment order.

If the order is to be community-based, the tribunal must identify the hospital to be responsible for appointing the person's responsible medical officer.[5]

If the mental health officer has applied for a hospital-based order, it is unlikely that the tribunal can grant an interim order based in the community. The Act does not contain a provision allowing the tribunal to modify the measures applied for in an interim order.[6]

---

[1] Mental Health (Care and Treatment) (Scotland) Act 2003, s 65(2).

[2] MH(CT)(S)A 2003, s 65(3).

[3] See comments of Deputy Minister for Health and Community Care, Mrs Mary Mulligan, in the Scottish Parliament, Health and Community Care Committee Official Report, Meeting No 3 (2003), Col 3668.

[4] MH(CT)(S)A 2003, s 65(6).

[5] MH(CT)(S)A 2003, s 65(6)(b).

[6] Contrast s 64(7), which gives the power to modify the measures in compulsory treatment orders.

Effect of order

14.24 The person cannot appeal against the making of an interim compulsory treatment order other than on a point of law.[1] See chapter 15 for appeals.

If at any time during the existence of the interim compulsory treatment order, either the person's responsible medical officer or the Mental Welfare Commission considers that the medical grounds for the compulsory treatment order do not apply to the person, they can cancel ('revoke') the interim compulsory treatment order.[2] They should give notice of this to the relevant people.[3] (The Mental Welfare Commission is unlikely to cancel an order. See above.)

If the tribunal later makes a compulsory treatment order, this replaces the interim compulsory treatment order.[4]

[1] Mental Health (Care and Treatment) (Scotland) Act 2003, s 320.
[2] MH(CT)(S)A 2003, ss 72 and 73.
[3] MH(CT)(S)A 2003, s 74.
[4] MH(CT)(S)A 2003, s 75.

EFFECT OF ORDER

Transfer to hospital

14.25 When an order authorises the detention of the person in hospital, this authorises taking the person to hospital within seven days of the date of the order.[1] If the person is already in hospital (as will often be the case), he or she is no longer entitled to leave.

[1] Mental Health (Care and Treatment) (Scotland) Act 2003, s 67(1).

Planning the transfer

14.26 All the bodies involved should attempt to ensure the transfer takes place as soon as possible. The psychiatric emergency plan (see 12.08) can be adapted for use when a person is admitted under a long-term order.[1]

[1] Code of Practice, vol 2, para 4.04.

Police involvement

14.27 See 12.09 for good practice on police involvement.

The police may be involved if someone subject to a compulsory treatment order or interim order absconds from the place he or she is held while waiting to be moved to hospital or if someone subject to a compulsory treatment order absconds while being moved to hospital.[1] A police offer may take the person into custody and take him or her to the hospital.[2]

If a court warrant authorises entry to the person's home, a police officer may effect entry. See 20.13, 30.08.

The police may also be involved if there is concern about a possible breach of the peace. This might be necessary if someone is likely to resist attempts to take him or her to hospital.

Use of the police should always be a last resort, in accordance with the principles of the Act.

[1]   Mental Health (Care and Treatment) (Scotland) Act 2003, ss 301 and 302.
[2]   MH(CT)(S)A 2003, s 303.

Transfer to community

14.28 A compulsory treatment order requiring someone to live in a certain place in the community authorises taking the person to that address within seven days of the date of the order.[1]

[1]   Mental Health (Care and Treatment) (Scotland) Act 2003, s 67(1).

Appeal rights

14.29 A patient or his or her named person may appeal to the sheriff principal against a compulsory treatment order. If the tribunal refuses to make an order, the mental health officer or the person's responsible medical officer, if he or she has one, may appeal to the sheriff principal.[1]

An appeal is possible only on a point of law or if there have been irregularities in the hearing.[2]

After three months, the patient or named person may appeal to the tribunal to have the order cancelled or to change some of its provisions.[3] For more details of reviews and appeals, see chapter 15.

[1]   Mental Health (Care and Treatment) (Scotland) Act 2003, s 320.
[2]   MH(CT)(S)A 2003, ss 320(1)(b) and 324(2).
[3]   MH(CT)(S)A 2003, s 100.

Impact on short-term detention

14.30 A compulsory treatment order replaces the short-term detention certificate.[1] See 12.24 for discussion of the options if the tribunal refuses to make an order.

1   Mental Health (Care and Treatment) (Scotland) Act 2003, s 70.

DUTIES OF HOSPITAL MANAGERS

Appointment of responsible medical officer

14.31 As soon as possible after the making of a compulsory treatment order or an interim compulsory treatment order, the managers of the hospital named in the order must appoint a responsible medical officer for the person.[1] If the person already has a responsible medical officer, that person may continue to act.

All people subject to compulsory treatment orders must always have a responsible medical officer, whether they are detained in hospital or subject to community-based orders. The compulsory treatment order names the hospital responsible for appointing the responsible medical officer when someone is subject to a community-based order.[2]

1   Mental Health (Care and Treatment) (Scotland) Act 2003, s 230.
2   MH(CT)(S)A 2003, s 65(2)(b).

Information giving

14.32 The hospital will also need to ensure that the person receives information about his or her rights.[1]

If the person has communication needs or his or her first language is not English, the hospital managers must make special arrangements for an interpreter.[2] For further details, see chapter 17.

1   Mental Health (Care and Treatment) (Scotland) Act 2003, s 260.
2   MH(CT)(S)A 2003, s 261.

DUTIES OF RESPONSIBLE MEDICAL OFFICER

14.33 As soon as possible after being appointed, the responsible medical officer must prepare a care plan for the person and place a copy with the person's medical records.[1] The care plan sets out the medical treatment intended for the person[2] and other information, as spelt out in regulations.[3]

The responsible medical officer should consult the mental health officer and the rest of the care team while preparing the care plan.[4] The care team presumably includes the person's primary carer.

The responsible medical officer may amend the care plan from time to time, and must do so if the tribunal varies or extends the order and in other circumstances stipulated in the regulations.[5] The responsible medical officer should keep the amended version with the person's records.

The responsible medical officer should give a copy of the care plan to the mental health officer, any community psychiatric nurse and other members of the care team, including community care providers. The patient and his or her named person should also receive a copy.[6]

The Mental Welfare Commission is taking a particular interest in care plans during the first year of the Act. It is examining plans in detail to check that they take account of individual needs and have been developed in partnership with the person they are designed to support.[7]

[1]   Mental Health (Care and Treatment) (Scotland) Act 2003, s 76.
[2]   MH(CT)(S)A 2003, s 76(2).
[3]   Mental Health (Content and amendment of care plans) (Scotland) Regulations 2005 (SSI 2005/309). ('The care plan regulations'.) See Code of Practice, vol 2, paras 4.14–20.
[4]   Code of Practice, vol 2, para 4.20.
[5]   Care plan regulations, reg 3. See Code of Practice, vol 2, para 4.18.
[6]   Code of Practice (above), para 4.19.
[7]   Monitoring priorities for 2005/6. See Commission's website.

DUTIES OF LOCAL AUTHORITY

Appointment of mental health officer

14.34 As soon as possible after the making of the order, the appropriate local authority must appoint a mental health officer for the person. It must ensure that the person has a mental health officer so long as he or she remains subject to an order under the Act.[1]

The appropriate local authority is the local authority for the area where the person will live, if the order is community-based. For a hospital-based order, the local authority is the one for the area where the person lived before he or she went into hospital.

For people living outside Scotland prior to admission, the local authority for the hospital appoints the mental health officer.[2]

[1]   Mental Health (Care and Treatment) (Scotland) Act 2003, s 229(1).
[2]   MH(CT)(S)A 2003, s 229(3).

Social circumstances report

14.35 Within 21 days of the making of the order, the mental health officer must draw up a social circumstances report for the person and send a copy to the responsible medical officer and the Mental Welfare Commission.[1] A form for the report is on the Scottish Executive's mental health law website.

If the mental health officer decides there would be little practical value in preparing such a report, he or she may record the reasons for this and send a copy to the responsible medical officer and the Commission.[2]

For more details on these reports, see 12.16.

[1]   Mental Health (Care and Treatment) (Scotland) Act 2003, s 231.
[2]   MH(CT)(S)A 2003, s 231(2).

Chapter 15

COMPULSORY TREATMENT ORDERS: REVIEWS, APPEALS AND SUSPENSION

OUTLINE OF PROCEDURES

15.01 This chapter looks at appeals and reviews, as well as varying and extending compulsory treatment orders and suspension of orders.

The responsible medical officer should keep the person's health and care needs under review at all times and may cancel ('revoke') the compulsory treatment order at any time.

The responsible medical officer may suspend some or all of the conditions of an order as part of someone's rehabilitation. The Mental Welfare Commission can set an order aside or, more likely, refer the case to the tribunal.

After six months, the responsible medical officer may extend the order, or may apply to the tribunal to extend and vary it. The responsible medical officer can apply to vary an order at any time. After the first six-month renewal, the responsible medical officer can renew the order for periods of 12 months at a time if the statutory grounds continue to apply.

The person subject to the order or his or her named person can appeal against the making of the order on legal grounds only, such as irregularities in the hearing. After three months, either may request the tribunal to cancel or vary the order, and either may appeal against any extension of an order. Either may request the tribunal to change any measures in the order.

In certain circumstances the tribunal automatically reviews an extension of an order. The tribunal also reviews every case where a person subject to an order does not receive a service which is a recorded matter. It may change the order or set it aside.

REVIEWS BY RESPONSIBLE MEDICAL OFFICER

Regular review

15.02 Whenever someone is subject to a compulsory treatment order, the responsible medical officer must keep the person's legal status under review and from time to time consider whether the statutory grounds for a compulsory treatment order continue to apply, bearing in mind the principles of the Act.[1]

The responsible medical officer must seek information on the person's condition from other members of the multi-disciplinary team.[2] The Code of Practice says all members of the care team should monitor the continuing need for a compulsory treatment order on a daily basis.[3]

If the responsible medical officer believes that all or any of the grounds no longer apply, he or she must discharge the person as soon as possible after reaching that decision.[4] It is not appropriate to allow an order to expire when it should be cancelled.[5]

A form for cancelling an order is available on the Scottish Executive's mental health law website.

1   Mental Health (Care and Treatment) (Scotland) Act 2003, s 80.
2   Code of Practice, vol 2, para 5.03.
3   Vol 2, para 5.15.
4   MH(CT)(S)A 2003, s 80(4).
5   Code of Practice, vol 2, para 5.19.

Formal review

15.03 Within two months before the end of the compulsory treatment order, the responsible medical officer must carry out a review.[1] The responsible medical officer must examine the person, or arrange for an approved medical practitioner to examine him or her. The responsible medical officer is the preferred choice.[2]

The responsible medical officer should consult the mental health officer and anyone proving medical and care services under the compulsory treatment order.[3] He or she should also consult the person subject to the order and any carers. Carers should be aware that they can contact the responsible medical officer at any time.[4]

The responsible medical officer should consider whether the grounds for a compulsory treatment order continue to apply, bearing in mind the principles of the Act.

The responsible medical officer has three alternatives:

- to discharge the order;
- to extend the order without any changes in the measures, or
- to apply to the tribunal to extend and vary the order.

Following the first review, subsequent formal reviews take place at 12 monthly intervals on the same basis as above.[5]

1   Mental Health (Care and Treatment) (Scotland) Act 2003, s 77.

2   Code of Practice, vol 2, para 5.09.

3   MH(CT)(S)A 2003, s 77(4).

4   Code of Practice, vol 2, para 5.13.

5   MH(CT)(S)A 2003, s 78.

DISCHARGE OF ORDER

15.04 If the responsible medical officer decides that the grounds for an order do not apply, he or she should cancel ('revoke') the order as soon as possible.[1]

If the responsible medical officer cancels the order following a regular review or a formal review (see below), he or she must notify the relevant people about the cancellation of the order and the reasons for it.

These people are the person subject to the order, the named person, any welfare guardian or attorney, the mental health officer, the tribunal and the Mental Welfare Commission.[2]

The responsible medical officer should notify the person and his or her representatives as soon as practicable, normally verbally.[3] The responsible medical officer should notify everyone within seven days of cancelling the order.[4]

A form is available on the Scottish Executive's mental health law website.

1   Mental Health (Care and Treatment) (Scotland) Act 2003, s 79.

2   MH(CT)(S)A 2003, s 82.

3   Code of Practice, vol 2, para 5.21.

4   MH(CT)(S)A 2003, s 82(4). Similar duties apply if the Commission cancels an order, (MH(CT)(S)A 2003, s 82(2).)

Discharge planning

15.05 Whenever the responsible medical officer cancels a compulsory treatment order or the tribunal sets aside an order, the responsible medical officer should oversee a full discharge plan for the person.[1] The person may go onto the care programme approach, which has specific requirements for discharge planning. (See chapter 6.)

1   Code of Practice, vol 2, para 5.24.

EXTENSION OF ORDER

15.06 If the statutory grounds for a compulsory treatment order continue to apply to a person, the responsible medical officer should reconsider whether an order is necessary, bearing in mind the principles of the Act. He or she should also reassess the person's needs for medical treatment.

Where the responsible medical officer considers an order should be extended, he or she must notify the mental health officer.[1]

1   Mental Health (Care and Treatment) (Scotland) Act 2003, s 84.

Duties of mental health officer

15.07 The mental health officer interviews the person (if this is practical).[1] He or she must advise the person of his or her rights and about independent advocacy and help the person access independent advocacy.[2]

The mental health officer should advise the responsible medical officer whether he or she agrees with any suggested changes to the order, and give his or her reasons, together with any other information the mental health officer considers relevant.[3]

1   Mental Health (Care and Treatment) (Scotland) Act 2003, s 85(3).
2   MH(CT)(S)A 2003, s 85.
3   MH(CT)(S)A 2003, s 85(2)(d).

Extension certificate

15.08 The responsible medical officer must bear in mind the views of the people consulted before deciding whether to extend the order.

If the responsible medical officer is satisfied that the person should remain subject to a compulsory treatment order, he or she may extend the order for six months from that date.[1] The form to record the decision is available on the Scottish Executive's mental health law website.

[1]   Mental Health (Care and Treatment) (Scotland) Act 2003, s 86(1).

Role of tribunal

Report to tribunal

15.09 If the responsible medical officer extends the compulsory treatment order, he or she must advise the tribunal as soon as possible and, in any event, before the expiry of the compulsory treatment order.[1]

The report should spell out why the responsible medical officer is extending the order and whether the mental health officer agrees or disagrees. If the mental health officer disagrees, the report should say why.

The report should specify the type(s) of mental disorder the person has (mental illness, learning disability or personality disorder). If these differ from the type(s) recorded in the compulsory treatment order, the report should note this.

The tribunal may call for further reports from the responsible medical officer or the mental health officer.[2]

[1]   Mental Health (Care and Treatment) (Scotland) Act 2003, s 87.
[2]   MH(CT)(S)A 2003, s 109(2). See the Mental Health (Compulsory treatment orders—documents and reports to be submitted to the Tribunal) (Scotland) Regulations 2005 (SSI 2005/366) ('The tribunal documents Regulations'), reg 6.

Review by tribunal

15.10 The tribunal reviews the responsible medical officer's decision if the mental health officer disagrees with the extension of the order or if the type of mental disorder specified in the compulsory treatment order differs from that in the responsible medical officer's report.[1]

It will also review the decision if the case has not come before the tribunal in the two years ending on the date the order was due to expire.[2] (This provision will not come into effect until the tribunal service has been in operation for two years.)[3]

The tribunal can confirm the extension or vary it.[4] It may revoke the extension of the order and, if it considers this appropriate, the order itself. It may also make interim orders.[5] For role of the tribunal, see 15.30.

For tribunal procedure, see chapter 23. All relevant parties will attend and have an opportunity to speak.[6]

1   Mental Health (Care and Treatment) (Scotland) Act 2003, s 101.
2   MH(CT)(S)A 2003, s 101(2).
3   The Mental Health (Care and Treatment) (Scotland) Act 2003 (Commencement No. 4) Amendment (No. 2) Order 2005 (SSI 2005/459).
4   MH(CT)(S)A 2003, s 102(1).
5   MH(CT)(S)A 2003, s 106.
6   MH(CT)(S)A 2003, s 102(2).

People to be informed

15.11 The responsible medical officer must notify the person subject to the order, the named person, the mental health officer and the Mental Welfare Commission that he or she has extended the order and send them a copy of his or her report.[1]

The responsible medical officer need not send a copy of the report to the person subject to the order if he or she believes this could lead to a risk of significant harm to the person or to other people.[2] The responsible medical officer must notify the tribunal and all other parties whether he or she is sending a copy of the record to the person, and if not, why not.

When the responsible medical officer sends the renewal forms to the Mental Welfare Commission, he or she should also advise the Commission about the medical treatment he or she has given to the person and about the person's condition.[3]

The hospital must ensure the person receives information about his or her rights[4] and has any communication needs met.[5]

1   Mental Health (Care and Treatment) (Scotland) Act 2003, s 87(2)(c).
2   MH(CT)(S)A 2003, s 87(3).
3   MH(CT)(S)A 2003, s 248.
4   MH(CT)(S)A 2003, s 260. See also the Mental Health (Provision of Information to Patients) (Prescribed Times) (Scotland) Regulations 2005 (SSI 2005/206), reg 2(a).
5   MH(CT)(S)A 2003, s 261. See chapter 17.

EXTENSION AND VARIATION

15.12 If, following a formal review, (see above) the responsible medical officer believes that the grounds for an order continue to apply, but that some of the measures should be changed or modified, he or she may apply to the tribunal for an order extending and varying the order.[1]

[1]   Mental Health (Care and Treatment) (Scotland) Act 2003, s 92.

Duties of mental health officer

15.13 The duties of the mental health officer are the same as his or her duties when the responsible medical officer is considering extending the order.[1] See above.

[1]   Mental Health (Care and Treatment) (Scotland) Act 2003, s 89.

Application to tribunal

15.14 The responsible medical officer must bear in mind the views of the people consulted, before deciding whether to apply to extend and vary the order.[1] He or she should apply to the tribunal for extension and variation as soon as possible after having decided it is necessary.[2] A form is available on the Scottish Executive's website. Together with the application, the responsible medical officer must submit to the tribunal a copy of the person's original care plan and any amendments to it.[3]

As soon as possible before he or she applies for the order, the responsible medical officer should notify the person subject to the order, the named person, any welfare guardian or attorney, the mental health officer and the Mental Welfare Commission that he or she intendeds to apply for an extension and variation of the order.[4]

[1]   Mental Health (Care and Treatment) (Scotland) Act 2003, s 90(1).
[2]   MH(CT)(S)A 2003, s 90(3).
[3]   MH(CT)(S)A 2003, s 92(b). Tribunal documents Regulations, reg 2.
[4]   MH(CT)(S)A 2003, s 91.

Powers of tribunal

15.15 For tribunal procedure, see chapter 23. All relevant parties may attend and have an opportunity to speak.[1] The tribunal may call for further reports from the mental health officer.[2]

The tribunal may extend the order and change its terms as requested by the responsible medical officer.

The tribunal may extend the order but refuse to change any measures. It may refuse the application and can revoke the compulsory treatment order with immediate effect.[3]

If the responsible medical officer applies for variation of the order, the tribunal may grant or refuse the application.[4] It can also set aside the original order.

The tribunal may make an interim order, either extending the original order for up to 28 days or extending and modifying it.[5] It may also vary an order for up to 28 days.[6] The tribunal cannot make interim orders exceeding 56 days in total.[7]

An interim order does not count in calculating when an order ends for the purposes of the duty to review the order at specific times.[8]

For role of the tribunal, see 15.30.

[1]   Mental Health (Care and Treatment) (Scotland) Act 2003, s 103(5).
[2]   MH(CT)(S)A 2003, s 109(2). Tribunal documents Regulations, regs 3 and 4. The regulations give more detail on content.
[3]   MH(CT)(S)A 2003, s 103(1).
[4]   MH(CT)(S)A 2003, s 104.
[5]   MH(CT)(S)A 2003, s 105.
[6]   MH(CT)(S)A 2003, s 106.
[7]   MH(CT)(S)A 2003, s 107.
[8]   MH(CT)(S)A 2003, s 110.

Review by responsible medical officer

15.16 If the tribunal extends the order, the responsible medical officer must carry out a formal review of the order within two months of the end of the extended period.[1] See above.

[1]   Mental Health (Care and Treatment) (Scotland) Act 2003, s 78.

VARIATION OF ORDER

Duties of responsible medical officer

15.17 The responsible medical officer may apply to vary the order at any time. The procedure is similar to the procedure for extending and varying the order.

The responsible medical officer should from time to time consider whether any of the terms of the order need modifying, and if he or she considers they might do, should consult the mental health officer and any other appropriate people.[1]

This consultation should be as wide as possible.[2]

1   Mental Health (Care and Treatment) (Scotland) Act 2003, s 94(4).
2   Code of Practice, vol 2, para 5.73.

Duties of mental health officer

15.18 The mental health officer's duties are the same as when the responsible medical officer is considering extending an order.[1] See above.

1   Mental Health (Care and Treatment) (Scotland) Act 2003 (as amended by the Mental Health (Care and Treatment) (Scotland) Act 2003 Modification Order 2004 (SSI 2004/533)), art 2(2).

Application to tribunal

15.19 The responsible medical officer should bear in mind the views of those consulted. If he or she considers a change is necessary, he or she should apply to the tribunal for the variation of the order as soon as possible.[1]

Together with the application, the responsible medical officer must send the tribunal a copy of the person's care plan and any amendments to it.[2]

1   Mental Health (Care and Treatment) (Scotland) Act 2003, ss 93(5) and (6).
2   MH(CT)(S)A 2003, s 95(b). Tribunal documents Regulations, reg 2.

Tribunal's powers

15.20 The tribunal may require the mental health officer to supply a report.[1] All relevant people are entitled to appear at the tribunal and make representations.[2]

The tribunal may vary the order or any recorded matter, refuse the application or refuse the application and set aside the order.[3] In modifying the order, the tribunal may amend or remove any measure or recorded matter, add a measure or recorded matter to the order or add a new recorded matter.[4] For role of the tribunal, see 15.30.

1   Mental Health (Care and Treatment) (Scotland) Act 2003, s 109(2). Tribunal documents Regulations, reg 4.
2   MH(CT)(S)A 2003, s 103(5).
3   MH(CT)(S)A 2003, s 103(4).
4   MH(CT)(S)A 2003, s 111.

PATIENTS' RIGHTS

Appeal against making of order

15.21 The person can appeal against the tribunal's initial decision to make an order only if he or she alleges the tribunal has made a legal mistake or that there were other irregularities in the hearing.[1]

Similarly, it is possible to appeal against the refusal of the tribunal to make an order only on a point of law.

1   Mental Health (Care and Treatment) (Scotland) Act 2003, s 324(2).

Application for discharge/variation

15.22 Once three months have passed from the making of the order (or from any subsequent order), the person subject to the order or his or her named person may apply to the tribunal to have the order set aside. They may also request the tribunal to vary one or more of the compulsory measures or recorded matters.[1] If the tribunal refuses the application, each can only make one further application during the relevant period.

The relevant period is six months, if the application was made between three and six months from the date of the making of the compulsory treatment order. Each party can make one other application in the next six months, and thereafter can make applications annually.[2]

1   Mental Health (Care and Treatment) (Scotland) Act 2003, s 100.
2   MH(CT)(S)A 2003, s 100(4).

Contacting Mental Welfare Commission

15.23 Either the person subject to the order or the named person can contact the Mental Welfare Commission.

The Commission can cancel the order, although it is unlikely to do so.[1] It may advise the person to contact the tribunal and may itself refer cases to the tribunal.[2] (See 12.19.)

1   Mental Health (Care and Treatment) (Scotland) Act 2003, s 81.
2   MH(CT)(S)A 2003, s 98.

Appeal against extension

15.24 If the responsible medical officer extends the order, the person subject to the order and his or her named person can appeal to the tribunal. In some cases the tribunal will automatically consider the extension of the order.[1]

If the tribunal makes an order confirming the extension of the order, neither party can appeal against the order until three months from the tribunal's decision[2] unless there was some procedural impropriety when the tribunal considered the matter.[3] The same rule applies where the tribunal varies the order or varies and extends it.

This provision is subject to human rights requirements that a person detained in hospital must have the right of 'speedy access' to a court or tribunal.[4] If a change in circumstances means it is urgently necessary that a person should be able to challenge his or her detention, the tribunal service might have to consider waiving this requirement.[5]

1   Mental Health (Care and Treatment) (Scotland) Act 2003, s 99.
2   MH(CT)(S)A 2003, s 100(5).
3   MH(CT)(S)A 2003, s 324.
4   European Convention on Human Rights, Art 5(4).
5   See *Kolanis v UK* [2005] ECHR 411 where the Mental Health Review Tribunal's inability to review K's detention, although in accordance with domestic law, was held in breach of K's rights under Art 5(4).

Powers of tribunal

15.25 The tribunal may call for further reports from the responsible medical officer or the mental health officer.[1] The tribunal can cancel the order or vary any measure in the order, including any recorded matter.[2] It can also make interim orders.[3]

When dealing with an application to vary an order, the tribunal may instead revoke the order.[4] All relevant parties may attend the tribunal and have an opportunity to speak.[5]

1   Mental Health (Care and Treatment) (Scotland) Act 2003, s 109(2). Tribunal documents Regulations, reg 5.
2   MH(CT)(S)A 2003, s 103(3).

3   MH(CT)(S)A 2003, s 106.
4   MH(CT)(S)A 2003, s 103(4).
5   MH(CT)(S)A 2003, s 103(5).

REFERENCE TO TRIBUNAL

15.26 The Mental Welfare Commission can refer a case to the tribunal.[1] This might be appropriate if, for example, someone is not receiving a service which is a recorded matter or if the Commission believes the tribunal should vary or discharge an order.

The Commission should give notice to the responsible medical officer and mental health officer, as well as to the person subject to the order, his or her named person, and any welfare attorney or guardian.[2]

Following such a reference, the tribunal may call for further reports from the responsible medical officer or the mental health officer.[3] It may vary the order or any recorded matters in it, or it may cancel the order altogether.[4] It may also make interim orders.[5]

All relevant parties may attend the tribunal and have an opportunity to speak.

1   Mental Health (Care and Treatment) (Scotland) Act 2003, s 98.
2   MH(CT)(S)A 2003, s 98(3).
3   MH(CT)(S)A 2003, s 109(2). Tribunal documents regulations, reg 8.
4   MH(CT)(S)A 2003, s 104.
5   MH(CT)(S)A 2003, s 106.

RECORDED MATTERS

15.27 If someone does not receive a service which the tribunal has made a recorded matter, the tribunal must be informed. The tribunal will then consider whether the order should remain in force, or whether the tribunal should change any of the measures in the order.

Duties of responsible medical officer

15.28 If the responsible medical officer believes that any recorded matter is not available to a patient, he or she must consult the mental health officer and any other appropriate people as soon as practicable.[1]

If one or more of the recorded matters are not available, the responsible medical officer must refer the case to the tribunal as soon as possible. A form is available on the Scottish Executive's website. The responsible medical officer must send the tribunal a copy of the person's care plan and any amendments to it.[2]

The responsible medical officer must notify the person subject to the order, his or her named person, any welfare attorney or guardian, the mental health officer and the Mental Welfare Commission as soon as possible.[3]

The responsible medical officer does not need to refer the case to the tribunal if he or she intends to cancel the order or to apply for a variation or an extension and variation.[4]

[1]   Mental Health (Care and Treatment) (Scotland) Act 2003, s 96.
[2]   MH(CT)(S)A 2003, s96(4)(b). Tribunal documents Regulations, reg 2.
[3]   MH(CT)(S)A 2003, s 97.
[4]   MH(CT)(S)A 2003, s 96(6).

Tribunal powers

15.29 Following the responsible medical officer's reference, the tribunal may call for a further report from the mental health officer.[1] It may then vary the order or any recorded matters in it, or it may cancel the order altogether.[2] It may also make interim orders.[3]

All relevant parties should have a chance to put their case at the tribunal.

[1]   Mental Health (Care and Treatment) (Scotland) Act 2003, s 109(2). Tribunal documents Regulations, reg 7.
[2]   MH(CT)(S)A 2003, s 104.
[3]   MH(CT)(S)A 2003, s 106.

ROLE OF TRIBUNAL

15.30 We have seen above that a case may be referred to the tribunal if there is a need to vary or extend an order, if a person appeals against an order or the Mental Welfare Commission refers a matter to the tribunal.

Unfortunately this part of the Act does not spell out the basis on which the tribunal should reach a decision. This is different from other provisions. For example, the tribunal must revoke a short-term detention certificate if it is not satisfied that the statutory grounds apply.[1] Similarly, the responsible medical officer must discharge the person if the statutory grounds for a compulsory treatment order do not apply.

The Act does not set out such clear statutory duties for the tribunal when it considers appeals, references and applications for extension or variation of orders. This may be because the Parliament wished to give the tribunal some discretion about what action to take. The tribunal has a variety of options.

This does not mean that, when considering an appeal or whether an order should be extended, the tribunal's discretion is unlimited. The tribunal must refer back to the statutory grounds. The House of Lords has said (in a case dealing with the discharge provisions of the 1984 Act) that when a court or tribunal considers whether it is appropriate for a person to be liable to be detained in hospital, it must refer back to whether the criteria for admission continue to apply.[2]

The Lords' decision reflects human rights concerns. Any review of compulsory detention must be wide enough to consider the lawfulness of the detention.[3] The law must not be arbitrary or uncertain. The Millan Committee, whose report influenced the Mental Health (Care and Treatment) Act, recommended that the 'entry' and 'exit' conditions for the use of compulsory measures should be the same.[4]

The responsible medical officer, in reaching a decision on what measures to recommend, has to consider whether the statutory grounds for compulsion apply. Although the Act does not specifically say that the tribunal should do the same, it may be possible to imply this. It is hard to think on what other basis the tribunal could reach a decision.

The case law is clear that it is for the mental health officer and responsible medical officer to satisfy the tribunal that the grounds apply, not for the patient to prove that they do not.[5]

[1]   Mental Health (Care and Treatment) (Scotland) Act 2003, s50(4).
[2]   *Reid v Secretary of State for Scotland*, 1999 SC(HL)17.
[3]   *X v United Kingdom* [1981] 4 EHRR 188.
[4]   *New directions*, para 28.30.
[5]   See *R (H) v MHRT North & East London Region* (2001) EWCA Civ 415, *L v Scottish Ministers* (IH) Court of Session, 17 January 2002; *Hutchison Reid v UK* [2003] ECtHR 94.

SUSPENSION OF ORDER

15.31 If a compulsory treatment order authorises detention in hospital, the person subject to the order can leave the hospital only if the responsible medical officer authorises this, by suspending the terms of the order. The person may need to leave the hospital for a specific event, such as a tribunal hearing, a medical appointment or for compassionate reasons, or may leave the hospital for a longer period as part of rehabilitation. The fact that staff will escort the person outside the hospital does not remove the need for a formal suspension of detention.

The responsible medical officer can also suspend the terms of a community-based compulsory treatment order.

The Scottish Executive has given detailed guidance on these provisions.[1]

[1]   Scottish Executive Health Department letter HDL (2006) 7, (6 February 2006).

Role of responsible medical officer

15.32 The responsible medical officer may suspend any term in a compulsory treatment order for such period as he or she thinks fit. He or she cannot suspend a compulsory treatment order for longer than nine months in any 12-month period.[1] A longer suspension requires variation of the order. See chapter 14.

The responsible medical officer should discuss the possible suspension with the person subject to the order and his or her named person, as well as the multi-disciplinary team. There may also need to be discussions with the person's carers. (The Code of Practice says that if a patient does not allow doctors to contact the people who may be caring for him or her outside the hospital, it is not appropriate to suspend the certificate.)[2]

The responsible medical officer remains responsible for the person's care while the measures are suspended and should ensure the relevant people understand how to contact him or her.[3]

[1]   Mental Health (Care and Treatment) (Scotland) Act 2003, s 127(2).
[2]   Code of Practice, vol 2, para 4.38.
[3]   Code of Practice, vol 2, para 4.44.

Suspension and variation

15.33 The Code of Practice gives advice on when it might be appropriate for the responsible medical officer to suspend an order and when he or she should apply to the tribunal for a variation of the order.[1]

Where the responsible medical officer considers that a person subject to a hospital-based order should remain subject to the order but live long-term in the community, he or she should apply to vary the order rather than rely on suspension provisions.[2] This reflects the principle of least restrictive alternative and allows the tribunal to monitor the person's care arrangements.

If the responsible medical officer is not sure whether the person is ready to return to the community and needs to keep the care arrangements under review, he or she should suspend the certificate.

[1]   Code of Practice, vol 2, paras 4.39–41.

[2]   Code of Practice, vol 2, para 4.39.

Suspension of detention

15.34 The responsible medical officer may suspend hospital detention under a compulsory treatment order or an interim compulsory treatment order,[1] either for a specific event, such as a hospital appointment or family event, or for a period, as part of rehabilitation.[2]

If the responsible medical officer intends to suspend detention for more than 28 days, (or if, taken with any other suspension, the suspension would exceed 28 days), he or she must notify the person subject to the order, the named person, the general practitioner and the mental health officer.[3] The Code of Practice recommends notifying these parties if a shorter suspension period is likely.[4]

The form of certificate authorising the suspension is on the Scottish Executive's mental health law website. The responsible medical officer may attach such conditions to the certificate as he or she considers necessary in the person's interests or for the protection of other people.[5] He or she may require the person to be kept in charge of someone named in the certificate or may impose other conditions, such as where the person should stay. The responsible medical officer should make sure all relevant people understand these conditions.[6]

Suspension of detention can last for up to six months.[7] For a person subject to an interim order, the suspension can last for any period until the end of the detention. The responsible medical officer may not grant a suspension certificate if the suspension of detention in the 12-month period preceding the end of the suspension certificate would exceed nine months.[8]

If the responsible medical officer suspends a person's detention in hospital for more than 28 days, he or she must notify the Mental Welfare Commission within 14 days of authorising the suspension.[9]

1   Including an interim order made by the tribunal following an application to extend or extend and vary an order. Mental Health (Care and Treatment) (Scotland) Act 2003 (as amended by the Mental Health (Care and Treatment) (Scotland) Act 2003 (Modification of Enactments) Order 2005 (SSI 2005/465)), s 127(3)(a).
2   MH(CT)(S)A 2003, s 127(1).
3   MH(CT)(S)A 2003, s 127(7).
4   Code of Practice, vol 2, para 4.48.
5   MH(CT)(S)A 2003, s 127(5).
6   Code of Practice, vol 2, para 4.34.
7   MH(CT)(S)A 2003, s 127(1).
8   MH(CT)(S)A 2003, s 127(2).
9   MH(CT)(S)A 2003, s 127(9).

Suspension of community-based order

15.35 The responsible medical officer may suspend any measures in a community-based compulsory treatment order for up to three months.[1] It is not possible to suspend the provisions of an interim community-based order.

Before suspending a measure in a community-based order, the responsible medical officer must write to the person subject to the order, the named person and the mental health officer. He or she should tell them the measures he or she intends to suspend, for how long he or she intends to suspend them and his or her reasons for proposing the suspension.[2]

The responsible medical officer cannot attach conditions to the suspension of community measures.

If the responsible medical officer suspends any measures in a community-based order, he or she must notify the Commission within 14 days.[3]

1   Mental Health (Care and Treatment) (Scotland) Act 2003, s 128.
2   MH(CT)(S)A 2003, s 128(3).
3   MH(CT)(S)A 2003, s 128(5).

Cancelling suspension

15.36 The responsible medical officer may cancel any suspension certificate if he or she thinks this necessary in the interests of the person or for the protection of other people.[1] He or she should generally discuss this with the person subject to the order and other relevant people.[2]

As soon as possible after cancelling suspension of detention, the responsible medical officer must give notice to the person subject to the order, the named person, the mental health officer, anyone authorised to be in charge of the person and the person's general practitioner.[3]

If the responsible medical officer cancels the suspension of a community-based order, he or she should give notice as soon as possible to the person subject to the order, the named person and the mental health officer and explain the reasons for cancelling the suspension.[4]

In both cases, the responsible medical officer should also notify the Mental Welfare Commission within 14 days of the cancellation.[5] There does not currently seem to be a form for notifying the Commission.

1   Mental Health (Care and Treatment) (Scotland) Act 2003, s 129(2).
2   Code of Practice, vol 2, para 4.59.
3   MH(CT)(S)A 2003, s 129(3).
4   MH(CT)(S)A 2003, s 129(4).
5   MH(CT)(S)A 2003, s 129(5).

Chapter 16

MEDICAL TREATMENT

16.01 One of the most significant effects of being subject to compulsion under the Mental Health (Care and Treatment) Act is that the people are usually subject to the compulsory treatment rules of Part 16 of the Act.[1] The rules mean that in certain circumstances a person subject to compulsory measures may receive medical treatment even though he or she does not consent to this. The Act contains a series of safeguards, according to the seriousness of the treatment.

The drafting of Part 16 is extremely complex. Many people will not find it easy to understand these important provisions when reading the Act. The Mental Health (Care and Treatment) Act is committed to principles of openness and accessibility. It is regrettable that the Parliamentary draftspeople appear to have found these principles so difficult.

---

[1]   A tribunal making a compulsory treatment order should consider whether it is necessary for the person to be subject to Part 16. The principle of minimum necessary intervention means that the tribunal should not include any measure in an order unless it is necessary. There may be occasions where the tribunal is satisfied that someone needs some degree of compulsion but is otherwise prepared to accept medical treatment. Such a person should not be subject to the Part 16 rules.

OUTLINE OF RULES

16.02 For the first two months of the order, a responsible medical officer can give drug treatment for the mental disorder if the person consents or if the responsible medical officer determines this is in the person's best interests. The responsible medical officer can authorise nursing and other medical care on this basis for the duration of the order.

Certain treatments require special safeguards. The responsible medical officer can give drug treatment after two months and certain other treatments if the person consents or a second opinion doctor approves the treatment.

There are special rules for electro-convulsive therapy (ECT). A doctor can never give ECT to a person who refuses it, if the person has the legal capacity to take treatment decisions.

Neurosurgery for mental disorder (a rare treatment) and other similar treatments require both the consent of the person and second opinions. These rules apply both to people subject to compulsory measure and to informal patients.

There are special rules for emergencies and special protections for children and young people.

SCOPE OF RULES

To whom rules apply

16.03 The Part 16 rules apply to:

- People subject to short-term detention, including extension of short-term detention by an extension certificate or following an application for a compulsory treatment order.
- People subject to compulsory treatment orders and interim compulsory treatment orders (provided the order contains such a power).
- People subject to compulsory measures under the Criminal Procedure (Scotland) Act 1995. (This includes people subject to compulsion orders and interim compulsion orders, people subject to hospital directions (as long as the person is in hospital) and people transferred to hospital under assessment or treatment orders and transfer for treatment directions. There are special safeguards for people who come to hospital under assessment orders, as a psychiatrist may not have authorised their admission.)

The rules do not apply to people subject to emergency detention certificates. A doctor may give urgent treatment under the Act (see below).

The treatments requiring both consent and second opinions apply not just to people subject to compulsory measures but also to informal patients.

People on probation

16.04 A person receiving psychiatric treatment as part of a probation order is not subject to Part 16 of the Mental Health (Care and Treatment)

Act. A person on probation does not have to accept any medical treatment. If someone on probation refuses treatment, he or she may have to return to court and satisfy the court that the refusal was reasonable.[1]

1   Criminal Procedure (Scotland) Act 1995, s 232(5).

Medical treatment

16.05 Part 16 authorises giving medical treatment. Medical treatment is treatment for mental disorder. The definition includes nursing and care, psychological treatments, rehabilitation and habilitation.[1] This section looks at what treatments these words cover.

The Court of Appeal in England has considered these issues in a case under the Mental Health Act 1983.[2] The definition of 'medical treatment' in that Act is very similar to that in the Mental Health (Care and Treatment) Act. The court said that medical treatment can also include a range of acts supplementing the core treatment that the person receives. Such subsidiary treatment could include nursing and care at the same time as the treatment, care that is a necessary part of such treatment and nursing (and care) to prevent someone from harming him or herself or to reduce the effects of the disorder.[3]

The courts in England have held that treatment for mental disorder can include giving food to someone with an eating disorder, so long as the doctor regards the food as treatment for the mental disorder.[4]

Difficult issues arise where blood tests are required for the giving of certain treatments. The Mental Welfare Commission has said that where blood tests are integral to the treatment, any authority to give the treatment includes the authority to give the blood test. One such drug is clozapine, where the manufacturers refuse to supply the drug if doctors fail to send it regular blood tests sent. The Mental Welfare Commission advised that blood testing came within any second opinion approval under the Mental Health (Scotland) Act 1984.[5]

The Mental Welfare Commission has advised that blood testing in connection with the prescribing of lithium and the administration of electro-convulsive therapy, while highly advisable, is not an essential part of the treatment, and could not be enforced under the 1984 Act.[6] If this legal advice is correct, there is no reason to think the situation would be different under the Mental Health (Care and Treatment) Act. This would mean that someone refusing consent to the blood tests might not be able to receive such treatments against his or her will.[7]

1   Mental Health (Care and Treatment) (Scotland) Act 2003, s 329.

2   *B v Croydon Health Authority* [1995] 1 All ER 683.

3   *B v Croydon Health Authority* (above) Lord Justice Hoffman, at p 687.

4   *Riverside Health NHS Trust v Fox* [1994] 1 FLR 614–22.

5   Mental Welfare Commission Annual Report 1996/97, para 10.6.

6   See Mental Welfare Commission Annual Report 1994–5, para 6.3.

7   The Mental Welfare Commission received legal advice to this effect when a detained patient refused to agree to the blood tests for the use of lithium. It advised that the person should not receive the treatment at that time. Annual Report 1987, para 6.6.

IMPACT OF PRINCIPLES

16.06 Anyone operating the Part 16 rules must bear in mind the principles of the Act.[1]

For someone subject to the consent to treatment rules, certain principles are particularly important. These are the importance of taking account of the person's past and present wishes and feelings, of encouraging the person to participate as far as possible in any decisions and of providing the person with adequate information.

Consent of the patient is always preferable to the use of compulsion, so a doctor should try to seek consent before seeking a second opinion, under the principle of least restrictive option.

Those involved should consider all options, within available resources. Even if Part 16 applies, doctors should attempt as far as possible to involve the person in decisions about treatment. It may also be appropriate to consult with the named person and carer, bearing in mind patient confidentiality.

An independent advocacy worker can help someone make decisions about medical treatment and care. The Code of Practice envisages that some people may wish an independent advocate to be present when a doctor is discussing treatment options.[2]

The principles represent good practice. They attempt to ensure that, even when someone is subject to compulsory measures, he or she does not lose all autonomy in relation to healthcare decisions.

The person's position is stronger if he or she has made an advance statement.

1   Code of Practice, vol 1, para 10.02.

2   Code of Practice, vol 1, para 10.19.

ADVANCE STATEMENTS

16.07 An advance statement sets out a person's wishes about treatment. Chapter 10 looks at the procedure.

In making any compulsory order, the tribunal must consider what the advance statement says.[1] If someone is subject to compulsory measures and has a valid advance statement,[2] anyone giving him or her medical treatment under Part 16 of the Mental Health (Care and Treatment) Act must take into account the person's wishes as expressed in the advance statement (provided the person has not withdrawn the advance statement and his or her ability to take treatment decisions is significantly impaired).[3]

Similarly, before a designated medical practitioner gives a second opinion that certain medical treatments are in the best interests of the person, he or she must take into account the person's wishes as set out in the statement.[4]

The person giving the treatment is not obliged to consider any advance statement if he or she is not aware of its existence, but the Code of Practice obliges doctors to make enquiries whether there is a valid statement.[5]

[1]   Mental Health (Care and Treatment) (Scotland) Act 2003, s 276(1).
[2]   An advance statement can be assumed to be valid, or validly withdrawn, unless there is any reason to think otherwise. (MH(CT)(S)A 2003, s 276(5).) If someone is subject to Part 16 following a tribunal decision, the person giving the treatment can rely on the tribunal's findings on the validity of the advance statement. (MH(CT)(S)A 2003, s 276(6).)
[3]   MH(CT)(S)A 2003, s 276(3).
[4]   MH(CT)(S)A 2003, s 276(4).
[5]   Code of Practice, vol 1, para 6.51.

Duties of doctors

16.08 Anyone giving treatment for mental disorder should ask the patient whether he or she has made an advance statement. If the person is unable to answer or remember, the health professional should enquire at the hospital, or ask the general practitioner, where the person is not in hospital. He or she should also ask the named person and carer.[1]

The advance statement may include the person's wish for certain treatments (such as counselling or other talking treatments) and a wish not to have other treatments (such as electro-convulsive therapy). It may not be possible to meet the person's wishes or a doctor may consider it necessary to overrule the person's wishes. He or she should bear the other principles of the Act in mind when reaching a decision.

The Code of Practice gives additional duties to a designated medical practitioner called upon to give a second opinion in respect of medical treatment. (See below.)

1   Code of Practice, vol 1, paras 6.51–54.

Where advance statement overruled

16.09 If a person gives medical treatment conflicting with a patient's wishes, he or she must notify the relevant people of the circumstances and reasons.[1] He or she should keep a copy of the record with the person's medical records. The relevant people are the patient, named person, any welfare attorney or guardian and the Mental Welfare Commission.[2]

The Mental Welfare Commission has said that it will pay close attention to cases where someone's advance statement has been overridden. It will look into why this has been the case and will challenge this if it is not satisfied.[3] The Commission says people providing care and treatment should 'think long and hard' before overruling an advance statement.

An advance statement cannot oblige health professionals to provide specific medical treatments. The Code of Practice says that if a patient does not receive the treatment he or she has requested, the people treating him or her should record this as an unmet need.[4]

1   Mental Health (Care and Treatment) (Scotland) Act 2003, s 276(7).
2   MH(CT)(S)A 2003, s 276(8).
3   *Monitoring priorities for 2005–6,* Mental Welfare Commission.
4   Code of Practice, vol 1, para 6.65.

TREATMENT REQUIRING CONSENT OR RMO AUTHORISATION

Relevant treatments

16.10 Certain treatments require special safeguards. We discuss these below. A person subject to Part 16 of the Act can receive other treatments either if he or she consents, or if the responsible medical officer authorises the treatment.[1]

This includes drug treatment for the first two months of the order. After two months, if the patient does not consent to the drug treatment, the responsible medical officer must seek a second opinion to see if it should continue.

Other medical treatment the responsible medical officer can authorise include nursing, care, psychological services, help with life skills (including education and training in work and social skills) and rehabilitation.[2]

In practice the responsible medical officer will not always be able to authorise such treatment if the person is not willing to accept it. Certain treatments, such as psychological services, require the patient's co-operation and consent.

[1]   Mental Health (Care and Treatment) (Scotland) Act 2003, s 242.
[2]   MH(CT)(S)A 2003, s 329.

Where person consents

16.11 If a patient is capable of consent and gives his or her consent, the responsible medical officer may give the treatment or authorise it.[1] The responsible medical officer must ask the person to sign a written consent form.[2] The doctor should keep the consent form with the person's medical records.[3]

A person may withdraw consent at any time. The responsible medical officer must seek a further written consent.[4]

[1]   Mental Health (Care and Treatment) (Scotland) Act 2003, ss 242(3) and (5).
[2]   MH(CT)(S)A 2003, s 242(3).
[3]   Code of Practice, vol 1, para 10.73.
[4]   Code of practice, vol 1, para 10.75.

Where person does not consent

16.12 If the person does not consent, is incapable of consenting, or does not sign the written consent form, the responsible medical officer may authorise the treatment if he or she considers it is in the person's best interests.[1] The responsible medical officer must record in writing the reasons for giving the treatment.[2]

In considering whether treatment is in someone's best interests, the question is not simply whether the treatment is likely to improve the person's condition or stop it getting worse. The responsible medical officer should bear in mind the principles of the Act (see above). This means he or she should attempt to find out the person's views and should try to ensure the person has enough information to reach a decision. He or she should take into account the person's reasons for refusing the treatment, if he or she knows these, and the views of the named person, as well as any advance statement.[3]

1   Mental Health (Care and Treatment) (Scotland) Act 2003, s 242(5).

2   MH(CT)(S)A 2003, s 242(5)(d).

3   MH(CT)(S)A 2003, s 242(5).

People subject to assessment orders

16.13 If a person in hospital under an assessment order does not give written consent to treatment, the responsible medical officer cannot authorise it. The responsible medical officer must seek a second opinion from another doctor who is an approved medical practitioner.[1]

The Code of Practice says that, to ensure the independence of the second opinion doctor, he or she should be in a clinical team separate from the team responsible for the patient. He or she should not have a line-management relationship to the responsible medical officer.[2]

The second opinion doctor must take into account the matters in 16.12 above when deciding whether to approve the treatment.[3] He or she should decide whether the treatment is in the best interests of the person, bearing in mind the principles of the Act. If the second opinion doctor approves the treatment, he or she should record the reasons in writing.[4]

If the second opinion doctor approves treatment conflicting with a valid advance statement, the responsible medical officer carrying out the treatment should inform the Commission.[5]

1   The doctor need not be on the Mental Welfare Commission's list of designated medical practitioners. See below.

2   Code of Practice, vol 1, para 10.80.

3   Mental Health (Care and Treatment) (Scotland) Act 2003, s 242(5)(b).

4   MH(CT)(S)A 2003, s 242(5)(e).

5   MH(CT)(S)A 2003, s 276(7)(b).

TREATMENTS REQUIRING CONSENT OR SECOND OPINION

Relevant treatments

16.14 A doctor may give certain treatments only if the person consents or an independent psychiatrist (known as a 'designated medical practitioner') confirms that the treatment should go ahead. These rules apply to the following treatments:[1]

- Drug treatment for mental disorder, once two months have passed since the person first received the treatment under an order.[2]
- Drugs to reduce sex drive (but not surgical implantation of hormones).
- Artificial nutrition where the person does not consent.[3] This does not include forcible feeding.[4]

Regulations may add to this list. At the date of writing, there are no such regulations.

[1] Mental Health (Care and Treatment) (Scotland) Act 2003, s 240(3).
[2] The Scottish Ministers may introduce regulations changing the length of this period. They must consult before they do so. MH(CT)(S)A 2003, ss 240(5) and 240(7).
[3] See *R v Collins, ex parte Brady* [2000] Lloyd's Rep Med 355. Feeding someone on hunger strike was held to be treatment for his mental disorder, as there was evidence mental disorder was partly responsible for the hunger strike.
[4] Code of Practice, vol 1, para 10.71.

If person consents

16.15 If the person agrees to the treatment, his or her responsible medical officer or an independent doctor appointed by the Mental Welfare Commission must certify that the person is capable of consenting and has consented in writing to the treatment. This independent doctor is called a designated medical practitioner. See 3.31.

 The doctor must also confirm that the treatment is in the person's best interests and is likely to make the person's condition better or at least stopping it getting worse.[1]

 The patient may consent to a specific treatment, or to a more general treatment plan, which involves more than one form of treatment.[2] If a patient later withdraws consent, the responsible medical officer must complete a new consent certificate or seek a second opinion.[3]

The medical certificate must be in the prescribed form, available on the Scottish Executive's mental health law website.[4] The doctor issuing the certificate must send a copy to the Mental Welfare Commission within seven days of issuing it.[5]

[1]   Mental Health (Care and Treatment) (Scotland) Act 2003, s 238(1).
[2]   MH(CT)(S)A 2003, s 247.
[3]   MH(CT)(S)A 2003, s 238(2).
[4]   Mental Health (Certificates for Medical Treatment) (Scotland) Regulations 2005 (SSI 2005/443) ('The medical certificate Regulations').
[5]   MH(CT)(S)A 2003 (as amended by the Mental Health (Care and Treatment) (Scotland) Act 2003 Modification Order 2004 (SSI 2004/533)), s 246(2).

If person does not consent

Role of designated medical practitioner

16.16 If a patient does not consent to a treatment, or is unable to consent, and the responsible medical officer wishes the treatment to go ahead, he or she must seek a second opinion to see whether the treatment can go ahead. The Mental Welfare Commission appoints a designated medical practitioner to interview the person and decide whether the treatment should be given despite the person's objections.[1]

The Commission tries to ensure that all designated medical practitioners have either special experience of the patient's condition or of the treatment the doctors propose. If a patient has a learning disability, the designated medical practitioner should specialise in this area.[2]

The Commission has a useful leaflet on the role of the designated medical practitioner.

[1]   Mental Health (Care and Treatment) (Scotland) Act 2003, s 233.
[2]   Code of Practice, vol 1, para 10.22.

Designated medical practitioner

16.17 The designated medical practitioner must consult with the patient and his or her named person, provided this is practicable.[1] He or she should also consult with the people principally concerned with the person's medical treatment.[2] This would presumably include the person's responsible medical officer and his or her key nurse.

The doctor can interview or examine the person, in private if necessary, and can ask to see the person's medical records.[3] The person may ask for an independent advocate, named person or carer to be present, and the doctor will generally agreed to this request.[4]

1   Mental Health (Care and Treatment) (Scotland) Act 2003, ss 245(3) and 245(4).
2   MH(CT)(S)A 2003, s 245(3)(b).
3   MH(CT)(S)A 2003, s 233(4).
4   Code of Practice, vol 1, para 10.19.

Where advance statement

16.18 In making a decision about whether the treatment should go ahead, the designated medical practitioner must bear in mind the principles of the Act (see above) and take account of any advance statement the person has made.[1]

The designated medical practitioner should ask the person if he or she has made an advance statement. If the person is unable to provide a copy, the doctor should ask if a copy is with the patient's hospital records. He or she should also check with the person's general practitioner, his or her named person and carers.

The Code of Practice says that the designated medical practitioner cannot certify that treatment is in someone's best interests under the Act until he or she has taken these steps.[2]

If the designated medical practitioner authorises any treatment conflicting with the wishes set out in a valid advance statement, he or she must write to the person explaining his or her reasons. He or she must send a copy to the named person, any welfare attorney or guardian and the Mental Welfare Commission. The person's doctor must keep a copy with the medical records.[3]

1   Mental Health (Care and Treatment) (Scotland) Act 2003, s 276(4).
2   Code of Practice, vol 1, para 6.87.
3   MH(CT)(S)A 2003, s 276(7).

Duties of designated medical practitioner

16.19 The designated medical practitioner should take account of the person's past and present wishes and feelings not expressed in an advance statement and to the views of the named person and of any carer, guardian or welfare attorney, unless it is unreasonable or impracticable to do so.[1]

If someone refuses treatment, the doctor should attempt to establish the reasons for the refusal and bear these in mind when considering whether to authorise the treatment.[2] This is particularly the case if the doctor considers the person is capable of taking treatment decisions.[3]

If the designated medical practitioner considers that the medical treatment is in the best interests of the person, because it is likely to improve the person's condition, or prevent it getting worse, he or she may sign a certificate to that effect. The responsible medical officer may then give the treatment.[4] The certificate may authorise a specific treatment or a more general treatment plan involving more than one treatment.[5]

The prescribed form[6] is available on the Scottish Executive's mental health law website. The designated medical practitioner doctor must send a copy of the certificate to the Mental Welfare Commission within seven days of issuing it.[7]

[1]   See Code of Practice, vol 1, para 6.87.
[2]   Mental Health (Care and Treatment) (Scotland) Act 2003, s 241(2). Code of Practice, vol 1, para 10.67.
[3]   Code of Practice, vol 1, para 10.67.
[4]   MH(CT)(S)A 2003, s 241(1).
[5]   MH(CT)(S)A 2003, s 247.
[6]   Medical certificate Regulations.
[7]   See MH(CT)(S)A 2003, s 245(5).

ELECTRO-CONVULSIVE THERAPY AND SIMILAR TREATMENTS

16.20 The Act contains special rules for electro-convulsive therapy (ECT).

A person subject to Part 16 can receive ECT if he or she consents or, if he or she is unable to consent, if a designated medical practitioner gives a second opinion recommending the treatment.[1] If the person has the ability to consent, but refuses consent, he or she cannot receive ECT, even in an emergency.[2]

Two other treatments have the same protections. These are transcranial magnetic stimulation and vagus nerve stimulation.[3] The Scottish Ministers may add other treatments.[4]

[1]   Mental Health (Care and Treatment) (Scotland) Act 2003, ss 237–239.
[2]   MH(CT)(S)A 2003, s 243(5).

3   Mental Health (Medical treatment subject to safeguards) (Section 237) (Scotland) Regulations 2005 (SSI 2005/292).

4   MH(CT)(S)A 2003, s 237(3)(b).

If person consents

16.21 When someone agrees to the treatment, either the responsible medical officer or a designated medical practitioner must certify that the person is capable of consent and has consented in writing.

The doctor must also confirm that the treatment is in the person's best interests, bearing in mind its likelihood of alleviating the person's condition or at least stopping it getting worse.[1] The doctor must use the prescribed form, available on the Scottish Executive's mental health law website.[2] The person may withdraw consent at any time.[3]

The doctor must send a copy of the certificate to the Mental Welfare Commission within seven days of issuing it.[4]

1   Mental Health (Care and Treatment) (Scotland) Act 2003, s 238(1).

2   MH(CT)(S)A 2003, s 246 and medical certificate Regulations.

3   MH(CT)(S)A 2003, s 238(2).

4   MH(CT)(S)A 2003, s 246(2).

If person unable to consent

16.22 If a person is unable to consent to treatment with ECT and the responsible medical officer believes the treatment is appropriate, bearing in mind the principles of the Act, he or she must seek a second opinion from a designated medical practitioner.

For the duties of the designated medical practitioner, see 16.19. The designated medical practitioner must bear in mind the principles of the Act. In particular, he or she must consider the wishes and feelings of the person, past and present, even if the person is unable to take the decision in question.

If the designated medical practitioner considers that the treatment is appropriate, he or she may sign a certificate authorising the treatment. The doctor must confirm that person is unable to understand the nature, purpose and likely effects of the treatment but that it is in the person's best interests for the person to receive the treatment, bearing in mind the likelihood that the treatment will alleviate the person's condition or prevent it from getting worse.[1] The prescribed form[2] is on the mental health law website.

If the person is unable to understand the treatment, but appears to resist or object to the treatment, the doctor can give the treatment only if a designated medical practitioner certifies that the treatment is necessary to save the person's life, to prevent serious deterioration in his or her condition or to prevent serious suffering.[3]

The designated medical practitioner must send a copy of the certificate to the Mental Welfare Commission within seven days of issuing it.[4] He or she must give additional notifications if the treatment conflicts with a valid advance directive. (See above.)

[1]   Mental Health (Care and Treatment) (Scotland) Act 2003, s 239(1).
[2]   MH(CT)(S)A 2003, s 245(2) and medical certificate Regulations.
[3]   MH(CT)(S)A 2003, s 239(2).
[4]   MH(CT)(S)A 2003, s 245(5).

If person refuses

16.23 If a person able to take a decision about electro-convulsive therapy refuses the treatment, the responsible medical officer cannot give the treatment.[1]

[1]   Mental Health (Care and Treatment) (Scotland) Act 2003, s 237.

TREATMENT REQUIRING CONSENT AND SECOND OPINION

16.24 Certain rare treatments require not just the consent of the person, but also second opinions. The second opinions look at whether the treatment is medically recommended and whether the person is able to consent and has consented.

These special protections are for anyone considering these treatments, not just people subject to compulsory measures under the Mental Health (Care and Treatment) Act. This reflects the seriousness of the procedures and the need to ensure they are appropriate for the individual.

These rules relate to neurosurgery for mental disorder, a procedure that is very rare in Scotland. Only one centre, in Dundee, offers these treatments. They also apply to a treatment known as deep brain stimulation.[1] The Scottish Ministers can make regulations adding further treatments.

[1]   Mental Health (Medical treatment subject to safeguards) (Section 234) (Scotland) Regulations 2005 (SSI 2005/291).

If person consents

16.25 If the person consents to the treatment, a designated medical practitioner must interview him or her and certify that the person is capable of consenting to the treatment and has consented in writing to it. In addition, the designated medical practitioner must certify that it is in the person's best interests that he or she should receive the treatment, bearing in mind the likelihood that it will improve his or her condition or stop it getting worse.[1] (For the duties of the designated medical practitioner on investigating these matters, see 16.19 above.)

In addition, two people appointed by the Mental Welfare Commission must confirm that the person is capable of consenting and has consented in writing to the treatment.[2] These people should not be doctors. They are usually lay members of the Commission.

In carrying out their functions, the lay Commissioners should comply with the principles of the Act. They must satisfy themselves that all other options have been considered and that the person has received enough information to enable him or her to make an informed decision. They may interview the person in private if necessary.[3] They should also ascertain the views of the person's named person if possible and of those principally responsible for the person's treatment.[4] This would include the person's consultant and his or her key nurse and might include psychologists and other specialists.

Within seven days of certifying the person's consent, those involved should send a copy to the Mental Welfare Commission.[5] Prescribed forms are available.[6] The Commission has the power to cancel either the medical or the lay certificate.[7]

The person may withdraw consent at any time.[8]

[1]   Mental Health (Care and Treatment) (Scotland) Act 2003, s 235(2).
[2]   MH(CT)(S)A 2003, s 235(3).
[3]   MH(CT)(S)A 2003, s 235(4).
[4]   MH(CT)(S)A 2003, s 245(3).
[5]   MH(CT)(S)A 2003, s 245(5).
[6]   MH(CT)(S)A 2003, s 245. See medical certificate Regulations (above).
[7]   MH(CT)(S)A 2003, s 248(2).
[8]   MH(CT)(S)A 2003, s 235(5).

People unable to consent

16.26 The Act provides a procedure for obtaining authorisation from the Court of Session in Edinburgh where someone is unable to consent.[1] It is very unlikely that this procedure will be used. The centre currently providing these treatments does not consider they are appropriate when a patient is unable to consent.[2]

In reaching a decision, the Court of Session should have regard to the principles of the Act.[3] It should also consider any advance statement of the person.[4] The Court of Session would require certain certificates. A designated medical practitioner, not the person's responsible medical officer or consultant, should certify that the person was not able to consent to the treatment but did not object to it. The designated medical practitioner should confirm that the treatment was in the person's best interests.[5] Two lay people should confirm that the person did not object to the treatment.[6]

If the Court of Session decided that the person did not object to the treatment and the treatment was in the person's best interests, it could authorise the treatment. The Court of Session would need to be persuaded that the treatment was likely to alleviate the person's condition or prevent its deterioration.[7]

[1]   Mental Health (Care and Treatment) (Scotland) Act 2003, s 236.
[2]   In Dundee Advanced Interventions/Neurosurgery for Mental Disorder Service Report to the Scottish Executive (January 2006), para 56.
[3]   MH(CT)(S)A 2003, ss 1–3.
[4]   The Act does not state this specifically. The principle of respect for the person's past and present wishes and feelings would mean that the Court should have regard to a valid advance statement which the person has not withdrawn.
[5]   MH(CT)(S)A 2003, s 236(2).
[6]   MH(CT)(S)A 2003, s 236(3).
[7]   MH(CT)(S)A 2003, s 236(5).

ROLE OF MENTAL WELFARE COMMISSION

16.27 We have seen that if the responsible medical officer issues a certificate confirming that someone has consented to treatment or is incapable of consenting to treatment, he or she must send a copy to the Mental Welfare Commission. The Mental Welfare Commission can ask a responsible medical officer to report to it about any treatment and a patient's condition. A responsible medical officer must always send the Commission such a report if he or she intends to extend an order or applies for an extension and/or variation of an order.[1]

The Mental Welfare Commission may make further enquiries. It has the power to cancel any certificate of consent or incapacity.[2] If a responsible medical officer continued to wish to give the treatment, he or she would need a second opinion from a designated medical practitioner. The Mental Welfare Commission can also cancel certificates in relation to neurosurgery and similar treatments (see above).

The Mental Welfare Commission must act in accordance with the principles of the Act. It will consider whether the person was truly able to consent or was incapable of making a treatment decision. Anyone concerned about the treatment of someone who is subject to Part 16 of the Act should contact the Mental Welfare Commission.

[1]   Mental Health (Care and Treatment) (Scotland) Act 2003, s 248(1).
[2]   MH(CT)(S)A 2003, s 248(2).

URGENT TREATMENT

Where treatment authorised

16.28 When someone is subject to detention in hospital under the Mental Health (Care and Treatment) Act or the Criminal Procedure (Scotland) Act, doctors may give urgent treatment without the patient's consent.[1]

The treatment must be urgently necessary. It must be intended to save the person's life, to prevent a serious deterioration in his or her condition or serious suffering or to prevent the person from behaving violently or being a danger to him or herself or other people.[2]

Except in a life saving situation, the treatment must not be likely to entail unfavourable irreversible physical or psychological consequences.[3] Treatment to prevent serious suffering or to reduce risk must not involve a significant physical risk to the person.[4]

In an emergency a doctor can treat a patient whether or not he or she has the capacity to consent to or refuse it and whether or not he or she consents or refuses. However if the person is competent and refuses electro-convulsive therapy, he or she cannot receive this even in an emergency.[5]

These urgent treatment rules do not apply to informal patients. Nor do they apply to people on community based community treatment orders or compulsion orders.[6] The doctors must rely on their common law powers to treat in an emergency. See chapter 8.

[1]   Mental Health (Care and Treatment) (Scotland) Act 2003, s 243.
[2]   MH(CT)(S)A 2003, s 243(3).
[3]   MH(CT)(S)A 2003, s 243(4).

4   MH(CT)(S)A 2003, s 243(4)(b).
5   MH(CT)(S)A 2003, s 243(5).
6   MH(CT)(S)A 2003, s 243(1).

Safeguards

16.29 The responsible medical officer must report details of any urgent treatment to the Mental Welfare Commission within seven days.[1] A form is available on the mental health law website.

The Code of Practice says that on the occasions where emergency treatment is given by force, staff should be appropriately trained in control, restraint and resuscitation techniques. Hospital managers should ensure staff skills are kept up-to-date. If a doctor has to administer treatment by force, he or she should include details in his or her report to the Mental Welfare Commission.[2]

1   Mental Health (Care and Treatment) (Scotland) Act 2003, s 243(6).
2   Code of Practice, vol 1, para 10.87.

PATIENTS LIVING IN COMMUNITY

16.30 A person may be subject to a compulsory order but living in the community, for example if the responsible medical officer suspends detention or if the person is subject to a community-based compulsory treatment order.

If someone living in the community refuses medical treatment, the doctors cannot give it to him or her by force.[1] If the person is living in the community on suspended detention, the responsible medical officer may cancel the suspension and require the person to return to hospital.[2] The person may then receive treatment, by force if necessary.

If someone on a community-based compulsory treatment order refuses to accept medical treatment, he or she may be brought back to hospital and receive treatment there. See chapter 20.

1   Mental Health (Care and Treatment) (Scotland) Act 2003, ss 239(4), 241(4) and 242(6).
2   Under MH(CT)(S)A 2003 ss 54(2), 129(2) and 179.

TREATMENT FOR PHYSICAL DISORDERS

16.31 The Part 16 rules apply only to treatment for mental disorders. If someone subject to a compulsory order refuses treatment for a physical disorder, the doctors must respect this. If they believe a patient is unable to make treatment decisions because of mental disorder, they may consider treating the person under the relevant provisions of the Adults with Incapacity Act. See chapter 8.

CHILDREN AND YOUNG PEOPLE

16.32 A child or young person can be subject to the compulsory treatment provisions of the Act, although this is rare.[1]

The Act provides additional safeguards for children and young people, including special safeguards if a doctor proposes electro-convulsive therapy (ECT) or similar treatments.

One of the most important safeguards gives a young person the right to hospital care appropriate for his or her age. The health board must provide services and accommodation suitable for the needs of any young person admitted to a psychiatric hospital as an in-patient, whether he or she is a voluntary patient, is admitted under the Mental Health (Care and Treatment) Act or has come from the criminal justice system.[2] A bed in an adult ward is unlikely to be suitable.[3]

Chapter 41 looks at children's rights in more detail.

---

[1]   In 2004–5, there were five episodes of short-term detention of young people aged under 14 and three episodes of long-term detention. In the 15 to 24-year old age group, the figures were much higher, 388 and 152 respectively. Mental Welfare Commission Annual Report 2004–5, p 40.
[2]   MH(CT)(S)A 2003, s 23.
[3]   Code of Practice, vol 1, para 1.50.

Where young person consents

16.33 We have seen that when an adult is subject to a Part 16 order, the responsible medical officer should generally seek the adult's consent to treatment before considering seeking a second opinion. The responsible medical officer may seek a second opinion if the person refuses treatment or is incapable of accepting treatment.

The same principle applies to children and young people. If the responsible medical officer is satisfied the patient can and does consent, he or she may rely on that consent. (See chapter 41 for rules about capacity and young people.)

The Code of Practice suggests that the responsible medical officer should consider whether a young person is capable of understanding and consenting to the proposed treatment if the young person is about 12 or older.[1] This is not the approach of the Age of Legal Capacity (Scotland) Act, which considers the maturity of the child rather than any age limit.

The Code suggests that if a child is unable to consent, a parent can consent.[2] This is incorrect. If someone (including a child or young person) is subject to compulsory measures under the Mental Health (Care and Treatment) Act, no-one can consent to medical treatment on his or her behalf.

Doctors will need to consider how far to involve parents where the child or young person is able to make his or her own treatment decisions. The Code recommends that parents are still involved if possible, but it appreciates that there may be issues of patient confidentiality.[3]

1   Code of Practice, vol 1, para 1.32.
2   Code of Practice, vol 1 para 1.30.
3   Code of Practice, vol 1, para 1.31.

Where young person does not consent

16.34 As with adults, if a child or young person is unable to consent or refuses consent, the responsible medical officer can give the treatment only if a second opinion authorises this. The child's parents (or the person with parental responsibility) have no role in authorising treatment.

The Mental Health (Care and Treatment) Act contains special protections for young people under the age of 18 who are subject to orders under the Act.

If the responsible medical officer wishes to give a young person medical treatment without consent, and the responsible medical officer is not a specialist in child and adolescent psychiatry, the designated medical practitioner who examines the young person must be a specialist in child and adolescent psychiatry.[1] If the responsible medical officer is a child specialist, the designated medical practitioner does not need special qualifications.

The Mental Welfare Commission determines the qualifications and experience required of child specialists.[2]

Any doctor considering the medical treatment of a child or young person subject to compulsory measures should bear in mind the principles set out in section 2 of the Act. The welfare of the child should be paramount. If a young person has made an advance statement, the doctor must consider this and report if he or she overrides the statement. (See above.)

1   Mental Health (Care and Treatment) (Scotland) Act 2003, ss 238(3), 239(3), 241(3), 239(3), 236(7) and 249.
2   MH(CT)(S)A 2003, s 249.

Rare treatments

16.35 The Act does not specifically prohibit neurosurgery for mental disorder for young people but good practice guidelines suggest that it is not appropriate for someone under the age of 20.[1]

Any such treatment requires the consent of the patient and second medical and lay opinions. If the young person's doctor is not a child specialist, the second opinion would be from a child specialist.[2]

These rules also apply to deep brain stimulation. They apply to both young people subject to compulsory measures under the Act and to informal patients.

1   *Neurosurgery for mental disorder,* report by good practice group of the CRAG Working Group on mental illness, Scottish Office (1996), para 115. Confirmed in Code of Practice, vol 1, para 10.27.
2   Mental Health (Care and Treatment) (Scotland) Act 2003, s 235(6).

HUMAN RIGHTS

16.36 There have been some human rights challenges to the giving of compulsory treatment for mental disorder.

At Strasbourg

16.37 In one case, a patient in France challenged the use of injectable old-style antipsychotic drugs. He said they resulted in inhumane and degrading side effects. The court accepted that the side effects were unpleasant, but held that this did not reach the minimum level of severity required under Article 3. However the court said the degree of seriousness of side effects would be taken into account in further challenges to Article 3.[1]

1   *Grare v France* [1992] 15 EHRR CD 100.

In English courts

16.38 In *Wilkinson*, a patient in a special hospital in England challenged the use of force to compel him to take medication against his will. He claimed this was a breach of his rights under Articles 2, 3 and 8 of the European Convention on Human Rights. He applied for authority to cross-examine the doctors in court, and alleged that the refusal to grant this was a breach of his human rights under Article 6.

The Court of Appeal said that, where such a serious breach of human rights was alleged, it was appropriate for the doctors to attend court to justify their decision to impose treatment under force.[1]

In a second case, a patient challenged his treatment with anti-psychotic drugs. The treatment had been approved by a second opinion appointed doctor, but not by his independent psychiatrist. He alleged a breach of Article 3 of the European Convention on Human Rights. The court followed *Wilkinson* and said that human rights required that it must be 'convincingly shown' that the treatment was medically necessary and in the person's best interests. In some cases it would be necessary to cross-examine the person's doctors but not in every case, if it was possible for the court to review the evidence.[2]

In a third case the patient argued that he should receive a full statement of the reasons why a second opinion doctor was certifying that he should receive medication against his will. The court agreed that human rights law required that doctors should tell him the reasons, unless this would be likely to cause serious harm to the physical or mental health of the patient or any other person.[3]

Such a case should not be necessary in Scotland. The relevant forms require doctors to give their reasons for overruling a patient's refusal.

[1] *R (on the application of Wilkinson) v Broadmoor Special Hospital Authority* [2001] EWCA Civ 1545.
[2] *R (on the application of N) v Dr M and others* [2002] EWCA Civ 1789.
[3] *R v Dr Graham Feggetter and the Mental Health Act Commission, ex parte JW* [2002] EWCA Civ 554.

In Scotland

16.39 A person in hospital in Scotland took a case based on *Wilkinson* to court. He claimed that treating him against his will with anti-psychotic drugs was a breach of his human rights. He argued that he should have had a right to appeal to an independent court and that the compulsory treatment rules in the 1984 Act were not 'necessary in a free and democratic society'.

His application was unsuccessful. The Court of Session held that the regime for authorising compulsory treatment in the 1984 Act was a proportionate response. If a person is subject to mental health legislation, Article 6 does not give him or her a right to appeal against the implications of the legislation.[1] It remains to be seen whether there will be further challenges to the rules in Scotland.

1   *M, Petitioner*, 2002 SCLR 1001.

Chapter 17

RIGHTS OF PATIENTS SUBJECT TO ORDERS

17.01 This chapter looks at people's rights when they are subject to compulsory orders and certificates. People must receive information about their rights. This is particularly important where someone's first language is not English.

Being obliged to live in hospital or in a certain place in the community may affect a person's right to family life. The Mental Health (Care and Treatment) Act requires that efforts are made to help people preserve relations with their children. This applies to everyone subject to compulsory measures, whether they are in hospital or living in the community.

INFORMATION TO PATIENTS

17.02 This section explains the duty to give people subject to compulsion information about their legal rights. In addition, like other patients, staff must ensure people receive proper information about their treatment and care plans. See chapter 7.

Information is of no use if it is not in an accessible format. The Act imposes specific duties on hospitals to meet the needs of people with communication difficulties, or whose first language is not English. This reflects the principle of respect for diversity.

Information about legal rights

17.03 Wherever a person become subject to compulsory measures under the Mental Health (Care and Treatment) Act or the Criminal Procedure (Scotland) Act, the hospital managers must take all reasonable steps to ensure that the person subject to the order understands the effect of the order, and his or her rights of appeal (if any).

They should tell the person about the role of the responsible medical officer, the Mental Welfare Commission and the tribunal and advise the person how to make appeals and get help from a lawyer.[1] They should tell him or her about advocacy and do what they can to help him or her find an independent advocate.[2]

The hospital must give information verbally and in writing (or another permanent format accessible to the person).[3] The hospital should copy the information to the named person, in a form appropriate to his or her needs.[4] For example, a person with a learning disability might require written information in Easy Read form.

The hospital should give this information as soon as possible after someone becomes subject to compulsory measures, or whenever he or she makes a reasonable request for information.[5]

The Code does not say what is a reasonable request for information, but in dealing with requests for information about advocacy, it says staff should generally assume a request is reasonable, unless there is some unusual circumstance suggesting otherwise. Staff should record any requests in the person's records and note how they responded.[6] This would seem the appropriate way to deal with all requests for information, bearing in mind the principles of the Act.

There are detailed regulations setting out the other occasions on which the person should receive information.[7] See table 3. These include the making or variation of an order or certificate, the suspension of an order and the revocation of suspension.

These rules do not apply to emergency certificates, because of the short time the detention lasts. Those involved must explain the position to the person. See 13.13.

The managers of the hospital specified in the order are responsible for information giving when someone subject to compulsion is not in hospital or is subject to a community-based order.[8]

Generally the person's keyworker or named nurse gives this information, but it remains the hospital's responsibility.

---

[1] Mental Health (Care and Treatment) (Scotland) Act 2003, s 260(2)-(5).

[2] MH(CT)(S) A 2003, ss 260(2)(a)(iii) and 260(2)(b).

[3] MH(CT)(S) A 2003, s 260(2)(a)(ii).

[4] MH(CT)(S) A 2003, s 260(4).

[5] MH(CT)(S) A 2003, s 260(3).

[6] Code of Practice, vol 1, para 6.137.

[7] Mental Health (Provision of Information to Persons) (Prescribed Times) (Scotland) Regulations 2005 (SSI 2005/206).

[8] MH(CT)(S) A 2003, s 260(5).

17.04

Table 3 Prescribed times for information giving	
Event	**Section**
RMO determination extending CTO	86(1)
Tribunal order confirming extension and varying CTO	102(1)(d)
Tribunal order extending and varying CTO	103(1)(a)
Tribunal order extending CTO	103(1)(b)
Tribunal order confirming extension and varying CTO	103(2)(d)
Tribunal order varying CTO	103(3)(b)/103(4)(a)/104(1)(a)
Interim order	105(2)/106(2)
RMO certificate where person in breach of CTO	114(2)
RMO certificate where person in breach of interim CTO	115(2)
Hospital managers' notice of proposed transfer	124(4)/124(6)(a)
Hospital managers' notice of transfer	124(6)(b)
RMO suspension certificate lasting more than 28 days	127(1)(b)/128(1)(b)
RMO cancellation of suspension	129(2)
RMO extension of compulsion order	152(2)
Tribunal order confirming extension and varying CO	166(1)(d)
Tribunal order extending CO	167(1)(a)
Tribunal order extending and varying CO	167(2)(a)
Tribunal order extending CO	167(2)(b)
Tribunal order confirming extension and varying CO	167(3)(d)
Tribunal order varying CO	167(4)(b)/167(5)(a)
Interim order extending/extending and varying CO	168(2)
Interim order varying CO	169(2)
Tribunal order varying CO	171(1)(a)/193(6)
Conditional discharge by tribunal	193(7)

Table 3 Prescribed times for information giving—*contd*	
Event	Section
Variation of conditions by Ministers	200(2)
Recall of patient to hospital by Ministers	
	202(2)
RMO suspension for more than 28 days	
of CO etc.	224(2)
RMO cancellation of suspension	225(2)
Ministers' cancellation of suspension	226(2)

Communication/interpretation help

17.05 If someone's first language is not English or a person needs help with communication, the hospital should give the person information about his or her legal rights in a form the person can understand. The Act requires the hospital to make all reasonable efforts to ensure the person understands his or her rights. The principles of respect for diversity means this must include respecting his or her special needs. It is also a human rights requirement.

Hospital managers must make extra help available to people subject to orders who have communication difficulties and people whose first language is not English. They must provide help with communication at certain times.[1] These are when a doctor is examining the person to assess him or her, when the responsible medical officer reviews detention and when there is a tribunal hearing relating to the person.

The Act does not require the hospital to make special arrangements when a responsible medical officer reviews a community-based compulsory treatment order. It would be hoped the hospital would see this as part of its duty under the principle of respect for diversity.

The hospital must keep a record of the steps it takes to comply with this duty.[2] The Code of Practice gives examples of the kind of help staff can provide.[3]

[1]   Mental Health (Care and Treatment) (Scotland) Act 2003, s 261(2).
[2]   MH(CT)(S) A 2003, s 261(4).
[3]   Code of Practice, vol 1, paras 4.32–39.

CONTACT WITH FAMILY

17.06 It may be difficult for someone subject to compulsory measures to maintain relations with his or her children. The person may be in hospital and it may be hard for children to visit, or the ward may not be suitable for children. A person living in the community may be temporarily unable to look after his or her children.

Assistance to maintain contact

17.07 In such circumstances there should be efforts to help the person keep contact with the children.

The Act says that if compulsory measures could impair someone's relations with his or her children or reduce the contact between the person and the children, the responsible person must take such steps as are practicable and appropriate to prevent this.[1] This applies to any children for whom the person has parental responsibilities.

[1]   Mental Health (Care and Treatment) (Scotland) Act 2003, s 278(2).

Where child subject to compulsion

17.08 The duty also applies when a child or young person is subject to compulsory measures.[1] There should be efforts to ensure that the child is able to keep contact with his or her parents or those having parental responsibilities. This reflects the principle of child welfare, set out in section 2 of the Act.

A 'child' for these purposes means someone under the age of 16.[2] Anyone involved in the compulsory measures should bear these duties in mind. The Code of Practice says that the mental welfare officer has an important role.[3]

[1]   Mental Health (Care and Treatment) (Scotland) Act 2003, s 278(2).
[2]   MH(CT)(S) A 2003, s 278(3).
[3]   Vol 1, par 1.47.

Limits to rights

17.09 The Mental Health (Care and Treatment) Act does not include any right for patients detained on long-term orders to receive conjugal visits from their spouses or partners. This may face challenges under Article 8 of the European Convention on Human Rights (right to family life).

In one case in England, a patient in a special hospital asked for facilities to artificially inseminate his wife. His claim failed. The court said the right to family life did not include the right to start a family.[1]

---

[1]   *R v Secretary of State for Home Department ex parte Mellor* [2001] 2 FLR 1158. See also *Aliev v Ukraine* [2003] ECHR 201, at para 188, a prisoner alleged that failure to provide conjugal visits was in breach of Article 8. The court said the restrictions were justified to prevent crime and disorder.

ADEQUATE SERVICES

17.10 One of the principles of the Mental Health (Care and Treatment) Act is reciprocity. This means if a person is subject to compulsory measures, he or she should receive adequate and appropriate care.[1]

It is concerning to note that the Annual Reports of the Mental Welfare Commission continue to report some very poor facilities and services for people in some hospitals.[2] Similarly there have been concerns that services will not be available to offer adequate support to people on community-based orders.

The responsible medical officer must report to the tribunal if services which are recorded matters are not available.[3] Anyone aware that a recorded matter is not available should ask the responsible medical officer to report this to the tribunal.

A person who believes that he or she is not receiving adequate services in hospital or on a community-based order may wish to ask the Mental Welfare Commission to investigate. See chapter 52.

A person may also want to put in a complaint[4] or take this up with an MSP or local councillor.

Very poor conditions could constitute a breach of the person's human rights, but it is difficult to prove this. In one case, the Court of Human Rights agreed that conditions in Broadmoor hospital at that time were 'deplorable' but said this was not a breach of patients' human rights.[5]

---

[1]   Mental Health (Care and Treatment) (Scotland) Act 2003, s 1(6).

[2]   See, for example, its Annual Report 2004–5, page 14.

[3]   See 15.27.

[4]   See chapter 50.

[5]   *B v UK* Application No 6870/75, 32 DR5 (1981).

APPEAL AGAINST EXCESSIVE SECURITY

17.11 There has been concern for many years about the situation of certain people 'entrapped' in the State Hospital.[1] These are patients who are in the State Hospital even though their doctors and other professionals consider they no longer require the degree of security the hospital provides. Because no suitable alternative facilities are available, these patients must remain at the State Hospital.

Guidance to the National Health Service in Scotland requires the creation of medium secure units based in local health board areas. These could provide care for people leaving the State Hospital as well as other people who need a secure environment but not the high security of the State Hospital.[2] Unfortunately, at the time of writing only one such unit exists, the Orchard Clinic in Edinburgh.

Both the Millan Committee and the Scottish Parliament were concerned about the apparent breach of human rights of people entrapped in the State Hospital. The Millan Committee recommended a right of appeal against excessive security for people held in the State Hospital and medium secure units.[3]

The Parliament resisted initial reluctance from the Scottish Executive and the Mental Health (Care and Treatment) Act gives State Hospital patients the right to appeal to the tribunal against the level of security.[4] If an appeal is successful, the relevant health board must arrange adequate services.

These provisions did not come into effect in October 2005, to allow health boards time to develop the necessary new facilities. The Act required that they must come into effect by 1 May 2006 at the latest.[5]

---

[1] See Annual Reports of Mental Welfare Commission 1999–2000, p 30 and 2004–5, para 3.7. In 2004–5, the Commission identified 20 individuals who had been entrapped in the State Hospital for up to a year and 12 who had been entrapped for over a year. Whilst some people had been discharged, including five people who moved to the Shannon clinic, a new medium secure unit in Northern Ireland, a number of other people have become entrapped in the meantime.

[2] *Health, social work and related services for mentally disordered offenders in Scotland* (1999) NHS MEL 5. *Services, care, support and accommodation for mentally disordered offenders in Scotland: care pathway document,* Scottish Executive Health Department (2001).

[3] *New directions,* recommendations 27.19–27.23.

[4] Mental Health (Care and Treatment) (Scotland) Act 2003, ss 264–273.

[5] MH(CT)(S)A 2003, s 333(2).

Application

People eligible to apply

17.12 The rules apply to anyone detained in the State Hospital on a compulsory treatment order, a compulsion order, a hospital direction or a transfer for treatment direction.[1] A person may apply even if he or she is currently living outside the hospital because of suspension of detention. Both restricted patients and non restricted patients can apply, although the rules are slightly different. (See below.)

The person cannot apply during the first six months of the original order. Only one application to the tribunal (by the person or someone on his or her behalf) is possible in the 12 months from the date of the order and in any subsequent 12-month period.[2]

[1]   Mental Health (Care and Treatment) (Scotland) Act 2003, s 264(1).
[2]   MH(CT)(S)A 2003, s 264(8).

Making the application

17.13 The patient, his or her named person and any welfare attorney or guardian may make the application. The Mental Welfare Commission may also refer a case to the tribunal.[1]

The application should be in writing. It must include details of the order, including details of any restriction order, and a brief statement of the reasons for the application.[2] A draft application is at Appendix 3. (Form 5.) Most people will wish to instruct a solicitor.

[1]   Mental Health (Care and Treatment) (Scotland) Act 2003, s 264(6).
[2]   Mental Health Tribunal for Scotland (Practice and Procedure) (No. 2) Rules 2005 (SSI 2005/229) (as amended by Mental Health Tribunal for Scotland (Practice and Procedure) (No. 2) Amendment Rules 2006 (SSI 2006/171)), r 17A.

Role of tribunal

The hearing

17.14 The tribunal must hold a hearing and must allow the patient, his or her named person, any welfare guardian or attorney and any curator *ad litem* the chance to speak, to make any written representations and to put evidence to the tribunal.[1]

The relevant health board, the responsible medical officer, the managers of the hospital, the mental health officer and the Mental Welfare Commission also have a chance to be heard, as do Scottish Ministers where a restricted patient makes an appeal.[2] Any other person with an interest in the case can ask the tribunal to allow him or her to make representations.

(For tribunal procedure, see chapter 23.)

1   Mental Health (Care and Treatment) (Scotland) Act 2003, s 264(9).
2   MH(CT)(S)A 2003, s 264(10).

Grounds for decision

17.15 The tribunal must consider whether it necessary for the person to be detained under the conditions of special security which only the State Hospital can provide.[1] (In a case dealing with similar wording in the 1984 Act, the sheriff principal said the court should not just look at general evidence about hospital facilities in Scotland, but should consider whether there was any other hospital in Scotland that could care for the person.[2])

If the tribunal is satisfied that the person does not need the special security of the State Hospital, it may make an order declaring that the person is being detained in conditions of excessive security. The order will specify a period of up to three months from the making of the order for the relevant health board to rectify the situation.[3]

1   Mental Health (Care and Treatment) (Scotland) Act 2003, s 264(2).
2   *Ferns v Management Committee and Managers of Ravenscraig Hospital*, 1987 SLT (Sh Ct) 76.
3   MH(CT)(S)A 2003, s 264(2).

Duties of health board

17.16 Within the period specified in the order, the relevant health board should identify a hospital whose managers agree they could care for the person and which has a place available for him or her.[1] If the person is a restricted patient, the health board must obtain Scottish Ministers' agreement to the change of hospital.[2]

Once it has identified a suitable hospital, the health board must notify the managers of the hospital where the person is detained.[3] When it has identified a suitable hospital and transferred the person, it should inform the tribunal.[4]

1   Mental Health (Care and Treatment) (Scotland) Act 2003, s 264(4).
2   MH(CT)(S)A 2003, s 264(3).
3   MH(CT)(S)A 2003, s 264(5).
4   MH(CT)(S)A 2003, s 265(2).

Relevant health board

17.17 If the person was ordinarily resident in Scotland before he or she was detained in hospital the relevant health board is the health board for the area where he or she was normally resident before going into hospital. In case of difficulty, Scottish Ministers may make statutory directions assigning particular classes of patients to particular health board areas. If it is not possible to ascertain the person's previous usual address, he or she will be treated as ordinarily resident in the area of the hospital.

If the person was not ordinarily resident in Scotland, the relevant health board is the health board for the area of the hospital.[1]

1   Mental Health (Relevant Health Board for Patients Detained in Conditions of Excessive Security) (Scotland) Regulations 2006 (SSI 2006/172) and Functions of Health Boards (Scotland) Order 1991 (SI 1991/570).

Further hearing(s)

17.18 If the person is not transferred within the period specified in the order, the tribunal holds a further hearing.

If the tribunal remains satisfied that the level of security is excessive for the person, it may make a further order requiring the relevant health board to find suitable accommodation for the patient. This second order may set a time limit of between 28 days and three months for compliance.[1]

If the health board still fails to comply, there will be a final hearing, requiring the health board to identify suitable accommodation within 28 days of the order.[2]

1   Mental Health (Care and Treatment) (Scotland) Act 2003, s 265(3).
2   MH(CT)(S)A 2003, s 266(3).

Enforcement of order

17.19 If a health board fails to comply with an order of the tribunal and the person remains detained in conditions of excessive security, it may be necessary to take further action to enforce the order. Such action would normally be by ways of proceedings for specific performance of a statutory duty.[1]

Specific performance is not available unless the tribunal has made an order requiring the health board to comply within 28 days. As well as the person and his or her named person or welfare attorney or guardian, the Mental Welfare Commission can initiate an action.[2]

The Mental Welfare Commission is not obliged to take legal action. It should bear in mind the principles of the Act. It might be less likely to use its powers if it is satisfied that the health board is making all reasonable efforts to make suitable provision in the near future.

The Commission's decision could itself be subject to judicial review.

[1]   Under the Court of Session Act 1988, s 45(b). See 51.04.

[2]   Mental Health (Care and Treatment) (Scotland) Act 2003, s 272(2).

Cancellation of order

17.20 At any time after the making of an order, the health board or the responsible medical officer may apply to the tribunal for a cancellation of the order. If the person is a restricted patient, Scottish Ministers may also apply.[1]

The tribunal must cancel the order if it is satisfied that the person now needs the special security only the State Hospital can provide.[2] It may cancel the order on any other grounds.[3]

The tribunal must hold a hearing and allow all the relevant people to attend and give evidence.[4]

[1]   Mental Health (Care and Treatment) (Scotland) Act 2003, s 267(4).

[2]   MH(CT)(S)A 2003, s 267(2)(a).

[3]   MH(CT)(S)A 2003, s 267(2)(b).

[4]   MH(CT)(S)A 2003, s 267(5).

Scope of appeal

17.21 The appeal against excessive security was primarily intended to protect the human rights of people detained in the State Hospital, where a particular problem had been identified.

The Act allows the Scottish Executive to make regulations extending the appeal rights to people held in conditions of excessive security in other hospitals.[1] This could extend to someone ready for rehabilitation who has to remain in the more restrictive environment of an admissions ward. It could give someone the right to appeal against being held in a locked ward or Intensive Psychiatric Care Unit (IPCU) because of lack of appropriate accommodation elsewhere in the hospital.

At the time of writing, the Scottish Executive is proposing to extend the right of appeal to people in medium secure units, but not further.[2]

The provisions for such appeals are almost identical to those governing appeals of people in the State Hospital. The person must satisfy the tribunal that the level of security to which he or she is subject is excessive in his or her case.[3]

[1]   Mental Health (Care and Treatment) (Scotland) Act 2003, ss 268–271.
[2]   *Appeals against detention under conditions of excessive security*, Scottish Executive Mental Health Division consultation document (9 December 2005).
[3]   MH(CT)(S)A 2003, s 268(2).

Chapter 18

RESTRICTIONS ON DETAINED PATIENTS

18.01 This chapter looks at the way in which a person's rights may be restricted because he or she is detained in hospital under a compulsory order or certificate.

On some occasions, in the interests of health and safety, hospital staff may consider it necessary to monitor someone's visitors or examine his or her correspondence.[1] They may wish to search a patient or test him or her for illegal drug use. There have been attempts in recent years to reduce the numbers of illegal drugs in psychiatric hospitals, due to concern that such drugs can lead to deterioration in a person's health.[2]

Previously many of these rules were left to the common law, but the Mental Health (Care and Treatment) Act and regulations made under the Act now spell out the rules in detail. Human rights law requires that the rules are open and transparent.

The special security rules apply to a small number of people detained in hospital, where the responsible medical officer considers there is a need for special security. The rules apply to all people detained in the State Hospital, and in some cases, to people detained in medium secure units, such as the Orchard Clinic in Edinburgh.

The Mental Welfare Commission has a special role in monitoring and reviewing the operation of these rules and may insist on changes in individual cases.

One set of rules deals with searches, the taking of samples, restrictions on possessions, surveillance and the control of visits. There are different rules for monitoring correspondence and the use of telephones.

This chapter does not look at the use of restraint, seclusion or time out. These issues are not just relevant for people subject to compulsory measures and are covered in chapter 9.

---

[1]   Mental Health (Care and Treatment) (Scotland) Act 2003, ss 281–6.
[2]   For a discussion of some of the issues, see the Annual Report of the Mental Welfare Commission 2000–1, pp 27–28.

SAFETY AND SECURITY CONTROLS

Use of special security

18.02 This section looks at the use of special security and surveillance. Special security measures must be authorised under the Mental Health (Care and Treatment) Act or subordinate legislation.[1] The responsible medical officer must confirm that a person detained in hospital is a person for whom such measures may be appropriate and that the measures are necessary in the interests of health and safety.

The Code of Practice stresses that the fact a person may be subject to the rules does not mean that he or she will automatically be subject to searches or other restrictions. The hospital should only carry out searches and other measures if it considers this necessary to ensure the safety and security of patients or of the hospital in general.[2]

[1] Mental Health (Safety and Security) (Scotland) Regulations 2005 (SSI 2005/464). ('The safety and security Regulations'.)

[2] Code of Practice, vol 1, para 12.41.

People subject to special security

18.03 The rules apply to everyone detained in the State Hospital and the Orchard Clinic in Edinburgh.[1] A person may also come within the rules if there is a specific concern that he or she is seeking to bring certain items into the hospital.

If the responsible medical officer believes that a patient has or is trying to obtain some item which could prejudice the health or safety of any person or the security or order of the hospital, he or she may record this in the person's notes. The responsible medical officer should set out the reasons for this opinion.[2] The special rules then apply to the person for six months from the date of recording.

The hospital should notify the person that the rules apply and what the possible impact will be (unless the responsible medical officer considers this would prejudice the person's health or treatment). The named person and the Mental Welfare Commission should also receive notice.[3]

The person should also receive information about his or her right to request a review[4] (see below). Although the rules do not say so, it is important that the person also understands his or her right to ask the Mental Welfare Commission to review the implementation of the rules.

1   Safety and security Regulations, reg 2(2)(a).
2   Reg 2(2)(b).
3   Reg 2(3).
4   Reg 2(4).

Use of special measures

18.04 Just because the rules apply to a person does not mean that special measures will always be appropriate. The decision to use a particular measure will depend on the risk in each case.

The responsible medical officer can authorise the use of a special security measure only if he or she believes it is necessary to avoid a significant risk to the health, safety or welfare of any person in the hospital or a significant risk to the security or good order of the hospital.[1]

Before staff use a special security measure, they should seek the person's consent, but they may implement the measure without consent if the responsible medical officer, having reassessed the risk, considers this necessary.[2]

1   Safety and security Regulations, reg 5(a).
2   Safety and security Regulations, regs 6, 7 and 11.

Measures which can be authorised

Searches

18.05 The responsible medical officer may authorise the search of a person to whom the rules apply. The Regulations contain detailed rules for searches, intended to preserve the person's dignity so far as possible.

The search must be by a person authorised by the hospital to carry out searches, who must be of the same sex as the person being searched. The person must show respect for the dignity and privacy of the person being searched. A witness should be present and should be of the same sex as the person being searched, wherever practicable.

Taking of blood/urine, etc, samples

18.06 A special member of staff should be authorised to take samples.[1] Staff should respect the person's privacy as far as possible, bearing in mind the need to prevent contamination of the sample. Staff should not use physical force when taking samples.[2]

Staff may carry out random sampling if they think this is necessary for the safety or security of the hospital. The Code of Practice anticipates that staff may wish to take samples where they consider someone may have been using illegal drugs.[3]

1   As listed in s 286(1)(a) of the Act.
2   Code of Practice, vol 1, para 12.47.
3   Code of Practice, vol 1, para 12.46.

Restrictions on possessions

18.07 The hospital can refuse to allow the person to have certain items in hospital, on the grounds of health and safety or in the interests of the security or good order of the hospital. The restriction should be the minimum necessary to achieve this aim.[1]

1   Safety and security Regulations, reg 8.

Surveillance

18.08 Staff can use surveillance where they consider this necessary. There may also be surveillance in visiting areas. The premises must display a conspicuous notice about the surveillance. If there is special surveillance of a particular person and his or her visitors, staff should attempt to obtain the person's consent.[1]

1   Safety and security Regulations, reg 11.

Restrictions on visitors

18.09 Generally, of course, hospitals will encourage visiting, as an important part of rehabilitation, but it may occasionally be necessary to monitor and restrict visiting.

If a person is subject to the special rules, there may be restrictions on his or her visitors. A visitor may be refused entry or a visit may be restricted if the visitor refuses to agree to a search.[1] The Regulations set out detailed rules about searching visitors.[2]

A person in a special hospital in England has challenged restrictions on visiting. The court held that the restrictions were not a breach of his human rights, because of the need to protect third parties.[3]

1   Safety and security Regulations, reg 9.
2   Safety and security Regulations, reg 10.
3   *R on the application of MC v Secretary of State for the Department of Health,* QBD
    11 October 2000. The hospital had a policy of refusing visits other than from
    close family. It refused to allow the person's nephew to visit. This was held
    not to breach the person's right to family life. The hospital had to balance
    patients' rights with the need to protect children. Its response was
    proportionate.

Safeguards

18.10 Staff must record any use of special measures in the person's
medical records, together with a note of the outcome. The hospital
managers must make a separate record.[1]

   The responsible medical officer should advise the patient and his or
her named person of the use of special measures, unless he or she
believes this would prejudice the person's health or treatment.[2]

1   Safety and security Regulations, reg 5(c).
2   Reg 5(d).

Review and/or reassessment of risk

18.11 A person subject to the special rules can request the responsible
medical officer to review whether he or she should be subject to the rules
at least once in every six months.[1] The responsible medical officer should
hear any representations the person and his or her named person wish to
make. The responsible medical officer should advise the person of the
outcome, unless he or she considers this would prejudice the person's
health or safety.

   If staff use special measures, the person or, if the measures relate to a
visitor, his or her visitor, may ask the responsible medical officer to re-
assess the risk. The responsible medical officer may change his or her
decision or modify the way in which staff use the special measures.[2]

1   Safety and security Regulations, reg 3.
2   Reg 5(b).

Reports to Scottish Ministers

18.12 Hospital managers must report to Scottish Ministers on request
about their use of security measures.[1] Scottish Ministers may make

legally binding directions about the implementation of the safety and security regulations.[2]

Reports should set out the hospital policy on safety and security, and how the hospital has implemented it. They should include details of any complaints and the outcome. They should not include information which could identify any patient.[3]

Copies of reports to Scottish Ministers should be available for inspection by the Mental Welfare Commission. The hospital managers must send a copy to the Mental Welfare Commission on request.

[1]   Safety and security Regulations, reg 12.
[2]   Mental Health (Care and Treatment) (Scotland) Act 2003, s 286(5).
[3]   Code of Practice, vol 1, para 12.61.

Role of Mental Welfare Commission

18.13 The Mental Welfare Commission has an important role to play in safeguarding people's interests. Anyone subject to the measures and anyone with an interest may ask the Commission to review whether the hospital is using a particular security measure appropriately. The Mental Welfare Commission may also take action on its own initiative.

The Commission may direct that for up to six months it will supervise the use of security measures in relation to a particular person. It may say that staff should seek prior permission of the Mental Welfare Commission before using any measure.[1]

The Commission may ask the hospital to notify a patient's named person that it has made such an order.

[1]   Safety and security Regulations, reg 13.

CORRESPONDENCE

Nature and scope of restrictions

18.14 Article 8 of the European Convention on Human Rights guarantees respect for private life, including freedom from interference with correspondence.[1] The majority of people in hospital, whether or not they are detained patients, will have no interference with their mail.

The European Convention on Human Rights allows interference with this fundamental human right where necessary, for the protection of health or morals, public safety, the prevention of crime or disorder, the economic well-being of the country and the protection of the rights and freedoms of others.[2]

Insofar as the Mental Health (Care and Treatment) Act allows interference with people' correspondence, it must be with these aims in mind. Any interference must be necessary and proportionate to the risk.[3]

The rules are contained in the Act[4] and in supplementary regulations.[5]

[1]   European Convention of Human Rights, Art 8.1.

[2]   ECHR, Art 8.2.

[3]   See Code of Practice, vol 1, introduction to chap 12.

[4]   Mental Health (Care and Treatment) (Scotland) Act 2003, ss 281–3.

[5]   The Mental Health (Specified Persons' Correspondence) (Scotland) Regulations 2005 (SSI 2005/408) ('The correspondence Regulations') and the Mental Health (Definition of Specified Person: Correspondence) (Scotland) Regulations 2005 (SSI 2005/466). ('The definition of specified person Regulations'.)

To whom rules apply

18.15 The rules apply only to people detained in hospital.[1] They apply to everyone detained in the State Hospital for so long as they are detained in the hospital.[2]

Other detained patients may come within the rules. A person will come within the rules if, within the last six months, the responsible medical officer has determined that:

- mail sent by the person may cause distress to the addressee or to any other person (other than a member of the staff of the hospital) or may put any person at risk, and/or

- mail addressed to the person may not be in the interests of his or her health and safety or may cause danger to any other person.[3]

The responsible medical officer must record the opinion, with his or her reasons, in the person's notes. In reaching a decision, he or she should consult with other members of the person's care team.[4]

The hospital must inform the patient, his or her named person and the Mental Welfare Commission when a patient comes within the rules.[5] If the responsible medical officer changes the person's status, he or she must also notify these people.[6]

Just because the rules apply to a person does not mean that staff will withhold his or her correspondence. The decision depends on the risk in each case.

1   Mental Health (Care and Treatment) (Scotland) Act 2003, s 281(9).
2   Definition of specified person Regulations, reg 2(2)(a).
3   Definition of specified person Regulations, reg 2(2)(b).
4   Code of Practice, vol 1, para 12.03.
5   Definition of specified person Regulations, reg 3.
6   Code of Practice, vol 1, para 12.15.

Withholding mail from person

Where third person request this

18.16 Where a person comes within the rules, staff may withhold mail sent by him or her if the recipient of the mail has notified the hospital that he or she does not want to receive mail from the person.[1]

For patients in the State Hospital, the request remains valid as long as the person remains detained in the hospital.

For people detained in other hospitals, the responsible medical officer must record the request. Staff will withhold the patient's mail to that person for six months. If the recipient of the mail does not renew the request, the responsible medical officer must decide whether mail from the patient is still likely to cause problems for the addressee. If this is likely, he or she may renew the certificate, as above.

Someone requiring a hospital to withhold mail from a detained patient may write to the hospital, to the person's responsible medical officer or to Scottish Ministers (in the case of a restricted patient).[2]

1   Mental Health (Care and Treatment) (Scotland) Act 2003, s 281(2).
2   MH(CT)(S)A 2003, s 281(4).

Where risk to others

18.17 The hospital managers may withhold mail from a patient if the person is within the rules because he or she is detained in the State Hospital or because the responsible medical officer has determined that there is a risk (see above).

They may withhold any mail they consider likely to cause distress to the recipient or to any other person (other than a member of the staff of the hospital). They can withhold mail they consider likely to cause danger to any person.[1] They can remove any enclosures sent with the mail.[2]

These rules apply to both letters and parcels.[3] They do not apply to emails, which are currently unregulated.[4] At the time of writing, few psychiatric hospitals in Scotland offer email facilities and internet use is generally restricted to educational facilities.

1   Mental Health (Care and Treatment) (Scotland) Act 2003, s 281(3)(b).
2   MH(CT)(S)A 2003, s 281(8).
3   MH(CT)(S)A 2003, s 281(9). A 'postal packet' is defined in the Postal Services Act 2000 as a letter, parcel, packet or other article which can be sent by post.
4   The Millan Committee recommended regulation of email and other electronic communication. *New Directions*, recommendation 11.12.

Withholding mail to person

18.18 The hospital managers may withhold mail to a person if he or she comes within the correspondence rules and they consider this necessary in the interests of the person's health or safety or for the protection of any other person.[1] They can also remove any enclosures sent with the mail.[2]

1   Mental Health (Care and Treatment) (Scotland) Act 2003, s 281(6).
2   MH(CT)(S)A 2003, s 281(8).

Where withholding not allowed

18.19 Mail to and from certain people cannot be withheld. These people are:[1]

- A government minister or Scottish Ministers.
- An MP, MSP or member of the National Assembly for Wales or the Northern Ireland Assembly.
- A UK member of the European Parliament.
- The Mental Welfare Commission or any Commissioner.
- The Parliamentary Ombudsman.
- The Scottish Public Services Ombudsman.
- A local authority.
- A judge or clerk of court.
- The Mental Health Tribunal for Scotland.
- The managers of the hospital where the person is detained.
- A health board or special health board, such as the State Hospitals Board for Scotland.
- The person's independent advocate.
- The person's lawyer.

- The European Court of Human Rights.
- The Scottish Information Commissioner.[2]

Regulations may add additional people to this list.

¹   Mental Health (Care and Treatment) (Scotland) Act 2003, s 281(5).
²   Correspondence Regulations, reg 3.

Implementing rules

Powers of hospital managers

18.20 The hospital authorities may inspect and open any mail to determine whether it is to or from a person to whom the rules apply and whether they should withhold it.[1] Staff will not need to open mail from and to the exempt bodies listed above if the sender and recipient are clearly identified on the envelope.[2]

A strict wording of the statute does not appear to allow staff to withhold mail to exempt bodies even the mail contains a dangerous item. It is likely that the staff would have a common law duty to withhold a dangerous item in such circumstances. They might also involve the police.

¹   Mental Health (Care and Treatment) (Scotland) Act 2003, s 281(7).
²   Code of Practice, vol 1, para 12.09.

Duties of hospital managers

18.21 The hospital should appoint a specific member of staff to be responsible for implementing these rules. For example, at the State Hospital, there is a person in charge of security matters, and other staff who check mail. Only staff specifically authorised by hospital management should implement the rules.[1]

The hospital must keep a written record if it withholds any mail or any enclosures addressed to or sent by the person.[2] Within seven days it must notify the Mental Welfare Commission, explaining the reasons (except where staff withhold mail at the request of the person to whom it is addressed).[3]

The hospital must notify the patient and the sender of the letter, if staff withhold mail to the patient and advise them of their right to request the Mental Welfare Commission to review the decision.[4] It should also ensure that the person can have an independent advocate to help with any application.[5]

1   Mental Health (Care and Treatment) (Scotland) Act 2003, s 282(6).
2   MH(CT)(S)A 2003, s 282(1).
3   MH(CT)(S)A 2003, s 282(2).
4   MH(CT)(S)A 2003, s 282(4).
5   Correspondence Regulations, reg 4.

Role of Mental Welfare Commission

18.22 The Mental Welfare Commission can review any decision to withhold mail. It may decide that mail should not be withheld, in which case the hospital managers must arrange delivery.[1]

The patient and the person whose mail has been withheld have six months to approach the Mental Welfare Commission for a review of the decision to withhold mail.[2] A phone call or letter to the Commission will suffice.[3]

If the Commission receives a request for a review, it notifies the hospital, which must deliver the correspondence to the Commission within 14 days of a request.[4] The hospital must keep any items of mail for at least nine months to allow time for review by the Commission.[5]

1   Mental Health (Care and Treatment) (Scotland) Act 2003, s 283(4).
2   MH(CT)(S)A 2003, s 283(3).
3   Code of Practice, vol 1, para 12.12.
4   Correspondence Regulations, reg 5.
5   Code of Practice, vol 1, para 12.18.

USE OF TELEPHONE

Scope of rules

18.23 In general, hospital staff should not restrict or stop any patient from making phone calls. Just because someone is detained in hospital should not mean that he or she cannot contact or be contacted by whomever he or she wishes. The Code of Practice says hospitals should provide all patients with reasonable access to a telephone, subject to any general policy on the use of telephones by patients.[1]

There may be occasions where phone calls may pose a risk. Regulations made under the Mental Health (Care and Treatment) Act set out detailed rules.[2]

These rules do not cover the use of mobile phones. If necessary, the hospital may stop or restrict a patient's access to a mobile phone under the safety and security regulations. See above.

The rules enable hospitals to restrict or prohibit telephone calls for certain categories of people. They potentially apply to all patients in the State Hospital. They also apply to other detained patients if the responsible medical officer authorises this.

If the responsible medical officer believes that telephone calls could cause distress to the person or other people (other than hospital staff) or could be a significant risk to the health, safety or welfare of a patient or to the safety of other people, he or she should record this in the person's notes.[3] The responsible medical officer's determination lasts for up to six months.

The responsible medical officer should consult with the care team and keep his or her decision under review, so that he or she can remove restrictions if he or she considers they are no longer necessary.[4]

The hospital managers should inform the person and his or her named person that the rules will apply and that the person's telephone use may be restricted (unless the responsible medical officer believes that telling the person would prejudice his or her health or treatment). They should tell them about the person's right to request a review (see below) and should inform the Mental Welfare Commission.[5]

[1]   Code of Practice, vol 1, para 12.19.
[2]   Mental Health (Use of Telephones) (Scotland) Regulations 2005 (SSI 2005/ 468). ('The use of Telephones Regulations'.)
[3]   Use of Telephones Regulations, reg 2(2).
[4]   Code of Practice, vol 1, para 12.22.
[5]   Use of Telephones Regulations, reg 2(3).

Restricting calls

18.24 Just because the rules apply to a person does not mean that staff will restrict his or her right to make and receive phone calls. This will happen only if the person's responsible medical officer considers that restrictions are necessary to prevent distress to the person or others (other than hospital staff) or to prevent a significant risk to the person's health, welfare or safety or the safety of anyone else.[1]

If the responsible medical officer considers there is such a risk, he or she may stop the person from making or receiving telephone calls or may restrict their use. The responsible medical officer may restrict or stop calls to a particular person or authorise a general restriction or prohibition on calls for up to three months.[2]

The responsible medical officer must act in accordance with the principles of the Act. He or she should attempt to reduce the impact on the person's rights, and ensure that any restrictions he or she imposes are in proportion to the risks he or she envisages.[3]

1   Use of Telephones Regulations, reg 5(2).
2   Use of Telephones Regulations, reg 5.
3   Code of Practice, vol 1, para 12.25.

Intercepting calls

18.25 The hospital managers can intercept a telephone call if it has previously been prohibited or restricted, or if the call would otherwise be unlawful (such as malicious or nuisance calls, or where there is a court order prohibiting contact).[1]

We saw above that there are certain privileged persons with whom any patient can correspond without interference.[2] Staff should not intercept phone calls to or from any of these people unless the person listed has requested this or the call would otherwise be unlawful.[3]

1   Use of Telephones Regulations, reg 7.
2   Mental Health (Care and Treatment) (Scotland) Act 2003, s 284(6).
3   Use of Telephones Regulations, regs 7(2) and 7(3).

Right to review

18.26 At least once in every six months the person can request the responsible medical officer to review his or her decision that the rules should apply.[1] The responsible medical officer should hear any representations the person and his or her named person wish to make.

The person can ask the responsible medical officer to review any restrictions on telephone calls lasting for seven consecutive days.[2] The responsible medical officer may either remove or reduce the restrictions or authorise their continued use for up to three months from the date of the review. He or she should consult with the care team.[3]

The responsible medical officer should advise the person, his or her named person and the Mental Welfare Commission of the outcome.

1   Use of Telephones Regulations, reg 3.

2   Use of Telephones Regulations, reg 6.
3   Code of Practice, vol 1, para 12.27.

Duty of hospital managers

18.27 The hospital managers must keep records of the operation of these rules in every patient's case and send the person a copy of the record (unless the responsible medical officer considers this would prejudice a patient's health or treatment). They should also send a copy to the named person and the Mental Welfare Commission.[1]

1   Use of Telephones Regulations, regs 8, 9.

Role of Mental Welfare Commission

18.28 A patient can request the Mental Welfare Commission to review any decision to restrict or prohibit his or her phone calls or to make him or her someone to whom the rules should apply.

The Mental Welfare Commission can direct the hospital to stop operating the rules in any particular case, can allow certain calls which the responsible medical officer had prohibited or restricted and can restrict the time for which the rules should apply.[1]

1   Use of Telephones Regulations, reg 10.

OTHER RESTRICTIONS

18.29 Any other restrictions on the life of a person detained in hospital will need to be in proportion to the possible risk and to be lawful and justifiable under Article 8 of the European Convention on Human Rights.

For example, the rules do not cover access to the internet and electronic communication. If a hospital provides internet facilities, it will need to consider what restrictions it can justify. The Millan Committee recommended that the law should make clear what restriction is permissible.[1]

Other restrictions require similar consideration. In a case in England, a male patient wished to wear female clothing. The hospital allowed this only in his room. He claimed this was a breach of his rights under Article 8. The court said that the hospital had a 'pressing and self evident need' to be able to control what patients wear. This power is implied in the hospital's power to detain a mentally ill offender. The court said the hospital's decision was rational and necessary and there was no breach of the person's human rights.[2]

In another English case, the court granted the hospital an order stopping a person publishing a book about himself, his crime and his fellow patients, on grounds that this could threaten the security of the hospital.[3]

[1] *New directions*, recommendation 11.2.
[2] *R (on the application of E) v Ashworth Hospital Authority* [2001] EWHC Admin 1089.
[3] *Broadmoor Hospital v R* [1999] EWCA 35, 20 December 1999.

Chapter 19

HOSPITAL TRANSFERS

19.01 This chapter deals with detained patients' right to request transfer to a different hospital and their right to appeal if the hospital managers wish to move them. It looks at transfers to hospitals outside Scotland and what happens when a person comes to a hospital in Scotland from outside the country.

The rules about transferring people out of Scotland apply to informal patients as well as those subject to compulsion.

TRANSFERS WITHIN SCOTLAND

People subject to short-term or emergency detention

19.02 There are no special legal requirements to transfer a person subject to an emergency detention certificate or a short-term detention certificate. The certificate authorises the person's detention in the hospital named in the order or another hospital.[1]

If a person subject to such an order wishes to move to another hospital, he or she should raise this with staff.

If hospital staff believe a person should move to another hospital, they should wherever possible, seek the consent of the person or his or her named person. The person should receive as much notice as possible of the move and all other relevant people should receive notice.[2]

[1]   Mental Health (Care and Treatment) (Scotland) Act 2003, ss 36(8), 45(5).

[2]   Code of Practice, vol 2, para 9.19.

People subject to compulsory treatment orders

19.03 Someone detained in hospital under a compulsory treatment order wishing to transfer to another hospital should raise this with the responsible medical officer, mental health officer or key nurse.

A hospital may wish to transfer a detained patient to a different hospital. It can do this if the hospital to which the person is to be transferred consents to the proposed move.[1]

1   Mental Health (Care and Treatment) (Scotland) Act 2003, s 124.

Procedure for transfer

19.04 Before transferring the person, the hospital managers must give him or her, his or her named person and primary carer at least seven days' notice of the proposed transfer[1] (unless the person needs to move urgently).[2] Urgency means there are strong clinical reasons for moving the person without notice.[3] Notice is not necessary if the person consents to the transfer.[4]

Even if notice is not necessary, the hospital managers must notify the named person and primary carer as soon as possible, unless the patient has consented to the transfer.[5]

If a proposed transfer does not take place within three months of this notice, another notice is necessary, unless the person consents to the move.[6] If the person needs moving urgently, he or she can be moved without notice, but the relevant people must be informed.[7]

Within seven days of the transfer, the hospital managers must inform the Mental Welfare Commission and advise them whether the person received notice. If they did not give notice, they must explain why an urgent move was necessary.[8] A form is available on the mental health law website.

1   Mental Health (Care and Treatment) (Scotland) Act 2003, s 124(4).
2   MH(CT)(S)A 2003, s 124(5).
3   Code of Practice, vol 2, para 9.04.
4   MH(CT)(S)A 2003, s 124(7).
5   MH(CT)(S)A 2003, s 124(6).
6   MH(CT)(S)A 2003, s 124(9).
7   MH(CT)(S)A 2003, s 124(11).
8   MH(CT)(S)A 2003, s 124(13).

Safeguards

19.05 The hospital should discuss any proposed transfer with the person and his or her named person and primary carer if possible.[1]

The patient and his or her named person can appeal to the tribunal against a transfer or proposed transfer. There is no form prescribed for the appeal. A suggested form is in Appendix 3, form 4.

The hospital must inform the patient and named person about these rights and how an advocate might help. They should assist him or her to access an independent advocate.[2] If the person making an appeal has special communication needs, the hospital must offer help with interpretation.[3]

The hospital cannot transfer the person before the appeal, unless the tribunal agrees to a temporary transfer.[4]

[1]   Under the principles of the Act.
[2]   Mental Health (Care and Treatment) (Scotland) Act 2003, s 260. The Mental Health (Provision of Information to Patients) (Prescribed Times) (Scotland) Regulations (SSI 2005/206), reg 2(g).
[3]   MH(CT)(S)A 2003, s 261.
[4]   MH(CT)(S)A 2003, s 125(4).

Appeals

19.06 There are strict time limits governing appeals.

When someone receives advance notice of a transfer, he or she may appeal at any time between the giving of the notice and 28 days after the transfer. If the transfer takes place on the same day as, or before, the person receives notice, he or she has 28 days from the date of the notice. If the person did not receive advance notice, he or she has 28 days from the date of the transfer.[1]

Similar notice periods apply for the named person.[2] For transfers to the State Hospital, the period is 12 weeks.[3]

For tribunal procedure, see chapter 23. The tribunal may order that the transfer should not take place or that the person return to the hospital from which he or she has been moved.[4]

The Act does not say on what basis the tribunal decides, but it must bear in mind the principles of the Act and any advance statement the person has made. It must allow the relevant parties to attend and give evidence and consider their views in deciding whether to approve the transfer.

A form for the tribunal's decision is on the mental health law website.

[1]   Mental Health (Care and Treatment) (Scotland) Act 2003, s 125(3)(a).
[2]   MH(CT)(S)A 2003, s 125(3)(b).

3   MH(CT)(S)A 2003, s 126(3).
4   MH(CT)(S)A 2003, s 125(5).

Transfer to State Hospital

19.07 If the proposed transfer is to the State Hospital, the tribunal must allow the appeal unless it is satisfied that the person needs to be detained in hospital under conditions of special security and that only a State Hospital can provide this special security.[1]

In a case concerned with similar wording of the 1984 Act, the sheriff principal held that the sheriff had to be satisfied that no other hospital in Scotland could provide suitable alternative treatment for the person.[2]

1   Mental Health (Care and Treatment) (Scotland) Act 2003, s 126(6).
2   *F v Management Committee and Managers, Ravenscraig Hospital* 1987 SLT (Sh Ct) 76 at p 80.

Restricted patients

19.08 The transfer rules apply also to people subject to compulsion orders, hospital directions and transfer for treatment directions imposed under the criminal justice system (see Part 12). If the person is a restricted patient, the transfer does not take place unless Scottish Ministers consent.[1]

1   Mental Health (Care and Treatment) (Scotland) Act 2003, ss 178 and 218.

CROSS-BORDER TRANSFERS

19.09 Detailed regulations cover the transfer of patients from Scotland to other parts of the UK and (provided the person is not subject to an order under the Mental Health (Care and Treatment) Act or the Criminal Procedure (Scotland) 1995 Act) to countries outside the UK.[1] A person subject to compulsory measures cannot be transferred outside the UK.

The rules also cover people subject to equivalent legislation within the UK who move to Scotland.

These rules do not permit the move of a person subject to temporary measures, such as a treatment order or an interim compulsion order.[2]

1   Mental Health (Cross-border transfer: people subject to detention requirement or otherwise in hospital) (Scotland) Regulations 2005 (SSI 2005/467). ('The cross-border transfer Regulations'.)
2   Cross-border transfer Regulations, reg 2(4).

Transfer out of Scotland

Who the rules apply to

19.10 These rules apply to both voluntary patients and people subject to orders under the Mental Health (Care and Treatment) Act or the Criminal Procedure Act.[1] The rules are complex and comprehensive. What follows is a summary.

[1] See Part II of the cross-border transfer Regulations.

Consultation required

19.11 The person's responsible medical officer or (for a voluntary patient, the doctor primarily responsible for treating the person) must consult the mental health officer and all relevant parties before considering moving the person. This will include the person and any carers, under the principles of the Act.

A voluntary patient does not have a mental health officer. The doctor must give notice to the relevant local authority[1] of the intention to move him or her. The local authority appoints a mental health officer. The mental health officer interviews the person and gives him or her advice about rights and access to advocacy services.

If, having heard the mental health officer's views, the doctor thinks the move should take place, he or she should give notice to the patient, the named person (or primary carer if there is no named person) and to any welfare guardian or attorney. The doctor should also notify the mental health officer.

Parties have seven days to give a response. The person should send a copy of his or her response to Scottish Ministers, as the transfer does not go ahead unless they approve.[2]

[1] If the patient was living in Scotland before he or she was admitted, the local authority where he or she was living, and if not, the authority for the hospital.
[2] Cross-border transfer Regulations, regs 3–6.

Application to Scottish Ministers

19.12 Having considered the views of the relevant parties, the responsible medical officer may then apply by warrant to move the person. The Scottish Ministers must take account of the best interests of the person, the availability of similar care and treatment for the person, the wishes of all concerned and any risk factors.[1]

If Scottish Ministers approve the transfer, they will grant a warrant to move the person. At least seven days' notice is required if the person is to be moved within the UK and at least 28 days' if the move is outside the UK, unless there is an urgent need to move the person more quickly. Scottish Ministers must obtain the approval of the Mental Welfare Commission to any urgent move.

1   Cross-border transfer Regulations, reg 8(2).

Appeal rights

19.13 The person (but not, apparently his or her named person) may appeal to the tribunal against a transfer.[1] The tribunal may decide that the person should not be transferred. It will take the principles of the Act into account as well as the criteria set out in the regulations.

There is an appeal against the tribunal's decision on a point of law. The person should not be removed from Scotland while the appeal is pending.

The Mental Welfare Commission can refer a proposed transfer to the tribunal.[2]

There have been human rights challenges to similar transfers by the Home Office in England. In one case, the European Court of Human Rights said that deporting a mentally ill person back to Algeria was not a breach of Articles 3 or 8, even though his care would not be as good as in England. The court said that what was alleged was not sufficiently serious to constitute inhumane or degrading treatment.[3]

In another case, the Court of Appeal in England said that it was not inhumane or degrading treatment for a person to have to return to hospital in Malta, provided there were adequate facilities for his treatment there.[4]

1   Cross-border transfer Regulations, reg 13. At the time of writing, the tribunal rules do not set out a procedure.
2   Cross-border transfer Regulations, reg 17.
3   *Bensaid v UK* 2001 [2001] ECtHR 82.
4   *R on the application of X v Secretary of State for Home Department* [2000] EWCA Civ 48 (CA 7 December 2000).

Duties of hospital managers

19.14 Following the person's transfer, the managers of the hospital where he or she was being treated must give notice of the transfer to the mental health officer and the Mental Welfare Commission.

If the person was subject to a short-term detention certificate, an interim compulsory treatment order, a compulsory treatment order or a compulsion order without a restriction order they must also notify Scottish Ministers.[1]

[1]   Cross-border transfer Regulations, reg 20.

Transfers to Scotland

19.15 These rules apply to the transfer to Scotland of people subject to compulsory detention in hospital in England and Wales, Northern Ireland, the Channel Islands or the Isle of Man.[1]

Part III of the cross-border transfer Regulations contains the detailed rules.

[1]   Cross-border transfer Regulations, reg 1.

Consent of Scottish Ministers

19.16 A person subject to detention in another part of the UK cannot transfer to a hospital in Scotland unless Scottish Ministers agree to the move.[1] Scottish Ministers must receive full information about the person.[2] They must bear in mind the principles of the Act when considering the request.

[1]   Cross-border transfer Regulations, reg 24(2).
[2]   Cross-border transfer Regulations, reg 24(4).

Duties of hospital managers

19.17 If Scottish Ministers accept the move and the person moves to a hospital in Scotland, the hospital managers must give notice to the relevant local authority so that it can appoint a mental health officer for the person. The hospital should appoint a responsible medical officer.

Admission to hospital

19.18 A person will become subject to the order which most closely corresponds to the order under which he or she was detained outside Scotland.[1] This could include being a restricted patient.

The mental health officer must give the person information about his or her rights and the responsible medical officer must examine the person within seven days of the person's arrival at the hospital.

The responsible medical officer must establish whether the appropriate grounds for admission apply to the person.[2] If they do not, he or she should revoke the order or, if the person is a restricted patient, make a report to Scottish Ministers.

As soon as possible, and in any event within 14 days of the person's arrival in Scotland, the responsible medical officer should inform the hospital managers whether the grounds for admission apply to the person, what type of mental disorder the person has and whether the responsible medical officer considers the order is necessary.

The hospital managers should notify the patient, his or her named person, the Mental Welfare Commission, the tribunal, (if the person has become subject to a compulsory treatment order or compulsion order), Scottish Ministers (if the person is a restricted patient) and the person's mental health officer.

The responsible medical officer must prepare a care plan. The hospital must ensure the person and his or her named person understand the person's rights. If the person has language or communication needs, these must be met. The Mental Welfare Commission must visit the person within six months of his or her arrival in Scotland.

If someone subject to guardianship under the Mental Health Act 1983 is admitted to a hospital or care home in Scotland, the relevant local authority from England or Wales must visit the person and take such other steps as would be expected of a parent.[3] This also applies where a local authority has taken over the functions of a nearest relative. The law is not clear what these duties are, but it could be argued they include regular visits, discussing the person's medical care with staff and helping with domestic arrangements while the person is in hospital.

---

[1] Cross-border transfer Regulations, reg 30.
[2] See detailed rules in cross-border transfer Regulations, reg 36.
[3] Mental Health (Scotland) Act 1984, s 10. Not repealed by the Mental Health (Care and Treatment) (Scotland) Act 2003. See Mental Health (Care and Treatment) (Scotland) Act 2003 (Consequential Provisions) Order 2005 (SI 2005/2078), Sched 3.

Chapter 20

BREACH OF ORDERS, UNAUTHORISED ABSENCES AND OFFENCES

OUTLINE OF PROVISIONS

20.01 This chapter deals with what happens if a person does not comply with the provisions of a community-based compulsory treatment order.

When a compulsory treatment order requires someone to attend a hospital or clinic for medical treatment and the person does not attend, the person may be taken to hospital for treatment, by force if necessary. The person can be detained for up to six hours for medical treatment.

If a person on a community-based compulsory treatment order fails to comply with any other term of the order, the responsible medical officer may arrange for the person to be brought to hospital and detained there for up to 72 hours. The person may be further detained for up to 28 days. The person may apply to the tribunal for discharge.

If someone absconds from the place where he or she is supposed to be, he or she may be taken into custody and returned there.

This chapter also looks at certain Mental Health (Care and Treatment) Act offences in connection with compulsory orders. Offences include encouraging a person to abscond, ill-treatment, and false statements.

BREACH OF COMPULSORY TREATMENT ORDER

Failure to attend for medical treatment

20.02 A community-based compulsory treatment order or interim order will generally require the person to attend a certain place to receive medical treatment.

If the person does not attend, the responsible medical officer may take the person into custody, or authorise someone else to do so. They can take the person to the place where he or she goes for medical treatment or to any hospital.[1]

Before exercising this power, the responsible medical officer must consult a mental health officer (if possible, the person's own mental health officer)[2] and obtain his or her consent to the person's removal.[3] The responsible medical officer should make all reasonable efforts to find out why the person is not complying with the order before using these provisions.[4]

If the person's order authorises the giving of medical treatment under Part 16 of the Act, the person may be detained in the hospital or other place for as long as necessary to give him or her medical treatment, but no longer than six hours.[5]

If the person's order does not contain the power to administer medical treatment under Part 16, the person may be detained as long as necessary (up to six hours) to decide whether he or she can consent to treatment and does so.[6]

A form for recording the admission is available on the mental health law website. The form requires the responsible medical officer to send a copy to the Mental Welfare Commission.

The Act does not allow a doctor to treat the person compulsorily in his or her own home or in a general practitioner's surgery. Any use of compulsory powers involves specialised mental health settings or hospitals. Treatment by force can only be given in hospital.[7]

If someone fails to comply with the medical treatment requirements of an order, the responsible medical officer should generally use this procedure. There may be occasions where a responsible medical officer needs to detain someone for longer, to assess the person's needs and review the order.[8]

[1]   Mental Health (Care and Treatment) (Scotland) Act 2003, s 112.
[2]   Code of Practice, vol 2, para 6.31.
[3]   MH(CT)(S)A 2003, s 112(2).
[4]   Code of Practice, vol 2, para 6.33.
[5]   MH(CT)(S)A 2003, s 112(5).
[6]   MH(CT)(S)A 2003, s 112(4).
[7]   See, for example, MH(CT)(S)A 2003, s 241(4).
[8]   Code of Practice, vol 2, para 6.03.

Breach of other provision(s)

Initial detention

20.03 If a person subject to a community-based compulsory treatment order or interim order does not comply with one of the measures in the order, the responsible medical officer (or someone authorised by him or her) may take the person into custody and then to hospital.[1] The person may be detained in the hospital for up to 72 hours.[2]

The responsible medical officer must be satisfied that he or she has taken reasonable steps to contact the person. If it is possible to contact the person, the responsible officer should give him or her a reasonable chance to comply with the order.[3] In an emergency, the responsible medical officer does not need to try to contact the person.[4]

The responsible medical officer should attempt to find out from the person and his or her named person, independent advocate, carers and relatives why he or she has not complied with the compulsory measure and should seek as much information as practicable about the person's mental health from the mental health officer and carers in the community.[5] Such people should feel free to contact the responsible medical officer if they have information to pass on.

The responsible medical officer should not exercise the power unless he or she considers it reasonably likely that if the person continues to breach the order, his or her mental health will deteriorate significantly.[6]

The detention suspends the provisions of the compulsory treatment order for period of the detention.[7] Any right to treat the person under Part 16 of the Act is not suspended.[8]

As soon as possible after the person has been taken to hospital, the responsible medical officer must examine him or her.[9] Another approved medical practitioner can carry out the examination, but the Code of Practice does not recommend this.[10]

[1]   Mental Health (Care and Treatment) (Scotland) Act 2003, s 113.
[2]   MH(CT)(S)A 2003, s 113(5).
[3]   MH(CT)(S)A 2003, s 113(2).
[4]   MH(CT)(S)A 2003, s 113(3).
[5]   Code of Practice, vol 2, para 6.08.
[6]   MH(CT)(S)A, s 113(2).
[7]   MH(CT)(S)A 2003, s 121(1).
[8]   MH(CT)(S)A 2003, s 121(2).
[9]   MH(CT)(S)A 2003, s 113(6).
[10]   Code of Practice, vol 2, para 6.14.

Subsequent detention

20.04 Following the medical examination, the responsible medical officer may detain the person for a further 28 days to consider whether any measures in the order should be varied.[1] The form of detention certificate is on the mental health law website.

The responsible medical officer must obtain the mental health officer's consent to any further detention[2] and should, if practicable, consult the named person.[3] The responsible medical officer can authorise further detention only if he or she believes it is reasonably likely that there will be a significant deterioration in the person's mental health if the person is not detained in hospital.[4]

The detention certificate suspends the provisions of compulsory treatment order for period of the detention,[5] but any right to give medical treatment under Part 16 remains.[6]

These provisions also apply to people on interim compulsory treatment orders. If the interim order is still in effect after the 72-hour detention, the responsible medical officer can further extend the detention until the expiry of the interim order.[7]

[1]   Mental Health (Care and Treatment) (Scotland) Act 2003, s 114.
[2]   MH(CT)(S)A 2003, s 114(3).
[3]   MH(CT)(S)A 2003, s 114(4).
[4]   MH(CT)(S)A 2003, s 114(1).
[5]   MH(CT)(S)A 2003, ss 122(1) and 123(1).
[6]   MH(CT)(S)A 2003, ss 122(2) and 123(2).
[7]   MH(CT)(S)A 2003, s 115.

Duty of hospital managers

20.05 As soon as possible after the responsible medical officer extends the detention, the hospital managers must notify the person, his or her named person and any guardian or welfare attorney, and send them a copy of the certificate.[1] Within seven days of the certificate, the hospital managers should notify the tribunal and the Mental Welfare Commission and send them a copy of the certificate.[2]

The hospital managers should also inform the person of his or her rights.[3]

[1]   Mental Health (Care and Treatment) (Scotland) Act 2003, s 116(1).
[2]   MH(CT)(S)A 2003, s 116(2).
[3]   MH(CT)(S)A 2003, s 260(3). See chapter 17.

Review of detention

20.06 The responsible medical officer should cancel the detention if he or she decides it is not necessary to vary the order[1] or if he or she no longer believes the person needs to be detained in hospital to prevent a significant deterioration in his or her mental health.[2]

The responsible medical officer should discuss options with the mental health officer and care providers and ensure that suitable care arrangements are available for the person in the community.[3]

The responsible medical officer must notify the person, his or her named person and any welfare attorney or guardian as soon as practicable. The responsible medical officer must notify the tribunal and the Mental Welfare Commission within seven days[4] and should notify the person's mental health officer.[5]

[1]   Mental Health (Care and Treatment) (Scotland) Act 2003, s 117(1).
[2]   MH(CT)(S)A 2003, ss 117 and 118.
[3]   Code of Practice, vol 2, para 6.24.
[4]   MH(CT)(S)A 2003, s 119.
[5]   Code of Practice, vol 2, para 6.26.

Appeal to tribunal

20.07 There is no appeal against detention in hospital for medical treatment or the initial 72-hour detention.

The patient and named person can apply to the tribunal for a review of the 28-day detention. A suggested form of application is at Appendix 3 (Form 7). The responsible medical officer must satisfy the tribunal that, unless the person is detained in hospital, it is reasonably likely that there will be a significant deterioration in his or her mental health. If not, the tribunal will cancel the certificate.[1] If the tribunal sets aside the certificate, the person continues to be subject to the community-based compulsory treatment order, but can return to live in the community.

[1]   Mental Health (Care and Treatment) (Scotland) Act 2003, s 120.

UNAUTHORISED ABSENCES

To whom rules apply

20.08 The Mental Health (Care and Treatment) Act contains detailed provisions ensuring that a person subject to a compulsory order or detention certificate cannot absent him or herself from the place where he or she is supposed to be living, whether in hospital or in the community.[1]

These powers apply to anyone detained or subject to detention under the Act or required under a compulsory treatment order to live in a certain place or to obtain approval to a change of address. The Code of Practice has a useful list of the relevant powers and procedures.[2]

A detained patient must not leave the hospital without consent. If someone leaves without the approval of the responsible medical officer, he or she may be taken into custody and returned to the hospital.

A person on a community-based compulsory treatment order can be returned to the place where he or she is required to be living under the order. A person who requires the approval of the mental health officer to any change of address and who moves without consent can be taken into custody and moved to such place as the responsible medical officer thinks appropriate.[3]

These powers are also available if a person absconds from any place where he or she is being kept before transfer to hospital, or if a person subject to a compulsory treatment order absconds during his or her transfer to the hospital or during a transfer to another hospital.[4]

They are available where a person's detention is suspended and he or she does not stay where he or she is meant to, or does not remain in the charge of the authorised person or return at the end of the suspension.[5]

[1] See Mental Health (Care and Treatment) (Scotland) Act 2003, ss 301–3.
[2] Code of Practice, vol 2, pages 220–222.
[3] MH(CT)(S)A 2003, s 301(4).
[4] MH(CT)(S)A 2003, s 301(1).
[5] MH(CT)(S)A 2003, s 301(2).

Breach of order or absconding

20.09 Wherever someone subject to a community-based compulsory treatment order or interim compulsory treatment order is absent without authority from the place he or she is supposed to live, he or she is in breach of the order. The responsible medical officer can use either the breach of order procedures set out above or the absconding provisions.

The Code of Practice gives guidance to professionals.[1] This suggests that it may be more appropriate to invoke the absconding provisions where the person's non-compliance with the order is likely to be temporary.

Sometimes it may be appropriate to use emergency detention. A person subject to a compulsory treatment order can be subject to emergency detention. The compulsory treatment order is suspended for the period of the emergency detention, but any powers of compulsory medical treatment remain.[2]

1   Code of Practice, vol 2, paras 8.6–8.9.
2   Mental Health (Care and Treatment) (Scotland) Act 2003, s 43.

Procedure

Taking person into custody

20.10 A person detained in hospital who leaves the hospital without the consent of the responsible medical officer may be taken into custody.

A mental health officer, a police officer, a member of staff of the hospital where the person is detained, a staff member from the place where the person is supposed to be living or anyone with written authority from the responsible medical officer[1] can retake the person.[2] They may use reasonable force to retake him or her.

The Code of Practice says that force should be a last resort, in accordance with the principles of the Act and good practice. Health boards and local authorities should have psychiatric emergency plans dealing with the use of force, taking into account relevant good practice guidelines.[3] The person should, if possible, have a chance to explain why he or she has absconded before a decision is made to take him or her into custody.[4]

The person should be returned to the hospital, to the place he or she absconded from, to the place where he or she was supposed to be living or, if this is not practical, to such other place as the responsible medical officer considers suitable.[5]

If a person on a suspended order absconds while in the charge of another person, that person may simply resume charge of the person. If this is not appropriate or practical, the responsible medical officer may authorise the person to take the patient to some other suitable place.[6]

1   This should be someone appropriately trained and qualified. Code of Practice, vol 2, para 8.11.
2   Mental Health (Care and Treatment) (Scotland) Act 2003, s 303(3)(a).
3   Code of Practice, vol 2, paras 8.14–15
4   Code of Practice, vol 2, para 8.0–5.
5   MH(CT)(S)A 2003, s 303(1).
6   MH(CT)(S)A 2003, s 303(1)(c).

Time limits

20.11 The authority to take into custody a person who absconds from a compulsory treatment order lasts three months from the date the person absconded,[1] even if the original order has lapsed.[2] For people on other orders, the authority lasts only so long as the person's liability to detention is current.[3]

If a person subject to a compulsory treatment order remains at liberty after three months, he or she cannot be retaken into custody under the original order and the order lapses.[4]

[1]   Mental Health (Care and Treatment) (Scotland) Act 2003, ss 303(4) and 304(3).
[2]   MH(CT)(S)A 2003, s 303(5).
[3]   MH(CT)(S)A 2003, s 303(4)(b).
[4]   MH(CT)(S)A 2003, ss 303(4) and 304(3).

Review of person's needs

20.12 When a person subject to a compulsory treatment order who has been on unauthorised absence for longer than 28 days returns within 14 days of the end of the compulsory treatment order, the compulsory treatment order continues for 14 days after his or her return.[1]

During this period the person's responsible medical officer reviews the need for the order.[2] The timing of subsequent reviews may be affected.[3]

Even when an order expires after a patient's return, it is deemed to continue for a period of 14 days to enable the responsible medical officer to carry out a review,[4] provided the person has not been absent for more than three months.

An order which has less than 14 days to run continues for 14 days after the person's return, to enable the responsible medical officer to review the need for a compulsory treatment order.[5] Such a review is not necessary if there has been a recent review.[6]

When a person who has absconded from short-term detention or detention following breach of a compulsory treatment order[7] returns to hospital in the last 13 days before the expiry of the detention, the measures specified in the certificate apply for a further 14 days.[8]

[1]   Mental Health (Care and Treatment) (Scotland) Act 2003, s 305(1).
[2]   MH(CT)(S)A 2003, s 305(2).
[3]   MH(CT)(S)A 2003, ss 305(3)-(6).
[4]   MH(CT)(S)A 2003, s 307.
[5]   MH(CT)(S)A 2003, s 306(1).
[6]   MH(CT)(S)A 2003, s 306(5).
[7]   MH(CT)(S)A 2003, ss 114(2) or 115(2).
[8]   MH(CT)(S)A 2003, s 308.

Obtaining a warrant

20.13 If a person who has absconded refuses to allow access to premises, a sheriff or justice of the peace can grant a warrant authorising access.[1] Anyone with authority under the Act to take the person to a specified place or into custody can apply for a warrant. He or she must satisfy the sheriff or justice that he or she needs to gain access and has failed to do so, or is unlikely to gain access.

A warrant authorises the person who made the application to enter the premises, together with a mental health officer and a police officer, if necessary.[2] A doctor or any authorised person may accompany them.[3] If any door is locked, the police officer can open it.[4]

A statutory form of application for the warrant is available on the mental health law website.[5]

[1]   Mental Health (Care and Treatment) (Scotland) Act 2003, s 292.
[2]   MH(CT)(S)A 2003, s 292(3).
[3]   MH(CT)(S)A 2003, s 292(4).
[4]   MH(CT)(S)A 2003, s 292(3)(b).
[5]   The Mental Health (Form of Documents) (Scotland) Regulations 2006 (SSI 2006/12).

Where criminal justice order

20.14 Separate rules made under section 310 of the Act apply to unauthorised absences by people who have come to hospital from the criminal justice system.[1] These specify in detail the situations where a person who absconds may be re-taken and to where he or she may be retaken.

The rules require the responsible medical officer to notify the appropriate persons of any unauthorised absences. These persons include the court which made the order, the Mental Welfare Commission and Scottish Ministers. If someone absconds before the court has sentenced him or her, the responsible medical officer must notify the prosecutor.

The responsible medical officer must review the person's condition on his or her return and may revoke any suspension of detention which he or she has previously granted.

[1]   Mental Health (Absconding by mentally disordered offenders) (Scotland) Regulations 2005 (SSI 2005/463).

MENTAL HEALTH ACT OFFENCES

Abuse

20.15 It is an offence for a member of the staff or management of a hospital or any carer in a residential or other setting to ill-treat or wilfully neglect anyone in their care.[1]

The Code of Practice gives guidance on good practice for the investigation of possible offences.[2]

[1]   Mental Health (Care and Treatment) (Scotland) Act 2003, s 315.
[2]   Code of Practice, vol 1, para 16.18.

People absent without leave

20.16 It is an offence knowingly to encourage or help a person subject to an order or detention certificate under the Act to be absent from the place where he or she is supposed to be, or to hide or protect a person who has absented him or herself[1] (including a person being removed or transferred under the cross-border Regulations).[2]

If professionals believe someone is obstructing them, they should explain to the person the impact of these rules.[3]

The person charged has a defence if he or she did not interfere with the performance of another person's statutory functions under the Act and was trying to protect the interests of the patient.[4]

[1]   Mental Health (Care and Treatment) (Scotland) Act 2003, s 316.
[2]   MH(CT)(S)A 2003 (as amended by the Mental Health (Care and Treatment) (Scotland) Act 2003 (Modification of Enactments) Order 2005 (SSI 2005/465)), s 316(1)(c).
[3]   Code of Practice, vol 1, para 16.21.
[4]   MH(CT)(S)A 2003, s 316(2).

Obstruction

20.17 It is an offence for anyone other than the patient[1] to obstruct a person carrying out his or her statutory functions under the Act without reasonable excuse by:

- Refusing to allow an authorised person access to premises or to a person subject to an order or detention certificate;

- Refusing to allow an authorised person to interview or examine a person subject to an order or detention certificate, or to examine or interview a person in private;
- Refusing to produce any document or records to a person authorised to request them; or
- Otherwise obstructing an authorised person in the carrying out of his or her functions under the Act.[2]

[1]   Mental Health (Care and Treatment) (Scotland) Act 2003, s 317(2).
[2]   MH(CT)(S)A 2003, s 317.

False statements

20.18 It is an offence to make a statement that is materially false in an application under the Act, any document submitted with an application or any other document used in connection with the Act, or to use any such false statement with intent to deceive.[1]

These rules do not apply to documents dealing with the nomination of a named person or declarations in relation to named persons or advance statements.[2]

[1]   Mental Health (Care and Treatment) (Scotland) Act 2003, s 318.
[2]   MH(CT)(S)A 2003, s 318(2)(b).

Chapter 21

TRANSITIONAL ARRANGEMENTS

IMPACT OF PROVISIONS

Continuation of orders

21.01 This chapter outlines the rules governing people who were subject to compulsory measures under the Mental Health (Scotland) Act 1984 or the Criminal Procedure (Scotland) Act 1995 on the date the Mental Health (Care and Treatment) Act came into effect, 5 October 2005. The regulations call these people '1984 Act' patients. Generally all 1984 Act patients are regarded as if they are subject to the appropriate order under the Mental Health (Care and Treatment) Act.[1]

A person liable to detention in hospital under section 18 of the 1984 Act is treated as if he or she was admitted to hospital under a compulsory treatment order made on the date of the admission. The order is deemed to authorise the person's detention in hospital and medical treatment under Part 16 of the Mental Health (Care and Treatment) Act.[2]

The rules make detailed provision for people subject to short-term and emergency detention under the 1984 Act, continuation of medical treatment under the new Act, appeals, etc. Most of these people will have moved over to new orders under the Mental Health (Care and Treatment) Act if necessary and this book does not cover the rules in detail. There is detailed guidance from the Scottish Executive.[3]

---

[1]   The Mental Health (Care and Treatment) (Scotland) Act 2003 (Transitional and Savings Provisions) Order 2005 (SSI 2005/452). ('The transitional provisions'.)

[2]   Transitional provisions, arts 3, 4.

[3]   See Scottish Executive Health Department (2005) NHS HDL 42 (28 September 2005). Available on the Scottish Executive's mental health law website.

Hospital orders

21.02 A person subject to a hospital order under the criminal justice system is treated as if he or she was subject to a compulsion order made on the same day as the hospital order.[1] Otherwise the rules are similar to those for people subject to civil orders.

1   Transitional provisions, art 9.

Community care orders

21.03 If someone subject to a community care order under the 1984 Act was previously compulsorily detained under section 18 of that Act, he or she is regarded as subject to a compulsory treatment order.[1] If previously detained under the Criminal Procedure (Scotland) Act, he or she is regarded as subject to a compulsion order.[2]

The measures in the compulsory treatment order will be as set out in the original order. These will not include authority to treat the person against his or her will. The person is not subject to the compulsory treatment provisions of Part 16 of the Mental Health (Care and Treatment) Act, as community care orders did not contains these powers.

1   Transitional provisions, art 14.
2   Transitional provisions, art 16.

Restricted patients

21.04 Someone who was a restricted patient before the commencement of the Mental Health (Care and Treatment) Act is treated as if subject to a compulsion order and a restriction order made on the date of the original hospital order.[1]

There are similar rules for people conditionally discharged from hospital, people subject to hospital directions and people transferred to hospital from prison under transfer directions.[2]

1   Transitional provisions, art 20.
2   See transitional provisions, arts 25–32.

DUTIES OF AUTHORITIES

Responsible medical officer

21.05 The responsible medical officer must prepare a care plan for each 1984 Act patient as soon as possible and keep a copy of the care plan within the person's medical records.[1] If the person is regarded as subject to a compulsion order, the responsible medical officer must prepare a Part 9 care plan.[2]

The responsible medical officer must advise the mental health officer if he or she is considering extending a deemed compulsory treatment order and must bear the mental health officer's views in mind before extending the order.[3]

If the responsible medical officer extends the order, he or she should send the tribunal a copy of the person's care plan and of the report made by the mental health officer (see below).[4] The responsible medical officer should also send a copy to the patient, the named person, the mental health officer and the Commission.[5]

The responsible medical officer need not send either document to the patient if he or she considers that this could cause a risk of significant harm to the patient or a third party.[6]

[1]   Transitional provisions, art 38.
[2]   See Mental Health (Care and Treatment) (Scotland) Act 2003, s 137(1).
[3]   MH(CT)(S)A 2003, s 84(2).
[4]   Transitional provisions, art 4(4).
[5]   Transitional provisions, art 4(5).
[6]   Transitional provisions, art 4(6).

Failure to deliver care plan

21.06 The Mental Welfare Commission advises that a number of doctors appear unaware of their duties to send a copy of the care plan and mental health officer reports to the tribunal on extension of a deemed compulsory treatment order.[1]

The Commission takes the view that this failure makes the extension of the order invalid. It advises that hospitals should advise people that their orders might not be valid and that responsible medical officers should consider making new orders.

[1]   Newsletter for mental health officers in Scotland, Issue 11, spring 2006, p 11.

Mental health officer

21.07 If the responsible medical officer extends the order, the mental health officer must prepare a formal report setting out:

- The mental health officer's views and the reasons for those views.

- The patient's and named person's views and their reasons for these views, if the mental health officer knows these.
- Details of the person's relevant personal circumstances.
- Details of any advance statement of which the mental health officer is aware.
- Any other information which the mental health officer considers may help the tribunal; and
- Any social circumstances report about the person.[1]

1 Transitional provisions, art 4(7).

Hospital managers

21.08 Hospital managers must give people information about their rights under the new Act.[1]

1 Transitional provisions, art 40.

ROLE OF THE TRIBUNAL

21.09 The tribunal does not have to consider the extension formally unless any party applies to the tribunal for revocation of the order.[1] The provisions for automatic review apply when two years have elapsed without reference to the tribunal.[2]

1 Under Mental Health (Care and Treatment) (Scotland) Act 2003, s 100.
2 MH(CT)(S)A 2003, s 101(2)(b). This part of the Act is not yet in effect. See Mental Health (Care and Treatment) (Scotland) Act 2003 (Commencement No 4) Amendment (No. 2) Order 2005 (SSI 2005/459).

TRANSFERS, LEAVE OF ABSENCE, ABSCONDING

21.10 The transitional provisions make detailed provision for the timescales for rights of appeal against transfer, for periods of leave of absence under the 1984 Act to be continued under the suspension provisions of the Mental Health (Care and Treatment) Act and for the return of 1984 Act patients who absconded prior to 5 October 2005. They also deal with the situation where an application for admission was made to the sheriff prior to the commencement date of the new Act but no determination made.[1]

1 Transitional provisions, art 8.

PART 4
THE TRIBUNAL

Chapter 22

REPRESENTATION AT THE TRIBUNAL

22.01 This part of the book looks at the role of the Mental Health Tribunal for Scotland. This chapter looks at the various parties who may attend the tribunal and their different roles in representing patients' interests. These include named persons, solicitors and independent advocacy workers. It also looks at the role of the curator *ad litem*, the person the tribunal may appoint if someone is unable to instruct a solicitor. Chapter 23 looks at tribunal procedure.

ROLE OF NAMED PERSON

Background

22.02 The role of the named person is significantly different from that of the nearest relative under the 1984 Act. (See chapter 4 for appointing a named person and who acts when a person does not appoint anyone.)

The nearest relative role dates from a time when it was automatic for family members to take a lead in arranging the affairs of someone living with mental illness or a learning disability. It has been suggested that this does not entirely correspond with modern ideas of autonomy and people to take their own decisions.[1]

Under the 1984 Act the nearest relative could apply for and consent to detention. The nearest relative could also start a formal review of the person's care by initiating discharge proceedings.

The Mental Health (Care and Treatment) Act removes these powers. The Millan Committee was told that they could lead to family friction.[2] Instead the Act attempts to define more clearly the roles of the various parties involved. It distinguishes between the carer, who may have information about the person's care needs, and the named person, who is there to receive information about proposed measures and take action if he or she thinks this is necessary to protect the person's interests.

---

[1] See P Bartlett & R Sandland, *Mental health law: policy and practice* (Blackstone Press, 2000), p 124ff.

[2] *New directions*, paras 7.5–11.

Current role

22.03 The role of the named person is now nearer to that of a safeguarder. The named person should be involved in discussions about care options and may take part in any legal proceedings for compulsory measures.

It may be that a person is unable or does not wish to take part in any compulsion proceedings. This does not mean that the proceedings should go ahead unchallenged. The named person can take action to protect the person's interests, such as organising a solicitor for someone who is unable to do this him or herself.

The named person receives information about any legal proceedings and can attend and give evidence at the hearing. He or she may also call witnesses, such as independent doctors.

The named person may also initiate appeals on behalf of the person and is eligible for legal aid. This is not means tested.

The named person receives information about the person's discharge from hospital. Anyone appointing a named person should be aware that the named person receives information that would otherwise remain confidential.

Nature of role

22.04 Chapter 4 deals with the ways in which someone may nominate a named person. In many cases the person will be happy for the named person to be his or her primary carer or, if there is no carer, for the nearest relative to act.

The role of the named person is not spelt out in the statute. While he or she is there to represent the person's interests, this does not mean that he or she is merely a mouthpiece for the person. A named person may disagree with the person about whether compulsory measures are necessary, and is entitled to state this at the tribunal. This may particularly be the case where the named person is the primary carer.[1]

This means that while the named person *represents the interests* of the person, he or she may not necessarily *represent* him or her. The person should have separate legal representation, both to ensure that the tribunal panel hears his or her views and to ensure that the legal case for an order is tested. The tribunal should appoint a curator *ad litem* if someone is not able to appoint a solicitor. See below.

[1]   See Code of Practice, vol 1, para 17.04.

INSTRUCTING SOLICITOR AND LEGAL AID

Importance of legal representation

22.05 Anyone wishing to challenge compulsion proceedings should seek legal advice. It is generally preferable for the person to have a solicitor representing him or her at the tribunal. The solicitor can interview the person and other relevant parties and seek independent medical reports (paid for by the legal aid system). A solicitor can put the person's case at the tribunal and question the people applying for compulsory measures.

While it is possible that other workers, such as independent advocacy workers or welfare rights officers, could obtain these skills with training, access to legal aid is not available to people outside the legal profession.

The European Court of Human Rights has stressed the importance of access to legal representation. This is particularly important where someone may be vulnerable because of his or her mental condition.[1] See 11.39. Any non-lawyer attempting to represent a service user could be inadvertently breaching the person's human rights.

1   See *Boumar v Belgium* (A 129 (1988)) para 60 (young person); *Megyeri v Germany* (A 237-A (1992)).

Ability to instruct solicitor

22.06 A solicitor cannot act for a client unless satisfied the client can give him or her instructions. The legal test is whether at the time of giving the instructions the client is able to understand the nature of the contract between the solicitor and the client.[1]

In testing capacity a number of factors are relevant, depending on the transaction.[2] Among the factors relevant to instructing a solicitor are whether someone can understand the nature of the decision, the choices he or she has and the relevant circumstances. The fact that someone may not accept that he or she has a mental illness should not affect the person's ability to instruct a solicitor, although it could mean he or she is unable to make decisions about medical treatment.

If someone is too ill to speak to a solicitor or to give a solicitor coherent instructions, the solicitor cannot act for him or her. The solicitor may be able to come back at a later stage and obtain instructions, but if there are concerns about a person's ability to instruct a solicitor, the solicitor may wish to notify the tribunal or the mental health officer. The tribunal can appoint a curator *ad litem* (see below) to represent the client's interests.

The question of whether someone is able to instruct a solicitor to represent him or her in tribunal proceedings is a legal one. In cases of difficulty, medical evidence, including psychological evidence may be necessary.[3]

1 W W McBryde,*The law of contract in Scotland* (2nd edn, W Green & Son, 2001), paras 6.69–73.
2 See Ward, *Adult Incapacity* (W Green & Son, 2003), para 1.30.
3 See Ward, *Adult Incapacity* (W Green & Son, 2003), para 1.32. Ward quotes several cases where the courts have taken the views of solicitors, rather than doctors, as to capacity.

Curator or solicitor

22.07 Just because someone appears to have a mental illness or learning disability does not mean the person is unable to instruct a solicitor. All patients, however disabled, should have the opportunity of knowing whether they are to be the subject of compulsion proceedings and of seeking legal representation. The only exception is where there would be a genuine and serious risk to the person's health or safety if he or she received this information.

It is generally preferable to have a solicitor rather than a curator *ad litem*. A solicitor represents the person and expresses his or her views to the tribunal. For example, even if a solicitor believes an order is in a person's best interests, he or she will oppose the order if the person wants this. By contrast, a curator *ad litem* tries to find out what is in the person's best interests and reports to the tribunal accordingly. The standard guide to sheriff court practice says the function of the curator is to protect and safeguard the interests of the person who is incapable of doing so him or herself.[1]

On civil liberties grounds, it is preferable that someone should have access to his or her own solicitor, who can test the legal basis of the application, formally question those proposing the application and clearly put the person's views to the tribunal. This does not mean that there should be a blanket restriction on appointing curators. The tribunal must consider in each case on its merits.[2].

1 I D MacPhail, *Sheriff court practice* (2nd edn, W Green & Son, 1998–2002), para 4.24.
2 See D Hanlon & K McGill, 'Safeguards before the MHTS' (4) 2006 Journal of Law Society of Scotland, p 28.

Capacity required

22.08 A solicitor considering whether the client can instruct him or her should bear in mind that the person's capacity might fluctuate and ask staff if there would be a better time when he or she can visit.

It is important that the test of capacity is not set too high. If a person can understand that a mental health officer is applying for a compulsory order and a solicitor can help him or her consider the options, he or she can instruct a solicitor.[1] Someone with a right of appeal who understands that a solicitor can seek a review of detention, is able to instruct the solicitor. The person does not have to be able to understand the precise nature of the proceedings or the precise effects of the various orders available.

Mental health hearings differ from, for example, criminal proceedings, which require a higher standard of capacity. Someone attending a mental health tribunal does not have to be able to give instructions throughout the tribunal hearing. Once the solicitor has the papers, he or she can instruct reports, and question the various parties without the need for significant intervention from the client.

This approach to assessing capacity is in accordance with the principles of both the Mental Health (Care and Treatment) Act and the Adults with Incapacity Act, both of which stress the importance of maximising the participation of the person in the hearing and of maximising capacity if possible.

For these reason, it is hoped that the appointment of curators *ad litem* in such cases will be required only occasionally and that generally people will have solicitors representing them.

[1]   A real life example recently was a woman with profound communication difficulties who appeared at a tribunal in England saying 'home, home'. It could be argued that her wishes were clear enough to allow a solicitor to represent her.

Tribunal representation in England and Wales

22.09 It is interesting to note that representation at tribunals in England and Wales is by solicitors, whether or not the person has legal capacity to instruct the solicitor. Guidance from the Law Society says that it sees no advantage in the appointment of a 'guardian *ad litem*' in such circumstances, as the guardian will be in no better position to protect the person's interests.

The Law Society of England and Wales says that an experienced solicitor should provide an adequate safeguard in most cases. When a client is unable to instruct a solicitor, the solicitor should act in accordance with the Law Society's guidance, bearing in mind Mental Capacity Act principles of respect for the person's wishes, the need to encourage the person's maximum possible participation in proceedings, the views of relevant others and the least restrictive option.[1]

It may be that this option would be attractive in Scotland. It relies for its effectiveness on the use of experienced and accredited solicitors. While the Law Society of Scotland now has a mental health accreditation scheme for solicitors, this is not obligatory, whilst it is in England and Wales.

[1] See Representation at Mental Health Review Tribunals: Guidelines for legal representatives, Law Society of England and Wales (2004), para 8.

Arranging legal representation

22.10 The medical reports submitted in connection with the application for a compulsory treatment order identify whether the person is able to appoint a solicitor. One of the approved medical practitioners must state whether the person can arrange for a solicitor to represent him or her in connection with the application.[1]

Either the mental health officer or the hospital should help the person gain access to legal assistance. The rules are not clear who should be responsible. Hospital managers must give patients key information about (among other things) how to get legal assistance at the relevant times.[2] One of the relevant times should clearly be when there is an application for a compulsory treatment order. Unfortunately this is not listed in the regulations.

Until the regulations are amended to include this key event, it would be hoped that hospitals and local authorities will agree who should be responsible for helping people arrange legal representation.

It is arguably preferable for hospital staff (usually the person's key nurse) to help the person contact a solicitor. The mental health officer may have a conflict of interest, in that he or she may be subject to rigorous scrutiny from the solicitor at the tribunal. This could affect the mental health officer's recommendations.

[1] Mental Health (Care & Treatment)(Scotland) Act 2003, s 57(5)(c).

²   MH(CT)(S)A 2003, s 260 and the Mental Health (Provision of Information to
     Patients) (Prescribed Times) (Scotland) Regulations 2005 (SSI 2005/206).

Role of solicitor

22.11 A solicitor is obliged to act in the 'best interests' of his or her client.¹
In mental health cases this is not a straightforward matter. For example,
there may be occasions where a client may wish to oppose an application
yet the solicitor believes that an order would be in the person's best
interests.

The Law Society of England and Wales has issued guidance to
solicitors acting in mental health hearings. The duty of the solicitor is to
act in accordance with the person's instructions, 'advocating the person's
views and wishes, even if those may be considered bizarre or contrary to
the person's best interests'.

The Law Society says it is not for the solicitor to represent what he or
she thinks the best outcome would be. That is a matter for the tribunal.
The solicitor should give the person good advice, which might include an
assessment of the chances of the person succeeding before the tribunal,
but the client has the right to reject that advice.²

It is suggested that this is a correct statement of the solicitor's
responsibilities in Scotland.

If a client wishes to oppose an order, the solicitor should do so, but it
has been argued it is not helpful for the solicitor to oppose an application
strenuously where someone does not understand that he or she is ill. A
solicitor should use his or her professional judgement.

¹   Law Society of Scotland Solicitors' Code of Conduct (June 2002), para 2.
²   *Representation at mental health review tribunals: guidelines for legal
     representatives*, The Law Society of England and Wales (June 2004), para 8.

Legal aid

22.12 Because mental health hearings deal with matters of such
importance to the civil liberties of the person, free legal aid without
means testing is now available to everyone who is the subject of a mental
health application. This was achieved partly as a result of considerable
lobbying from the Law Society of Scotland and the Mental Welfare
Commission.

Legal aid is by means of the Advice by Way of Representation
(ABWOR) scheme.¹ The scheme covers advice and representation at the

tribunal and is regardless of means. Legal aid and representation at the tribunal is available to the patient and his or her named person.

1   Advice and Assistance (Assistance by Way of Representation) (Scotland) Regulations 2003 (SSI 2003/179), (as amended by the Advice and Assistance (Assistance by Way of Representation) (Scotland) Amendment (No. 2) Regulations 2005 (SSI 2005/482)), reg 9.

CURATORS *AD LITEM*

Appointment of curator

22.13 A curator *ad litem* is someone appointed to take part in legal proceedings if one of the parties to the proceedings is unable to do this him or herself. The tribunal appoints curators, who are usually experienced mental health solicitors.

The tribunal rules envisage three situations where a curator may be appointed. Firstly, if the person lacks the legal capacity to instruct a solicitor to represent him or her in the proceedings.[1] Secondly, if the tribunal has withheld certain documents from the person and he or she does not have a solicitor.[2] Thirdly, if the tribunal excludes the person from the hearing, or part of it, and the person has no solicitor.[3]

Unlike the previous rules, the tribunal has no discretion to appoint a curator in any other circumstances and the tribunal cannot appoint a solicitor if a person says he or she would like legal representation but has not appointed anyone.[4] In the latter case, the tribunal may have to adjourn the hearing to enable the person to arrange for a solicitor.

The tribunal may appoint an expert to help it consider whether to appoint a curator.[5] At the time of writing, the tribunal service appears to be using the services of 'men of skill' to make these assessments. These people are generally experienced mental health solicitors, but they do not have medical expertise. If the 'man of skill' decides the person can instruct a solicitor, he or she or a member of the firm will offer to act. If not, the man of skill acts as curator *ad* litem.

1   Tribunal rules, r 47(9).
2   Tribunal rules, r 68(8).
3   Tribunal rules, r 69(6). The rules refer to whether the person has a 'representative'. The rules are subject to human rights law, which emphasises the importance of legal representation.

⁴   Act of Sederunt (Mental Health Rules) 1996 (SI 1996/2149), rules 5(2)(b) and 6.

⁵   Mental Health Tribunal for Scotland (Practice and Procedure) (No. 2) Rules 2005 (SSI 2005/519), r 55(3).

President's practice guidance

22.14 A major concern of the tribunal service has been the frequency of requests for the appointment of curators *ad litem*. A practice note from the President (available on the Mental Health Tribunal for Scotland's website) stresses that the fact that someone may have a mental disorder is not of itself a reason to say that he or she cannot appoint a solicitor. The tribunal must be satisfied that there is proper evidence (usually medical evidence) justifying the appointment of a curator.

The primary aim should be to ensure that the person has a solicitor. If the person has not arranged for a solicitor, the mental health officer, the independent advocate or the named person may approach a solicitor on the person's behalf.[1]

If a solicitor decides someone is unable to give him or her instructions, it may be appropriate for the solicitor to approach the tribunal and request the appointment of a curator.

1   The Scottish Independent Advocacy Alliance advises independent advocacy services to have lists of solicitors in their area who specialise in these matters. Independent advocates should not recommend a particular solicitor (SIAA newsletter: December 2005).

Concerns about curators

22.15 There has been concern that some tribunals have failed to appoint curators *ad* litem even where people appear to lack the capacity to instruct a solicitor.[1] It appears that some tribunals appear to have read the President's guidance as saying that if a person has a named person or independent advocate representing him or her at the tribunal, legal representation through a solicitor or curator *ad litem* is not necessary.

It is doubtful if this satisfies human rights requirements. The named person or independent advocate is unlikely to be legally qualified or to possess the necessary knowledge and skills to conduct the proceedings adequately on the person's behalf.

This appears to be a less satisfactory situation than under the 1984 Act, where the sheriff generally appointed a curator when someone was unable to instruct a solicitor.

¹   See D Hanlon & K McGill, 'Safeguards before the MHTS' (4) 2006 Journal of Law Society of Scotland, p 28.

Duties of curator ad litem

22.16 The tribunal rules say that the curator should represent the person's interests at the tribunal hearing.[1] A curator protects the person's interests at the hearing and must advise the tribunal about the person's views and concerns.

Some curators have felt that civil liberties concerns mean they should always oppose the application. Yet not all people faced with compulsory measures wish to oppose them. A better statement of the duties of the curator is that he or she should:

- Meet with the person and attempt to identify his or her concerns, in accordance with the principles of the Act.[2]
- Talk to health and social care staff, carers and the named person to establish the person's background and social circumstances.
- Obtain an independent psychiatric report on the person's condition.
- Establish whether the Mental Health (Care and Treatment) Act grounds, as set out in the relevant part of the Act, appear to apply and whether an order is appropriate in the light of the principles of the Act.
- Consider whether in the light of the above to oppose the application.
- Put the person's views or concerns to the tribunal, even though it may not be appropriate to oppose the application.[3]

¹   Rule 55(5).
²   The curator is not legally bound by the principles of the Act, (Mental Health (Care and Treatment) (Scotland) Act 2003, s 1(7)), but the tribunal must consider the principles. The curator should ensure that the person's wishes and feelings, past and present, are put to the tribunal.
³   See guidance given by the Mental Welfare Commission, approved by the Association of Sheriffs and the Scottish Courts Administration, on the role of curators *ad litem* under the 1984 Act. Mental Welfare Commission Annual Report 1998–9, para 12.1.

Paying curators

22.17 There is no provision in the tribunal rules for paying curators. (The previous rules provided that the person, or if appropriate the tribunal, should pay the curator *ad litem*, in accordance with directions from the President.)[1] The Mental Health (Care and Treatment) Act says the tribunal may pay a person's allowances and expenses in connection with attendance at hearings, as directed by the President.[2] This could enable the tribunal to pay curators' fees.

The Scottish Legal Aid Board is unwilling to pay curators' fees, arguing that the curator *ad litem* is an officer of the court and does not provide a legal service to his or her client within the meaning of the Legal Aid Regulations. Under the 1984 Act, the Scottish Legal Aid Board paid for curators where it was satisfied that the curator's task was essentially providing legal services to the person.

The Scottish Legal Aid Board says that in the absence of any statutory payment scheme, or a direction under a rule of court as to who should pay, the payment position reverts to the common law. The court (or in this case the tribunal) should find someone to pay.[3] This would normally be the party seeking the order. (This does not deal with who should pay when someone is appealing against an order.)

This is a clearly unsatisfactory situation and may require reconsideration of the way in which people's human rights can best be protected at tribunals.

[1] Mental Health Tribunal for Scotland (Practice and Procedure) Rules 2005 (SSI 2005/420), r 55(6).
[2] Mental Health (Care and Treatment) (Scotland) Act 2003, Sched 2, Part 4, para 16.
[3] Correspondence with the author.

INDEPENDENT PSYCHIATRIST

22.18 A solicitor or curator *ad litem* generally arranges for an independent psychiatric report on the person's condition for the purposes of any appeal the person may wish to make. (See 23.12 for making the report available to the tribunal.) A doctor authorised by the person subject to the order or his or her named person can visit the person at any reasonable time and examine him or her in private.[1]

The person subject to the order can cancel the doctor's authority if he or she has the legal capacity to do so.[2]

The independent doctor can ask to see the medical records relating to the person's detention in hospital or medical treatment.[3]

1   Mental Health (Care and Treatment) (Scotland) Act 2003, s 262.
2   MH(CT)(S)A 2003, s 262(5).
3   MH(CT)(S)A 2003, s 263.

INDEPENDENT ADVOCACY

22.19 A person may wish an independent advocacy worker to support him or her at the hearing even where the person also has a legal representative. The principle of participation requires the tribunal to ensure that the person can participate as fully as possible in the hearing and that the person receives such information and support as is necessary to achieve this. An independent advocacy worker may be able to help the person, both before the tribunal and in dealings with the solicitor and the tribunal.[1]

The role of the independent advocacy worker should be to support the person and to ensure that the tribunal hears the person's views, from the person him or herself, from the solicitor or, if the person is unwilling to speak, from the advocacy worker. The advocacy worker will usually agree in advance with the person what the worker will say. The independent advocacy worker can ensure that the solicitor raises any issues the person has. The advocacy worker will also support the person after the hearing and help the person recall what the tribunal decided.

An advocacy worker does not replace any legal representative the person may have.[2] The tribunal should not ask advocacy worker for his or her views on the application. The rules do not list independent advocates as entitled to attend the hearing.[3] This is because their function is to support the person, not give their own evidence to the tribunal.

Solicitors and independent advocacy workers should discuss the advocacy worker's role before the hearing.

1   Code of Practice, vol 1, para 6.143.
2   Code of Practice (as above).
3   See, for example, s 64(3) of the Act.

Chapter 23

TRIBUNAL PROCEDURE

23.01 This chapter deals with tribunal procedure relating to applications, appeals and references to the tribunal. The powers of the tribunal to deal with a particular application or reference are set out in the relevant chapter.

The tribunal procedure is set out in detailed rules.[1] In addition, the tribunal may develop its own procedures.[2] The President may also make practice directions.[3]

Part I of the tribunal rules sets out the overriding objective: that the tribunal should handle proceedings as fairly, expeditiously and efficiently as possible.[4]

Parts II to VI set out the detailed rules of procedure for making an application, appeal or reference to the tribunal. Parts I to IV deal with applications, appeals and references to the tribunal. Part V deals with reviews by the tribunal and Part VI deals with cases remitted back to the tribunal following a successful appeal to the sheriff principal or Court of Session.

The procedures are all very similar. This chapter concentrates on the procedure for applying for a compulsory treatment order. The other procedures are set out in detail in the rules.

Part VII contains general rules of procedure, dealing with such matters as evidence, case management and procedure at the hearing.

---

[1]   Mental Health Tribunal for Scotland (Practice and Procedure) (No. 2) Tribunal Rules 2005 (SSI 2005/519). (The 'tribunal rules'.) These replace the previous rules (SSI 2005/420). Purchasers of the previous rules can obtain a copy of the replacement free of charge. The rules have been further amended by the Mental Health Tribunal for Scotland (Practice and Procedure) (No. 2) Amendment Tribunal Rules 2006 (SSI 2006/171), which deal with appeals against excessive security.

[2]   Tribunal rules, r 52(1).

[3]   Mental Health (Care and Treatment) (Scotland) Act 2003, Sched 2, para 11.

[4]   Tribunal rules, r 4.

PARTIES AND 'RELEVANT PERSONS'

23.02 The Act lists certain people who are entitled to attend the hearing, to give and produce evidence and to make oral or written representations at the hearing. They are the person who is the subject of the proceedings and his or her named person and primary carer.

If there is a welfare guardian, a welfare attorney authorised to act because of the person's incapacity[1] or a curator *ad litem,* he or she has the right to attend. The mental health officer, the doctors who submitted the mental health reports and the responsible medical officer are also entitled to appear and give evidence.[2]

Any other person with an interest may apply to the tribunal for permission to take part in the proceedings.[3]

Because of concerns about patient confidentiality, the tribunal rules attempt to restrict the number of people who receive all the papers and reports in the case. They do this by distinguishing between the parties to the case and other 'relevant persons' who are notified of the case and entitled to attend and give evidence but do not receive all the papers.

This chapter uses these terms.

[1] Mental Health (Care and Treatment) (Scotland) Act 2003, s 64(3)(d).
[2] MH(CT)(S)A 2003, s 64(3).
[3] Tribunal rules, r 48. See 23.24 below.

Parties

23.03 The parties are the person who is the subject of the proceedings, his or her named person, the person who brought the application before the tribunal (in the case of a compulsory treatment order, the mental health officer), and anyone whose decision is being considered by the tribunal.[1] In addition, someone may become a party under rule 48 (below).

[1] Tribunal rules, r 2.

Relevant persons

23.04 The 'relevant persons' are the parties and other people from the list above who notify the tribunal under Parts II, IV or V of the Rules that they wish to give evidence to the tribunal.

If one of the relevant persons fails to give notice within the appropriate timescale, he or she may have to seek permission from the tribunal to take part.[1] The tribunal may waive the time limits to avoid prejudice to any relevant person.[2] If a named person, primary carer, attorney, or guardian is unable to attend, this is likely to prejudice the person's interests. Any such person should apply to the tribunal for permission to attend the hearing.

[1]   Under r 75.
[2]   Tribunal rules, r 75(2).

MAKING APPLICATIONS

23.05 Forms for applications and submissions to the tribunal are available on the Scottish Executive's mental health law website. The Scottish Executive advises applicants to use these forms wherever possible to assist the Mental Welfare Commission to monitor the Act. They are also on the Mental Welfare Commission's website.

Applications by email are possible but not telephone applications. Applications must be in writing.

Most of the forms are for people making applications. There are no forms for appeal against orders. Some suggested forms are at Appendix 3.

APPLICATION FOR COMPULSORY TREATMENT ORDER

Notifying parties

23.06 The tribunal sends a copy of the application, together with the medical reports, the mental health officer's report and a copy of the proposed care plan, to the person and his or her named person.[1]

The other relevant persons receive notice of the application, but do not receive the supporting documentation, because of patient confidentiality. The person may, of course, agree to share the contents with them.

The relevant persons have up to 14 days to notify the tribunal whether they wish to make any representations or to lead or produce evidence at the hearing. The notice of application may specify a period of less than 14 days, but this must be reasonable. For example, 48 hours' notice will be adequate only in the most extreme circumstances.[2]

[1]   Tribunal rules, r 6(2).
[2]   *EB v Mental Health Tribunal for Scotland*, Glasgow Sheriff Court B2606/05.

Where person subject to short-term detention

23.07 If an application for a compulsory treatment order is for someone subject to short-term detention, the order is extended to enable the tribunal to hold a hearing. The extension lasts for up to five working days beyond the time when the 28-day period would have ended.[1] The tribunal must hold a first hearing within this period.[2]

The tribunal may not have sufficient information at this stage to consider the case for the order. It can use the first hearing to consider whether it is appropriate to make an interim compulsory treatment order. Anyone can make a request for an interim compulsory treatment order. The request can be oral, at the hearing, or in writing.[3]

There is then a further hearing to deal with the application for the compulsory treatment order.[4]

The tribunal uses the first hearing to give directions to the parties as to the management of their case, to identify what witnesses and information the tribunal may wish to see, to set deadlines for the production of further evidence and reports and to deal with any preliminary requests or applications.[5]

If the tribunal considers someone needs a curator *ad litem*, it could appoint one at the first hearing (although current practice appears to be to seek a report from a 'man of skill'. See chapter 22). If the person's lawyer is seeking an independent medical report, the tribunal will wish to know how long this is likely to take.

If an interim compulsory treatment order is not appropriate, the tribunal must determine the application, either by granting a compulsory treatment order or by dismissing the application.[6]

1   Mental Health (Care and Treatment) (Scotland) Act 2003, s 68.
2   Tribunal rules, r 8(2). See 12.22.
3   Tribunal rules, r 7.
4   Tribunal rules, r 8(2).
5   Tribunal rules, r 8(4).
6   Tribunal rules, r 8(2).

Where appeal pending

23.08 If a mental health officer applies for a compulsory treatment order application and the patient has applied to the tribunal for cancellation ('revocation') of a short-term detention certificate, the tribunal may suspend either of the proceedings until it has determined the other. It may also suspend one of the proceedings for a certain period, or it may hear the two proceedings together, if appropriate.[1]

[1] Tribunal rules, r 52(5).

Where person not subject to detention

23.09 If a mental health officer has applied for a compulsory treatment order for someone who is not subject to detention, the time limits do not apply.

The tribunal may hold a 'preliminary hearing'. It may decide certain preliminary matters prior to the hearing, on giving the relevant persons appropriate notice and time to respond.[1] The tribunal has wide powers to issue directions setting out time limits for the production of evidence and more generally setting out its requirements for evidence.[2]

A relevant person may request the tribunal for a direction about any matter listed in the regulations, for example a direction asking that someone produce a medical report. The request must be in writing.[3]

Failure to comply with a direction of the tribunal could lead to the tribunal directing that the relevant person should take no further part in the tribunal,[4] but it is unlikely to do this if any other relevant person could be prejudiced.[5] The tribunal can extend time limits in the patient's interests.[6]

[1] Tribunal rules, r 43.
[2] Tribunal rules, r 49(1).
[3] Tribunal rules, r 49(2).
[4] Tribunal rules, r 51.
[5] Tribunal rules, r 75.
[6] Tribunal rules, r 52(2)(a).

OTHER APPLICATIONS, REFERENCES ETC

23.10 The procedure for notifying the parties, responding to notices, etc., are broadly as in the application for the compulsory treatment order, although different time limits may apply to different cases. There is no first hearing, but as with the compulsory treatment order, there may be a preliminary hearing where the tribunal can take case management decisions.

There are no time limits for the holding of hearings, but the tribunal must hold a hearing as soon as possible, for example, where there is an application for the cancellation of short-term detention or where the Mental Welfare Commission or Scottish Ministers make a reference to the tribunal.[1]

Even if the rules do not provide for a swift hearing of the case, this is a requirement of human rights law.[2]

[1]   Tribunal rules, r 5(5).
[2]   European Convention on Human Rights, Art 5(4). Anyone deprived of his or her liberty must have 'speedy access' to a court to determine the legality of the continued confinement.

BEFORE THE HEARING

Exchange of documents

23.11 Once a hearing has been set, each relevant person should deliver to the tribunal the documents he or she will rely on at the hearing (together with a list of the documents), a list of the witnesses he or she is calling and send any written representations he or she wishes to make.[1]

In the case of the compulsory treatment order application, the mental health officer generally does this on behalf of the doctors who gave the medical reports. The patient's legal representative delivers the list for the patient.

The tribunal should receive this information at least seven days before the hearing, but the tribunal may specify a different date. The tribunal can allow someone to rely on documents which he or she has not submitted within the appropriate timescales if there is a good reason for this and the tribunal thinks it would be fair to allow their admission.[2]

The tribunal distributes all documents it receives to the parties. It may distribute them to other people if the tribunal considers this appropriate.[3]

[1]   Tribunal rules, r 45.
[2]   Tribunal rules, rules 45(2) and 45(3). See also r 63(4). A relevant person can introduce new material if the tribunal considers this is just and reasonable.
[3]   Tribunal rules, rules 46(1)-(2).

Independent medical reports

23.12 If a relevant person has obtained an expert report (for example if a person's solicitor has obtained an independent psychiatric report), he or she must deliver this to the tribunal at this time.[1] This is a controversial

341

provision, which could be subject to challenge under Article 8 of the European Convention on Human Rights as an unwarranted interference with a patient's rights to confidentiality.

The relevant person can request the tribunal to waive this requirement, but must give reasons. The final decision remains with the tribunal.[2] The tribunal must allow the person a chance to state his or her case, either to the Convener or to the Convener and other panel member(s).[3] The tribunal must consider the principles of the Act when reaching a decision. This should include respect for the person's wishes and respect for patient confidentiality. It may be that only part of the document should be seen, because of patient confidentiality.

In one early case under the Act, the sheriff principal remarked that a tribunal should waive this requirement only in very exceptional circumstances, and only if the applicant can establish a specific reason why this is appropriate. The sheriff principal said that the tribunal is concerned with what is best in the interests of the patient and it was in the interests of justice for it to see any independent medical report.[4] These remarks of the sheriff principal were not part of his decision and do not bind other courts, but it will be interesting to see how the tribunal service responds to future requests.

1   Tribunal rules, r 62(5).
2   Tribunal rules, r 62(6).
3   Tribunal rules, r 62(7).
4   Sheriff Principal Lockhart in *SB v Peter Dunbar, Mental Health Officer and Mental Health Tribunal for Scotland*, B1013/05.

Restricting disclosure

23.13 Any party may request the tribunal to withhold a document (including a medical report), or any part of it, from one or more of the parties or from anyone else entitled to see a copy.[1]

The tribunal may, but need not, notify other parties of this request and may seek their views.[2] If the tribunal decides to restrict disclosure, it may ask the person to supply an edited version of the document.

The tribunal must interpret this provision in accordance with human rights law. It is a fundamental rule of human rights law that parties to an action should be able to hear and question the evidence before the court or tribunal.[3]

The rules also allow the tribunal (or a Convener) to withhold all or part of a document if it is satisfied that the disclosure could cause serious harm to the patient or any other person, and it is not unfair for the tribunal to consider the document.[4]

Before deciding this, the tribunal or Convener must give the parties notice of this intention and an opportunity to make written representations.[5] A party may request an oral hearing on the matter.[6]

If the tribunal withholds a document from the patient or any other relevant person, the tribunal will explain the reasons to the patient's representative. If the tribunal withholds a document from a patient with no legal representative, the tribunal may appoint a curator *ad litem* for the person.[7]

[1]   Tribunal rules, r 46(3).

[2]   Tribunal rules, r 46(5).

[3]   For discussion of some of the issues in the context of children's hearings, see *Dosoo v Dosoo (No.1)*, 1999 SCLR 905, *McGrath v McGrath*, 1999 SCLR 121 and *Oyeneyin v Oyeneyin*, 1999 GWD 38–1836.

[4]   Tribunal rules, r 47.

[5]   Tribunal rules, r 47(4).

[6]   Tribunal rules, r 47(5).

[7]   Tribunal rules, r 47(9).

Merging two actions

23.14 If there are two or more sets of proceedings before the tribunal (such as an appeal against short-term detention and an application for a compulsory treatment order), the tribunal may hear the two proceedings at the same time. It can take this decision or at the request of any relevant person.[1]

[1]   Tribunal rules, r 52(5).

PRELIMINARY DUTIES OF TRIBUNAL

Checking paperwork

23.15 The tribunal service should check the paperwork connected with the application. If the paperwork is inaccurate, any order the tribunal makes may be subject to challenge. In one case the sheriff principal held that accidental omissions in paperwork did not make the application invalid.[1]

1 Sheriff Principal Lockhart in *SB v Peter Dunbar, Mental Health Officer and Mental Health Tribunal for Scotland*, B1013/05. A page of one of the medical reports was missing. The doctor had also failed to shade a box on the form confirming the order was necessary.

Communication needs

23.16 The tribunal must make arrangements to meet the needs of anyone participating in the hearing who has communication difficulties or whose first language is not English, if the person is not entitled to communication help under the Act.[1] Anyone aware that someone appearing before the tribunal has such needs should notify the tribunal as soon as possible.

These provisions will be relevant only when someone not subject to an order has communication needs, for example, where there is an application for a compulsory treatment order direct from the community or when another relevant person has needs. If someone subject to a compulsory order or certificate has communication needs, the hospital managers should arrange for interpretation or communication help at the tribunal hearing.[2] See 17.05.

1 Tribunal rules, r 53(4).
2 Mental Health (Care and Treatment) (Scotland) Act 2003, s 261(3).

Conflict of interest

23.17 The tribunal must ensure that no member of the panel has any conflict of interest in connection with the case.

A member cannot sit on the panel if he or she works at the hospital where the person is or may be detained, if he or she provides any medical or social care services to the person or if he or she has personal or professional connection with the person.[1]

There may be other situations where a panel member considers it inappropriate to act, for example, if he or she is doctor to another member of the person's family or related to the mental health officer.[2]

The President can make practice rules setting out other occasions where it would be inappropriate for members to act.

1   Tribunal rules, r 42.
2   For example, for solicitors, *Cleland v Morrison* (1878) 6 R 156 says that the knowledge of one partner is assumed to be the knowledge of all the partners. It would not be appropriate for someone to act as Convener of the tribunal if a solicitor in his or her firm will be appearing before the tribunal.

Information

23.18 The tribunal service must give all relevant parties information about the tribunal procedure and the rights of the various parties attending.[1]

Anyone can contact the tribunal service for general procedural advice.

1   Tribunal rules, r 56(4).

Curator ad litem

23.19 It is advisable for the tribunal to consider whether to appoint a curator *ad* litem before the hearing. The tribunal may appoint a curator if a patient is unable to appoint a solicitor, is excluded from the proceedings and has no solicitor or if certain documents are withheld from a patient who has no solicitor.[1]

See chapter 22 for further discussion.

1   Tribunal rules, r 55.

ATTENDANCE AT HEARING

Ensuring patient participation

23.20 Under the 1984 Act it was rare for people to attend their hearings. Research commissioned by the Millan Committee established that they attended court in only around 28% of cases.[1] They gave evidence in only around 18% of cases. In just over half the cases, the person neither attended nor had legal representation.

The Mental Health (Care and Treatment) Act has participation and respect for the wishes and feelings of the person as two of its key principles. One of its aims is that people will feel able to attend and take part in their tribunal hearings. The rules attempt to assist this process. We look at how they do this below.

Early indications are that the tribunal service is succeeding in its aim of maximising participation. In the three months to February 2006, people attended their hearings in an average of 71% of cases.[2]

1   *An evaluation of s 18 of the MH(S) Act 1984,* Scottish Executive Central Research Unit (2001).
2   Correspondence from the Mental Health Tribunal for Scotland.

Duties of tribunal service

23.21 The tribunal service has a duty to maximise the patient participation, in accordance with the principles of the Act. If someone has not attended or is not able to attend, the Convener should attempt to consider how best to conduct the hearing to ensure the tribunal is clear as to the person's wishes and feelings.

The hearing can continue even if one of the parties or a relevant person is not present, provided the tribunal is satisfied that the person has received proper information about the hearing and there is good reason for his or her absence.[1] If the person has made any representations in writing, the tribunal must consider these.[2]

If one of the parties fails to attend, the tribunal should give him or her a chance to meet either with the Convener or with other panel members to explain why he or she has not attended and whether he or she wishes to proceed.[3]

There may be occasions where someone is too ill to attend the hearing. The Convener may have to consider how best to hear the case in the person's absence.[4] It may be possible to arrange for a video-link with the tribunal,[5] or it may be possible for the person to make a signed statement or to ask if witnesses can speak for him or her. The rules also envisage the use of telephone links and other means of communication as appropriate.[6]

If a patient is unable to arrange for legal representation, a mental health officer, independent advocate or the named person may be able to arrange for a solicitor to represent the person. If the person is unable to instruct a solicitor, the tribunal should appoint a curator under Rule 55.

1   Tribunal rules, r 70(1).
2   Tribunal rules, r 70(2).
3   Tribunal rules, r 70(3).
4   Tribunal rules, r 71.
5   Tribunal rules, r 71(2).
6   See Tribunal rules, r 52(2)(c).

Assistance for person

23.22 An independent advocacy worker or other helper may support a patient at the hearing.[1] The tribunal service should provide any interpretation or communication services any relevant person may need.[2]

The patient should be encouraged to appoint a solicitor. A relevant person may conduct his or her own case (with assistance if necessary) or may use a representative, legal or non-legal.[3] As far as the patient is concerned, legal representation is the only guarantee of a fair hearing in accordance with human rights law.[4] While an independent advocacy worker may be present to support the person, he or she cannot advise on the person's legal rights.

[1]   Tribunal rules, r 66(6)(d).
[2]   Tribunal rules, r 53.
[3]   Tribunal rules, r 54(3).
[4]   See *Megyeri v Germany* [1992] ECtHR 49.

Attendance of other people

23.23 The parties to a case depend on the nature of the proceedings. On an application for a compulsory treatment order, the parties are the mental health officer, the patient and the named person. On an application to cancel the extension of a compulsory treatment order, the parties are the patient, named person and responsible medical officer.

It is not clear what legal representation other parties will seek. Some local authorities appear to be considering legal representation for all hearings. This may be less necessary when an application is not opposed. There could be concerns that inappropriate use of lawyers could make the process unduly legalistic.

It is for the tribunal to decide how and when the various relevant persons should attend the hearing.[1] Relevant persons (if they are not parties) have the right to make representations to the tribunal, either in person or in writing, and to and lead or produce evidence.[2] They do not have the right to hear all the evidence or to cross-examine the various parties. That is for the parties alone.

There may be cases where a tribunal considers the relevant persons should all attend the whole hearing. In other cases, the tribunal may decide that relevant persons should simply attend to give or lead their evidence and make any statements they wish to make.

There may be issues of confidentiality or other reasons why certain witnesses should not attend throughout. The tribunal must decide what is fair in all the circumstances.

1   Tribunal rules, r 63(7).
2   Tribunal rules, r 63(3).

Application to attend

23.24 A person with an interest in the proceedings, such as another relative of the person or a close friend, may apply to attend the hearing, either as a party or as a 'relevant person'. The person must demonstrate to the tribunal why it is appropriate for him or her to be involved.[1]

1   Tribunal rules, r 48.

Excluding people from hearing

On safety grounds

23.25 The tribunal may exclude the patient or any other person from the hearing, or any part of it, if the person's attendance could cause serious harm to the patient or another person.[1] The tribunal should give all relevant persons a chance to make representations before making a decision to exclude anyone. The action taken by the tribunal should be the minimum necessary to remove the risk.[2]

If the patient is excluded, the tribunal will suggest an adjournment so that he or she can obtain legal representation.[3] Alternatively it might appoint a curator *ad litem*. The rules give no right to appeal against exclusion from the hearing.

1   Tribunal rules, r 68(1).
2   Tribunal rules, r 68(7).
3   Tribunal rules, r 68(6).

To avoid disruption

23.26 The tribunal may also exclude someone from the hearing, or part of it, if he or she has disrupted the hearing or is likely to. In addition, the tribunal may exclude someone if his or her presence is likely to make it difficult for anyone to make representations or present evidence, or if his or her conduct has in some other way interfered with 'the administration of justice' or is likely to do so.[1]

Before making such a decision the tribunal will consider the interests of the relevant persons and will give them a chance to make representations. It will attempt to consider alternatives to allow the person to participate.

If the tribunal excludes a patient who has no solicitor, the tribunal will adjourn to allow the person to seek legal representation or to allow the tribunal to consider appointing a curator *ad litem*.[2]

It may be possible for the excluded person to give evidence by video link or some other means.[3]

[1]   Tribunal rules, r 69.
[2]   Tribunal rules, r 69(4).
[3]   Tribunal rules, r 69(5).

Tribunal's powers regarding attendance

23.27 The tribunal can:

- Require a witness to attend and give or produce evidence in person.[1] Signed statements can also be admissible in evidence. The person must receive at least 48 hours' notice.

- Order ('cite') a witness to attend and produce any documents the tribunal wishes to examine.[2] It is a criminal offence not to attend following such a notice.[3]

  If someone ordered to attend is concerned about disclosing certain documents, he or she may request the tribunal to vary the citation. The tribunal must bear in mind the need to protect confidentiality.[4]

- Require any relevant person, the named person or their legal representatives to attend the hearing.[5] The tribunal cannot require a patient to attend[6] and it would not be appropriate to cite him or her to attend, although the rules do not state this explicitly.

[1]   Tribunal rules, r 60.
[2]   Tribunal rules, r 59(1).
[3]   Tribunal rules, r 59(6).
[4]   Tribunal rules, r 59(7).
[5]   Tribunal rules, r 52(2)(b).
[6]   Tribunal rules, r 52(2)(b).

HEARINGS IN UNCONTESTED CASES

23.28 The tribunal can dispense with oral hearings if it considers it has sufficient evidence to enable it to come to a decision. It must obtain the written agreement of all parties. The tribunal must be satisfied that dispensing with an oral hearing would not prejudice the interests of the patient.[1] The author understands that the current intention is to have oral hearings in every case.

There are some situations where the Act requires an oral hearing, for example when considering an appeal against excessive security. See chapter 17.

1   Tribunal rules, r 58(2).

PROCEDURE AT HEARING

23.29 While the procedural rules set out certain requirements, the tribunal regulates its own procedure.[1] It can conduct the hearing in the way it thinks most appropriate for the clarification of the issues.[2]

The rules envisage the hearing being as informal as possible, bearing in mind that the tribunal is dealing with matters of very significant impact on the lives of people coming before it.[3]

The Convener explains the procedure at the start of the hearing.[4] If people at the hearing use legal language which is not easily understood, the Convener should explain the terms used.[5]

1   Tribunal rules, r 52(1).
2   Tribunal rules, r 63(2).
3   Tribunal rules, r 63(2)(a).
4   Tribunal rules, r 63(1).
5   Tribunal rules, r 63(5).

Private hearings

23.30 Human rights law has a presumption in favour of public hearings, for obvious reasons. Justice should be seen to be done. Mental health cases are a recognised exception to this rule, because of the sensitivity and the need to preserve confidentiality.[1] Consequently the rules of procedure provide that in most cases hearings will be in private.[2]

The patient may submit a written request for a public hearing, but even then this may be refused (as to all or part of the hearing) if the tribunal considers such a hearing would not be in the person's interests or would prejudice the fair hearing of the case or the interests of justice.[3]

Even if a hearing is public, the tribunal may limit the amount of publicity given to it, if it considers this necessary in the interests of the welfare of the patient or of any other person or to protect the private life of anyone.[4] One way of limiting publicity is to allow reporting but require anonymity.[5]

Any relevant person may make representations to the tribunal about the need to limit publicity.[6]

It is unfortunate that, at the time of writing, some published reports of cases appealed to sheriff principals identify the patients involved. It is hoped this practice will soon cease. Some sheriff principals anonymise their reports. The Scottish Court Service is currently consulting with sheriffs and judges to see if they can agree a standard practice.[7] (Similar issues arise with incapacity cases, where practice is also inconsistent.)

[1]   Hearings in private may be justified under Art 6 European Convention on Human Rights where this is necessary for (among other reasons) the protection of the private life of the parties: *B and P v UK* (2002) 34 EHRR 529 at para 39. See also *R (on the application of Mersey Care NHS Trust) v Mental Health Review tribunal* EWHC [2004] 1749 QBD (Admin) where the English rules were tested on this point. The judge held that there were special circumstances to justify hearings in private.

[2]   Tribunal rules, r 66(1).

[3]   Tribunal rules, r 66(4).

[4]   Tribunal rules, r 67.

[5]   Tribunal rules, r 67(3).

[6]   Tribunal rules, r 67(1)(c).

[7]   Correspondence with the author.

Nature of process

23.31 There has been much debate about whether tribunal procedure is 'adversarial' or 'inquisitorial'. In an adversarial system, each side puts its own case and then faces questions from the other side. In an inquisitorial system, the judge (or tribunal) questions the parties to establish the facts.

In a mental health case there are not really two 'sides', as even if the patient opposes the application, any decision made is intended to be for his or her benefit. This makes mental health cases unique in the Scottish legal system. To comply with human rights law, some elements of an adversarial system have to be in place. This is an essential part of ensuring there is a 'fair hearing'.[1]

The rules provide this. Each relevant person is entitled to give evidence, to call witnesses and to make representations to the tribunal on the evidence and on the case.[2]

The rules also envisage an element of inquisitorial procedure. Panel members may question the parties and all relevant persons to resolve any disputed facts, and the rules envisage that this may particularly be necessary where a relevant person does not have a solicitor.[3]

It is important to note that, just because the procedure is described as adversarial, this does not mean that it should become aggressive or unpleasant.

The adversarial system is simply a way of establishing the facts of the case and there is no reason for it to become either unduly legalistic or combative. This could increase the stress for the person and could make it less likely people will want to attend their hearings. This would be contrary to the Act's principles, which stress the importance of the person's participation in decisions.

It is for the Convener to establish the appropriate tone for the hearing. As a last resort, he or she could exclude an unduly aggressive legal representative from the hearing.[4]

---

[1] DJ Harris, M O'Boyle & C Warbrick, *Law of the European Convention on Human Rights* (Butterworths, 1995), p 150.
[2] Tribunal rules, r 63(4).
[3] Tribunal rules, r 63(5).
[4] Tribunal rules, r 69(1)(a).

Procedural matters

Oath or affirmation

23.32 The tribunal can require anyone appearing before it to take an oath or make an affirmation to confirm he or she is telling the truth.[1] At the time of writing, it seems unlikely that tribunals will require oaths. In any event, anyone relying on false statements in any application or document submitted under the Act is committing an offence.[2]

---

[1] Tribunal rules, r 63(6).
[2] Under the Mental Health (Care and Treatment) Scotland Act 2003, s 318.

Recording of proceedings

23.33 The tribunal may give directions restricting the reporting and recording of the hearing.[1] It does not have statutory powers to record proceedings, but has general powers to make directions as to the conduct of the proceedings.[2]

The tribunal service intends to make tape recordings of the proceedings. The intention was originally to ensure that a transcript would be available in case of appeal, and the tribunal advised the parties of this at the time of the hearing. In an early case under the Mental Health (Care and Treatment) Act, the tribunal opposed handing over a transcript, on the grounds of cost. The sheriff principal upheld this refusal.[3] The sheriff recommended that the tribunal make it clear from the outset that transcripts of the proceedings are not necessarily available for appeal purposes.

[1] Tribunal rules, r 49(1)(f).
[2] Tribunal rules, r 49(1).
[3] *AG against a decision of the Mental Health Tribunal dated 18 November 2005,* Sheriff Principal Bowen (11 January 2006).

Appointment of experts

23.34 The tribunal can appoint experts to advise it in certain circumstances.[1] See para 22.13 for 'men of skill'.

[1] See, for example, r 55(3).

Adjournment

23.35 The tribunal may adjourn the hearing to allow a relevant person to obtain further information or evidence.[1] The tribunal may set time limits for the production of such evidence.

Failure to adjourn proceedings to enable someone to instruct his or her lawyer could be in breach of the person's human rights.[2] In an early appeal under the Mental Health (Care and Treatment) Act, the sheriff principal overturned a compulsory treatment order made where the tribunal refused to allow an adjournment to allow the person time to brief her lawyer.[3]

The English courts have said that, while a tribunal can adjourn in order to obtain further information about a restricted patient's state of health, it cannot adjourn to allow a responsible medical officer to monitor the person's mental state. It is not appropriate for a tribunal to adjourn for a 'trial period' to decide whether a discharge should be absolute or conditional.[4]

Nor is it appropriate for a tribunal to adjourn if the sole purpose is to help it decide whether to recommend a patient's transfer to a less secure hospital. It can adjourn to obtain further information or for such other purposes as it thinks appropriate.[5]

[1]   Tribunal rules, r 65.

[2]   See *Re CB (A Child)* [2004] EWCA Civ 1517 where this was held to breach the claimant's Art 6(1) rights in childcare proceedings.

[3]   *EB v Mental Health Tribunal for Scotland*, Glasgow Sheriff Court B2606/05.

[4]   *R v Nottingham Mental Health Review Tribunal ex parte Secretary of State for the Home Department* [1989] COD 165–248.

[5]   *R v Mental Health Review Tribunal for NE Thames Region ex parte Secretary of State for the Home Department* (2002) 63 BMLR 181.

Absence of member of panel

23.36 All three members of the panel should be present throughout the hearing. If a member is absent the tribunal should adjourn the hearing.[1] If a member is absent after the hearing has commenced, the hearing can continue in his or her absence only if all the parties agree.[2]

No party should feel under any pressure to agree. The balanced make up of the tribunal ensures that the tribunal can properly consider all aspects of the case.

[1]   Tribunal rules, r 64(1).

[2]   Tribunal rules, r 64(3).

Late evidence

23.37 While each party should give as much notice as possible of the matters on which they wish to rely at the hearing, inevitably the person's health may change or new matters may arise between the date of the application and the date of the hearing.

The tribunal can allow someone to raise new matters or to bring in new evidence if it is satisfied that this would be just and reasonable.[1]

[1]   Tribunal rules, r 63(4).

Transfer of case

23.38 The President may transfer a case to a hearing in another area if this appears appropriate.[1]

1   Tribunal rules, r 79.

DECISION OF TRIBUNAL

Reaching decision

23.39 In general, the statute requires that in reaching its decision the tribunal is 'satisfied' as to the matters set out in the application or appeal. The test is the civil test of the balance of probabilities, not the criminal law test of beyond reasonable doubt.

All members of the tribunal should take part in the decision-making process. If this is not possible, the tribunal should adjourn or refer the case to another tribunal, unless the parties have agreed that the case should continue in the absence of one of the panel members.[1]

The tribunal can take a majority decision and the Convener has a casting vote.[2] This is necessary only if one of the panel members is absent.

1   See above.
2   Mental Health (Care and Treatment) (Scotland) Act 2003, Sched 2, para 13.

Announcing decision

23.40 The tribunal may announce its decision at the end of the hearing or at a later stage.[1] In the majority of cases the tribunal gives an oral decision soon after the hearing.

The tribunal must notify the parties of the decision as soon as possible and may notify certain other relevant persons.[2] The tribunal must also give information about any appeal rights and of the relevant time limits.[3]

As well as any written order it makes, the tribunal must produce a written document setting out the full facts found by the tribunal and the reasons for its decision.[4] It sends a copy to the parties as soon as possible after completion.[5]

The tribunal service also sends a copy of its decision to the Mental Welfare Commission.[6]

1   Tribunal rules, r 72(1).
2   Tribunal rules, r 72(3).
3   Tribunal rules, r 72(4).
4   Mental Health (Care and Treatment) (Scotland) Act 2003, Sched 2, para 13(3) and tribunal rules, r 72(7).
5   MH(CT)(S)A 2003, (as amended by the Mental Health (Care and Treatment) (Scotland) Act 2003 (Modification of Enactments) Order 2005 (SSI 2005/465)), Sched 2 para 13(4).
6   Tribunal rules, r 72(5).

Publication of decision

23.41 The tribunal can publish its decisions, but in anonymised form.[1] The tribunal may edit the decisions as necessary to protect the privacy of the parties.

1   Tribunal rules, r 73.

LEGAL CHALLENGES

Appeal to sheriff principal

23.42 The patient, his or her named person, or any welfare guardian or attorney may appeal against the granting of an order or the refusal of an application to cancel an order.[1] The mental health officer and responsible medical officer may appeal against the tribunal's refusal to make an order or its cancellation of an order or certificate.

A person can appeal only if he or she alleges the tribunal has made a legal mistake or that there were irregularities in the hearing. This would include a claim that the tribunal acted unreasonably in the exercise of its discretion or that its decision could not be justified on the facts established at the tribunal.[2]

The appeal is to the sheriff principal, a senior sheriff. This is the sheriff principal of the area where the person lives when he or she lodges the appeal, or, if the person is detained in hospital, the sheriff principal of the area of the hospital.[3] The appeal must be submitted within 21 days of the tribunal's determination.[4]

The tribunal may be a party to the appeal,[5] and the sheriff principal may require the tribunal to have legal representation at the appeal.[6] In an early case, the sheriff principal said that he regarded it as unusual for a tribunal whose decision is the subject of an appeal to be a party to the appeal. This should not be the norm.[7]

1   Mental Health (Care and Treatment) (Scotland) Act 2003, s 320(5).
2   MH(CT)(S)A 2003, s 324(2).
3   MH(CT)(S)A 2003, s 320(3).
4   Act of Sederunt (Summary Applications, Statutory Applications and Appeals etc. Tribunal rules, rules) 1999 (as amended by the Mental Health (Care and Treatment) (Scotland) Act 2003 (Modification of Subordinate Legislation) Order 2005 (SSI 2005/445)), para 2.6.
5   MH(CT)(S)A 2003, s 324(3).
6   MH(CT)(S)A 2003, s 324(4).
7   *Appeal by AG against a decision of the Mental Health Tribunal dated 18 November 2005,* Sheriff Principal Bowen, (11 January 2006).

Effect of appeal

23.43 If the sheriff principal allows the appeal, he or she will set aside the decision of the tribunal and either substitute his or her own decision (if this is possible on the facts established by the tribunal) or send the case back to the tribunal for reconsideration.[1]

If the sheriff principal sends the case back to the tribunal, he or she may require the tribunal to be comprised of different panel members from those when it made the decision or issue directions to the tribunal about how it should consider the case.[2]

1   Mental Health (Care and Treatment) (Scotland) Act 2003, s 324(5).
2   MH(CT)(S)A 2003, s 324(6).

Appeal to Court of Session

23.44 If the sheriff principal considers the appeal raises an important or difficult point of law he or she may pass the appeal on to the Court of Session, at his or her own instance or if any party to the appeal requests this.[1]

A party may appeal a decision of the sheriff principal to the Court of Session.[2] The Court of Session has similar powers to those of the sheriff principal. The appeal must be on a point of law.

The appeal must be within 21 days of the date on which the party received the decision from the sheriff principal. If the sheriff principal issued written reasons for the decision later than the date on which the decision being appealed was given, the time is 21 days from the date on which the party received the written reasons. If the sheriff principal granted leave to appeal, the time is 21 days from the date on which the sheriff principal granted leave to appeal.[3]

1   Mental Health (Care and Treatment) (Scotland) Act 2003, s 320(4).
2   MH(CT)(S)A 2003, s 321.
3   Rules of Court of Session, r 40.4.

PART 5
ADULTS WITH INCAPACITY

Chapter 24

ADULTS WITH INCAPACITY ACT

24.01 A person may be unable, because of mental disorder, to take certain decisions, such as where to live or whether to agree to medical treatment. The person may be unable to manage aspects of his or her finances or property. The Adults with Incapacity Act provides a hierarchy of measures for decision-making where someone is unable to do this him or herself.[1] Separate measures deal with welfare, medical and financial decisions.

The Adults with Incapacity Act aims to ensure that solutions concentrate on the needs of the individual. A person may be unable to manage his or her money, but clearly able to demonstrate where he or she wishes to live. He or she may be able to take simple medical decisions but not weigh up the options for complex medical treatment. The Act gives powers to take only those decisions the person is unable to manage him or herself.

There are different procedures for different types of decision-making. This book deals with medical decisions in chapter 8. Chapters 25 and 26 deal with welfare and financial decisions. This chapter covers some general matters, common to all procedures.

This chapter deals solely with people over the age of 16 who are unable to take some or all decisions about their lives and/or property. The law is different for children and young people. A parent (or person with parental authority) usually has authority to act if the child or young person cannot. See chapter 41.

The Adults with Incapacity Act describes a person unable to take a certain decision as an 'adult'. This part of the book does the same.

---

[1]   For background, see chapter 2.

PRINCIPLES OF ACT

24.02 The principles in the Adults with Incapacity Act express the ethical basis for intervening in the life of someone unable to take his or her own decisions. The principles represent agreed good practice and appear generally well accepted.[1] Research indicates a need to extend understanding of the principles to people providing continuing care and support for adults.[2]

As with the Mental Health (Care and Treatment) Act, the principles influence the structure of the Act, with its hierarchy of measures, involvement of the adult and significant others at all stages, and its emphasis on tailor-made solutions. The principles are more than pious platitude. They are clearer and more strongly worded than the corresponding principles in the Mental Health (Care and Treatment) Act. Anyone taking action under the Act has a clear legal duty to implement the principles.[3]

This applies both to interventions and to decisions not to intervene.[4] For example, having weighed up the options and consulted with the relevant people, a doctor might decide that burdensome medical treatment would not benefit someone who is unconscious and has a terminal illness. A social worker might decide that it is better for a person to remain in his or her home, perhaps with some extra care, despite some risk to the person from poor self-care. The doctor or social worker should make his or her decision by weighing up the various issues according to the principles of the Act.

Application of the principles may lead to contradictory results. A person may resist certain care measures in his or her home, but the sheriff may decide these measures will benefit the person and are less restrictive than the only other alternative, a move to residential care. Adrian Ward has helpfully suggested that reference to the principles can often help resolve difficulties in interpreting the Adults with Incapacity Act.[5]

Applying the principles will necessarily lead to a weighing up of the options in the light of individual circumstances. This highlights one of the central themes of the Adults with Incapacity Act. All action should stem from the needs of the adult.

---

[1]   See Jan Killen, Fiona Myers and Others, *The Adults with Incapacity (Scotland) Act 2000: Learning from Experience* (Scottish Executive, October 2004), para 3.73.

[2]   *Learning from experience*, (above) paras 3.74 and 6.4.

[3]   Adults with Incapacity (Scotland) Act 2000, s 1(1).

[4]   See Ward, *Adult incapacity* (W Green, 2003), para 4.3.

[5]   *Adult incapacity* (W Green, 2003), para 4.2.

Benefit

24.03 The first, and central, principle is that no one should take action ('intervene') under the Adults with Incapacity Act unless he or she is satisfied that the action will benefit the adult. The person must also be satisfied that this action is the only reasonable way of achieving the benefit. If, for example, someone could remain in his or her own home with extra help, a court should not grant an order moving him or her to residential care. Intervention under the Adults with Incapacity Act is not the only reasonable way of achieving the benefit.

This does not mean that an intervention under the Act can never be a benefit in itself. If there are too many informal controls over someone's life, it may be in his or her interests to have these on a formal footing and subject to monitoring by the appropriate bodies.[1]

---

1   See *Report on Incapable Adults*, Scottish Law Commission, para 2.53 and Hilary Patrick, 'When is guardianship appropriate?' in *Authorising significant interventions for adults who lack capacity* (Mental Welfare Commission, 2004), p 26, para 2.

What is benefit?

24.04 The Act uses the test of 'benefit' rather than 'best interests'. The difference is probably not significant in practice.[1] The Scottish Law Commission originally recommended that the test should be best interests.[2] It later changed the test to benefit, following criticism that a best interests test was too paternalistic in the context of adult welfare.[3] It believed that 'best interests' did not give enough emphasis to the wishes and feelings of the adult.

Academics discuss whether benefit/best interests is an objective test or should be the decision the person would have made if able to. The Adults with Incapacity Act takes a more pragmatic approach. Benefit is not simply what might be in an adult's best interests, but must take into account the other principles of the Act. A person intervening should consider the adult's wishes and feelings, past and present, (if it is possible to establish these). He or she should consider the views of carers and significant others, attempt to encourage the adult to use the skills he or she has and ensure that the intervention is the least restrictive option.

Taken together, the principles mean that a decision on behalf of an adult takes account of more than just what is 'best' for him or her. This approach reflects good practice and reflects current concerns about human dignity and autonomy.

People working with the Adults with Incapacity Act have had some difficulty in defining and assessing benefit in individual cases.[4] Assessing benefit in the light of all the principles may help. It is interesting to note that this is the approach used in the Mental Capacity Act.[5]

1   See JK Mason and GT Laurie, *Law and Medical Ethics* (6th edn, Oxford University Press, 2005), para 12.26.
2   *Mentally disabled adults: Legal arrangements for managing their welfare and finances* (Scottish Law Commission Discussion Paper 94, 1991), proposal 38.
3   *Report on incapable adults*, para 2.50.
4   *Learning from Experience* (above) para 5.131.
5   Mental Capacity Act 2005, s 4.

Least restrictive option

24.05 The second principle is that any action taken should be the minimum necessary to achieve the purpose.[1] A person intervening must be able to justify his or her action in accordance with this principle. If a carer can access a bank account, financial guardianship is not appropriate. If an adult has appointed a welfare attorney with power to approve treatment, it should not generally be necessary to ask the Court of Session to approve the treatment.

Other measures outside the scope of the Act may remove the need for intervention under the Adults with Incapacity Act. A Department of Work and Pensions appointee may manage state benefits. If that is the only source of income, Adults with Incapacity Act procedures are not necessary. A social work department may arrange an adult's move to residential care using its powers under the Social Work (Scotland) Act 1968. There may be no need for welfare guardianship.

This very important principle is subject to the other principles of the Act. If an adult objects to a Department of Work and Pensions appointee or is not happy with the informal care he or she receives, intervention under the Act may be necessary.

There remains concern about the operation of the least restrictive option principle. Scottish Executive research highlights cases where guardians appear to have applied for powers in excess of what the evidence suggested was necessary.[2] There is also a growing number of guardianships granted for indefinite periods.[3]

To avoid excessive legal costs, someone applying for guardianship must anticipate those powers reasonably likely to be necessary in the near future.[4] The court has to weigh up whether it is appropriate to grant such powers in the light of the principle of minimum necessary intervention. An order of indefinite duration requires similar justification.

[1]   Adults with Incapacity (Scotland) Act 2000, s 1(3).

[2]   *Learning from Experience* (above), paras 3.74 and 6.30.

[3]   One third of welfare guardianships in 2004–5. Mental Welfare Commission Annual Report 2004–5, p 60.

[4]   Scottish Law Commission, *Report on incapable adults*, para 2.55.

Ascertaining adult's views

24.06 The third principle is that anyone determining whether to intervene, and if so, how, should consider the present and past wishes and feelings of the adult.

A prospective intervener should use all reasonable means to find out the adult's views and feelings.[1] This may involve the use of communication or interpretation facilities, including the use of advocacy. A person intervening should enquire whether the adult has expressed a view on the matter or made a living will. It may be necessary to ask carers and/or relatives.[2]

It may be that, having attempted to establish an adult's views and feelings, those involved may consider the adult is able to take the decision. The Adults with Incapacity Act is no longer relevant. If using interpretation facilities, non-verbal communication and advocacy can enable someone to take his or her own decisions, this is clearly in line with the principles of the Act.

Research shows professionals are generally familiar with this principle and operate it well. The principle works well when a significant intervention, such as guardianship, is being considered, but perhaps less well on a day-to-day basis.[3]

[1]   Adults with Incapacity (Scotland) Act 2000, s 1(4).

[2]   See, for example Part 5 Code of Practice, para 2.28.

[3]   *Learning from experience*, paras 5.134 and 6.4.

Views of significant others

24.07 The principles require everyone intervening under the Adults with Incapacity Act to consider the views of the adult's nearest relative, named person and primary carer, if this is reasonable and practicable.[1]

The nearest relative is as defined in the Mental Health (Care and Treatment) Act.[2] See 4.06. An adult can apply for the removal of the nearest relative. See 24.28. The list now includes the named person appointed under the Mental Health (Care and Treatment) Act.[3] See chapter 4. This could be useful if someone has a specific person he or she wants to be involved.

Other people should also be consulted. These include any guardian or attorney of the adult. The sheriff should consider the views of anyone else who has contacted him or her who appears to have an interest in the adult's affairs. The sheriff may require an intervener to consult other people.

While the obligation to consider the adult's views is an absolute one, (if the person intervening can find these out), the duty to consult other people is limited to what is reasonable and practicable in the circumstances.

The Codes of Practice give further guidance.[4] What is reasonable and practicable depends on the circumstances. If there is an emergency and one of the people on the list is away, for example, it would not be reasonable to wait for his or her views before acting.

1 Adults with Incapacity (Scotland) Act 2000, s 1(4).
2 AWI(S)A 2000 (as amended by the Mental Health (Care and Treatment) (Scotland) Act 2003, Sched 4), s 87(1).
3 AWI(S)A 2000, (as amended by the Mental Health (Care and Treatment) (Scotland) Act 2003 (Modification of Enactments) Order 2005 (SSI 2005/465)), s 1(4).
4 See for example Part 6 Code for guardians and people authorised under intervention orders, para 5.23. Part 5 Code, para 2.30.

Participation

24.08 The Adults with Incapacity Act requires a guardian, continuing attorney, welfare attorney or manager of an establishment to encourage the adult to exercise whatever skills he or she has and to develop new skills, as far as this is reasonable and practicable.[1]

Research indicates less awareness of this principle. The researchers heard concerns about the lack of opportunity for some adults to develop their skills, either because of a lack of resources within a particular environment and/or because of lack of sufficient support.[2]

This is largely a question of education and resources. It is important that the Scottish Executive makes available good practice guidance for people carrying out Adults with Incapacity Act functions.

[1]   Adults with Incapacity (Scotland) Act 2000, s 1(5).

[2]   *Learning from Experience*, (above) para 5.139.

Impact of principles

24.09 Everyone intervening under the Adults with Incapacity Act must be able to justify his or her action in accordance with the principles. The principles apply at three stages, when someone is considering whether to take action under the Act, when he or she considers how to act and the way in which an intervener acts when carrying out his or her day-to-day functions.

A local authority social worker should consider whether it is necessary to apply for an order or whether to put in measures to help the adult stay in his or her home. A sheriff considering an order must consider whether he or she could make a less restrictive order and whether all the powers requested are necessary.

An attorney acting under a welfare power of attorney should consider how far he or she could encourage the adult to take his or her own decisions over certain matters. A guardian authorised to decide where the adult should live should bear in mind not just the adult's present feelings but any views the adult has expressed in the past. The Office of the Public Guardian uses the principles as a fundamental guide in all its dealings.

Principles and indemnity

24.10 The Adults with Incapacity Act appreciates that carrying out the duties of an attorney or guardian is onerous. Compliance with the principles is a defence to criticisms of the person's action. It is not possible to allege breach of duty of care if someone acting under the Adults with Incapacity Act can show he or she has acted or failed to act reasonably, in good faith and in accordance with the principles.[1]

The indemnity is available to financial and welfare guardians, welfare and continuing attorneys, people acting under intervention orders, people given authority to withdraw money from an adult's bank account and managers of establishments dealing with residents' finances.

1   Adults with Incapacity (Scotland) Act 2000, s 82(1).

INCAPACITY

24.11 A person is incapable for the purposes of the Adults with Incapacity Act if he or she is unable to take a relevant decision because of mental disorder (or cannot communicate because of physical disability.[1] This could apply to someone who is unconscious following an accident or a stroke as well as to someone with communication difficulties).[2]

'Mental disorder' means mental illness, learning disability or personality disorder, with the exclusions set out in the Mental Health (Care and Treatment) Act.[3] See 11.13.

A person who can communicate with help, such as through interpretation services and technological aids should not be regarded as unable to communicate.

1   Adults with Incapacity (Scotland) Act 2000, s 1(6).
2   See, for example, *Fraser v Patterson*, 1987 SLT 562.
3   AWI(S)A 2000, (as amended by Mental Health (Care and Treatment) (Scotland) Act 2003, Sched 4, para 9(5)), s 87(1).

ASSESSING INCAPACITY

24.12 The Adults with Incapacity Act does not explain how to assess capacity, but says that the person is incapable of taking a decision if he or she cannot act, make a decision, communicate a decision, understand a decision or remember a decision made because of mental disorder.[1]

Any one of these elements may be critical, depending on the nature of the decision in question.

Whether someone has capacity to take a particular decision is a legal question, although often doctors or social workers will make an assessment or provide reports to the court.

Adrian Ward gives a useful checklist of relevant factors, such as understanding the nature of the decision, the available choices, etc.[2] The Scottish Executive is compiling a list of resource materials on assessing capacity,[3] following concerns from doctors, particularly general practitioners, that they need extra training.[4] It intends to produce further guidelines on communication and assessment of capacity to supplement the information provided in the Codes of Practice.[5]

The English Law Society and the British Medical Association have prepared very useful guidance, but this relates to English law.[6] The Scottish section of the British Medical Association and Scottish Law Society held a seminar on the same issue in 1997. The papers from that seminar may have some useful information for practitioners.

[1] Adults with Incapacity (Scotland) Act 2000, s 1(6).
[2] Adrian Ward, *Adult incapacity* (W Green, 2003), para 1.30.
[3] See helpful guidelines produced by Highland Council and Highland Health Board (January 2006).
[4] See Shirley Davidson, Heather Wilkinson and others *Review of the implementation of Part 5 of the Adults with Incapacity (Scotland) Act 2000: A qualitative study of implementation and early operation* (Scottish Executive, 2004).
[5] At the date of writing, NHS Education Scotland is developing accredited training for certain other health care professionals, and this will be open to medical practitioners.
[6] *Assessment of mental capacity: guidance for doctors and lawyers* (2nd edn, British Medical Association, 2004).

Status not test

24.13 Use of the Adults with Incapacity Act is not dependent on a person's status. No one should make assumptions of incapacity.[1] Adults with Incapacity Act procedures may be appropriate for people living at home, in hospital or in residential care. Some people who are subject to compulsory orders under the Mental Health (Care and Treatment) Act may fall within the Adults with Incapacity Act, as may some informal patients in hospital and some people receiving care from a general practitioner or in a nursing home.

The test is whether there is a decision the person is unable to take, a need to take the decision and the Act's principles require an intervention under the Adults with Incapacity Act.

[1] See, for example, Part 5 Code of Practice, para 2.41.

Capacity linked to tasks

24.14 There is no all-purpose test of incapacity. The test depends on the decision to be taken. A person may be able to decide about medical treatment but not manage his or her finances. A person may be able to organise day-to-day spending but not deal with investments.

The capacity test for guardianship, for example, is different from whether someone can appoint an attorney or consent to medical treatment. A guardian may be appointed if an adult is unable to act, or unable to protect his or her own interests, (if guardianship is necessary to safeguard the person).[1] The court may make an order even when someone is quite clearly able to state his or her own views, if it decides the person is unable to manage his or her own affairs or to protect him or herself from risk.

On the other hand a person can sign a power of attorney provided he or she understands the nature of the transaction. The person may no longer be able to manage his or her own affairs by this stage. See chapter 25.

Chapter 7 deals with capacity to take medical decisions. The test is whether the person can comprehend, believe and retain the necessary information and can weigh up and balance the risks and needs to make a true choice.[2] The higher the level of risk, the greater degree of competence required.[3]

The principles of least restrictive alternative and maximising the person's capacity underline the importance of not making blanket assessments of incapacity and recognising any residual capacity an adult has.

[1]   Adults with Incapacity (Scotland) Act 2000, s 58(1).
[2]   *Re C (patient: refusal of medical treatment)* [1994] 1 All ER 819 (Fam Div).
[3]   *Re T (patient: refusal of medical treatment)* (1992) 9 BMLR 46.

Standards of capacity

24.15 The test of capacity is linked to the task to be done. It is more difficult to manage a complex financial portfolio than to decide about spending weekly welfare benefit money. The test should not be set so high as to exclude people from making decisions they can properly make.

For example, when a person with a learning disability moves out of hospital as part of a closure programme, the person may visit the house in the community and know and accept the staff. Provided those involved in planning the move are satisfied that the move will benefit the person and there is no other reason to apply for a guardianship order, it is surely in accordance with the principles of the Adults with Incapacity Act that, if the person can assent to a process, this assent should be recognised. A Part 6 order would not be appropriate. (This does not mean that it would be appropriate to presume capacity and assent in such a situation. There must be proper efforts to establish the person's wishes and feelings. Failure to be satisfied that the person truly assents deprives the person of appropriate protections under the Adults with Incapacity Act.)

The Mental Capacity Act for England and Wales says a person is not unable to take a medical decision if he or she can understand a broad explanation in simple terms or if he or she could understand with the use of proper communication methods.[1] Such an approach is clearly in accordance with the principles of the Adults with Incapacity Act. Setting too high a test of capacity undermines the autonomy of the person.

Adrian Ward has suggested that good practice involves balancing the principles of empowerment and respect against those of protecting vulnerable people.[2] While the Act should not set too high a standard of capacity for routine decisions, it may require a higher standard for decisions which could pose significant risk, such as rejecting medical advice, or where the financial or other implications may otherwise be serious, such as changing a will, making a gift or otherwise doing something to one's prejudice.

[1]   Mental Capacity Act 2005, s 3.
[2]   *Adult Incapacity* (W Green, 2003), para 1.31.

MAXIMISING CAPACITY

24.16 There is guidance on how to maximise a person's ability to participate in the decision making process.[1] The way in which information is given and the setting in which it is given may mean that a person is able to take his or her own healthcare decisions, or at least some of them.

A person should not be treated as unable to take a decision because of failures in the communication skills of people working with him or her. Improved use of communication skills can help establish the person's wishes and feelings.[2]

Some local authorities have improved the use of non-verbal communication (such as demeanour, body language and the use of pictorial aides) to establish an adult's wishes and feelings. Scotland is pioneering good practice. For example, the City of Edinburgh Council has published guidance for its staff on assessing capacity.[3] The guidance emphasises the need to overcome barriers to communication.

The use of an independent advocacy service may help a person make an informed decision about treatment. Even if someone is unable to take medical decisions, the use of advocacy can be helpful. The advocacy worker can make sure that the person's wishes and feelings are heard and taken into account in the decision-making process.

1   See British Medical Association guidance, (above). Part 5 Code of Practice, above and guidance from Highland Health Board and Highland Council, (above).
2   See, for example K Allan, *Communication and consultation: exploring ways for staff to involve people with dementia in developing services* (Bristol: The Policy Press, 2001) and Heather Wilkinson (ed.), *The perspectives of people with dementia: research methods and motivations*, (Jessica Kingsley, 2002).
3   Published summer 2005.

SUPERVISORY BODIES

24.17 A number of bodies have a role in under the Adults with Incapacity Act. For more detail, see chapter 3.

The Public Guardian registers all documents and is responsible for supervising and monitoring the operation of the financial powers.[1] The Public Guardian supervises financial guardians and people authorised under financial intervention orders. She investigates financial concerns and gives advice to people with financial authority under the Adults with Incapacity Act.

The Mental Welfare Commission monitors the operation of the welfare powers.[2] The Mental Welfare Commission can investigate complaints. The Commission should bring to the attention of relevant bodies the welfare of anyone for whom it has concerns. It offers information and advice to welfare attorneys, people acting under welfare intervention orders and welfare guardians.

Local authorities can investigate if someone is at risk. The local authority supervises welfare guardians. Its chief social work officer may be appointed welfare guardian. The local authority is the primary body charged with investigating complaints about welfare guardians, welfare attorneys or people acting under welfare intervention orders. The authority should provide these people with advice and information to help them promote the adult's welfare.[3]

The courts have the final supervisory role. The Court of Session deals with disputes over medical treatment. The sheriff courts deal with a wide range of matters, including appeals against a finding of incapacity, concerns about attorneys, guardians or people acting under intervention orders and appeals against decisions of the Public Guardian. More details are in the relevant sections of this book.

¹   Adults with Incapacity (Scotland) Act 2000, s 6.

²   AWI(S)A 2000, s 9.

³   AWI(S)A 2000, s 10.

THE SHERIFF COURT

24.18 The sheriff court hears applications for guardianship or intervention orders and has a supervisory role in connection with powers of attorney and other matters under the Act. More details are in the relevant sections of this book.

Powers of sheriff

24.19 The sheriff can make any order or direction he or she considers necessary when considering an application or hearing other proceedings under the Adults with Incapacity Act.¹ He or she may call for reports, require a further assessment or interview of the adult, make further inquiries or ask for extra information. The sheriff may impose conditions or restrictions on any order and may make interim orders if necessary.²

The adult and anyone authorised under an order or entitled to apply for an order may ask the sheriff to vary an order.³

In exercising his or her powers, the sheriff must comply with the principles of the Adults with Incapacity Act.

¹   Adults with Incapacity (Scotland) Act 2000, s 3(1).

²   AWI(S)A 2000, s 3(2).

³   AWI(S)A 2000, s 3(6).

Directions from sheriff

24.20 Anyone with an interest in the property, financial affairs or personal welfare of an adult (including the adult him or herself and anyone with authority under the Act) may ask the sheriff to give directions to a person carrying out functions under the Adults with Incapacity Act.

The sheriff may tell the person how to exercise his or her powers under the Act, or require the person to make a decision or take some action.[1]

¹   Adults with Incapacity (Scotland) Act 2000, s 3(3).

Legal aid and solicitors

24.21 A private individual applying for financial or welfare guardianship must generally bear the legal costs of the application, but can recover the costs from the adult's estate if the court so orders. A local authority applying for its chief social work officer to be guardian must meet the cost.[1]

The court can require the adult or any other person to pay the legal expenses of other hearings involving a local authority, the Mental Welfare Commission or Public Guardian.[2] An example would be where the Public Guardian seeks an order for the supervision of an attorney. The court might order the attorney to pay the court expenses.

The local authority must pay for any subsequent applications to the court while the chief social worker is acting as guardian, unless these relate to financial or property matters, in which case the adult's estate will bear the cost. If a subsequent application relates to welfare and financial or property matters, the sheriff decides what proportion the adult's estate should bear.

Most people use solicitors for applications for guardianship or intervention orders, but this is not always necessary. The applicant can represent him or herself or use a worker from an independent advocacy service.[3] The sheriff clerk at the sheriff court can assist and the Office of the Public Guardian will give advice. Anyone wishing to oppose an application for guardianship or an intervention order should employ a solicitor.

Legal aid is available for most proceedings under the Adults with Incapacity Act. The amount of financial assistance depends on the resources of the adult, not the resources of the person bringing or defending the action.[4]

The Scottish Executive has made a commitment to provide free legal aid for welfare guardianship proceedings.[5] On 9 June 2006, it laid new Civil Legal Aid and Advice Regulations before the Scottish Parliament.[6] These regulations should come in force on 1 August 2006 and will give entitlement to free legal aid, regardless of the adult's means, for welfare guardianship and for joint financial and welfare guardianship applications.

1   Adults with Incapacity (Scotland) Act 2000, s 68(3).
2   AWI(S)A 2000, s 8.
3   Act of Sederunt (Summary Cause Rules) 2002 (SSI 2002/132), r 2.1.
4   Civil Legal Aid (Scotland) Amendment Regulations 2001 (SSI 2001/82), Civil Legal Aid (Scotland) Amendment Regulations 2002 (SSI 2002/88), Advice and Assistance (Scotland) (Amendment No 3) Regulations 2005 (SSI 2005/339).
5   Letter from Deputy Minister for Justice to Convener of Scottish Parliament Justice 2 Committee, 28 October 2004.
6   The Civil Legal Aid (Scotland) Amendment (No. 2) Regulations 2006 (SSI 2006/325).

Curators and safeguarders

24.22 If an adult is unable to instruct a solicitor, the court may appoint a curator *ad litem*. A curator *ad litem* is usually a solicitor with experience in mental health law issues. The curator interviews all the relevant people and reports to the court. He or she considers whether there is a legal case for the order and reports on the welfare or financial issues under consideration.

A curator *ad litem* can be in addition to, or instead of a safeguarder, according to the needs of the adult.

Whenever a sheriff considers a case under the Adults with Incapacity Act, he or she should consider whether it is necessary to appoint a safeguarder for the adult.[1] The safeguarder's role is to represent the interests of the adult. This includes advising the sheriff of the adult's views so far it is possible to ascertain them.

If the sheriff does not think it appropriate for one safeguarder to act both to protect the adult's interests and to advise the sheriff of the adult's views, he or she may appoint a second safeguarder to give him or her information about the adult's views.[2]

Research about the use of curators *ad litem* and safeguarders shows that practice varies. Some sheriffs appoint curators *ad litem* and others safeguarders.[3] The Scottish Law Commission recommended sheriffs should have flexibility to appoint according to the circumstances.[4]

1   Adults with Incapacity (Scotland) Act 2000, s 3(4).
2   AWI(S)A 2000, s 3(5).

3   *Learning from Experience* (above), para 5.86.

4   *Report on incapable adults*, para 2.36.

Payment of safeguarders/curators

24.23 There have been problems in remuneration of safeguarders and curators and difficulties in obtaining payment from the Scottish Legal Aid Board.[1]

The Scottish Legal Aid Board agree to pay a curator or safeguarder if it is satisfied that the curator's task is essentially to represent the interests of the adult and can be seen as providing legal services to the adult within the meaning of the legal aid regulations. A statutory scheme to authorise payment of curators' fees would resolve this matter.[2]

1   See comments of sheriff in *Muldoon*, Glasgow Sheriff Court AW 37/04.

2   An article by Helen McGinty in the Mental Health Officers' Newsletter (2 February, 2003), p 10 suggests that this problem is now resolved, but the Scottish Legal Aid Board advise the author that it remains unresolved.

Attending sheriff court

24.24 A person subject to proceedings generally receives notice of the proceedings and is entitled to attend the court hearing. If the adult is unable to attend court, the sheriff may appoint a safeguarder to find out the adult's views.

It may very occasionally be inappropriate to give an adult notice of the proceedings or to notify him or her about any decisions of the court. The court can dispense with notice if satisfied that this would be likely to pose a serious risk to the health of the adult.[1]

The court must see two medical certificates stating that giving notice would be likely to pose a serious risk to the adult's health.[2] The doctors giving the certificates must be independent of each other. If the reports allege incapacity because of mental disorder, one of the doctors must be an approved medical practitioner. The medical reports must give sufficient information to enable the court to reach a decision. A mere statement that notice is likely to threaten the adult's health is unlikely to satisfy the court, if the doctor does not explain his or her reasoning.[3]

A decision not to give notice must be in accordance with the principles of the Act and with human rights law. This would happen only in exceptional circumstances.[4] Excluding someone from the hearing or failing to give someone the chance to appoint a solicitor is on the face of it a breach of the person's right to a fair trial under Article 6(1) of the European Convention on Human Rights.

1   Adults with Incapacity (Scotland) Act 2000, s 11, and Act of Sederunt (Summary Applications, Statutory Applications and Appeals etc Rules) 1999 (SI 1999/929) (as amended) r 3.16.4(1)(a).
2   Act of Sederunt, above, r 3.16.5.
3   See comments of the sheriff in *Application in respect of Mrs L C*, Glasgow Sheriff Court AW 38/05.
4   See Ward, *Adult Incapacity* (W Green, 2003), para 5.9.

Human rights

24.25 Everyone facing proceedings about his or her civil rights and obligations is entitled to a fair hearing.[1] This generally means that the person should have the right to attend the hearing in person, have his or her say and question witnesses.

Special procedural guarantees are necessary when someone is vulnerable.[2] A legally qualified person should be present to protect the adult's interests. Guardianship orders can contain powers which severely restrict someone's civil liberties.[3] A curator *ad litem* or safeguarder will usually be necessary if someone is unable to instruct a solicitor.

1   European Convention on Human Rights, Art 6(1).
2   *Winterwerp v The Netherlands* [1979] ECHR 4, para 60.
3   See *McVicar v UK* [2002] ECtHR 436, *Airey v Ireland* [1979] (2 EHRR 305), *P v UK* (2002) 35 EHRR 31 where failure to provide legal representation deprived the person of a fair hearing.

Court hearings

24.26 There has been concern that sometimes applications for guardianship are heard in open court. This can mean that personal information about a person's family circumstances or health can become public knowledge.[1] The Mental Welfare Commission points out that, while there is nothing in the Adults with Incapacity Act to prevent a hearing being held in open court, hearings under the 1984 Act were always held in closed court. It hopes this practice will continue under the Adults with Incapacity Act.

Anyone concerned that a hearing is to be in open court can formally request the sheriff to hear the case in private.

Tribunal hearings under the Mental Health (Care and Treatment) Act are always held in private. While human law is generally in favour of public hearings, it recognises that mental health cases are an exceptional case, because they raise matters of sensitive personal information. See 23.30.

There are also concerns about the reporting of Adults with Incapacity cases on the Scottish Courts' website. See 23.30.

[1] See Annual Report of Mental Welfare Commission 2002–3, para 3.3.

APPEALS

Against finding of incapacity

24.27 Anyone found incapable for the purposes of the Adults with Incapacity Act may appeal to the sheriff against the finding. The adult him or herself or anyone with an interest in the subject matter of the decision may make the appeal.[1]

A person can also appeal to the sheriff principal against a sheriff's decision about incapacity. There is a further appeal, with permission of the court, to the Court of Session.

[1] Adults with Incapacity (Scotland) Act 2000, s 14.

Changing nearest relative

24.28 A person wishing to remove a nearest relative, or restrict his or her involvement, can apply to the sheriff court for an order.

The court can order that the nearest relative should not receive information, including notice of certain applications under the Adults with Incapacity Act. The sheriff may appoint someone else as nearest relative, provided the person is entitled to act, willing and suitable. Alternatively the court may order that, for a certain period, the adult shall not have anyone acting as nearest relative.[1] In reaching its decision, the court must consider the principles of the Act and satisfy itself that its order will benefit the adult.[2] Any nearest relative who is also primary carer will remain involved in that capacity.[3]

The court may vary an order, if the adult requests this.[4]

(The Adults with Incapacity Act says that a person cannot apply for the removal of his or her nearest relative unless at the time of the application the adult is incapable, as defined in the Act.[5] As the Act's definition of incapacity is always linked to particular decisions, it is not clear what this means. If it means that someone can make an application only when he or she is unable to do so, it is not, perhaps, one of the more enabling provisions of the Act. This provision is subject to human rights law, which says everyone is entitled to remove an unsuitable nearest relative.[6]

The Scottish Executive proposes to allow anyone with an interest in the affairs of the adult to apply for an order to remove an unsuitable nearest relative. It also proposes that the court should have power to make an order on its own initiative. The court would notify the adult and any other person with an interest.[7])

In the meantime, a person making plans for future incapacity can appoint a 'named person' to receive information. See chapter 4. The nomination form could include a provision that the person does not wish his or her nearest relative to receive any information. Alternatively the person could make an advance statement stating that he or she does not want the nearest relative to receive confidential information, and perhaps giving some reasons. People intervening under the Act would have to consider whether it would be reasonable to consult the nearest relative in such circumstances.

A person with a progressive condition which might lead to incapacity may wish to challenge the current law on human rights grounds, by applying to the sheriff for an order to relieve the nearest relative of his or her functions.

1   Adults with Incapacity (Scotland) Act 2000, s 4.
2   AWI(S)A 2000, s 4(1).
3   AWI(S)A 2000, s 4(2).
4   AWI(S)A 2000, s 4(3).
5   AWI(S)A 2000, s 4(5).
6   *JT v UK* [2000] ECtHR 133.
7   *Improving with Experience: Adults with Incapacity (Scotland) Act 2000 Consultation*, Scottish Executive (August 2005), para 5.6. This provision in the Adult Support and Protection (Scotland) Bill, clause 52.

Other appeals

24.29 There are rights to appeal certain decisions or actions to the sheriff. Some decisions of the sheriff are final. In other cases there is an appeal is to the sheriff principal and with leave to the Court of Session.[1] Certain complex medical decisions go straight to the Court of Session. The Court of Session may appoint a safeguarder.

¹   Adults with Incapacity (Scotland) Act 2000, s 2(3).

INDEPENDENT ADVOCACY

24.30 Independent advocacy services can help a person voice his or her wishes and feelings or may help ascertain what the person wishes. The use of an advocacy worker may mean that someone is able to communicate and can take a decision him or herself.

Some advocacy services specialise in working with people who lack the legal capacity to appoint an advocacy worker. Even though the person may be unable to instruct an advocacy worker or express a view, the advocacy worker may feel able to take a view as to the person's feelings or interests. The advocacy worker may wish to pass this information to a court, local authority or care provider, as the case may be.

Under the Mental Health (Care and Treatment) Act, everyone with a mental disorder (not just those subject to Mental Health Act measures) is entitled to the services of an independent advocate.[1] The Code of Practice is clear that a person should not be discriminated against because he or she is unable to appoint an advocacy worker. Those responsible for making advocacy available should consider how to involve an advocacy worker, bearing in mind the adult's past wishes, the views of carers and any advance statement the person has made.[2]

It is essential that advocacy projects working with this client group have policies about accountability and standards, as the person for whom they act may not be able to call an advocacy worker to account.[3]

[1]   Mental Health (Care and Treatment) (Scotland) Act 2003, s 259.
[2]   Mental Health (Care and Treatment) Act Code of Practice, vol 1, para 6.140.
[3]   For discussion of the issues see Jan Killeen, *Advocacy and Dementia* (Alzheimer Scotland, 1996), and *Hear what I say: developing dementia advocacy services* (Dementia North, Northumbria University).

EMERGENCIES

24.31 One of the criticisms of the Adults with Incapacity Act legislation is that it does not allow emergency action when someone is at risk. The Adults with Incapacity Act was not originally intended to deal with adult protection, but to provide a framework for decision-making.

There is provision for interim guardianship and for the sheriff to make ancillary orders or directions following an application to him or her.[1] There has been concern that these powers are not sufficient, or sufficiently flexible to cover all circumstances where someone unable to protect him or herself is at risk.

There have been rare cases where a relative has removed an adult from the place where he or she was living, to the adult's detriment. It has sometimes proved difficult to return the adult home. Families may disagree about care options. While it is preferable that such matters are not resolved in the courts, the courts must be able to deal with these situations.

The Mental Welfare Commission advises that the local authority may wish to seek guardianship in such a situation. Those involved may need to go to court to seek a court order prohibiting the removal of an adult. If an adult is removed from his or her home in this way, the local authority should assess his or her needs, with a view to welfare guardianship.[2]

It may be that adult protection legislation should deal with these matters, rather than incapacity legislation. See Part 7.

1   Adults with Incapacity (Scotland) Act 2000, s 3(2)(d).
2   Annual Report 2004–5, para 3.6.

CROSS BORDER ISSUES

24.32 Complex legal issues can arise if an adult moves out of Scotland or a person with incapacities comes to Scotland and is in need of help. France, Germany, the Netherlands and the United Kingdom have signed the Hague Convention on the International Protection of Adults (2000), which attempts to deal with some of these issues for vulnerable adults.

For example, Article 5 of the Convention states that the state which is the habitual residence of the adult has jurisdiction to take measures to protect an adult's person or property. If the person moves, and his or her habitual residence becomes another contracting state, the authorities of that state have jurisdiction. The state which has jurisdiction may ask another state to take action to protect an adult's interests.[1] Any contracting state can take action in an emergency to protect an adult or his or her property.[2]

The Convention also deals with questions of the applicable law and recognition and enforcement powers. It imposes a duty on contracting states to co-operate in adult protection measures and to share information as necessary.[3]

The Hague Convention does not deal with issues between Scotland and the rest of the United Kingdom, which is treated as one state for these purposes. There appears to be a shortage of regulation to deal with mutual recognition of guardianship powers throughout the United Kingdom. By contrast, there are detailed regulations dealing with cross border issues under the Mental Health (Care and Treatment) Act. See chapter 19.

1   Hague Convention, Art 8.
2   Hague Convention, Art 10.
3   Hague Convention, Chap V.

RELATIONSHIP WITH MENTAL HEALTH (CARE AND TREATMENT) ACT

24.33 This section looks at the complex relationship between the Adults with Incapacity Act and the Mental Health (Care and Treatment) Act.[1] Most people facing mental health challenges will not need to be familiar with much of the Mental Health (Care and Treatment) Act or the Adults with Incapacity Act. They retain legal capacity to take all decisions, so the Adults with Incapacity Act is not relevant. They agree with doctors and social workers about the help they need. There is no question of using the compulsory measures contained in the Mental Health (Care and Treatment) Act.

Everyone with a mental disorder in Scotland is entitled to the protections offered by the Mental Health (Care and Treatment) Act, whether or not they are subject to measures under that Act or the Adults with Incapacity Act. These rights include the right to independent advocacy, appropriate healthcare services and care and support services.[2] The Mental Health (Care and Treatment) Act offers protections for vulnerable people[3] and creates new sexual offences where a victim has a mental disorder.[4]

The Mental Welfare Commission's role covers everyone with a mental disorder in Scotland, whether or not the person is subject to an order under the Adults with Incapacity Act or the Mental Health (Care and Treatment) Act.[5]

The thresholds imposed by the two Acts are not exclusive. A person can move from one to another, as his or her condition fluctuates. A person may need measures under both Acts. For example, a person subject to an order under the Mental Health (Care and Treatment) Act may need a financial guardian under the Adults with Incapacity Act.

It is important to understand the different criteria for the use of the two Acts, and in particular, to understand that just because someone is subject to compulsory measures under the Mental Health (Care and Treatment) Act does not mean he or she is automatically incapable of taking other decisions.

1   For further reading, see Jean Gordon, *A comparison of the Adults with Incapacity (Scotland) Act 2000 and the Mental Health (Care and Treatment) (Scotland) Act 2003* (Scottish Executive, 2004).
2   Mental Health (Care and Treatment) (Scotland) Act 2003, ss 23–27.
3   MH(CT)(S)A 2003, Pt 19.
4   MH(CT)(S)A 2003, ss 311–315.
5   See chapter 3.

Grounds for intervention

24.34 Both Acts require the presence of mental disorder, as defined in the Mental Health (Care and Treatment) Act.[1] The Adults with Incapacity Act may be relevant if someone is unable to take a decision because of mental disorder. A person without a mental disorder may also come within the Adults with Incapacity Act if a physical disability means he or she cannot communicate.[2] This could cover someone unconscious following a stroke or an accident.

The tests are not wholly exclusive. Some Adults with Incapacity tests are similar to the Mental Health (Care and Treatment) Act grounds. For example, guardianship or an intervention order may be appropriate if someone is unable to act to promote his or her interests in financial or welfare matters. Like the Mental Health (Care and Treatment) Act, this involves issues of risk. Similarly, capacity is among the issues considered under the Mental Health (Care and Treatment) Act. Compulsion is appropriate only if the person's ability to take treatment decisions is significantly impaired.

1   Adults with Incapacity (Scotland) Act 2000 (as modified by Mental Health (Care and Treatment) (Scotland) Act 2003), s 1(6).
2   AWI(S)A 2000, s 1(6).

Carers, relatives and appointees

24.35 The same people may be involved in Adults with Incapacity Act and Mental Health (Care and Treatment) Act procedures. The Mental

Health (Care and Treatment) Act definition of nearest relative applies for both Acts. Both Acts recognise the primary carer, although the definition is different. A paid carer or worker for a voluntary organisation is not a primary carer for Mental Health (Care and Treatment) Act purposes, although he or she could have a role under the Adults with Incapacity Act.

Anyone exercising Adults with Incapacity Act functions should consult any named person within the meaning of the Mental Health (Care and Treatment) Act. See chapter 4. The appointment of a named person removes the nearest relative for Mental Health (Care and Treatment) Act purposes, but not for Adults with Incapacity Act purposes.

Both Acts require the involvement of all relevant people if possible. If someone is subject to a Mental Health (Care and Treatment) Act order, those involved must seek the views of any welfare guardian or attorney appointed under Adults with Incapacity Act, as far as this is reasonable and practical. The welfare guardian or attorney can take part in any proceedings before the tribunal, but does not have any role in approving medical treatment given under Part 16 of the Act. See chapter 16.

Which Act is appropriate?

24.36 The decision whether to use the Adults with Incapacity Act, the Mental Health (Care and Treatment) Act or neither does not relate to the severity of the mental disorder as such but to the ability and willingness of the person to take decisions about care and treatment.

One person with a serious mental disorder may be unable to take medical decisions. It may be appropriate to authorise treatment under the Adults with Incapacity Act. Another, with a very similar diagnosis, may retain capacity. That person may agree with the need for treatment and no legal interventions will be necessary. If the person refuses treatment, doctors must respect this, unless the person has significantly impaired decision-making and the other Mental Health (Care and Treatment) Act grounds apply.

General rules

24.37 This section suggests some general rules, summarised at table 4.

- If a person does not have a mental disorder, neither Act is appropriate. This can be an issue in some cases of self-harm or attempted suicide. If a doctor does not consider the person has a mental disorder, for example, depression or a personality disorder, he or she cannot intervene. Carers may find this difficult to understand. (The only exception is where someone is unable to communicate and thus comes within the Adults with Incapacity Act.)

- When someone is able to take a decision about medical care and treatment, the Adults with Incapacity Act is not appropriate. It may be appropriate to consider whether the Mental Health (Care and Treatment) Act criteria apply.

- If an adult is unable to take a decision or unable to protect or promote his or her own interests, Adults with Incapacity Act procedures may be appropriate. A health professional may be able to treat using the general authority. In social care, a Part 6 order may be appropriate.

- If the Adults with Incapacity Act authorises treatment for mental disorder and the person does not resist or object to the care or treatment, it may not be appropriate to consider using compulsory measures under the Mental Health (Care and Treatment) Act. An order is not 'necessary' if the Adults with Incapacity Act can provide a less restrictive alternative.

- When someone capable of taking treatment decisions agrees to treatment for mental disorder, the Mental Health (Care and Treatment) Act is not appropriate.

- If someone does not agree to treatment for mental disorder, the Mental Health (Care and Treatment) Act may be appropriate if there is treatment available, risk and the person's decision-making about the treatment is significantly impaired because of the mental disorder.

- If the person does not have significantly impaired decision-making, Mental Health (Care and Treatment) Act measures are not available, even if the person is at risk and there is appropriate treatment available.

- If someone treated under the Adults with Incapacity Act is likely to resist or object to treatment for mental disorder and the doctor envisages that force or detention may be necessary to give the treatment, the doctor should consider using Mental Health (Care and Treatment) Act procedures.

- The Mental Health (Care and Treatment) Act cannot authorise treatment for physical disorders. Where someone subject to Mental Health (Care and Treatment) Act measures needs treatment for a physical disorder, the health professional must consider whether the person is able to consent.

If the person has legal capacity to consent, the health professional must respect his or her views. If he or she does not have legal capacity, any treatment will require authorisation under the Adults with Incapacity Act (other than in an emergency).

- In an emergency, a doctor may treat under common law powers or, when someone needs treatment for mental disorder, admit the person under a short-term or emergency certificate. The latter does not authorise medical treatment unless the urgent treatment rules of the Mental Health (Care and Treatment) Act apply. The Code of Practice gives guidance.[1]

[1]   Code of Practice, vol 2, paras 7.27–29.

Children and young people

24.38 If someone is under 16, the Adults with Incapacity Act is not relevant. It applies only to people over the age of 16. Any welfare decisions will have to be authorised under the Children (Scotland) Act 1995. A person under 16 can become subject to compulsory measures under the Mental Health (Care and Treatment) Act if necessary.

Use of force and detention

24.39 Where force or detention may be necessary on a regular basis, a doctor cannot rely on his or her general authority under the Adults with Incapacity Act. Nor can it be used to admit someone to psychiatric hospital against his or her will.[1]

In the latter case, it may be appropriate to use Mental Health (Care and Treatment) Act authority. In the former case, if the care or treatment proposed does not relate solely to the mental disorder, it may be more appropriate to use a Part 6 order under the Adults with Incapacity Act.

It may be inappropriate to use Adults with Incapacity Act authority to treat someone's mental disorder where the adult resists or objects to the treatment. The doctor may have general authority to carry out such treatment under the Adults with Incapacity Act, but the Mental Health (Care and Treatment) Act provides a regime for authorising treatment for mental disorder when someone objects. It provides more safeguards (in particular, second opinions for long-term drug treatment).

[1]   Adults with Incapacity (Scotland) Act 2000, s 47(7).

Community treatment order and welfare guardianship

24.40 Both the Adults with Incapacity Act and Mental Health (Care and Treatment) Act can authorise care and treatment on a compulsory or non-consensual basis in hospital and in the community. A community based compulsory treatment order can be very similar in its terms to a guardianship order under the Adults with Incapacity Act.[1] Both orders may impose considerable restrictions on the person's life. Which is the preferred option in particular circumstances will be a matter of developing good practice.

It is suggested that if the primary reason to seek powers is to authorise medical treatment for mental disorder, the Mental Health (Care and Treatment) Act, with its comprehensive range of safeguards for treatments, is the appropriate option. If the primary focus is to provide community based support and social care within a restricted setting, such as secure residential care, the Adults with Incapacity Act might be more appropriate.

Another consideration is the remedies for breach of an order. Breach of a compulsory treatment order may lead to the person's return to hospital and re-consideration of the order, perhaps replacing it with a hospital-based order or a different community-based order. Breach of guardianship might require a return to the sheriff for variation of the order or for an order that the adult complies with the order.

In certain circumstances, the choice of order will be clear. For example, guardianship cannot be used to admit an adult to hospital for treatment for mental disorder against the person's will. Mental Health (Care and Treatment) measures would be necessary, if appropriate.

[1]   In a March 2006 application for a Mental Health (Care and Treatment) Act compulsory treatment order, the mental health officer did not seek power to compel treatment but simply residence, attendance and access requirements. (Similar to guardianship powers.) In this case, the tribunal inserted a Part 16 requirement because it was not satisfied the person understood his ability to refuse treatment. (Unreported case.)

Impact of principles

24.41 Consideration of the principles may assist people unclear whether to invoke the Adults with Incapacity Act or Mental Health (Care and Treatment) Act. For example, if medical treatment does not require the use of force or compulsion and someone is unable to agree to treatment, the Adults with Incapacity Act may be a less restrictive option. On the other hand, it does not provide the benefits of second opinions on, for example, long-term drug treatment, which might offer better protection to the person.

Mental Health (Care and Treatment) Act duties of reciprocity and involvement and information to carers might lead towards that option rather than an Adults with Incapacity Act order. The wishes of the person and his or her carers and welfare guardian/attorney may also be relevant in the choice of order, if any.

The Millan Committee recommended that, eventually, the Scottish Parliament should consolidate mental health and incapacity law into one Act.[1] This would clearly resolve some of the difficulties in operating two Acts. In the meantime, good practice will have to develop under the guidance of the Scottish Executive.

Integration of the two Acts could also result in adults with incapacity cases moving away from the sheriff court to mental health tribunals. Research indicates some unhappiness about the appropriateness of a court environment for such cases.[2]

[1]   *New directions*, recommendation 2.1.

[2]   *The Adults with Incapacity (Scotland) Act 2000: Learning from experience* (Scottish Executive 2004), paras 6.22–6.23.

24.42

Table 4—Use of Mental Health (Care and Treatment) Act or Adults with Incapacity Act	
Person needing treatment for mental disorder	**Appropriate Act**
Capable*/accepts treatment	Neither
Capable/refuses treatment/not at risk	Neither
Capable/refuses treatment/at risk/no impaired decision-making*	Neither
Capable/refuses treatment/at risk/ treatment available/impaired decision-making	MH(CT)(S)A
Incapable/accepts treatment	AWI(S)A
Incapable/resists treatment	Consider MH(CT)(S)A

Table 4—Use of Mental Health (Care and Treatment) Act or Adults with Incapacity Act—*contd*	
Person needing treatment for mental and physical disorders	**Appropriate Act**
Capable/impaired capacity/resists treatment	MH(CT)(S)A but no treatment for physical disorder
Incapable/resists all treatment	MH(CT)(S)A/ AWI(S)A for physical disorder
* 'Capable' means the person is able to take the decision in question and 'impaired decision-making' means the person's ability to take the decision is significantly impaired by mental disorder.	

FURTHER INFORMATION AND ADVICE

24.43 Information and advice about the Adults with Incapacity Act is available on the Scottish Executive's Adults with Incapacity website, and on the easily accessible websites of the Mental Welfare Commission and Public Guardian.

Anyone with an interest in the welfare or finances of an adult can telephone or write to the Mental Welfare Commission or the Public Guardian for advice and assistance. The remit of the Public Guardian is limited to financial and property matters. Local authority mental health officers should be able to give detailed help on individual welfare matters.

Chapter 25

AUTHORISING WELFARE DECISIONS

25.01 This chapter looks at how the Adults with Incapacity Act deals with decision-making for people unable to take certain welfare decisions, such as where to live or what day-care to have. It does not look at authorising medical decisions, which is in chapter 8. There will often be an overlap. Welfare powers often include the power to take medical decisions.

Financial and welfare matters are often closely connected. Financial constraints influence welfare decisions. Chapter 26 deals with the different procedures for financial decision-making. The same person may have financial and welfare powers, depending on the circumstances.

Under the common law, no one (even a spouse or civil partner) can take welfare decisions on behalf of another adult. A parent can take decisions for a child or young person under the age of 16, if the child is unable to take the decision him or herself. See chapter 41.

The Adults with Incapacity Act has three procedures for substituted decision-making in welfare matters. A person can appoint a welfare attorney, who can take welfare decisions in the event of his or her future incapacity. The court can grant a one-off intervention order. A local authority or private individual may apply for full or partial welfare guardianship.

WELFARE POWERS OF ATTORNEY

Granting power of attorney

25.02 A power of attorney is a document appointing someone to take decisions for a person who is unable to take these decisions him or herself. The person who grants the power is known as the granter and the person appointed is the attorney.

Powers of attorney can deal with financial matters and/or welfare matters. The Adults with Incapacity Act calls a financial power of attorney a 'continuing' power of attorney. Chapter 25 deals with continuing powers of attorney.

The granter can appoint the same person to deal with financial matters and welfare matters or different people. Of course many welfare decisions, such as where someone should live, have financial implications, so if there are two attorneys they need to co-operate.

A welfare power of attorney gives power to take such welfare decisions as the granter thinks appropriate. It might also cover medical matters, allowing the attorney to discuss medical treatments with the granter's doctors and other healthcare staff.

Anyone anxious to make plans for the future should consider making a power of attorney. Anyone could become incapacitated, perhaps following an accident. Many solicitors advise the making of a power of attorney at the same time as making a will.

A power of attorney can be useful both for someone anticipating permanent incapacity or to deal with periods of temporary incapacity. This could be relevant for someone with a fluctuating condition.

Who can be attorney

25.03 The granter may appoint any individual his or her welfare attorney, but cannot appoint someone who works for a local authority or statutory body in his or her official capacity.[1] A granter can appoint such a person in a personal capacity, unless the attorney would have a conflict of interest. Similar considerations apply to appointing, for example, the manager of a care establishment. The Adults with Incapacity Act does not disqualify such a person, but acting as attorney might be a conflict of interest.

The writer understands independent advocates do not generally agree to act as attorneys, as they do not consider this compatible with their duties as advocates.

Bankruptcy, either of the granter or the attorney, is not a bar to acting as welfare attorney, although it is to acting as continuing attorney.

The granter can appoint one or more attorneys. The deed should indicate whether the attorneys can act alone or must always act jointly. The granter may wish to appoint a substitute attorney in case the first attorney cannot act.[2] This is preferable to giving the attorney the right to appoint a successor.[3]

Before granting a power of attorney, the granter should establish that the attorney is prepared to act. The Public Guardian, who has to register the power (see below), will not register it unless she is satisfied the attorney will act.[4]

¹   Adults with Incapacity (Scotland) Act 2000, s 16(5).
²   See, for example, the model form of power of attorney set out in Ward, *Adult Incapacity* (W Green, 2003), Appendix 5.
³   Because of the legal principle which says that someone given delegated powers cannot delegate them further.
⁴   AWI(S)A 2000, s 19(2). There is an appeal against the Public Guardian's decision to the sheriff. The sheriff's decision is final (AWI(S)A 2000, s 19(6)).

Ability to sign

25.04 Anyone can sign a power of attorney if he or she has the legal capacity to do so. The test is whether the granter understands the 'nature and effect' of the document.[1]

A granter may be able to understand the nature and effect of a power of attorney even though he or she is not able to manage his or her own affairs. In an English decision, the court said that the test is whether the granter can understand the extent of the powers he or she is granting to the attorney and that, should the granter lose capacity, the power will remain in effect and the granter will be unable to revoke it.[2]

It is not essential to use a solicitor to draw up a power of attorney, but a solicitor, a member of the Faculty of Advocates or a doctor must sign a certificate confirming that the person understands the nature and effect of the document. This person must also confirm that he or she has no reason to believe that the granter is acting under undue influence or that any other factor could make the signing of the power ineffective.[3] There is a prescribed form.[4] The person certifying cannot sign the certificate if he or she is to be the attorney.[5]

The Scottish Executive's Adults with Incapacity website contains good practice guidance for certifiers. The person signing the certificate must interview the granter immediately before the granter signs the power of attorney and must confirm that the person understands the nature and effect of the document. The interview must be conducted face-to-face and not by telephone or other remote means.[6] If there is any doubt about a granter's ability to sign, it may be necessary to seek the opinion of a doctor, psychologist or another person or persons. Changes in the Adult Support and Protection (Scotland) Bill make it clear only one other person need be consulted.[7]

Regulations prescribe the form of certificate. If the deed contains a welfare and continuing power, two certificates are needed.[8] The Scottish Executive is proposing just one supporting certificate when a power of attorney contains both continuing and welfare powers.[9]

1 Adults with Incapacity (Scotland) Act 2000, s 16(3).
2 *Re K, Re F* [1988] Ch 310.
3 AWI(S)A 2000, s 16(3).
4 Adults with Incapacity (Certificates in Relation to Powers of Attorney) (Scotland) Regulations 2001 (SSI 2001/80). ('The power of attorney certificate Regulations'.)
5 AWI(S)A 2000, s 16(4).
6 Scottish Executive guidance note, para 3.1.
7 Adult Support and Protection (Scotland) Bill, clause 53(2).
8 Power of attorney certificate Regulations, regs 2 and 3.
9 *Improving with Experience: Adults with Incapacity (Scotland) Act 2000 Consultation* (Scottish Executive August 2005), para 4.8. See Adult Support and Protection (Scotland) Bill, clause 53(3).

Establishing incapacity

25.05 Unlike continuing powers of attorney, welfare powers do not come into effect unless a granter is unable to take the decision in question.[1] An attorney can act only when he or she reasonably believes the person has lost capacity to take a relevant welfare decision.

A person signing a welfare power of attorney should consider what steps (if any) his or her attorney should take to establish that the granter is no longer able to act.[2] The Act does not require an attorney to obtain a medical certificate of incapacity. An attorney may seek medical advice, perhaps if there may be disputes about whether the granter has lost capacity. Some powers of attorney do require welfare attorneys to seek a medical opinion about the granter's capacity or impose some other condition, such as that the Public Guardian should not register the power until she has received evidence that certain people have had a chance to object.[3] This is an additional safeguard against misuse.

What safeguards are required is a matter for the granter. No one should grant a power of attorney unless there is someone he or she can trust to take decisions for him or her.

No one should feel any pressure to sign a power of attorney. Anyone feeling under pressure should discuss this with his or her solicitor. The safeguards and checks on attorneys are less than, for example, those on guardians. This is because the law assumes that a person appointing an attorney expects him or her to act in the granter's interests.

1 Adults with Incapacity (Scotland) Act 2000, s 16(5).
2 The Scottish Executive intends to include a check in the registration process to ensure that the granter has considered how and by whom incapacity is to be

determined. *Improving with Experience: Adults with Incapacity (Scotland) Act 2000 Consultation* (Scottish Executive, August 2005), para 4.6. See Adult Support and Protection (Scotland) Bill, clause 53.

³   AWI(S)A 2000, s 19(3).

Powers granted

25.06 The document should list the powers given to the attorney. These could include power to:

- Make decisions about the granter's future care arrangements (in residential care, hospital or at home).
- Make decisions about the granter's clothes, personal appearance, diet, leisure activities or holidays.
- Decide where the granter should live.
- See confidential or personal information about the granter's welfare, such as health or social work records.
- Consent to or refuse medical treatment.
- Consent to the granter taking part in research.
- Bring or defend legal actions concerning the granter's welfare.

Certain decisions are too personal to allow delegation to an attorney. Examples include consenting to marriage,¹ freeing a child for adoption and making a will for the granter.²

The granter should grant only those powers he or she is happy to grant. No one should feel under any pressure to grant a power of attorney or to include certain powers in it. If at a later stage an attorney does not have the powers he or she needs, the attorney can apply to the sheriff court for an intervention order (see below) to fill the gap. The sheriff will decide what is in the granter's interests.

The Adults with Incapacity Act imposes certain limits on the attorney's powers in relation to medical treatment. See chapter 8.

¹   Although a welfare guardian can have powers in connection with divorce. Adults with Incapacity (Scotland) Act 2000, s 64(1).
²   See Ward, *Adult Incapacity* (W Green, 2003), para 6.24.

Fees

25.07 A welfare power usually allows the attorney to recover expenses. A fee for acting as welfare attorney is unusual, but it might be appropriate if a professional is the best person to act.

Duties of solicitor

25.08 A solicitor preparing a power of attorney must ensure that the client understands the transaction and wishes to proceed.

The Law Society of Scotland gave guidance to solicitors before the commencement of the Adults with Incapacity Act. The guidance highlighted the case of a solicitor who did not satisfy himself that the granter had the capacity to grant a power of attorney. The solicitor allegedly prepared the paperwork and passed this on to the family, who obtained the signature from their elderly relative in hospital.

The Law Society reminds solicitors that a solicitor must have instructions from his or her client. The solicitor's client is the granter of the power of attorney. Solicitors are not the judges of mental capacity. The solicitor should seek the advice of a medical professional if there is any doubt as to a client's capacity.[1]

The Scottish Law Commission has suggested that whether someone can understand the legal effects of a power of attorney is primarily a legal question.[2] The correct position is, perhaps, that in cases of doubt the lawyer should explain the legal implications to the doctor and the doctor should assess whether the client understands the transaction.

[1]   Law Society of Scotland Professional Practices Committee July 1998.
[2]   *Mentally Disabled Adults,* Discussion Paper No 94, (1991), para 5.19.

Registration

25.09 The power of attorney is not effective until registered with the Public Guardian.[1] It is advisable to register as soon as the granter has signed. If the Public Guardian discovers any errors, the granter can remedy them. This will not be possible if a granter subsequently loses capacity.

The Public Guardian enters details of the power of attorney in the register. This register is a public document and any member of the public can examine it. The Public Guardian sends a copy of the registered document to the person registering, the granter and up to two other people named in the document.[2] The attorney does not automatically receive a copy. The Mental Welfare Commission and the local authority[3] receive a copy of every welfare power of attorney, but not of documents containing only financial powers.[4]

[1]   Adults with Incapacity (Scotland) Act 2000, s 19(1).

2   AWI(S)A 2000, s 19(5).

3   Prospective change in Adult Support and Protection (Scotland) Bill, clause 53(5).

4   AWI(S)A 2000, s 19(2).

Impact of welfare powers

Authority to act

25.10 Once registered, a welfare power of attorney comes into effect when the granter is unable to take welfare decisions.[1] If it is reasonable for the attorney to believe the person is incapable, he or she does not have to seek medical reports, unless the terms of the deed require this. The attorney should bear in mind the principles of the Act when considering both whether the time has come for him or her to act and how to act.

Registration may be dependent on the Public Guardian being satisfied that a certain event has occurred, such as the attorney producing a valid certificate of incapacity. Anyone with an interest may appeal against the Public Guardian's decision. The sheriff's decision is final.[2]

1   Adults with Incapacity (Scotland) Act 2000, s 16(5).

2   AWI(S)A 2000, s 19(6).

Attorney and medical treatment

25.11 See para 8.20 for how a doctor should deal with an attorney with powers to consent to or refuse medical treatment. Para 8.31ff deal with the attorney's role in relation to research.

An attorney cannot place the granter in hospital for treatment for mental disorder against his or her will.[1] If the granter is unable to consent and does not appear to resist or object to admission, the attorney can lawfully admit him or her to hospital. This would be a 'lawful procedure' within human rights rules (see 11.36).

Certain medical treatments require additional safeguards under the Adults with Incapacity Act (see chapter 8). The attorney cannot give formal consent to such treatments on behalf of the granter,[2] but doctors should consult the attorney in accordance with the principles of the Act. The attorney may seek information and advice from the local authority or the Mental Welfare Commission in connection with his or her duties and powers.[3]

[1] Adults with Incapacity (Scotland) Act 2000, s 16(6)(a).

[2] AWI(S)A 2000, s 16(6)(b).

[3] AWI(S)A 2000, ss 9(1)(g) and 10(1)(e).

Mental health act proceedings

25.12 If someone has become unable to act and a welfare power is in effect, the attorney should be involved in any discussions about the use of compulsory measures. The attorney should have an opportunity to speak, to make representations and to lead and produce evidence at the mental health tribunal. See chapter 25.

An attorney cannot consent to treatment given under the Mental Health (Care and Treatment) Act, but doctors should bear in mind his or her views, under the principles of that Act.

Duties of attorney

25.13 An attorney should always bear in mind the principles of the Adults with Incapacity Act. These apply when an attorney is carrying out his or her duties and when the attorney considers whether and how to intervene. An attorney failing to consider the principles may lose the benefit of the indemnity provisions. (See 24.10.)

An attorney must keep a record of his or her actions.[1] The Code of Practice sets out requirements for record keeping.[2] An attorney should attempt to familiarise him or herself with the Code. Disregard of the Code could be relevant if there are allegations of negligence. An attorney owes a duty of care to the granter and could be liable if he or she fails to protect the granter's interests. It is a criminal offence for someone with welfare powers to ill-treat or wilfully neglect the adult.[3]

Acting as a welfare attorney is, therefore, a potentially onerous task. It involves not merely acting on request, but taking active steps to protect the granter's interests, in so far as the attorney has power under the power of attorney to do so. No one should agree to act as attorney if he or she is not prepared to accept this burden.

An attorney does not have to do anything which would be within his or her powers if it would be unduly burdensome or expensive in relation to the possible benefits.[4]

[1] Adults with Incapacity (Scotland) Act 2000, s 21.

[2] *Code of Practice for continuing and welfare attorneys* (Scottish Executive, March 2001), ('the Part 2 Code') paras 2.27, 3.28–29.

3   AWI(S)A 2000, s 83.

4   AWI(S)A 2000, s 17.

Supervision and reporting

25.14 There is no routine supervision of attorneys by local authorities, the Public Guardian or the Mental Welfare Commission. An attorney is not generally required to submit accounts or records, although he or she must keep records, which he or she may have to deliver on request.

Those drafting the legislation considered regular reporting and supervision would be unduly burdensome on attorneys. The granter has chosen the attorney to act on his or her behalf and the state should not make this too difficult a task.[1]

If there is a complaint about a welfare attorney, the sheriff may order the local authority or some other body to supervise him or her and/or may order the attorney to provide regular reports to the court.[2] The local authority will then visit both the adult and the attorney at least monthly. It may require the attorney to report to it on a regular basis.[3]

The Mental Welfare Commission may visit if it is concerned about the welfare of a granter. The attorney must grant access.[4]

1   Scottish Law Commission *Report on Incapable Adults*, para 3.54.

2   Adults with Incapacity (Scotland) Act 2000, s 20. See below.

3   The Adults with Incapacity (Supervision of Welfare Attorneys by Local Authorities) (Scotland) Regulations 2001 (SSI 2001/77).

4   AWI(S)A 2000, s 9(2).

Reporting to Public Guardian

25.15 After the Public Guardian has registered the power of attorney, the attorney must advise the Public Guardian of any change in his or her or the granter's address. The attorney must notify the Public Guardian if the granter dies or if the power of attorney ends for any other reason.[1] The Public Guardian notifies the local authority, the Mental Welfare Commission, and the granter, if appropriate.

1   Adults with Incapacity (Scotland) Act 2000, s 22.

Complaints

Local authority

25.16 Anyone concerned about the welfare of the granter of a welfare power of attorney can contact the local authority for advice. It may be necessary to make a formal complaint. The local authority must investigate if there is a complaint or if an adult may be at risk.[1]

[1]   AWI(S)A 2000, s 10.

Mental Welfare Commission

25.17 The Mental Welfare Commission can give help and advice. If the Mental Welfare Commission is not satisfied with a local authority's action, it will investigate.[1] It has a duty to investigate when someone may be at risk and it is not satisfied with a local authority's action, it should make enquiries.

[1]   Adults with Incapacity (Scotland) Act 2000, s 9.

Application to sheriff

25.18 Anyone with an interest in the welfare of an adult may approach the sheriff court. The granter, the attorney or anyone with an interest may ask the sheriff to give directions to the attorney.[1] This could be useful if there is a dispute about an attorney's powers or the way an attorney is exercising his or her powers.

Anyone with an interest (including a granter) may apply to the sheriff for an order restricting or limiting an attorney's powers.[2] The applicant may ask the sheriff to cancel the power of attorney, to restrict the attorney's powers in some areas, or to order supervision or monitoring of the attorney.

If the sheriff is satisfied a granter cannot take welfare decisions or cannot protect his or her welfare in areas covered by the welfare power of attorney, he or she may make an order. The sheriff can order the local authority to supervise the attorney and may order the attorney to submit reports to the sheriff. The sheriff can cancel any of the powers in the welfare power of attorney or set aside the attorney's appointment.[3]

An attorney can appeal against any cancellation or limitation of his or her powers, but not against supervision or reporting requirements.[4]

[1]   Under s 3(3) of the Act. See 24.20.

2   Adults with Incapacity (Scotland) Act 2000, s 20.
3   AWI(S)A 2000, s 20(2).
4   AWI(S)A 2000, s 20(4).

Termination

Cancellation of power

25.19 A granter can cancel ('revoke') a welfare or continuing power of attorney at any time, so long as he or she has the capacity to do so. There is no requirement that anyone witness the cancellation, to confirm the person's ability to cancel the power of attorney, but in case of dispute, this might be a sensible precaution.

The author is not aware of any court decisions in Scotland about the capacity required to cancel a power of attorney. We saw above that the test to create a power of attorney is not that the granter can manage his or her affairs, but that he or she can understand that someone could help with this management. Similarly, the test for cancelling a power should be linked to whether the granter understands that the attorney will no longer be able to act for him or her and that this may mean guardianship will be necessary in the future.

The Court of Protection in England and Wales (which has a role similar to that of the Public Guardian) has advised that a person can cancel a financial power of attorney if he or she knows who the attorney is and understands the attorney's authority. The person should know why he or she considers it necessary or expedient to cancel the power and what the consequences will be.[1]

The test of capacity should not be set too high. If a granter is no longer happy for a certain person to act as attorney, the law should respect this, in accordance with the principles of respect for the person's wishes. The Mental Capacity Act specifically states that a person is not deemed unable to take a decision simply because the decision is unwise.[2] The Adults with Incapacity Act does not incorporate this protection (although it does say that a person does not have a mental disorder simply because he or she makes an unwise decision).[3]

The scheme of the Act envisages lesser protections available when an attorney is appointed, because the granter chooses to appoint an attorney, as someone he or she trusts. If that trust is no longer present, this lack of protection could be unfortunate. The law should generally respect a person's cancellation of a power of attorney unless there is clear evidence he or she is not able to take the decision.

If a granter's attempt to cancel a power of attorney is not recogised because of the person's incapacity, the granter can apply to the court for the cancellation of the power. The court should consider the adult's wishes as well as what would benefit him or her. See below.

The Adult Support and Protection (Scotland) Bill proposes amendments to the Adults with Incapacity Act. These will require granters to send notice of cancellation to the Public Guardian, who will amend the register and notify the appropriate people. The cancellation takes effect once registered by the Public Guardian. At the time of writing, the Bill does not make it clear whether the Public Guardian would be obliged to register a cancellation where she receives evidence that the granter lacks the capacity to revoke the power.

1   D Lush (ed), *Heyward and Massey: Court of Protection Practice* (13th edn, Sweet and Maxwell, 2002), para 6-042.
2   Mental Capacity Act 2005, s 1(4).
3   Adults with Incapacity (Scotland) Act 2000, s 87.

Divorce or separation

25.20 If an attorney and granter are married to each other, the power of attorney ends if they divorce or officially separate or if they obtain a decree of nullity.[1] If they are in a civil partnership, the power of attorney ends if the couple separate or obtain a decree of dissolution or nullity of the civil partnership.[2]

A granter can exclude this provision, to enable a power of attorney to continue after divorce.

1   Adults with Incapacity (Scotland) Act 2000, s 24.
2   AWI(S)A 2000 (as amended by Family Law (Scotland) Act 2006), s 24(1A).

Appointment of guardian

25.21 A power of attorney ends if the court appoints a guardian with powers relating to the matters in the power of attorney.[1]

1   Adults with Incapacity (Scotland) Act 2000, s 24(2).

Resignation of attorney

25.22 An attorney wishing to resign must notify the granter, the Public Guardian and any guardian, such as a financial guardian. If there is no guardian, he or she must notify the granter's primary carer, and the local authority, if it is supervising the attorney.[1]

The resignation takes effect 28 days after the date the Public Guardian receives the notice. If there is a remaining joint or substitute attorney, the resignation takes effect on the date the Public Guardian receives the notice. The notice must indicate that the remaining attorney is willing to act.[2]

The Public Guardian notifies the local authority and the Mental Welfare Commission.[3]

1   Adults with Incapacity (Scotland) Act 2000, s 23(1).
2   AWI(S)A 2000, s 23(4).
3   AWI(S)A 2000, s 23(3).

Death of granter or attorney

25.23 A power of attorney ends on the death of the granter. Any ongoing obligations are for the people responsible for the granter's will or intestacy.

The attorney's death also terminates the power of attorney. Neither the court, nor anyone else can appoint a substitute.[1] The granter can appoint a substitute if he or she has the legal capacity to do so. The granter signs a new document and registers it with the Public Guardian.

If the attorney dies after registration, his or her personal representatives should notify the Public Guardian, if they know about the power of attorney. The Public Guardian notifies the adult, the local authority and the Mental Welfare Commission.[2]

1   See Scottish Law Commission, *Report on incapable adults*, para 3.45.
2   Adults with Incapacity (Scotland) Act 2000, s 22(2).

COURT ORDERS

25.24 There will always be occasions when it is not possible to appoint a welfare attorney. A granter may not have the legal capacity to sign the documentation or there may be no one he or she trusts sufficiently to appoint.

Guardianship and intervention orders also allow substituted decision-making for someone unable to take decisions him or herself. The Adults with Incapacity Act creates a one-off 'intervention order' and a form of flexible guardianship, tailored to the needs of the individual.[1]

Guardianship and intervention orders can deal with both financial and welfare matters, including medical matters. This section deals with welfare matters. Chapter 26 deals with financial matters.

¹   Adults with Incapacity (Scotland) Act 2000, s 64.

INTERVENTION ORDERS

25.25 A welfare intervention order authorises a specific transaction such as a medical procedure, a welfare decision or the signing of a contract for care.¹ The court may order an action or authorise someone to take the action or make a decision.²

The principle of least restrictive alternative means that someone considering a guardianship order should always consider whether an intervention order would be sufficient.

¹   Adults with Incapacity (Scotland) Act, s 53.
²   AWI(S)A 2000, s 53(5).

Application

25.26 Anyone with an interest in the welfare of an adult (including the adult him or herself) may apply to the sheriff for a welfare intervention order.¹ The local authority must apply if it considers an intervention order is necessary to protect the adult's welfare and no one else has applied or is likely to apply.²

The applicant must obtain two medical reports, carried out not more than 30 days before the making of the application. At least one of the reports must be from an approved medical practitioner.³

A mental health officer must also supply a report. An applicant other than the local authority must notify the chief social work officer of the proposed application. The mental health officer must report within 21 days of the date of the notice.⁴

The mental health officer must interview and assess the adult not more than 30 days before the lodging of the application and confirm whether the order would be appropriate and the person nominated is suitable. If the adult's incapacity is because of communication needs rather than mental disorder, the chief social work officer reports instead of the mental health officer.⁵

There are prescribed forms for the doctors' and mental health officer's reports.⁶

1   Adults with Incapacity (Scotland) Act 2000, s 53(1).
2   AWI(S)A 2000, s 53(3).
3   AWI(S)A 2000 (as amended by Mental Health (Care and Treatment) (Scotland) Act 2003), s 57(3).
4   AWI(S)A 2000, s 57(4).
5   AWI(S)A 2000, s 57(3)(b).
6   Adults with Incapacity (Reports in Relation to Guardianship and Intervention Orders) (Scotland) Regulations 2002 (SSI 2002/96).

Role of sheriff

25.27 The sheriff may make further inquiries or call for further information and may appoint a safeguarder. See 24.22.

The sheriff may make an order if he or she is satisfied the adult is incapable of taking the action or making the decision to which the application relates.[1] The sheriff should bear in mind the principles of the Act.[2] The sheriff must take into account any existing intervention order or guardianship order, and any variations of an order.[3]

The sheriff may require an insurance policy (called 'caution' and pronounced 'kayshun') from the intervener.[4] This is not essential for welfare powers. Changes in the Adult Support and Protection (Scotland) Bill will give the sheriff a discretion to dispense with insurance in financial cases.

The court notifies the adult, the Public Guardian and the Mental Welfare Commission of the order.[5] (It may not be necessary to notify the adult if this could harm him or her. See 24.24.)

1   Adults with Incapacity (Scotland) Act 2000, s 53(1).
2   See discussion of 'benefit' in a Glasgow Sheriff Court decision *Application in respect of Mrs H T AW* 58/04, where the sheriff held that it could benefit the adult to authorise the making of a codicil to her will.
3   AWI(S)A 2000, s 53(2).
4   AWI(S)A 2000, s 53(7).
5   AWI(S)A 2000, s 53(10).

Matters which cannot be authorised

25.28 An intervention order cannot authorise admitting the adult to a psychiatric hospital against his or her will. It cannot authorise the intervener to consent to medical treatments subject to special regulations.[1] See chapter 8.

1   Adults with Incapacity (Scotland) Act 2000, s 53(14).

Appeals

25.29 Anyone with an interest may appeal against the making of an intervention order. Appeal is to the sheriff principal.[1]

[1]   Adults with Incapacity (Scotland) Act 2000, s 2(3).

Duties of intervener

25.30 The intervener should always bear in mind the principles of the Act. These apply when an intervener is carrying out his or her duties and when he or she is considering whether and how to intervene. An intervener who fails to consider the principles may lose the benefit of the Act's indemnity. See 24.10.

An intervener owes a duty of care to the adult and could be liable if he or she fails to act to protect an adult's interests or negligently decides what those interests are. It is a criminal offence for someone acting under an intervention order to ill-treat or wilfully neglect an adult.[1] The Code of Practice contains guidance. Disregard of the Code of Practice could be relevant if someone alleges an intervener has been negligent.[2]

An intervener must keep records of his or her actions.[3] The Code of Practice sets out requirements for record keeping.[4]

The intervener must keep the Public Guardian advised about any change in his or her or the adult's address. The Public Guardian notifies the local authority and the Mental Welfare Commission.[5] The Adult Support and Protection (Scotland) Bill requires the intervener to notify the Public Guardian within seven days of any change of address.[6]

The intervener must report to the local authority on request. The local authority must act reasonably in asking for information.[7]

If an intervener dies, changes introduced by the Adult Support and Protection (Scotland) Bill will require his or her personal representatives to notify the Public Guardian, who will notify the adult, the local authority and the Mental Welfare Commission, where an order relates to welfare matters.[8]

[1]   Adults with Incapacity (Scotland) Act 2000, s 83.
[2]   *Code of Practice for people authorised under intervention orders and guardians* (Scottish Executive, March 2002) ('The Part 6 Code of Practice').
[3]   AWI(S)A 2000, s 54.
[4]   Part 6 Code of Practice, para 2.89.
[5]   AWI(S)A 2000, s 55.

6   Adult Support and Protection (Scotland) Bill, clause 60.
7   The Adults with Incapacity (Supervision of Welfare Guardians etc. by Local Authorities) (Scotland) Regulations 2002 (SSI 2002/95), reg 3.
8   Adult Support and Protection (Scotland) Bill, clause 60.

Supervision

25.31 There is no routine supervision of people acting under welfare intervention orders (unlike financial orders), but an intervention order may require the local authority to supervise the intervener. If the local authority is required to supervise, it will visit the adult and the person authorised under the intervention order.[1]

A local authority must investigate if it receives a complaint or has concerns about an adult's welfare.[2]

The Mental Welfare Commission may also request a visit.[3] The intervener must grant access.[4] The Commission should offer information and advice to interveners.[5]

1   The Adults with Incapacity (Supervision of Welfare Guardians etc. by Local Authorities) (Scotland) Regulations 2002 (SSI 2002/95), reg 2(3).
2   Adults with Incapacity (Scotland) Act 2000, s 10.
3   Mental Health (Care and Treatment) (Scotland) Act 2003, s 13(2)(e).
4   AWI(S)A 2000, s 9(2).
5   AWI(S)A 2000, s 9(1)(g).

Complaints

25.32 Anyone concerned about the welfare of an adult subject to an intervention order can complain to the local authority and, if dissatisfied, to the Mental Welfare Commission. The local authority and the Mental Welfare Commission can give advice.

Cancellation of order

25.33 A person authorised under an intervention order, an adult and anyone with an interest in his or her welfare may apply to the sheriff for an order varying or cancelling an intervention order.[1] There is an appeal against the sheriff's decision to the sheriff principal and, with leave, to the Court of Session.

1   Adults with Incapacity (Scotland) Act 2000, s 53(8).

GUARDIANSHIP ORDERS

25.34 Welfare guardianship may be appropriate where someone is unable to take welfare decisions, or is unable to protect his or her own welfare, and an intervention order will not suffice. The guardian may have full or partial powers, according to the needs of the adult and the principle of least restrictive intervention. The Adults with Incapacity Act envisages a flexible form of guardianship, with powers tailored according to the needs of the adult.

Depending on the circumstances, the guardian can be a relative or carer of the adult, the chief social work officer of the local authority or a professional person. The local authority cannot provide a financial guardian, only a welfare guardian.[1]

Guardianship orders can be granted for up to five years, or if cause is shown, indefinitely.[2]

[1] Adults with Incapacity (Scotland) Act 2000, s 59(1).
[2] AWI(S)A 2000, s 58(4).

Where guardianship appropriate

25.35 A discussion paper published by the Mental Welfare Commission suggests that guardianship might be appropriate in the following situations:[1]

- *Personal guardianship* This is based on a personal relationship with the adult. The guardian can assist the adult with decision-making, in accordance with the principles of the Act. A carer, family member or member of a voluntary organisation[2] can be guardian. The local authority chief social work officer can act, if the local authority has the resources to support him or her.

- *To replace informal controls* Where an individual is exercising a series of informal controls over the life of the adult, the adult lacks legal protections if no formal powers exist.[3] What constitutes a 'control' and when it is appropriate to seek formal authorisation is a question of judgement in each case.

- *To grant legal authority* A relative or carer may want or need legal authority and status to take decisions and negotiate on the adult's behalf.[4] A local authority may wish to seek such legal authority. The court needs to be satisfied that this will benefit the adult and is in accordance with the other principles of the Act.

- *To authorise a legal transaction* There may be specific financial, medical or welfare transaction(s) requiring authorisation, such as the approval of a medical procedure, the sale of a house or the signing of an occupancy agreement. For only one transaction, an intervention order will generally be more appropriate.

- *To protect an adult at risk* A local authority (or private individual) may apply for guardianship where someone is unable to protect his or her own interests because of mental disorder.[5]

  Guardianship may be appropriate for a person who is vulnerable because of mental disorder even if the person remains legally capable of taking decisions about where to live and what care to accept, for example.[6] The local authority may consider it needs the power to move an adult from an unsuitable living situation, to protect him or her against abuse, or to prevent him or her consorting with certain individuals.

  If the adult or his or her relatives or carers oppose the local authority's views and agreement cannot be reached between the relevant parties, it may be necessary to make a guardianship application so that the sheriff can resolve the matter.

  Guardianship may also be used to establish care arrangements in the community necessary for an adult's protection. Even though an adult may resist such care, it could be less restrictive than a move to residential care.[7]

  Guardianship used to protect a person at risk may contain quite restrictive powers, such as the power to control where the adult lives or with whom he or she should consort. This is generally seen as a less restrictive alternative than applying for compulsory measures under the Mental Health (Care and Treatment) Act. It remains to be seen whether the new compulsory treatment orders are less or more restrictive than some forms of guardianship.

- *As an option under the criminal justice system.* See 46.19.

- *Where detention, force or confinement is likely* If an adult may need restraining or close supervision on a regular basis, or if his or her care arrangements could constitute a deprivation of liberty, a guardianship order is necessary. See below.

The wide powers available under guardianship and the variety of situations which may arise, mean that there will be a number of different situations where a guardianship order may be appropriate. Adults with

Incapacity Act guardianship can cover personal welfare decisions by family members and situations where local authorities take action to protect adults at risk. Prior to the implementation of the Adults with Incapacity Act, different legal proceedings were necessary to meet these various aims.[8]

1   Hilary Patrick, *Authorising significant interventions for adults who lack capacity* (Mental Welfare Commission, August 2004).

2   See Scottish Law Commission *Report on Incapable Adults*, para 6.48.

3   See Ward, *Adult Incapacity* (W Green, 2003), para 10.37.

4   Prior to the Adults with Incapacity Act, the person might have applied to become the adult's 'tutor-dative'. Guardianship has replaced the tutor-dative system.

5   This was the main use of guardianship under the Mental Health (Scotland) Act 1984. Guardianship under the Adults with Incapacity Act has replaced Mental Health Act guardianship.

6   In its Annual Report 2004–5, pp 5–6, the Mental Welfare Commission highlighted a case where guardianship should have been, and was eventually, used to protect a vulnerable woman with learning disabilities. The Commission found major deficiencies in Ms D's care by the local authority, based partly on the authority's failure to understand that it could seek guardianship to protect Ms D from serious abuse. The fact that Ms D had the legal capacity to state where she wished to live did not mean that she was able to take action to protect her own interests.

7   See, for example, Mental Welfare Commission Annual Report 2001–2, p 49. The Commission highlights a case where guardianship was sought to move a woman to residential care against her will. The Commission believed that guardianship could have been used earlier to insist that Mrs K, whose living conditions were unsatisfactory, accepted more help at home.

8   Family members sometimes sought to be appointed 'tutors dative' to take decisions on behalf of adults. Local authorities could seek guardianship powers under the Mental Health (Scotland) Act 1984. If financial powers were necessary a 'curator *bonis*' might be appointed. See Adrian Ward, *The Power to Act* (Enable, 1990).

Scottish Executive guidance

25.36 Some legal experts believe that an Adults with Incapacity Act order is necessary whenever someone admitted to hospital or moved to residential care is unable to consent to the move. Failure to obtain an order, they argue, is an unlawful deprivation of liberty and a breach of human rights.[1]

Other lawyers (including the author) take a somewhat different line. It is usually possible, and appropriate, to admit an adult to hospital using the general treatment authority (see chapter 8). The treatment authority does not authorise admitting the adult to a psychiatric hospital against his or her will. Mental Health (Care and Treatment) Act measures may be appropriate.

Scottish Executive Guidance, based on legal advice it has received, is that where an adult seems compliant with a move and a rigorous application of the principles gives no indication an order is otherwise necessary, a local authority can consider authorising a move using its powers and duties under the Social Work (Scotland) Act 1968.[2]

If a carer without a valid power of attorney wishes to move an adult, the local authority may authorise this under the Social Work Act, or the carer may seek an order. If the local authority considers an order is necessary, it may apply for one. For further discussion, see 9.15, 42.14.

[1] See comments of Sheriff Baird, Glasgow Sheriff Court, in *Muldoon*, W 37/04, and *Docherty*, AW 56/04. Discussed in Hilary Patrick, *When to invoke the Act* (Mental Welfare Commission, 2005).

[2] *Interventions under the Adults with Incapacity (Scotland) Act 2000*, letter from Chief Inspector, Social Work Services Inspectorate, 30 July 2004. The Scottish Executive is consulting on further guidance in the light of the *Bournewood* judgement. See letter from Lorna Brownlie, 29 September 2005. Draft Guidance for local authorities on when to invoke the Act was circulated in May 2006.

Application for order

25.37 A guardianship application can name either an individual or the chief social work officer of the local authority.[1] An individual may seek financial and welfare powers. The chief social work officer may seek only welfare powers.

The procedure and timescales are very similar to those for intervention orders and are set out in more detail in that section. See above. The application is to the sheriff court. The adult him or herself may apply.[2] The local authority must apply for an order if this appears necessary.[3] Two medical reports are required, one of them from an approved medical practitioner.

If the application relates to welfare matters, a report is required from a mental health officer confirming that the order is appropriate and the person nominated is suitable.[4] If the applicant is not the local authority, he or she must notify the chief social work officer of the proposed application. The mental health officer must report within 21 days of the date of the notice.[5]

It can be difficult to co-ordinate the production of the three reports within the timescale. The courts have been prepared to accept late reports.[6] The Scottish Executive proposes to give sheriffs discretion to extend the time limit if satisfied that an adult's condition is unlikely to have improved since the date of the medical reports.[7]

There are prescribed forms for the doctors' and mental health officer's reports.[8]

Two or more people can apply to be joint guardians.[9] If the proposed people are not the parents, brothers, sisters or children of the adult, the sheriff must consider whether it is appropriate to appoint joint guardians.[10]

Where there is an existing guardianship, someone may apply to be joint guardian with the existing guardian. The rules are as for an application for guardianship.[11]

---

[1]   Adults with Incapacity (Scotland) Act 2000, s 59(1). Ward, *Adult Incapacity* (W Green, 2003), suggests styles.

[2]   AWI(S)A 2000, s 57(1).

[3]   AWI(S)A 2000, s 57(2).

[4]   AWI(S)A 2000, s 57(3)(b).

[5]   AWI(S)A 2000, s 57(4).

[6]   See Adrian Ward, 'Managing the timetable: Some practical advice on the procedural requirements relating to guardianship applications' (2004) 3 Journal of the Law Society of Scotland, p 55.

[7]   See Adult Support and Protection (Scotland) Bill, clause 61.

[8]   The Adults with Incapacity (Reports in Relation to Guardianship and Intervention Orders) (Scotland) Regulations 2002 (SSI 2002/96).

[9]   AWI(S)A 2000, s 62.

[10]   AWI(S)A 2000, s 62.

[11]   AWI(S)A 2000, s 62(1)(b).

Interim order

25.38 In urgent cases, an applicant may ask for an interim order. Interim guardianship can last for up to three months.[1] At the time of writing, the Scottish Executive is proposing to give the sheriff discretion to extend this period for up to six months.[2]

An interim welfare guardian must report to the local authority's chief social work officer each month.[3]

[1] Adults with Incapacity (Scotland) Act 2000, s 57(5).
[2] *Improving with Experience: Adults with Incapacity (Scotland) Act 2000 Consultation* (Scottish Executive, August 2005), para 4.22. Adult Support and Protection (Scotland) Bill, clause 61.
[3] AWI(S)A 2000, s 64(8)(b).

Grounds for guardianship

25.39 The sheriff should bear in mind the principles of the Act. He or she must take into account any existing intervention order or guardianship order and any variations of such an order.[1] The sheriff may make further inquiries or call for further information and may appoint a safeguarder.[2] See 24.22.

Three tests have to be satisfied before the sheriff can appoint a welfare guardian.

Firstly, the sheriff must be satisfied that the adult is incapable of making decisions about his or her welfare or incapable of acting to safeguard his or her welfare, and is likely to continue to be so.[3] See 24.11 for incapacity. A person may be unable to safeguard his or her welfare if, because of his or her mental disorder, the person takes decisions which are rash or unwise.[4] The sheriff needs to consider both risk and benefit in accordance with the principles of the Act, including giving appropriate respect to the adult's wishes.

The second test relates to the minimum necessary intervention principle. The sheriff has to be satisfied that the Adults with Incapacity Act offers no other measures for protecting the person's welfare.[5] If, for example, an intervention order would be sufficient, the sheriff should grant this.[6] (The minimum necessary intervention principle is also relevant to the powers granted to the guardian. The sheriff should grant only those powers that are necessary or likely to be in the near future. See discussion at 24.05.)

The third test relates to the suitability of the proposed guardian. The sheriff must be satisfied that the proposed guardian is aware of the adult's circumstances and needs and of the duties of a guardian. The sheriff must consider whether the applicant would be a suitable guardian.[7] The sheriff should consider all the circumstances and, in particular, the applicant's accessibility to the adult and primary carer, the applicant's ability to act, any possible conflict of interest and/or undue concentration of power and any adverse effects the appointment might have on the adult.[8]

Caution (insurance) is not required for welfare guardians.[9]

[1]   Adults with Incapacity (Scotland) Act 2000, s 58(2).
[2]   AWI(S)A 2000, s 3.
[3]   AWI(S)A 2000, s 58(1)(a).
[4]   See the case of Ms D, at 25.39, footnote 6.
[5]   AWI(S)A 2000, s 58(1)(b).
[6]   AWI(S)A 2000, s 58(3).
[7]   AWI(S)A 2000, s 59(1).
[8]   AWI(S)A 2000, s 59(4). The fact that the applicant is a relative of the adult or lives with the adult is not of itself a conflict of interest or undue concentration of power. AWI(S)A 2000, s 59(5).
[9]   AWI(S)A 2000, s 58(6).

Effect of order

25.40 A guardianship order lasts for three years. The guardianship order may be for a shorter period, and the sheriff may grant an indefinite order if satisfied there is a case for this.[1] The sheriff may renew the order for periods of five years at a time or indefinitely.[2] The local authority must apply for renewal if it considers this necessary.[3]

The adult cannot enter into any transaction relating to a matter within the scope of the guardian's authority, unless the guardian authorises this.[4] This does not affect the adult's ability to deal with matters not specified in the guardianship order. These could be welfare, medical or financial matters.

The adult, the Public Guardian and the Mental Welfare Commission receive details of the order.[5] The Public Guardian registers the order and delivers a certificate of appointment to the guardian.[6]

[1]   Adults with Incapacity (Scotland) Act 2000, s 58(4).
[2]   AWI(S)A 2000, s 60(4)(b).
[3]   AWI(S)A 2000, s 60(2).
[4]   AWI(S)A 2000, s 67(1).
[5]   AWI(S)A 2000, s 58(7).
[6]   AWI(S)A 2000, s 58(7).

Powers of guardian

25.41 The guardian may have the power to deal with specific matters relating to the welfare of the adult or to deal with all aspects of the adult's welfare.[1] The order may allow the guardian to authorise the adult to take certain decisions or types of decisions.[2]

Unless the guardianship order states otherwise, the guardian is authorised to act as the adult's legal representative in relation to any matter within the scope of the guardianship order.[3] The guardian may be authorised to start or defend an action for divorce, separation or nullity of marriage on behalf of the adult.[4] As any legal action is expensive, a welfare guardian should seek authority from any financial guardian.

A guardian exercising welfare powers can claim reimbursement for any expenses incurred,[5] but would not normally expect to receive a fee, unless there is some special reason.[6] The local authority cannot receive payment for acting as guardian or be reimbursed for providing items which would normally be provided free of charge.[7]

A guardian may exercise welfare powers even though the adult is not in Scotland at the time.[8]

1   Adults with Incapacity (Scotland) Act 2000, s 64(1).
2   AWI(S)A 2000, s 64(1)(e).
3   AWI(S)A 2000, s 64(3).
4   AWI(S)A 2000, s 64(1)(c).
5   AWI(S)A 2000, s 68.
6   AWI(S)A 2000, s 68(4)(a).
7   AWI(S)A 2000, s 68(4)(b).
8   AWI(S)A 2000, s 67(3).

Limits to guardian's powers

25.42 There are certain powers a sheriff cannot grant. The guardian may not place the adult in a hospital for the treatment of mental disorder against his or her will.[1] Mental Health (Care and Treatment) Act measures may be used. The guardian cannot consent on behalf of the adult to certain forms of medical treatment (see chapter 8). For restraint, force and detention, see chapter 9. The Scottish Executive can issue regulations further defining guardians' powers.[2] To date there have been no such regulations.

1   Adults with Incapacity (Scotland) Act 2000, s 64(2)(a).
2   AWI(S)A 2000, s 64(11).

Enforcement powers

25.43 If an adult does not comply with a guardian's decisions, the guardian can seek to compel compliance.[1]

If a guardian has the power to decide where the adult should live and the adult leaves, the guardian can apply to the sheriff court for a warrant. This authorises a police officer to return the adult to the place where he or she is supposed to be living.[2] The police officer can use reasonable force if necessary.[3] The guardian, or someone authorised by the guardian, must be present when the police officer executes the warrant.

If an adult (or another person) fails to comply with some other decision of the guardian, the guardian can apply to the sheriff court for an order. The application can name the adult and/or someone else, provided it is reasonable to expect the other person to comply with the guardian's decision.[4] The Adult Support and Protection (Scotland) Bill proposes removing guardians' power to require people other than the adult to comply.[5]

The adult has 21 days to object to the application. The sheriff must allow him or her and anyone named in the application a chance to give evidence.[6] The sheriff may dispense with notice if appropriate, if Adult Support and Protection (Scotland) Bill changes are introduced.[7] Failure to comply with a court order is contempt of court, although it may not be in the public interest to prosecute the adult in such circumstances. It is more likely that the guardian will review the guardianship order.

[1]   Adults with Incapacity (Scotland) Act 2000, s 70.
[2]   For form of application, see Adults with Incapacity (Non-compliance with Decisions of Welfare Guardians) (Scotland) Regulations 2002 (SSI 2002/98). ('The non-compliance Regulations'.)
[3]   AWI(S)A 2000, s 70(5).
[4]   AWI(S)A 2000, s 70(1)(a).
[5]   Adult Support and Protection (Scotland) Bill, clause 61.
[6]   AWI(S)A 2000, s 70(3). Non-compliance Regulations, reg 3.
[7]   Adult Support and Protection (Scotland) Bill, clause 61.

Duties of guardian

25.44 The guardian should bear in mind the principles of the Act. If a guardian fails to consider the principles, he or she may lose the benefit of the indemnity provisions and may forfeit any remuneration due.[1] The Code of Practice contains guidance. Disregard of the Code of Practice could be relevant if there are allegations of negligence against a guardian.

A guardian owes a duty of care to the adult and could be liable if he or she fails to act to protect the adult's interests or negligently decides what those interests are. It is a criminal offence for a guardian to ill-treat or wilfully neglect the adult.[2] A guardian must keep records of the exercise of his or her powers.[3] The Part 6 Code of Practice gives further guidance.[4]

A guardian may delegate some or all of his or her duties but cannot surrender or transfer any part of them.[5] This means that a guardian can allow someone else to carry out day-to-day duties for the adult, but the guardian remains responsible.[6] The Code of Practice says the guardian remains responsible for ensuring staff exercise the powers properly.[7] (This is an onerous responsibility where, for example, the chief social work officer is guardian.)

A guardian must, so far as reasonable and practicable, encourage the adult to exercise whatever skills he or she has and should encourage the adult to develop new skills.[8] When the local authority's chief social work officer is guardian, he or she must give the adult the name of the person who will be exercising guardianship powers within seven days of the appointment[9] (unless the sheriff has said the adult should not receive notice).[10] The guardian must also inform the Public Guardian and the Mental Welfare Commission.

Guardians must, upon request, give the local authority a report on the welfare of the adult, or on their exercise of their welfare powers. The local authority must act reasonably in asking for information.[11]

A guardian must keep the Public Guardian advised about any change in his or her address or in the adult's address. The Public Guardian notifies the local authority and the Mental Welfare Commission.[12] Changes in the Adult Support and Protection (Scotland) Bill will require the personal representatives of a guardian who has died to notify the Public Guardian of the death, if they are aware of the guardianship.[13]

1   Adults with Incapacity (Scotland) Act 2000, s 69. Remuneration for a welfare guardian would be unusual.
2   AWI(S)A 2000, s 83.
3   AWI(S)A 2000, s 65(1).
4   Part 6 Code of Practice, paras 5.43 and 5.57.
5   AWI(S)A 2000, s 64(6).
6   See Scottish Law Commission, *Report on incapable adults, para* 6.151 ff.
7   Part 6 Code of Practice, para 5.21.
8   AWI(S)A 2000, s 1(5).

9   AWI(S)A 2000, s 64(9).
10 AWI(S)A 2000, s 64(10).
11 The Adults with Incapacity (Supervision of Welfare Guardians etc. by Local Authorities) (Scotland) Regulations 2002 (SSI 2002/95), reg 3.
12 AWI(S)A 2000, s 64(4).
13 Adult Support and Protection (Scotland) Bill, clause 61.

Duties of joint welfare guardians

25.45 Joint welfare guardians may act individually, but are liable not just for any breach of their own duty of care, but also to take reasonable steps to ensure that the other guardian does not breach his or her duty of care to the adult.[1]

If practicable, a joint guardian should consult other guardian(s) before acting under guardianship powers, unless the joint guardians agree this is not necessary.[2] If joint guardians disagree on how to act, either or both of them may apply to the sheriff for directions.[3]

1   Adults with Incapacity (Scotland) Act 2000, s 62(6).
2   AWI(S)A 2000, s 62(7).
3   AWI(S)A 2000, s 62(8).

Supervision and controls

Duties of local authority

25.46 The local authority's duties are set out in regulations.[1] If the sheriff appoints a welfare guardian for a period of a year or more, the local authority must visit the adult within three months of the guardianship order and then at intervals of not more than six months. It must visit the guardian at similar intervals, except where the chief social work officer is guardian. If guardianship is for less than a year, the local authority must visit the adult and guardian within 14 days of the midpoint of the period of appointment, and not more than 14 days before the end of the period of appointment.

If the local authority chief social work officer is guardian for an adult who moves to the area of another local authority, the local authority must notify the chief social worker of the other authority, who then becomes guardian.[2]

1   Adults with Incapacity (Supervision of Welfare Guardians etc. by Local Authorities) (Scotland) Regulations 2002 (SSI 2002/95), (as amended by the

Adults with Incapacity (Supervision of Welfare Guardians etc. by Local Authorities) (Scotland) Amendment Regulations 2005 (SSI 2005/630)).

2   Adults with Incapacity (Scotland) Act 2000, s 76.

Role of Mental Welfare Commission

25.47 The Mental Welfare Commission's duties are set out in the Mental Health (Care and Treatment) Act and the Adults with Incapacity Act.

The Mental Welfare Commission should visit adults subject to welfare guardianship.[1] The timing of such visits is a matter for the Commission. It should offer information and advice to welfare guardians.[2]

It also has important powers to cancel guardianship (see below).

The Commission has produced helpful leaflets explaining its role in welfare guardianship and the purpose of its visiting programme.

1   Mental Health (Care and Treatment) (Scotland) Act 2003, s 13(2)(c).
2   AWI(S)A 2000, s 9(1)(g).

Replacement or removal of guardian

25.48 An adult can appeal against a guardianship order or a finding of incapacity. The adult and anyone with an interest in his or her welfare may apply to the sheriff for a variation in the order. The sheriff can replace or remove a guardian.[1] The sheriff will not remove a guardian unless satisfied that there is a suitable substitute or that the remaining joint guardian is prepared to act.[2]

The sheriff can vary the terms of the guardianship[3] or cancel the order.[4]

The sheriff may also appoint a substitute guardian if a guardian is unable to act for a period, perhaps because of illness.[5]

1   Adults with Incapacity (Scotland) Act 2000, s 71(1).
2   AWI(S)A 2000, s 71(1)(b).
3   AWI(S)A 2000, s 74.
4   AWI(S)A 2000, s 71. See below.
5   AWI(S)A 2000, s 63.

Resignation

25.49 Strict rules govern the resignation of guardians.[1] A sole guardian wishing to resign must apply to the sheriff for the appointment of a replacement.[2] Greater flexibility is available if joint guardians are appointed, but even in this case, a guardian cannot resign unless the other agrees to continue to act.

The guardian must give notice to the Public Guardian, the local authority and, if the guardian has welfare powers, the Mental Welfare Commission. The notice should confirm that the remaining guardian(s) is willing to act.[3]

[1] Adults with Incapacity (Scotland) Act 2000, s 75.
[2] AWI(S)A 2000, s 75(5).
[3] AWI(S)A 2000, s 75(2).

Recall of guardianship

25.50 Guardianship ends when the grounds for the appointment of a guardian no longer apply or when it is possible to protect the interests of the adult satisfactorily without guardianship.[1]

[1] Adults with Incapacity (Scotland) Act 2000, ss 71(1)(c) and 73(3).

Local authority/Mental Welfare Commission

25.51 The local authority and the Mental Welfare Commission can cancel ('recall') welfare guardianship.[1] At the time of writing, a local authority cannot recall guardianship if its chief social work officer is guardian. The Scottish Executive is considering allowing the local authority to recall a guardianship if this is in accordance with the principles of the Act.[2] At the date of writing this in not included in the proposed amendments to the Act in the Adult Support and Protection (Scotland) Bill.

An adult under guardianship or anyone with an interest may apply to the Mental Welfare Commission and/or to the local authority for discharge of welfare guardianship.[3] If the local authority or Mental Welfare Commission proposes to refuse the application, it must give the applicant and the adult a chance to express their views.[4] They have up to 21 days from application to voice any objections.[5] If they propose to recall the guardianship they must give the adult, primary carer, named person and nearest relative a chance to voice any objections.[6]

The Mental Welfare Commission or the local authority may refer a case to the sheriff. Anyone with an interest may ask them to transfer the matter to the sheriff. Alternatively they can await the decision of the local authority or the Mental Welfare Commission and appeal to the sheriff if necessary.[7] The sheriff's decision is final.[8]

[1] Adults with Incapacity (Scotland) Act 2000, s 73(3).
[2] *Improving with Experience: Adults with Incapacity (Scotland) Act 2000 Consultation* (Scottish Executive, August 2005), para 4.23.
[3] AWI(S)A 2000, s 73. For application forms, see Sched 1 and 2 of the Adults with Incapacity (Recall of Guardians' Powers) (Scotland) Regulations 2002 (SSI 2002/97). Where the applicant claims the adult has regained capacity, he or she should obtain a medical report as set out in Sched 3.
[4] AWI(S)A 2000, s 73(7).
[5] Adults with Incapacity (Recall of Guardians' Powers) (Scotland) Regulations 2002 (SSI 2002/97).
[6] AWI(S)A 2000, s 73(5) (as modified by the Mental Health (Care and Treatment) (Scotland) Act 2003 (Modification of Enactments) Order 2005 (SSI 2005/465)), Sched 1 para 28(8).
[7] AWI(S)A 2000, s 73(9).
[8] AWI(S)A 2000, s 73(8).

Recall by sheriff

25.52 Anyone with an interest (including the adult) may apply to the sheriff for recall of guardianship.[1] The sheriff may recall the guardianship and at the same time make an intervention order.[2] An intervention order will generally be less restrictive than guardianship. There is an appeal against the decision of the sheriff to the sheriff principal and, with his or her permission, to the Court of Session.[3]

[1] Under Adults with Incapacity (Scotland) Act 2000, s 71(1).
[2] AWI(S)A 2000, s 71(4).
[3] AWI(S)A 2000, s 2(3).

Human rights considerations

25.53 The sheriff, local authority and Mental Welfare Commission must consider human rights requirements when they consider whether to recall guardianship. If an adult remains incapable of taking decisions and his or her care arrangements could be a deprivation of liberty (see 9.15), human rights law requires a regular assessment of his or her need for detention and access to a legal forum. See 11.34. An adult not subject to guardianship does not have these rights. Recall of guardianship in these circumstances could be a breach of the adult's human rights under Article 5 of the European Convention on Human Rights.

Chapter 26

FINANCIAL MANAGEMENT

26.01 This chapter looks at planning for future incapacity by granting a financial ('continuing') power of attorney. It examines the procedures available if an adult is unable to manage some or all aspects of his or her finances or property. Most procedures are under the Adults with Incapacity Act, but this chapter also looks at Department of Work and Pensions appointees and informal management.

INFORMAL MANAGEMENT

26.02 A person may be unable to manage aspects of his or her property or finances, either temporarily or permanently. Someone may lack the mental capacity to manage or may be absent from home, for example, in hospital. Another person can take over on an informal basis, if he or she has reasonable grounds for believing the person would have authorised this.

This common law rule, which comes from Roman law, is called *negotiorum gestio* (management of affairs) and the person who acts is called the *gestor* (manager). The Adults with Incapacity Act did not abolish the rule, but replaces it for most practical purposes.[1]

The manager must act prudently and will be liable for any negligent damage to the person's estate. A manager should keep a record of transactions and account to the person for income and expenditure. He or she can reclaim any expenses incurred on the person's behalf.

This rule allows someone to give practical help, such as ensuring a person's home is secure or dealing with his or her pets. It could also be useful if there is an emergency, or while Adults with Incapacity Act procedures are under way. It is unlikely to be of use for most financial transactions. The manager has no written authority. Bank and building societies require a power of attorney or some other Adults with Incapacity Act authority.

Although this common law rule is not part of the Adults with Incapacity Act, anyone concerned about a manager can contact the Public Guardian.

[1] See discussion in Ward, *Adult Incapacity* (W Green, 2003), para 12.18–20.

MANAGING WELFARE BENEFITS

26.03 If welfare benefits are a person's only source of income, there may be no need to use the Adults with Incapacity Act. Department of Work and Pensions (DWP) agency or appointeeship may be adequate.

Agents

26.04 Anyone unable to collect his or her benefits may appoint an agent to collect them. The DWP can pay the money into a bank. Agency is not appropriate when someone is not mentally able to manage his or her own benefits.

Appointees

26.05 If someone is unable to manage his or her own finances, a Department of Work and Pensions appointee can manage benefits. The appointee receives the benefits and pays bills, etc. The appointee is responsible for advising the DWP about any changes in the person's circumstances.

An appointee usually deals with all aspects of the person's benefits. This can include welfare benefits, housing and council tax benefits, tax and pension credits. If the DWP accepts someone as appointee, the local authority and Inland Revenue usually accept the appointment.

Procedure

26.06 The Department of Work and Pensions may appoint someone if a benefit claimant is unable to act.[1] The DWP needs to be satisfied that the person cannot manage his or her own affairs, because of mental disability or, for example, following a stroke.[2] If there is a financial guardian or an attorney with relevant powers, the DWP expects him or her to act.

Anyone over 18 can apply to act as appointee. An official from the DWP visits the claimant and the proposed appointee to establish that an appointee is necessary and the person is suitable. The DWP may require medical or other evidence that the claimant cannot manage his or her affairs.

Although a formal certificate of incapacity is not necessary, the Mental Welfare Commission regards it good practice for managers or others to arrange a formal assessment of the person's capacity before they apply to become appointees.[3]

1   Social Security(Claims and Payments) Regulations 1987 (SI 1987/1968), reg 33, Housing Benefit (General) Regulations 1987 (SI 1987/1971), reg 71(3), Council Tax Benefit (General) Regulations 1992 (SI 1992/1814), reg 61(3).

2   *Agents, Appointees, Attorneys and Receivers,* Department of Work and Pensions Information for Professionals and Advisers, para 5170.

3   Annual Report of Mental Welfare Commission 2004–5, para 4.1.2.

Duties of appointee

26.07 The appointee deals with claims and receives benefits on behalf of the claimant. He or she must report any changes in the claimant's situation to the DWP, local authority or Inland Revenue, as appropriate.

Removing appointee

26.08 If a claimant becomes able to manage benefits, he or she should contact the DWP and it will cancel the appointment.

The DWP may remove an appointee at any time if he or she is not acting in the claimant's best interests.[1] Anyone concerned should contact the DWP. The Office of the Public Guardian can also give advice and will investigate if someone's finances could be at risk.

An appointee who becomes unable to act should notify the DWP. It will make a new appointment.

1   Social Security (Claims and Payments) Regulations (above), reg 33.

ADULTS WITH INCAPACITY ACT MEASURES

26.09 The Adults with Incapacity Act contains a hierarchy of measures for managing all or part of an adult's finances or property. These include changes in the law relating to joint bank accounts, allowing access to bank accounts, financial ('continuing') powers of attorney, financial management by care homes and hospitals, intervention orders and full or partial financial guardianship.

Many of the Adults with Incapacity Act financial provisions are similar to the welfare provisions. The principles of the Act apply. The procedures for granting a power of attorney, applying for an intervention order or appointing a financial guardian are broadly similar in financial and welfare matters. This chapter highlights the differences. See chapter 25 for further details.

Supervisory regime

26.10 One major difference from welfare measures is the supervisory regime. The Office of the Public Guardian is responsible for supervising property and financial transactions. See chapter 3 for background information about the Public Guardian.

The Mental Welfare Commission has a minor role. It must investigate if it considers someone's property is at risk because of mental disorder, but will generally do this only if there are also significant welfare concerns.[1]

The role of local authorities is also different. The chief social work officer cannot act as financial guardian.[2] A separate financial guardian may be necessary.

[1]   Mental Health (Care and Treatment) (Scotland) Act 2003, s 11(2). See Annual Report of Mental Welfare Commission 2001–2, para 4.2.

[2]   Adults with Incapacity (Scotland) Act 2000, s 59(2).

Public Guardian investigations

26.11 Unlike the Mental Welfare Commission, the Public Guardian does not have power to compel anyone to co-operate with her investigations. If someone exercising functions under the Adults with Incapacity Act does not co-operate, the Public Guardian may request the sheriff to direct the person to do so.[1]

If an adult's property or finances are at risk and there is no Adults with Incapacity Act appointee, the Public Guardian may contact the local authority. The local authority can apply for the appointment of a financial guardian or for an intervention order to gain access to records. See below.

[1]   Under Adults with Incapacity (Scotland) Act 2000, s 3(3).

Notification by Public Guardian

26.12 The Public Guardian usually notifies the adult of any proceedings or applications. The Public Guardian may dispense with notice if she considers it is likely to pose a serious risk to the adult's health.[1]

Before reaching such a decision, the Public Guardian must receive two independent medical certificates confirming the risk.[2] At least one of the doctors must be a Mental Health (Care and Treatment) Act approved medical practitioner. The doctors should give their reasons for their views.

It would be very unusual to withhold notice, because of the human rights implications. See discussion at 24.24 for 'serious risk'.

[1]   Adults with Incapacity (Scotland) Act 2000, s 11(2).
[2]   Adults with Incapacity (Evidence in Relation to Dispensing with Intimation or Notification) (Scotland) Regulations 2001 (SSI 2001/79), reg 2.

CONTINUING POWERS OF ATTORNEY

26.13 A power of attorney is one of the most useful ways of planning for future incapacity. It enables a person to choose someone he or she trusts and to set out the terms on which that person should manage the granter's property and finances.

Many people now grant powers of attorney.[1] Chapter 24 dealt with welfare powers. Financial powers of attorney are more widely known. The Adults with Incapacity Act reforms the law relating to these 'continuing' powers of attorney.

The rules are generally the same as for welfare powers of attorney.[2] This chapter highlights the differences.

[1]   Over 20,000 powers of attorney were registered with the Public Guardian between April 2001 and February 2006 (Office of the Public Guardian).
[2]   Adults with Incapacity (Scotland) Act 2000, s 15 deals with the creation of a continuing power of attorney.

Granting continuing power of attorney

Who can be appointed

26.14 Unlike welfare powers of attorney, the granter of a continuing power of attorney can appoint an individual, the holder of a statutory office or a corporation as attorney. Someone who is bankrupt cannot accept the appointment,[1] although he or she can act as welfare attorney.

[1] Scottish Law Commission, *Report on incapable adults*, para 3.20. (The Adult Support and Protection (Scotland) Bill proposes changes to the Adults with Incapacity Act which will clarify this rule of law. See Clause 53(1)).

Drafting matters

26.15 A financial power of attorney may authorise an attorney to sign a commercial document or to manage a person's affairs while he or she is away. This type of power of attorney does not continue after incapacity unless the document makes clear this is the intent, and the document complies with Adults with Incapacity Act requirements.[1]

A granter must consider when the continuing power of attorney should come into effect. This could be on registration, at a later date, or on the granter's incapacity. Unlike a welfare power of attorney, a continuing power of attorney can start to operate before a granter loses the capacity to manage his or her affairs. A person who is frail or worried about money matters could authorise an attorney to take over. A continuing power of attorney can also be useful for someone experiencing periods of temporary incapacity, perhaps due to a fluctuating condition, such as bipolar disorder.

A professional person acting as continuing attorney is likely to charge a fee. The granter should seek clarification of fees before signing.

[1] Adults with Incapacity (Scotland) Act 2000, ss 15(3) and 18.

Powers granted

26.16 The document should list the powers of the continuing attorney. These could include a general right to deal with all the granter's financial affairs, or might list the specific powers the granter wants to give. These could include power to:

- Deal with day-to-day bills and expenses.
- Collect pensions and welfare benefits.
- Manage bank or building society accounts.
- Deal with tax returns.
- Have access to business correspondence.
- Buy and sell investments in stocks and shares.
- Buy and sell a house or other property.

- Sign legal documents and enter contracts on the granter's behalf.
- Bring or defend legal actions.
- Make gifts of specified amounts to named people.

The attorney cannot take welfare decisions unless the document includes these powers. An attorney cannot make a will for the grantor.

A granter should grant only those powers he or she is happy to grant. No one should feel under any pressure to grant a continuing power of attorney or to include certain powers in it.

Duties of solicitor and registration

26.17 As for welfare powers.

Duties of attorney

26.18 The attorney's duties are as for welfare attorneys. The attorney must act in accordance with the principles of the Act. The attorney owes a duty of care to the granter and is in a position of trust when dealing with the granter's assets. This means that he or she must be sure that he or she uses the assets for the granter's benefit.

The Code of Practice sets out detailed duties.[1] Attorneys should be familiar with the Code. An attorney has protection against legal liability if he or she can show he or she has acted reasonably, in good faith and in accordance with the principles of the Act.[2] Having regard to the Code of Practice is a reasonable requirement.

[1]   *Code of Practice for continuing and welfare attorneys* ('The Part 2 Code') (Scottish Executive, March 2001), chap 5.
[2]   Adults with Incapacity (Scotland) Act 2000, s 82.

Supervision

26.19 As with welfare powers of attorney, there is no routine supervision of attorneys by local authorities, the Public Guardian or the Mental Welfare Commission. An attorney is not generally required to submit accounts or records on a regular basis, but must keep records and may have to submit these to the Public Guardian on request.

Following a complaint about a continuing attorney, the sheriff may order an attorney to accept supervision from the Public Guardian. The sheriff may order the attorney to submit regular accounts to the Public Guardian.[1]

The attorney must report changes of address, etc, to the Public Guardian, as with welfare powers.

[1]   Adults with Incapacity (Scotland) Act 2000, s 20(2).

Complaints

Public Guardian

26.20 Anyone concerned about the property or finances of a person who has granted a continuing power of attorney can contact the Public Guardian for advice. It might be necessary to make a formal complaint.

The Public Guardian investigates complaints about continuing powers of attorney and must investigate wherever it considers the property or financial affairs of an adult may be at risk.[1] The Mental Welfare Commission also has a duty to investigate if someone's finances or property may be at risk,[2] but the Public Guardian has particular responsibilities for financial matters.

[1]   Adults with Incapacity (Scotland) Act 2000, s 6.
[2]   Mental Health (Care and Treatment) (Scotland) Act 2003, s 11(2).

Sheriff court

26.21 As with welfare powers of attorney, anyone with an interest may apply to the sheriff court if there are concerns about the operation of a continuing power of attorney.

The applicant can request the sheriff to give directions to the attorney or can request the sheriff to restrict or limit the attorney's powers.[1] If the sheriff is satisfied that the granter is unable to take financial decisions or to protect his or her own property and finances in an area covered by the continuing power of attorney, he or she may make an order cancelling the continuing power of attorney or restricting the attorney's powers in some areas.

The sheriff can order that the Public Guardian supervise the continuing attorney and/or that the continuing attorney issues reports to the Public Guardian.

The attorney can appeal against any cancellation or limitation of his or her powers, but not against a supervision or reporting requirement.[2]

An attorney who misuses any of the granter's funds or who acts outside the scope of his or her authority may be required to repay the granter with interest.[3]

1   Adults with Incapacity (Scotland) Act 2000, s 20.

2   AWI(S)A 2000, s 20(4).

3   AWI(S)A 2000, s 81.

Termination

26.22 As for welfare powers, with the differences below.

Resignation of attorney

26.23 It is not necessary to notify the local authority or the Mental Welfare Commission if the power relates only to financial matters.[1]

1   Adults with Incapacity (Scotland) Act 2000, s 23.

Bankruptcy of grantor or attorney

26.24 A continuing power of attorney (but not a welfare power of attorney) ends on the bankruptcy of the attorney or grantor.[1]

1   Scottish Law Commission, *Report on Incapable Adults*, paras 3.20–21. (The Adult Support and Protection (Scotland) Bill clarifies this rule of law in Clause 53.)

JOINT BANK ACCOUNTS

26.25 One of the simplest ways of helping someone manage his or her finances is to open a joint bank account with him or her. The person's savings, pension or other benefits go into the account. Either party can draw on the fund. If the person becomes unable to manage his or her money, the remaining account holder takes over the account.

This arrangement offers no safeguards against abuse, but if both parties trust each other, they may consider they do not need such safeguards.

Prior to the Adults with Incapacity Act, some banks said that a joint bank account terminated on the incapacity of one account holder. The Adults with Incapacity Act reversed this rule. The other joint account holder(s) may continue to operate the account, unless the terms of the account provide otherwise or there is a court order preventing this.[1]

The remaining account holder owes a duty of care to the person who is unable to operate the account, and will be liable if he or she misuses the funds. He or she should act in accordance with the principles of the Act.[2]

Anyone concerned about the way in which someone is operating a joint bank account can contact the Public Guardian.

[1]   Adults with Incapacity (Scotland) Act 2000, s 32.
[2]   Ward, *Adult incapacity* (W Green, 2003), para 7.2.

WITHDRAWALS FROM BANK ACCOUNTS

26.26 A person cannot set up a joint bank if he or she is unable to manage the account. It is not possible to change an account to a joint account if the account holder has already lost capacity. The Adults with Incapacity Act allows access to a bank or building society account if the account holder is no longer able to manage the account.

This procedure is helpful if an adult's finances are relatively uncomplicated and predictable. It allows an authorised person to withdraw sums from the adult's account to meet regular spending commitments. The withdrawer may access funds in bank, building society and post office accounts.

The procedure is for individual carers. Local authorities and other public officials cannot use it,[1] although changes in Adult Support and Protection (Scotland) Bill will allow local authorities and other bodies to access accounts.[2] The procedure does not allow access to a joint account.[3]

It is not possible to access an account if there is a continuing attorney with powers relating to the account or an intervention or guardianship order in relation to the account, unless the guardian applies to access the account.[4]

A useful leaflet is available from the Public Guardian's office.

[1]   Adults with Incapacity (Scotland) Act 2000, s 25.
[2]   Adult Support and Protection (Scotland) Bill, clause 54.
[3]   AWI(S)A 2000, s 25(1).
[4]   AWI(S)A 2000, s 34 (prospectively amended by Adult Support and Protection (Scotland) Bill, clause 59).

Procedure

Application

26.27 The person wishing to access the account applies to the Public Guardian. (The application form is on the Public Guardian's website.) Someone who knows the adult and has known the applicant for at least two years must countersign the form. This person confirms the information in the application and certifies that the applicant is suitable.[1]

A wide class of people can countersign, including local councillors, MSPs, mental health officers, ministers, nurses, other health professionals, social workers, teachers and solicitors.[2] A person cannot countersign if he or she is related to the applicant or the adult or lives with either of them, works for the relevant bank or is the adult's or any other relevant person's solicitor.

The applicant must obtain a medical certificate confirming that the adult cannot operate the account or cannot manage the money. The form is set out in regulations.[3] If the applicant gains authority to operate the account, he or she can recover the cost of the certificate.

The Act lists the type of purposes for which the account may be used. This includes heating, food, clothing, council tax, care fees, etc.[4] The applicant must estimate the sums he or she is likely to need for specific items. Only one certificate can be in force at any one time and it is not possible to vary the certificate. The applicant must estimate how the sums might increase (for example because of inflation) over the period of the certificate.

The application form should list the adult's nearest relative, primary carer and named person, if the applicant knows this.[5] The applicant must deliver the form to the Public Guardian no later than 14 days after it is countersigned.

---

[1]   Adults with Incapacity (Scotland) Act 2000, s 26(1).

[2]   The full list is set out in the schedule to the Adults with Incapacity (Countersignatories of Applications for Authority to Intromit) (Scotland) Regulations 2001 (SSI 2001/78) (as amended by the Adults with Incapacity (Countersignatories of Applications for Authority to Intromit) (Scotland) Amendment Regulations 2005 (SSI 2005/631)).

[3]   Adults with Incapacity (Certificates from Medical Practitioners) (Accounts and Funds) (Scotland) Regulations 2001 (SSI 2001/76).

[4]   See list in AWI(S)A 2000, s 28.

5   AWI(S)A 2000 (as amended by the Mental Health (Care and Treatment) (Scotland) Act 2003 (Modification of Enactments) Order 2005 (SSI 2005/465)), s 26(1)(d).

Role of Public Guardian

26.28 The Public Guardian notifies the adult, nearest relative, primary carer and named person and anyone else with an interest.[1] They have 21 days to object. The Public Guardian must give anyone who objects an opportunity of giving evidence.[2] Regulations from the Scottish Executive may set out requirements for approval of applications.[3]

If the Public Guardian intends to refuse the application, he or she must notify the applicant and allow him or her 21 days to make representations.[4]

Any party can appeal to the sheriff against a decision of the Public Guardian.[5] The sheriff's decision is final. (The Public Guardian may, on request or on her own initiative, refer the matter to the sheriff.)[6]

1   Unless giving notice could be a serious risk to the person's health, see 24.24.
2   Adults with Incapacity (Scotland) Act 2000, s 26(3).
3   Changes to be introduced in Adult Support and Protection (Scotland) Bill, clause 54.
4   AWI(S)A 2000, s 26(7).
5   AWI(S)A 2000, s 26(9).
6   AWI(S)A 2000, s 26(8).

Effect of authority

26.29 If the Public Guardian grants the application, she issues a certificate authorising the applicant to withdraw sums from the account.

From the date of the certificate the only dealings on the account will be those authorised by the certificate.[1] The authorised withdrawer must open a special account for receiving the money. The bank/building society transfers regular sums to this designated account.[2] Standing orders and direct debits can continue to be paid from the original account.

The withdrawer can apply to the Public Guardian at any time for permission to change the adult's account, for example to an account paying a higher rate of interest.[3]

The certificate lasts for three years, but the Public Guardian may reduce or extend this.[4]

1 Adults with Incapacity (Scotland) Act 2000, s 26(6).
2 AWI(S)A 2000, s 29.
3 AWI(S)A 2000, s 33.
4 AWI(S)A 2000, s 31.

Duties of withdrawer

26.30 The withdrawer must comply with the principles of the Act. A withdrawer owes a duty of care to the adult and must use the moneys to benefit him or her. If the adult and withdrawer live in the same house, the funds can go towards household expenses.[1] The Code of Practice gives guidance.[2]

The withdrawer must use the money for the purposes set out in his or her authority from the Public Guardian. A withdrawer needing extra amounts must ask the Public Guardian to cancel the certificate and grant a new one. A new medical report will be necessary. An alternative would be to apply for an intervention order (see below).

The withdrawer must not allow the adult's account to be overdrawn. If it is, the bank can recover the money from the withdrawer.[3]

The withdrawer must keep records, as requested by the Public Guardian, and receipts. The Code of Practice gives guidance.[4] The Public Guardian may ask to see the withdrawer's records and may ask for a report on the withdrawer's actions.[5] If the adult or withdrawer changes address, the withdrawer must notify the Public Guardian.[6]

The withdrawer cannot charge expenses, but may recover the costs associated with making the application.

1 Adults with Incapacity (Scotland) Act 2000, s 28(4).
2 *Code of Practice for people authorised under Part 3 to access funds of an adult* (Scottish Executive, 2001) ('the Part 3 Code of Practice'), paras 4.15–18.
3 AWI(S)A 2000, s 26(4).
4 Part 3 Code of Practice, para 4.20- 24. The Public Guardian also issues guidance.
5 AWI(S)A 2000, s 30(2).
6 AWI(S)A 2000, s 27.

Complaints

26.31 The Public Guardian investigates any complaints and can terminate or suspend the authority. If a withdrawer misappropriates any funds or acts outside the scope of his or her authority, he or she may have to repay the funds with interest.[1]

1   Adults with Incapacity (Scotland) Act 2000, s 81.

Termination of authority

26.32 Normally the authority ends when the certificate expires. The withdrawer may apply for a new authority. The Public Guardian can extend the certificate for such period as she thinks fit, including indefinitely.[1] A withdrawer wishing for an extension should apply to the Public Guardian in good time before the certificate expires.

The Public Guardian normally requires medical evidence that the adult remains unable of managing his or her finances. The withdrawer must provide new details of the sums she wishes to withdraw and the Public Guardian then considers whether to issue a new certificate.

The Public Guardian may terminate or suspend a withdrawer's authority for such period as she thinks fit.[2] Anyone with an interest may appeal to the sheriff against this. The sheriff's decision is final.[3]

The authority ends if the account holder dies, if there is a financial guardian or continuing attorney with powers relating to the account, or if the court grants an intervention order relating to the account.[4]

1   Adults with Incapacity (Scotland) Act 2000, s 31(2).
2   AWI(S)A 2000, s 31(3).
3   AWI(S)A 2000, s 31(6).
4   AWI(S)A 2000, s 31(7).

Proposals for reform

26.33 This scheme has not been well used.[1] The Scottish Executive plans a number of changes to make it more accessible.

Changes in the Adult Support and Protection (Scotland) Bill will allow anyone who has known the withdrawer (and not necessarily the adult) for at least a year to countersign the form, providing he or she is not barred as above and is not the adult's welfare or financial guardian or attorney or authorised under an intervention order.[2]

The Scottish Executive plans other measures to make the arrangements more flexible and accessible and proposes allowing local authorities and other organisations to manage accounts. These include giving a potential withdrawer the right to access information about the accounts before making an application[3] and allowing joint withdrawers and reserve withdrawers for circumstances where the principal withdrawer cannot act.[4]

1   *Improving with Experience: Adults with Incapacity (Scotland) Act 2000 Consultation* (Scottish Executive, August 2005), para 3.11.

2   Adult Support and Protection (Scotland) Bill, clause 54.

3   Adult Support and Protection (Scotland) Bill, clause 55.

4   Adult Support and Protection (Scotland) Bill, clause 56.

MANAGEMENT BY HOSPITALS AND CARE SERVICES

26.34 Some adults living in hospitals and care homes do not have anyone who could act as attorney or access a bank account. The sums involved may not be large enough to justify the costs of financial guardianship. It may be appropriate for the hospital or care home to manage the adult's money.

Care homes and hospitals can now manage all or part of their residents' finances if a resident is unable to do this him or herself. The body must be an 'authorised establishment', either registered with the Care Commission as a care home service or an NHS or private hospital, including the State Hospital.[1]

A body which is not a registered care home service may seek limited registration to enable it to manage residents' finances.[2]

The Care Commission supervises care homes, private hospitals and limited registration establishments. The relevant health board supervises National Health Service hospitals. The State Hospitals Board for Scotland supervises the State Hospital.[3] Scottish Ministers may pass regulations amending the list of supervisory bodies.

No service is obliged to manage residents' finances. A service may opt out by giving notice to its supervisory body.[4]

1   Adults with Incapacity (Scotland) Act 2000 (as amended by Regulation of Care (Scotland) Act 2001), s 35. The Adults with Incapacity (Management of Residents' Finances) (Scotland) Regulations 2005 (SSI 2005/610)).

2   Regulation of Care (Scotland) Act 2001, s 8.

3   AWI(S)A 2000 (as amended by Registration of Care (Scotland) Act 2001), s 40.

4   AWI(S)A 2000, s 35(2).

Procedure

26.35 The managers of an authorised establishment must consider all the options in the light of the principles of the Adults with Incapacity Act. If they believe it would be appropriate to manage a resident's finances, they must arrange for a doctor to examine him or her.

The doctor must not be related to the resident, to any manager of the establishment or have any financial interest in the establishment.[1] If a resident is unable to manage because of mental disorder, the doctor must be an approved medical practitioner.[2]

The doctor certifies whether the resident is able to manage or protect his or her interests in the relevant aspect of his or her finances. There is a prescribed form.[3]

The establishment must notify the resident, his or her nearest relative and the named person of its intention to seek a medical examination.[4] If the doctor grants a certificate, the managers must send a copy to the resident and to the relevant supervisory body. The notification should explain what other courses of action the managers considered and why they were not appropriate.[5] The supervisory body notifies the nearest relative and named person.[6]

If the manager consider giving notice to the resident at any stage would be likely to pose a serious risk to his or her health, they may apply to the supervisory body to dispense with notice.[7] The supervisory body must receive two medical certificates in the prescribed form before considering dispensing with notice.[8]

[1] Adults with Incapacity (Scotland) Act 2000, s 37(6).
[2] Adults with Incapacity (Management of Residents' Finances) (No 2) (Scotland) Regulations 2003 (SSI 2003/266), ('The management of residents' finances Regulations'), reg 3(5).
[3] Management of residents' finances Regulations, Sched 1.
[4] AWI(S)A 2000, s 37(3).
[5] AWI(S)A 2000, s 37(5).
[6] AWI(S)A 2000, s 37(4).
[7] AWI(S)A 2000, s 37(8).
[8] Management of residents' finances Regulations, reg 3.

Authority and duties of managers

26.36 A certificate lasts for three years.[1] The managers must review it on the request of the resident, the doctor who provided the certificate or anyone else with an interest. A review could be necessary because there is a change in the resident's health or if his or her circumstances have changed.[2]

The certificate authorises the managers of the establishment to manage a resident's pensions and benefits, any money to which a resident is entitled and any possessions of the resident. They may dispose of such possessions (bearing in mind any sentimental value).[3] They cannot deal with any house or other property.

They cannot deal with claims for income support, retirement pensions and other state benefits. The Department of Work and Pensions appointee system deals with these matters. Managers can apply to be appointees. See above.

Before the managers withdraw any money from the resident's account, they must obtain a certificate of authority from the supervisory body.[4] If the managers wish to sell any item for more than £100, they must obtain the consent of the supervisory body. They must obtain consent to manage assets if the value of assets to be managed exceeds £10,000.[5]

[1]   Adults with Incapacity (Scotland) Act 2000, s 37(7).
[2]   AWI(S)A 2000, s 37(7).
[3]   AWI(S)A 2000, s 39.
[4]   AWI(S)A 2000, s 42.
[5]   AWI(S)A 2000, s 39(3), Management of residents' finances Regulations, reg 4.

Duties of managers

26.37 Managers must bear in mind the principles of the Act. If, for example, a resident is able to look after any of his or her possessions it is not appropriate for the managers to take over. They should consider the wishes and feelings of the resident and act only for the resident's benefit.[1] They should encourage the resident to use his or her skills. The Code of Practice gives further guidance.[2]

The managers have the following specific duties:

* To deal with and make claims for all pensions and benefits to which the resident is entitled (other than claims for state benefits, see above).

* To keep the funds of the resident separate from the funds of the establishment. The supervisory body may impose detailed requirements.

- To place any resident's money exceeding £500 in an interest-bearing account.
- To keep records of all transactions on the resident's account. The details of the balance and any interest due to each resident should be available at all times.
- To give a copy of the records to the resident, his or her nearest relative, named person or the supervisory body on request.
- To spend the money only on items which benefit the resident (not the general establishment).[3]
- Not to spend the money on items or services the establishment provides as part of its normal service.
- To arrange indemnity insurance.[4]

[1]   Adults with Incapacity (Scotland) Act 2000, s 39(2).
[2]   *Code of Practice for managers of authorised establishments under part 4 of the Act* (Scottish Executive, July 2003) ('The Part 4 Code of Practice'.).
[3]   See discussion in Part 4 Code of Practice, paras 7.66–70.
[4]   AWI(S)A 2000, s 41, Management of residents' finances Regulations, reg 5.

Change in resident's circumstances

26.38 If the resident's circumstances change, the managers must prepare an account of their dealings on the account.

If a resident becomes capable of managing his or her affairs, the managers must give the account to him or her. If a resident moves to another authorised establishment, they give it to the managers of the new establishment. If a resident moves to a place which is not an authorised establishment, they give it to the person likely to manage the resident's affairs.[1]

The managers may continue to manage a resident's affairs for up to three months from the date of any such change in the resident's circumstances. At the end of this period, they must prepare another account.[2]

The managers must notify the supervisory body if a resident leaves. If he or she is not moving to another authorised establishment they must also notify the local authority where the person is to live.[3]

[1]   Adults with Incapacity (Scotland) Act 2000, s 43.
[2]   AWI(S)A 2000, s 44.
[3]   AWI(S)A 2000, s 44(4).

Appeals, supervision and complaints

Appeals

26.39 A resident or anyone with an interest can appeal against the doctor's finding that the resident is unable to manage his or her finances. See 24.27. They can ask the relevant supervisory body to cancel the certificate. See below.

Supervision of establishments

26.40 Supervisory bodies must carry out enquiries from time to time about the operation of the scheme and the managers' compliance with their legal duties.[1] They must also investigate complaints.[2]

The Code of Practice for supervisory bodies gives detailed guidance.[3]

1   Adults with Incapacity (Scotland) Act 2000, s 40(2).
2   AWI(S)A 2000, s 40(3).
3   *Code of Practice for supervisory bodies under Part 4 of the Act* (Scottish Executive, 2003) ('The supervisory bodies' Code of Practice').

Complaints

26.41 Complaints about management of residents' finances are to the authorised body and from there to the supervisory body. The Code of Practice gives detailed guidance on investigating complaints.[1]

The Public Guardian can give advice. The Public Guardian has a general power to investigate where an adult's property or financial affairs seem to be at risk, even though she does not have a formal role in investigating complaints about management of residents' finances.[2] The Mental Welfare Commission has a similar role.[3]

An establishment which misuses an adult's funds or acts outside the scope of its authority may be required to repay any sums lost with interest.[4]

1   Supervisory bodies' Code of Practice, chap 8.
2   Adults with Incapacity (Scotland) Act 2000, s 6(1)(d).
3   Mental Health (Care and Treatment) (Scotland) Act 2003, s 11(2)(e).
4   AWI(S)A 2000, s 81.

Termination of authority

26.42 The appointment of a financial guardian or attorney terminates managers' authority. The authority ends if the court grants an intervention order relating to the funds or if anyone obtains powers over the funds.[1]

The supervisory body may cancel an establishment's authority to manage a specific resident's, or all residents', funds.[2] This could be because an establishment has ceased operating, has failed to carry out its duties under the Adults with Incapacity Act, or because for any other reason it is no longer appropriate for it to manage funds. The supervisory body may set aside this cancellation if satisfied the grounds no longer apply.[3]

There is an appeal to the sheriff against a supervisory body's decision. The sheriff's decision is final.[4]

An establishment may inform the supervisory body that is ceasing to manage residents' finances. When the establishment ceases to manage, the supervisory body can manage the funds for up to three months, until it can pass them on to another body.[5]

[1]   Adults with Incapacity (Scotland) Act 2000, s 46(1).
[2]   AWI(S)A 2000, s 45(1).
[3]   AWI(S)A 2000, s 45(5).
[4]   AWI(S)A 2000, s 45(6).
[5]   AWI(S)A 2000, s 45(4).

COURT ORDERS

26.43 Guardianship and intervention orders are discussed in detail in chapter 25. This chapter highlights differences for financial and property matters. Proposed reforms covered in chapter 25 will affect financial orders as well as welfare orders.

INTERVENTION ORDERS

26.44 A one-off intervention order can authorise various financial and property matters, such as selling a house or surrendering a lease, signing a legal document such as a contract for care, or taking out or defending legal proceedings.

An intervention order should normally be for a finite period or have a clear termination point, even if this is some time in the future. It might be appropriate, for example, to grant an order authorising the sale of a house and the opening of a bank account to receive the proceeds of the sale. If on-going management of these funds may be necessary, financial guardianship offers more protection to the adult, because of the enhanced supervisory role of the Public Guardian.[1]

¹   See Part 6 Code of Practice, paras 2.12, 2.37–2.40.

Application

26.45 Anyone with an interest in the property or financial affairs of an adult can apply for an intervention order.[1] This includes the adult him or herself. As with welfare guardianship, the local authority must apply if it considers an order is necessary and no one else has applied or is likely to apply[2] (although its chief social work officer cannot act as financial guardian).

Instead of a mental health officer's report, the applicant must obtain a report from someone who can confirm that the intervention order is appropriate and the person nominated in the application is suitable.[3] This person must interview and assess the applicant within 30 days before the lodging of the application. There is a prescribed form for the report.[4]

It is not necessary to notify the chief social work officer of an application for a financial or property order.

¹   Adults with Incapacity (Scotland) Act 2000, s 53(1).
²   AWI(S)A 2000, s 53(3).
³   AWI(S)A 2000, ss 53(4) and 57(3).
⁴   Adults with Incapacity (Reports in Relation to Guardianship and Intervention Orders) (Scotland) Regulations 2002 (SSI 2002/96), Sched 10.

Role of sheriff

26.46 The sheriff requires a bond of caution (insurance policy) from the intervener. The sheriff may waive this requirement if the person authorised under the intervention order cannot obtain caution and the sheriff considers he or she is a suitable person to act.[1] Proposed changes in the Adult Support and Protection (Scotland) Bill would allow the sheriff discretion in every case.[2]

The sheriff clerk notifies the Public Guardian, who notifies the adult.[3] The Mental Welfare Commission does not receive notice of financial intervention orders.

1   Adults with Incapacity (Scotland) Act 2000, s 53(7).
2   Adult Support and Protection (Scotland) Bill, clause 60.
3   AWI(S)A 2000, s 53(10).

Protection of third parties

26.47 If an order authorises dealings with a house, land or other similar property, the intervener should register it at the General Register of Sasines or the Land Register and send a copy of the registration certificate to the Public Guardian.[1]

The Adults with Incapacity Act protects anyone who deals in good faith with someone authorised under an intervention order. A transaction for value between a third party and the intervener remains valid even if the intervener exceeds his or her authority or is in breach of the order.[2]

If a third party buys a house, land or other property from an intervener, the transaction remains valid despite any irregularities in the making of the order or the fact that the intervener acted outside his or her authority.[3] The buyer must check that the intervener has complied with the requirements of the Adults with Incapacity Act and with any conditions imposed by the sheriff or the Public Guardian.

If an intervener enters into a transaction and does not disclose that he or she is acting under an intervention order, the intervener is personally liable under the transaction. The intervener is also liable for any transactions outside the scope of the intervention order. He or she can seek reimbursement from the adult's estate if he or she has not breached any other provisions of the Act relating to the order.[4]

An intervention order ends on the adult's death. A transaction with someone acting in good faith without notice of the death is not prejudiced.[5] Similarly, if someone buys a house or other property in good faith from an intervener, it remains valid notwithstanding that the authority has ended.[6]

1   Adults with Incapacity (Scotland) Act 2000, s 56.
2   AWI(S)A 2000, s 53(11).
3   AWI(S)A 2000, s 53(13).
4   AWI(S)A 2000, ss 53(14) and 67(4).

5   AWI(S)A 2000, s 77(3).

6   AWI(S)A 2000, s 77(4).

Supervision

26.48 There is no routine supervision of people acting under welfare intervention orders, but the Public Guardian supervises everyone acting under a financial intervention order.[1] The Public Guardian requires the intervener to provide reports and/or accounts. If the intervener does not comply, the Public Guardian may refer the matter to the court and may request cancellation of the order.

An intervention order may authorise an intervener to sell the house where an adult lives or buy accommodation for an adult. The intervener must obtain the Public Guardian's consent to the price received or paid.[2]

The intervener's accounts are public documents, open to inspection.[3]

1   Adults with Incapacity (Scotland) Act 2000, s 6. Part 6 Code of Practice, paras 2.91–2.97.

2   AWI(S)A 2000, s 53(6).

3   Part 6 Code of Practice, para 2.96.

Complaints

26.49 Complaints and advice about financial or property intervention orders go to the Public Guardian. An intervener who misuses an adult's funds or acts outside the scope of his or her authority may be required to repay any sums lost with interest.[1]

1   Adults with Incapacity (Scotland) Act 2000, s 81.

Cancellation

26.50 A person authorised under the intervention order, an adult and anyone with an interest in his or her finances or property may apply to the sheriff for an order varying or cancelling an intervention order.[1]

1   Adults with Incapacity (Scotland) Act 2000, s 53(8).

FINANCIAL GUARDIANSHIP

26.51 Financial guardianship may be appropriate if an adult is unable to manage all or part of his or her property or finances. A guardian may have full or partial guardianship powers.

If an adult's finances are very complex, a professional person may be a suitable guardian. The professional could be joint guardian with a relative or carer.

Financial guardianship imposes a heavy burden of accounting and reporting, but a lay guardian can employ professional help. This option leaves the relatives and carers with the power to take important decisions.

The local authority chief social work officer cannot act as financial guardian, but the local authority can assist people considering whether to make an application. If an order is necessary and no one else is likely to apply, the local authority must apply, possibly naming a professional guardian.[1]

Chapter 25 deals with welfare guardians. This chapter highlights the differences for financial guardians.

[1] Adults with Incapacity (Scotland) Act 2000, s 57(2).

Application

26.52 The procedures are as for welfare guardianship. Anyone with an interest in the adult's property or finances may apply.[1]

[1] Adults with Incapacity (Scotland) Act 2000, s 57(1). For suggested form of application, see Ward, *Adult Incapacity* (W Green, 2003).

Interim orders

26.53 An interim guardian must report to the Public Guardian on a monthly basis.[1]

[1] Adults with Incapacity (Scotland) Act 2000, s 64(8)(b).

Role of sheriff

26.54 The sheriff should bear in mind the principles of the Act. The principle of least restrictive option is particularly important in financial matters. Someone may be able to manage day-to-day finances but not more complex investment decisions.

While the Code of Practice advises a prospective guardian to 'foresee' the powers he or she might need,[1] a sheriff must not deprive an adult of powers in areas where he or she is still able to manage.

The tests for financial guardianship are as for welfare guardianship. The sheriff must be satisfied that the person is incapable in relation to decisions about, or of acting to safeguard his or her property or financial affairs, and is likely to continue to be so incapable.[2]

The sheriff must be satisfied that the Adults with Incapacity Act does not provide any other ways of protecting the adult's finances or property.[3] For example, an intervention order might suffice. The adult might still be able to sign a power of attorney or employ a professional to manage his or her investments. It might be possible to use the Department of Work and Pensions appointee scheme to manage welfare benefits.

The sheriff must be satisfied that the proposed guardian is suitable. Conflicts of interest can be particularly important where a relative or carer is seeking to exercise financial powers.

As with financial intervention orders, the sheriff will require a bond of caution (insurance policy) from the guardian, but may waive this requirement.[4] The Scottish Executive is proposing to give sheriffs discretion to dispense with insurance bonds in all cases and to allow the Public Guardian to vary the amount of cover.[5]

[1]   Part 6 Code of Practice, para 3.53.
[2]   Adults with Incapacity (Scotland) Act 2000, s 58(1)(a).
[3]   AWI(S)A 2000, s 58(1)(b).
[4]   AWI(S)A 2000, s 53(7).
[5]   *Improving with Experience: Adults with Incapacity (Scotland) Act 2000 Consultation* (Scottish Executive, August 2005), para 5.18. See Adult Support and Protection (Scotland) Bill, clause 61.

Effect of order

26.55 As with welfare guardianship, once the sheriff makes an order, the adult cannot enter into any transaction relating to a matter within the guardian's authority.[1] The order may allow the guardian to authorise the adult to enter into certain transactions or types of transactions.[2] The guardian might, for example, authorise the adult to run a post office savings account.[3]

The adult retains capacity in relation to matters not specified in the order.

Once a guardian has received a certificate of appointment from the Public Guardian, he or she is entitled to deal with all the adult's property and assets within the scope of the order. This includes debts due to the adult. Debtors should now pay these to the guardian.[4]

1   Adults with Incapacity (Scotland) Act 2000, s 67(1). See below.
2   AWI(S)A 2000, s 64(1)(e).
3   Provided the post office would allow the person to operate it. The AWI(S)A 2000 provides that such a contract will not be set aside on the grounds of incapacity (s 67(5)).
4   AWI(S)A 2000, s 67(2).

Protection of third parties

26.56 Third parties acting in good faith are entitled to deal with guardians. The fact that a guardian exceeds his or her authority or breaches any term of the order or any requirement of the Public Guardian does not affect a transaction for value between a third party and the guardian acting in his or her role as guardian.[1]

If a guardian enters into any transaction and does not disclose that he or she is acting as guardian, the guardian is personally liable. This is also the case if a transaction is not authorised under the guardianship order. The guardian can seek reimbursement from the adult's estate if he or she has not breached any other provision of the Act relating to the guardianship order.[2]

If a guardianship order authorises a guardian to deal with a house, land or other similar property, the guardian should apply to register the order at the General Register of Sasines or Land Register of Scotland and send a copy of the registration to the Public Guardian.[3] If the guardian is replaced or removed, the guardianship is cancelled or the adult dies, the Public Guardian notifies the appropriate register(s).[4]

There are additional protections for people buying property from guardians. If a third party acquires a house, land or other property from a guardian, the transaction remains valid notwithstanding any irregularities in the making of the guardianship order or the fact that a guardian has acted outside his or her authority.[5]

Guardianship ends on the death of the adult, but a third party acting in good faith without notice of the death is not prejudiced.[6] Similarly, if a third party buys a house or other property from a guardian in good faith, the transaction cannot be challenged solely on the basis that the guardian's authority has ended.[7]

1   Adults with Incapacity (Scotland) Act 2000, s 67(6).
2   AWI(S)A 2000, s 67(4).
3   AWI(S)A 2000, s 61.
4   AWI(S)A 2000, s 78.
5   AWI(S)A 2000, s 79.
6   AWI(S)A 2000, s 77(3).
7   AWI(S)A 2000, s 77(4).

Powers and duties of guardian

Powers

26.57 The guardian may have the power to deal with specific financial or property matters or with all aspects of the adult's property and finances.[1] The guardian is authorised to act as the adult's legal representative in relation to any financial or property matter within the scope of the guardianship order, unless the order states otherwise.[2]

The guardian can claim reimbursement for any expenses incurred.[3] A financial guardian can charge a fee for acting, unless the order prohibits this.[4] When deciding whether to restrict fees, the sheriff should take into account the value of the estate and the likely difficulties in managing it.[5]

The Public Guardian fixes fee levels. The guardian can appeal to the sheriff against a decision of the Public Guardian on fee levels, on the payments of fees to account or on the amount of expenses he or she can recover.[6]

1   Adults with Incapacity (Scotland) Act 2000, s 64(1).
2   AWI(S)A 2000, s 64(3).
3   AWI(S)A 2000, s 68.
4   AWI(S)A 2000, s 68(4)(b).
5   AWI(S)A 2000, s 68(5).
6   AWI(S)A 2000, s 68(8).

Duties of guardians

26.58 The principles of the Act apply to financial guardians. A guardian exercising financial powers might consider it his or her duty to preserve the value of the adult's estate, but the principles make it clear that he or she should use the money to benefit the adult.

The Adults with Incapacity Act is clear that a guardian can use both capital and income to buy items, services or accommodation that will enhance the adult's quality of life. This is subject to any restrictions in the guardianship order. The guardian must comply with the terms of any management plan for the estate and the Act's restrictions on guardians' buying and selling of accommodation.[1]

The guardian should also try to encourage the adult to exercise whatever skills he or she has to deal with his or her finances and property and should try to encourage the adult to develop new skills.[2]

A financial guardian owes a duty of care to the adult, not just to his or her property. A guardian could be liable if he or she fails to act to protect the adult's interests. Any aggrieved person may apply to the sheriff for the withholding of a guardian's remuneration.[3] A guardian who misuses any funds of the adult or who acts outside the scope of his or her authority may be required to recompense the adult with interest.[4]

A guardian must keep records of the exercise of his or her powers.[5] The Part 6 Code of Practice gives further guidance.[6]

As with welfare guardianship, a financial guardian may delegate day-to-day functions, but remains liable for the proper performance of guardianship duties.[7]

A guardian must comply with any order or demand made by the Public Guardian in relation to the property or financial affairs of the adult, if he or she has power to do so within the guardian order.[8] If the guardian fails to comply, the Public Guardian may apply to the sheriff for an order. Any decision of the sheriff will be final.[9]

Guardians must keep the Public Guardian advised about any change in the adult's or guardian's address and the Public Guardian notifies the local authority.[10]

For duties of joint guardians, see chapter 25.

[1] Adults with Incapacity (Scotland) Act 2000, Sched 2, para 6.
[2] AWI(S)A 2000, s 1(5).
[3] AWI(S)A 2000, s 69.
[4] AWI(S)A 2000, s 81.
[5] AWI(S)A 2000, s 65(1).
[6] Part 6 Code of Practice, paras 4.70 –74.
[7] AWI(S)A 2000, s 64(6).
[8] AWI(S)A 2000, s 64(7).
[9] AWI(S)A 2000, s 64(7).
[10] AWI(S)A 2000, s 64(4).

Financial management

26.59 The guardian has the following duties:[1]

- *To prepare an inventory of the estate*[2] The guardian must prepare an inventory as soon as possible and in any event within three months of registration of the guardianship order. The Public Guardian prescribes the form of inventory.

- *To draw up a financial management plan*[3] The Public Guardian must approve the plan. The guardian should send the Public Guardian a draft plan within one month of submitting the inventory. The guardian must review the plan from time to time and if appropriate ask the Public Guardian to approve a variation. The Public Guardian may also suggest variations.

  A guardian who disagrees with any decision of the Public Guardian may apply to the sheriff for a determination. The sheriff's decision is final.[4]

- *To open a bank account*[5] The guardian must open a separate bank account for the adult's money. If a guardian holds over £500, this must be an interest-bearing account.

- *To seek approval of investments*[6] The guardian may keep existing investments, but must get advice from an independent financial adviser if the investments are in excess of a certain figure, currently £25,000. A guardian wishing to make new investments must set out details in the management plan or ask the Public Guardian for specific consent. The Public Guardian may direct the guardian to sell an investment.

- *To submit financial statements*[7] The guardian must submit regular financial statements to the Public Guardian for approval. The guardian has up to 18 months to submit the first financial statement. The Public Guardian prescribes the form of statement.

  The Public Guardian can require the submission of audited accounts. The Public Guardian may approve the accounts notwithstanding minor errors or inconsistencies if satisfied that a guardian has acted reasonably and in good faith.[8] If accounts reveal any shortfall, the Public Guardian may require a guardian to reimburse the adult's estate.[9]

---

[1]   Spelt out in more detail in the Adults with Incapacity (Scotland) Act 2000, Sched 2.

[2]   AWI(S)A 2000, Sched 2, para 3.

3   AWI(S)A 2000, Sched 2, para 1.

4   AWI(S)A 2000, Sched 2, para 2.

5   AWI(S)A 2000, Sched 2, para 4.

6   AWI(S)A 2000, Sched 2, para 5.

7   AWI(S)A 2000, Sched 2, para 7.

8   AWI(S)A 2000, Sched 2, para 8(2).

9   AWI(S)A 2000, Sched 2, para 8(6).

Sale/purchase of dwelling house

26.60 The Public Guardian must consent to any purchase of a house for an adult or to the sale of any property which an adult is for the time being using as a dwelling house.[1] When a sheriff gives a guardian power to sell property, the sheriff should consider whether the property is for the time being used as the adult's dwelling house. The sheriff may specify in the order that the sale requires the consent of the Public Guardian.

The Public Guardian informs the adult, nearest relative and primary carer of any proposed sale or purchase, (unless he or she decides notice might cause serious harm to the adult's health. See above.) The Public Guardian may decide to notify other people and will generally notify any named person.[2]

Anyone with an interest may object to the sale or purchase. If anyone objects, the Public Guardian remits the matter to the sheriff, whose decision is final.[3]

If the Public Guardian decides to refuse an application, she must give the guardian a chance to state a case. Either the guardian or the Public Guardian may then refer the matter to the sheriff.

Any decision of the Public Guardian may be appealed to the sheriff, whose decision will be final. It is not possible to appeal against the Public Guardian's approval of the purchase or sale price of the house.[4]

Further guidance is available from the Public Guardian.[5]

1   Adults with Incapacity (Scotland) Act 2000, Sched 2, para 6.

2   Correspondence between Public Guardian and author.

3   AWI(S)A 2000, Sched 2, para 6(3).

4   AWI(S)A 2000, Sched 2, para 6(9).

5   Guidance from Public Guardian, 5 March 2003.

Making gifts

26.61 A financial guardian wishing to make a gift out of an adult's estate must seek authority from the Public Guardian.[1] The Public Guardian may give a general authority (for example, to make regular presents at Christmas or birthdays) or may authorise a specific gift.

The Public Guardian notifies all the relevant parties and gives them a chance to object. There are rights of appeal to the sheriff.[2] The Public Guardian need not give notice if the value of the proposed gift does not warrant it.[3]

[1]   Adults with Incapacity (Scotland) Act 2000, s 66. The Public Guardian has a prescribed form for applications.

[2]   The procedure mirrors that for the sale or purchase of a dwelling house (above).

[3]   AWI(S)A 2000, s 66(4).

Supervision and controls

26.62 We have seen that the Public Guardian is the primary body responsible for monitoring financial guardians. Other bodies must co-operate with the Public Guardian.

The local authority should consult with the Public Guardian on matters of common interest[1] and the Public Guardian may refer a case to the local authority.

The Mental Welfare Commission visits people subject to welfare guardianship and their guardians. If, following a guardianship visit, the Mental Welfare Commission is concerned about a financial or property matter it generally refers this to the Public Guardian. The Mental Welfare Commission must consult the Public Guardian on matters of common interest.[2]

Similarly, if the Public Guardian is concerned about the welfare of someone subject to financial guardianship, she should consult the local authority or the Mental Welfare Commission.[3]

[1]   Adults with Incapacity (Scotland) Act 2000, s 10(1)(b).

[2]   AWI(S)A 2000, s 9(1)(c).

[3]   AWI(S)A 2000, s 6(2)(f).

Changes to order

26.63 If a sheriff varies financial guardianship or replaces a financial guardian, he or she may require a new bond of caution (insurance).[1]

Only the Public Guardian or the sheriff can cancel ('recall') financial guardianship. Neither the local authority nor the Mental Welfare Commission has any jurisdiction.[2] The procedure is as for cancellation of welfare guardianship.

Anyone with an interest may apply to the Public Guardian for cancellation.

[1] Adults with Incapacity (Scotland) Act 2000, ss 63(7), 71(2) and 74(2).
[2] AWI(S)A 2000, s 73(3).

Death of adult

26.64 Guardianship orders end on the death of the adult. The guardian is not liable if he or she continues to act after the death or after any other event terminating his or her authority, provided the guardian acts in good faith.[1]

[1] Adults with Incapacity (Scotland) Act 2000, s 72(2).

Discharge of guardian

26.65 Following the cancellation of financial guardianship, the resignation, removal or replacement of a financial guardian or the death of an adult, the guardian may apply to the Public Guardian for discharge of the guardian's liabilities in respect of the adult's estate.[1] If the guardian has died, his or her personal representatives may apply.

The Public Guardian gives notice to the relevant parties and must hear any objections. If the Public Guardian intends to reject the application, she must give the applicant a chance to make representations.

Any decision of the Public Guardian may be appealed to the sheriff, whose decision is final. The Public Guardian may also remit the matter to the sheriff.

[1] Adults with Incapacity (Scotland) Act 2000, s 72.

PART 6
CARE IN THE COMMUNITY

Chapter 27

COMMUNITY CARE

27.01 Most people living with mental health challenges or learning disabilities live in the community. When someone needs help to continue to stay in his or her home, local health services and the local authority social work department should provide help under the community care system.

Whereas a patient in hospital is entitled to expect a minimum standard of service, fewer guarantees are available to people living in the community. We will see later how few legal rights to services people have. Voluntary organisations and advocacy groups must be vigilant to ensure that community care provides at least as good a quality of life as care in hospital.

This chapter looks at how to access community care services, carers' rights, and the direct payments system. The next chapter looks at legal rights to community care services.[1]

For services for children, see chapter 41.

[1]   For a fuller discussion, see Hilary Patrick 'Community care' in *Butterworth's Scottish Older Client Law Service* (Tottel Publishing).

PROVIDING COMMUNITY CARE

27.02 The Community Care and Health (Scotland) Act 2002 has paved the way for changes in the relationship between local authorities and the National Health Service in Scotland. This is reflected in the 'Joint Futures' policy, which aims to encourage joint working between health, housing and social services. The aim is to provide a better service, with sharing of information and resources.

National Health Service bodies may make payments to local authorities towards expenditure in connection with health projects.[1] Similarly local authorities may transfer funds to National Health Service bodies, as prescribed in regulations.[2]

Local authorities and National Health Service bodies can delegate their functions to each other, make payments to any delegated bodies[3] and transfer staff to each other.[4] Scottish Ministers may direct such delegation if they consider it would improve services.[5]

New bodies can take over the main functions of local authorities or health services and local authorities can jointly commission services.[6]

This reform could lead to a major shift in the way people in Scotland receive health, housing and community care services.

[1] Community Care and Health (Scotland) Act 2002, s 13.

[2] CCH(S)A 2002, s 14. For details of the functions which can be delegated, see the Community Care (Joint Working etc.) (Scotland) Regulations 2002 (SSI 2002/533).

[3] CCH(S)A 2002, s 15.

[4] CCH(S)A 2002, s 16.

[5] CCH(S)A 2002, s 17.

[6] See the Community Care (Joint Working etc.) (Scotland) Regulations 2002 (SSI 533/2002).

Community care plans

27.03 Local authorities must prepare community care plans for their areas.[1] They must consult relevant people and groups, including voluntary organisations representing users of services and carers.[2] As well as community care needs, the plans should look at housing options[3] and implementation of the local authority's carers' strategy.[4]

Anyone concerned about the provision, or lack of it, in an area should examine the community care plan. In certain circumstances if a public authority moves too far away from its publicly stated policy, there may be grounds for judicial review of its actions. See chapter 51.

If, for example a community care plan says a local authority will consult with carers before taking a decision to close a care home or if it says that the authority will give priority in community care assessments to people with severe mental illness and this does not happen, legal challenge might be a possibility.

[1] Social Work (Scotland) Act 1968, s 5A(1).

[2] SW(S)A 1968, s 5A(3).

[3] *Community care: the housing dimension* (SW7/1994).

[4] *Community care planning* (Scottish Executive Health Department, CCD 3/2000).

ACCESSING COMMUNITY CARE

Community care assessment

27.04 One of the keys to the community care system is the assessment of needs.[1] The local authority has a legal duty to make a formal assessment of a community care client's needs and, having done that, formally to record how it proposes to meet those needs.

The community care assessment aims to improve practice in both assessment and planning. The person assessing the client should record not just those needs the local authority can meet but also those needs it cannot meet. Details of unmet needs should feed into the planning process and help the development of future services.

Where a person has health or housing need, the local authority should carry out the assessment jointly with health or housing services.[2] This is called the single shared assessment. Originally for elderly people, it is now extending to other community care groups.

The Scottish Executive has given guidance on how to carry out assessments. The original guidance[3] has been expanded and refined.[4]

[1]   Social Work (Scotland) Act 1968, s 12A.
[2]   *Guidance on single shared assessment of community care needs* (Scottish Executive circular, CCD 8/2001). ('The single shared assessment guidance.')
[3]   *Assessment and care management* (Scottish Office circular, SWSG 11/91).
[4]   *Care management in community care* (Scottish Executive, CCD 8/2004). ('the Care Management guidance')

Requesting assessment

27.05 If someone does not appear to be receiving the help he or she needs, the person, a carer or anyone with an interest should formally request the local authority to assess the person's need for community care services.

('Community care services'[1] are the services a local authority has a power or duty to provide under the Part II of the Social Work (Scotland) Act[2] and services the local authority must provide under the Mental Health (Care and Treatment) Act. See chapter 28.)

A local authority must assess a person's needs for community care services if it appears the person may be eligible.[3] An individual who is eligible for an assessment of needs but who does not receive one can challenge this in the courts.[4]

A local authority should not refuse to carry out an assessment because it knows or suspects that it will not have the resources to meet needs identified.[5] It should not consider a person's resources when considering whether to assess his or her needs.[6]

1   Social Work (Scotland) Act 1968 (as amended by the Mental Health (Care and Treatment) (Scotland) Act 2003), s 5A(4).
2   SW(S)A 1968, s 94.
3   SW(S)A 1968, s 12A(1)(a).
4   *McGregor v South Lanarkshire Council*, 2001 SLT 233. Lord Hardie said that otherwise local authorities could 'ignore their statutory duty with impunity'.
5   *R v Bristol City Council ex parte P*enfold (1998) 1 CCLR 315 QBD (on similar wording in the English Act).
6   *R v Sefton Metropolitan Borough Council, Ex p Help the Aged* [1997] 4 All ER 532.

New rights under Mental Health (Care and Treatment) Act

27.06 Anyone with a mental illness, learning disability or personality disorder can insist on having a community care assessment, whether or not the person is subject to compulsory measures under the Mental Health (Care and Treatment) Act.

If a local authority receives a written request for an assessment from a person with a mental disorder or his or her advocate, named person or primary carer, it must respond within 14 days of the request.[1] It should generally involve a mental health officer in any assessment, if the person has one.[2]

If the local authority does not intend to carry out an assessment, it should advise the applicant of its reasons.[3] It cannot refuse a request if it has a legal obligation to provide an assessment under the community care legislation.

1   Mental Health (Care and Treatment) (Scotland) Act 2003, s 228.
2   MH(CT)(S)A Code of Practice, vol 1, para 7.09.
3   MH(CT)(S)A 2003, s 228(3). The procedure is as for healthcare assessments. For more detail see 5.15.

Carrying out the assessment

27.07 The local authority decides how to carry out the assessment, depending on the complexities of the case. It may carry out a full comprehensive assessment, or simply assess a person's needs for a specific service. The law gives it the discretion to decide what is appropriate in the circumstances.

Scottish Executive guidance distinguishes between care management, for people with complex needs, and care co-ordination, for less complex cases.[1]

The single shared assessment means that the local authority may not carry out the assessment. It may be more appropriate for a National Health Service or housing department employee to assess the person. All references to 'local authority' in this section refer to the person who carries out the assessment.

The local authority must involve the client in the needs assessment and take account of his or her views.[2]

[1]   Care management guidance (CCD 8/2004) (above), paras 21–22.
[2]   Social Work (Scotland) Act 1968 (as amended by Community Care and Health (Scotland) Act 2002), s 12A(1)(b)(ii). Care management guidance (CCD 8/2004), para 18.

Urgent situations

27.08 In an emergency, the local authority can provide services and carry out an assessment of needs later.[1] It should carry out the assessment as soon as possible.[2]

[1]   Social Work (Scotland) Act 1968, s 12(5).
[2]   SW(S)A 1968, s 12(6).

Involving carers

27.09 The community care legislation recognises the importance of carers. A carer is any person who gives a substantial amount of care on a regular basis.[1] (The Scottish Executive has given statutory guidance on how to interpret this.)[2] A paid carer or a volunteer working for a voluntary organisation is not treated as a carer under the community care legislation.

In making an assessment, the local authority must take into account the amount of care the carer provides. The local authority must consider the views of the carer as far as reasonable and practical.[3] The carer and user of services should be seen separately if their needs or wishes conflict.[4]

The use of an independent advocate might be helpful if the user of services and carer have conflicting views or if a user of services is unable to agree to the arrangements because of mental incapacity.[5]

The local authority should advise any carer of his or her right to request a separate carer's assessment.[6] (See below.)

1   Social Work (Scotland) Act 1968, ss12A and 12AA.
2   *Community Care and Health (Scotland) Act 2002: New statutory rights for Carers* (Scottish Executive Health Department circular, CCD2/2003) ('The Carers' guidance') para 3.5. Particular consideration should be given to the needs of older carers, young carers, carers who provide support at a distance and carers of people with fluctuating conditions.
3   It will rarely be impractical. Carers' guidance, para 7.6.
4   *R v North Yorkshire County Council ex parte Hargreaves*, May 1997, The Times, 12 June 1997.
5   Single shared assessment guidance (CCD8/2001), paras 10 and 12.
6   SW(S)A 1968, s 12AB.

Legal requirements for assessment

27.10 If someone appears to need health or housing services, the local authority must contact the health board or housing authority (if it is not the local authority) to establish what help they can provide.[1]

Before the local authority decides someone needs nursing care it must consult a doctor.[2] When the person being assessed is 'disabled'[3] the authority must carry out an assessment of his or her needs under the Chronically Sick and Disabled Persons Act 1970.[4] See chapter 28.

(This should happen automatically if there is a single shared assessment.)

The local authority should advise a disabled parent that he or she can ask the local authority to assess his or her children's needs for services.[5]

1   Social Work (Scotland) Act 1968, s 12A(3).
2   SW(S) A 1968, s 12A(2). This could be a GP, psychiatrist or other appropriate doctor, such as a geriatrian.
3   SW(S) A 1968, s 12A(4). This includes mental health problems and learning disability. (Disabled Persons (Services, Consultation and Representation) Act 1986, s 16.)
4   SW(S) A 1968, s 12A(4).
5   *Scotland's children: support and protection for children and their families* (Scottish Office, 1995), p 33.

Carer's assessment

27.11 A carer may request the local authority to assess his or her ability to provide care or to continue to provide care in the future.[1] The local authority must assess the carer's ability to care and take the results of the assessment into account when considering the needs of the person requiring care.

A carer may ask for an assessment of his or her needs at any time, not just during a community care assessment.

Health Boards must prepare Carer Information Strategies, to ensure carers receive information about their rights.[2]

¹ Social Work (Scotland) Act 1968 (as amended by the Community Care and Health (Scotland) Act 2002), s 12AA.

² CCH(S)A 2002, s 9.

Care programme approach

27.12 People with severe long-term mental illness or dementia and 'complex health and social care needs' should be included in the care programme approach arrangements. The care programme approach attempts to ensure that clients receive a comprehensive package of services, based on joint working between health and social services.

A user of services and relevant carer(s) should be fully involved in discussions about the person's care programme approach needs. A person on the care programme approach should receive a copy of his or her care plan and have a key worker.[1] The person should generally receive a single shared assessment, involving health and social work bodies.[2]

¹ See *Care Programme Approach for people with severe and enduring mental illness including dementia* (Scottish Office circular, SWSG16/96).

² Care management guidance (CCD 8/2004), para 20.

Delays

27.13 If there is undue delay in carrying out a community care assessment a complaint may be necessary. The Scottish Public Services Ombudsman (see chapter 50) could investigate delay. There may be occasions where a lengthy delay could be the basis for legal action. The local authority may be failing to comply with its statutory duties.

Outcome of assessment

Decision about services

27.14 Following the assessment of needs, the local authority must take a formal decision about the services it will provide.[1] If there are various ways of meeting the person's needs, the local authority is entitled to consider costs. It should bear in mind the views of the person and his or her carer.[2]

1   Social Work (Scotland) Act 1968, s 12A(1)(b).
2   *R v Lancashire County Council ex parte RADAR and another* [1996] AER 421. A woman needing 24 hour nursing care wanted this in her own home. The court said the local authority was entitled to consider the cost and could meet her needs by offering care in a residential care home.

Care plan

27.15 The local authority writes up its decision about services in a care plan. It should give the person a copy of the plan. The plan should include a timetable for implementation and ensure that the user of services and any carer(s) can have a role in monitoring and reviewing the care provided.[1]

1   Care management guidance (CCD 8/2004), Annex, para 11.

Relevance of resources

27.16 When considering whether someone's needs call for the provision of services, the local authority should not take into account the person's ability to pay for them.

The House of Lords has said that the delivery of community care services must not depend on the ability of the person to meet the costs. The assessment of need and the decision whether to provide a service come first. The assessment of means comes afterwards.[1]

1   Lord Hope in *Robertson v Fife Council* [2002] UKHL 35, at para 53.

Local authority resources

27.17 The Court of Session has said that in assessing what an individual 'needs', the local authority's own resources are irrelevant.[1] The local authority should assess the person's needs without reference to what it may be able to provide.

The law recognises that a local authority may not be able to meet all the needs of the person as shown in the assessment. The local authority's duty is to decide whether the needs 'call for' the provision of services.[2] What services the local authority provides depends, at least partly, on the local authority's resources.

The courts in Scotland have said that this does not mean that a local authority can abdicate its responsibility to people in need. A local authority assessed an elderly man with complex needs as needing 24-hour nursing home care. Because of pressure on its resources, the local authority put his name on a waiting list. The Court of Session said that this was not enough. The local authority must take some action in the short term to meet his needs.

Once a local authority has determined that the needs of an individual in their area require the provision of a particular service and that these needs cannot be met in any other way, the authority must provide the necessary assistance, if no other individual or body can do so (such as the person's family).[3]

The English courts have also confirmed that the local authority must act in a reasonable way. The court may intervene if it considers a care plan inadequate.[4]

[1]   *McGregor v South Lanarkshire Council*, 2001 SLT 233. Lord Hardie said that '...the only relevant issues are the particular circumstances of the individual, including his or her ability to care adequately for himself or herself without any assistance from any outside agency.' Contrast the House of Lords decision in *Barry*, 28.20 below.

[2]   Social Work (Scotland) Act 1968, s 12A(1)(b).

[3]   Lord Hardie in *McGregor v South Lanarkshire Council*, 2001 SLT 233.

[4]   See *R v Sutton LBC ex parte Tucker* (1998) 1 CCLR 251QBD and *R v Birmingham City Council ex parte Killigrew* (2000) 3 CCLR 109, where the court set aside a community care assessment because the local authority had failed to consider relevant information from the client's medical reports or discuss the case with the client's GP.

Challenging assessment

27.18 There is no formal appeal or review procedure. Someone dissatisfied with an assessment of need or the proposed services to meet the needs can ask the local authority to review its decision.

If the review is unsatisfactory, the person can make a complaint under the local authority's social work complaints procedure. See chapter 50.

People unwilling to be assessed

27.19 The community care legislation does not provide a mechanism for assessing needs of when someone is unwilling to have an assessment.

If an individual refuses to co-operate with an assessment, a local authority may carry out an independent carer's assessment to find out more about the person's needs. If the person's health and safety, or that of others, could be at risk, the local authority may decide to use Mental Health (Care and Treatment) Act powers of compulsory admission to hospital or an order under the Adults with Incapacity Act.

DIRECT PAYMENTS

27.20 When a local authority assesses someone as needing care it may, instead of providing care itself, make a payment to the client to enable him or her to buy the care.[1] This is called making a direct payment.[2]

The scheme can help people remain independent by enabling them to buy the care they need. Many people prefer to do this, rather than have care provided by the local authority.

Local authorities have a legal obligation to arrange direct payment schemes[3] and the scheme now covers all community care groups.[4] A parent can receive a direct payment if a child needs services under the Children (Scotland) Act 1995.[5]

The Scottish Executive is particularly keen to see mental health user of services making use of direct payments.[6]

---

[1]   Social Work (Scotland) Act 1968, s 12B.

[2]   For more details see Social Work (Scotland) Act 1968 , ss 12B and 12C; *Direct Payments: Policy and Practice Guidance* (Scottish Executive circular, CCD 4/ 2003).

[3]   Community Care and Health (Scotland) Act 2002, s 7.

[4]   Community Care (Direct Payments) (Scotland) Regulations 2003 (SSI 2003/ 243), as amended by the Community Care (Direct Payments) (Scotland) Amendment Regulations 2005 (SSI 2005/114) and the Mental Health (Care and Treatment) (Scotland) Act 2003 (Modification of Subordinate Legislation) Order 2005 (SSI 2005/445) ('The direct payments regulations')

5   SW(S)A 1968, s 12B(1)(a). This does not extend to services under any other sections of the Children (Scotland) Act 1995 or services provided by local authorities under the Education (Scotland) Act 1980.

6   See *Roll out of direct payments to older people* (Scottish Executive circular, CCD 3/2005), para 5.

Outline of scheme

27.21 The local authority should assess the person's needs as above and then provide him or her with the money to buy the care. The local authority deducts the client's financial contribution from the amount of the direct payment.

The client employs his or her own carers and may need advice about PAYE, National Insurance, contracts of service, interviewing carers, etc. Independent living centres can provide such advice. Information is also available from Direct Payments Scotland. See Appendix 2.

Some people are not eligible for direct payments. This includes detained patients living in the community, restricted patients on conditional discharge and people living in the community subject to conditions prescribed by the criminal courts.[1]

1   For the full list, see the direct payments regulations, reg 2.

Eligibility

27.22 The local authority must satisfy itself that the person will be able to manage the scheme, either on his or her own or with assistance.[1] The local authority can make a direct payment even when someone is unable to consent to the scheme him or herself, if the person's guardian or attorney consents.[2] A parent may consent on behalf of a child.

A direct payment cannot pay a spouse or close relative (as defined in the regulations) to provide care. It cannot pay for residential accommodation, although it can pay for respite care for up to four weeks in a year.[3]

A direct payment cannot pay for care normally provided by the National Health Service,[4] but local authorities can offer joint funding packages with the National Health Service.[5] The local authority can delegate its direct payments scheme to an NHS body.[6]

1   Direct payments regulations, reg 2(b). For discussion about how to help people manage direct payments, see Scottish Executive circular, CCD 4/2003 (above), para 91.
2   SW(S)A 1968, s 12B(1)(B), Direct payments regulations, reg 3.
3   Direct payments regulations, reg 6.
4   See Scottish Executive circular, CCD4/2003, para 63. Available on the Scottish Executive website www.show.scot.nhs.uk.
5   CCD4/2003, para 70.
6   Community Care (Joint Working Etc.) (Scotland) Regulations 2002 (SSI 2002/533).

Chapter 28

DUTY TO PROVIDE SERVICES

28.01 This section looks at local authorities' legal obligations to provide community care services and considers how far an individual client can enforce those obligations.

Local authorities must provide some services by law. These are:

- General welfare services.
- Support services for children and young people.
- Services under the Mental Health (Care and Treatment) (Scotland) Act 2003.
- Help for families affected by mental disorder or other disability.
- Home help services.
- Services under the Chronically Sick and Disabled Person Act 1970.
- Residential accommodation.
- Accommodation in nursing homes.

We look at these in more detail below.

Nature of statutory duties

28.02 If a local authority has a duty under statute, it must comply with that duty. A duty to do something is different from a power to do something. For example, the Social Work (Scotland) Act says that if a local authority provides employment for people in need it 'may' help them sell any items they make.[1] There is no legal obligation on the local authority to do this.

Even where a local authority has a statutory duty, someone who does not receive a service does not necessarily have the right to take legal action to enforce the duty. The way in which a statutory duty is worded influences how far individuals can enforce its provisions.

The courts are aware that local authorities operate with finite resources.[2] If a statute gives local authorities a 'discretion' to act or allows them to make such provision as they consider 'reasonable', 'suitable' or 'appropriate'[3] the courts recognise that a local authority can take its resources into account when providing services.

This does not mean that it can provide no services or manifestly inadequate services, but it does mean that an individual affected by a failure to provide a specific service may not be able to challenge this in the courts.

If a statute is expressed in very general terms, the courts may say it represents a 'target' duty, rather than one imposing a duty in individual cases. An example is the requirement to ensure there is adequate provision of nursing homes in a local authority area.[4]

A duty to provide services 'designed to minimise', 'designed to reduce' or to 'encourage' or 'avoid' something also leave some discretion to the local authority.[5]

The more specific and precise the wording of the statute, the more likely it is to be enforceable. For example, a local authority is under a clear statutory duty to assess a person's needs for community care services and to assess his or her carer's needs.[6] Once the needs are assessed, the law may require the local authority to meet all or some of them.

We will look at this in more detail below.

[1] Social Work (Scotland) Act 1968, s 13.
[2] For a clear explanation of the law, see remarks of Lord Nicholls in *R v London Borough of Barnet, ex parte G* [2003] UKHL 57, paras 10–15
[3] See, for example, the general welfare duty under Social Work (Scotland) Act, s 12.
[4] Under SW(S)A 1968, s 13A.
[5] See services under Mental Health (Care and Treatment) (Scotland) Act 2003 and Children (Scotland) Act below.
[6] See chapter 27.

WELFARE SERVICES FOR ADULTS AND CHILDREN

28.03 The general duties to provide services are set out in the Social Work (Scotland) Act 1968 and the Children (Scotland) Act 1995.

Under Social Work (Scotland) Act

28.04 The Social Work (Scotland) Act gives local authorities the power and the duty to promote the social welfare of adults living in their areas.

Local authorities should make available advice, guidance and assistance on such a scale as may be appropriate for their area. They should provide such facilities (including residential facilities) and make such other arrangements as they consider suitable and adequate.[1]

They may make assistance in kind, such as providing meals or a home help, and may make cash payments to a person in need, in exceptional circumstances.[2]

[1]   Social Work (Scotland) Act, s 12(1).
[2]   SW(S)A 1968, s 12(2). The test of whether it is appropriate to give such assistance is whether it will avoid greater expenditure to the local authority in the future.

Under Children (Scotland) Act

28.05 Local authorities must safeguard and promote the welfare of children in need in their area.[1]

They must promote the upbringing of children in need by their families,[2] by providing a range and level of services appropriate to the children's needs.[3]

[1]   Children (Scotland) Act 1995, s 22(1)(a).
[2]   Provided this is in the individual child's interests.
[3]   C(S)A 1995, s 22(1)(b).

Effect of duties

28.06 It is generally accepted that these are very wide duties, giving considerable discretion to local authorities. In an important judgement, the House of Lords considered the scope of similarly worded provisions in England and Wales.[1] The judgement is relevant to the interpretation of both section 22 of the Children (Scotland) Act and section 12 of the Social Work (Scotland) Act.

In considering the corresponding section of the Children Act 1989, the House of Lords held that the duty to provide childrens' services is owed to each child in need within the local authority's area. Although described as a general duty and although expressed in broad terms, the duty is enforceable by an individual child. Local authorities must provide a range of services to meet the needs of children in their area.

However the House of Lords said that this did not mean that a local authority has to meet all the assessed needs of every child who is in need, whatever those needs may be. Assessing a child's needs is a question of degree and judgement. There could be differing views on the child's needs and how to meet them.

Cost is also an element which may properly be taken into account in deciding what is 'appropriate' in a particular case. How far cost and a local authority's resources can be taken into account depends upon all the circumstances, including the nature of the person's assessed needs, the ease of meeting them, and the consequences of not meeting them. In any individual case, the local authority must act reasonably, bearing in mind all the circumstances of the case.[2]

This judgement of the House of Lords would be strongly influential if a case came before the Scottish courts.[3]

McGregor v South Lanarkshire Council (see 27.17) is an example of a case where the Scottish courts were prepared to insist that a local authority could not abandon its responsibilities to a person in need.

[1]   *R v London Borough of Barnet, ex parte G* [2003] UKHL 57.

[2]   See Lord Nicholls at para 30.

[3]   Judgments of the House of Lords on statutes which have similar wording to Scottish statutes are 'persuasive' in the Scottish courts, but not binding on them.

MENTAL HEALTH (CARE AND TREATMENT) ACT DUTIES

28.07 The Mental Health (Care and Treatment) Act imposes statutory duties on local authorities to provide services for people with mental disorders in their area. Local authorities must provide care and support services and a wide range of services to promote well being.

These services are for any adult with mental health difficulties, a learning disability, dementia or a personality disorder. They are also for children with mental disorders, in addition to the local authority's duties under the Children (Scotland) Act.[1]

Local authorities must either provide these services themselves or arrange for a voluntary or other organisation to provide them. A local authority should co-operate with local health boards and voluntary organisations[2] and may formally request a health board to provide it with assistance. The health board must comply, provided this is compatible with its own functions and would not excessively prejudice its performance of those functions.[3]

Local authorities do not have to provide services for people in hospital, but may do if they wish. A person does not have to have been in hospital to qualify for help.

Either the person themselves or anyone with a concern, such as a carer or a GP, can contact the local authority to see what help is available. A local authority must consider the person's needs for these services when it makes a community care assessment, but should bear in mind a person's need for these services at other times.[4]

Local authorities may charge for services they provide,[5] but services should not be withheld if a person is unable (or refuses) to pay.[6] Even if a fixed sliding scale applies, a person may ask the local authority to consider his or her special circumstances.[7]

1   Mental Health (Care and Treatment) (Scotland) Act 2003, s 29(2).
2   MH(CT)(S)A 2003, s 30.
3   MH(CT)(S)A 2003, s 31.
4   Code of Practice, vol 1, para 5.07.
5   Social Work (Scotland) Act 1968, s 87(1) (amended by MH(CT)(S)A 2003, s 28). See chapter 29.
6   See *Charging for adult non-residential sector care* (Social Work Services Group circular, SWSG1/97), para 36. The local authority may go to court to seek to recover any unpaid charges.
7   MH(CT)(S)A Code of Practice, vol 1, para 5.12.

Support services

28.08 Local authorities must provide care and support services for people with mental disorders.[1] These should be designed to minimise the impact of the person's mental disorder and aim to give the person the opportunity to lead as normal a life as possible.[2] Services should also be available for people recovering from mental disorders.

These services should include both residential accommodation and personal care and/or support services.[3] Personal care is help with day-to-day physical tasks and needs and with the mental processes (such as memory or motivation) related to those tasks and needs. Personal support is counselling, or other help, provided as part of a planned programme.[4]

Nursing is not included. Local authorities have no statutory powers to provide nursing care,[5] but must help others to do so (see below).

1   Mental Health (Care and Treatment) (Scotland) Act 2003, s 25.
2   MH(CT)(S)A 2003, s 25(2).

3   MH(CT)(S)A 2003, s 25(3).
4   As defined in the Regulation of Care (Scotland) Act 2001, s 2(28).
5   Although it may arrange with a health board to provide this under Joint Futures (see 27.02).

Personal development services

28.09 Local authorities must provide services designed to promote the well-being and social development of people who have or have had a mental disorder.[1] This includes people with learning disabilities, mental health difficulties, personality disorders and dementia. It also includes people recovering from a mental disorder.

These provisions are wide enough to encourage the development of innovative services which could enhance people's lives. The services the local authority should provide include:

- Services providing social, cultural and recreational activities.
- Training for people aged 16 and over; and
- Employment help for people aged over 16 (including helping people to find jobs and helping them to carry out the job).[2]

These duties[3] are in addition to the local authority's duties to provide education for people of school age[4] and to Scottish Ministers' duties to provide further education.[5] Even though the education statutes contain the primary responsibility for implementing educational programmes, the social work department can facilitate the provision of suitable education and training schemes in schools and colleges. The Mental Health (Care and Treatment) Act reinforces this.[6]

1   Mental Health (Care and Treatment) (Scotland) Act 2003, s 26.
2   MH(CT)(S)A 2003, s 26(2).
3   MH(CT)(S)A 2003, s 26(3).
4   Education (Scotland) Act 1980, s 1.
5   Further and Higher Education (Scotland) Act 1992, s 1.
6   See *New Directions*, para 13.54.

Transport

28.10 To help people attend services, a local authority must provide transport facilities or help with travel costs, as it considers necessary.[1]

1   Mental Health (Care and Treatment) (Scotland) Act 2003, s 27.

Nature of obligations

28.11 The wording of these obligations gives some discretion to local authorities as to how they meet the need for services in their areas.

The local authority's duty is to provide services 'designed to minimise' distress or 'designed to promote' well being. The courts have said that this wording[1] leaves a great deal to the judgement of the local authority.[2] A local authority can probably consider its resources in considering what social and recreational facilities it provides, for example.

Once a local authority has assessed a person as needing a service, it must consider how and whether it can meet the need.

A local authority must act reasonably. The courts are unlikely to be sympathetic if a local authority's failure to provide services leaves someone at risk.[3] This could also be challenged under human rights legislation.[4]

---

[1] Also seen in the Children (Scotland) Act, s 23, (below).

[2] See *R v London Borough of Barnet ex parte G* [2003] UKHL 57, Lord Hope at para 81.

[3] See *McGregor and Robertson* (below).

[4] Art 2 (right to life), Art 3 (inhumane and degrading treatment), Art 8 (respect for family and private life).

Case law

28.12 The personal support duties in the Mental Health (Care and Treatment) Act replace the duty to provide after-care in the 1984 Act.[1] There have been some cases looking at the obligations of local authorities to provide after-care in England and Wales.

The current English and Welsh Act gives a very limited right to after-care. The legal duty extends only to patients who have been compulsorily detained in hospital for at least six months.[2] Yet even in these circumstances the duty to provide after-care is not unlimited.

In one case, the court held that a person who did not receive after-care could not enforce even this limited statutory duty.[3] The claimant alleged that it was lack of such after-care which led him to kill a stranger in the street. (This case may have turned on its particular facts and, in particular, on the unwillingness of the courts to compensate a person for his criminal act.)

In a more instructive case,[4] the Court of Appeal said that the duty to provide after-care was not absolute. A mental health review tribunal gave K a conditional discharge from hospital. The hospital and local authority were unable to arrange suitable after-care for her. She remained in hospital. The court said that the authorities had to decide what was appropriate in the circumstances. It was not a breach of K's human rights for her to remain in hospital if no suitable facilities could be found in the community. K took her case to the Court of Human Rights, which upheld the Court of Appeal's findings (although it did find for K on other grounds).[5]

This case clearly illustrates how, even where a statute appears to impose an unequivocal duty on a local authority, the courts may not regard this as a matter of strict liability. The courts recognised that the local authority had a legal duty to provide after-care, but accepted that it must exercise its discretion in deciding how to provide suitable care.

1   Mental Health (Scotland) Act 1984, s 8.
2   Mental Health Act 1983, s 117.
3   *Clunis v Camden and Islington Health Authority* (1998) 1 CCLR 215.
4   *R on the application of K v Camden and Islington Health Authority* [2001] EWCA Civ 240.
5   *Kolanis v UK* [2005] ECtHR 411.

SUPPORT FOR CHILDREN AND YOUNG PEOPLE

Under Children (Scotland) Act

28.13 See chapter 41. Local authorities have general duties to provide services for children in their area, including pre-school and after-school care.[1] The Court of Session has held these duties are not enforceable by individual children. Local authorities have discretion as to what services they should provide.[2]

Local authorities have a legal duty to provide services 'designed to minimise' the effect of disability on young people living with disabilities.[3] We saw above that this wording gives local authorities discretion as to how they meet this obligation, but this provision imposes a more specific obligation owed to an individual child than the general duties above.[4]

A local authority must assess a young person's needs for services if requested by his or her parent or guardian. This duty is likely to be enforceable in the courts.[5] Having assessed the child's needs, the local authority must act reasonably in deciding how to meet them. See 28.06 above.

1   Children (Scotland) Act 1995, ss 22 and 27.
2   *Crossan v South Lanarkshire Council* [2006] CSOH 28 (14 February 2006).
3   C(S)A 1995, s 23.
4   See 28.11 for the effect of similar wording in the Mental Health (Care and Treatment) Act.
5   In a case in England, a judge ordered a local authority to carry out a full assessment of a child's needs in accordance with the guidance given by the Secretary of State. *R (on the application of AB and SB) v Nottinghamshire County Council* [2001] EWHC Admin 235 (2001) 4 CCLR 295.

Under Mental Health (Care and Treatment) Act

Contact with family

28.14 If a child is subject to a compulsory order under the Mental Health (Care and Treatment) Act, the local authority must 'take such steps as are practical and appropriate' to enable him or her to maintain contact with his or her parents.[1]

The Mental Health (Care and Treatment) Act again gives the local authority some discretion as to how it might meet this need, but this provision is expressed as a very clear duty owed to individual children, and an individual child could seek to enforce the duty in the courts.

1   Mental Health (Care and Treatment) (Scotland) Act 2003, s 278.

Education

28.15 The Mental Health (Care and Treatment) Act modifies the Education (Scotland) Act 1980. If a child subject to a compulsory order under the Mental Health (Care and Treatment) Act or the Criminal Procedure (Scotland) Act 1995 is unable to attend school, the local authority must arrange to provide school education for him or her.

This obligation is likely to be enforceable in the courts.[1]

1   See *R v East Sussex County Council, ex p Tandy* [1998] AC 714 where the House of Lords upheld a young person's right to home tuition. The local authority had a duty to provide 'suitable education' for children unable to attend school. This meant education suitable for each child. See also *G (a child) v Bromley* LBC [1999] ELR 356. (A local authority owed a duty of care to meet the special educational needs of a profoundly disabled pupil.)

HELP FOR FAMILIES

28.16 Local authorities must also provide services 'designed to minimise' any adverse effect for a young person of having a family member with a disability.[1]

If a parent is subject to a compulsory order, the local authority must 'take such steps as are practical and appropriate' to enable him or her to maintain contact with his or her children.[2]

See comments at 28.11 above.

---

[1]   Children (Scotland) Act 1995, s 23.

[2]   Mental Health (Care and Treatment) (Scotland) Act 2003, s 278.

HOME HELPS

28.17 Each local authority should ensure that there are 'adequate' domiciliary services in its area for people in need.[1] It may provide services itself or arrange for others to provide them.[2]

Domiciliary services are services in the home which the local authority considers necessary to help a person live as independently as possible.[3] They could include help with cooking, cleaning or home-care services, such as help with budgeting or emotional support.

This general provision is likely to be regarded as a 'target duty'. The question of what are adequate services for the needs of the area is partly a matter of judgement and partly a matter of resources.

Anyone needing help in the home should seek an assessment of his or her needs. The local authority should then consider what help it can provide. A person who is chronically sick or disabled should also receive an assessment under the Chronically Sick and Disabled Persons Act.

---

[1]   This includes people with a mental disorder. Social Work (Scotland) Act 1968, s 94(1).

[2]   SW(S)A 1968 (as amended by the National Health Service and Community Care Act 1990), s 14.

[3]   SW(S)A 1968, s 94(1).

WELFARE SERVICES

Chronically Sick and Disabled Persons Act

28.18 If a local authority determines that a disabled person[1] needs certain services, it must provide these or arrange to provide them if no one else is doing this.[2]

The services include:

- Practical help at home.
- Radio, television, books or similar leisure facilities.
- Games, lectures, outings or similar recreational facilities.
- Help in using any educational facilities which may be available.
- Help with transport to local authority services, or similar services run by another organisation.[3]
- Home adaptations or other facilities which would improve the person's safety, comfort or convenience.
- Holidays (which may be organised by the local authority, the person him or herself[4] or by a carer).[5]
- Meals at home or at a day centre.
- Telephone and equipment to help to use it.

Some of these services could be particularly helpful to a person living with mental health challenges or a person with a learning disability or dementia. If a local authority decides someone needs such services and no other arrangements can be made to provide them, it must provide them. The local authority cannot argue lack of resources.

---

[1] This includes a person with physical disability, a person who is chronically sick and a person with a mental disorder.

[2] Chronically Sick and Disabled Persons Act 1970, (as amended by the Chronically Sick and Disabled Persons (Scotland) Act 1972) and the Disabled Persons (Services, Consultation and Representation) Act 1986), s 2(1).

[3] The local authority has discretion whether to pay for transport to services it has not provided or arranged.

[4] In *R v Ealing London Borough Council ex p Leapman*, The Times, 10 February 1984, the court said that a local authority cannot refuse to fund a holiday simply because it has not arranged it.

[5] The amount to be paid is the whole cost of the holiday, not just any extra costs caused because of the person's disability. *R v North Yorkshire County Council ex parte Hargreaves*, The Times, 12 June 1997.

Obtaining an assessment

28.19 A person needing services or his or her carer may request their local authority to assess the person's need for services under the Act. The local authority must comply with the request.[1] The local authority may assess the client's needs at the same time as it carries out a community care assessment.

The local authority may charge for any services it provides under the Chronically Sick and Disabled Person Act.[2] Its charges must be reasonable and it may not withdraw the services if the person later becomes unable to pay.[3]

1   Disabled Persons (Services, Consultation and Representation) Act 1986, s 4.
2   Social Work (Scotland) Act 1968, s 87(1).
3   The duty to provide services is not subject to the payment provisions. See *Barry* below.

Extent of duty

28.20 The duty under the Chronically Sick and Disabled Person Act is enforceable in the courts, but in a limited way. The House of Lords has clarified the extent of the local authority's duty. The court said that:

- In deciding what a person 'needs' for the purposes of the section, a local authority can take into account its own resources to meet those needs. This means that a local authority can set its own eligibility criteria for services.
- Once a local authority has decided it should make arrangements to meet a person's needs, it is under an absolute duty to do so. It cannot argue that it does not have the resources. The time for considering resources is when it considers how to set eligibility criteria.
- When a local authority assesses someone as needing a service, it cannot withdraw the service without a reassessment of the person's needs.[1]

There may be some circumstances where no reasonable authority could refuse to consider meeting a person's needs. For example, a person might be at serious risk if he or she does not have assistance in his or her home.

The lower courts said that in such circumstances the local authority must help, and cannot argue it does not have the money in its budget. An authority could not be said to be acting reasonably if it refuses help in such circumstances.[2]

1   See *R v Gloucestershire County Council, ex parte Barry* [1997] 2 All ER 1.
2   *R v Gloucestershire County Council, ex parte Mahfood and others R v Gloucestershire CC, ex parte Mahfood* (1995) 8 Admin LR 180.

RESIDENTIAL CARE

Duty to arrange

28.21 Local authorities must establish and maintain residential and other establishments to fulfil their duties under the Social Work (Scotland) Act, the Mental Health (Care and Treatment) (Scotland) Act and the Children (Scotland) Act.[1]

A 'residential establishment' is accommodation managed by a local authority, voluntary organisation or other body.[2] It does not include a private house.[3]

Local authorities may run such establishments themselves or jointly with other local authorities or may arrange for voluntary or other organisations to provide suitable accommodation.[4] They are not obliged to run residential establishments themselves.[5]

Accommodation can be provided outside Scotland if clients need this. This could include care in residential care homes or in hospitals south of the border.[6]

1   Social Work (Scotland) Act 1968, s 59. This duty supplements the general duty in SW(S)A 1968, s 12, to assist people in need, which also requires the provision of residential establishments.
2   SW(S)A 1968, s 94.
3   *Assessor for Edinburgh v Brodie*, 1976 SLT 235.
4   SW(S)A 1968, s 59(2).
5   See *R v Wandsworth London Borough Council, ex parte Beckwith*. CA, Times Law Report, 29 June 1995. The court said (on similar wording in the English Act) that nothing in the legislation prevented a local authority from closing its homes if adequate provision was available elsewhere.
6   Community Care and Health (Scotland) Act 2002, s 5.

Choice of accommodation

28.22 Local authorities must arrange for a people assessed as needing residential care to go to the care homes of their choice, provided the local authority considers the accommodation is suitable for the person's needs, it is available and it does not cost more than what the local authority would expect to pay.[1]

Authorities can arrange for more expensive care if a third party (but not the client) is willing to pay the difference.

If someone cannot go to the care home of his or her choice within six weeks of leaving hospital, a local authority may arrange an intermediate placement.[2] The process may (and usually will) take considerably longer if those involved need to seek an order under the Adults with Incapacity (Scotland) Act.

1   Social Work (Scotland) Act 1968 (Choice of Accommodation) Directions 1993. Social Work Services Group circular, SWSG 5/93.
2   *Choice of accommodation: discharge from hospital* (Scottish Executive Health Department circular, CCD8/2003).

Effect of duties

28.23 The Choice of Accommodation Directions are legally binding on local authorities. Taken together with section 59 of the Social Work (Scotland) Act, it does appear that if an individual is assessed as needing residential care there is a legal obligation on a local authority to make arrangements for this.[1]

This does not mean that the local authority must make residential accommodation available to anyone who might wish this. The legal duty appears to be owed only to people who are assessed as needing residential care.[2]

1   In a case in England the court said that a 'target' duty to a group of people could be 'crystallised' for an individual following an assessment of his or her needs. *R v Kensington and Chelsea Royal London Borough Council, Ex p Kujtim* [1999] 4 All ER 161. (See also *McGregor* case below.)
2   *R v London Borough of Barnet, ex parte G* [2003] UKHL 57.

NURSING HOMES

28.24 Local authorities must make such arrangements as they consider appropriate to ensure that adequate nursing home accommodation is available. This is a separate and distinct duty from local authorities' general legal duties under section 12 of the Social Work (Scotland) Act.[1] Nursing homes should be provided for people who need care because of infirmity, age, illness, mental disorder, disability or dependency on drugs or alcohol.[2]

Local authorities are not under a legal obligation to provide nursing homes themselves, but can now do so under the Joint Futures programme with the National Health Service.[3]

This provision requires local authorities to make adequate provision for nursing home services within their geographical area, but its wording gives a wide discretion to local authorities.

It is unlikely this section, on its own, would give rights to an individual who does not receive nursing home care services.[4] It is different if the person is assessed as needing nursing.[5]

[1]   Lord Nicholls in House of Lords judgement in *Robertson v Fife Council* [2002] UKHL 35.
[2]   Social Work (Scotland) Act, s 13A.
[3]   See 27.02.
[4]   See comments of Lord Hardie in *McGregor v South Lanarkshire Council*, 2001 SLT 233, para 7.
[5]   *McGregor* (above). See 27.17.

Chapter 29

PAYING FOR CARE

29.01 While care in the National Health Service is free, someone who receives help arranged through the local authority must pay, according to the person's means. Different rules apply according to whether the care is day care or residential care.

In this chapter we look at charging for day care; respite care; paying for residential care; liability of relatives to pay for care and planning for future care.

Scottish Ministers can make regulations requiring local authorities to charge or not to charge for social care, including care in the home or personal support services.[1] They can cap charges and can specify the amount local authorities can take into account when calculating charges.[2] The Convention of Scottish Local Authorities ('COSLA') is evaluating charging for non-residential services. The Scottish Executive has said that it will not exercise these powers until it has evaluated the working of the COSLA guidance.[3]

[1]   Community Care and Health (Scotland) Act 2002, s 1(4). These provisions do not extend to charging for residential care. CCH(S)A 2002, s 22(2).
[2]   CCH(S)A 2002, s 1(5).
[3]   Circular CCD4/2002, para 3.3. For COSLA guidance, see 29.03 below.

WHERE NO CHARGE PERMITTED

29.02 Certain local authority services do not attract charges. Local authorities cannot charge for general advice and assistance, for carrying out community care assessments or for managing a client's care.

The Scottish Executive has advised local authorities not to charge for services involved in providing 'supervision' to some psychiatric patients discharged into the community.[1] Someone subject to a compulsion order (formerly a hospital order), guardianship order or a supervision and treatment order should not have to pay for social work services he or she receives.[2]

Nursing and personal care for people over 65 is free (see below).[3]

[1]   *Charging for adult non-residential sector care* (Circular SWSG1/97), para 8.

²   Circular SWSG1/97, para 9.
³   Community Care and Health (Scotland) Act 2002, s 1.

NON-RESIDENTIAL SERVICES
Making charges

29.03 Local authorities may recover reasonable charges for services they provide under the Social Work (Scotland) Act, the Children (Scotland) Act and the Mental Health (Care and Treatment) (Scotland) Act. These include day care, domiciliary services, childrens services, wardens in sheltered housing and aids and adaptations. They can charge for services they provide themselves and for services they contract to other agencies, such as voluntary organisations.[1]

Local authorities fix their own charging rates. There is considerable variation throughout the country. Guidance from the Convention of Scottish Local Authorities recommends local authorities set the income threshold for charges at 125 per cent above Income Support levels.[2] Councils do not charge for day care or for aids and adaptations.[3]

A local authority should not make an assessment of needs dependent on a client's ability to pay for services. While a financial assessment will be carried out, this should be a separate process from the needs assessment.[4]

All local authorities should provide information about their charging policies and people should be told as quickly as possible about the possible cost of services they are to receive.[5]

¹   Social Work (Scotland) Act 1968, s 87(1).
²   *Guidance on charging policies for non-residential services that enable older people to remain in their own home* (May 2002), ('the 'COSLA guidance') paras 49–50. At the time of writing, COSLA was revising this guidance.
³   COSLA guidance, para 62.
⁴   See chapter 27.
⁵   *Charging for adult non-residential sector care* (Circular SWSG 1/97), paras 37 and 38. COSLA guidance (above), para 68.

Challenging charges

29.04 A client can appeal against any charges imposed.[1] The local authority must then look into the client's financial circumstances and cannot require him or her to pay more than a reasonable amount.[2]

If a client receives a service the local authority is under a legal obligation to provide (see above), it cannot withdraw the service if a client later becomes unable to pay or refuses to pay. The statutory duty to provide the service is not subject to the ability of the authority to recover charges. The local authority can take action in the sheriff court to recover any unpaid charges.

Scottish Executive guidance says that local authorities should consider waiving charges for support services for a disabled child where the cost of supporting the child imposes significant extra costs on a parent.[3]

1   Social Work (Scotland) Act, s 87(1A).

2   The local government ombudsman for England criticised one council which failed properly to look into its client's ability to pay. *Report by the local government ombudsman into complaint No 90/A/2675, 2025, 1702 and others against Essex County Council* (October 1991). See *Avon County Council v Hooper* [1997] 1 WLR 1605 for what might be 'reasonable'. A local authority must take into account its general obligations to ratepayers and council taxpayers.

3   *New statutory rights for carers* (Scottish Executive Health Department, circular CCD2/2003), para 8.9.1.

Free day care

29.05 People aged 65 or over who need home care after leaving National Health Service in-patient care are now entitled to up to four weeks' free care.[1] This includes social care in the person's home, such as domiciliary services or minor home adaptations, and services provided under the Mental Health (Care and Treatment) Act.

Services provided wholly outside the person's home, such as lunch clubs, are not covered, but the care can include help with shopping, as the need originates in the home.

1   Scottish Executive circular CCD2/2001.

Relatives' liability

29.06 Local authorities should not ask relatives or carers to contribute towards the cost of day care. Relatives have no legal liability to pay for such items.

This general rule is modified where a spouse receives day care. Spouses have a legal duty to maintain each other, subject to proposed changes in the Adult Support and Protection (Scotland) Bill. See 29.14.

Unfortunately, the law is unclear whether the duty to maintain includes a duty to pay day care charges. Some local authorities have attempted to recover day care fees from spouses. The amounts involved can be quite considerable.

A local authority can go to court to recover residential day care fees from a spouse who refuse to pay,[1] but there is no provision empowering them to recover day care fees. In the absence of such authority, it would appear that Parliament did not intend spouses to pay each other's day care fees. Any financial assessment made should look solely at the resources of the person receiving day care.

The Scottish Executive confirms that it is not appropriate for local authorities to charge spouses for the cost of day care. It states that in certain circumstances a person might have 'access to resources' which could be taken into account in considering their own resources. This is most likely to happen in the case of married or unmarried couples.[2]

COSLA guidance suggests that spouses' income should be taken into account. With the advent of free personal and nursing care, COSLA suggests these charges will cover only non-personal care. It says both partners benefit from these domestic services and the resources of both should be taken into account.[3]

Spouses required to contribute to day care costs should take legal advice. If a spouse refuses to pay, the local authority can start court action. The court would have to make a judgement about whether a spouse should pay and, if so, what would be a reasonable contribution.

[1]   National Assistance Act 1948, s 43.

[2]   *Charging for adult non-residential sector care* (Circular SWSG1/97), para 29.

[3]   COSLA guidance, para 51.

RESPITE CARE

29.07 Respite care may involve a carer coming into a person's home to allow a carer to get out, or it may involve a cared-for person going to stay in residential care, a hospital or even with another family. Charges depend on the kind of respite care.

• *Respite care received in the home* A charge may be made following the rules in 29.03 above.

- *Respite care provided in a day centre* Local authorities can make a 'reasonable' charge. See 29.03.
- *Respite care in hospital* This is free of charge. Respite care in hospital is becoming increasingly unusual, but is appropriate when someone has special nursing or medical needs which can be met only in a health setting.[1]
- *Respite care in a nursing home or residential care for less than eight weeks at a time* Local authorities can charge what they consider a reasonable amount.[2] They may charge the full cost of the care and carry out a full financial assessment, but can charge a nominal amount. Scottish Executive guidance says that charging policies which discourage the use of respite care are not in anyone's interests and may ultimately lead to greater expense for local authorities.[3]
- *Residential respite care for longer than eight weeks at a time* Local authorities must charge the full rate for the accommodation, depending on clients' means.[4] They must carry out a full financial assessment according to the rules for residential accommodation (see below). The value of a client's home and regular expenses connected with the home are not taken into account, nor are certain welfare benefits.[5]

Going into respite care can affect welfare benefits. Specialist welfare rights advice should be sought on how best to arrange this.

[1] For the criteria see *Guidance on Respite Care* (Scottish Executive circular SWSG 10/96), para 21. ('The respite care guidance'.) The guidance says it is up to health boards and local authorities to arrange who should provide what forms of respite care. Care which is needed to give the carer a break should be organised by the local authority and paid for by them, even if it is provided in a hospital. Care which is needed for the health needs of the person being cared for should be organised by the health service and be free to the recipient. Arrangements under Joint Futures (see 27.02) may deal with the arrangement and funding of respite care.
[2] National Assistance Act 1948, s 22(5A).
[3] Respite Care Guidance (SWSG10/96) para 45.
[4] National Assistance Act 1948, s 22, Social Work (Scotland) Act 1968, s 87(3).
[5] National Assistance (Assessment of Resources) Regulations 1992 (SI 1992/2977), as amended.

RESIDENTIAL CARE

29.08 A person moving into a care home must pay the full cost of the care, dependent on his or her means.[1] The local authority assesses the person's means according to a statutory formula. Whilst in general only the resources of the person moving into care are assessed, a contribution may also be required from a spouse. Other relatives may agree to make an additional contribution so that their family member can go to the home of his or her choice.

The health board should meet the costs of nursing home care for people who need medical supervision or specialist nursing care.[2]

1   National Assistance Act 1948, s 22, Social Work (Scotland) Act 1968, s 87(3).
2   The person is treated as a hospital patient for Income Support purposes and is not eligible for housing benefit. *Botchell v Chief Adjudication Officer*, Times Law Report, 8 May 1996.

Charging for residential care

The charging rules

29.09 This section gives an outline of the rules for charging for residential care.[1] The rules are particularly complex if people are also receiving welfare benefits, because both the Department of Work and Pensions and the local authority must make financial assessments. Each has slightly different rules.

A resident's income and capital are taken into account.

Income includes most welfare benefits.[2] When a resident has a pension and a spouse or civil partner still alive, the local authority disregards 50 per cent of the pension, provided the resident actually gives this money to the spouse or partner.[3] A resident with an unmarried partner of either sex can ask the local authority to consider increasing the personal expenses allowance to give the partner access to the pension.[4]

Residents are always left with a small amount of money to meet personal expenses. At the time of writing this amount is £19.60 a week.[5]

The value of any capital over £20,000 owned by a resident is taken into account in full.[6] 'Capital' includes the family home, stocks and shares and money in the bank. Capital between £12,250 and £20,000 is taken into account on a sliding scale. The local authority can put a mortgage, or charge, on any property(ies) of a person who fails to pay his or her contribution.[7]

The income and capital limits change each April, in line with inflation.

1   For more information see *The Paying for Care Handbook* (Child Poverty Action Group). The guidance from the Scottish Executive, see footnote 4 below, also sets out the rules in very clear and readable language. However it is not a

statement of the law and its guidance to local authorities (for example on deprivation of capital) is just that.

2   The main exception is the mobility component of Disability Living Allowance.

3   National Assistance (Assessment of Resources) Regulations 1992 (SI 1992/2977), as amended, ('The Assessment of Resources Regulations') Sched 3, para 10A.

4   *Charging for residential accommodation guidance* attached to Scottish Executive Health department circular CCD1/2006, ('the Residential charges guidance') paras 8.024C and 5.005.

5   National Assistance (Sums for Personal Requirements) (Scotland) Regulations 2005, (SSI 2005/84).

6   National Assistance (Assessment of Resources) Amendment (Scotland) Regulations 2005 (SSI 2005/82).

7   Health and Social Services and Social Security Adjudications Act 1983, s 23. For the form of the order see the Charging Orders (Residential Accommodation) (Scotland) Order 1993 (SI 1993/1516).

Family home

29.10 A person's capital includes any house or share in a house she owns. The house may have to be sold to pay for care. It may be possible to raise money on the value of the property by an equity release scheme and use this to finance an insurance policy to pay for care fees. Professional advice is necessary.

The value of the resident's share may not be large when a house is jointly owned. This is because the value is taken as what the resident's half interest in the property would be worth, not the value of half the home.[1] This is generally not a large amount, as there is unlikely to be a market for a part share in a house.

1   Assessment of Resources Regulations, reg 27(2).

Disregarding value of home

29.11 The home is not treated as part of a person's capital if the person's spouse, partner or certain other people are still living there. These are any relative or member of the resident's family (as defined) who is aged over 60, a former partner of the resident who is a lone parent, a child under 16 whom the resident is eligible to maintain and a member of the resident's family who is 'incapacitated' (a term which is not defined).[1]

The local authority may decide to disregard the value of the property in certain other circumstances.[2] Scottish Executive guidance says it might be reasonable to disregard the value of the home where it is the sole residence of someone who has given up his or her home to care for the resident, (whether or not they are a relative of the person going into care). It might also be reasonable to disregard the value if an elderly companion of the resident or a same sex partner is living in the house.[3]

1   Assessment of Resources Regulations 1992 (SI 1992/2977), Sched 4, para 2.
2   Assessment of Resources Regulations 1992, Sched 4, para 18.
3   See the Residential charges guidance (CCD1/2006), para 7.007.

Anti-avoidance provisions

29.12 The rules say that anyone who disposes of income or capital in order to reduce charges for residential care is treated as if he or she still owns the item in question.[1] Scottish Executive guidance says that avoiding charges may not have been the only reason for the transaction, but it should be a significant one.[2] If, for example, a transfer is made for inheritance tax purposes, it might be thought that this should not be regarded as an attempt to avoid care home charges.

A local authority which decides there has been a deprivation of capital or income may treat the asset as 'notional capital or income' of the person and levy the full charge.

If the transaction took place within six months of the person moving into residential care, the local authority may require the third party to pay.[3] The test is that the resident made the transfer knowingly with the intention of avoiding or reducing liability for charges.

1   Assessment of Resources Regulations 1992 (SI 1992/2977), regs 17 and 25.
2   Residential charges guidance, para 6.061.
3   Health and Social Services and Social Security Adjudications Act 1983, s 21.

Extent of anti-avoidance provision

29.13 Any arrangements, however complex, may get caught by these anti-avoidance provisions. Some advisers suggest setting up trusts, or leases and other complex schemes. If the motive, or a significant part of the motive, for such a scheme is to prevent the proceeds of the sale of the house to pay for residential care, it could be caught under this provision.[1]

The local authority may treat a transaction as a deliberate deprivation of capital whenever it was made. There is no time limit on how far back the local authority can go. Clearly, the longer the time gap between the making of the decision to transfer the asset or the income and the person's going into residential care, the less likely it is that the local authority could establish that the motive was to avoid charges which might never arise.[2]

The guidance says that it is not reasonable for a local authority to bring a transaction within the rules if the person made it when he or she was fit and healthy and could not have foreseen the need to move.[3] However if it is reasonable to infer from the circumstances that a person must have made the transaction at least in part to avoid care charges, the fact that he or she was fit and healthy at the time will not be enough to avoid being caught by the rules.[4]

Anyone having problems with these rules needs legal advice.

1   See *Yule v South Lanarkshire Council (No 1)*, 1998 SLT 490, *Yule v South Lanarkshire Council (No 2)*, 2000 SLT 1249.
2   There is a six-month time limit on tracking the money to third parties, however, see above.
3   Residential charges guidance, para 6.063.
4   *Yule* (above).

Spouses' liability

29.14 Husbands and wives (but not unmarried partners or divorced couples) are legally obliged to maintain each other.[1] If either of them is unable to pay residential care charges from their own resources, the local authority may require the other to make a reasonable contribution.

Scottish Executive guidance says that this would not be appropriate if the supporting spouse was living on income support, nor is it appropriate to expect the spouse's income to be reduced to income support levels to pay maintenance.[2]

A local authority cannot insist that a spouse has a financial assessment. If a spouse refuses to give details of his or her income and capital or refuses to pay the amount the local authority requires, the local authority can go to court to seek an order for the spouse to maintain the other spouse. The court can then fix a reasonable amount.[3]

The Scottish Executive intends to remove the liability of spouses to contribute to each other's care costs.[4] In the meantime, it encourages local authorities to base charges for residential care solely on the resources of the person moving to care.[5]

1   National Assistance Act 1948, s 42.

2   *Charges for Residential Accommodation- Guidance Amendment No 8* (Circular 6/ 98), para 11.0006.
3   National Assistance Act 1948, s 43.
4   See Adult Support and Protection (Scotland) Bill, clause 62.
5   See circular CCD6/2004, Annex C.

Relatives

29.15 While spouses remain legally liable to maintain each other, other relatives are never legally obliged to do so, although they may want to help.

No one is ever legally liable to pay for day care, domiciliary services or residential care for a relative other than their spouse *unless* the person has transferred assets or income to him or her to reduce charges (see above).

Anyone moving to residential care has the right to choose a care home, provided it is suitable and available.[1] The person cannot insist the local authority provides accommodation that costs more than it would usually expect to pay, but a relative may be prepared to contribute the extra amount. The relative can agree with the local authority to pay the extra amount.[2] The local authority must be satisfied that the relative has the ability to pay and will be able to continue to pay for as long as the resident is likely to remain in residential care.

The relative will generally have to sign a contract. He or she should obtain legal advice on the contract and check with local organisations that the local authority is accurately stating the amount it would usually pay for care.

Spouses cannot make extra payments under this provision.[3]

1   Social Work (Scotland) Act 1968 (Choice of Accommodation) Directions 1993, para 3. See Scottish Executive circular SW05/1993.
2   Social Work (Scotland) Act 1968 (Choice of Accommodation) Directions 1993, para 4(1). See Social Work Services Group circular SWSG5/93.
3   Choice of accommodation directions (above), para 4(2).

Deferred payments

29.16 A resident can defer the cost of care home fees by entering into an agreement with the local authority to pay the charges on a deferred basis. The person gives the local authority a mortgage over the house[1] and the charges can be deferred until 56 days after the person's death.[2]

No interest is payable until the date for repayment is past. Thereafter the local authority may charge a reasonable rate of interest.[3] Local authorities should make this scheme available for any resident whose capital (excluding the value of his or her home) is at, or below, the lower capital limit for paying care, currently £12,250.

Uptake of deferred payment schemes has not been high. All local authorities must give details of the scheme to people who might be eligible.[4] The Scottish Executive has powers to make the scheme compulsory if local authorities do not set up appropriate schemes voluntarily.[5]

It appears that local authorities in England and Wales can make loans to residents to enable them to pay care fees, secured by a mortgage on the resident's house.[6] Such a scheme could be available to any resident, regardless of capital or income. It is not known whether this would be an attractive option for Scotland.

[1]   Called a 'standard security'.

[2]   Community Care and Health (Scotland) Act 2002, s 6.

[3]   Scottish Executive Health Department Letter HDL 2003/6. The rate should not be 'punitive' in a situation where a property takes some time to sell.

[4]   *Deferred payments and other funding arrangements which allow care home residents to delay selling their homes* (Scottish Executive circular 13/2004).

[5]   Community Care and Health (Scotland) Act 2002, s 6(1).

[6]   See *Paying the fees of a care home in England* (Counsel and Care, 2005/6) para 3.7.

DISCHARGE FROM LONG-TERM CARE

29.17 While National Health Service care is free, social care arranged by local authorities may not be. This means that when someone moves from National Health Service care to residential care, there may be financial implications.

Residents of long stay wards may be moved out of hospital with little opportunity for relatives to be involved. Because of public concern about the implications, the National Health Service has a system allowing patients to appeal against the decision to discharge them from National Health Service care.[1]

[1]   See 6.14.

PLANNING FOR FUTURE CARE

29.18 A person needing to plan for future residential or nursing home care for themselves or a member of their family needs independent financial advice, either from an accountant or solicitor or from an independent financial adviser. Schemes which promise a way to avoid residential care home fees should be regarded with caution.

It may be possible to maximise a person's income and avoid having to sell the family home. Alternatively, if there are other good reasons to dispose of a family house, for inheritance tax planning reasons, for example, or if a person is no longer able to manage his or her house because of a mental disorder, it might be possible to argue that the anti-avoidance legislation should not come into play.

PART 7
PEOPLE AT RISK

Chapter 30

PEOPLE AT RISK

30.01 This chapter looks at people at risk and considers the legal protections available to them. A person might be at risk because of illness, abuse or lack of care. Abuse may be physical, financial or sexual. The protection available depends on the nature of the risk.

There is no single law protecting people against abuse. The common law, the criminal law, the Mental Health (Care and Treatment) Act and/or the Adults with Incapacity Act may be relevant. All have different principles and procedures, and people working in this field must become familiar with various different legal remedies.

The Scottish Law Commission has proposed a comprehensive package of reforms to protect vulnerable people.[1] Its report covers people vulnerable due to age, mental or physical illness or infirmity and people with physical disabilities.

The Commission recommended that local authorities should have a duty to investigate any situation where a vulnerable adult might be at risk. They should be able to gain access to a vulnerable person's home, to interview him or her and arrange for a medical examination, if necessary. They should be able to remove a person at risk to a place of safety or seek a court order removing an alleged abuser.

The Mental Health (Care and Treatment) Act implemented some of these recommendations. It did not go as far as the Scottish Law Commission recommended.

In April 2006 the Scottish Executive introduced the Adult Support and Protection (Scotland) Bill to the Scottish Parliament. The Bill gives local authorities more powers to investigate abuse along the lines of the Scottish Law Commission report. It proposes setting up local Adult Protection Committees to develop policies to help protect people from abuse and to investigate abuse.[2]

This chapter deals solely with adults at risk. The rules for children and young people are different. Appendix 1 suggests further reading.

[1]   *Vulnerable Adults,* Scot Law Com No 158, 1997.
[2]   *Protecting Vulnerable Adults—Securing their safety* (Scottish Executive Health Department, July 2005).

INVESTIGATING ABUSE

30.02 Just as there is no single Act of Parliament protecting people against abuse, so there is no one body responsible for investigating it. The responsibility for investigation depends on the nature of the alleged abuse and the place where it takes place.

The people investigating could include the Care Commission (where a registered service is involved), a health board (where someone claims to have been abused in an NHS service), a police (if the alleged conduct is a criminal offence), a local authority or the Mental Welfare Commission (for welfare concerns) and the Office of the Public Guardian (for financial and property matters). The Scottish Public Services Ombudsman could become involved if a complaint is made.

The relevant bodies should agree protocols for enquiries.[1] The Public Guardian and the Mental Welfare Commission have signed a Memorandum of Agreement clarifying their roles in investigating complaints.[2]

The Mental Welfare Commission generally refers complaints about financial matters to the Public Guardian, although if there are significant and complex welfare issues involved, it may be appropriate for the Commission to investigate. Either the Public Guardian or the Mental Welfare Commission can ask a local authority to investigate. It may be appropriate for the Public Guardian to investigate the financial aspects of a case, while the local authority investigates welfare matters.

The Mental Welfare Commission receives copies of the Public Guardian's reports into cases involving welfare issues and of local authorities' reports of welfare investigations. It may make further enquiries.

[1] Mental Health (Care and Treatment) (Scotland) Act 2003 Code of Practice, vol 1, para 15.11.
[2] See Mental Welfare Commission Annual Report 2001–2, para 4.2.1.

WELFARE RISK

30.03 The Adults with Incapacity Act and the Mental Health (Care and Treatment) Act give local authorities duties to investigate wherever a person with a mental disorder may be at risk. The Mental Welfare Commission has similar responsibilities. It generally refers the matter to a local authority, unless there is some reason why this would not be suitable.

Duties of local authorities

Under the Adults with Incapacity Act

30.04 Local authorities supervise welfare guardians and investigate complaints about welfare attorneys and other people operating welfare powers under the Adults with Incapacity Act. See chapter 25. They must also investigate whenever they are aware that someone with a mental disorder may be at risk.[1]

The Code of Practice gives guidance on good practice.[2] The local authority should generally arrange to visit the adult, and should consider the principles of the Act when carrying out its investigations. A local authority should bear in mind the need to safeguard the person's welfare and property, perhaps by seeking an order from the sheriff.[3]

A local authority can take action under the Adults with Incapacity Act only if its investigations reveal an adult lacks capacity in relation to the matter in question. Other powers, such as Mental Health (Care and Treatment) Act powers, might be appropriate in some circumstances.

The local authority may do what is necessary to protect the welfare of an adult at risk.[4] This could include making an application to a sheriff for a guardianship or intervention order or asking a sheriff for directions.[5] Urgent action might include applying for an interim order or removing the person to a place of safety (see below). If the person at risk is away from home, the local authority where he or she is living must investigate.[6]

The local authority should copy its investigation report to the Mental Welfare Commission.[7]

Anyone concerned that a person is at risk should feel free to contact the local authority social work or community services department.

[1] Adults with Incapacity (Scotland) Act 2000, s 10(1)(d).
[2] Code of Practice for local authorities exercising functions under the Act (March 2001) ('The local authority Code of Practice'), Part 4.
[3] AWI(S)A 2000, s 12.
[4] AWI(S)A 2000, s 12.
[5] Under AWI(S)A 2000, s 3. See 24.20.
[6] AWI(S)A 2000, s 10(2).
[7] Local authority Code of Practice, para 4.38.

Under Mental Health (Care and Treatment) Act

30.05 The local authority must investigate where it is aware that someone over 16 who may have a mental illness, personality disorder or learning disability may be at risk.[1] The risk might be:

- Ill-treatment, neglect or inadequate care (other than care in hospital), either currently or in the past.
- Someone appearing to be living alone or without care is unable to look after him or herself or his or her property or finances.
- Risk to other people because of a person's mental disorder (unless the person is in hospital).
- Risk of loss or damage to a person's property because of his or her mental disorder.

The Mental Health (Care and Treatment) Act gives local authorities new powers to carry out these duties (see below).

[1] Mental Health (Care and Treatment) (Scotland) Act 2003, s 33.

Co-operation with local authority

30.06 When a local authority carries out an enquiry under the Adults with Incapacity Act, it may seek help from the Mental Welfare Commission or the Public Guardian as necessary. These bodies should co-operate with the local authority.[1]

The local authority can ask a wider range of bodies to co-operate with Mental Health (Care and Treatment) Act investigations. These include the Mental Welfare Commission, the Public Guardian, the Care Commission and any health board.[2] These bodies must co-operate with the local authority, except in the unlikely event that this would prejudice their other duties.[3]

[1] Adults with Incapacity (Scotland) Act 2000, s 12(2).
[2] Mental Health (Care and Treatment) (Scotland) Act 2003, s 34.
[3] MH(CT)(S)A 2003, s 34(4).

Local authority powers

30.07 The Mental Health (Care and Treatment) Act gives local authorities enhanced powers to investigate where people may be at risk. If necessary, an authority can obtain a warrant to enter premises, to authorise a medical examination or to gain access to medical records. It can apply to move someone to hospital or a care home for assessment and medical examination.

The local authority should bear in mind the principles of the Act. It should not seek these powers if a less restrictive alternative is possible. It should try to involve the person at risk and any carers as far as possible when carrying out investigations, and bear in mind the wishes of the person. This may mean having to balance respect for the person's autonomy against risks to the person or other people. Human rights concerns, such as respect for privacy, are also relevant.

The Act's Code of Practice gives further advice on how these powers should operate in practice.[1]

[1]   See Code of Practice, vol 1, chap 15.

Application for warrant

30.08 A mental health officer can usually gain access and interview the person at risk and should always attempt this before using enforcement methods.[1]

Where someone at risk or others in the house are unwilling to allow a mental health officer to enter, the mental health officer may apply for a warrant. The application is to the sheriff or justice of the peace for the area where the premises are situated.[2]

There are three separate warrants. These authorise entry to the premises, the medical examination of the person and access to a person's medical records. The mental health officer may apply for all or any of these warrants.

For a warrant to enter premises, a mental health officer employed by the local authority where the premises are situated should make the application. For other warrants, the mental health officer must be an employee of the local authority conducting the enquiries.[3]

There are prescribed forms for the application and warrant.[4] These are available on the Scottish Executive's mental health law website.

[1]   See Code of Practice, vol 1, para 15.16.
[2]   Mental Health (Care and Treatment) (Scotland) Act 2003, s 35(3).
[3]   MH(CT)(S)A 2003, s 35(12).
[4]   Mental Health (Form of Documents) (Scotland) Regulations 2006 (SSI 2006/12).

Warrant to enter premises

30.09 A mental health officer must satisfy the court on oath that a warrant is necessary and that he or she has been unable to gain access (or will be unable to gain access).[1]

A warrant authorises the mental health officer and anyone named in the warrant to enter the premises within eight days of the warrant.[2] A police officer may attend and can make a forcible entry, if necessary.[3] If forced entry is used, the mental health officer must take steps to protect the person's premises and belongings.[4] The Code of Practice contains guidance to minimise the impact on the person.[5]

[1] Mental Health (Care and Treatment) (Scotland) Act 2003, s 35(1).

[2] MH(CT)(S)A 2003, s 35(2).

[3] MH(CT)(S)A 2003, s 35(2)(b).

[4] Code of Practice, vol 1, para 15.24.

[5] Code of Practice, vol 1, para 15.25.

Warrant for medical examination

30.10 The court may grant a warrant authorising a medical examination. The mental health officer must satisfy the court that a person needs to see a doctor and the mental health officer cannot obtain the person's consent.[1] (This could be because the mental health officer has been unable to speak to the person or because the person has refused consent.)

The application is to the sheriff or justice for the area where the person is living.[2]

The warrant authorises the detention of the person for up to three hours to enable the doctor named in the warrant to examine him or her.[3] The three hours runs from the time of the detention, not the time of the warrant. The procedure should be in accordance with the local psychiatric emergency plan.[4]

[1] Mental Health (Care and Treatment) (Scotland) Act 2003, s 35(4).

[2] MH(CT)(S)A 2003, s 35(6).

[3] MH(CT)(S)A 2003, s 35(5).

[4] Code of Practice, vol 1, para 15.28.

Access to medical records

30.11 The mental health officer may also apply for a warrant to allow access to someone's medical records. The application is to the sheriff or justice for the area where the person is living.

The mental health officer must satisfy the court that it is necessary for a doctor to see the records and the mental health officer cannot obtain the person's consent.[1]

If the court grants the warrant, any person who has the medical records must allow the doctor named in the warrant to inspect them.[2]

[1]   Mental Health (Care and Treatment) (Scotland) Act 2003, s 35(7).
[2]   MH(CT)(S)A 2003, s 35(8).

After the hearing

30.12 As soon as possible after the hearing, the mental health officer must notify the Mental Welfare Commission of the outcome.[1]

It is not possible to appeal against the decision of the sheriff or justice to grant or refuse a warrant.[2] Judicial review (see chapter 51) is available to challenge any errors in the legal process.

[1]   Mental Health (Care and Treatment) (Scotland) Act 2003, s 35(10).
[2]   MH(CT)(S)A 2003, s 35(11).

Removal orders

30.13 The local authority may consider that a person at risk needs to go to hospital or clinic for assessment. If the person or his or her carers do not agree, the local authority may apply for a removal order.[1]

A removal order is suitable only for people who are a risk to themselves or at risk from others. Short-term (or emergency) detention might be appropriate where someone may pose a risk to others. A removal order does not authorise medical treatment under Part 16 of the Mental Health (Care and Treatment) Act.

The application is to the sheriff of the area where the person at risk is living. In an emergency, a justice of the peace may grant an order.

The local authority must decide whether to use its powers to assess the person in his or her home (above) or to remove him or her to a place of safety. The Code of Practice says this generally depends on the risk.[2] It may be difficult for a mental health officer to satisfy a sheriff that a removal order is necessary unless the mental health officer has been able to gain some access and establish that the risk factors exist.

This means that as a matter of practice, where someone at risk will not grant entry, the local authority should generally seek a warrant to make enquiries at the person's home before it applies for a removal order, unless it considers the situation requires more urgent action.

1 Mental Health (Care and Treatment) (Scotland) Act 2003, s 293.
2 Code of Practice, vol 1, para 15.04.

Making the application

30.14 The mental health officer making the application should be an employee of the local authority for the area where the person is living.[1] The application is to the sheriff for that area.[2] A statutory form[3] is available on the Scottish Executive's mental health law website.

The mental health officer must satisfy the sheriff that the person is aged over 16 and has a mental disorder, that he or she is likely to suffer significant harm if he or she does not go to a place of safety, and that:

- The person is being ill-treated or neglected or is receiving inadequate care or treatment.
- Because of mental disorder the person's property is lost or damaged or is at a risk of loss or damage; or
- The person is living alone or without care and is unable to look after him or herself or his or her property or financial affairs.[4]

1 Mental Health (Care and Treatment) (Scotland) Act 2003, s 293(8).
2 MH(CT)(S)A 2003, s 293(4). For procedure, see Act of Sederunt (Summary Applications, Statutory Applications and Appeals etc. Rules) Amendment (Mental Health (Care and Treatment) (Scotland) Act 2003) 2005 (SSI 2005/504).
3 Under the Mental Health (Form of Documents) (Scotland) Regulations 2006 (SSI 2006/12).
4 MH(CT)(S)A 2003, ss 293(1) and 293(2).

Involving the parties

30.15 The sheriff must bear in mind the principles of the Act. The sheriff should give the person and his or her nearest relative, primary carer and any welfare guardian or attorney the opportunity of making representations to the sheriff (orally or in writing) and of leading, or producing, evidence.[1]

It is the responsibility of the mental health officer to find out who these people are, if possible. Anyone involved may want to seek legal advice.

The sheriff may dispense with a hearing if he or she considers this would cause delay likely to prejudice the interests of the person at risk.[2]

The mental health officer can ask the sheriff to dispense with notice to the relevant parties. The relevant parties should generally receive notice unless this is likely to prejudice the person's welfare.[3] Even if a sheriff decides not to hold a hearing, the relevant people might wish to supply him or her with written evidence or statements.

Statutory forms for notifying the parties are on the Scottish Executive website.[4]

[1] Mental Health (Care and Treatment) (Scotland) Act 2003, ss 293(5) and 293(6) and the Mental Health (Removal Order) (Scotland) Regulations 2005 (SSI 2005/381).
[2] MH(CT)(S)A 2003, s 293(7).
[3] Code of Practice, vol 1, paras 15.37–15.38.
[4] Form mental health officer 5a.

Urgent applications

30.16 If it is impracticable to apply to the sheriff and the mental health officer considers that delay could prejudice the person at risk, he or she may apply to a justice of the peace for the area where the person is living.[1]

The Mental Health (Care and Treatment) Act does not require the justice to hear from the relevant parties, although he or she should do this if possible, in accordance with the principles of the Act. For human rights reasons, the mental health officer should approach a justice of the peace only in an emergency.[2]

[1] Mental Health (Care and Treatment) (Scotland) Act 2003, s 294.
[2] Code of Practice, vol 1, para 15.40.

Effect of order

30.17 A removal order authorises the mental health officer and anyone named in the order to enter the place specified in the order within 72 hours of the making of the order. A police officer may accompany them and may use reasonable force to gain access.[1] They can take the person to a place of safety within 72 hours of the order. The person can be detained there for up to seven days, as specified in the order.[2] In accordance with the principles of the Act, if less than seven days is sufficient, the mental health officer should apply for a shorter period.

There is no appeal against the sheriff or justice's decision to make or refuse to make a refusal order,[3] but the person and anyone with an interest may apply for a variation or recall of the order. See below.

The mental health officer must notify all relevant parties of the outcome of the application and advise them of their rights to apply for variation or recall.[4] The mental health officer must also notify the Mental Welfare Commission.

[1]   Although the Code of Practice does not specifically state this, presumably, the mental health officer should take steps to protect any property or possessions of the person. See 6.10 above.
[2]   Mental Health (Care and Treatment) (Scotland) Act 2003, s 293(3).
[3]   MH(CT)(S)A 2003, s 296.
[4]   Code of Practice, vol 1, paras 15.44–15.45.

Place of safety

30.18 The removal order specifies the address of the place of safety. The place of safety should be a hospital, a care home service[1] or any other suitable place.[2] A police station should not be used as a place of safety (although it may be necessary to do so in an emergency. See below).

An accident and emergency department is not a suitable place, unless the person has significant physical health problems, perhaps because of self harm. A place of safety should have qualified mental health staff. It should generally be a specialist assessment unit linked to, or with access to, a psychiatric hospital or clinic.[3]

[1]   As defined in the Regulation of Care (Scotland) Act 2001, s 2(3).
[2]   Mental Health (Care and Treatment) (Scotland) Act 2003, s 300.
[3]   Code of Practice, vol 1, para 15.86.

Cancellation or variation of removal order

30.19 A person subject to a removal order and any person with an interest in his or her welfare may apply to a sheriff (not a justice of the peace) to set the order aside.[1] They may also apply to move the person to a different place.[2]

There is a form on the Scottish Executive mental health law website.[3] The form goes to the sheriff court for the area from where the person was moved.[4]

The sheriff must give the relevant people a chance to make representations and to lead or produce evidence. These people are the mental health officer who applied for the removal order, the nearest relative of the person, any guardian or welfare attorney of the person and the person's primary carer.[5] The sheriff cannot dispense with this requirement on grounds of urgency.[6]

When a sheriff cancels ('recalls') a removal order, the sheriff may order the local authority to return the person to the place from where he or she was removed or to another suitable place chosen by the person.[7]

It is not possible to appeal against a sheriff's decision to cancel or vary a removal order or to refuse to do so.[8]

[1] Mental Health (Care and Treatment) (Scotland) Act 2003, s 295(1)(a).

[2] MH(CT)(S)A 2003, s 295(1)(b).

[3] Form mental health officer 7.

[4] MH(CT)(S)A 2003, s 295(3).

[5] Mental Health (Recall or Variation of Removal Order) (Scotland) Regulations 2006 (SSI 2006/11).

[6] MH(CT)(S)A 2003, s 295(4)-(5).

[7] MH(CT)(S)A 2003, s 295(6).

[8] MH(CT)(S)A 2003, s 296.

POLICE AND PLACES OF SAFETY

30.20 The police may be the first people a person is in contact with if he or she is mentally disturbed. A person may be in the street in a disorientated state or neighbours may phone the police because of disturbances. The police can arrange to take the person to a place of safety.

These powers apply only if a person is in a public place. A public place is any place to which the public have access. It includes places such as cinemas, which charge for entry. It specifically includes common stairs and hallways.[1]

[1] Mental Health (Care and Treatment) (Scotland) Act 2003, s 297(4).

People not in public place

30.21 The police must rely on their common law powers when people are at risk in private places, such as their homes. The police can enter only if there is a serious disturbance or if they are in pursuit of someone they suspect of having committed a crime.

These general powers are unlikely to be of much use in the majority of cases. If police help is needed to gain access to someone in a private place, a mental health officer must apply to a sheriff for a warrant under the Mental Health (Care and Treatment) Act.

People at risk in public

30.22 If a police officer reasonably suspects that someone in a public place has a mental disorder and is in immediate need of care and treatment, the officer can remove the person to a place of safety.[1] There need be no immediate danger to the public. The police officer can remove the person either because he or she thinks there is a risk to the public or because it is in the person's interests to do so.

A place of safety is a hospital, a care home service or any other suitable place willing to take the person temporarily.[2] The police officer can take the person to a police station only if no suitable place of safety is immediately available.[3]

A police station is clearly an unsuitable place to keep someone who appears to be at risk. It should be rare for the police to use a police station, and if they do, they should take the person to a place of safety as soon as possible.[4]

1   Mental Health (Care and Treatment) (Scotland) Act 2003, s 297.
2   MH(CT)(S)A 2003, s 300.
3   MH(CT)(S)A 2003, s 297.
4   Code of Practice, vol 1, paras 15.82 and 15.63.

Arranging medical examination

30.23 The police may keep the person in the place of safety for up to 24 hours from the time they removed him or her from the public place. Should the person attempt to abscond from the place of safety, the police can return him or her there.[1]

The police officer should arrange for a doctor to examine the person as soon as possible to make any necessary arrangements for the person's care or treatment.[2] (The police need to know how to contact police surgeons and mental health professionals, such as mental health officers, community psychiatric nurses and psychiatrists.)

A doctor may have to consider the use of short-term or emergency detention if a person is at risk and is unwilling to accept help.

As soon as possible after the person has arrived at the place of safety, the police officer should contact the person's nearest relative and the local authority for the area where the place of safety is situated.[3] The police officer should inform these people when and why the person was removed by the police, where the place of safety is situated and if a police station has been used, the reason why.[4]

Regulations may require the report to cover other matters. At the date of writing, there are no such regulations.

If it is impractical to inform the nearest relative, or if the nearest relative does not live with the person, the police officer should inform anyone living with the person, or the person's carer.[5]

The police officer should notify the Mental Welfare Commission within 14 days.[6] There is a form on the Scottish Executive's mental health law website.

[1]   Mental Health (Care and Treatment) (Scotland) Act 2003, s 297(3).
[2]   MH(CT)(S)A 2003, s 297(2). Code of Practice, vol 1, para 15.67.
[3]   MH(CT)(S)A 2003, s 298(2).
[4]   MH(CT)(S)A 2003, s 298(3).
[5]   MH(CT)(S)A 2003, s 298(5).
[6]   MH(CT)(S)A 2003, s 298(2)(b).

Problems with places of safety

30.24 There have been concerns that suitable places of safety are not always available, with the result that mentally disordered people who have committed no crime are being kept in police cells, or even in police vans, due to lack of suitable alternatives.[1]

The Code of Practice requires local agencies to work together to provide sufficient places of safety within their area.[2] This work should be part of the development of Psychiatric Emergency Plans. (See chapter 12). Guidance on standards is in the Code of Practice.[3]

[1]   See Annual Report of the Mental Welfare Commission 2000–1, p 50.
[2]   Code of Practice, vol 1, para 15.84.
[3]   Vol 1, paras 15.85–88.

Police training

30.25 There is also concern the police are not as familiar with their powers as they could be. Sometimes the police arrest people at risk and keep them in prison cells overnight rather than seek access to medical help. In rural areas it may be time-consuming for the police to take someone to a hospital some distance away.

Sometimes the police find it difficult to distinguish mental disorder from alcohol or substance abuse. There have been calls for greater training for the police to enable them better to deal with mentally ill people with whom they come in contact.[1]

The Mental Welfare Commission monitors how various bodies meet the needs of people with a mental illness, personality disorder or learning disabilities.[2] Their remit now includes the police.[3] Anyone concerned that the police have not acted appropriately in a particular case may wish to contact the Commission.

[1] See the comments of the Mental Welfare Commission in its report of its enquiry into the care and treatment of Philip McFadden (August 1995).
[2] See chapter 3.
[3] Mental Health (Care and Treatment) (Scotland) Act 2003, s 8.

MENTAL WELFARE COMMISSION

30.26 The Mental Welfare Commission's duties to investigate people at risk are in the Mental Health (Care and Treatment) Act.[1] The Mental Welfare Commission has a duty to investigate ill treatment, neglect, inadequate care or treatment and risk to property or finances. It must also investigate if someone living alone or without care is unable to look after him or herself or his or her property or financial affairs.[2]

The Commission may pass enquiries to a local authority. It may ask the local authority to advise it of the outcome. Many cases will not require formal enquiries, but the Commission has carried out several far-reaching enquiries into deficiencies of care.[3] See chapter 52.

The Mental Welfare Commission has a user and carer helpline. Anyone concerned about the welfare of a person with a mental illness, personality disorder or learning disability can contact the Mental Welfare Commission for advice.

[1] Mental Health (Care and Treatment) (Scotland) Act 2003, s 11. Duties previously contained in Adults with Incapacity (Scotland) Act 2000 were

removed by the Mental Health (Care and Treatment) (Scotland) Act 2003, Sched 5, Part 1.

2   MH(CT)(S)A 2003, ss 11(2)(d)–(f). (For other duties of Mental Welfare Commission, see chapter 3.)

3   For details, see Annual Reports of Mental Welfare Commission and the Commission's website.

HARASSMENT

30.27 Many people with disabilities suffer from harassment. This is particularly a problem for people with mental disabilities.[1] The victim should report the incident to the police, who may be able to offer advice on security measures.

A victim who believes he or she may face intimidation if the case comes to court, should advise the police or prosecution services. There is protection for vulnerable and intimidated witnesses. See chapter 35.

A person who has been harassed may go to court to seek a court order ('interdict') requiring the harassment to stop.[2] 'Harassment ' includes behaviour causing alarm and distress. This need not include physical violence. The court does not make an order unless there have been at least two acts of harassment.

Instead of an interdict, the court may make a 'non-harassment order'. Breach of the order is a criminal offence carrying a prison sentence of up to five years. The court can also make a non-harassment order where someone is found guilty of a crime involving harassment. This can offer some protection for the victim in the future.[3]

A victim of harassment can also request the local authority to apply for an anti-social behaviour order.[4] One advantage is that the local authority conducts the court case and the victim does not have the stress of court proceedings.

'Anti social behaviour' includes speech or conduct likely to cause alarm or distress. There must have been at least two incidents. The local authority must consult with the police before it applies for an order. This again emphasises the importance of reporting incidents to the police.

1   See *An exploration of harassment of people with mental health problems living in Scottish communities* (Nuffield Centre for Community Care Studies, Glasgow University with the National Schizophrenia Fellowship (Scotland) and the former Scottish Users' Network, 1991). See also KM Berzins, A Petch and JM Atkinson, 'Prevalence and experience of harassment of people with mental health problems living in the community' (2003) 183 British Journal of Psychiatry 526–533.

2   Protection from Harassment Act 1997, s 8.

3   PFHA 1997, s 11.

4   Under the Crime and Disorder Act 1998, s 19.

SEXUAL ABUSE

30.28 This section looks at sexual offences under the common law and the Mental Health (Care and Treatment) Act. Rape and other sexual offences were dealt with in a discussion paper published by the Scottish Law Commission in 2006.[1] The paper proposed re-stating the law of sexual offences, based on defects in a victim's consent. If these new offences are adopted, they will replace some of the offences in the Mental Health (Care and Treatment) Act.[2]

The local authority and Mental Welfare Commission can investigate an allegation of sexual abuse. Anyone concerned can report it to the police.

New powers to protect vulnerable witnesses and to preserve evidence given by vulnerable people may mean that there is increasing chance of successfully prosecuting such offences. See chapter 35. Local authorities will have new powers to investigate under the Adult Support and Protection Bill.

1   *Rape and Other Sexual Offences*, Scot Law Com Discussion Paper No 131.

2   See paras 5.80–5.87.

Mental Health (Care and Treatment) Act offences

30.29 Under the Mental Health (Care and Treatment) Act, a non-consensual sexual act with a person with mental illness, learning disability or personality disorder is a statutory criminal offence, quite apart from any crime that it may comprise at common law or under any other statute.[1]

The offence applies to any sexual act[2] including intercourse.[3] Such an act is an offence if the mentally disordered person does not consent to the act or is incapable of consenting.[4] Apparent consent is not a true consent if it is as a result of a person being placed in a state of such fear, or subjected to such threat, intimidation, deceit or persuasion, that consent is ineffective.[5]

A person is incapable of consenting if he or she is unable to understand what the act is, to form a decision as to whether the act should to take place or whether the person should engage in it, or to communicate such a decision.[6]

A person accused of such an offence may, in defence, prove that at the time of the sexual act he or she did not know (and could not reasonably have been expected to know) that the other person had a mental disorder and was incapable of consenting.[7] (This applies only to the issue of capacity to consent and not whether the victim gave consent or whether consent was ineffective.)

[1]   Mental Health (Care and Treatment) (Scotland) Act 2003, s 311 and see Code of Practice, vol 1, chap 16. Other statutory sexual offences are in the Criminal Law (Consolidation) (Scotland) Act 1995, Sexual Offences Amendment Act 2000 and Sexual Offences Act 2003 (insofar as they apply in Scotland), and the Protection of Children and Prevention of Sexual Offences (Scotland) Act 2005. For time limits and effects, see 30.30 below.
[2]   Being any activity which a reasonable person would in all the circumstances, regard as sexual. Mental Health (Care and Treatment) (Scotland) Act 2003, s 311(8).
[3]   MH(CT)(S)A 2003, s 311(2).
[4]   MH(CT)(S)A 2003, s 311(1).
[5]   MH(CT)(S)A 2003, s 311(3).
[6]   MH(CT)(S)A 2003, s 311(4).
[7]   MH(CT)(S)A 2003, s 311(5).

Offences by carers

30.30 There are further offences in the Mental Health (Care and Treatment) Act dealing with sexual conduct involving carers. If a person entrusted with caring for a person with mental illness, learning disability or personality disorder engages in sexual conduct with that person, this is presumed to be exploitative, whether or not the person appears to consent.

Engaging in a sexual act with a person with mental disorder is an offence regardless of consent if the other person is a person providing care services to the mentally disordered person, or is involved in the hospital care of such a person, whether as a manager, employee, volunteer or service contractor.[1]

There are defences to cover spouses who are carers. A care provider who was in a sexual relationship with the person immediately before providing care services or before the person's last admission to hospital also has a defence.[2]

It is also a defence to prove that, at the time of the sexual act, the person charged did not know (and could not reasonably have been expected to know) that the person had a mental disorder.[3]

In common with all statutory crime, these statutory offences are subject to a six-month time limit for prosecution. To take account of the fact that there may be delay in reporting or establishing the evidence, the time runs from the time when prosecution services obtain sufficient evidence to commence proceedings, rather than from date the crime was committed.[4]

A person convicted of an offence under the Mental Health (Care and Treatment) Act may be included on the Sex Offenders Register, and his or her personal details may be given to the police under the Sexual Offenders Act 1997 Part I.[5]

[1]   Mental Health (Care and Treatment) (Scotland) Act 2003, s 313.
[2]   MH(CT)(S)A 2003, s 313(3).
[3]   MH(CT)(S)A 2003, s 313(3)(a)(i).
[4]   MH(CT)(S)A 2003, s 319, Criminal Law (Consolidation) (Scotland) Act 1995, s 4.
[5]   MH(CT)(S)A 2003, s 313.

Other offences

30.31 There are additional statutory sexual offences aimed at protecting people against incest and protecting young people under 16 from sexual abuse or exploitation. These offences are largely based on the age or relationships of the people involved rather than personal intent.

For example, it is an offence for anyone over the age of 16 to have sexual intercourse with a child under 16 who is a member of the same household, if the person over 16 is in a position of trust or authority in relation to that child.[1] Such offences exist alongside the specific protections contained in the Mental Health (Care and Treatment) Act.

Homosexual activity between consenting parties of 18 or over is not an offence, but when a male person has a 'mental deficiency' of such a nature or degree that he is incapable of living an independent life or guarding himself against serious exploitation, the law says he is incapable of giving this consent.[2] A homosexual act is an offence in such circumstances.

A person who has relied on such apparent consent can avoid conviction if able to prove that he did not know and had no reason to suspect the other person had such a mental 'deficiency'. It appears that this means that a person's knowledge of a mental 'deficiency' is not fatal to the defence if the person charged did not know (and had no reason to suspect) that the deficiency was of a nature and degree to make the other person's consent ineffective.[3]

1   Criminal Law (Consolidation)(Scotland) Act 1995, s 3.
2   CL(C)(S)A 1995, s 13(3).
3   CL(C)(S)A 1995, s 13(3).

Investigating sexual abuse

30.32 The Code of Practice suggests particular vigilance in respect of sexual relationships involving vulnerable people, particularly in care provided or commissioned by health or social work services, but also in family or other settings.[1]

Staff must balance respect for sexual autonomy and self-determination with managing risk of exploitation or abuse. Suspected exploitation or abuse, or complaints of behaviour, must be taken seriously and dealt with appropriately after discussion, and having regard to the principles of the Mental Health (Care and Treatment) Act.[2]

Close liaison with police and prosecution agencies is desirable both for dealing with cases generally and for the appropriate management of individual cases. Relevant professional and disciplinary bodies, such as the Scottish Social Services Council and the Care Commission should be involved.

1   Code of Practice, vol 1, paras 16.12–16.18.
2   For discussion of the background to some of the issues, see Colin McKay, *Sex, laws and red tape: Scots Law, Personal Relationships and People with Learning Difficulties* (Enable, 1991).

FINANCIAL ABUSE

30.33 The law provides remedies in both the criminal and civil courts for people who have suffered financial abuse. Unfortunately, the very nature of people's vulnerability may mean that such abuse does not become known.

Since the passing of the Adults with Incapacity Act and the Mental Health (Care and Treatment) Act, there is more possibility of investigating financial abuse. The role of the Public Guardian under the Adults with Incapacity Act is particularly important.

Duties of Public Guardian

30.34 The Public Guardian supervises financial guardians and investigates complaints about attorneys and others operating the financial provisions of the Adults with Incapacity Act (see Part 5 of this book). The Public Guardian has a specific duty to investigate whenever she becomes aware that the property or financial affairs of an adult may be at risk.[1]

If the investigation reveals cause for concern, the Public Guardian may do what she thinks necessary to safeguard the property or financial affairs of the adult.[2] The Public Guardian may pass the matter on to the local authority, with a recommendation that it applies for financial guardianship. The Public Guardian may apply to the sheriff for an intervention order or for further directions[3] and can contact the police in cases of possible fraud, misappropriation or theft.

The local authority and the Mental Welfare Commission should co-operate with the Public Guardian's investigation.[4] If the investigation reveals welfare concerns, the Public Guardian passes these on to the local authority.

Anyone concerned may contact the Investigations Section at the Office of the Public Guardian. The Public Guardian normally requires some written evidence before she can investigate.

1   Adults with Incapacity (Scotland) Act 2000, s 6(2)(e). The Public Guardian can investigate only where the person is over 16.
2   AWI(S)A 2000, s 12.
3   AWI(S)A 2000, s 3(3).
4   AWI(S)A 2000, s 12(2).

Co-operation with Public Guardian

30.35 Local authorities and the Mental Welfare Commission also have a legal duty to investigate financial risks (see chapter 3). Local authorities, the Mental Welfare Commission and the Public Guardian should agree how best to share these responsibilities and are developing local investigation protocols.[1]

The Public Guardian is primarily concerned with financial matters and the Commission and local authorities primarily concerned with welfare matters, but it is not always easy to disentangle the two. It may sometimes be appropriate for the local authority to lead an investigation even where there are financial concerns. The Commission should investigate where a case highlights a failure of services or structures.

In any event, anyone concerned about someone's financial affairs may contact the local authority or the Mental Welfare Commission, in addition to or instead of the Public Guardian. These bodies can explain how they will discharge their duty to investigate.

1   Code of Practice, vol 1, paras 15.09 and 15.11.

POLICE CHECKS

Disclosure

30.36 Anyone who intends to work with people with mental illness, learning disability or personality disorder, whether as an employee or as a volunteer, should obtain a certificate of criminal record, commonly known as a disclosure certificate. Such a certificate reveals any information available from criminal records about the person to which the certificate relates.

There are two types of disclosure. Standard Disclosure is for people who have regular contact with children and vulnerable adults. Enhanced Disclosure is for people whose work regularly involves caring for, training, supervising or being in sole charge of children or vulnerable adults in certain settings. These are care home services, service providing personal care or support in the home, private hospitals and clinics, social care services and services for people with learning difficulties. 'Vulnerable adults' include people with mental and physical disabilities and disorders, people who have abused alcohol or drugs and frail elderly people.[1]

Organisations working with children and vulnerable adults will seek police checks on all managers, employees and volunteers.[2] Disclosure Scotland now provides this service for the police. For more information, see their website.

Care standards generally require that organisations carry out police checks before they employ a member of staff or a volunteer. It is for the employer, having received the disclosure, to decide whether to employ someone with a conviction as an employee or volunteer, but no one convicted of an offence punishable by three months' imprisonment or more and sentenced to imprisonment can act as the manager or provider of a care service, even if sentence was deferred or suspended.[3]

¹   And other people with 'reduced physical and mental capacity'. The Police Act 1997 (Enhanced Criminal Record Certificates) (Protection of Vulnerable Adults) (Scotland) Regulations 2002 (SSI 2002/217).
²   Under the Police Act 1997.
³   The Regulation of Care (Requirements as to Care Services) (Scotland) Regulations 2002 (SSI 2002/114), regs 6 and 7.

Working with children

30.37 Scottish Ministers also keep a list of people unsuitable to work with children.¹ A person can be on the list even if he or she has not been convicted of a crime, if Scottish Ministers receive a report of conduct which calls into question the person's suitability to work with children.

Employers and employment agencies must report any cause for concern to Scottish Ministers, and certain other bodies may do so.

A person with a mental illness, learning disability or personality disorder can be included on the list if the person has demonstrated behaviour which makes him or her unsuitable. The fact that the behaviour may be because of a person's mental condition is not enough to prevent inclusion, if other risk factors exist. A person who is to be listed can make representations opposing his or her inclusion on the list.

¹   The Disqualified from Working with Children List was established under the Protection of Children (Scotland) Act 2003.

Proposals for reform

30.38 The Scottish Executive consulted in 2004 and again in 2006 concerning new procedures for keeping a list in relation to those who are unsuitable to work with vulnerable adults. The 2006 proposals are for a Vetting and Barring system, and merging the lists of those unsuitable for work with children and vulnerable adults.¹

In the meantime, when steps are taken to engage a person to work with an adult with a mental illness, learning disability or personality disorder, particularly if that work is as a carer in the adult's own home, utmost care must be taken in selection and vetting of the carer. This includes obtaining the relevant disclosure certificate and calling up references from those for whom the person has worked before.

¹   *Consultation on protecting vulnerable groups: Scottish vetting and barring scheme* (Scottish Executive, February 2006).

CRIMINAL OFFENCES

Mental Health (Care and Treatment) Act

30.39 It is an offence under the Mental Health (Care and Treatment) Act for a member of the staff or management of a hospital or any carer in a residential or other setting to ill-treat or wilfully neglect any person in their care.[1] This applies whether or not the person is subject to compulsory measures under the Mental Health (Care and Treatment) Act.

An employee of a hospital or care service, an independent contractor, an individual who provide cares voluntarily for a voluntary organisation or an unpaid carer can be charged with this offence.[2]

The extent of this provision reflects the role that the voluntary sector now plays in the care. The 1984 Act was more focused on hospital and care home settings, but it also expressly included ill-treatment by a friend or family member, in relation to a person on a community care order. Given the more restricted scope of the Mental Health (Care and Treatment) Act, it would be necessary to use the common law, broader statutory offences or civil remedies, if there were allegations of ill-treatment or neglect by a family member.

[1] Mental Health (Care and Treatment) (Scotland) Act 2003, s 315.
[2] MH(CT)(S)A 2003, s 315(1)(d)(ii).

Adults with Incapacity Act

30.40 It is an offence for anyone exercising personal welfare powers under the Adults with Incapacity Act to ill-treat or wilfully neglect the adult.[1] This could apply to a welfare guardian, a welfare attorney or someone acting under an intervention order.

A person who holds only financial powers may not commit the offence. Again it would be necessary to have resort to common law or broader statutory offences or civil claims if there were allegations of ill-treatment or neglect on the part of, for example, a financial guardian.

A person is not liable for breach of his or her duties when acting under the Adults with Incapacity Act if the person has acted in good faith and in accordance with the general principles of the Act.[2]

[1] Adults with Incapacity (Scotland) Act 2000, s 83.
[2] AWI(S)A 2000, s 82.

PART 8
THE IMPACT OF MENTAL DISORDER

Chapter 31

PERSONAL LIFE

31.01 This chapter looks at the effects a mental illness or learning disability might have on a person's family life, including his or her sexual relationships and relations with children.

SEXUAL RELATIONSHIPS

Capacity to enter relationships

31.02 The right to marry and to found a family found in Article 12 of the European Convention on Human Rights (ECHR), and respect for private and family life in Article 8 of the ECHR, apply whether or not a person has a mental disorder. These rights may be limited by domestic law, including for the prevention of disorder or crime, the protection of health or morals, or the protection of the rights and freedoms of others.

All adults (ie people over 16) are entitled to have sexual autonomy and to enter into sexual relationships should they wish, regardless of mental disorder. The emphasis of the Mental Health (Care and Treatment) Act is on autonomy and the protection of the person and others from sexual abuse. Special provisions applying to sexual conduct with a mentally disordered person are considered in chapter 30.

For the common law, the matter is essentially one of capacity to consent, which may be called into question in cases of certain mental illnesses or learning disabilities. A person can retain capacity despite mental illness, although it might be lost from time to time during periods of severe mental ill-health. A person with a learning disability or diminishing capacity may not have or may lose the ability to consent.

The question of capacity to consent may become an issue under the general law, in the context of criminal proceedings for rape or other sexual offence, or in civil proceedings arising from personal relationships such as divorce or nullity of marriage. Chapter 30 looks at the criminal law.

Impact of mental disorder

31.03 Mental disorder, or medication used to treat it, may have the side-effect of inhibiting the ability or desire for sexual activity. Conversely, mania or hypomania may induce the person to indulge in promiscuous activity. When either of these situations occurs, or if a mental disorder otherwise affects a person's sexual behaviour, relationships may be put under extreme strain. It is important for the partner of a person with such mental disorder to be aware of the extent to which problems in the relationship may have roots in the mental disorder or in medication or other treatment of it.

If a marriage has not been consummated at all, because of impotence caused by the mental disorder directly or indirectly, the marriage may be declared void. Alternatively, an order for separation or divorce may be sought on the basis of unreasonable behaviour. This could include lack of sexual activity within the marriage or other breakdown of sexual compatibility or fidelity. See below.

Sexual vulnerabilities

31.04 Even though a mentally disordered adult may have the capacity to consent, a person might be at increased risk of sexual coercion or of promiscuity because of mental disorder. Unwanted pregnancy, or concealment of pregnancy might also be a risk.[1]

In extreme cases of vulnerability or risk to self, or of risk to others, doctors or others might seek authority to inhibit a person's sexual activity by drug treatment, or to limit by abortion or sterilization the potential for procreation, if this would not be sustainable emotionally or physically by the person with mental disorder.[2] Such interventions have been considered at common law in England, and have been the subject of academic legal debate in the past.[3]

The common law conclusions were that the court would have to be satisfied in cases involving sterilization that pregnancy was likely. In cases of sterilization and abortion, the court would have to be satisfied that if the procedure was not carried out, this would cause serious damage to the person's physical or mental health.

Reliance on common law tests is now less likely, given the new statutory regimes for dealing with incapacity and mental disorder, under the Adults with Incapacity Act and the Mental Health (Care and Treatment) Act.

In the case of abortion these must be read alongside the provisions of the Abortion Act 1967, which creates the range of situations in which abortion will not give rise to a criminal charge.[4]

1   The criminal law is explained in Gordon, *Criminal Law* (3rd edn, W Green & Son, 2001), Vol 2, chap 27. It is only an offence if the child dies after a concealed pregnancy. Although the criminal law on this is old (an Act of 1809) there have been a number of criminal prosecutions in recent years arising from concealment, where the mental state of the accused mother has been an issue.

2   For further information see Mason and McCall-Smith, *Law and Medical Ethics* (6th edn, Oxford University Press, 2006).

3   J Blackie and H Patrick, *Mental Health: A guide to the law in Scotland* (1990, Butterworths), p 79, and materials quoted there.

4   Abortion Act 1967, s 5(2). See Gordon, *Criminal Law* (3rd edn, W Green & Son, 2001), Vol II, chap 28.

MARRIAGE

Capacity test

31.05 At common law, people with mental disorder may marry if they have the capacity to consent to the marriage ceremony. Marriage has been said to be a 'simple contract'.[1] Lack of capacity is a legal impediment to the marriage ceremony,[2] and should be considered by the Registrar both at the point of application for a marriage schedule and at the point of marriage.[3]

Anyone objecting to an application for a marriage schedule on the ground of incapacity must produce evidence of lack of capacity.[4] The incapacity could be due to mental illness,[5] mental disability[6] or other cause, including a short-term incapacity to embark upon the contract of marriage.[7]

Mental disorder and compulsion under the Mental Health (Care and Treatment) Act are not of themselves a basis for incapacity, but those caring for a person who is vulnerable because of mental disorder may consider whether to object to an application to the Registrar on the grounds of the person's lack of capacity. This is particularly important now that an amendment to the Marriage (Scotland) Act 1977[8] expressly includes issues of capacity to consent impaired by force or threats. See below.

When the person applying for a marriage schedule is a restricted patient, Scottish Ministers have indicated they will communicate to the

Registrar any doubts about that person meeting the test of capacity. The responsible medical officer must advice Scottish Ministers of any restricted patient's impending marriage plans in order that they can decide whether to raise an objection.[9]

1   Thomson, *Family Law in Scotland* (4th edn, Butterworths, 2002), 37.
2   Marriage (Scotland) Act 1977 s 5(4).
3   Clive, *The Law of Husband and Wife in Scotland* (4th ed, W Green & Son, 1997), para 03.004.
4   Marriage (Scotland) Act 1977 s 5(1).
5   *Park v Park* 1914 1SLT 88, *Calder v Calder* 1942 SN 40.
6   *Blair v Blair* 2 (1747) Mor 6293, *Long v Long* 1950 SLT (Notes) 32.
7   See *Gall v Gall* (1870) 9M 177.
8   Section 20A added by Family Law (Scotland) Act 2006
9   *Memorandum of Procedure on Restricted Patients*, Scottish Executive October 2005, para 4.26.

Effect of lack of capacity

31.06 At common law, if a person whose capacity is under challenge entered into a marriage, the marriage was voidable and could be set aside, but it was not clearly void, unless either party was incapable of understanding the nature of marriage and giving consent to it at the time of the marriage ceremony. At common law, the burden of proof was firmly on the person alleging lack of capacity to prove it. Mental disorder or learning disability was not equated with lack of capacity,[1] nor was 'facility and circumvention'.[2] See below.

Either party to the marriage could raise proceedings for nullity based on lack of capacity to consent. It is likely that a third party with an interest could also raise proceedings.[3]

There is no mention in the marriage statutes of defences to proceedings for nullity. The interaction between common law and statute is still open to test.[4] Practically, the concern must be that a person who has entered into and acted in good faith upon the purported existence of such a marriage (whether the person of questioned capacity or the other person) should be dealt with fairly and with regard to his or her contribution to the relationship. For example, in proceedings for nullity the person may seek financial provision.

1   *Long v Long*, 1950 SLT (Notes) 32.
2   *Scott v Kelly*, 1992 SCLR 646.

³   *Blair v Blair*, 2 (1747) Mor 6293.

⁴   Clive comments that the law on defective consent has not been affected by statute—but there is now express provision for defective consent to marriage and civil partnership, and no mention of defences to proceedings to declare that the marriage is void.

Temporary incapacity

31.07 Permanent incapacity at the time of the marriage clearly strikes at a person's capacity for marriage in general. The situation is less clear if there is a temporary incapacity, followed by apparently normal living as husband and wife. The underlying law is one of contract, and it has been suggested that

> 'although the law cannot be said to be clear, a marriage which is void because of some temporary defect of consent can be validated … after the impediment has been removed. [This] …. would normally be inferred from voluntary cohabitation as husband and wife on the faith of the void ceremony after the vitiating factor has ceased to operate.'¹

Living together as husband and wife in such circumstances might bar a person from starting proceedings for nullity.²

The introduction of a statutory test for void marriage or civil partnership, discussed below, throws the focus on to capacity to understand and consent at the time that the relationship is entered into, regardless of whether that is a permanent state of affairs.

¹   Clive, *The Law of Husband and Wife in Scotland* (4th edn, W Green & Son, 1997), para 07.062, after scholarly consideration of the underlying church law and common law.

²   Whether subsequent cohabitation as husband and wife is able to ratify consent affected by temporary lack of capacity, or bar proceedings for nullity following temporary lack of capacity, is still a moot point, see Clive, *The Law of Husband and Wife in Scotland* (4th edn, W Green & Son, 1997), para 07.062, which contains scholarly consideration of the underlying church law and common law, but its inter-relationship with the new statutory provisions has yet to be tested.

Void marriages

31.08 *Statutory test*—The common law has now been replaced with a statutory test. With effect from 1 May 2006, the law provides expressly for two situations affecting consent which render a marriage void.¹ These are that (1) at the time of the marriage ceremony a party who was capable of consenting to marriage purported to give consent but did so by reason only of treats, force or error, or (2) at the time of the marriage ceremony one of the parties was incapable of understanding the nature of marriage and consenting to the marriage.

The second ground may seem more directly relevant to the situation of a person with mental disorder, but the former could also be relevant. A person's mental disorder may lead or contribute to error, or susceptibility to threats or force.

If a person with apparent capacity, albeit with mental disorder, enters into a marriage, that marriage is valid, and it can be dissolved only by divorce or by action of nullity if the circumstances fall into the new statutory void categories.

It is suggested that the same burden of proof of incapacity to consent as is established at common law will apply to the new statutory ground, as will issues of a person's ability to sue. No assumptions as to incapacity can be drawn from mere mental disorder. In proceedings for nullity where the parties have been living as husband and wife, there are provisions for financial provision similar to those arising on divorce as explained below.

[1]   Marriage (Scotland) Act 1977 (as amended by the Family Law (Scotland) Act 2006, s 2), s 20A.

Impotency

31.09 Lack of capacity for sexual intercourse (impotency) is not an impediment to marriage, but a marriage is voidable on the ground of impotency. It is a very limited ground for nullity proceedings, and to succeed there must be proof that as at the date of the marriage the person did not have the capacity for full and complete sexual intercourse, and the impotency is permanent and incurable.

The impotency may be due to physical causes, but psychological causes have been recognised[1] so this may arise in the case of person with mental disorder who has entered into marriage but is not able to engage sexually.

As usual, medical evidence is key. Whether a person may be barred from success in proceedings for nullity by acceptance of the situation or by engagement in procuring a child by surrogacy or adoption is a moot point, and various texts on family law come to different conclusions reviewing the same case law.

Sexual problems may be a ground for divorce or separation. See below.

1   Clive, *The Law of Husband and Wife in Scotland* (4th edn, W Green & Son, 1997), para 07.064 and cases cited there including: *G v G*, 1924 SC (HL) 42 and *Paterson v Paterson*, 1958 SC 141, which mention the term the term 'invincible repugnance' to sexual intercourse.

CIVIL PARTNERSHIP

Nature of partnership

31.10 With effect from December 2005, people of the same sex can enter into civil partnerships with consequences akin to marriage.[1] People of opposite sexes are not eligible. The Civil Partnership Act is an Act of the UK parliament, which contains special provision for Scotland.[2] It provides for a process of registration of civil partnerships, and contains conditions of eligibility for participation in that process.[3]

Civil partnership carries rights of succession and occupancy, and to seek interdict and power of arrest, and for financial provision, linked to provisions for separation and dissolution, discussed below.[4]

1   Civil Partnership Act 2004, s 1.
2   CPA 2004, Pt 3.
3   CPA 2004, s 85.
4   CPA 2004.

Capacity

31.11 People cannot enter civil partnerships if either is incapable of understanding the nature of civil partnership, or validly consenting to its formation.[1]

Any person may object to the registration. If a person objects on the basis that either of the intended civil partners does not have the capacity to understand or validly consent, he or she must submit a supporting certificate signed by a registered medical practitioner.[2]

For civil partnerships in England or Wales, there are special provisions applying to detained patients, including those detained under certain provisions of the Mental Health Act 1983, but there is no equivalent for Scotland. It could be argued that objection to registration in respect of people subject to compulsory measures under the Mental

Health (Care and Treatment) Act or Criminal Procedure Act (discussed at 31.05 above) could be considered equally in relation to civil partnerships.

Indeed it might be argued that the concept of civil partnership, in its novelty, is more complex in its nature than marriage, and scope for objection may be greater. However there should not be discrimination between those who wish to enter a civil commitment to a homosexual relationship rather than a heterosexual one via marriage.

1   Civil Partnership Act 2004, s 86(1)(e).
2   CPA 2004, ss 92(1)-(2).

Nullity

31.12 Proceedings for nullity of the civil partnership are available, and the partnership is void if, and only if, the people were not eligible to register, or thought they were so eligible, either of them did not validly consent to its formation.[1]

This leaves scope for argument about a person's incapacity to consent, even if information about that incapacity at the time of consent was not available when the consent was given, or during the process of the registration.

A civil partner falls within the definitions of nearest relative for Mental Health (Care and Treatment) Act and Adults with Incapacity Act purposes.[2]

1   Civil Partnership Act 2004, s 123.
2   Mental Health (Care and Treatment) (Scotland) Act 2003 (as amended by CPA 2004, Sched 28, para 69), s 254.

COHABITATION

31.13 Many people do not go through the formalities of registering a marriage or a civil partnership but live together as a couple, whether of the same or opposite sexes. Until 1 May 2006, such couples were treated as strangers in terms of the law of property, succession and financial provision, unless they had made wills or contractual arrangements regulating their affairs. For a person with a mental disorder in such a relationship, issues of capacity to marry, make a will or enter into a contractual agreement with the other party might have arisen.

From 1 May, people who have been living together as if husband and wife or civil partners,[1] may apply to the courts to be regarded as cohabitants. The court may make a determination, having regard to the length of the period during which the couple have lived together, the nature of the relationship during that period, and the nature and extent of any financial arrangements having subsisted during that period.[2]

A determination that a couple have been cohabitants gives rise to a number of rights on termination of the cohabitation. The other cohabitant may have rights to the other party's estate if the person died without making a will[3] and there are provisions to assist in determining the contributions that have been made to meeting the costs and acquiring household goods during the period of cohabitation.

It does not appear that capacity to consent to the nature of the relationship is a factor, if the nature of the relationship appears to be one of cohabitation. This means that a cohabiting relationship between, for example, a person with dementia and a person with no mental disorder could fall to be classed as a cohabiting one. If a person is considered by the court to be a cohabitant, he or she may apply for occupancy rights and for interdict and power of arrest.[4]

Voluntary arrangements made by the cohabitants to regulate their affairs by will or contract take precedence, although their validity could be challenged on common law grounds if the capacity of one of the parties is in doubt.

There is no statutory provision for financial support between the cohabitants, but there is provision for capital payments and for financial support of a child parented by the cohabitants.

The statutory recognition of separating cohabitants provides a new set of potential safeguards and remedies for people with mental disorder who have been living as cohabitees. The criteria are entirely based on factual living arrangements and may thus avoid the consent and capacity issues that are key to valid marriage or civil partnership.

---

[1]   This simply means that they are in a domestic setting akin to that of married couples or civil partners. The partners do not have to hold themselves out, unlike the common law marriage of 'cohabitation by habit and repute' (which is itself abolished for the future by s 3 of the Family Law (Scotland) Act 2006).

[2]   Family Law (Scotland) Act 2006, s 25.

[3]   FL(S)A 2006, s 29.

[4]   FL(S)A 2006, ss 31–34.

DIVORCE, SEPARATION AND DISSOLUTION OF CIVIL PARTNERSHIP

31.14 For more than 30 years, the basis for separation and divorce has been in the Divorce (Scotland) Act 1976, section 1. The general ground of irretrievable breakdown of marriage may be established by non-cohabitation for specified periods, with or without consent of the other party,[1] adultery,[2] and by the defender having at any time behaved (whether as a result of mental abnormality and whether such behaviour has been active or passive)[3] in such a way that the pursuer cannot reasonably be expected to live with the defender.[4]

The behaviour and separation grounds are repeated as a basis for dissolution in the Civil Partnerships Act 2004.[5]

[1]   Divorce (Scotland) Act 1976, ss 1(1)(d) and (e).
[2]   D(S)A 1976, s 1(1)(a).
[3]   D(S)A 1976, s 1(2)(b).
[4]   D(S)A 1976, s 1(1)(b).
[5]   Civil Partnership Act 2004, ss 117–122.

Divorce based on separation

31.15 The periods of separation required for non-fault divorce have been amended from 4 May 2006. The period for no consent divorce is reduced from five years to two years and in divorce with consent from two years to one year.[1]

Proof of separation in cases not requiring consent could include separation while a person is detained in a hospital or prison, or while a person is a voluntary patient in a psychiatric hospital, care home or other address away from the matrimonial home.

The test for separation does not depend on the *will* of the separated defender. Questions asked in the proceedings about the mental state of the defender, are relevant only to that person's capacity to deal with the proceedings, rather than to the test for irretrievable breakdown of marriage.

This means that two spouses placed in different care establishments by the local authority could technically be in the situation of having grounds for divorce, because of a separation brought about outside the will of either of them.

[1]   Family Law (Scotland) Act 2006, s 11.

Unreasonable behaviour

31.16 Behaviour grounds are based partly on an objective interpretation of whether a reasonable person could have tolerated the other party's behaviour within the marriage and partly on the subjective test of whether the behaviour is tolerable to the person seeking the divorce.

Mental disorder may feature heavily in the motives of a person pursuing divorce proceedings (called the pursuer). At one end of the spectrum a person seeking divorce may be delusional about the behaviour of the other spouse, and believe him or her to be involved in behaviour destructive of the marriage, for which there is no objective evidence. At the other end of the spectrum, a spouse with a history of mental disorder may be particularly susceptible to and affected by undermining behaviour by the other spouse, which a person with no such history might find innocuous.

It is a great strength of Scottish law that it can deal with a very wide range of situations and attempt to balance objective and subjective tests. However it can make for a lack of predictability, because of the number of different domestic contexts.

One certainty is that behaviour triggered by mental disorder can be included as behaviour which can be complained about by a spouse seeking dissolution of a marriage or civil partnership.

A person may feel morally aggrieved to be blamed for marriage breakdown on the strength of behaviour over which the person has, at best, limited control. On the other hand, the other person in that relationship has the certainty that the existence of a mental health reason for the behaviour does not exclude the behaviour from consideration.

Although there may be no basis on which to defend a divorce based on unreasonable behaviour, the existence of mental disorder may be highly relevant to orders supplementary to divorce, such as financial provision or orders in relation to a child of the relationship.

Mental disorder also plays a large part in the procedures that must be followed for notification of the proceedings and in ensuring that the views of the person affected by mental disorder are taken into account in the proceedings.

Adultery

31.17 Voluntary sexual intercourse[1] outside marriage establishes the adultery ground for divorce or separation, whether or not it was the actual cause of the breakdown of the marriage.

Where the person engaging in such activity has a mental disorder, the issue of whether sexual intercourse was voluntary may be blurred. The behaviour might not have occurred but for the mental disorder.

The general understanding is that only forced sexual intercourse (as in rape) will fall outside the definition, but it might equally be argued that if the situation is one in which consent or capacity is questioned[2] then the conduct could not have been voluntary.

Even if adultery was in doubt due to the lack of voluntariness, sexual activity outside the marriage could satisfy the unreasonable behaviour ground above.

1   At least one act of sexual activity between the defender and a person of the opposite sex. (Sexual activity with a person of the same sex does not found an action of adultery, but can satisfy the behaviour ground.)
2   As in the definition of the offence under Mental Health (Care and Treatment) (Scotland) Act 2003, s 311.

Mental disorder in family actions

Simplified divorce procedure

31.18 Do it Yourself Divorce, using forms available from the sheriff clerk, is not available if either party to the marriage has a mental disorder.[1] This simplified procedure where the parties have been separated for the requisite period and no ancillary orders are sought, has the advantage of simplicity, speed and low cost.

The application form requires the applicant to certify whether or not the other spouse has any mental disorder (whether mental illness or learning disability) and to give details.[2]

Despite the rule requiring that neither party suffers from mental disorder (without specification as to the effect of that disorder), the form does not require the applicant to declare that he or she has no mental disorder.[3]

The form includes a document known as an affidavit, which the applicant must sign in the presence of a justice of the peace or notary public, and swear that the contents of the application are true. The person countersigning the affidavit might refuse to do so if it is apparent that the applicant has a mental disorder which means that he or she is unable to manage such affairs.

The clerk of court might also query a person's capacity, but all dealings could be by post rather than personal attendance at the clerk's office. These checks apart, there seems to be no way of ascertaining whether an applicant meets the requirement of having no mental disorder, and the presumption of capacity would prevail.

If the form discloses mental disorder, the sheriff clerk is likely to reject it, unless it is clear that this does not affect a spouse's ability to manage his or her affairs. The applicant will have to use the ordinary family action procedures instead, which contain safeguards for the person with a mental disorder.

[1]   Ordinary Cause Rules 1993, r 33.73(1)(f).

[2]   Ordinary Cause Rules 1993, Forms F31 and F33.

[3]   The applicant is asked to read an information leaflet before completing the form which states 'there must be no sign that your husband or wife is unable to manage his or her affairs because of mental illness or mental handicap'. (Available from sheriff courts and www.scotcourts.gov.uk/library/civil/divorce/index.asp.)

Family actions

31.19 Family actions are subject to special procedures if the person defending the proceedings (the defender) has a mental disorder.[1] These actions include actions of divorce, separation, nullity of marriage or civil partnership, parentage and actions concerning parental responsibilities and rights under the Children (Scotland) Act 1995, Part 1.[2]

If the person defending such an action has or appears to have a mental disorder and is living in a hospital or similar place, the normal notifications that accompany the action[3] are not sent to the defender direct, but to the medical officer in charge of the hospital or other place.

The medical officer should deliver the documents to the defender and explain the contents to him or her, unless satisfied that such delivery or explanation would be dangerous to the person's health or mental condition.[4] There is a specified form of request.[5]

The medical officer must complete an accompanying certificate[6] to the effect that he or she has carried out the delivery and explanation, or reporting why this has not been done, and return that to the pursuer or the pursuer's solicitor.

There is no provision for the medical officer at that stage to certify the defender's fitness to deal with the remainder of the action. If the medical officer has not delivered and explained the papers, the court can but, it seems, is not required to, order a further medical inquiry, service or notification as it thinks fit.[7]

1   Ordinary Cause Rules 1993, r 33.13 and r 33.16.
2   The full list is in OCR 1993, r 33.1(1).
3   Special forms of notification, information notices, forms of consent etc are specified throughout Ordinary Cause Rules 1993, Chap 33.
4   OCR 1993, Form F17.
5   OCR 1993, r 33.13.
6   OCR 1993, Form F18.
7   OCR 1993, r 33.13(4).

Divorce and separation

31.20 Actions of divorce and separation (but not other family actions) are subject to specific rules providing for the appointment of a curator *ad litem*, if it appears to the court that a defender has a mental disorder.[1]

The court must appoint a curator *ad litem* in such a case,[2] and, if the case is based on two years separation with the consent of the defender, must order notification of the action to the Mental Welfare Commission. The Commission reports to the sheriff clerk (who in turn will pass it to the pursuer, any solicitor for the defender and the curator *ad litem*), indicating whether the Mental Welfare Commission considers the defender is capable of deciding whether or not to consent to the granting of decree.[3]

The curator holds office until discharged, and may apply for discharge if the defender no longer has a mental disorder.[4] The pursuer is responsible for the preliminary cost of the curator's involvement, up to the point of the curator lodging any of the relevant documents, or being discharged due to the absence of a mental disorder in the defender.[5]

The main purpose of this rule is to bring a curator into the proceedings as a temporary safeguard, to be replaced with a longer term appointment at common law if needed. (The court's power to appoint a curator *ad litem* where a party lacks capacity is considered in more detail at 35.16.)

The court must also have regard to the existence of a proxy for the defender, such a guardian or person holding a power of attorney, who may be able to defend or pursue a family action.

1   Ordinary Cause Rules 1993, r 33.16.
2   OCR 1993, r 33.16(2)(a).
3   OCR 1993 rr 33.16(2)(b) & (4).
4   OCR 1993 r 33.16(8).
5   OCR 1993 r 33.16(9).

MENTAL DISORDER AND PARENTAL RESPONSIBILITIES

31.21 A child whose parent has a mental disorder has the full range of common law and statutory rights and entitlements in respect of that parent. A parent's responsibilities and rights in respect of the child and a child's succession rights arise automatically in accordance with law.[1]

Parental rights flow from parental responsibilities to the child,[2] which arise regardless of mental disorder on the part of a parent. A mother automatically has these rights, as does a father who is married to the mother at any time between the child's conception and birth. (For unmarried fathers certain additional criteria must be met before parental responsibilities exist.)[3] Parents who are not married can create parental responsibilities for the father.[4]

Mental disorder may affect a person's capacity to enter into arrangements concerning the child, such as a parental responsibility agreement or a will. Mental disorder may be relevant to the ability of a parent to care for a child, to have contact with a child and to maintain the child financially. The court may grant or adjust the parental responsibilities of a parent in respect of a child.[5]

[1]　Children (Scotland) Act 1995, Succession (Scotland) Act 1964, and see Thomson, *Family Law in Scotland* (4th edn, Butterworths, 2002), Sutherland, *Family Law* (2nd edn, W Green & Son, 2005).

[2]　There is disagreement between Sheriffs Principal as to whether the law allows rights unless they flow from parental responsibility, see *D v H*, 2004 SLT (Sh Ct) 73 (refuses contact application by sibling aged 15), *E v E*, 2004 Fam. L.R. 115; 2004 GWD 26–548 (grants contact application by half-sibling aged 14).

[3]　Children (Scotland) Act 1995, s 3 and Family Law (Scotland) Act 2006, s 23.

[4]　By signing an agreement under the Children (Scotland) Act 1995, s 4.

[5]　Under the Children (Scotland) Act 1995, s 11.

Maintaining relationships

Private care arrangements

31.22 If mental disorder prevents a parent who cares for a child from performing that function to an adequate standard, temporarily or permanently, various options exist. Informal arrangements may be made within families for care while the parent is unable to provide care, either on a temporary or longer term basis.

A person over 16 having effective care and control of a child must exercise it in a manner consistent with the parental responsibilities to safeguard and protect the child. The person may consent to medical or dental treatment if the child cannot do so and the person considers that a parent would not withhold consent.[1]

1   Children (Scotland) Act 1995, s 6(1).

Local authority help

31.23 If local authority support for care is required, this may be offered informally to the family under the general duties to provide advice in the Social Work (Scotland) Act 1968,[1] or in accordance with the Children (Scotland) Act 1995 in particular. This may be dealt with by the local authority in consultation with the family.

A parent with a mental disorder needing help to look after his or her children may seek help from the local authority during a community care assessment. (See Part 6.) Anyone carrying out a community care assessment should consider any childcare issues the person might have. See 27.10.

A child whose parent has a mental disorder is a 'child in need' for the purposes of the Children (Scotland) Act.[2] A parent may ask the local authority if it can provide any children's services.

The local authority has a duty to promote the welfare of children in need in its area and to do what it can to help children in need stay with their families.[3] A child in need is automatically entitled to statutory services, such as care for pre-school children and after-school care for older children.[4]

The child is also a 'child affected by disability'. The local authority has a duty to provide services aimed at minimising the effects of the disability and helping the child lead as normal a life as possible.[5] This could involve giving the parent help to care.

The child's parent or guardian is entitled to a formal assessment of the child's needs.[6] It might be possible to argue that, having identified the child's needs, the local authority is under a statutory duty to meet at least some of them.[7]

The local authority may meet a child's needs by providing services to the child, a parent or another member of the family.[8]

The local authority may help facilitate an arrangement whereby gaps in ability to care are filled by (extended) family members[9] and this is normally the preference when a parent's impaired ability to care is an intermittent effect of mental illness. The local authority may provide accommodation for the child from its own resources in foster care or residential care.[10]

1   Social Work (Scotland) Act 1968, s 12.
2   Children (Scotland) Act 1995, s 93.
3   C(S)A 1995, s 22(1).
4   C(S)A 1995, s 27.
5   C(S)A 1995, s 23.
6   C(S)A 1995, s 23(3).
7   See *McGregor v South Lanarkshire Council*, 27.05.
8   C(S)A 1995, s 22(3).
9   Under C(S)A 1995, s 26.
10   Under C(S)A 1995, s 25.

Where parent subject to compulsory measures

31.24 If a parent (or person with parental responsibilities), become subject to compulsory measures under the Mental Health (Care and Treatment) Act, those involved in his or her care must do what they can to minimise the disruption of family life and to help the child to maintain contact with his or her parent.[1] The mental health officer should liaise with colleagues in the social work children and families team.[2]

1   Mental Health (Care and Treatment) (Scotland) Act 2003, s 278.
2   Code of Practice, vol 1, para 1.47.

Adjusting parental responsibilities and rights

Attitude of the courts

31.25 In proceedings concerning the child between parents and family members, mental disorder may be a relevant factor, but not necessarily a determining one, since the welfare of the child is paramount in decision-making. Mental disorder of itself does not prevent a parent from retaining and exercising parental responsibilities. The other parent may fear the ability of the parent to participate in caring for the child. Medical evidence will be influential in this respect.[1]

Principles from the UN Convention on the Rights of the Child and the European Convention on the Exercise of the Rights of the Child underpin an inclusive approach, promoting maintenance of relationships for the welfare of the child, and having regard to the views of a child who is old enough to express them.

A child of 12 is presumed old enough to express a view,[2] although younger children often do, whether directly or through an older sibling. If the court is to intervene to limit those relationships, their reasons must be supported by child welfare considerations.

1   As in *CR or D v ARD*, Lord Macphail, Outer House, 28 June 2005.
2   Children (Scotland) Act 1995, s 6.

Order for parental responsibilities and rights

31.26 The court can make an order for parental responsibility in favour of a private individual or individuals who will provide care (such a grandparent or any other person claiming interest).[1] It may also, if necessary in the interests of the child, restrict the responsibilities and rights of a parent with mental disorder.

In deciding whether to make an order, the court must have regard to the need to protect a child from abuse or the risk of abuse within the household.[2] It must consider the effect such abuse or risk might have on the child, the ability of the abuser or potential abuser to care for, or otherwise meet the needs of the child and the effect of the abuse on the ability of someone else in the household to care for or otherwise meet the needs of the child. This is designed to address the effects of domestic abuse upon child care, even when the abuse is not directed towards the child.

1   Under the Children (Scotland) Act 1995, Pt 1.
2   C(S)A 1995 (as amended by the Family Law (Scotland) Act 2006), ss 11(7B) and (7C).

Need for order

31.27 The court should not make an order unless it will be better for the child than no order at all.[1] This is well illustrated by a recent case. A Russian father married to a Scottish woman had taken their child to live in Russia after the marriage broke down. The mother, who remained in Scotland, sought a residence order. The matter came before the court three years after the child had moved to Russia.

The mother had schizophrenia, but her illness was relatively well controlled and her treating psychiatrist confirmed that she could give adequate care to the child in Scotland. The court refused an order for residence in favour of the mother, indicating that there was not evidence to satisfy the court that such an order (which would require the child to be returned from Russia, and the father's responsibilities limited as a consequence) would be better for the child than no order. The child was settled with the father in Russia, and it was not possible on the evidence to say where the child's best interests would be served.

The court did make an order for contact and for other specific issues, since they were necessary and better for the child than no order. The court ordered that the child could come to visit his mother in Scotland periodically at the father's cost, and the father should have the child's school reports translated into English and sent to the mother. The mother's parental responsibilities in law in relation to this child remained intact despite the separation and divorce of the parents and the mother's mental illness.[2]

---

1   C(S)A 1995, s 11(7)(a).
2   *CR or D v ARD*, Lord Macphail, Outer House, 28 June 2005. The judge was unwilling to accept sweeping and unsupported criticisms of the mother by the father and his Russian advocate, linked to her mental illness.

Children at risk

Children's hearing

31.28 If a parent needs help with caring for children and is unwilling to agree to, or is unhappy with, proposed arrangements, the matter may be referred to a children's hearing. If the children's hearing is satisfied that grounds for referral exist, it may make a supervision requirement, requiring a parent to accept support for care within the family home, or ordering the local authority to look after the child.[1] The parent has the right to attend the hearing.

It is essential that the children's hearing is aware of and has regard to any mental disorder a parent may have, and oversees appropriate levels of support for parenting. Ultimately, the paramount consideration of the hearing is the welfare of the child, and if the interests of the child conflict with those of the parent, the child's interest must prevail.

The children's hearing may appoint a safeguarder to the child if there is a conflict of interest between the child and the child's interest, as viewed by the parent. The parent may dispute that the factors presented by the local authority to the children's are correct, and if so, the factual resolution of these is referred to the sheriff. Once the grounds of referral are established or agreed the matter goes back to the hearing for a determination on what support is necessary for the child.

Grounds which may arise because of mental disorder on the part of a parent include lack of parental care, exposure to moral danger, or the child being beyond the parent's control.[2]

If the local authority raises child protection issues, the parent should seek immediate legal advice. The parent should also insist that the local authority carries out a formal assessment of the child's needs.

1   Children (Scotland) Act 1995, Pt II.
2   C(S)A 1995, s 52(2).

Care after childbirth

31.29 If a local authority is aware before a child's birth that a parent's ability to care for a child may be impaired by mental disorder, the local authority may seek involvement of the hearing from the point of birth, so that the potential risk to the child is recorded and care is monitored under the oversight of the hearing.

The local authority has duties to a parent with mental disorder as well as the child, and separate social workers should be allocated to parent and child. It is often the case that support is offered to the parent for a period, to allow parent and child to bond and to ascertain the person's parenting ability. This may be in the parent's own home or in a setting where care support is on hand, such as a specialist mother and baby unit.

Regular reviews should be undertaken. If care is of a good enough standard, with any risk to the child being managed, the child can remain with the parent, and may be discharged from supervision. Risk factors arising in the future can lead to another referral by the local authority to the children's hearing. Where care continues to be of concern, local authorities must, in the paramount interests of the child, consider whether they should plan for permanent resettlement of the child other than with that parent.

The normal means of securing that permanence for a young child is by adoption. See below.

Adoption is generally associated with a clean break between parent and child, and contact after adoption is still relatively unusual, although adoptive parents are now encouraged to ensure that the child is made aware, and kept aware, of birth family heritage in an age-appropriate manner. An older child who has developed a greater bond with the birth parent before circumstances have impaired that parent's caring ability, may be more suitably placed in foster care rather than adoption, to allow for retention of family identity and relationships.

Under proposals in the Adoption and Children (Scotland) Bill, a new 'permanence order' may be sought in such a situation.

Parties to family proceedings

31.30 In any proceedings to regulate responsibilities and rights in relation to the child, it is essential that the court or hearing has effective access to the views of the parent. The parent may be represented by a lawyer or, in the children's hearing, by any person admitted by the hearing.

In the absence of clear evidence that the parent's views have been sought and presented in a way that the parent/person could engage in and understand, a curator *ad litem* should be appointed for that person. In proceedings involving children, the court must also ensure that the child's views are obtained and regard had to them, taking into account the age and maturity of the child.

Children are entitled to instruct their own legal representatives. If a child is below the age of ability to give views directly or via a solicitor, the court must consider if any steps are needed to obtain the views of the child. For children with mental disorder this is a more complex process, considered below.

Children in court proceedings

31.31 A child with mental illness or learning disability may require special provision for his or her view to be heard in proceedings concerning his or her welfare. This may arise in dispute over parental responsibility within a family action, or in care proceedings brought by the Reporter to the children's hearing.

The court or hearing must obtain and have regard to the child's views in connection with any decision between individuals concerning the welfare of the child.[1] The child is entitled to separate representation if he or she is of the age and maturity to instruct a legal representative. This is presumed at age 12, but the contrary can be proved.

If the court perceives that there may be a conflict of interest between the child and a parent or other applicant, or if the consequences of an order sought are particularly significant for the child (such as a finding that the child has engaged in criminal conduct) it may be necessary for the court or hearing to rule that the child should be separately advised before any final order is made.

It appears that a court or children's hearing can still appoint a curator *bonis* (a financial manager) to a child, if the circumstances are appropriate for general assumption of responsibilities for the child's decision-making. When the child attains the age of 16 the curator automatically becomes a financial guardian.[2] The appropriateness of this depends on the extent of the child's mental disorder and incapacity.[3]

If a child's capacity to offer a view or instruct a legal representative is impaired by mental disorder, the court or children's hearing may appoint a curator *ad litem*. The curator *ad litem* may make enquiries and make recommendations to the court in the best interest of the child, or may attempt to ascertain the child's views and wishes so far as possible and communicate those to the court, either directly or through a legal representative appointed by the curator.

1   Children (Scotland) Act 1995, s 6.
2   In terms of the Adults with Incapacity (Scotland) Act 2000, Sched 4, para 1(2).
3   Wilkinson and Norrie, *Parent and Child* (2nd edn, W Green & Son, 1999), para 15.64.

ADOPTION

31.32 In some cases where a person with a mental disorder is facing long term inability to look after a child or children, the local authority may propose adoption, and this must be considered as a plan for the future by the children's hearing. If adoption is endorsed as an appropriate plan for the child, there must be an application to the court, since only the court can make an order under the Adoption (Scotland) Act 1978.

There may be an outright application for adoption in favour of the proposed adoptive parents, or an application may be preceded by an application to 'free' the child for adoption. In the latter case, the application is made by the local authority which, if the freeing application is granted, assumes the role of parent pending an application and order for adoption.

Before an adoption order is made, the court must have reports from the local authority and from an independent curator *ad litem* for the child. The curator *ad litem* normally also acts as reporting officer, and obtains, and relates to the court, the views of birth parents and the child.

Consent of child

31.33 A child aged from 12 to 18 (the maximum age at which adoption is permitted) can be the subject of an adoption order only if he or she consents to that adoption.[1] This consent is sought by the curator *ad litem* appointed under the legislation to any child in respect of whom an adoption order is sought.

There may be an issue of capacity to consent if a young person has a mental disorder or developmental delay, and the court may dispense with the agreement of that child where satisfied that the child is incapable of giving consent.[2] At common law, the court may appoint a curator *ad litem* for the distinct purpose of informing the court as to the capacity, understanding and wishes of a child.

[1]   Adoption (Scotland) Act 1978, s 12(8).
[2]   A(S)A 1978, s 12(8).

Consent of parent

31.34 Any birth parent who can be found must be approached for agreement to adoption, and agreement must have been given freely and with full understanding of what is involved.[1] The reporting officer appointed by the court must ensure that the parent understands the meaning and effect of adoption. The local authority must also provide information to the parent.

A parent with mental disorder may be temporarily or permanently inhibited by the disorder from having full understanding, or may be open to undue pressure to agree without full understanding. The fact that someone refuses to take notice of the information offered does not mean that he or she should be taken not to have understood the information.

Every effort should be made to enhance a parent's understanding and to include the parent fully in the process of adoption. Where a parent offers agreement, but the reporting officer is unclear whether the parent can fully understand, the parent should be permitted to sign the agreement form, and the reporting officer should report any concerns to the court. The court can dispense with the agreement of a parent who lacks capacity to give agreement. See below.

[1]   Adoption (Scotland) Act 1978, s 16(1)(b)(i).

Dispensing with parental consent

31.35 In the absence of agreement, adoption can only be granted if grounds for dispensing with parental agreement are made out.

The statutory grounds for dispensing with agreement at present[1] are that the parent:

(a) is not known, cannot be found or is incapable of giving agreement;

(b) is withholding agreement unreasonably;

(c) has persistently failed without reasonable cause, to fulfill one or other of the following parental responsibilities in relation to the child

    (i) the responsibility to safeguard and promote the child's health, development and welfare, or

    (ii) if the child is not living with that parent, the responsibility to maintain personal relations and direct contact with the child on a regular basis; or

(d) has seriously ill-treated the child and the child's reintegration into the same household as the parent or guardian is unlikely, because of the serious ill-treatment or for other reasons.

[1] Adoption (Scotland) Act 1978 as amended by the Children (Scotland) Act 1995, s 16(2). Adoption law has been the subject of review between 2003 and 2006 and, at the time of writing, an Adoption of Children (Scotland) Bill is before the Scottish Parliament.

Incapacity to consent

31.36 It has been suggested that the incapacity element of ground (a) refers to mental or physical incapacity, but that it should be invoked only if the incapacity is likely to be long term, since:

> '[t]he deprivation of the right to withhold agreement to the adoption of one's child is so significant that it should not be permitted because of a mere temporary or short-term incapacity at the critical time.'[1]

There may well be an issue of capacity to consent if a parent has a mental disorder or developmental delay, and the court may separately at common law appoint a curator *ad litem* for the distinct purpose of informing the court as to the capacity, understanding and wishes of a parent.

The fact that agreement of a parent can be dispensed with on the ground of incapacity does not deflect from the importance of the court ensuring that the views of that parent are sought as fully and effectively as circumstances permit before the decision is made.

[1] Wilkinson & Norrie, *Parent and Child* (2nd edn, W Green & Son, 1999), para 4.43.

Failure of care

31.37 The grounds (c) and (d) are factual and relate to events in the child's past care, which represent failings in key aspects of parenting or serious ill-treatment. The test for both requires that the parental behaviour has been without reasonable cause.

Many instances of failures in parenting, less so serious ill-treatment, may be attributable to the effects of mental disorder, at times aggravated by substance abuse. The question of whether the effects of mental disorder constitute reasonable cause have not been considered expressly, but in a child protection case involving a mother who was in an abusive relationship and suffered ill-health, the court, considering a similar test, stressed that what is reasonable must be considered objectively rather than in the subjective circumstances of the parent.[1]

Lack of means to provide adequate parental care due to restriction of liberty or lack of funds have not been held to be reasonable cause,[2] and it is not necessary for the persistent failure to be intentional. Instead the test is whether the persistence is likely to have enduring significance.[3]

Serious ill-treatment, even a single instance, is sufficient ground to dispense with agreement, if it is without reasonable cause and the reintegration of the child in the household of the parent is unlikely. (The unlikelihood does not have to be directly linked to the ill-treatment). Delusional grounds for ill-treatment are unlikely to be considered reasonable cause, because they are detached from both the reason of the parent and from objective standards of reasonableness.

[1] *Central Regional Council v B*, 1985 SLT 413 at 418.
[2] Wilkinson and Norrie, *Parent and Child* (2nd edn, W Green & Son, 1999), para 4.53 and cases cited there.
[3] *G v M*, 1999 SCLR 648 (IH).

Unreasonable withholding of consent

31.38 Reliance for dispensing with parental agreement is commonly placed on ground (b), that the parent is withholding consent unreasonably at the time of the adoption hearing. This ground has led to more judicial interpretation than the other grounds, and there have been contradictory comments on this by the courts over the years, particularly in relation to its relationship to the best interests of the child, which is key to the separate test for granting an adoption order.[1]

The reasonableness of withholding agreement is measured by the objective test of whether or not a reasonable parent would *in all the circumstances* withhold agreement. If it would have been within the bounds of an objectively reasonable parent's decision-making to withhold agreement to adoption, the basis for the ground of dispensation is not made out.

Unlike grounds (c) and (d) where the view is entirely based on past events, this ground may be available where a parent claims ongoing improvement or future realistic expectation of improvement in his or her parenting capacity, since the decision on reasonableness is made at the point of hearing (or appeal) in the adoption proceedings. On the other hand, the case for securing the position of the child in the home of prospective adopters may have become stronger with passage of time.

1   For a review of the issues see Wilkinson and Norrie, *Parent and Child* (2nd edn, W Green & Son, 1999), paras 4.44–4.50 and cases cited there.

Proposals for reform

31.39 Many people with mental disorder report severe psychological trauma following the adoption of their children. Children report trauma and loss of identity following adoption, (even when adoption has been preceded by periods of inadequate care, neglect or even abuse and care by adoptive parents has been loving and successful). For children adopted after a period of care by the birth parent, increasingly consideration is given to openness in the adoption, although most commonly this is via letterbox contact between a birth parent and the child.

Proposed changes in adoption law include a new option for permanent substitute parenting. This would be free of the bureaucratic limitations of fostering and does not include the severance of all legal (and normally practical) links with birth relatives that are typical of adoption.[1]

As the law stands at present, a person whose parental responsibilities are removed by adoption or freeing for adoption is absolutely barred from seeking any parental responsibilities in relation to the child thereafter, although any other person claiming an interest can claim.

This provides certainty for adopters that the birth parent will not attempt to re-enter the child's life, for example by making an application for contact when the parent's life is more stable, but review of adoption law has led to proposals that the birth parent may, with the express leave of the court, so apply. This would allow at least for the situation that if adoptive parents are unable to care for the child, birth parents may be competently, although exceptionally, considered alongside other potential carers.

1   Adoption and Children (Scotland) Bill, introduced to the Scottish Parliament 28 March 2006.

Applying to adopt or foster

31.40 A person with a mental illness or learning disability may apply for adoption. If the adoption application follows upon private arrangements, such as the remarriage of birth parent of the child, the application must be accompanied by a certificate from a doctor to the effect that there is no medical reason why the person would be unable to fulfill the role of adoptive parent to the child.

If a child is placed for adoption through an adoption agency, such as a local authority, the person who applies for adoption must go through the process of selection as an adopter, and issues of health and capacity are investigated.

Similar processes of selection apply to people who seek to become foster parents to take children who are looked after by the local authority. Families or friends occasionally enter into private fostering arrangements, but there is an obligation, often overlooked, to inform the local authority of that private fostering arrangement so that the authority may inquire into the suitability of the person chosen as private foster carer.

Chapter 32

HOUSING

32.01 This chapter looks in outline at some of the legal issues surrounding housing for people with mental health challenges and learning disabilities.[1] It does not attempt to give practical advice about housing.

People need a range of housing options, from occasional support in ordinary living, through to supported accommodation, residential and nursing care and 24 hour staffed care.[2] Many of these options now exist, but provision is patchy. An independent advocate might be able to help a person establish what housing support is available in his or her area.

Research in England and Wales shows that most people with severe and enduring mental health problems live in mainstream housing, with only around one in five living in supported accommodation or specialist housing.[3]

Adequate housing is crucial to mental health. Lack of access to stable, adequate housing is a problem for many people living with mental health challenges, who, compared with the general population, are more likely to live in rented housing, to be dissatisfied with their accommodation and to consider their home in a poor state of repair.[4] Lack of stable housing is also a problem, with one in four tenants with mental health challenges having serious rent arrears.[5]

This chapter looks in outline at the general duties of local authorities and health bodies to support people's needs and to ensure adequate housing is available. It looks at accessing housing and at opposition to community care projects. A high level of those who are homeless have mental health issues[6] and this chapter considers local authorities' duties to provide adequate accommodation and support. For the duty of local authorities to provide residential care homes and nursing homes, see 28.21.

---

[1] Shelter, the housing campaign, has a helpful website which covers the issues in more detail, including a specialist legal service for Scotland, available on subscription.

[2] *Framework for Mental Health Services in Scotland* (Scottish Office, 1995), s 2.

[3] *Mental health and social exclusion* (Social Exclusion Unit, 2004).

4   H Meltzer, N Singleton, A Lee, P Bebbington, T Brugha and R Jenkins, *The social and economic circumstances of adults with mental disorders* (The Stationery Office, 2002).

5   *House Keeping: preventing homelessness though tackling rent arrears in social housing* (Shelter, 2003).

6   The Social Exclusion Unit found that between 30% and 50% of rough sleepers had mental health issues. Around 88% of them became ill before they became homeless. Only a third of single people who were rough sleepers were receiving any treatment. *Rough sleeping* (Social Exclusion Unit, 1998).

OBTAINING HOUSING

Waiting lists

32.02 A person may wish to move to an area to be near family members or others who could offer support. A person may have been resident in a hospital in an area for many years and wish to remain living near the hospital for after-care.

Local authority housing waiting lists are generally limited to people who reside in the area. A person can apply to go on a waiting list for another area if, among other things, he or she wishes to move into the area to be near a relative or carer or has special social or medical reasons for wishing to be housed in the area.[1]

Once on the waiting list, allocation of housing depends on the number of points the applicant has, based on his or her needs. Medical needs generally count highly. Unsuitable housing also attracts points.[2] Housing which might otherwise seem suitable may not be suitable for a person with a mental disability and the person should make sure the housing authority is aware of any factors making his or her housing unsuitable.

1   Housing (Scotland) Act 1987, as amended by the Housing (Scotland) Act 2001 and the Homelessness (Scotland) Act 2003, s 20(2).

2   H(S)A 1987 (amended as above), s 20(1)(a).

Homelessness

32.03 People with mental disorders who are homeless or threatened with homelessness should receive help from the local authority and health services.

In addition to local authorities' obligations as housing providers, health authorities should have homelessness action plans, negotiated in consultation with local authorities, to ensure that people who could otherwise be discharged from hospital have appropriate discharge plans for housing.[1]

People who live with mental health challenges or learning disabilities who find themselves homeless are owed special duties by the local authority housing department, because they will nearly always be regarded as 'vulnerable'. The rules are complex, and dealt with here only in outline. The person should seek specialist advice from a Citizens Advice Bureau or specialised housing advice centre.

If a housing department has reason to believe that a person is (1) homeless (or threatened with homelessness), (2) in 'priority need', (3) not intentionally homeless and (4) has no local connection with any other housing department (which would then be required to house him or her), it must make accommodation available for the person.[2]

Such accommodation may be special housing which the housing department use for housing homeless people, and may be bed and breakfast accommodation. When allocating tenancies from the ordinary council waiting list, the housing department must give 'reasonable preference' to people who are homeless.[3]

[1]   Scottish Executive Code of Guidance on Homelessness (May 2005), para 2.30–2.31.
[2]   Housing (Scotland) Act 1987, ss 31 and 32.
[3]   H(S)A 1987, s 20(1)(b).

Establishing homelessness

32.04 The homelessness legislation applies not just to people who have no home but also, in some circumstances, to people who have accommodation which is unsuitable. A person is homeless if there is no accommodation that the person can occupy as of right[1] or if he or she has accommodation but it is not reasonable for him or her to occupy it.[2]

Someone who cannot secure entry to his or her accommodation, or who is subject to the risk of violence, is also regarded as homeless.

Whether it is unreasonable for a person to occupy accommodation is a question of fact and depends on the circumstances of the case. If the conditions in the house are such that they are causing a person with a mental disability additional stress or danger, it could be argued that it is unreasonable for the person to occupy that house.

A person in such a situation has the option of applying for a transfer (if he or she is already in local authority accommodation) or applying for re-housing as a homeless person. The decision will be partly based on the seriousness of the situation in the person's home.[3]

1   Thus a person whose only home is sleeping on the floor of a friend's flat is regarded as homeless.
2   Housing (Scotland) Act 1987, s 24.
3   Scottish Executive Code of Guidance on Homelessness (May 2005), Chap 5.

Priority need for re-housing

32.05 Certain homeless people are regarded as having a priority need for accommodation. Among them are people who are vulnerable because of a mental illness or learning disability, people who are vulnerable because of old age and people who are otherwise vulnerable, for example because of their youth.[1]

A person is also regarded as in priority need if he or she lives, or might reasonably be expected to live, with a person who is in priority need.[2] Thus a carer could apply for housing, if the person him or herself is unable to do so.

The housing department must make temporary housing available for person in priority need, while it makes inquiries into the case.[3]

1   Housing (Scotland) Act 1987, s 25.
2   H(S)A 1987, s 25(1)(c). Scottish Executive Code of Guidance on Homelessness (May 2005), Chap 6.
3   H(S)A 1987, s 29(1).

Intentional homelessness

32.06 Where a person has deliberately done something which has led to him or her giving up accommodation which was available to him or her, the person is treated as 'intentionally homeless'.[1]

If the housing department decides that someone in priority need is intentionally homeless, it has no duty to offer permanent housing, but it must give the person temporary accommodation and advice and assistance to help him or her find somewhere else.[2]

A person whose mental health problems or learning disabilities caused him or her to have difficulties maintaining a tenancy would have a strong case for arguing that he or she should not be treated as intentionally homeless.[3]

1   Housing (Scotland) Act 1987, s 26(1).

2   H(S)A 1987, s 31(3).

3   Scottish Executive Code of Guidance on Homelessness (May 2005), para 7.8. In an English case, a person was evicted because of anti-social behaviour. She had mental health problems and the local authority claimed she was intentionally homeless. The court said the local authority should have given her a community care assessment and should have made absolutely clear to her the consequences of refusing its offer of alternative accommodation. *R v Newham LBC ex parte P* (2000) 4 CCLR 48.

Local connection

32.07 A person can have a local connection with an area because he or she has lived there, because he or she works there, because of family connections or for other special reasons.[1] The person must have lived in the area by choice. Residence as a long-term patient in an area qualifies, but not if the patient was in the hospital as a detained patient.[2]

When a person has no local connection with a housing department's area and has a local connection with another housing department's area, the department to which he or she has applied may notify the other department. It is then the duty of the other department to house the applicant.[3]

If someone has particular reasons for wanting to live in the first area, he or she will have to persuade the housing department that there are special circumstances giving him or her a local connection with the area. This could include the need for access to specialist health care available in that area.[4] If this fails, the person can still put his or her name on the first council's waiting list under the rules described above.

1   Housing (Scotland) Act 1987, s 27, and Scottish Executive Code of Guidance on Homelessness (May 2005), Chap 8.

2   H(S)A 1987, s 27(2)(a).

3   Provided that the applicant is not at risk of domestic violence in the other area. H(S)A 1987, s 34.

4   Scottish Executive Code of Guidance on Homelessness (May 2005), para 8.16.

Making the application

32.08 In an English case, the House of Lords held that only a person who is mentally able to make an application for housing can do so.[1] A carer who does not him or herself qualify for housing, for example if he or she is intentionally homeless, cannot use an application made on behalf of a person without mental capacity to get round the rules.

[1] *R v Tower Hamlets London Borough Council ex parte Ferdous Begum* [1993] 2 All ER 65.

Carers and tenancies

32.09 People who rent accommodation from a local authority or registered social landlord usually have a form of tenancy known as a Scottish secure tenancy. A person who gives up his or her home to care for such a tenant may be entitled to inherit the tenancy on the tenant's death.

On the death of a tenant, the tenancy passes by operation of law to a qualified person. On his or her death, the tenancy passes to another qualified person and on his or her death, the tenancy ends. If there is no qualified person, or a qualified person declines the tenancy, the tenancy ends.[1] There are detailed rules dealing with the situation where more than one person qualifies.

A person qualifies if he or she is the spouse or civil partner of the person who has died, holds a joint tenancy with the tenant or is an adult member of the tenant's family who was living in the house. A non-related carer can also qualify. The carer must be providing, or have provided, care for the tenant or a member of the tenant's family and must be aged at least 16 years. The house must be the carer's only or principal home at the time of the tenant's death, and the carer must have given up his or her home.[2]

If the house has been specially adapted for the tenant's needs, a carer (or adult member of the tenant's family other than a spouse or civil partner) can qualify only if he or she has special needs which mean he or she requires similar accommodation.[3]

[1] Housing (Scotland) Act 2001, s 22.
[2] H(S)A 2001, Sched 2, para 4.
[3] H(S)A 2001, Sched 2, para 5.

Tenancy and other agreements

32.10 People living under conditions of comparative security as residents of long-stay hospital wards may move to accommodation in the community as part of a planned closure of the ward. The new resident may be asked to sign a tenancy or occupancy agreement drawn up by the voluntary or independent organisation offering housing. There are concerns about whether people receive proper advice about their rights and the implications of such agreements. There are also concerns about what is good practice when a resident is not able to understand the terms and conditions of such an agreement.[1]

As a matter of good practice, a potential resident should have the terms of any new agreement explained. The person should also be advised about his or her rights of security of tenure, which are different according to whether the property is rented from the local authority or a housing association, or if the person is entering into residential care.

It may not be appropriate for the staff of the new accommodation to give such explanations, as it could be argued they have a conflict of interest. This might be a matter for the social worker or care manager at the hospital arranging the person's discharge. The involvement of an independent advocate may help ensure the person understands his or her legal rights.

[1]   In one case of which the writer is aware (before the Adults with Incapacity Act), a woman with profound learning disabilities moved from good provision in a learning disability hospital to unsuitable accommodation in the community. When the placement broke down, she had to return to hospital. The original ward, which offered a range of facilities, had gone and she was returned to a locked facility in a psychiatric hospital. If she had been independently advised about her lack of security of tenure at the time of the original placement, she might have refused the move, or insisted on adequate safeguards.

Adults with incapacities

32.11 If a resident is unable to sign a tenancy or occupancy agreement, no one else can sign for him or her, unless the resident has signed a power of attorney. Some organisations ask relatives to sign, as an indication that they have seen the terms of the new accommodation and agree with them. It should be made clear that the relatives are signing in this capacity. In some cases it may be appropriate to obtain an order under the Adults with Incapacity Act to authorise the signing of the agreement. See Part 5.

Similar problems can arise when a person needs to give up a tenancy because he or she is moving to new accommodation, perhaps residential care. If a person has not appointed an attorney, no one else can give up the tenancy, unless a guardian or person authorised under an intervention order is appointed. Sometimes those working with the person will simply notify the local authority that the person is leaving, and the authority will later treat the accommodation as abandoned.

HOUSING SUPPORT

Local housing strategies

32.12 Housing authorities and social work authorities must plan to meet the needs of their areas. Local authorities should carry out an assessment of the housing needs of their area, and must in particular consider the availability and need for housing for people with special needs.)[1] The housing strategies they submit to Scottish Ministers must set out the authority's housing plans for these special needs groups,[2] but local authorities may delegate their duties to provide housing to Registered Social Landlords (formerly housing associations).[3]

The housing department clearly needs information from the social work department before it can assess the needs for special housing in its area. Similarly social work departments drawing up their community care plans (see 27.03) need information from the housing department on housing provision in the area. Government guidance stresses the need for co-operation when drawing up plans.[4] It regrets that such co-operation has not always existed in the past.

[1] Housing (Scotland) Act 2001, s 89(2).
[2] H(S)A 2001, s 89.
[3] H(S)A 2001 s 89(4).
[4] See *Community care: the housing dimension* (Scottish Office circular SWSG7/94).

Meeting needs

32.13 When an individual needs help from the housing department or from the social work department, it is essential that the other department co-operates to provide the information and help the person needs. When a local authority carries out a community care assessment, the person's housing needs often need to be investigated. When a housing department assesses a person for housing, it may become obvious that the person has more profound needs, and needs on-going support from social work.

Government guidance stresses the importance of housing departments co-operating in the process to ensure that the person's needs are looked at as a whole.[1] Similarly the housing department may call in the social work department to help a person manage a tenancy and remove the need for the person to move house. The single shared assessment can help departments to co-ordinate this.[2]

A person who does not receive the appropriate help may wish to put in a complaint to the local authority or the Scottish Public Services Ombudsman, or may even have grounds for legal action.

In a case in England, a person with mental health challenges was living in crowded and unsuitable accommodation. The local authority carried out a community care assessment which concluded he needed better accommodation. The housing department failed to supply this. The court said that once the person's need had been assessed under the community care system, and a particular need identified, the local authority was under a duty to provide appropriate accommodation for the person, and could not take into account its own lack of resources.[3]

---

[1]   Scottish Executive Code of Guidance on Homelessness (May 2005), para 4.45, *Community care: the housing dimension* (Scottish Office circular SWSG7/94), section 4.

[2]   Scottish Executive Code of Guidance on Homelessness, (above), para 4.47.

[3]   *R v Islington LBC ex parte Banatu* (2001) 4 CCLR 445. (This was distinguished in *R (on application of Walid) v Tower Hamlets LBC* (2003) HLR 2, where, in the absence of a particular need being identified, there was no such obligation. *See also R (on application of G) v Barnet LBC* (2004) 2 AC 208, where, in considering whether to fund housing adaptations for disabilities in children, the local authority was entitled to take account of family resources and their ability to contribute towards the cost.)

Supporting People

32.14 Local authorities can arrange some support for people in their homes through the Supporting People framework, introduced from April 2003. Supporting People allows local authorities to use money provided by the Scottish Executive to fund schemes to enable people to stay in their homes.

It cannot be used to provide services such as personal care and personal support services[1] or employment services, which could be funded through the community care budget, but it can be used to provide general counselling, befriending, help with community involvement and help with 'resettlement', among other things.[2]

Local authorities should assess the overall levels of need in their area and commission appropriate services to meet those needs. They should involve health agencies, service providers and service user groups in this assessment. The local authority then funds services on a contract basis.

The local housing strategy should show how the local authority proposes to meet the needs of people in its area through Supporting People. For more information, see the Scottish Executive's Supporting People website.

[1]   As defined in the Regulation of Care (Scotland) Act 2001, s 2(28).

[2]   The full list of what it can cover is in the Housing (Scotland) Act 2001 (Housing Support Services) Regulations 2002 (SSI 2002/444).

Adaptations

32.15 Grants to adapt a house to meet the needs of a person with a disability are available.[1] The local authority may be obliged to help a person arrange adaptations under the Chronically Sick and Disabled Persons Act. See 28.18.

A disabled person can apply for a grant whether or not he or she is the owner or tenant of the property. If the person is a private tenant, he or she should seek the approval of the landlord, but the landlord cannot unreasonably withhold approval.[2]

[1]   See *Housing Grants, an applicant's guide to improvement and repair grants for private housing* (Scottish Executive 2003). Available on the Scottish Executive's website.

[2]   Housing (Scotland) Act 2006, s 52. Disability includes mental and physical disability, as defined in the Disability Discrimination Act 1995 (H(S)A 2006, s 194.)

PROBLEMS WITH TENANCY

32.16 Problems may arise for a tenant in maintaining a tenancy. The person may suffer harassment from neighbours or other occupiers in a house, or the person's condition might prompt behaviour that neighbours or landlords find alarming or unacceptable.

Harassment

32.17 If a tenant is subject to harassment, the landlord should attempt to deal with this, so that the tenant can enjoy the tenancy without harassment. If that is not achieved by discussion, the landlord should consider alternatives, such as a community mediation service, or an application to the court for an Anti-Social Behaviour order (ASBO), by which the court orders the person to cease the harassment under threat of further penalty or loss of tenancy. An ASBO is considered a last resort, and where the landlord is a registered social landlord, it should first attempt to achieve an Acceptable Behaviour Contract.

The landlord might also seek to evict a tenant if there is persistent breach of tenancy conditions, such as excessive noise, failure to keep the property in habitable condition, or abuse of neighbours.

A tenant affected by such behaviour is also entitled to apply to the court for a court order (interdict) to stop the offensive behaviour, or may take proceedings on the grounds of discrimination.

Housing advice agencies suggest that a tenant who is suffering harassment or anti-social behaviour by a neighbour should keep a diary of the events. If noise is the problem, local authorities can provide noise-recording equipment to assist in gathering evidence and can advise whether noise is excessive.

Problems for tenant

32.18 If a person's mental disorder leads to his or her conduct of the tenancy being unacceptable to neighbours, the neighbours or landlord have the same remedies, but the role that the disorder plays in bringing about that behaviour must be taken into account.[1]

If the landlord takes eviction proceedings, the court must balance the interests involved, and even if a tenant's behaviour is because of mental disorder, the grounds for eviction may still be made out. However the landlord may be required to offer alternative accommodation, and the rights to housing on homelessness might assist the person who has been evicted, on the argument that the homelessness was due to the effects of illness rather than intentional behaviour. See above.

A landlord might seek to evict a tenant who does not comply with conditions for payment of rent. If the tenant receives housing benefit or the local authority equivalent, the tenant can request that benefit is paid direct to the landlord, particularly if there is a history of rent arrears.

[1] See *Langstane Housing Association Ltd v Morrow*, 2005 GWD 34–647.

NEIGHBOUR OPPOSITION AND DISCRIMINATION

32.19 Unfortunately the development of community care projects has not met with a unanimous welcome from prospective neighbours of new projects. Some take legal advice to attempt to thwart new developments. Any organisation wishing to open a new project must check the legal situation, including planning restrictions, conditions in law restricting use of the property and the licensing requirements for Homes in Multiple Occupancy (properties where three or more people share one house).

Planning permission is necessary if properties are being adapted or extended or if there is a change of use. Planning permission is needed for conversion to flats, no matter what the number of residents.

Guidance for organisations wishing to open community care projects stresses the importance of making contact with neighbours and allaying neighbours' concerns, but it also stresses the need to respect the confidentiality of prospective residents.[1]

The laws outlawing discrimination in housing may help remove the scope for ill-informed opposition to community care projects. See Part 9.

[1] *Community care accommodation: public awareness and local discussion* (Scottish Office circular SWSG8/94).

Chapter 33

EDUCATION AND EMPLOYMENT

EDUCATION

33.01 Children with learning disabilities or mental health difficulties should hope to receive help from their local educational authority in meeting their needs for education.

The Education (Scotland) Act 1980 places a duty on parents to secure appropriate educational provision for their children. Local authorities must provide education to which parents can secure access, at school and pre-school level, and by further education, although there is no absolute right to secure access to a chosen educational facility at school or pre-school level. The test is whether the provision offered meets the minimum requirement placed on the parent by the law.

Local authorities' general duty to provide a suitable school education for children in their area includes a duty to provide for the needs of children who have needs for additional support for learning.[1] It is the expectation that children will be educated wherever possible in mainstream schools, rather than special schools.[2]

Education authorities, and the proprietors and managers of independent or grant-aided schools, must have written disability strategies. These should aim to increase the extent to which school pupils and potential[3] pupils with a disability[4] can participate in the curriculum, take advantage of the services provided in schools, and improve timely and effective communication with pupils in ways which take account of pupils' needs and preferences.[5]

The obligation of education authorities to provide education includes meeting the ongoing educational needs of those with mental disorder whose need for education extends into adulthood.[6] Authorities are not obliged to provide free out of school care[7] and can make charges for providing education and training to adults.[8]

---

[1] Education (Additional Support for Learning)(Scotland) Act 2004, s 1.
[2] Standards in Scotland's Schools Act 2000, s 15.
[3] Education authorities have further duties in relation to pre-school provision, for some after school care and for education for those of school age who are travelling people.

4   Defined according to the Disability Discrimination Act 1995.
5   Education (Disability Strategies and Pupils' Educational Records) (Scotland) Act 2002.
6   Mental Health (Care and Treatment) (Scotland) Act 2003, s 26, see below.
7   *Crossan v South Lanarkshire Council*, Outer House (Lady Smith) 14 February 2006, interpreting the relevant provisions of the Social Work (Scotland) Act 1968, Education (Scotland) Act 1980 and Children (Scotland) Act 1995.
8   Mental Health (Care and Treatment) (Scotland) Act 2003, s 28.

Private education

33.02 Parents may choose private suppliers of education facilities at pre-school and school level, or may choose to educate at home. Local authorities are not obliged to provide support for children with additional education needs who are privately educated or home educated, but may agree to do so.[1] A private education provider may be the subject of complaint if the school does not adequately safeguard or promote the welfare of a pupil attending the school.[2]

Where a child has additional support needs for education, recorded as such under the relevant legislation, or a coordinated education support plan, a parent may make a placing request which includes an educational establishment anywhere in the UK.

There are no private providers of university or further education in Scotland, but private health facilities and/or specialist education provision may be available for adults on a fully costed basis. Usually the cost must be sought from a local authority under statutory duties. See below.

1   Education (Additional Support for Learning) (Scotland) Act 2004, s 5.
2   Standards in Scotland's Schools Act 2000, s 15, inserting Education (Scotland) Act 1980 s 99(1)(aa).

Support for learning before November 2005

33.03 Local authorities' duty to provide a suitable school education for children in their area with mental disorder or learning disability was until November 2005 defined in terms of the child having 'special educational needs'.[1]

A child had 'special educational needs' if he or she had a 'learning difficulty' which meant that provision for special educational needs was necessary.[2] A learning difficulty included both difficulty in learning and a disability which hindered or prevented a child from making use of the educational facilities available in his or her area.

If a child or young person appeared to have a learning difficulty, the school would assess his or her needs, to see whether a formal record of needs should be opened. A child might have needs which could be met without opening a record of needs. A record of needs was appropriate only if the child needed a long-term strategy to meet his or her educational needs.

The young person had a legal right to request an assessment of needs, and had a statutory right to information, to have his or her views taken into account and to challenge the decision about what provision was appropriate. If a young person was unable to exercise this right, the parents might act on his or her behalf. A decision on whether to draw up a record of needs had to be made within six months of a request for an assessment.[3]

[1]   Education (Scotland) Act 1980, s 1.

[2]   E(S)A 1980, s 1(5)(d).

[3]   *Children and young persons with special educational needs, Assessment and recording* (Scottish Office Education and Industry circular 4/96).

Effect of record

33.04 A child with a record of needs has to have that taken into account. A child with a record of needs moving out of education and children's services might be entitled to assessment by social work or health authorities for provision of support in adulthood. Whether this would be necessary depends entirely upon the nature of the needs.

For example, in the case of children whose need was assessed on the ground of an autistic spectrum disorder, support might be necessary through adult services. If an assessment was on the ground of dyslexia, it might be necessary to communicate that to a provider of university or further education, so that appropriate provision could be made within that education context, but there might be no need to call upon adult services in health or social work for mental health or learning disability.

It was necessary to note that that the autonomy of a young person or adult moving into education allowed that person to decide what to disclose to university or further education providers about prior assessed needs, but providers of education could not make adjustments if unaware of the needs.

Consumers of services for those with learning disability or delayed development may prefer to use the term 'learning difficulty' when discussing needs. In the education context (particularly the regime applying before November 2005), the term 'learning difficulty' has a statutory meaning, which takes in a much broader range of obstacles to learning than a clinical assessment of learning disability itself.

Additional support for learning

33.05 The 'record of needs' process has been replaced with a new statutory regime with effect from 14 November 2005.[1] The term 'Additional Support Needs' was introduced by the Education (Additional Support for Learning) (Scotland) Act 2004. A useful guide to the new provisions has been prepared by the Disability Rights Commission in Scotland.[2]

This does not mean that the record of needs is defunct. Local authorities must retain information about existing records of needs, and provide education in accordance with that record, at least at the level applying before the change in the law, for up to two years from 14 November 2005.

Within those two years the local authority must establish whether the child requires a coordinated support plan (a feature of the new Act), or has a significant change in support needs from that contained in the record. If the child is found not to require a coordinated support plan, the record of needs is deemed to be the additional support need under the new Act, but there are rights of appeal against a finding that the child does not require a coordinated support plan.

The local authority has many duties under the legislation. It must make adequate and efficient provision for such additional support as is required by a child or young person; and must make appropriate arrangements to keep under consideration those needs and the adequacy of support (unless that provision is outside the power of the local authority, or would result in unreasonable public expenditure being incurred).[3]

There are also duties of examination and assessment, and preparation of coordinated support plans for children with complex factors contributing to their needs. The requirement to make provision is that which is 'adequate and efficient' rather than ideal, and it must be within the authority's general powers and not an unreasonable public expenditure.

1   At the time of writing there is a special section on the Scottish Executive website concerning the implementation of these new provisions, see www.scotland.gov.uk. See also Education (Additional Support For Learning) (Scotland) Act 2004 Circular 5/2005.

2   Accompanying guidance for the Disability Rights Commission's Code of Practice for Schools (Scotland) (Disability Rights Commission, 2006).

3   Education (Additional Support for Learning) (Scotland) Act 2004, s 4.

Qualifying for additional support

33.06 A child or young person[1] has additional support needs for the purposes of that Act where, for whatever reason, the child or young person is, or is likely to be, unable to benefit from school education without the provision of additional support. This includes education directed to the development of the personality, talents and mental and physical abilities of the child or young person to their fullest potential.[2]

Clearly a mental illness or learning disability may mean additional support will be necessary in some cases. The test is now directed to the role of additional support in meeting the developmental outcomes a child can expect from education, rather than the nature of qualifying learning difficulty, although if a coordinated support plan is appropriate, the factors leading to it must be recorded.

Support is 'additional' when it is more than, or otherwise different from, the educational provision made generally for children or young persons of the same age in local authority schools and pre-schools (other than special schools).[3]

1   As defined in the Education (Scotland) Act 1980, s 135(1).

2   Education (Additional Support for Learning) (Scotland) Act 2004, ss 1(1) and (2).

3   Education (Additional Support for Learning)(Scotland) Act 2004, s 1(3)(b).

Assessing needs

33.07 Children with mental illness or learning disability should, if possible, participate in requesting an assessment of their additional support needs and participate in decisions regarding the assessment. Indeed the child's views should be taken into account in all decisions made under this legislation.

Where a child or young person lacks capacity because of mental illness, developmental delay or learning disability or cannot communicate because of physical disability,[1] a parent or other person can speak on behalf of the child or young person.

A local authority must deal with a request for an assessment, provided that the request is not unreasonable, and it must provide the opportunity to determine the request and the support to which the child or young person will be entitled, in a speedy and effective manner.

There are a number of aspects to the new system aimed at inclusive decision making and integrated provision of support which are novel to the education law, although familiar in mental health and incapacity contexts.

It is a novel expectation of local authorities to allow any relevant person (the child, young person or parent) to have a supporter and an advocate at any discussions about the additional support needs. The local authority must also provide for independent mediation in situations where agreement cannot be reached by direct discussion.[2]

A relevant person who is not happy with any decision of the local authority under this Act may take the matter first to a new specialist tribunal, the Education (Additional Support for Learning) (Scotland) Tribunal[3] and then there is a right of appeal on a point of law to the Court of Session.

Local authorities must share information with other local authorities and agencies which might assist in meeting the additional support needs of the child. If a child whom a local authority has a duty to educate has needs which arise from complex or multiple factors, which needs are likely to last for more than a year and cannot be met within education resources alone, the local authority must prepare a 'coordinated support plan'.[4]

This should identify the factors giving rise to the additional support needs, the outcomes for the child, the support required and who will provide it or parts of it. The local education authority is responsible for leading the efforts to implement the plan, although other agencies or arms of local government may be part of that plan.

---

[1] Incapacity cannot be assumed from physical inability to communicate, and steps must be taken to assist communication including with mechanical means.

[2] Education (Additional Support for Learning) (Scotland) Act 2004, ss 14–15.

[3] E(ASFL)(S)A 2004, s 17 and Sched 1.

[4] Additional Support for Learning (Coordinated Support Plan) (Scotland) Regulations 2005 (SSI 2005/266).

HELP FOR SCHOOL LEAVERS

33.08 Since November 2005, not later than 12 months before the child is due to leave school education, the local authority should seek information from other agencies likely to be involved with the person after he or she leaves school.

At least six months before the child leaves school, education authorities must liaise with other agencies, including other local authority departments, to consider and plan for the support of that child in adult services.[1]

Transfer of information to other agencies about the young person should be with his or her consent, or, if a young person is unable to give or withhold consent, the consent of his or her parent.

1   Education (Additional Support for Learning) (Scotland) Act 2004, ss 12–13.

FURTHER AND HIGHER EDUCATION

33.09 The Special Educational Needs and Disability Act 2001, Part 2, added a new Part 4 to the Disability Discrimination Act 1995 which came into full effect in October 2005 and requires providers of further and higher education not to discriminate on the grounds of disability in their admission procedures and in teaching and learning provision, including physical access to teaching accommodation.

Students with learning disabilities qualify for help under these provisions, but also students who have other disabilities which make it more difficult for them to use the facilities of the college.[1] This could apply to some students with mental health problems, who might need extra support or a re-arrangement of the timetable, for example.

Colleges' proposals for meeting the needs of students with special needs are set out in their development plans, and all colleges should be able to give potential students the name of the person responsible for co-ordinating help for students with special needs. Disabled Students' Allowance, a bursary from the Scottish Executive, may also be available in some cases.

Universities and other higher education institutions are also now required to publish disability statements, giving details of the facilities they have available for disabled students, including those with mental disabilities.[2] The Scottish Funding Council must consider such matters when considering the funding of such institutions.[3] It has issued guidance to institutions[4]

1   Further and Higher Education (S) Act 1992, s 1(4).

2   Disability Discrimination Act 1995, s 37(3).

3   DDA 1995, s 37(2).

4   *Disability self-evaluation tool: improving equality for disabled people in Scotland's colleges and universities* (Circular SFC/17/05, 16 December 2005).

HELP FROM SOCIAL WORK DEPARTMENT

Children and young people

33.10 A young person who needs additional support for learning may also need additional help from the local authority social work department to help continue his or her education. Guidance from the Scottish Executive requires local authority departments to co-operate in providing the whole range of services to children in need, but the Education (Additional Support for Learning) (Scotland) Act 2003 places the education authority in the lead in coordinating support for learning.

When an education department carries out a needs assessment, the local authority should consider carrying out an assessment under the Children (Scotland) Act. See 31.12. Similarly, if the social work department is carrying out a childrens' services assessment, the education department should be informed, to see if the two assessments could be combined. The aim is to reduce the number of assessments and professionals visiting and interviewing the young person.[1]

1   See Scotland's Children, The Children (Scotland) Act 1995 Regulations and Guidance, Vol 1, Chapter 6, para 14.

Adults

33.11 The local authority social work department can also help adults who may need help furthering their education. When a person receiving a community care assessment[1] appears to have educational needs, the education department should be told so that they can see what help they can offer.[2]

If a local authority decides that a person needs help to take advantage of the educational help available to them, they are under a legal duty to provide arrange this help if it cannot be organised elsewhere, for example by some voluntary body or trust.[3] It would be up to the local authority to see what other help might be available.

1   See chapter 27.

² *Assessment and Care Management* (Scottish Office circular SWSG11/91), para 12.3.

³ Chronically Sick and Disabled Persons Act 1970, s 2(1). For more details, see 28.18.

Education and training for adults

33.12 The local authority is under a legal duty to provide services designed to promote the well-being and social development of people with mental illnesses, personality disorders and learning disabilities. This should include social, cultural and recreational activities, training for those who are over school age and assistance in obtaining and undertaking employment.[1] The local authority should also make sure that the necessary transport to such training is available.[2] It is up to them to decide what is necessary.

These statutory obligations are additional to the obligations to provide school education, and further and higher education generally,[3] and to provide social work support generally.[4] All obligations to provide education are subject to the Disability Discrimination Act, and the obligation is on education providers to make provision to accommodate any additional disabilities a person might have.

The local authority is responsible for providing development, training and occupation only for people who are living in the community, not for people living in hospital.[5] They have discretion to provide it in hospital, but this would be a matter for discussion at a service or individual level between local authorities and health care providers. The local authority can charge for any of the services including training and travel.[6]

The statutory duty to provide suitable training and occupation was very clearly set out in the 1984 Act and expanded upon in the Mental Health (Care and Treatment) Act. As far as the author is aware, there have been no legal test cases to enforce the duty under either Act, but if a person is not receiving suitable training or occupation, legal action could be considered. See chapter 28.

¹ Mental Health (Care and Treatment)(Scotland) Act 2003, ss 26(1)(a) and (2).
² MH(CT)(S)A 2003, s 27.
³ MH(CT)(S)A 2003, s 26(3), referring to Education (Scotland) Act 1980, s 1 and Further and Higher Education (Scotland) Act 1992, s 1.
⁴ MH(CT)(S)A 2003, s 29.
⁵ MH(CT)(S)A 2003, s 26(1)(b).
⁶ MH(CT)(S)A 2003, s 28.

EDUCATION

33.13 Part 4 of the Disability Discrimination Act relates to education providers, and its provisions have been phased in over the three years to October 2005, following amendment by the Special Educational Needs and Disability Act 2001. Since October 2005 there has been specific provision making it illegal for schools or educational facilities to discriminate against disabled students, including students with mental health problems or learning disabilities. See Part 9.

EMPLOYMENT

33.14 Fewer than four in 10 employers would employ a person with a history of mental health problems. Only 24 per cent of adults facing mental health challenges are in work.[1] Yet the evidence is that, generally speaking, work is good for mental health.[2] The Social Exclusion Unit found that many people want to work but are restrained by an inflexible welfare benefits system and an unwelcoming job market.

The law deals with these issues in a variety of ways:

- By outlawing discrimination in employment and requiring employers to make 'reasonable adjustments' to their working practices to meet the needs of employees with disabilities. Part 9 of this book looks at protection against unfair discrimination.
- By protecting people against unfair dismissal. This could include dismissal because of conduct or absence caused by a mental condition. See below.
- By obliging local authorities to develop schemes to support people in employment. See above.
- By imposing new disability equality duties on public sector employers. See 36.44. The duty to promote equality of opportunity includes a duty to consider the make up of the employer's workforce. A public sector employer may wish to take positive steps to employ people with mental disabilities.
- By setting up various employment schemes through Job Centres to help people back to work, such as Jobcentre Plus's New Deal for Disabled People, (which can help people find work and support them in the early stages of work) and the Access to Work scheme, which can fund adjustments in the workplace.

One of the major ways in which the law could make a difference is through the welfare benefits system. People are sometimes unwilling to take up employment opportunities because they risk losing their benefits and the difficulty in recovering benefits should the job not work out. A more flexible benefits system would help people feel more able to access job opportunities.

Disability Living Allowance can continue even if someone is in work, and a person can qualify for Working Tax Credit, but anyone seeking work should seek welfare rights advice. See Appendix 1 for further reading.

[1]   *Mental health and social exclusion* (Social Exclusion Unit, 2004).
[2]   Reseach from Ireland quoted by Social Firms Scotland indicates a 98% reduction in use of in-patient facilities, day centres and day hospitals and a 47% reduction in use of medication. See *Time for a change* (Social Firms Scotland, 2005).

Statutory protections

33.15 The trend in employment has been away from separate, sheltered employment towards attempting to ensure that more disabled people can take their place in the workplace. The quota system, which obliged employers to employ a certain percentage of workers with disabilities and which restricted certain employments to disabled workers[1] has been abolished.[2] Instead attempts have been made to reduce discrimination against disabled people.[3]

While the sheltered placement scheme[4] has been useful for some people with mental disabilities, there is no statutory obligation on the Department of Work and Pensions to fund such schemes. Local councils can establish sheltered employment projects[5] but, again, there is no duty on them to do so. A disabled person wishing to obtain a sheltered placement has no legal right to such a placement.

There is a government initiative to promote social firms across the UK. Social firms are commercial businesses developed to provide employment opportunities for people with a disability or other disadvantage in the labour market, and at least 25% of their employees must have that disability or disadvantage. For contact information for Social Firms Scotland see Appendix 1.

The local Jobcentre Plus gives advice on what help might be available. Employers can also contact Jobcentre Plus for advice about meeting the needs of disabled employees.

[1]   Set out in the Disabled Persons (Employment) Act 1944.

2   By the Disability Discrimination Act 1995.
3   See Part 9.
4   Established under DP(E)A 1944, s 15.
5   Under DP(E)A 1958, s 3.

Unfair dismissal

33.16 Dismissal because of a mental health condition or learning disability, or failing to make appropriate adjustments to a person's needs may constitute unfair dismissal.[1] This is in addition to any protection the person may have under the Disability Discrimination Act. A person in this situation needs legal advice.

1   See *Greenhof v Barnsley Metropolitan Borough Council* [2006] IRLR 98, *Rowden v Dutton Gregory* [2002] ICR 971.

VOLUNTEERING

33.17 Volunteering can be a useful way back into employment and may not affect welfare benefits. The Scottish Executive is funding Volunteer Development Scotland to help encourage greater awareness of the benefits of volunteering for improving mental health and well-being, and supporting improved opportunities for people with mental health problems to become volunteers.

Chapter 34

CONSUMER RIGHTS

34.01 This chapter looks at the effects a mental disorder may have on a person's ability to enter into contracts and other commercial transactions. A contract is a legally enforceable agreement between two people (or a person and an organisation). Buying an item in a shop, opening a bank account, buying a house and signing a tenancy agreement are all kinds of contracts. Marriage and civil partnership are particular kinds of contract, covered in chapter 31.

A person cannot sign a contract or enter into a transaction if he or she lacks the legal ability to do so. Moreover, someone with mental disorder may be vulnerable to being pressurised into making a contract or a will. The basis for challenging this is discussed below.

This chapter also looks at special concerns about bank accounts, travel and driving.

CONTRACTS

Capacity to contract

34.02 A person who lacks capacity is unable to enter into a valid contract. Any apparent contract with a person who lacks capacity is null and void. It is irrelevant whether the other party to the contract was aware of the person's disability.[1]

Having a mental disorder does not automatically mean that a person is unable to enter into a particular contract. It is only if a mental condition undermines the person's ability to enter into the contract that it does so.

Each party to a contract must satisfy him or herself that the other party has capacity to enter into the contract, because the purported contract is void if the other party lacks capacity to enter into it. The law presumes that a person has capacity and is mentally well until the contrary is proved.[2] This means that it is up to the person challenging the contract to establish that one of the parties lacked the capacity to enter into it.

There is a real tension between these conflicting legal responsibilities, and many situations call for a practical approach to resolution. The increase in telesales and internet purchase opportunities make this an increasingly complex area, but the position in law is that if the person lacked the legal capacity to make the contract, the contract is void. A void contract creates no responsibilities or rights.

Some mental disorders which are intermittent in the severity of their effects, may lead to periods of incapacity to enter into contracts, and some may mean that a person enters into transactions which are unrealistic or inappropriate. For example, a person with mania may enter into purchases or other contractual situations which he or she is unable to sustain, even though to a third party that person may appear confident and fully in command of his or her affairs.

Such a contract has no legal validity if it can be established that the person lacked the capacity to make the contract, at the time he or she entered into the contract, even though the other party to the contract may have been unable to detect that incapacity.

1   *John Loudon & Co v Elder's curator bonis*, 1923 SLT 226. The position is different in England and Wales, where the contract can be set aside only if the other party knows of the effect of the mental impairment. *Imperial Loan Co v Stone* [1892] 1 QB 599, *Gore v Gibson* (1845) 13 M & W 621.

2   *Lindsay v Watson* (1843) 5 D 1194.

Establishing capacity

34.03 The capacity required to enter into a contract depends on the contract involved.[1] A person may lack capacity for some forms of contract but not others. For example, the person may be able to make a small purchase from a shop, but not to take out insurance or rent a property, which requires more complex understanding.

The test is the person's ability to understand the nature of the contract involved.[2] A person may be unable to enter a contract if mental disorder means he or she is unable to act, make a decision, understand, communicate a decision (if this cannot be remedied by communication services or mechanical aids) or remember a decision.[3] Illiteracy is not incapacity, although it may be evidence of incapacity.[4]

In the context of some mental disorders, such as mania and hypomania, the question of capacity is complex. For example, a person who engages in excessive spending during a period of mania may be able to understand the nature of the contract and intend to enter into it, but is not acting as he or she would have acted when well.

There does not appear to be any case law in Scotland considering these matters. Case law in England and Wales links the test to whether the person is able to manage his or her property and affairs. This includes the ability to:

'recognise a problem, obtain and receive, understand and retain relevant information, including advice; the ability to weigh the information (including that derived from advice) in the balance in reaching a decision, and the ability to communicate that decision.'[5]

A person with mania may not have this ability. The person may be unable to appreciate his or her true situation and financial circumstances and weigh the relevant information in the balance. The effects of a mental disorder on mood must also be considered.[6]

It is suggested that if a mental disorder means that a person cannot give the free consent to a contract which the law requires, the person should be regarded as unable to enter into the contract. This distinction has been recognised in the context of both medical law and criminal law. See 7.11 and 43.13.

1   *Masterman- Lister v Brutton & Co* [2003] 1 WLR 1511.
2   Stair I x 13(2); Erskine I vii 48; Bell's Comm II ii 8; *Gall v Bird*, 17 D 1027.
3   Adults with Incapacity (Scotland) Act 2000, s 1(6). Adrian Ward suggests that short-term memory failure should not, of itself, mean that a person is unable to make a decision if, whenever the question is raised the person makes the same decision. The person's consistency should render the decision valid, provided the person does not lack capacity under one of the other criteria. *Adult Incapacity* (W Green & Son, 2003), para 1.30.
4   *Barclays Bank Plc v Schwartz*, Court of Appeal The Times, 2 August 1995.
5   *Masterman- Lister v Brutton & Co* [2003] 1 WLR 1511 at para 26. Followed in *Bailey v Warren* [2006] EWCA Civ 51.
6   See *Sharp v Adam* [2006] All ER (D) 277, discussed at 34.11 below.

Effect of lack of capacity

34.04 Under Scots law, an apparent contract with a person who lacks capacity is void from the start. (In England and Wales such a contract is voidable and remains valid unless a court sets the contract aside.) A void contract creates no responsibilities or rights. Only a voidable contract can give rights to either party, or to a third party who acts in reliance on the contract. The courts will uphold some terms of voidable contracts if it is not possible to undo their effects completely, particularly to preserve the rights of third parties.

Even when a contract is void due to lack of capacity, in practice efforts should be made to restore both parties to the position they were in before they entered into the void 'contract'. So if a person who is in a manic phase of illness purchases goods or instructs services, if the goods can be returned or the services cancelled, this should be done as soon as possible, to minimise the loss to the other party. This is only fair, particularly when it was not easy for the other party to detect the person's incapacity.

It may not be possible to undo the situation if purchases have been consumed, such as expensive restaurant meals or hotel accommodation, or the goods have now passed to a third party. In that situation it is wise to offer some recompense for the goods or services, failing which it is necessary to fall back on the legal argument, supported by medical evidence, that the person did not have the capacity to enter into the contract and the contract is void. If it is void, neither party can enforce it.

The only exception to this rule is if the contract was to supply 'necessaries' and these are delivered, in which case the person must pay a reasonable price (not necessarily the contract price) for the goods.[1]

It is not normally necessary to go to court over a void contract, it is simply a case of making clear that it never existed. If one party wants to hold the other party to terms of the contract, or refuses to accept that it is void, it may be necessary to take the matter to court.

[1] Sale of Goods Act 1979, s 3.

Remedies

34.05 If the person with whom the 'contract' was entered into has suffered loss through the transaction but has no contract to enforce, and the person lacking capacity has benefited, the loser might argue that the person who has benefited should pay for what was received.

It might be possible for such a person to succeed on the expanding legal principle of unjustified enrichment. A detailed text on the subject should be consulted on this complex area.[1] What is clear is that the person has no rights to enforce any part of the contract as such, because it did not exist.

[1] McBryde, *Contract* (2nd edn, W Green & Son, 2001); Evans-Jones, *Unjustified Enrichment* (W Green/Scottish Universities Law Institute, 2003).

Authorising transactions

34.06 Clearly there are situations in which contractual relationships are necessary to provide goods or services to a person who lacks capacity. The power to contract for such person must be established by a power of attorney (granted before the onset of incapacity), by guardianship, or by an intervention order, as regulated by the Adults with Incapacity (Scotland) Act 2000. See Part 5.

For someone who lacks capacity, certain essential services may be contracted for, not in the name of that person, but in the name of a responsible authority, such as a local authority or health authority, which can commission accommodation or care services to fulfil a statutory duty to that person.

Pre-existing contracts

34.07 A person may lose capacity while being bound by the terms of a domestic contract, such as a lease or credit agreement, or by a business contract, such as agency or partnership. The termination of an ongoing consumer contract in such circumstances requires the intervention of an attorney, guardian or court order, since if the person had capacity when he or she entered into the contract, the other party is entitled to assume this capacity is continuing.

When one other party to a contract is aware that the other party now lacks capacity, he or she may take the initiative to end the contract, by application for an intervention order or guardianship under the Adults with Incapacity Act or by any other available means.

For example, a landlord might apply to the court for an order for recovery of a tenancy of a person who is no longer able to fulfill the tenancy obligations because of mental incapacity. The family of a person who has, for example, moved into long-term hospital care might ask the landlord to do so. The court normally appoints a curator *ad litem*. See 35.21.

Special contracts

Agency

34.08 A person might appoint an agent for various purposes, such as buying or selling a house, or to deal with a business transaction. The person who appoints the agent is called the principal.

A contract of agency can continue only so long as the principal retains capacity. A person who lacks capacity cannot contract legally, whether through an agent or directly. So if a person who lacks capacity employs an agent to sell his or her house, the contract of agency, and any agreement the agent enters into with others (such as with a newspaper for advertising, or with a surveyor for a valuation) is void.

This is a harsh rule in situations where the person contracting with the agent may have no means of knowing whether the principal instructing the agent has capacity. If the third party provides services or goods for value, he or she may be able to recover under the doctrine of unjustified enrichment. See above.

Where it is the agent who lacks capacity, this appears not to be relevant in relation to claims by third parties, provided the principal, who is the main contracting party and will be liable to the third party, has capacity and has authorised the transaction or the transaction is within the apparent scope of the agent's authority.[1] In a contractual dispute between the principal and agent, lack of capacity on the part of the agent makes the agency contract void.

[1]   Gloag and Henderson *The law of Scotland* (11th edn, W Green & Son, 2001) paras 21.27 –28.

Partnership

34.09 A contract of partnership continues notwithstanding that one of the partners loses capacity. Contracts entered into by the partnership remain valid, since they are contracts of the partnership rather than an individual partner.

The mental incapacity of a partner entitles another partner to seek to end the partnership.[1] In practice the remaining partner or partners may seek to have a more practical solution than statutory dissolution of the partnership, if there is someone with power, under a power of attorney or an order under the Adults with Incapacity Act, to agree the terms of dissolution in place of the partner who has lost capacity.

A partnership agreement may contain express provision to deal with the loss of capacity of a partner, such as excluding that partner's power to bind the partnership during a period of incapacity. This regulates the situation only between the partners. Third parties who contract with the partnership through a partner who lacks capacity have a valid contract with the partnership.

1   Partnership (Scotland) Act 1890, ss 35(a) and 35(b).

WILLS AND TRUSTS

34.10 A person may make a will or grant a deed of trust to give bequests or property rights to third parties. A will creates rights that will arise only on the person's death. A trust deed creates rights linked to some other event, for example, a third party reaching a particular age. The will or trust deed usually gives power to someone (an executor or trustee) to put the bequests or trust provisions into effect.

As the words 'will' and 'trust' imply, the act of setting out these instructions requires that the person has the capacity to make the decisions as to who will receive what from his or her property or estate. If a person does not have the capacity to make the decision, due to severe learning disability or mental illness, the will or trust deed, just like the contracts described earlier, is null and void from the outset.

Capacity to make will

34.11 The law supports a person's right to make his or her own will, even if others do not like what the will says. If the terms of the will appear to be ill-judged or perverse, or even delusional, that is not conclusive of lack of capacity, but might be used in support of the argument.

A person must be able to understand that he or she is making a will and its likely effects. (This includes being able to understand the extent of his or her property and the possible claimants under the will.)[1] The fact that the person suffers from delusions because of a mental disorder is not relevant unless the delusions influence the terms of the will.[2] A will made in a lucid interval is valid.[3]

Forgetfulness or confusion are not of themselves enough to mean that a person does not have capacity, if he or she understands the nature and effect of making a will.[4]

The English courts have spelt out the law in England and Wales very clearly. When considering whether a person can make a will it essential that the person:

'[a] shall understand the nature of the Act and its effects; [b] shall understand the extent of the property of which he is disposing; [c] shall be able to comprehend and appreciate the claims to which he ought to give effect; and, with a view to the latter object, [d] that no disorder of the mind shall poison his affections, pervert his sense of right, or prevent the exercise of his natural faculties—that no insane delusion shall influence his will in disposing of his property and bring about a disposal of it which, if the mind had been sound, would not have been made.'[5]

In a recent English case, a person with multiple sclerosis made a will which totally excluded his daughters from benefit, despite there being no evidence of any problems in the relationship between them. The Court of Appeal held his decision should not stand.[6] The multiple sclerosis had deprived him of the necessary clarity of thought to enable him to make a rational decision and had affected his natural feelings for his daughters and his sense of right. Although he satisfied tests (a) to (c), he did not satisfy test (d). The court said that when considering capacity, it was appropriate to consider the effect of a condition on the person's mood as well as on his or her cognitive functions.[7]

1   See AR Barr, JMH Biggar, AMC Dalgleish, HJ Stevens, *Drafting wills in Scotland* (Butterworths, Law Society of Scotland, 1994), para 2.03.
2   *Jenkins v Morris* (1880) 14 Ch D 674.
3   *Sivewright's trustees v Sivewright* 1920 SC (HL) 63.
4   *Rennie v Stephen*, GWD 26–1559.
5   *Banks v Goodfellow* (1870) LR 5 QB 549.
6   *Sharp v Adam* [2006] All ER (D) 277.
7   At para 93.

Effect of lack of capacity

34.12 If someone has made a will or granted a trust deed, the law presumes capacity and mental health, and that formal documents are valid (provided they appear to be completed according to the required formalities).[1] This means that the burden of producing evidence that a person did not have capacity when he or she signed the document is on the person challenging the will or trust deed.

Mental disorder or learning disability do not of themselves render a will void, and wills made during lucid intervals in severe mental illness have long been recognised as valid. Standard forms of will or trust deed often contain a declaration that the person granting the deed is of sound mind, but this could be challenged by evidence to the contrary.

Where a will or trust deed is challenged successfully on the ground of incapacity, the document is treated as if it has never been written. In the case of a will or trust that is intended to come into effect on the death of a person, the situation will be as if the person left no will. The law of intestacy applies on that person's death, unless the document is challenged during the person's lifetime and there is a period when the person has the capacity to make a new will. If the person who died has made a previous will, that revives.

Because a person may choose not to reveal the terms of a will or trust deed during his or her lifetime, it is often only after death that the validity of the will is questioned on grounds of lack of capacity. Someone challenging the will may want the law of intestacy to apply, but it may not be what would have been the desire of the person.

If a will or trust is challenged during the person's lifetime, or shortly after death, it may not be to the benefit of the person that the will is declared null, but this is the effect of a successful challenge on grounds of incapacity (or reduction on the grounds described below).[2]

1   For formalities of execution see Requirements of Writing (Scotland) Act 1995. For formalities of validity see Macdonald, *Succession* (3rd edn, W Green & Son, 2001) or Hiram, *The Scots Law of Succession* (Butterworths, 2002).

2   Often a will is challenged on the ground of incapacity to make it, with an alternative case that there was unfair advantage taken and/or undue influence. See, for example, *Boyle v Boyle's Exr*, 1999 GWD 12–584. Whilst these other challenges have the benefit of not requiring proof of actual incapacity, there are additional factors to those tests which make them difficult to satisfy. See below.

Authorisations under Adults with Incapacity Act

34.13 In one case under the Adults with Incapacity Act, a sheriff granted an application for an intervention order to allow a guardian to write a specific codicil to the will of an adult with incapacity. The sheriff believed that this was within the principles of the Act and would benefit the adult.[1]

In theory the terms of the Adults with Incapacity Act seem sufficiently broad to permit the court to authorise a guardian under that Act to make a will for an adult with incapacity or revoke a will that had been made, although the Scottish Law Commission rejected this in principle in its Report on Succession,[2] but this conflicts with the general principle of the law of succession that testamentary powers cannot be delegated to a third party.

Adrian Ward suggests that where there is clear evidence that injustice would result if the court does not grant such powers, (for example in a situation where the person had shown his or her wishes and was prevented by supervening incapacity) and the intervention would be otherwise in accordance with the principles of the Act, the courts should have such a discretion.[3]

1   *T, Applicant*, 2005 SLT (Sh Ct) 97.
2   Scottish Law Commission No 124 (1990) paras 4.78–4.80.
3   *Adult incapacity* (W Green & Son, 2003), para 10.34.

CHALLENGES TO CONTRACTS AND WILLS

34.14 The validity of a contract or will made by a person who has mental disorder, but has capacity, may be challenged on other grounds. Some may arise most commonly when there is mental disorder or infirmity on the part of the person who entered into the contract or made the will.

A party may argue that a contract was entered into as a result of undue influence on the part of a trusted person who has benefited from the contract, that a person was subject to force or fear, or that the person was vulnerable and advantage was taken to mislead him or her into a contract or action which caused him or her loss (facility and circumvention). If any of these grounds of objection are proved, a contract may be declared invalid.

The more complex the contract or obligation, the more likely that such an argument, taken to court, will make the contract invalid under one of these grounds. Marriage is a contract in which these grounds of attack have been resisted, and now incapacity at the date of marriage is the prevailing test for validity of that contract. (See 31.08.) A will or trust deed challenged on this basis is valid until the ground of challenge is proved, at which point it is declared null and void. The usual remedy is to seek the cancellation ('reduction') of the document in the Court of Session.

Good faith

34.15 Recent case law brings into Scots law the requirement of good faith in contract, at least if a person is being asked to grant security over his or her property to benefit not the person but a spouse or third party.[1] The case arises out of a wife agreeing to grant a mortgage over the family home to secure additional funding for her husband's business, without being fully and independently advised. The court said that the husband owed an obligation of good faith to the wife in that situation, but if mental disorder existed too, the contract would no doubt be rendered invalid, unless there was clear evidence that the person understood the effect and showed unconditional willingness to enter into the arrangement.

There is no general obligation of good faith in contract in Scotland and generally people are deemed fit to protect themselves in making contracts. The presumptions of mental health and capacity apply. The situations listed below are the main exceptions that have evolved at common law or by statute to allow the setting aside of a contract. These contracts are valid at the time of making, but rendered invalid if the situations described can be proved.

1   *Smith v Bank of Scotland*, 1997 SC (HL) 111.

Effect of challenge

34.16 A contract can be set aside only if it is possible to undo the situation and restore the parties to their original situation.[1] So, where a contract concerns goods or property which have passed to a third party in good faith for a price before the contract is challenged, it is not possible to set the contract aside.

Since making a will or granting a trust deed was an act of one party in the first place, there is no need to consider whether another party is prejudiced by the challenge to it, but in fact third parties may indeed stand to lose as a result of cancellation of the will or trust deed. For example, a person who hoped to inherit but was not mentioned in a will may challenge the will to bring about intestacy, or to revert to an earlier will which will benefit the challenger, but this outcome may be to the detriment of those named in the challenged will. The court's only concern should be whether the ground of challenge is proved, rather than the consequences of the successful challenge.

If a will has been amended by a later document, (a 'codicil'), a challenge to either the will or the codicil usually leads to the whole document being set aside.[2] As to the scope for adding a codicil after the person who made the will has lost capacity, see above.

1   What the law calls '*restitutio in integrum*'.

2   The exception seems to be *Horsburgh v Thomson's Trs* (1912) 1 SLT 73, where the codicil was reduced on a successful challenge, but the will, which was valid, was allowed to stand.

Unfair advantage

34.17 If a person is in a vulnerable ('weak and facile') state and someone takes the opportunity to mislead him or her unfairly into entering a contract or taking a unilateral step such as making a will or a gift, the contract or act is open to challenge, and may be declared invalid. The law calls this 'facility and circumvention'.

Vulnerability is a matter of fact depending both on the person's mental state and his or her circumstances. It has been held that physical illness in hospital is not sufficient vulnerability in itself[1] but mental illness or learning disability could well be. Elderly people or young people might be at particular risk.

This ground for challenge of a contract applies in situations where a person has capacity, but (a) is vulnerable in the circumstances, (b) unfair advantage has been taken of the person by or on behalf of the other party to the contract, and (c) as a result the vulnerable person has suffered disadvantage.

The three elements are interlinked. So the greater the vulnerability, the lower the level of unfairness that may be necessary to establish the ground of challenge, and *vice versa*. Unfairness can be through threat, or more subtle persuasion.[2] There must be unfair advantage to give rise to this ground in contract. So if the same deal was offered to all parties, and a vulnerable individual took it up, then the ground may not apply and the contract is valid unless the person lacked capacity.

In consumer contracts there are now statutory protections against some situations which might have given rise to this ground of invalidity. Legislation provides for certain contracts not to be valid until the stronger (commercial) party has given the consumer the chance to think about it and decide not to go ahead. This applies when contracts are entered into at a distance (for example, phone or internet) or by doorstep selling of certain products.[3]

1   *Mackay v Campbell*, 1967 SC (HL) 53.
2   MacQueen & Thomson, *Contract Law in Scotland* (Tottel, 2000), at para 4.28 give the examples of a relative who persuades an old person to sell him a house at a low price by charm, and one who threatens that he will remove her from the home if she refuses, both of which could meet the test for this ground of invalidity.
3   For a list of the applicable situations and legislation see Woolman, *Contract* (3rd edn, W Green & Son), para 6.12.

Wills

34.18 A will can be cancelled on the grounds of unfair advantage, but the case law suggests that it must be clear that the person was persuadable because of his or her mental weakness.[1]

Evidence that a person has declining mental health or a learning disability does not of itself satisfy these grounds, since that decline may have made the person more resistant to persuasion than more open to it. Also the persuasion need not be as deceitful or dishonest as the case law in contract expects.

More emphasis is placed on the fact of persuasion or suggestion having brought about a particular set of instructions concerning the will or trust (usually a change in a will). The unfair advantage may be inferred from the circumstances and the timing of the changes to an earlier will.

1   For further discussion see Macdonald, *Succession* (3rd edn, W Green & Son, 2001), paras 8.17–8.24, Hiram *The Scots Law of Succession* (Butterworths, 2002), paras 9.22–9.29.

Undue influence

34.19 A contract may be challenged on the ground that A entered into the contract as a result of B (who was in a position of authority or trust over A) abusing that position to influence the terms of the contract ('undue influence').

There is undue influence if B (who may be one or more persons) has had a material benefit from the contract (directly or indirectly) to the prejudice of A, that B did not give any value under the contract and that A did not have independent advice in relation to the contract.

B might be a formal agent for A, such as a solicitor or accountant, but could equally be an influential family member, a doctor or a carer. The influence could be exerted by B directly, or through a third party, such as a mutual friend.

Wills

34.20 A similar ground exists for challenging a will. Anyone in a position of authority or trust, who stands to gain directly or indirectly from the terms of the will, could exert undue influence.

Particular attention applies to lawyers who have drafted wills, if the lawyer, or a person connected to the lawyer, stands to benefit from the will. In that situation undue influence will almost certainly be raised, and the facts may raise a presumption of undue influence that the lawyer will have to contradict. Indeed the lawyer will also face professional complaints procedure and possible disciplinary action.

A will is not automatically invalid if, after evidence is heard, the circumstances do not disclose that there was undue influence.[1]

[1]   Macdonald, *Succession* (3rd edn, W Green & Son, 2001), paras 8.25–8.33, Hiram, *The Scots Law of Succession* (Butterworths, 2002), paras 9.16–9.21.

Extortionate contracts

34.21 A contract may be declared invalid if it was entered into only because the person was put in fear (for him or herself or for another person close to him or her) by the unlawful threats of the other party or someone acting on that party's behalf.

This normally applies to threats which would influence the decision of the 'reasonable person' viewed objectively, but it has been suggested that it is more appropriate to consider instead whether a reasonable person would infer that the party to the contract was put in fear by the threats made.[1]

It is certainly preferable for those who are vulnerable because of mental disorder that the test allows for consideration of the impact of a threat upon that person in particular.

[1]   MacQueen & Thomson, *Contract Law in Scotland* (Tottel, 2000), para 4.23.

BANK ACCOUNTS

34.22 Mental disorder is not a bar to opening a bank account, provided the person has the legal ability to understand the nature of the transaction and to operate the account. It would be unlawful discrimination for a bank to attempt to prevent a person who is able to open an account from so doing. See chapter 36.

Capacity to open account

34.23 The degree of understanding partly relates to the complexity of the account. For example, a person may be able to operate a savings account, but not understand the terms and conditions of a more complex cheque and overdraft account.

A new form of Basic Bank Account has been introduced, to make bank accounts more generally available. The account is intended to be simple to operate. It does not provide a cheque book or allow a person to go into overdraft, but employers and the government can pay wages and benefits directly into the account, and the account holder or a carer can pay cheques and cash into the account. The person can withdraw cash at ATMs and can set up direct debits to pay regular bills.

A basic bank account could be suitable for some people, but research shows that bank staff are not always familiar with the accounts and continue to offer people accounts which are more sophisticated than they need.[1]

[1]   Roger Knight, *Survey of subscriber institutions on basic bank accounts* (Banking Code Standards Board, June 2003).

Identification

34.24 People living with mental health challenges can find it difficult to access bank accounts.[1] A major problem has been providing adequate identification. Standard requirements are a passport, driving licence or utility bill. A person may have none of these.

Guidance from the Financial Services Authority confirms that other acceptable items include a benefits book or original letter from a benefits agency, and, as proof of address, a tenancy agreement or rent book.

If none of these is available, the person should discuss with bank staff what might be acceptable. A letter from a teacher, doctor or religious leader may suffice.[2] Presumably a letter from a social worker or care provider would also be acceptable.

The Department for Work and Pensions can provide written confirmation that a customer is receiving a benefit or pension, and the banks can accept this if the customer does not have any other acceptable documentation to prove his or her identity.[3]

Unfortunately bank and building society staff are not always aware that the rules allow for flexibility where a potential customer may not have the formal identification required.[4] Other problems revealed include inflexibility in dealing with attorneys and people authorised under incapacity legislation.[5]

Anyone with a complaint about how a bank or building society has dealt with them can contact the Disability Rights Commission or the Financial Services Ombudsman for advice.

1   *Mental health and social exclusion* (Social Exclusion Unit, 2004), paras 7.15–16.

2   Joint Money Laundering Steering Group and the Financial Services Authority Guidance Notes, as explained in *Checking your identity*, leaflet to public from Financial Services Authority.

3   Parliamentary Under-Secretary of State, Department for Work and Pensions House of Lords, 19 June 2006 [HL 6131].

4   Knight (above) concluded that only 38% of institutions appeared to offer flexibility over identification requirements. Staff gave inaccurate, conflicting and unhelpful advice to applicants, especially people who could not produce the 'primary' documents, including asking a blind researcher for his driving licence.

5   See *Giving all customers equal access to bank accounts* (Financial Services Ombudsman newsletter May/June 2004), where the ombudsman dealt with a case, supported by the Disability Rights Commission, where a bank had refused to allow a customer's attorney to open an internet banking account. The case was settled, with the bank allowing the attorney internet banking.

DEBT

34.25 One in three adults facing serious mental health challenges has debt problems, three times the national average.[1] The Royal College of Psychiatrists has produced a booklet to help health workers advise and support people.[2]

In many cases the person will need advice from a professional debt counsellor. The Citizens Advice Bureau can advise.

1   *Social and economic circumstances of adults with mental disorders* (Office for National Statistics, 2002).

2   *Final Demand: Debt and Mental Health* (Royal College of Psychiatrists and First Step Trust, 2006).

INSURANCE

34.26 Many kinds of insurance, from life assurance to holiday and car insurance, make special provision for people with pre-existing conditions, including mental disorder or disabilities. There may be attempts to exclude them from its cover, or people may be charged extra for insurance. Insurance provision is now influenced by the Disability Discrimination Act (see Part 9) but key insurance issues are mentioned here separately.

Obtaining insurance

34.27 The terms on which any insurance is offered are set out in the insurance policy. The contract is based on the information provided in the proposal form by the person seeking insurance. Any failure to declare information that would potentially affect the insurance company's assessment of the risk (to issue the policy and fix the premium) allows the insurance company to refuse to pay out in the event of a claim.

Anyone with a history of mental illness or mental disability who is planning to take out any insurance should ask to see a copy of the specimen policy before signing. Most insurance companies now have these on their webpages. The person should read the small print very carefully to see if any mental or medical conditions are excluded from cover.

Policies may also exclude cover for 'pre-existing conditions' or for people travelling against medical advice, all of which might be relevant. Anyone with concerns, particularly about whether an expensive insurance policy is appropriate, should seek advice from an insurance broker registered with the British Insurance Brokers' Association. The Association of British Insurers has offered good practice guidance to its members and it may be helpful to consult this in cases of difficulty.[1]

The Disability Discrimination Act says that in certain circumstances it is not unlawful for an insurer to impose different conditions when insuring a disabled person (including a person with a mental disability) if (but only if) the increased costs can be justified. See 36.27.

These rules are of importance to people with disabilities who have experience of being charged higher premiums. Some people take out specialised insurance policies which aim to cater for the particular needs of disabled people, but these specialist policies are often expensive. The Disability Discrimination Act changes mean that insurers must be able to justify any additional charges they impose on clients with mental disabilities.

[1]   *An insurer's guide to the Disability Discrimination Act* (Association of British Insurers, 2003). Available on their website.

Renewing insurance

34.28 Commonly people renew insurance annually on the same terms as before, confirming to insurance companies or brokers that no change has arisen in the information that is held on file about the person's medical condition. If a person has experienced a mental disorder since the last renewal, he or she should bring this to the attention of the insurer without delay.

Insurers often agree to maintain to the agreed premium for the remainder of the year for which it was quoted, and recalculate at the end of that year, but they are not obliged to do so.

An insurer can review the premium, or its willingness to provide cover at all, with effect from the date when the person's condition was diagnosed. An insurer can refuse to pay out in a claim on the policy if the person insured has not informed them of all relevant and material circumstances.

Insuring against effects of mental disorder

34.29 Reading the terms of the specimen policy before any insurance is taken out will reveal whether the future effects of mental disorder can be covered by insurance. If unsure, a person should take advice from a broker registered with the British Insurance Brokers' Association.

If there are strong risk factors, such as with genetically determined conditions, an insurer may refuse to insure the person or quote a premium at a prohibitive cost. It is only obligatory to disclose what is known about risk factors for onset of a condition, such as a family history of a medical condition.

Insurers follow the Association of British Insurers' policy on genetics and insurance, which does not require that the outcome of predictive genetic testing is declared, unless the policy is for over £500,000 life insurance or £300,000 critical illness insurance.[1] Applicants may choose to declare negative results from genetic testing, to show insurers that risk is reduced, but insurers normally check the impact of results with a clinical geneticist.

The following are the most common situations in which insurance might cover the effects of mental disorder.

---

[1]   If the cover is above these limits there is guidance for applicants as to which test results must be declared, see http://www.abi.org.uk/public/consumer/codes/disclosure.asp.

Permanent health insurance/critical illness insurance

34.30 Policies of insurance provide additional income or capital support if the person insured develops a condition which impairs his or her ability to work or enjoy anticipated financial security. Examples are permanent health insurance and critical illness insurance.

Such insurance can be used to mitigate the financial effects of the onset of mental disorder as well as physical deterioration, accident or injury, but if a condition is pre-existing, insurance is not normally available.

Treatment for medical conditions or accident

34.31 Insurance to provide private medical care can include treatment for mental disorder, but facilities in Scotland are limited for privately funded provision of such services. Accident insurance may lead to cover for effects of mental impairment, such as, for example, the effects of serious head injury in a car crash or at work.

Loss of life/terminal illness

34.32 Policies paying out on loss of life (whole life or endowment policies) historically provided that payment would not be made if death was as a result of suicide. Now that exclusion is normally limited to suicide within 12 months of the policy being taken out.

A number of life policies now provide for payment before death, but on diagnosis of certain terminal illnesses.

DRIVING

34.33 Whether or not a person with a mental disorder can have a driving licence depends on the nature of the person's condition, the treatment, and its effectiveness. The Driver and Vehicle Licensing Agency (DVLA) website provides considerable information about psychiatric conditions (including learning disability) and driving.[1]

[1]   www.dvla.gov.uk/at_a_glance/ch4_psychiatric.htm.

Applying for a licence

34.34 A person applying for a driving licence must complete the medical section of the application form. The person must advise whether he or she has any disability or prospective disability, including any disease, or persistent misuse of alcohol or drugs.

The DVLA require further medical reports if an applicant confirms he or she has any of these conditions. Their medical advisers contact the person's doctors and may require an opinion from a consultant. There are stricter medical rules for gaining and keeping licences for driving lorries and buses (Group 2 vehicles), than there are for cars and motorcycles (Group 1 vehicles).

Impact of mental disorder

34.35 Mental disorders are notifiable conditions for applicants and existing licence holders. A person seeking to continue to hold a licence to drive must notify the DVLA if he or she is diagnosed with a mental health condition, and of the steps being taken to treat that condition. Among the conditions included are severe mental handicap, severe mental illness or disorder and chronic neurological conditions.[1]

Doctors should remind patients of their responsibilities to notify the DVLA. A person is entitled not to report a condition that is not expected to last more than three months. A first onset of depression, for example, could fall within this exception.

Any severe mental illness should be reported. It is a criminal offence to knowingly make a false declaration about health.[2]

The DVLA's medical advisers approach the person's doctor and may call for an independent consultant's report before deciding what conditions should apply to the licence.

When someone is unable to notify the DVLA, or if someone refuses to give up driving and the doctor considers this is not safe, the doctor responsible for the patient's care should inform the DVLA, and is empowered to breach confidentiality to do so.[3] The doctor should inform the patient that he or she will be contacting the DVLA, if it is practicable to do so.

An insurer who has refused to issue motor insurance to any person because of, or at least partly because of, unsatisfactory health, must notify the DVLA of that refusal and of the full name, address, sex and date of birth of that person, as given to the insurer.[4]

[1] Road Traffic Act 1988, s 92(1).
[2] RTA 1988, s 92(10).
[3] GMC Confidentiality Guide, quoted in www.dvla.gov.uk/at_a_glance/ch4_psychiatric.htm.
[4] RTA 1988, s 95.

DVLA options

34.36 The DVLA may grant a licence, grant one for a limited period only or restricted to a particular class of vehicle, or refuse the application for a licence. A person can appeal to the sheriff court against the refusal of a licence. The appeal is by way of a summary application.

The DVLA include information about rights of appeal with any decision to refuse, suspend or revoke a licence. A person wishing to appeal should seek legal advice.

It is a criminal offence to drive if a licence has been cancelled on medical grounds.[1]

[1]   Road Traffic Act 1988, s 94A.

Medical standards

34.37 The DVLA has published a guide to its current medical standards, including information about medications that will affect the ability to hold a driving licence.[1]

A driving licence is not necessarily withdrawn after a depressive illness. A person must cease driving if he or she has an episode of acute psychosis or mania, and re-issue of a licence requires evidence of stability for at least three months, together with treatment compliance, recovery of reasonable insight (although not necessarily absolute insight) and a favourable report from a consultant. If the condition is a recurring one, evidence of longer period of stable health may be required. When the application relates to a class 2 vehicle, such as a lorry or bus, the DVLA normally requires evidence of three years' good health before it re-issues or grants a licence following mania or any psychotic episode.

Similarly with a diagnosis of schizophrenia, the DVLA requires the driver to be stable for at least three months, compliant with treatment, free from any side effects of medication which would impair driving and requires a favourable report from a specialist. Again, recurring illness will need to be followed by longer periods of good health before a licence is reissued or renewed, and normally three years' good health before issuing or renewing a licence for a class 2 vehicle, even after a single episode of illness.

Mild learning disability or autism does not of itself prevent the issue of a driving licence, if the person can demonstrate his or her ability to drive by passing the driving test.

Deteriorating conditions, such as dementia, may require annual renewal in the early stages, but short-term memory loss is not considered consistent with safe driving.

Where specific conditions are not listed in the guide, doctors are advised that patients should report to the DVLA any conditions which cause impairment of consciousness, or any symptoms that either distract from the task of driving or prevent the driver from operating the controls of the vehicle safely.

Declared or reported misuse of controlled drugs co-existing with mental disorder normally prevents the issue or re-issue of a licence. Indeed persistent misuse of drugs or alcohol, whether or not amounting to dependency is a notifiable disability.[2]

Additional requirements and extended suspensions apply to Group 2 licences for lorries and buses.

[1]   *At a glance guide to the current medical standards for fitness to drive: a guide for medical practitioners* (DVLA, revised February 2006).
[2]   Road Traffic Act 1988, s 92(2).

Impact of medication

34.38 The effects of medication and an individual's tolerance of medications are relevant to decisions about medical fitness to hold a licence. This is also relevant to the general offence of driving while unfit through drugs. It is an offence to drive while unfit through the effects of drugs.[1] A person can be guilty of this offence even if the drugs were properly prescribed by a doctor for a psychiatric condition.

[1]   Road Traffic Act 1988, s 4. There is also an offence of being unfit through drink or drugs to be capable of proper control of a bicycle, s 30.

TRAVEL AND HOLIDAYS

Concessionary travel

34.39 People aged over 60 and people with disabilities are entitled to free bus travel for most buses and coach services throughout Scotland.[1] The person receives an entitlement card from the local authority or Passenger Transport Executive, who can give advice.

Not everyone with a mental health condition or learning disability qualifies for a card. To qualify, the person must show that his or her ability to travel is impaired by a mental disorder, that he or she has had the condition for more than a year, and needs to travel to keep health or social care appointments or to take part in activities as part of a treatment, care or rehabilitation programme.[2] A psychiatrist, educational psychologist, mental health officer, community psychiatric nurse, occupational therapist, social care manager or special needs school head teacher should confirm the conditions apply.

People can also qualify if they have been refused a driving licence on medical grounds[3] or if they live in a residential home or hospital and are eligible for the higher or middle rate of the care component of Disability Living Allowance or Attendance Allowance. Certain carers are also entitled to a pass.[4]

Disabled people can purchase a disabled person's railcard, which gives entitlement to reduced rail fares. A person qualifies if he or she receives Disability Living Allowance (either higher rate for help with getting around, or in the higher/middle rates for help with personal care), Attendance Allowance, Severe Disablement Allowance or long-term Incapacity Benefit.

[1]   The National Bus Travel Concession Scheme for Older and Disabled Persons (Scotland) Order 2006 (SSI 2006/107). For relevant services see the National Bus Travel Concession Scheme for Older and Disabled Persons (Eligible Persons and Eligible Services) (Scotland) Order 2006 (SSI 2006/117), ('The eligible persons order') art 5.

[2]   Eligible persons order, art 3(h).

[3]   Unless the reason for the refusal is persistent misuse of drugs or alcohol.

[4]   SSI 2006/117 (above), art 3(k).

Help with holidays

34.40 A person who has a mental disorder may be able to receive help with the cost of a holiday as a form of respite care. See 28.18. Penumbra, the mental health charity, has two respite care guest houses, in Edinburgh and Aberdeen. Some charitable trusts help fund holidays for people with disabilities and these may include mental health conditions and learning disabilities. Enable has a leaflet.

Travel abroad

34.41 Unfortunately, having a mental health condition (but not, so far as the author is aware, a learning disability) may affect a person's ability to travel. Some countries require a person to be 'in good health' before they will issue a temporary visa, even for tourist entry.[1] Other countries may restrict the person from bringing medications into the country.

Travellers to the United States complete a visa waiver form on the aeroplane. A person with a mental disorder associated with harmful behaviour (to self or others) is not eligible to travel under the Visa Waiver Programme.[2] The person must apply for a visa and a waiver of ineligibility.

A traveller with a mental illness diagnosis can travel visa free under the Visa Waiver Programme if he or she can satisfy immigration officials that the condition does not render the person a danger to him or herself or others. US immigration advice is to carry a letter from a doctor to that effect, to facilitate entry into the United States. If immigration officials refuse entry, there is no right of appeal.

Within the European Union there is free movement of persons, which generally means that nationals of member states can move freely within the EU.[3] However a country may restrict even this free movement to refuse entry to a person with acute mental illness.[4]

A person intending to travel abroad should seek advice from a travel agent about visa and entry requirements. The person may need a doctor's confirmation that he or she is fit for travel. The person should also check that he or she will be free to bring any necessary medications into the countries he or she is visiting.

[1]   For example, for an automatic entry visa to Australia, the person must be 'in good health'. If an automatic visa is not available, the person must apply for a full visa. A person applying for a visa for New Zealand and Canada must be in 'good health'.

[2]   Under the Immigration and Nationality Act 1952, s 212.

[3]   Treaty Establishing the European Economic Community, Rome 1957, Art 56(2).

[4]   Council Directive 64/221/EEC allows member states to refuse entry or residence to a person who is experiencing obvious symptoms of psychotic disturbance with agitation, delirium, hallucinations or confusion. (Art 4 and Annex.)

Chapter 35

CIVIL RIGHTS AND PUBLIC LIFE

35.01 This chapter looks at the rights of people with mental disabilities to take part in the public, legal and political processes of the country.

APPOINTMENTS

Fitness for office

35.02 Mental disorder is not a bar to appointment to a profession, to directorship of a company, or to public or elected positions. The appointment depends on the person's ability to understand and carry out the obligations of the office. The person's fitness is assessed according to the published standards and regulations affecting that particular office. Automatic disqualification on the grounds of mental disorder is not appropriate and might be challenged on Disability Discrimination or human rights grounds. See Part 9.

Joining a private business partnership or taking up employment in the private or public sector is essentially a matter of contract, and is dealt with at chapter 34. This section concentrates on particular offices and public settings to which special rules apply.

Company directorships

35.03 Fitness for appointment to a company directorship is presumed, subject to a minimum age, but mental disorder is relevant to the question of unfitness and period of disqualification from holding future directorships

Companies' constitutions are contained in their articles of association. The model articles of association attached to the 1948 Companies Act say that a director loses office if he or she becomes of 'unsound mind'.[1] The articles attached to the 1985 Companies Act say that a director loses office if he or she is admitted to hospital under the Mental Health (Scotland) Act 1960 or a court appoints someone to manage his or her affairs.[2]

Neither provision is suitable. The 1948 Act test is too vague. The 1985 Act refers to outdated legislation, and should include a reference to the

Adults with Incapacity Act. It is suggested that an appropriate provision would be that a person should cease to be a director if he or she has a mental disorder and the directors determine the person is permanently or temporarily unable to carry out the duties of a director.

A person may be removed as a director in proceedings under the Company Directors Disqualification Act 1986.[3] Usually the reason is mental illness, but it could include diminished capacity due to a degenerative condition of the brain or severe head injury. When proceedings are taken in respect of a director's acts or omissions, the effect of a director's mental illness may be a relevant mitigating factor, but will not normally prevent a finding of unfitness, which could lead to disqualification. The fact that a director was mentally ill at the time might affect the length of the order.

A director might argue that, but for the disorder, breaches of the director's duties would not have occurred, but the assumption tends to be made that a person holding office should be alert to the onset of any impairment to fitness. The Secretary of State might argue that a director should have resigned if he or she was becoming unable to carry out a director's duties and failure to do so in itself indicates the person's unfitness.[4]

Whether a mental illness is likely to remain a factor or to recur will be taken into account. Those involved must balance the interest of the individual in being restored to office and the interest of ensuring that directors can carry out their duties.

[1]   Table A, para 88(d).

[2]   Table A, para 81(c).

[3]   Company Directors Disqualification Act 1986, s 6. *Secretary of State for Trade and Industry v Mitchell*, 2001 SLT 658 (OH).

[4]   *Secretary of State for Trade and Industry v Mitchell*, 2001 SLT 658 (OH), (an argument supported by the stance taken by the English courts in applications where mental illness is an issue (eg *Re Stoneacre Ltd*, 22 August 1997, unreported) and for discussion see Mithani, *Directors' Disqualifications* (Lexis Nexis Butterworths), Chap IX paras 300–305.

Members of professions

Admission to profession

35.04 A professional body can refuse to admit a person who has not established his or her fitness to be a member of that profession. Certain professional bodies require applicants for admission to provide a certificate of their fitness to be admitted.

The process of assessing 'fitness' varies across professional bodies. For example, the Law Society of Scotland asks referees to comment on the fitness of an applicant to enter practice, and to declare anything which would call that fitness into question, such as previous convictions or matters of dishonesty. A mental disorder could call fitness into question, if it is serious or its symptoms are not well managed.

Entrants to the medical profession require a certificate of fitness to practice. This may be withheld if there is evidence supporting concerns about fitness (expressly including physical or mental ill health).[1]

Such requirements to establish fitness are two-fold in purpose. On the one hand, they seek to maintain the professionalism of the members of that body, and it is in the nature of a profession that it should seek to set the highest professional standards for itself. On the other hand, they are for the protection of those members of the public who commit important issues concerning their lives, health or property to members of those professions.

This does not mean that professional bodies can discriminate unfairly against people on the grounds of mental disorder. The Disability Discrimination Act outlaws such discrimination by professional bodies. See chapter 36.

1   The General Medical Council (Fitness to Practise) Rules Order of Council 2004 (SI 2608/2004).

Disciplinary procedures

35.05 In addition to the general civil and criminal law, members of professions are liable to investigation, complaints procedures and disciplinary action by their professional body in connection with any acts or omissions calling their fitness to practice into question. (See, for example, chapter 49 for action by the General Medical Council and the Nursing and Midwifery Council.) Mental disorder may feature in those acts or omissions. Usually the disorder referred to in such proceedings is mental illness, but it could include diminished capacity due to a degenerative condition of the brain or severe head injury.

This section draws some general points from material relevant to the professional regulation of lawyers, (and there are common features with the approach to mental disorder in the disqualification of company directors).

There are differences between professions, so the situation must always be checked by reference to the standards, regulations and precedents of the profession of which the person with mental disorder is a member.[1]

1   Available from the website of the relevant regulatory body, or by contacting the chief office of that body. Telephone numbers are usually available in regional directories.

Support systems

35.06 Professions tend to assume that once a member has been admitted, it is the responsibility of that member to be alert to his or her ongoing fitness to practice in that profession. Nowadays most professions have expectations of continuing professional development and education, which may include mentoring, appraisal or re-registration processes.

Most professions have in place some means of offering support to those who personally, or through colleagues, become aware of actual or potential impairment. Recent reports indicate that there is growing use by Scottish Solicitors of the LawCare scheme which offers a confidential helpline to solicitors suffering stress, depression or addiction.[1]

There is no requirement at present in Scotland[2] for solicitors to inform the Law Society, as professional regulatory body,[3] if there is concern about the impaired professional capacity of another member of the profession whether as a result of mental disorder or otherwise. If the Law Society receives such information, it must promptly investigate the solicitor's professional activities.

1   *Rise in Calls to Lawyer Helpline*, http://www.journalonline.co.uk/news, 10 April 2006, reports a 70% increase over the previous two years, with depression and stress accounting for 75% of the calls. For a history of the models of support offered to Scottish Solicitors since 1975 see Paterson, *Professional Ethics* (Law Society of Scotland and W Green & Son) para 1.16.

2   Although 'whistle blowing' is expected in some other jurisdictions, and many employers now have policies concerning this.

3   The Legal Profession and Legal Aid (Scotland) Bill before the Scottish Parliament for stage 1 in Spring 2006 proposes an independent body for receiving complaints and handling those about service issues. Conduct issues are to be referred back to the Law Society for determination.

Investigating misconduct

35.07 Each profession is the guardian of its own professional standards. The professions appear reluctant to prescribe what misconduct is and the situations when it can arise. Instead misconduct is seen as any conduct which members of that profession would find serious and reprehensible.[1] It is assumed that members of professions will be alert to the onset of any mental illness or other condition which might impair their fitness to practise.

In dealing with complaints or disciplinary proceedings in respect of a professional person, the fact that the person may have a mental disorder is a relevant mitigating factor, but will not normally prevent a finding of blame or unfitness. If a person's mental disorder causes failures in professional service or conduct, it is just possible this may deflect or mitigate a finding of inadequate professional service or professional misconduct.[2]

If a person is found unfit to practice, the disciplinary body may mitigate the penalty or restriction to apply for the future if the person has a mental disorder,[3] but this is not guaranteed. Indeed it may aggravate the restriction.[4]

Sanctions have the dual purpose of showing the profession's disapproval of the past behaviour and protecting the public (and profession) from it in the future. If it is likely that a professional person's fitness to practice will be impaired in the future and that the person will be unable to maintain professional standards (particularly where the person intends to work unsupervised), the balance between the interests of the individual member of the profession and the public tilts towards public protection.

Private conduct, as compared to professional activities, if sufficiently disreputable and destructive of the reputation of the profession, can also lead to a finding of professional misconduct. It is suggested that when mental disorder is at the root of that private conduct it may be more difficult to infer the necessary blame than it is in the case of acts or omissions in professional life caused by mental impairment. Of course, there will always be issues of fact around the cause and effect of mental impairment and breaches of professional standards, and these must be matters of evidence in the relevant professional body.

1   *Sharp v Council of the Law Society of Scotland*, 1984 SC 129.
2   See Paterson, *Professional Ethics* (Law Society of Scotland and W Green & Son) paras 1.12–1.13.

3   As in Disciplinary Tribunal Decision *Hetherington*, 19/09/02 as cited by A
     Paterson, *Professional Ethics* (Law Society of Scotland and W Green) in
     para 1.13.

4   As in *Shaw*, Solicitors Disciplinary Tribunal Decision reported in Journal of
     Law Society of Scotland, April 1998, p 9 and cited by A Paterson, *Professional
     Ethics* (above) in para 1.13.

Elected political office

35.08 There is no statutory restriction against a person with a mental
illness, learning disability or personality disorder holding office in an
elected position at European, central, devolved or local government
levels. The disqualifying provisions under the relevant pieces of
legislation[1] are aimed at holders of other offices whose interests may be
seen to conflict with elected office rather than at individual capacities to
perform the task.

At common law in England, those with severe learning disability are
disqualified from election and those with mental illness are disqualified
during non-lucid intervals,[2] but most grounds of disqualification do not
prevent a candidate from being nominated or standing for election. If a
disqualified candidate is elected, this is open to challenge. The challenge
is the Election Court, which in Scotland consists of two judges of the
Court of Session.[3]

Clearly, matters of health and fitness to fulfil the duties of an elected
representative are issues for party selection committees, who would be
expected to perform the selection process without discrimination on
grounds of disability, including mental impairment.[4]

Behaviour in the performance of elected office is subject to Standing
Orders of the elected body. If behaviour contrary to expected standards is
a result of mental disorder, this would be a factor in any ruling on the
matter. Generally it would be expected that if such behaviour was
because of mental disorder this would mitigate any sanctions imposed. A
mental disorder would not necessarily be a defence to the behaviour,
since the standards are set in the broader interests of effective
government.

1   Such as in the House of Commons Disqualification Act 1975, Representation
     of the People Act 1981, Scotland Act 1998.

2   The Electoral Commission Factsheet: Candidates at a general election,
     available from www.electoralcommission,gov.uk.

3   Representation of the People Act 1983, s 125; Rules of the Court of Session 1994, Chap 69.
4   The Sex Discrimination Act was held to apply in the case of *Jepson and Dyas-Elliot v The Labour Party and others* [1996] IRLR 116.

Public appointments

35.09 Public appointments, that is appointments to certain public bodies including non-executive members of public bodies and agencies, are made at Scottish and UK level. The process of selection for and fulfilment of public appointment is subject to principles determined by the Nolan Committee, and there is an express commitment to appointment that is transparent and inclusive, and representative of the skills that exist across the public at large.[1]

A Commissioner for Public Appointments oversees the process, and each selection committee includes an independent assessor selected and trained by the Commissioner's office, to uphold the standards within the appointments process.

There is no disqualification of those with mental illnesses, learning disabilities or personality disorders. Indeed, applicants with a disability who otherwise meet the selection criteria as set out in person and job specifications are guaranteed an interview.

The nature of many public appointments requires specialist knowledge of the context. For example, an appointee to the Mental Welfare Commission for Scotland may need to show that he or she has been a user of mental health or learning disability services in order to satisfy the person/job specification.

Membership of the Mental Health Tribunal for Scotland is not a public appointment as such, but the standards applicable to public appointments have been applied to the first round of appointments to the tribunal. One of the potential qualifying criteria for appointment as a general member of the tribunal is that the person has experience of a mental disorder and of using mental health services.[2]

It is not only in the mental health and care context of public appointments that people with mental disorder can make a valuable contribution, and it should be noted that all public appointments are open for application by a person with living with mental health challenges or a learning disability, provided the applicant meets other criteria in the person specification. If a person became unfit for office during the period of appointment he or she could be removed.

1   Details at http://www.scotland.gov.uk/Topics/Government/public-bodies/public-appointments.
2   Mental Health Tribunal for Scotland (Appointment of General Members) Regulations 2004 (SSI 2004/375).

Judges

Appointment

35.10 There is no statutory disqualification from appointment to judicial office based on mental disorder. A mental illness which could impair a person's ability to act as a judge is likely to become known prior to appointment, and thus to prevent appointment.

Since the introduction of a judicial appointments process, applicants for office of sheriff (including part-time or floating sheriffs) and for judges are asked whether they suffer from any medical condition that could affect their ability to carry out the duties associated with the post. If so, the candidate must provide details and authorise enquiries with a medical practitioner.[1]

Members of the District Court bench at present hold appointment via the local authority responsible for establishing a district court for their area, and mental illness or impairment might be taken into account in the selection or re-appointment of District Court justices.

Many other tribunals exist in Scotland and those which apply UK-wide legislation are now governed by the Tribunals Service, an agency of the Department of Constitutional Affairs. All processes of appointments to such UK wide tribunals are subject to review by the Commission for Judicial Appointments.

In Scotland, procedures for appointment to tribunals are not standardised, and are found within the legislative framework establishing the tribunal. All appointments to tribunals are directed to the skills of the applicant, and there are no disqualifying provisions based on mental disorder.

1   Selection criteria and application forms are published on
     www.judicialappointmentsscot.gov.uk.

Removal

35.11 A person may develop a mental illness which impairs his or her ability to carry out the duties of a judge, sheriff or tribunal member. Members of tribunal systems are usually appointed for fixed periods, and reappointment is subject to continued ability to perform the duties of the office. If a person were to become unfit for office during the period of appointment he or she could be removed.

Where judges are concerned this is a complex area. Judges must be, and be seen to be, independent, and politicians must not interfere in this.[1] This restricts the scope for routine performance appraisal such as exists in other walks of life. Sheriffs and judges hold office until retirement age (maximum 70), resignation (unusual) or removal (very unusual). The sole basis for removal[2] is unfitness for office on the grounds of inability, neglect of duty or misbehaviour, although different procedures exist for removal of sheriffs[3] and judges.[4]

It is possible that any one or more of these failings in judicial office might result from mental disorder. 'Inability' has been interpreted as including, but not being restricted to, physical or mental infirmity.[5]

The existence of mental disorder is no doubt a relevant factor in consideration of the case for removal of a sheriff or judge from office, both as a potential ground for removal and a potential explanation for judicial conduct. Because of the need to ensure the system of justice and the importance of sound judgement of individual judges, the fact that a person's behaviour may be explained because of a mental disorder is not likely to prevent a person's removal from office if the person has shown repeated failings.

[1]   *Starrs v Ruxton*, 2000 SLT 42.
[2]   Proposals have been made by the Scottish Executive to place the Lord President in the role of head of the judiciary in Scotland, with a remit to deal with judicial discipline short of the removal process, *Strengthening Judicial Independence in a Modern Scotland* (Scottish Executive, February 2006).
[3]   Sheriff Courts (Scotland) Act 1971, ss 11C and 12.
[4]   Scotland Act 1998, s 95, and Scotland Act 1998 (Transitory and Transitional Provisions) (Removal of Judges) Order 1999 (SI 1999/1017).
[5]   *Stewart v Secretary of State for Scotland (No 7)*, 1998 SC (HL) 81, where inability had been found by the investigating judges to be due to 'an underlying defect in character.'

PUBLIC LIFE

Voting

35.12 There are no general statutory restrictions on voting in Scotland in European, Westminster, Scottish Parliamentary or Council elections for people with a mental disorder. The European Court of Human Rights has stressed recently that voting is a right rather than a privilege.[1]

Under common law, someone with a learning disability or mental illness may not be allowed to vote if, on polling day, the person is incapable of making a reasoned judgement about the election. Election officials can refuse to allow an individual to vote on grounds of reduced capacity at the polling station (including through intoxication).

At the point of registration as a voter, there is no onus to prove capacity of that person, and the issue of capacity only arises if there is a doubt about the ability to make a reasoned judgement at the point of voting. The presumption of capacity acts in favour of the inclusion on the electoral register of all people over the age of 18 who are not disqualified on other grounds.

If a person resides in a psychiatric or learning disability hospital or other place in which care is offered to people with mental disorder, whether or not that is by way of statutory compulsion,[2] he or she can be registered to vote using that registration address. Alternatively he or she can choose a home residential address, or if he or she does not have a residential address, choose a place with which he or she has local connection.

A person detained in hospital under a compulsion order, an interim compulsion order, or temporary compulsion order, is legally incapable of voting at any parliamentary or local government election.[3] There is a similar statutory restriction on voting by convicted prisoners during the detention period of the sentence,[4] which has been challenged as contrary to the European Convention on Human Rights. The European Court of Human Rights held that a blanket restriction on prisoners' voting was not a proportionate response and was a violation of the right to free elections.[5] As yet the domestic law has not changed.[6] Similar arguments could apply to a blanket restriction on voting by patients detained in psychiatric hospitals by the criminal justice system. A legal challenge to such a ban would clarify the human rights position.

[1]   *Hirst v United Kingdom* [2005] 19 BHRC 546.

[2]   Representation of the People Act 1983, s 4 as substituted by Representation of the People Act 2000, s 4.

[3]   Representation of the People Act 1983, (as amended by the Representation of the People Act 2000), s 3A.

[4]   Representation of the People Act 1983, s 3.

[5]   *Hirst v United Kingdom* [2005] 19 BHRC 546.

6   The Millan Committee made no recommendation for change on the issue of registration for voting by those with mental disorder detained under Criminal Procedure Act orders, but this was prior to the decision in *Hirst*, above.

Jury service

Eligibility

35.13 Anyone aged between 18 and 65 and on the register of electors with five years' residence in the locality may be called to serve on a jury.[1]

Certain people are ineligible to serve on juries. A person who is receiving medical treatment for mental disorder and is detained in hospital under the Mental Health (Care and Treatment) Act or the Criminal Procedure (Scotland) Act is ineligible,[2] as is a person who is subject to guardianship under the Adults with Incapacity Act.[3] A person subject to a community based compulsory treatment order remains eligible. When a person detained in hospital leaves hospital under suspended detention, the person becomes eligible to act as a juror.

Jurors are called from a database ('list of assize') kept by the clerk of court in each sheriff court area.[4] It is possible that a person will be called for jury service while ineligible, although if a person's address for electoral register purposes is in a hospital or other care facility, he or she might be less likely to be called inappropriately.

A juror who fails to respond to the order to attend for jury service could face a fine, unless excused.[5] It is important to let the clerk of court know if someone called to serve may not be eligible,[6] so that the ineligibility is recognised before the jury is balloted and starts to hear the case. A verdict is not rendered unsafe merely because a member of the jury was ineligible.[7]

A carer or member of staff should help the person inform the clerk of court if a person who falls within the ineligible category is called to act as a juror. If a person being treated in hospital or subject to guardianship fails to respond to a call for jury service and becomes subject to a fine, the court should be asked to remit the fine, on being made aware of the circumstances.[8]

1   Law Reform (Miscellaneous Provisions) (Scotland) Act 1980, s 1.
2   LR(MP)(S)A 1980 (as amended by Mental Health (Care and Treatment) (Scotland) Act 2003 (Modification of Enactments) Order (SSI 2005/465), Sched 2 para 1), s 1.
3   LR(MP)(S)A 1980, s 1 and Sched 1, Pt I, para 1(3)(b).

4   Criminal Procedure (Scotland) Act 1995, ss 84–85.

5   CP(S)A 1995, s 85(6).

6   And indeed it is an offence not to do so, LR(MP)(S)A 1980, s 3.

7   LR(MP)(S)A 1980, s 1(4).

8   CP(S)A 1995, s 85(7).

Being excused jury service

35.14 A person who is not ineligible may nevertheless be excused from jury service. People with mental illnesses or learning disabilities have no right to ask to be excused.[1] A juror must be able to understand the charges, the oath and the evidence, to concentrate and be able to attend throughout the trial. If a person called for jury service would find this difficult, the clerk of court should be told and the person can apply to be excused jury service.[2] If the clerk refuses, the person can apply to the court, but the reasons will be declared in open court.[3]

A person could also ask to be excused jury service if the effect of serving could have an adverse impact on his or her mental health. The clerk might ask for medical confirmation.

1   Which is restricted to those categories of person mentioned in the Law Reform (Miscellaneous Provisions) (Scotland) Act 1980, s1(2) and Sched 1, Pt III.

2   LR(MP)(S)A 1980, s 1(5). Excusal is for the current case only, and it is expected that a juror excused by the clerk will, unless it is inappropriate, be recalled in the future, s 1(5A). The clerk should be told whether the condition is likely to be permanent or not.

3   LR(MP)(S)A 1980, s 1(6), *Hughes Petr*, 1990 SLT 142.

Objecting to jurors

35.15 A prosecutor or an accused person can object to a juror, but in Scotland some reason must be shown.[1] At common law 'insanity', deafness, dumbness, blindness and being under the age of majority fall within recognised examples of appropriate reasons,[2] so there could be objection to a juror because of learning disability or mental illness even when that juror has not sought to be excused.

All parties in a criminal case may make a joint application for a juror to be excused, and the court must grant this even where no reason is stated.[3] Any such objections and excusals should be made before the juror is sworn, and before the first witness is sworn, since at that point the remaining jurors called for possible service are discharged and it is not possible to replace an excused juror.[4]

If a juror becomes unwell during the trial, the trial judge must consider whether this will affect the juror's fitness to proceed to fulfil the expectations of a juror, and may excuse that juror.[5]

[1]   Criminal Procedure (Scotland) Act 1995, s 86(2).

[2]   Renton & Brown, *Criminal Procedure* (6th edn, W Green & Son), para 18–36.

[3]   CP(S)A 1995, s 86(1).

[4]   Excusal may only occur later in the trial if a juror becomes ill, suddenly recognises some connection with the subject matter or witnesses, or because there is some allegation of improper conduct by the juror rendering him or her unfit, CP(S)A 1995, s 90(1)(b). For further discussion, see Sheehan & Dickson, *Criminal Procedure* (2nd edn), para 255.

[5]   CP(S)A 1995, s 90(1)(b). The trial may proceed with a jury reduced in size, but the jury may not fall below 12 in number.

CIVIL RIGHTS

Instructing a solicitor

35.16 The Disability Discrimination Act requires solicitors to make reasonable adjustments to their policies and procedures to make sure that people with mental disabilities have appropriate access to them. This could include making arrangements to ensure that a person can understand any legal documents and procedures which apply to him or her. (See chapter 36 for further details.) Financial assistance towards the solicitor's charges may be available from the Scottish Legal Aid Board, (see below for further details.)

Duties of solicitor

35.17 The fact that a person has a mental disability is not a bar to employing a solicitor, although in certain circumstances it will be a practical bar. Before a solicitor can agree to act for a client, he or she must be certain that the client has the ability to give the solicitor instructions. A mental disability might be so severe that the solicitor cannot ascertain what the client wishes to do. Alternatively it might not be clear if what the client says represents his or her true intentions or is the result of some mental lapse. In either of these circumstances, a solicitor would not be able to act for the client.

Generally a solicitor is entitled to assume that a client is able to give instructions. This is because of the presumption of capacity (see 34.02). It may be difficult for a solicitor to act on that presumption if he or she is aware a potential client has a mental disability or if there is other cause for concern. Throughout his or her dealings with the client, the solicitor must make a judgement as to whether the client can give instructions.

A solicitor will be open to criticism if he or she acts for a person later found to lack capacity. A solicitor with grounds for concern can raise this with the client, and if he or she remains unsatisfied, can insist on receiving a medical opinion before following the instructions. An assessment of capacity is not ultimately a matter for a lawyer but for a medical person, and if in doubt the lawyer should seek medical advice.[1]

In some cases a client may be giving apparently coherent instructions but such instructions are so out-of-character[2] or far-fetched as to raise questions of the person's mental capacity. This could happen, for example, if a person with manic depression attempts to purchase an expensive property during a period of mania, or a person with dementia wishes to write a completely new will and destroy the old one.

Any purchase by the client during a period of mania would run the risk of being set aside on the grounds of the person's lack of capacity at the time (see chapter 34), as might a new will made during failing capacity.[3]

[1]   'Professional Practice Committee Guidance' (2002) 7 Journal of Law Society of Scotland 51.
[2]   This may be very difficult for the solicitor to identify if the person is a new client. Requirements to know the client for money laundering prevention do little to assist in terms of highlighting whether they are providing instructions that are out of character.
[3]   See Scobbie, 'Executry practitioners run daily risks' (2003) 6 Journal of Law Society of Scotland 33.

Identifying the client

35.18 Difficulties can be compounded when a third party, such as a relative or carer, helps to explain the instructions of the person with mental disorder. While on the one hand this may help to alert the solicitor to concerns about mental health issues or incapacity, it is vital for the solicitor to be clear as to who the client is—the third party consulting the solicitor or the person on whose behalf he or she appears to seek legal assistance.

It is quite possible that there may be, or appear to be, a conflict of interest between the person communicating the instruction and the person whose instructions they are said to be. The solicitor must identify and then focus on who is the client, if necessary referring the other party to a different solicitor should there appear to be a conflict of interest.[1]

A solicitor may take instructions from a financial or welfare attorney, a financial guardian or a person authorised under an intervention order on receipt of evidence that the person has authority to act on behalf of the adult for the transaction in respect of which the solicitor is instructed. In accordance with the principles of the Adults with Incapacity Act, the solicitor should seek to involve the adult to the extent that his or her capacity permits.

If a solicitor also acts for an attorney or guardian as a individual, potential conflict of interest must be carefully considered, and advice may be sought from the Public Guardian (see chapter 3).

If a person with mental disorder who is under 16 seeks to consult a solicitor, all of the above may apply, but so too do factors particular to taking instructions from a child. The Law Society has issued guidance about acting for a child and taking instructions from a representative or guardian of a child in relation to a money claim.[2]

1   Code of Conduct for Scottish Solicitors 2002, arts 3 and 5(a).
2   'Destiny's child' (2004) 8 Journal of Law Society of Scotland 38, Guidance approved by the Society's Professional Practice and Civil Procedure Committees.

Ability to instruct solicitor

35.19 There is very little case law in Scotland[1] about the degree of capacity required to enable a client to give instructions to a solicitor. The writer would argue that a functional test should be applied.[2] This would mean that a different degree of ability is required for different transactions.

For example, a client defending a criminal case must be able to remember the event in question, follow the proceedings at the trial and discuss options and pleas with his or her solicitor. This requires a relatively high degree of ability. It may require much less ability to merely instruct that a not guilty plea is lodged (as a preserving step in the procedure).

Concern has been raised about solicitors taking instructions to prepare powers of attorney for elderly persons who are losing their mental abilities. Sometimes family members, rather than the elderly person themselves, instruct the solicitor. The Adults with Incapacity Act requires solicitors to certify that the person understands the nature of the power of attorney and does not appear to be under any undue pressure to sign.[3] The Law Society's Discipline Tribunal has held that the cancellation of a power of attorney is also a matter on which a solicitor must obtain instructions direct from the client.[4]

A patient may wish to be represented in a mental health tribunal (see Part 3). In such a case the majority of information before the tribunal will come from others: psychiatrists, social workers and perhaps the patient's nearest relative or named person as well as from the patient him or herself. There is a limited amount of information that the client has to give to the solicitor that is not available from other people or documents before the tribunal.

If a solicitor is content that a client understands that he or she is in hospital, that he or she is not happy to go along with the proposed care options, and that a solicitor can help put the case, there is probably not a need for a high degree of ability in such a case, at least to instruct the solicitor to oppose the application. It could be argued, for example, that it is not crucial to the conduct of the case that the client should be able to follow all the proceedings at the tribunal. See chapter 22.

Some solicitors, concerned about clients' ability to instruct them in mental health tribunal hearings, apply for the appointment of curators *ad litem* to represent the client's instructions in such cases. Consideration should always be given as to whether a curator's appointment in practice is in a client's best interests, if the solicitor is able to get some instructions from the client.

The curator does not act solely according to the client's instructions, as a solicitor would, but instead takes a view on what is in the client's best interests, which may be different from what the client says he or she wants.[5] On the other hand, there should not be blanket restriction of such appointment, and every case requires careful consideration of the issues of capacity and need for a curator as well as any other representative.[6]

---

[1]   In England a test case was taken around the extent of capacity required to instruct an Enduring Power of Attorney, see *Re K, Re F* [1988] Ch 310. The court's guidance is focussed upon understanding of the nature of the enduring power of attorney (for example, the fact that it could be permanent and continue in effect beyond the loss of capacity, and the role of the court in overseeing the power) and the court stressed that it was not necessary for the granter of that power to have the capacity to do all of the things which she was authorising the attorney to do.

2   Following research evidence such as in Gunn, Michael et al, 'Families and New Medical Dilemmas—Capacity to Make Decisions' (2001) Child and Family Law Quarterly 383.

3   Adults with Incapacity Act 2000, ss 15(3) and 16(3).

4   *Dawson*, Solicitors Disciplinary Tribunal Decision reported in (2006) 6 Journal of Law Society of Scotland 45. The tribunal took account of the potential seriousness of the consequences of the cancellation.

5   MacPhail, *Sheriff Court Practice* (2nd edn, W Green & Son, 1998–2002) paras 4.23–4.28.

6   For concern that curator appointments may be curtailed and others expected to represent the client, and arguments against curtailment see Hanlon & McGill, 'Safeguards before the MHTS' (2006) 4 Journal of Law Society of Scotland 28.

Mediation and arbitration

35.20 Parties to a dispute may agree that they will approach its resolution without resorting to legal action, or, if a court action has already started, may agree to attempt to resolve the matter by agreement. There are many options operating in different contexts. The Scottish Executive publishes a guide entitled *Resolving disputes without going to court*.[1]

Mediation is often a chosen method of dispute resolution in family, neighbour or employment disputes, and in the last of these it is now expected that parties will have attempted dispute resolution within employment procedures or via the conciliation service, ACAS, before the matter is to be determined by an employment tribunal.

In neighbour disputes, the police often make referrals to mediation, local authority housing officers or housing association staff. Courts in family actions involving children may order the parties to attempt mediation concerning the children, but many couples choose to have all issues arising from separation settled via a mediation process.

Such an option may be attractive to a person with a mental illness or learning disability, who may find the prospect of litigation too intimidating. On the other hand such an option may cause concern, since its form is not familiar and the point of the process is to assist the parties to reach a resolution rather than for the mediator to produce or impose a solution. A person may fear that the other party is more powerful and will impose an outcome.

Mediators are trained to remain impartial, but at the same time to manage the process in such a way that power imbalances (real or perceived) are addressed as well as possible. They may be legally qualified but most are not, and it is not necessary for them to be so, since their focus is effective dispute management between the parties, who may separately have or seek legal advice as to their rights and obligations.

Mediation allows parties to describe the dispute in a more personal way than is possible in court, and to talk confidentially to the mediator about what matters to the party in terms of achieving a settlement, which may include steps that are outside the range of orders a court is able to grant.

Mediation may not be appropriate in certain situations, such as where there has been violence within the family, or one or other party lacks capacity to consent to enter into the process, or to reach agreement in it. However it could be a powerful and empowering option for a person with mental disorder.

Arbitration clauses in contracts are common for building or engineering services and in certain consumer situations. Some credit card companies' conditions of contract state that arbitration will be used for any dispute arising under the contract. A person who has entered into such a contract is bound by the arbitration clause, and the courts have no jurisdiction in any disputes.[2]

There has been considerable concern in the USA around consumers being drawn into these contracts and then bound to meet a share of the costs of expensive arbitration, or concede the dispute. Anyone entering into such a contract should check whether it contains an arbitration clause.

If a person with mental disorder has entered into such a contract and it appears to provide for onerous and complex arbitration procedure, it may be possible to challenge the contract on the basis that the person did not have the capacity to agree to it (see chapter 34).

[1]   Available from public libraries, courts and www.scotland.gov.uk.
[2]   Hunter, *The Law of Arbitration in Scotland* (2nd edn, Tottel, 2002); Ross, 'Commercial Dispute Resolution' in Forte (ed) *Scots Commercial Law,* chap 1.

Being a party to litigation

Capacity to instruct

35.21 At common law, a person deemed 'insane' has no standing in court[1] and can neither commence a legal action in person or via a legal representative. A person with a mental disorder may instruct or defend a legal action in person or as client instructing a solicitor, provided he or she has the capacity to make the decisions necessary to the litigation process.

When a person's capacity to conduct litigation is in doubt, the lawyer should act only as urgently necessary to secure the person's position in the litigation, until the person's capacity is clarified and any steps necessary to involve a proxy are taken.

To take part in litigation a person must have the capacity to enter into a contract for legal services (which is considered above), and be able to provide information to allow the solicitor to advocate his or her case. The person must be able to provide instructions in connection with the settlement of the case, based on understanding of legal advice.

A person's capacity may fluctuate as the case proceeds. If a solicitor or legal advocate for a person, (or any other party to the litigation) suspects that the person is unable to take part in the litigation or give instructions, he or she may ask the court to consider this. If necessary, the court can order a medical assessment specifically for the purpose of determining the issue of capacity.

The law presumes that a person has full capacity and good mental health. Anyone wishing to challenge this must establish an initial case and must then lead evidence on which it may be determined.[2] If the court is satisfied a person is unable to take part in legal proceedings or fully to instruct a legal representative, the court may allow any guardian, person holding a power of attorney or intervention order (if they have relevant powers) to initiate, defend or step into the shoes of the person lacking capacity.

The court might adjourn the case to allow for an intervention order or guardianship order to be sought, or for a curator *ad litem* to be appointed.[3] Although this allows a substitute to act for the person, it is expected in accordance with the principles of the Adults with Incapacity Act that the views and wishes of the person will be heard and taken into account.

---

1   See MacPhail, *Sheriff Court Practice* (2nd edn, W Green & Son, 1998–2002), para 4.07, but references there to curator *bonis* have been superceded by the Adults with Incapacity Act, Pt 6.

2   *AB v CB*, 1937 SC 408.

3   See MacPhail, *Sheriff Court Practice* (2nd edn, W Green & Son, 1998–2002), para 4.07 and paras 4.23–4.28.

Special protections

35.22 When proceedings in the sheriff court result in an award of damages for a person aged 18 or above who has a legal disability, special rules apply for the payment or management of those damages.[1]

When the action is a family action and the person defending the action is in hospital because of mental disorder, special notification requirements apply.[2] When the action is for divorce or separation and the defender is suffering from mental disorder, a curator *ad litem* must be appointed. If the ground of divorce or separation is separation with consent, the Mental Welfare Commission receives notice and is required to report whether the defender has capacity to consent.[3] The effect of mental disorder in family actions is considered in more detail at 31.19.

[1]   Sheriff Court Ordinary Cause Rules 1993 as amended, Chap 36, Pt III.
[2]   Ordinary Cause Rules 1993, r33.13.
[3]   OCR 1993, r33.16.

Domicile and residence

35.23 In order to establish jurisdiction in most civil proceedings it is necessary to establish that one or both of the parties to the proceedings is domiciled or resident in Scotland. A person's domicile is the country the person considers his or her permanent home.

The most general ground, (which may have different meanings according to domestic law and European standards) is domicile of the defender, but other grounds exist. For example, in family actions, the test is habitual residence of either party or of a child. Some actions take their jurisdiction from the place where the action complained of took place (such as the place where the negligent act was committed or the place where the contract was to be performed). Consumer actions depend on the domicile of the consumer.

The technicalities of jurisdiction are profound and ever changing, and definitely outside the scope of this text,[1] but they may be relevant to someone resident in hospital or another place offering care, which may not be in the place of that person's choice or in an area with which the person has any chosen connection.

A person's domicile is established by an element of intention to settle, and remain in the place, such as the place of the family home, even though the person is accommodated long term in a distant place. Residence, by comparison, is much more factual in nature, and a hospital address could be used as the residence for the purposes of jurisdiction and citation.

1   For much more detail see MacPhail, *Sheriff Court Practice* (2nd edn, W Green & Son, 1998–2002), chap 3, but with the warning that significant changes have been made since that text was written, as a result of European activity. For example, the Brussels II Convention in family actions led to many changes to primary legislation, listed in European Communities (Matrimonial and Parental Responsibility Jurisdiction and Judgments) (Scotland) Regulations 2005 (SSI 2005/42) which came into force in March 2005. A new edition of Anton & Beaumont, *Civil Jurisdiction in Scotland* (W Green & Son), is awaited.

Legal aid

Outline of scheme

35.24 Financial assistance with legal expenses is provided through the systems of Legal Aid for civil or criminal court proceedings, Legal Advice and Assistance for advice and limited court representation via Advice by way of Representation (ABWOR). In some instances there are relaxations on normal tests (such as means testing) for those with mental disorder in mental health or incapacity proceedings. More information on legal aid or advice and assistance for mental health proceedings is contained in chapter 22.

These systems for financial support for legal services assume that an individual will apply for support specific to a piece of legal work, and if granted, the solicitor's fee for that work will be met from the Legal Aid fund at a prescribed rate. Only registered practitioners can offer work under that scheme, and registration exists separately for civil and criminal work.

Another option exists in certain parts of Scotland for obtaining representation through a Law Centre whose employees have been funded by the Scottish Legal Aid Board to assist individuals, including those with mental disorder, without the person having to apply to fund the individual piece of work. For example, the Legal Services Agency is funded to offer legal assistance which includes mental health and housing matters. At the Fife Rights Forum Project, the solicitor provides specialised legal advice and representation to mental health clients in Fife, including young people and children. The Scottish Legal Aid Board maintains a comprehensive website, including an updated version of the Scottish Legal Aid Handbook.

Most situations in which legal aid or advice and assistance may be required are subject to means testing, and may be refused if the applicant's income or capital is above a stated threshold. In some situations support is available, but the person must contribute a specified sum.

Even if someone is eligible on financial grounds, legal aid will not always be available. In civil and criminal proceedings heard without a jury, it is also necessary to show that there is a reasonable case to put forward via the legal representative, and that it is reasonable for the Legal Aid Board to contribute to the costs of legal representation. The Board also considers whether the person is able to present his or her case without legal help. A client with a mental illness or learning disability is unlikely to be able to conduct his or her own case.

Capacity

35.25 A person's capacity to understand and complete a legal aid or legal advice and assistance form can be presumed, and the solicitor is on hand to assist with this in any event. If a client does not have the capacity to apply or to sign the form, consideration must be given to whether a proxy can be appointed to complete the application. Express power might be specified within a power of attorney, an intervention order or guardianship order.

Legal Aid Regulations allow an application for legal aid by a person with mental disorder to be signed by a person having parental responsibilities in relation to a child, a judicial factor or a person authorised to act on an adult's behalf under the Adults with Incapacity (Scotland) Act 2000.[1]

A named person, or other person who pursues or defends legal proceedings as a representative for a person with mental disorder can apply for legal aid. The representative's own income and resources are not taken into account, but the Legal Aid Board takes into account the value of any property or fund on which the applicant is entitled to call for compensation and the income and capital of anyone (including the applicant, if appropriate) who might benefit from the outcome of the proceedings.[2]

In such a situation, the Scottish Legal Aid Board also takes account of the rights any such representative has to recover from a third party or another source (such as insurance), and grants legal aid only if these sources would not be able to meet the expenses of the case.[3]

Applications for legal aid for proceedings under the Adults with Incapacity (Scotland) Act 2000 are calculated on the resources of the adult with incapacity, not the person who applies for the order.[4] See chapter 24.

The Legal Aid Board must recover charges made to the Fund from any money or property recovered or preserved as a result of the legally aided proceedings, subject to certain savings and exemptions. If proceedings on behalf of a legally aided person are not successful, the court can modify the person's liability for the opponent's court costs and may modify the amount to nil.

1   The Civil Legal Aid (Scotland) Regulations 2002 (SI 2002/494), regs 2 and 5(1)(a)(iii).
2   SI 2002/494 (as amended by Civil Legal Aid (Scotland) Amendment (No. 2) Regulations 2005 (SSI 448/2005)), reg 14(1).
3   SI 2002/494, (as amended), reg 14(2).
4   SI 2002/494, (as amended) reg 14(3).

Other funding of legal action

35.26 Increasingly people who wish to litigate in the civil courts use claims management firms to pursue a claim on a 'no win—no fee' basis. These arrangements usually involve the firm taking a success fee based on the level of settlement of the claim, called a 'contingency fee'.

Solicitors cannot currently use this type of fee charging arrangement, but they may enter into a written agreement with a client to waive fees if the action fails and to charge a fee of up to 100% more than that normally charged if it succeeds.

There are insurance policies available that cover legal expenses exclusively or as part of broader cover, for example motor insurance or home insurance.

All of these options are open to people with mental disabilities, so long as the person has the capacity to enter into the contract for that service. All these options involve a degree of risk assessment on the part of the provider or funder of the service, and the impact of a person's mental disorder on the prospects of a claim arising and being successfully pursued are relevant to the assessment of risk.

These funding options are most commonly associated with claims for personal injury, but are available in a variety of contexts, and have been used, for example, in employment and discrimination cases.

IN THE COURTS

Acting as a witness

35.27 The contents of this section applies to both civil and criminal cases.

Capacity at common law

35.28 A person with a mental disorder is presumed to be a competent witness, and it has long been accepted that a person, even while resident in a hospital for compulsory treatment, can give evidence of what he or she saw and is able to recount.[1]

The court will presume a witness has the capacity to give evidence unless there is evidence to the contrary. The final decision is for the judge. It may not be appropriate for a judge to raise the issue of the capacity if a witness's ability to give evidence is not challenged.[2]

Until 1 April 2005, prior to admitting the witness to give evidence, if the witness' capacity was the subject of challenge, the court could make enquiries. The judge could hear medical evidence,[3] and the witness could be questioned,[4] all before the court made a decision on whether or not the person should be allowed to give evidence in the cause.

It was not necessary for the witness to be able to understand the relevance of the evidence—indeed it could be helpful to truth if the witness had not understood the importance of what he or she had seen, since there was less risk that the witness had interpreted the evidence before recounting it.[5]

---

[1]   *HM Advocate v Stott* (1894) 1 Adam 386.
[2]   *McAvoy v HM Advocate*, 1991 JC 16.
[3]   *HM Advocate v Stott* (1894) 1 Adam 386, *HM Advocate v McKenzie* (1869) 1 Coup 244.
[4]   *O'Neil and Gollan* (1858) 3 Irv 93.
[5]   *HM Advocate v Skene Black* (1887) 1 White 365.

Competence test abolished

35.29 This process of assessing the competence of the witness before giving evidence[1] appears now to be swept away in both civil and criminal cases by the Vulnerable Witnesses (Scotland) Act.[2] This prohibits any step being taken, any time before the witness gives evidence, intended to establish whether the witness understands the nature of the duty of a witness to give truthful evidence, or the difference between truth and lies. The evidence of a witness can be heard even if the witness is unable to understand the nature of the duty of a witness to give truthful evidence, or the difference between truth and lies.

It is rather early to tell how this prohibition will apply. It does not say expressly that the witness' mental capacity cannot be the subject of enquiry (just as the capacity of a party can be challenged at any stage, as discussed above). However to avoid the prohibition, it will be necessary to raise broader questions of capacity than whether the witness understands the need to tell the truth. If the question is so limited, this can be raised only after the witness has given evidence or begun to give evidence.

It is likely that the courts will continue to administer the oath or affirmation to any witness who appears able to understand it,[3] and it would seem, to advise the witness to tell the truth (even without first inquiring whether the witness understands what truth means).

1   Which applied also to young children who were not presumed to be competent witnesses.
2   Vulnerable Witnesses (Scotland) Act 2004, ss 24(1)-(2).
3   This was done in *McAvoy v HM Advocate*, 1991 JC 16 and is the current test for administering the oath to children between 12 and 14, *Quinn v Lees*, 1994 SCCR 159. See MacPhail, *Sheriff Court Practice* (2nd edn, W Green & Son, 1998–2002), para 16.63 regarding the oath in situations of questioned understanding.

Facilitating evidence

35.30 The removal of the competence test may resolve a dilemma that has existed for some time for those with mental disabilities who may be witnesses to or victims of crimes. Prosecutors, carers or defence lawyers working with such people could not be reassured that the evidence would come before a court.

All would depend upon the outcome of the competence test administered by the judge. Cases have been withheld or dropped because of fears about the ability of the mentally disordered witness to give the necessary evidence in the case.[1] Information about the witness's ability came more from evidence about the witness (from experts or, less commonly by family members or carers) than from the witness herself, adding to the marginalization of the potential witness.

However, the new situation may raise other dilemmas. Will prosecutors or defence solicitors, or legal representatives in civil cases, be willing or able to interpret and present positively the evidence of a witness whose mental capacity may be in doubt?[2] Will they communicate effectively with the witness in a way that the witness can understand?

Assistance may be found in a pack *Special Measures for Vulnerable Adult and Child Witnesses,* which has been developed by the Scottish Executive in partnership with justice agencies and voluntary organisations and issued to professionals and others connected with court proceedings.[3]

This ostensibly provides guidance in relation to special measures for dealing with vulnerable witnesses (discussed below), and in fact makes no mention of capacity at all, but it has more general information about getting to know the witness and his or her needs for giving best evidence, both before and during the proceedings.

There is guidance in the Law Society's Code of Conduct for Criminal Work to the effect that it is the duty of a solicitor taking witness statements personally or through a third party such as an employee or an independent agent (called a 'precognition agent') , to take into account any disability or vulnerable status of a witness.[4] There are many other multi-agency information packs at the time of writing, but with the exception of *Good Practice Guidance: Information about child, young and vulnerable adult witnesses to inform decision-making in the legal process,* most are directed to dealing with child witnesses.[5]

Some publications have been developed for witnesses and for the carers of vulnerable witnesses. There are leaflets and a CD about 'Being a Witness' for child and vulnerable adult witnesses. These are all accessible from the Scottish Executive website as well as court buildings and other agencies,[6] where general information for witnesses is also available.[7]

Vulnerable witness support officers are being established in most court venues. Meantime, Victim Support Scotland also provides a Witness Service in all sheriff courts and high courts in Scotland[8] where advice is available to witnesses generally, particularly on the day when the witness attends to give evidence.

---

1   The most high profile of these preceded *H v Sweeney,* 1983 SLT 48, where the Lord Advocate did not object to the case proceeding as a private prosecution but could not cooperate in it because he had already renounced the right to prosecute after the complainer had been too unwell to give evidence at a number of trials.

2   One of the grounds of appeal in *McBrearty v HM Advocate,* 2004 SLT 917 was that the defence advocate had failed to make use of evidence from experts as to the mental state of one of the complainers.

3   *Special Measures for Vulnerable Adult and Child Witnesses* (Scottish Executive, 2005), on the Scottish Executive Justice Department's website. Especially chap 3: Vulnerable Witnesses with Special Needs.

4   Art 13.

5   A Guidance pack *Supporting Child Witnesses* contains guidance on interviewing child witnesses, and on questioning child witnesses in court, the Lord Justice General's Memorandum on Child Witnesses, child witness court familiarisation visits, a Code of Practice for therapeutic support for child witnesses and guidance on conducting identification parades with child witnesses. These contain some interesting information about effective, straightforward communication methods that might be of use with some, but not all, adult witnesses who have mental disorder. These are all available from www.scotland.gov.uk.

6   Details on the Scottish Executive Website, www.scotland.gov.uk/Topics/Justice/criminal/17416/InformationMaterials and the Crown Office Website www.copfs.gov.uk/Witnesses/WitnessesattendingCourt.

7   www.copfs.gov.uk/Witnesses/WitnessesattendingCourt.

8   See www.victimsupportsco.demon.co.uk/main/witnesses.html.

Special arrangements for witnesses: common law

35.31 Where a witness has a mental disorder, certain steps are available at common law or under statute to help the witness give evidence. At common law, the courts have permitted special arrangements to help witnesses give evidence more freely.

Witnesses have been allowed to give evidence from behind a screen[1] provided that arrangements are in place to ensure that the accused person's right to a fair trial is not denied.[2]

In one case, a witness had paranoid psychosis with secondary depression and obsessive compulsive disorder, and a consultant psychologist expressed serious doubts about her ability to give evidence from the witness box. The court allowed a screen to be placed between her and the accused person.[3] The accused person was able to see and hear her give evidence by a camera and television screen, but she could not see him.

This measure was permitted at common law since the witness did not meet the test for statutory special measures under the relevant provisions of the Criminal Procedure (Scotland) Act applicable at that time.

The court has also allowed vulnerable adult witnesses to have a supporter present in court and near the witness while giving evidence.[4]

In civil cases, similar common law options would exist but have been rarely requested. In civil cases a witness (including a party) with a mental disorder who is ill, infirm or in a hospital and unable to attend a hearing might be able to give evidence to a specially appointed Commissioner.[5] Evidence might also be taken in advance when the witness is at serious risk of deteriorating mental health or developing incapacity.[6]

1   *Hampson v HM Advocate*, 2003 SLT 94.
2   *HM Advocate v Smith* 2000, SCCR 910.
3   *Hampson v HM Advocate*, 2003 SLT 94.
4   *McGinley v HM Advocate*, 2001 SLT 198. In that case the supporter was the witness's boyfriend, in a case where the accused was charged with sexual crimes against the witness alleged to have been committed years before. The court commented that it might have been preferable to have a different supporter in all the circumstances, but the trial was not unfair.
5   See MacPhail, *Sheriff Court Practice* (2nd edn, W Green & Son, 1998–2002) paras 15.26 and 15.27. MacPhail's comments about the Commissioner reporting on the capacity of the witness are affected now by the prohibition on prior enquiry as to 'competence' contained in the Vulnerable Witnesses (Scotland) Act 2004, s 24, discussed above.
6   See Ross, *Walker & Walker's Law of Evidence in Scotland* (2nd edn) para 14.2.1.

Special measures: statute

Prior to implementation of Vulnerable Witnesses (Scotland) Act

35.32 Since 1997 a vulnerable person, that is an adult subject to a Mental Health (Scotland) Act order or a child, has been entitled to apply for special measures for giving evidence in criminal cases.[1] The special arrangements provided for under a developing variety of statutory measures have been, until 2005, giving evidence via live television link,[2] by evidence to a Commissioner,[3] or from behind a screen.[4] The law also allowed the court to receive evidence of a witness's earlier identification, even where the witness might no longer be able to identify the person in court.[5]

An application for special measures would have to show why they would be appropriate and the court was obliged to take into account the possible effect on the vulnerable person of giving evidence without special measures, whether the person would be better able to give evidence if special measures were granted, and the views of the person.[6] The court might also have regard to the nature of the alleged offence or of the evidence the witness would have to give and any relationship with the accused (for example, if the accused is a family member or former partner).[7]

There was no equivalent general civil provision, but a similar provision existed in relation to child witnesses in care proceedings.[8]

The statutory power to allow special measures did not remove the common law power,[9] and once measures were allowed (although they had to be applied for as individual alternatives), the court would adjust the conduct of the trial accordingly in balance with fairness to the accused. Thus, when a vulnerable witness was allowed to give evidence via live television link, identification of the accused was allowed by the witness viewing the court room through a camera, rather than being brought into court just for the purpose of identification.[10]

A new version of the section together with additional related sections has been devised for criminal cases, and a civil equivalent introduced through the Vulnerable Witnesses (Scotland) Act 2004. This Act is being implemented in stages and at the time of writing those stages are not yet complete.[11] The description here of the statutory situation prior to the commencement of the 2004 Act is given, since it applies in criminal cases until the relevant stage of implementation has been reached. The common law is preserved by the 2004 Act.[12]

[1]   Criminal Procedure (Scotland) Act 1995, s 271, as substituted by the Crime and Punishment (Scotland) Act 19997, s 29. Measures had been introduced for children in 1990 by the Law Reform (Miscellaneous Provisions)(Scotland) Act 1990, ss 55–59.

[2]   Criminal Procedure (Scotland) Act 1995, s 271(5).

[3]   CP(S)A 1995, s 271(1).

[4]   CP(S)A 1995, s 271(6).

[5]   CP(S)A 1995, s 271(11).

[6]   CP(S)A 1995, s 271(7).

[7]   CP(S)A 1995, s 271(8).

[8]   Act of Sederunt (Child Care and Maintenance Rules) 1997 (SI 1997/291), r 3.22.

[9]   *Hampson v HM Advocate*, 2003 SLT 94.

[10] *Brotherstone v HM Advocate*, 1996 SLT 1154.

[11] For the implementation timetable see Scottish Executive, *Vulnerable Witnesses (Scotland) Act 2004 Information Guide* (2005), also available from www.scotland.gov.uk.

[12] CP(S)A 1995, s 271G.

Vulnerable Witnesses (Scotland) Act 2004

35.33 The Vulnerable Witnesses (Scotland) 2004 creates a new range of special measures for vulnerable witnesses, and creates a new definition of vulnerable witness. It does so by making major amendments to the Criminal Procedure (Scotland) Act, and by specifying certain measures for civil cases and cases arising out of the children's hearing system.

Qualifying as vulnerable witness

35.34 The courts automatically treat all children under the age of 16 as vulnerable witnesses.

The court may decide to regard an adult as a vulnerable witness. This may be because of a person's fear and distress about giving evidence, (perhaps because of intimidation) or because of vulnerability due to the person's mental health needs. The court must decide whether there is a significant risk that fear, distress or mental disorder will affect the quality of the person's evidence to the court.[1]

The court will consider all the circumstances in deciding whether a witness is vulnerable. These include the nature of the alleged offence, the evidence the witness is likely to give, the witness's age and maturity, the relationship between the witness and the accused person and whether there has been any (intimidating) behaviour towards the witness by the accused person or others connected with him or her or with the case. The court should also consider any social and cultural issues and issues of race, gender, religion and physical disability that may be relevant.[2]

The fact that giving evidence in court might damage a witness's mental health does not of itself mean that the court will use special measures. It must be satisfied there is a risk to the completeness, clarity or accuracy of the person's evidence.[3]

If the court decides someone is a vulnerable witness, it must consider the possible effect on the person of giving evidence without special measures and whether it would be easier for the person to give evidence using special measures.[4] This means that the court can consider the effects on the person at this stage.

[1] Criminal Procedure (Scotland) Act 1995 (as amended by Vulnerable Witnesses (Scotland) Act 2004), s 271(1).

[2] CP(S)A 1995, s 271(2), VW(S)A 2004, s 11. Hereafter the CP(S)A 1995 reference gives the source for criminal proceedings and the VW(S) A 2004 reference, the source for civil proceedings.

[3] CP(S)A 1995, s 271(4).

[4] CP(S)A 1995, s 271C(8).

Application for special measures

35.35 Someone who believes he or she is a vulnerable witness should tell the person calling him or her to give evidence. That person must consider the best interests of the witness and consider his or her views.[1] If the prosecution or defence consider special measures are appropriate, they should submit an application to the court.

In the High Court, the application must be within 14 days of the first hearing. For proceedings on indictment in the sheriff court, the period is within seven days of the first hearing. In all other cases, it is within 14 days of the first hearing.[2]

The application should include a summary of the views of the witness.[3]

If the prosecution or defence fail to apply for special measures, the witness (or someone on his or her behalf) can approach the court.

The court hears the application in private. It should decide whether it agrees to the use of special measures or whether it requires the parties to attend the court.[4]

The witness will not generally be required to attend the court, but may request to do so. The court has regard to the possible effect on the witness of being required to give evidence with no special measures, and whether the witness is likely to be better able to give evidence with them.[5]

The court and the party making the application must take account of the views of the witness, and have regard to the witness's best interests.[6] The court must decide whether the witness is a vulnerable witness, and what special measure or measures will be most appropriate The final decision is with the court, and there is no right of appeal.[7]

[1] Criminal Procedure (Scotland) Act 1995, s 271E(2).
[2] CP(S)A 1995, s 271C.
[3] CP(S)A 1995, s 271C(3).
[4] CP(S)A 1995, s 271C(5).
[5] CP(S)A 1995, s 271C(8), Vulnerable Witnesses (Scotland) Act 2004, s 12(7).
[6] CP(S)A 1995, s 271E; VW(S)A 2004 s 15.
[7] CP(S)A 1995, s 271C(7); Vulnerable Witnesses (Scotland) Act 2004, s 12(6). For young children as witnesses to specified serious crimes, it is presumed, unless contrary application succeeds, that evidence will be given from outside both the court room and the court building, CP(S)A 1995, s 271B.

Special measures available

35.36 The special measures include the use of screens to protect the person from having to see the accused person, the use of live television links between the person and the court, and the taking of evidence by a specially appointed Commissioner, recorded on video camera.

The rules also envisage the use of witness supporters[1] and the giving of evidence in advance of the trial in the form of a statement (which could be a written statement or one recorded by any means such as film, audio or DVD).[2] Ministers may specify other special measures in regulations.

The needs of the witness must be kept under review during the proceedings.[3] Clearly more than one measure may be authorised by the court, and measures may be adjusted or cancelled as the case proceeds.[4]

A special measure may be cancelled entirely if a witness chooses to give evidence without the authorised measure and it is appropriate for him or her to do so. It may also be cancelled if using or continuing to use a measure would significantly risk prejudicing the fairness of the proceedings or the interests of justice and such prejudice significantly outweighs the possible prejudice to the interests of the vulnerable witness.[5]

These provisions in relation to adults have been in operation only since April 2006 and only in cases involving trial by jury commencing after that date. There will be phased implementation thereafter in relation to other criminal cases and civil cases. They now apply, with the exception of use of a screen, to an accused person who is to be a witness and who meets the qualifying criteria.[6]

[1]   A supporter may attend as well as an appropriate adult, if necessary. See Criminal Procedure (Scotland) Act 1995, s 271L.
[2]   CP(S)A 1995, s 271H. For the detailed rules, see ss 271I–271M. Special measures for civil cases are potentially the same and are set out in Vulnerable Witnesses (Scotland) Act 2004, s 18.
[3]   CP(S)A 1995, s 271D.
[4]   CP(S)A 1995, ss 271D(2)–(3), VW(S)A 2004, ss 13(1)–(3).
[5]   CP(S)A 1995, s 271D(4); VW(S)A 2004, s 13(4).
[6]   CP(S)A 1995, s 271F.

Impact on witness

35.37 A witness may feel that the easiest thing would be to give a written statement to the court. The witness may find defence or prosecution lawyers put him or her under pressure to attend court and give evidence, particularly if his or her evidence is vital to the case.

Generally, the court prefers to see the best evidence it can. The evidence of a witness in person is stronger and more convincing than a written statement. Evidence is also stronger if the witness will agree to be cross-examined. Special measures will reduce the strain of a court appearance but cannot remove it altogether.

Implementation

35.38 Whilst these provisions are very detailed, and complex to distil, it is likely that in reality the vulnerability and needs of the witness will be quite obvious if more thought is given to this than in the past, and that in appropriate cases there will be more access to suitable means for giving evidence.

The Scottish Executive, which has been advised by a number of multi-interest implementation groups, has put much effort into pre-implementation publicity and many publications exist to inform professionals about the new provisions, although most are focused on the child witness rather than the vulnerable adult.[1] Vulnerable Witness support officers have been appointed for court areas.

It is to be hoped that raised awareness amongst professionals directly and indirectly involved with the justice system, will prompt them to put forward suitable candidates for special measures.

Some special measures may add to the cost of the proceedings. The Scottish Legal Aid Board has indicated that it will expect the cost of using a screen, live television link within the court building or supporter to be within normal bounds in a solemn criminal case, and that any additional cost, up to £2,000, will not require prior authority. However if the special measure is a live television link from outside the court or evidence on commission, prior sanction for special expenditure will be needed.[2]

It will be important to make clear to vulnerable witnesses that:

- If a court authorises the use of a screen or taking of evidence by a Commissioner, arrangements will still need to be made for the accused person or other party to see and hear the witness giving evidence;[3]

- Another witness in the case may act as supporter only if he or she has given evidence first;[4]

- The supporter is not permitted to prompt or influence the witness when giving evidence;[5] and

- Whilst a prior statement replaces giving evidence in court in criminal cases, the witness is still open to cross-examination by normal means, or via another special measure.

1   See above and www.scotland.gov.uk.
2   Letter from SLAB to all Legal Aid practitioners, 30 March 2006, available from www.slab.org.uk.
3   Criminal Procedure (Scotland) Act 1995, ss 271I(3) and 271K(2); Vulnerable Witnesses (Scotland) Act 2004, s 21(2).
4   CP(S)A 1995, s 271L(2); VW(S)A 2004, s 22(2).
5   CP(S)A 1995, s 271L(3); VW(S)A 2004, s 22(3).

Credibility and reliability of witnesses

35.39 Although the Vulnerable Witnesses Act has removed the test of competence before a person gives evidence, a witness's ability to understand the need to tell the truth remains clearly relevant when the witness is being examined and when the judge or jury assess the witness's reliability and credibility.

A witness with a mental illness or learning disability may be questioned to establish his or her credibility and reliability, although special arrangements, described above, may be made to enable the witness to give evidence more comfortably and effectively than by standing in the witness box.

Challenges to a witness's credibility are particularly, but not exclusively, important in criminal cases, to which most of this paragraph refers. In civil cases, rules as to admissibility of evidence tend to be less restrictive,[1] and it is in the criminal context that issues have arisen in relation to evidence concerning the credibility and reliability of witnesses with mental disorders.

Vulnerable witnesses are protected from examination or cross-examination by the accused personally, so in cases involving a vulnerable witness the court insists that the defence is conducted through a legal representative.[2]

Evidence from one witness about the credibility or reliability of another witness has not previously been admitted[3] but the situation has begun to change. The law now allows expert psychological or psychiatric evidence relating to any subsequent behaviour or statement of an alleged victim. This is allowed where it is necessary to remove any adverse effect on the person's credibility or reliability as a witness which the behaviour or statement might otherwise have caused.[4]

More generally, the courts have begun to take account of expert evidence suggesting that the evidence given by a witness is outside the bounds of reliability[5] or likely to be impaired by pathology,[6] all as assessed in objective terms.

A witness's expectation of being listened to in court may be dashed by demeaning cross-examination, and expert evidence challenging the witness' capacity for reliable or truthful account. In the end of the day it may still be competent to ask the court to rule that, having taken some evidence from the witness, the evidence is so unreliable due to the state of mind of the witness at the time of the events under recall or at the time of giving evidence, that it should be disregarded.

1   The Civil Evidence (Scotland) Act 1988 allows for hearsay evidence (evidence of what a third party said) to be admitted as proof of its contents, and removes the requirement for evidence to be corroborated. *M v Kennedy*, 1993 SCLR 69, is an example of the court taking great pains to ensure that it received the evidence of a person unable to speak.

2   Criminal Procedure (Scotland) Act 1995, s 288F, adding to the protection that already existed from this in cases of a sexual nature, s 288C-D.

3   *HM Advocate v Grimmond*, 2002 SLT 508, but its relevance went without question in *Green v HMA*, 1983 SCCR 42.

4   Criminal Procedure (Scotland) Act 1995, s 275C inserted by Vulnerable Witnesses (Scotland) Act 2004.

5   *Campbell v HM Advocate*, 2004 SCCR 220 (Evidence from linguists that it was unlikely that anyone would have made a statement in the precise combination of words said to have been used in an admission to police.)

6   *McBrearty v HM Advocate*, 2004 SLT 917 (Evidence that someone may be a pathological liar.)

Evidence of witness's character

35.40 Witnesses are in general open to attack on their past character in so far as this might be relevant to their credibility or reliability. For example, evidence may be led that a witness is a known drug user whose recollection is dimmed, or is of argumentative nature and may have provoked an alleged attack.[1] This in turn may open up scope for attack on the past character of the accused person in criminal cases.[2]

An attack on a witness's character may be only about the witness's general character rather than individual incidents (since it is not the witness who is on trial) but could include reference to behaviour or offending resulting from mental disorder or learning disability.

In cases involving offences against a child, or sexual crime, there is statutory protection from reference to the past character of the alleged victim and of the behaviour of the victim at any time other than the offence itself.[3] Some protection has attached to the complainer in a sexual case for many years, but the provisions were expanded greatly in 2002.[4]

Nevertheless, there are detailed grounds on which this protection may be over-ridden.[5] These are linked to the relevance and importance value of the evidence that sought and the 'proper administration of justice'.

The court may allow evidence demonstrating any condition or predisposition to which the complainer is or has been subject'[6] and this could include mental disorder. However the 'proper administration of justice' expressly includes considering the dignity and privacy of the witness, and the judge must bear this in mind when considering whether to admit the evidence. If such evidence is allowed, it is assumed that the court will allow evidence of the accused person's previous character, unless the accused can establish this is not appropriate.[7]

1   *Brady v H.M.Advocate*, 1986 SLT 686, *Walker v McGruther & Marshall*, 1982 SLT 345.
2   Under Criminal Procedure (Scotland) Act 1995, ss 266 or 270.
3   CP(S)A 1995, s 274.
4   CP(S)A 1995, ss 274–275A were introduced by the Sexual Offences (Procedure and Evidence) (Scotland) Act 2002. The previous prohibition applied only to the introduction by the defence of evidence of past sexual character of the complainer, and the provisions were considerably less detailed.
5   CP(S)A 1995, s 275.
6   CP(S)A 1995, s 275(1)(a)(ii).
7   CP(S)A 1995, s 275A.

Hearsay evidence

35.41 If a witness is not eligible for special measures or is unable to give evidence in court, there are other ways to help him or her give evidence. If someone is likely to be too ill to give evidence or cannot give it adequately, the prosecution or defence can apply to the judge for permission to allow previous statements of the witness as evidence. This kind of evidence is called hearsay evidence. This is when a witness gives evidence of what someone else has told him or her.

In civil cases all hearsay evidence (other than that in a witness statement) is now allowable in court.[1] Hearsay evidence is not normally allowed in the criminal courts. At common law hearsay evidence was allowed if the original maker of the statement was dead or permanently 'insane',[2] although whether it was allowed when the original speaker was permanently disabled was left open.[3]

Hearsay is now admissible in criminal cases if the person who made the statement is unable to give evidence in a competent manner because of his or her physical or mental condition.[4]

There are now many ways in which a person may give evidence in a competent manner, so it might be considered that use of hearsay evidence in criminal cases, at least under this general provision, is only for situations where other competent means of giving evidence are ruled out.[5]

The statement must be contained in a 'document', which includes any form of audio, visual or digital recording as well as statements recorded on paper, and heard by the person making the document.[6] The statement is allowed if the witness would have been a competent witness at the time when the statement was made.[7]

Other statutory exceptions allow for hearsay in a document to be admitted if the witness refuses to take the oath or affirm, or having taken it refuses to give evidence,[8] and a witness who gives evidence may adopt an earlier statement in a document[9] or record of identification[10] to fill a gap in recollection.[11]

These relaxations of the hearsay rule may be useful in some cases, but they are not as useful as having the witness in court giving evidence. These measures could be useful if a witness might not remember the events by the time of the trial or might be unable to give evidence at the trial.

1   Civil Evidence (Scotland) Act 1988, s 2.

2   *HM Advocate v Manson* (1897) 21 R (J) 5.

3   *McKie v Western SMT Co*, 1952 SC 206.

4   Criminal Procedure (Scotland) Act 1995, s 259(2)(a).

5   In practice this provision is little used, except when there is no other means of access to the evidence, or the evidence is uncontroversial, in which case it is likely to be the subject of agreement under ss 257–258. If all sides of a criminal case agree, the evidence can be admitted as hearsay even if the statutory grounds for admission are not made out. Criminal Procedure (Scotland) Act 1995, s 259(7).

6   CP(S)A 1995, s 262.

7 CP(S)A 1995, s 259(1)(c). It is thought that the reference to 'competence' may have been left by oversight rather than amended out when the competence test was removed by the Vulnerable Witnesses (Scotland) Act 2004.

8 CP(S)A 1995, s 259(2)(e).

9 CP(S)A 1995, s 260.

10 *Muldoon v Herron*, 1970 JC 30.

11 Or indeed to replace a denial of identification of the accused person in court, as in *Muldoon v Herron*, 1970 JC 30, *Smith v HM Advocate*, 1986, *Maxwell v HM Advocate* [1990 JC 340.

PART 9
DISCRIMINATION

Chapter 36

PROTECTION AGAINST DISCRIMINATION

36.01 The Disability Discrimination Act 1995 offers people with long-term mental disabilities protection against unfair discrimination in areas such as employment and education. For example, mental illness, or a history of mental illness, should not be a barrier to employment if the person is able to do the job in question. The law goes some way to reflecting this.

Unfortunately the legislation is somewhat complex, though the relevant Codes of Practice issued by the Disability Rights Commission help explain it. Although the Codes do not have statutory force, they are useful in helping establish what might be considered discriminatory practice and can be used as evidence in court or tribunal proceedings.

SOURCES OF INFORMATION

36.02 People who consider they have experienced discrimination should seek specialist advice. In employment claims, Legal Aid is available in the form of advice and assistance, and in a limited number of more complex cases for representation before tribunals.

For other claims Legal Aid advice and assistance is available and full Civil Legal Aid may be available for raising court action.

To qualify for Legal Aid, a claimant has to qualify financially and must satisfy the Scottish Legal Aid Board that there is a legal basis for the case, that it is reasonable in the particular circumstances of the case that he or she should receive Legal Aid and that financial help is not available from someone else, such as a trade union or insurance company.

A Law Centre may be able to offer advice, as can some Citizens Advice Bureaux.

ROLE OF DISABILITY RIGHTS COMMISSION

36.03 The Disability Rights Commission is the statutory body charged with reviewing the implementation of the Disability Discrimination Act and is responsible for the Codes of Practice.

The Commission provides Helpline Assistance, arranges independent conciliation and in limited cases may offer casework and legal assistance.

Copies of the legislation, Regulations and Codes of Practice, and some of the cases referred to in this chapter are all available on the Commission's website. At the end of 2007, the Commission for Equality and Human Rights will take over the powers and functions of the Disability Rights Commission.

CHANGES TO DISABILITY DISCRIMINATION ACT

36.04 The Disability Discrimination Act 1995 has been substantially amended since it was first introduced. Further changes to the legislation come into effect in December 2006, covering public authority functions and introducing the new disability equality duty.

This chapter looks at the definition of disability, discrimination in employment, the provision of goods, facilities and services, including insurance and housing, public authority functions, education and the disability equality duty.

DEFINITION OF DISABILITY

36.05 The definition of disability used in the Disability Discrimination Act is not the same as that which applies in other areas such as disability benefits. It may cover some people who would not ordinarily think of themselves as disabled, but equally may exclude some who do consider themselves to be disabled. The definition applies to all parts of the legislation. If someone wants to claim discrimination under the Disability Discrimination Act, he or she must be able to show that all parts of the definition apply.

A disabled person, including those with mental illness or learning disabilities, is covered under the legislation if he or she meets the statutory definition. This says that a person has a disability if he or she has a physical or mental impairment which has a substantial and long-term adverse effect on the person's ability to carry out normal day-to-day activities.[1]

Further details on each aspect of the definition is available in the Guidance on matters to be taken into account in determining questions relating to the definition of disability.[2]

Of particular importance in the case of mental illness, is the provision that people qualify for protection if they have in the past met the requirements of the definition, even if they are no longer disabled.[3]

1   Disability Discrimination Act 1995, s 1.
2   SI 1996/1455.
3   DDA 1995, s 2(1).

Substantial effect

36.06 An impairment does not count as a disability for the purposes of
the Disability Discrimination Act unless it has a substantial and long-
term adverse effect on a person's ability to carry out normal day-to-day
activities. 'Substantial' only means more than trivial. In this context, it
does not mean 'very large'.[1] 'Long-term' means that the illness must have
lasted or be likely to last for at least 12 months.[2]

This has the unfortunate result that it can be difficult for people who
are dismissed or otherwise discriminated against because of an episode
of illness to show that the definition applies.[3] In that event, it may be
possible to show that the condition is a recurring one.[4]

A mental impairment is taken to affect a person's ability to carry out
day-to-day activities only if it affects one or more of the broad categories
of capacity listed in the legislation. This list includes, amongst other
activities, a person's speech, mobility (which can include ability to leave
home), memory or ability to concentrate or understand, or perception of
risk of physical danger.[5] Most mental disabilities have these kinds of
effects.

The list does not specifically include work or social and leisure
activities. However the Court of Session has held that the impact of an
impairment on a person's duties at work can be considered if they
include any of the listed 'normal day-to-day' activities.[6]

1   *Goodwin v Patent Office*, 1999 IRLR 4 EAT.
2   Disability Discrimination Act 1995, Sched 1, para 2.
3   In *Cruickshank v VAW Motorcast Ltd*, 2002 IRLR 24 it was held that the material
     time at which to assess the applicant's disability is at the time of the alleged
     discriminatory act, in this case the dismissal, rather than at the time of the
     tribunal hearing.
4   See below.
5   Disability Discrimination Act 1995, Sched 1, para 4.
6   *Law Hospital NHS Trust v Rush*, 2001 IRLR 611.

Effects of medication

36.07 A person may take medication, or have other treatment, to relieve
the symptoms of an illness. When deciding whether that person is

covered by the definition, the effects of the medication or other treatment must be excluded when assessing whether the illness has a substantial effect.[1] In other words, what would the effect of the illness be if, for example, he or she stopped taking anti-depressants or stopped therapy or counselling?

Where an impairment ceases to have a substantial adverse effect on a person's ability to carry out normal day-to-day activities, it is treated as continuing to have that effect if that effect is likely to recur.

In a case where a senior cargo assistant had been off work because of depression, the tribunal held that at the time of the alleged discrimination, the condition was not likely to recur. Overturning the decision on appeal, the Employment Appeal Tribunal held that in considering recurring conditions, the tribunal must consider the actual adverse effects the claimant had had up to the time of the hearing.[2]

The illness does not have to recur, only the effect of it.

[1]   Disability Discrimination Act 1995, Sched 1, para 6.
[2]   *Greenwood v British Airways plc*, 1999 IRLR 600.

Progressive conditions

36.08 For progressive conditions there are two different rules. People diagnosed with HIV, multiple sclerosis or cancer are deemed to be disabled, irrespective of whether the definition is met.[1] For all other progressive conditions, a disabled person is covered only once it can be shown that the condition has had some effect on his or her day-to-day activities and the condition is likely to have a substantial adverse effect in the future.[2]

[1]   Disability Discrimination Act 1995, Sched 1, para 6A (as added by the Disability Discrimination Act 2005, s 18).
[2]   DDA 1995, Sched 1, para 8.

People who do not qualify

36.09 Certain conditions are excluded from meeting the definition of disability by the Disability Discrimination (Meaning of Disability) Regulations 1996.[1] These conditions include addiction to alcohol, nicotine or any substance (except as a result of medically prescribed treatment), a tendency to set fires, a tendency to steal, exhibitionism, voyeurism, and a tendency to physical or sexual abuse of other persons. The fact that a person has one of these conditions does not necessarily exclude him or her from being a disabled person by virtue of another impairment. It does not matter whether the other impairment was caused by the excluded condition or indeed if it was the cause of the excluded condition.[2]

The Act gives no protection to people who are not disabled, except for protection against victimisation.[3] This means that a person who has been treated less favourably because someone wrongly believes she or he is mentally ill or has a learning disability, is not covered by the Disability Discrimination Act.

1   SI 1996/1455.
2   Guidance on matters to be taken into account in determining questions relating to the definition of disability, paras A8 and A14.
3   See below.

EMPLOYMENT

36.10 The Disability Discrimination Act requires employers not to discriminate against disabled employees in advertising posts, recruitment, terms of employment, promotion, provision of training, dismissal,[1] or in any relationship after dismissal, for example in providing references.[2]

As well as applying to all workers, the employment provisions of the legislation include contract workers,[3] office holders, e.g. councillors,[4] occupational pension schemes,[5] partners in partnerships,[6] advocates,[7] and work placements.[8] Most voluntary work is not covered, and members of the armed forces are excluded.

The types of discrimination which are outlawed by the Disability Discrimination Act in relation to employment are direct discrimination; failure to make a reasonable adjustment; disability related discrimination, and harassment or victimisation.

An employer discriminates against an employee if he or she treats the person less favourably because of his or her disability (direct discrimination); treats the person less favourably for reasons relating to his or her disability (disability-related discrimination); fails to comply with a duty to make reasonable adjustments; or harasses or victimises someone.

1   Disability Discrimination Act 1995, s 4(2).
2   DDA 1995, s 4(5).

3   DDA 1995, s 4B.
4   DDA 1995, ss 4C–4F, and see ss 15A–15B.
5   DDA 1995, ss 4G–4K.
6   DDA 1995, ss 6A–6C.
7   DDA 1995, ss 7C–7D.
8   DDA 1995, ss14C–14D.

Direct discrimination

36.11 An employer's conduct amounts to direct discrimination if the employer treats a disabled person less favourably than a person not having that particular disability is (or would be) treated; the reason for the treatment is the person's disability; and the relevant circumstances of the person with whom the comparison is made are the same or not materially different from those of the disabled person.[1]

To show that treatment is on the grounds of disability, the disabled employee has to show that but for the disability, he or she would not have been treated in that way. This may be because the employer has made stereotypical assumptions about the disability or its effect, or because of prejudice about disability. For example, it would be direct discrimination to advertise an internal promotion stating that people with a history of mental illness would not be suitable for the post.

Direct discrimination can never be justified.[2]

1   Disability Discrimination Act 1995, s 3A(5).
2   See below for justification.

Reasonable adjustments

36.12 As well as the duty not to treat a person unfairly because of his or her disability, there is a more positive duty on employers to do what is reasonable to accommodate disabled employees. If working practices or a physical feature of premises put an employee at a substantial disadvantage in relation to other employees, the employer should make changes which are reasonable in the circumstances.[1] The Act gives some examples of reasonable adjustments, such as changing hours of work, changing the place of work, giving training and support and moving someone to another job.[2]

In a landmark case involving the Disability Rights Commission in Scotland, the House of Lords held that to the extent that the duty to make reasonable adjustments requires it, the employer is not only permitted to, but is obliged to treat a disabled person more favourably than others.

Transfer to an alternative post, when provided as a reasonable adjustment, can include a move upwards, downwards, or sideways.[3]

In the case of people with mental illness, adjustments to working arrangements might include moving the employee to a less stressful environment, allowing time off for medical appointments, and arranging flexible working hours, or providing a quiet room, for example. A person with a learning disability might require extra training or supervision to help him or her do the job.

What it is reasonable for an employer to provide depends on the circumstances of the case. A large employer has more resources to make adjustments than a small employer. Again the Disability Discrimination Act gives a list of issues to consider when thinking about what is reasonable, such as the extent to which taking the step would prevent the effect in relation to which the duty is imposed, the extent to which it is practicable, as well as the financial and other costs that would be incurred and the resources of the employer.[4]

[1]   Disability Discrimination Act 1995, s 4A(1).
[2]   DDA 1995, s 18B(2).
[3]   *Archibald v Fife Council* [2004] IRLR 651 HL.
[4]   DDA 1995, s 18B.

Disability-related discrimination

36.13 An employer's conduct amounts to disability-related discrimination[1] if it is for a reason related to the disabled employee's disability; and the treatment is less favourable than the way in which the employer treats or would treat others to whom that reason does not or would not apply; and the employer cannot show that the treatment is justified in one of the ways permitted by the law.[2]

An example of disability-related discrimination would be the dismissal of a disabled man after a long period of sick leave. The reason for the treatment would be the sickness absence rather that the disability itself (so it does not amount to direct discrimination).[3] The employer can, however, justify this type of discrimination if the employer has a material and substantial reason, and has complied with the duty to make reasonable adjustments.[4]

[1]   Disability Discrimination Act 1995, s 3A(1).
[2]   For justification see below.

638

3 *Clark v Novacold*, 1999 IRLR 318, considered whether dismissing a person who had been off sick with a disability-related illness constituted less favourable treatment under the Disability Discrimination Act.

4 See above.

Job applications

36.14 One of the difficulties for people who have a psychiatric history is deciding whether they should reveal details when they apply for jobs. On the one hand, people now have protection against discrimination, on the other discrimination can be hard to prove especially at recruitment stage, if an application is refused on an apparently legitimate ground, such as lack of experience or academic qualifications.

There is nothing in the Disability Discrimination Act prohibiting employers from asking if an applicant has a disability. If a person answers questions about his or her medical history dishonestly, this could be a ground for dismissing him or her, though an employer cannot use disability related information to discriminate against someone.

There is no easy answer, but one factor to bear in mind is that employers cannot be held accountable for not adjusting working practices to assist an employee if they did not know, and it cannot be shown that they ought to have known, of the employee's disability.[1]

1 Disability Discrimination Act 1995, s 4A(3).

Justified discrimination

36.15 If direct discrimination is established or if there has been a failure to make reasonable adjustments, these can never be justified under the law. Justification is permitted in disability-related discrimination only, if the reason for the treatment is both material to the circumstances of the particular case and substantial[1] and the employer has complied with the duty to make reasonable adjustments.[2]

'Material' means that it must relate to the individual employee and not be a blanket justification and 'substantial' means it must be more than trivial. For example, health and safety grounds may justify less favourable treatment, but only if there has been an individual assessment of the circumstances, including a suitable risk assessment by a properly qualified person, if necessary.

1 Disability Discrimination Act 1995, s 3A(3).

2 DDA 1995, s 3A(6).

Harassment

36.16 Unlawful harassment occurs where an employer, for a reason which relates to a disabled person's disability, engages in unwanted conduct which has the purpose or effect of violating the disabled person's dignity or creating an intimidating, hostile, degrading humiliating or offensive environment for him or her.[1]

An example of this would be an employee with a history of mental illness being called offensive and humiliating names by work colleagues.

[1]   Disability Discrimination Act 1995, s 3B.

Victimisation

36.17 It is unlawful victimisation for an employer to treat someone less favourably because the employer believes that the person has made a complaint, raised proceedings or given evidence in connection with proceedings under the Disability Discrimination Act.[1]

The person need not himself or herself be disabled to be protected against victimisation. This is the only part of the Disability Discrimination Act which protects disabled and non-disabled people.

[1]   Disability Discrimination Act 1995, s 55.

Remedies

36.18 Efforts should always be made to resolve employment disputes within the workplace, but inevitably, in some cases a claim to an employment tribunal may be necessary.

Under the Disability Discrimination Act, the usual time limit is three months, subject to extension where the tribunal considers this is just and equitable in all the circumstances.[1]

There are also detailed rules under the Employment Act 2002 which require that in certain circumstances, an employee must first make a complaint in writing under the statutory grievance procedure before the employee can proceed to a tribunal.

The way the legislation works is complicated. In cases where the rules require a written grievance to be made, the usual time limit is extended by three months. This written grievance requirement is not necessary, for example, if the employee has been dismissed. Further advice should be sought about the circumstances in which the grievance procedure has to be used and how the time limits are calculated.

1   Disability Discrimination Act Sched 3, para 3.

TRADE ORGANISATIONS AND QUALIFICATIONS BODIES

36.19 The law also recognises that people who are mentally ill or who have a learning disability may be discriminated against by trade organisations and bodies which confer professional or trade qualifications. Such discrimination can affect a person's prospects of getting a job or keeping a job, or of getting promotion. An example might be a nursing organisation refusing to admit a woman with a history of mental health problems without further enquiry. This is likely to be unlawful.[1]

The Disability Discrimination Act places duties on such organisations not to discriminate. These are similar to the types of duties on employers.

The Act makes it unlawful for a trade organisation to discriminate against a disabled person in relation to membership of the organisation or access to membership benefits. This covers arrangements for deciding who should be offered membership, the terms of membership offered, or the refusal to accept, or deliberately not accepting, an application for membership.

A trade organisation is defined as an organisation of workers or of employees, or any other organisation whose members carry on a particular profession or trade for the purposes of which the organisation exists. Examples are trade unions, employers' associations, the Royal College of Nursing, the Law Society and the British Computer Society.[2]

The Act also makes it unlawful for a qualifications body to discriminate against a disabled person in relation to conferring professional or trade qualifications. This covers the way members are given or denied access to any benefits, or depriving the member of membership or varying the terms of membership, or subjecting the member to any other detriment.

A qualifications body is defined as an authority or body which can confer, renew or extend a professional or trade qualification. Examples would be the General Medical Council, City and Guilds, or the Driving Standards Agency.[3]

The forms of discrimination which are unlawful are like those covered in employment: direct discrimination; failure to make reasonable adjustments; disability-related discrimination; victimisation.

1   Code of Practice Trade Organisations and Qualifications Bodies, para 7.5.
2   Code of Practice, para 3.8.
3   Code of Practice, para 3.9.

GOODS, FACILITIES AND SERVICES

36.20 It is unlawful for providers of goods, facilities and services to discriminate unfairly against disabled people in the way in which they provide goods or offer facilities[1] or services.[2] Providers of goods, facilities and services also have a duty under the legislation to make reasonable adjustments for disabled people.[3] The term 'service provider' is used here to cover those providing goods, facilities and services covered by the Disability Discrimination Act.

The legislation applies to all those who provide services to the public, including voluntary organisations, and applies whether or not services are provided free of charge.[4] It extends to, for example, shops, leisure facilities, banks, telecommunications, sports facilities, hotels and guest houses, employment agencies, professions, trades and local and other public authorities.[5] This would include GPs' surgeries, hospitals, local authority social work departments and sheriff courts, amongst many others. There are some services which are specifically excluded.[6] Insurance and domestic housing are dealt with separately below.

1   The word 'facilities' is not defined in the legislation or in the Code of Practice, but covers, for example, the provision of facilities by way of banking or insurance or for grants, loans, credit or finance' and 'facilities for entertainment, recreation or refreshment' in terms of the Disability Discrimination Act 1995, s 19(3).
2   See DDA 1995, s 19.
3   DDA 1995, s 21.
4   DDA 1995, s 19(2).
5   DDA 1995, s 19(3).
6   See below.

Less favourable treatment

36.21 The Disability Discrimination Act says that service providers must not discriminate against a disabled person by refusing to provide services, by providing services of a worse standard or on worse terms.[1] Discrimination means treating the disabled person less favourably for a reason related to his or her disability, in circumstances that are not justified.[2]

The following is an example of less favourable treatment in the terms of service provided. A person who has a diagnosis of schizophrenia is booking a holiday. The travel agent asks her for a larger deposit than the travel agent asks for from other customers. The travel agent believes, without good cause, that because of her disability she is more likely to cancel her holiday. This is likely to be against the law.

[1]   Disability Discrimination Act 1995, s 19(1).

[2]   DDA 1995, s 20.

Reasonable adjustments

36.22 In addition to the duty not to discriminate by providing less favourable treatment, the Disability Discrimination Act imposes a positive duty on service providers to adjust practices to make facilities more accessible to disabled people.[1] There are three types of reasonable adjustment: changes to policies, practices and procedures; provision of auxiliary aids and services; and changes to physical features.

Service providers must make reasonable adjustments to their policies, practices or procedures if these make it impossible or unreasonably difficult for disabled people to use their services.[2] It is important to note that the question is whether the service provider made a reasonable adjustment and not whether a person who is not disabled would have been treated in the same way in similar circumstances. The same policies can be applied to everyone, but they are still discriminatory if disabled people cannot use the service, or find it unreasonably difficult.

Service providers must also take reasonable steps to provide auxiliary aids or services to make use of the service easier.[3] An example of this would be the provision of an interpreter for a meeting with a doctor, or supplying information in EasyRead form for people with learning disabilities.

[1]   Disability Discrimination Act 1995, s 21.

[2]   DDA 1995, s 21(1).

[3]   DDA 1995, s 21(4).

Physical adaptations

36.23 Service providers must overcome barriers created by physical features which make it impossible or unreasonably difficult for disabled people to make use of the service. The service providers must take reasonable steps to remove the feature, alter or avoid it, or provide services by alternative methods.[1]

The question of what is reasonable depends on the circumstances of the case. Some of the factors which may be taken into account include the cost of the adjustment and the number of people likely to be affected, as well as the size of the service provider's organisation. The Code of Practice[2] explains in more detail what is meant by reasonable steps.

1   Disability Discrimination Act 1995, s 21(2).
2   Code of Practice: Rights of Access: Services and Premises, chap 7.

Exemptions

36.24 Some services are excluded from the Disability Discrimination Act. The 'use of any means of transport' is not covered, but related services such as booking facilities, ticketing, timetables, stations and waiting rooms are covered. From December 2006 a series of gradual changes to the rules covering public transport is being made by way of regulations.[1]

The legislation does not apply to private clubs who have less than 25 members. Clubs with 25 members or more must not treat a disabled member less favourably for reasons relating to his or her disability. From December 2006, these private clubs must also make reasonable adjustments.[2]

Clubs which are essentially commercial organisations, but which impose a membership fee, are included in the same way as any other service provider.[3]

1   Disability Discrimination Act 2005, s 5.
2   DDA 1995, ss 21F–21J as added by DDA 2005, s 12.
3   The examples given in the Code of Practice are of video and leisure clubs, para 3.11.

Justification

36.25 In limited circumstances, the Disability Discrimination Act permits a service provider to justify less favourable treatment of a disabled person or a failure to make a reasonable adjustment.[1] The test of justification is twofold. It depends on the service provider believing one of the relevant conditions listed applies,[2] and it being reasonable for the service provider to believe that.

The Act lists five conditions which may be satisfied before the service provider can show that the discrimination was legally justified:

- Different treatment of disabled people can be justified if there is an objective health or safety consideration for refusing or modifying the service given. To use this justification, the service provider must have carried out a qualified audit to identify the risk.

- If a disabled person is unable to give informed consent to a transaction, it is not discrimination to refuse to deal with him or her. This depends on the type of transaction involved. For example, if a jeweller refuses to sell a pair of earrings to a person with a learning disability whose order is clear and who is able to pay for the earrings, this is unlikely to be justified.[3]

  If there is a person who is legally entitled to act on behalf of the disabled person (such as an attorney or guardian), discrimination cannot be justified in this way.[4]

- It is not discrimination to charge more for a service if there is a greater cost involved in providing the service to the disabled person. However, a service provider cannot charge for reasonable adjustments.

- Discrimination can also be justified if otherwise the service could not be provided to the public or if it is a way of ensuring that the service can be given to the public.

- Service providers do not have to make changes that would fundamentally change the nature of the service in question.

[1]   Disability Discrimination Act 1995, s 20.
[2]   DDA 1995, s 20(4).
[3]   Code of Practice Access to Services: Services and Premises, para 8.20.
[4]   Disability Discrimination (Services and Premises) Regulations 1996 (SI 1996/ 1836).

Remedies

36.26 An action can be raised in the sheriff court alleging discrimination by a service provider.[1] The action can ask the court for damages (compensation), for a declaration by the court that there has been discrimination, for a court order (interdict) to stop further discrimination, or for an order requiring a reasonable adjustment to be carried out (order for specific implement).

The court proceedings must be started within six months of the alleged discrimination.[2] This is a very tight time limit when compared to other court proceedings. The time limit is extended to eight months if parties use the Disability Rights Commission's independent conciliation service.

A person who considers that he or she has been discriminated against or subjected to harassment can use a questionnaire procedure.[3] This procedure, which is similar to that available in employment tribunal proceedings, allows the person to seek relevant information from the service provider, to help decide whether to institute proceedings and if he or she does so, to formulate and present the case in the most effective manner.

1 Disability Discrimination Act 1995, s 25.

2 DDA 1995, Sched 3, para 6.

3 Under DDA 1995, s 56.

INSURANCE

36.27 The Disability Discrimination Act governs insurance, and although it is included in the Code of Practice dealing with Rights of Access: Services and Premises, it has its own particular rules, for example regarding justification. The special rules on insurance only apply to insurance services provided by an insurer.

Anyone with a history of mental illness or mental disability may be concerned that the small print of insurance policies may exclude cover, for example, for 'pre-existing conditions' or for people travelling against medical advice, all of which might be relevant.

Regulations made under the Disability Discrimination Act recognise that in certain circumstances it is not unlawful discrimination for an insurer to impose different conditions when insuring a disabled person (including a person with a mental disability).[1]

The rules say that less favourable terms may be justified if they are based on information which is relevant to the assessment of the risk to be insured and it is reasonable to rely on the source of information. The insurer must also be able to prove that the less favourable treatment is then justified by the information they have received and any other relevant factors.[2]

The Code of Practice gives an example of a man with manic depression applying for motor insurance. The insurer may have statistical evidence that his type of illness involves a greater risk. However if there is medical evidence that his condition is stable and his driving is unimpaired the Code says the insurer would not be justified in charging a higher premium.[3]

The kind of information on which insurers are entitled to rely includes statistical or actuarial data and medical reports. The information must be current and applicable. An insurer cannot rely on general impressions and assumptions.[4] See chapter 34 for further discussion.

1   Disability Discrimination (Services and Premises) Regulations 1996 (SI 1996/1836).
2   Disability Discrimination (Services and Premises) Regulations 1996 (SI 1996/1836), reg 2(2).
3   Code of Practice Rights of Access: Services and Premises, para 9.4.
4   Disability Discrimination (Services and Premises) Regulations 1996 (SI 1996/1836), reg 2(2)(b).

HOUSING

36.28 The Disability Discrimination Act 1995 covers selling, letting and management of domestic housing, referred to in the Act to as 'premises'.[1] The law makes it unlawful for a person selling or leasing property to refuse to sell or let to a disabled person, or to do so only on worse terms.[2] Nor must disabled people be discriminated against when waiting lists are being drawn up.[3]

Managers of property are also barred from discriminating against disabled people in the way they offer any benefits and facilities (or denying the use of these benefits or facilities) at the property, or in their eviction policies.[4]

Discrimination in this area means treating the person less favourably for reasons relating to his or her disability in a way which cannot be justified.[5] The tests for justification are similar to those in the provision of goods and services.[6] There must be reasonable grounds for believing that the decision is justified.

An example of discrimination in housing is given in the Code of Practice.[7] A housing association has a blanket policy of requiring all new tenants with a history of mental health problems to have only a short-term tenancy in the first instance. This is so that the association can see whether such tenants are suitable. This policy is not applied to other tenants and is likely to be unlawful.

1   Disability Discrimination Act 1995, ss 22–24L.
2   DDA 1995, ss 22(1)(a) and (b).
3   DDA 1995, s 22(1)(c).
4   DDA 1995, s 22(3).
5   DDA 1995, s 24(1).
6   DDA Act 1995, ss 24 (2)–(5). See above and the Code of Practice Rights of Access: Services and Premises, chap 17.
7   Code of Practice Rights of Access: Services and Premises, para 14.6.

Reasonable adjustments

36.29 From December 2006, there is a duty to make reasonable adjustments in relation to a disabled person who rents or lawfully occupies premises. This includes a duty to provide auxiliary aids or services, or to change policies, practices or procedures which make it impossible or unreasonably difficult for a disabled person to enjoy the premises or make use of any benefit or facility.

Exemptions

36.30 These rules do not apply to private transactions where the seller lives on the premises, unless the seller uses an estate agent or publishes an advertisement about a sale.[1] They do not apply to small premises where the owner or occupier shares accommodation with people who are not members of his or her household.[2]

1   Disability Discrimination Act 1995, s 22(2).
2   DDA 1995, s 23.

Improvements

36.31 Tenants in the social rented sector can ask their landlords for consent to carry out improvements in their home and landlords cannot unreasonably withhold consent.[1]

From December 2006, private landlords are prohibited from unreasonably withholding consent to improvements to the premises which are needed to accommodate disability, if requested by the tenant in writing. Improvements include any addition to or alteration in the fittings and fixtures or to the provision of services.[2]

1   Housing (Scotland) Act 2001, s 28.
2   H(S)A 2006, s 52.

Remedies

36.32 A claim of unlawful discrimination under the premises part of the Disability Discrimination Act is made by taking out an action in the sheriff court, in a similar way to claims in relation to goods and services. The action must be started within six months of the act complained of.

An action under the Housing (Scotland) Act 2006 is slightly different, and the person should seek legal advice.

PUBLIC AUTHORITY FUNCTIONS

36.33 Public authorities are covered by the Disability Discrimination Act insofar as they are employers, or education authorities, or service providers or in relation to premises. From December 2006,[1] the Disability Discrimination Act prohibits discrimination by public authorities in carrying out their functions.

A public authority includes any organisation certain of whose functions are of a public nature. An example of a public authority exercising a function would be the police arresting a suspect. Some public authorities are excluded, such as the security services.[2]

A public authority exercising its functions discriminates against a disabled person, if, for a reason relating to the person's disability, it treats that person less favourably than it treats or would treat others to whom that reason does not or would not apply, and it cannot show any justification.[3]

It is also discrimination if a public authority fails to make reasonable adjustments for a disabled person, without justification, and that makes it impossible or unreasonably difficult for the person to benefit from the function being carried out, or means that the person is subjected to an unreasonably adverse detriment.[4]

The principles applying to these two types of discrimination (less favourable treatment and the duty to make reasonable adjustments) are similar to those set out above in relation to discrimination by service providers.

Treatment is justified where the public authority has a genuine belief that one of the conditions in the Disability Discrimination Act applies and it is reasonable to hold that belief.[5] Treatment is also justified where it is a proportionate means of achieving a legitimate aim.

1 Disability Discrimination Act 2005, s 2 added ss 21B–21E to Disability Discrimination Act 1995.
2 DDA 1995, s 21C.
3 DDA 1995, s 21D(1).
4 DDA 1995, s 21D(2).
5 DDA 1995, s 21D.

EDUCATION: PEOPLE UNDER 16

36.34 It is unlawful for education authorities and independent and grant-aided schools[1] to discriminate against pupils and prospective pupils who are disabled. Schools and education authorities cannot discriminate when deciding whom they will admit to school, in the education and associated services provided nor in whom and how they exclude from school.[2]

This means that activities such as school sports, clubs and trips are covered by the Disability Discrimination Act, as well as homework, lunchtime arrangements and exams.

There are two main duties on education authorities and independent and grant-aided schools, the duty not to treat disabled pupils less favourably;[3] and the 'reasonable adjustment duty'.[4]

1 Disability Discrimination Act 1995, Sched 4A.
2 DDA 1995, s 28A.
3 DDA 1995, s 28B(1).
4 DDA 1995, ss 28B(2) and 28C.

Equal treatment

36.35 The duty not to treat disabled pupils less favourably occurs if for a reason relating to his or her disability, a disabled child is treated less favourably than a pupil to whom that reason does not apply.[1]

For example, it may be discrimination to exclude a child who has been behaving badly in school, if that behaviour was because of a mental disability.

1 Disability Discrimination Act 1995, s 28B(1).

Reasonable adjustments

36.36 The second duty is to take reasonable steps to avoid placing disabled pupils at a substantial disadvantage, in comparison with those who are not disabled.[1] For example, a school may have a duty to allow a mentally ill pupil more time to sit her exam if her illness causes her to take longer to complete tasks.

What is reasonable depends on the individual circumstances of each case. The Code of Practice lists some of the factors which may be relevant in considering whether a particular adjustment might be reasonable.[2]

This duty applies only to adjusting policies, practices and procedures. A school does not have to provide auxiliary aids or services or to remove or alter physical features.

The reasonable adjustment duty requires schools to make reasonable adjustments in anticipation of any child having a need for the adjustment.

Education authorities and independent and grant-aided schools must review their policies, practices and procedures to ensure they do not discriminate, well in advance of any child with a disability coming to the school. Discrimination occurs where there has been a failure to make reasonable adjustments and this leads to a detriment for an individual child.

[1]   Disability Discrimination Act 1995, s 28C(1).

[2]   Code of Practice for Schools Disability Discrimination Act 1995: Part 4, chap 6.

Justification

36.37 Less favourable treatment of a disabled child may be justified if it is the result of a permitted form of selection. Both less favourable treatment and a failure to make reasonable adjustments may be justified where the reason for the treatment or failure is both material to the circumstances of the particular case and substantial.[1]

This means the reason must relate to the particular child and must be more than trivial. In the example at 36.35 above, the school may argue that if the child's behaviour was violent, it can justify the pupil's exclusion on the grounds of the health and safety of other pupils and staff.

However, an education authority, independent or grant-aided school can only use this justification defence if they have made all reasonable adjustments which may be required. So, in the example, if the school had not trained the staff in how to deal with the child's needs, the school may not be able to justify its actions.

¹   Disability Discrimination Act 1995, ss 28B(6) and (7).

Access strategy

36.38 There is a further duty on education authorities, independent and grant-aided schools to prepare and implement accessibility strategies to improve access for disabled pupils.[1]

The strategies must include improvements in access to the curriculum, improvements to the physical environment to increase access to education and associated services and improvements in communication with disabled pupils. These strategies should be made available for parents to see.

Education authorities also have duties to children under the Education (Additional Support for Learning) (Scotland) Act 2004. See chapter 33. Disabled pupils may have rights under this legislation, along with other children who are not disabled.

The Act introduces the concept of 'additional support needs', covering children or young people who, for whatever reason, require additional support for learning. Additional support needs include needs arising from any factor which causes a barrier to learning, whether that relates to disability or to social, emotional, or other circumstances.

Education Authorities have a duty to make adequate and efficient provision of additional support for children and young people with additional support needs. Some disabled children may also be eligible for a co-ordinated support plan if significant additional support is needed from, for example, social work services. The education authority has an additional duty to pupils who have a co-ordinated support plan, to try to make sure that additional support is also provided by the other relevant agencies.

¹   Education (Disability Strategies and Pupil's Educational Records) (Scotland) Act 2002.

Remedies

36.39 Parents can pursue claims of discrimination, as can pupils over the age of 16 in their own right. A pupil under the age of 16 can also pursue a claim, including raising a court action, if the pupil has a general understanding of what it means to do so. There is a presumption that children over the age of 12 have sufficient age and maturity to instruct a solicitor. Children under the age of 12 may instruct a solicitor if they can show sufficient understanding.

A court action can be raised in the sheriff court claiming unlawful discrimination. It must be raised within six months of the date of the discrimination. This period is extended to eight months if parties use the Disability Rights Commission's independent conciliation service.

The action can ask the court for a declaration by the court that there has been discrimination, for a court order to stop further discrimination, or for an order that the education authority, independent or grant-aided school take action to comply with their statutory duties. The court cannot award any financial compensation.

EDUCATION: PEOPLE AGED OVER 16

36.40 The Disability Discrimination Act[1] prohibits disability discrimination in the provision of post-16 education. The provisions cover higher education institutions, colleges of further education, schools providing education for adults and education authorities securing community education.

These education providers are referred to in the Disability Discrimination Act as 'responsible bodies'. The rules do not cover other education providers, such as private colleges.

The law relating to discrimination in education for people aged over 16 mirrors that for people aged under-16 education in the activities covered by the duty. It is unlawful to discriminate when deciding who will be admitted to a college or institution, in the education and associated services provided and in how disabled students are excluded. Associated services might include, for example, exams, graduation ceremonies, counselling services, childcare facilities, or campus shops.

Again, like in the law relating to pre-16 education, there are two key duties on responsible bodies, the duty not to treat disabled students less favourably and the reasonable adjustment duty.

[1]   Sections 28R–31A and Sched 4C paras 1 and 5.

Equal treatment

36.41 The duty not to treat disabled students less favourably arises if for a reason relating to his or her disability, a disabled student or potential student is treated less favourably than someone to whom that reason does not apply.[1]

For example, it may be discrimination to refuse an application from a dyslexic student to do a distance learning degree in English. The treatment is less favourable when compared to other students and the reason for the treatment relates to the disability.

Less favourable treatment of a disabled student may be justified by the responsible body where the reason for the treatment or failure is both material to the circumstances of the particular case and substantial. This means the reason must relate to the particular student and must be more than trivial.

A responsible body can use this justification defence only if they have made all reasonable adjustments which may be required. In the example of the dyslexic student, these steps could include, for example, allowing the student more time and providing a scribe to help the student complete any assessments required.

[1]   Disability Discrimination Act 1995, ss 28R and 28S.

Reasonable adjustments

36.42 Responsible bodies, the educational institutions referred to above must also take reasonable steps to avoid placing disabled students at a substantial disadvantage, in comparison with those who are not disabled.[1]

For example, a student with depression might, because of the effects of her medication, find it difficult to attend a work placement that requires attendance early in the morning. A reasonable adjustment would be for the college to arrange for this student's placement to take place later in the day.

What steps are reasonable depends on the individual circumstances of each case. The Code of Practice lists some of the factors which may be relevant to considering whether a particular adjustment might be reasonable.[2] These include the need to maintain academic and other prescribed standards, the body's financial resources, the financial assistance which might be available, the cost of taking a particular step, and health and safety requirements.[3]

In education for people over 16, the reasonable adjustment duty extends not only to adjusting policies, practices and procedures, but also to providing auxiliary aids or services and removing or altering physical features.

The reasonable adjustment duty is a duty owed to disabled students and the public at large. Responsible bodies must review their policies, practices and procedures well in advance, to ensure they do not discriminate, as well as address any need for auxiliary aids or services or any need to make adjustments to physical features of premises. Discrimination occurs where there has been a failure to make reasonable adjustments and this leads to a detriment for an individual student.

1   Disability Discrimination Act 1995, ss 28S and 28T.
2   Code of Practice Post-16 Disability Discrimination Act 1995: Part 4, chap 6.
3   DDA 1995, s 28T(2).

Remedies

36.43 An action can be raised in the sheriff court alleging discrimination by the responsible body, in a similar way to that in respect of claims against service providers.[1] The action can ask the court for damages (compensation), for a declaration by the court that there has been discrimination, for a court order to stop further discrimination, or for an order that a reasonable adjustment is carried out (specific implement).

The court proceedings must be started within six months of the alleged discrimination.[2] This period is extended to eight months if the parties use the Disability Rights Commission's independent conciliation service.

1   See above.
2   Disability Discrimination Act 1995, Sched 3, paras 12 and 13.

DISABILITY EQUALITY DUTY

36.44 So far, this chapter has looked at the rights and remedies of individuals who have been the victims of discrimination. The Disability Discrimination Act 2005 introduced a new and very different type of duty which seeks to prevent discrimination from happening in the first place.

From December 2006 all public authorities[1] when carrying out their functions, must have due regard to the need to eliminate unlawful disability discrimination, eliminate unlawful harassment, promote equality of opportunity, promote positive attitudes towards disabled people and encourage the participation of disabled people in public life.[2]

The duty builds on the Disability Discrimination Act, but at the same time is a new approach, as it is not about individual entitlement. Instead, the duty focuses on organisational change rather than individual adjustments.

The aim of the duty is to avoid circumstances arising in which disabled people are discriminated against, by making sure that consideration is given, at an early stage, to how the way that organisation's policies, practices and procedures affect disabled people.

1   Disability Discrimination Act 1995, ss 49A–49F, as added by the Disability Discrimination Act 2005, s 3.
2   DDA 2005, s 49A.

Specific duties

36.45 In addition to this general duty, certain public authorities are subject to what are known as specific duties.[1] The regulations set out specific steps which must be taken to assist these public authorities fulfil the general duty.

This includes a duty to publish a Disability Equality Scheme demonstrating how the authority intends to fulfil its general and specific duties, involve disabled people in the development of the Scheme, carry out impact assessments, make arrangements for gathering relevant information, develop an 'action plan', take the steps set out in its action plan within three years and publish a report.

1   Disability Discrimination Act 1995, s 49D, Disability Discrimination (Public Authorities)(Statutory Duties)(Scotland) Regulations 2005 (SI 2005/565).

Effect of duty

36.46 The public authority duty does not give any individual rights to disabled people, but an individual, as well as the Disability Rights Commission, could seek to challenge by judicial review any public authority considered in breach of the general duty.

The Commission also has the power to serve a compliance notice, if satisfied that a public authority is failing to comply with the specific duty and the Commission can enforce the notice through proceedings in the sheriff court.[1]

1   Disability Discrimination Act 1995, ss 49E and 49F.

PART 10
PEOPLE WITH ADDITIONAL NEEDS

Chapter 37

RESPECT FOR DIVERSITY

37.01 This chapter looks at how the mental health and community care systems should respond to the differing needs of people using mental health or community care services.

The Millan Committee highlighted issues of concern.[1] It recommended that, as well as prohibiting discrimination, the law should impose a positive duty on services to consider the needs and backgrounds of users of services. The Mental Health (Care and Treatment) Act principles of equality and respect for diversity reflect these recommendations.

[1]   *New directions*, chap 18.

GENERAL EQUALITY DUTIES

Non discrimination

37.02 UK anti-discrimination laws (the Sex Discrimination Act 1975, Race Relations Act 1976 and Disability Discrimination Act 1995) outlaw discrimination and impose a general duty on all public authorities to promote equality.[1] We look at these duties in outline below.

Discrimination law is a matter for the Westminster Parliament. The Equality Act 2006, which is expected to come into effect in 2007, established a new single Commission for Equality and Human Rights. The Commission brings all six strands of discrimination; race, age, gender, disability, religion and sexual orientation, into one unified organisation. There is concern that people less able to speak up for their rights may miss out.

The Equality Act outlaws discrimination on grounds of religion and belief. The Secretary of State can pass regulations outlawing discrimination on grounds of sexual orientation.

The Commission for Equality and Human Rights has a duty to work to reduce prejudice against people on the grounds of age, gender, gender reassignment, religion and/or belief and sexual orientation.[2]

[1]   There is a duty to promote gender equality in the Equality Act 2006.
[2]   Equality Act 2006, s 3.

Respect for equality

37.03 Although the Scottish Parliament is not able to legislate on discrimination matters, it has passed laws showing its commitment to anti-discriminatory practices.[1] These laws oblige local authorities and the National Health Service in Scotland to respect equal opportunities, as defined in the Scotland Act 1998 (the Act giving Scotland devolved government).

All these authorities must act in a way that encourages equal opportunities.[2] This means they must try to prevent discrimination on the grounds of sex, marital status, race, language, social origin, or personal attributes, (for example, religious beliefs or political opinions).[3] This applies to health boards, special health boards and the Common Services Agency of the National Health Service in Scotland. The local authority duty extends to the police and some other organisations.[4]

These duties do not cover the Mental Welfare Commission, the Public Guardian or the Mental Health Tribunal for Scotland, but they are subject to the laws on race, sex and disability discrimination and the racial and disability equality duties referred to above. The Commission and the tribunal are subject to additional duties under the Mental Health (Care and Treatment) Act. See below. These bodies may commit to anti-discriminatory practice that meets or surpasses their legal obligations.

[1]   Local Government in Scotland Act 2003, National Health Service Reform (Scotland) Act 2004.
[2]   LGISA 2003, s 59. National Health Service (Scotland) Act 1978, as amended, s 2D.
[3]   Scotland Act 1998, Sched 5, Pt II, s L2.
[4]   LGISA 2003, s 16(1).

MENTAL HEALTH ACT DUTIES

Principles

37.04 The Mental Health (Care and Treatment) Act obliges authorities to consider needs arising from a person's disability, gender, religious or ethnic origins.

These duties apply wherever a person is exercising functions under the Act. This includes decisions about the use of compulsion but also, for example, access to independent advocacy and local authority welfare services.

Two of the Act's principles underline this commitment. These are non-discrimination and respect for diversity.

Non-discrimination

37.05 Anyone carrying out functions under the Mental Health (Care and Treatment) Act must do so in a way that encourages equal opportunities and the observance of the equal opportunity requirements.[1] See above. This obliges them to carry out their functions in a way that attempts to reduce discrimination.

The duty applies to the Scottish Ministers, the Mental Welfare Commission, local authorities, health boards, special health boards (such as the State Hospitals Board for Scotland), hospital managers, mental health officers, responsible medical officers, doctors and nurses.[2]

[1]   Mental Health (Care and Treatment) (Scotland) Act 2003, s 3(2).
[2]   MH(CT)(S)A 2003, s 3(3).

Respect for diversity

37.06 This positive duty supplements the duty not to discriminate. Anyone carrying out functions under the Act must consider the abilities, background and characteristics of the person receiving services. This includes the person's age, sex, sexual orientation, religion, racial origin, cultural and linguistic background and membership of any ethnic group.[1]

This duty extends to everyone exercising functions under the Mental Health (Care and Treatment) Act. A hospital admitting someone subject to a compulsory order should consider the person's needs for a special diet, for religious observance requirements or single sex facilities. An independent advocacy service should consider how to work with someone with communication difficulties.[2] The Code of Practice gives other examples.[2]

The Mental Health Tribunal for Scotland must consider these matters when approving orders. It must ensure interpreters are available, that its literature is available in different languages and formats and that its premises and procedures are accessible to people with disabilities. It should consider whether a proposed care plan respects the person's needs and background.

There are similar examples for mental health officers and doctors. A doctor must consider whether a patient would prefer to see a member of his or her own sex and what interpretation/communication services the person might need. Local authorities and health boards must fund services to meet these needs.

These duties are onerous. They respect the Millan principle of *reciprocity*. If society deems it appropriate to use compulsory measures for someone with a mental disorder, it should ensure that services go some way to meeting his or her needs.

It is to be hoped that good practice developed under the Mental Health (Care and Treatment) Act will eventually extend to everyone receiving mental health and community care services in Scotland.

1   Mental Health (Care and Treatment) (Scotland) Act, s 1(3)(h).
2   MH(CT)(S)A 2003, s 259. The Mental Welfare Commission reports a shortage of appropriate advocacy services for people from the black and minority ethnic communities. Annual Report 2003–4, p 13.
3   Code of Practice, vol 1, para 4.04.

Monitoring equality

37.07 The Mental Welfare Commission monitors the operation of the Mental Health (Care and Treatment) Act and gives guidance on good practice.[1] Anyone concerned about poor practice can contact the Commission for advice.

1   See chapter 3.

Accessible information

37.08 Everyone subject to compulsory measures under the Mental Health (Care and Treatment) Act should receive information about his or her rights at certain specified times and on request. See chapter 17. The hospital must ensure that the person giving the information takes all reasonable steps to ensure the person understands his or her rights.[1]

Read in conjunction with the principle of respect for diversity, this means that the person giving information must consider whether interpretation/communication services are necessary.

The hospital must also supply written material in a form appropriate for the person's needs.[2] For example, a visually impaired person who does not speak English might need a tape in his or her first language.

1   Mental Health (Care and Treatment) (Scotland) Act 2003, s 260(2)(a).
2   MH(CT)(S)A 2003, s 260(2)(a)(ii).

Communication/interpretation

37.09 Hospital managers must take steps to meet patients' communication needs at certain stages of the compulsion procedure. See chapter 17.

They must take all reasonable steps to help the person communicate with doctors at such times, by making the appropriate arrangements or by giving the person appropriate assistance or written materials.[1]

This duty extends only to people subject to orders under the Act. It does not apply to people who are not subject to orders, who could equally benefit from the use of interpreters and help with communication.

[1]   Mental Health (Care and Treatment) (Scotland) Act 2003, s 261(2).

MEETING NEEDS

People from minority ethnic communities

37.10 People from black and minority ethnic communities may face discrimination and/or services which fail to consider their needs.

The Race Relations Act 1976 affects all health service and social care providers, voluntary organisations and private providers. It is relevant for voluntary patients and people subject to orders, and people receiving hospital and community-based services.

There are two strands to the Act. The first is the outlawing of discrimination. This applies to public and private bodies. It is unlawful to discriminate, either directly or indirectly, in the provision of services.[1]

Secondly, there is a duty to promote racial equality. This applies to public authorities, such as the National Health Service in Scotland, local authorities, the Mental Welfare Commission and the Public Guardian. When a public body carries out its functions, it must consider the need to eliminate unlawful discrimination and to promote racial equality and good race relations.[2]

This means public authorities should take what steps are necessary to ensure their policies and practices do not disadvantage any racial or ethnic groups. They must draw up schemes and policies setting out their arrangements for meeting the race equality duty.

[1]   Race Relations Act 1976, s 3(1).

2   RRA 1976 (as amended by Race Relations (Amendment) Act 2000), s 71(1). This is in addition to the new equality duties set out above.

Good practice

37.11 The Commission for Racial Equality has published a statutory Code of Practice for all public authorities in Scotland.[1] Any legal action concerning an authority's compliance with its legal obligations will consider whether the authority complied with the Code.

There is also a primary health care services Code of Practice.[2] Local health boards, when planning services, should consider how they will meet the needs of people from their local minority ethnic communities and should consult with members of the communities when drawing up plans. All these bodies should have race equality policies and procedures for reviewing them.

The National Health Service in Scotland is monitoring progress through the Scottish Executive's *Fair for all* initiative.[3]

1   *Code of practice on the duty to promote racial equality in Scotland* (Commission for Racial Equality, 2002).
2   Commission for Racial Equality (1992). (Published before the racial equality duty was introduced.)
3   Scottish Executive (2002).

Monitoring progress

37.12 Progress towards implementing racial equality policies in Scotland appears to be patchy.[1]

Before the implementation of the Mental Health (Care and Treatment) Act, the Mental Welfare Commission reviewed mental health services for people from minority ethnic communities. It found a number of barriers to care. These included a lack of interpreting services and culturally appropriate accommodation, and a failure to provide culturally appropriate assessment and follow up services. There was also a lack of dedicated advocacy services.[2]

The National Resource Centre for Ethnic Minorities (see Appendix 2) surveyed mental health services across Scotland. In the overwhelming majority of National Health Service, it found that little indication that race equality issues influenced services.[3]

1   See *Public sector complacency about promoting race equality must end*, Commission for Racial Equality (Scotland), press release, 22 February 2006.

2   Annual Report 2003–4, p 3. For the Commission's role in promoting racial
     equality, see Annual Report 2000–1, p 17.
3   *Equal services* (National Resource Centre for Ethnic Minorities, 2005).

Remedies

37.13 Anyone concerned about discrimination or institutionalised racism
in the National Health Service or any public authority may want to make
a complaint to the body concerned. See chapter 50. A person can also
contact the Commission for Racial Equality, a local Race Equality Council
or law centre.

The Mental Welfare Commission can also give advice.

People with physical and sensory impairments

37.14 The Disability Discrimination Act 1995 prohibits discrimination
against people with physical and sensory impairments. Organisations
must make reasonable adaptations to their services and procedures to
meet the people's needs. This could involve changes to policies,
procedures and some changes to premises.

The 1995 Act applies to local authorities, GPs, hospitals, day centres
and services run by voluntary and independent organisations. It also
applies to the Mental Health Tribunal for Scotland, the Mental Welfare
Commission and the Office of the Public Guardian.

Public authorities are also under a Disability Equality Duty, to take
positive steps to address discrimination and promote equality on the
grounds of disability. See chapter 36. There is a considerable amount of
good practice guidance available from the Disability Rights Commission.

All such bodies must consider their policies and procedures to ensure
that they avoid discrimination and take positive steps to reduce
inequality. For more detail, see chapter 36.

Anyone who receives services which do not respect his or her needs,
or who faces discrimination or poor disability awareness by staff, may
wish to put in a complaint. The person can also contact the Disability
Rights Commission.

Women

37.15 Women patients and users of services want to know that services
do not discriminate against them[1] and take into account any special
needs they may have. They need to be reassured that there are adequate
protections against sexual harassment in hospitals and care settings.[2]

The Equal Opportunities Commission can give advice on good practice, or if a woman alleges sex discrimination or sexual harassment.

1   Illegal under the Sex Discrimination Act 1975.
2   An offence under SDA 1975, s 41.

Single sex accommodation

37.16 A major issue for women is single sex accommodation in hospital. This can be an issue for religious or other reasons. Women who have experienced sexual or other abuse often find mixed wards threatening. Hospitals owe a duty of care to protect all patients against abuse or inappropriate behaviour from other patients.

In 1999 the then Scottish Health Secretary gave a commitment to phase out mixed wards in psychiatric hospitals in Scotland by 2002.[1] Almost all acute psychiatric wards now offer single-sex facilities.

The Scottish Executive says it is committed to making the remaining wards compliant as quickly as possible. Where mixed wards remain, hospitals should have a policy to respect patients' dignity and privacy. They should have obtained the local health council's approval of this policy.[2]

Some mixed wards remain.[3] The Mental Welfare Commission continues to find a lack of single sex facilities (other than sleeping accommodation) on acute wards and says that a significant proportion of women patients continue to feel unsafe in acute wards in Scottish psychiatric hospitals.[4]

Women patients with concerns should raise them with the staff, with an independent advocacy organisation or with the Mental Welfare Commission.

1   *Priorities and Planning Guidance for the National Health Service in Scotland* (Scottish Office, 1999). See also *Our national health* (Scottish Executive Health Department, 2000).
2   See comments of Deputy Minister for Community Care, Scottish Parliament Health and Community Care Committee Official Report Meeting No 1, 2002, Col 3610. (Local health councils no longer exist. They have been replaced by advisory bodies. See 50.03.)
3   'Health chiefs told to abolish mixed wards' *Edinburgh Evening News*, 3 August 2004. At that time there were still mixed wards in Edinburgh, Grampian and Glasgow.
4   *Unannounced visits 2005, Our impressions of mental health acute admissions wards in Scotland* (Mental Welfare Commission, 2005), p 4.

Mothers and children

37.17 One provision in the Mental Health (Care and Treatment) Act is solely for mothers. This follows pressure in the Parliament to recognise the needs of women with post-natal depression.

Hospitals must provide suitable services and accommodation for mothers with post-natal depression. Where a woman is admitted to hospital for treatment for post-natal depression, whether voluntarily or under an order, the hospital should ensure that its facilities enable the woman to care for the child in hospital if she wishes to do so.[1]

This applies to any woman with post-natal depression who cares for a child (including an adoptive child) under the age of one, so long as it is not likely she will put the child at risk. Health boards may extend these services to cover any woman needing care in the weeks or months leading up to or following a birth.[2]

Health boards should collaborate with other health boards to meet these obligations.[3] The Scottish Executive has given guidance to health boards, including service specifications.[4] There is a SIGN guideline on the management of post-natal depression. See chapter 49 for SIGN.

[1]   Mental Health (Care and Treatment) (Scotland) Act 2003, s 24.

[2]   Code of Practice, vol 1, para 4.20.

[3]   MH(CT)(S)A 2003, s 24(2).

[4]   See Scottish Executive HDL (2004) 6.

Lesbian, gay, bisexual and transgender people

Respect for diversity

37.18 The equality reforms give local authorities and health boards a legal duty to recognise the needs lesbian, gay, bisexual and transgender people.

The Scottish Executive Health Department has set up an Inclusion Project to give guidance on good practice in the National Health Service in Scotland.[1]

[1]   See *Fair for all—The wider challenge. Good LGBT practice in the National Health Service* (National Health Service Inclusion Project, 2005).

Recognising relationships

37.19 The Adults with Incapacity Act was one of the first Acts of the Scottish Parliament to recognise gay and lesbian relationships, by saying that a gay or lesbian partner can be an adult's nearest relative.[1]

The Mental Health (Care and Treatment) Act goes further in respecting patient autonomy. It allows someone to nominate the person he or she wishes to act as named person to represent his or her interests.[2] See chapter 4. To avoid dispute, it is always advisable to nominate a named person.

If someone does not nominate a named person, any primary carer is named person. This could be a gay or lesbian partner. If there is no named person, the nearest relative acts as named person. Spouses and civil partners are top of the list, followed by partners of either sex.[3]

A named person should be consulted about any intervention under the Adults with Incapacity Act.[4] For this reason, anyone anticipating incapacity may wish to nominate a named person.

[1] Adults with Incapacity (Scotland) Act 2000, s 87(2). Its definition of nearest relative now mirrors that in the Mental Health (Care and Treatment) (Scotland) Act 2003. AWI(S)A 2000 (as amended by the Mental Health (Care and Treatment) (Scotland) Act 2003), s 87(1).

[2] Mental Health (Care and Treatment) (Scotland) Act 2003, s 250.

[3] MH(CT)(S)A 2003, s 254(7).

[4] AWI(S)A 2000, (as amended by the Mental Health (Care and Treatment) (Scotland) Act 2003 (Modification of Enactments) Order 2005 (SSI 2005/465)), s 1(4).

Clarification of law

37.20 It should be unnecessary to state that issues of sexual orientation are not indications of mental disorder. However the Millan Committee found that some diagnostic manuals continue to treat certain sexual behaviours and gender issues as mental disorders. For this reason, the Committee recommended a clear statement in the law that sexual orientation or behaviour is not a mental disorder.[1]

The Mental Health (Care and Treatment) Act states that a person is not to be regarded as mentally disordered solely because of his or her sexual orientation, or the fact that he or she is transsexual or a transvestite.[2]

[1] *New directions*, Recommendation 4.13.

[2] Mental Health (Care and Treatment) (Scotland) Act 2003, s 328(2).

Chapter 38

ISSUES FOR PEOPLE WITH DEMENTIA

38.01 This chapter highlights sections of this book that may be of particular relevance to people diagnosed with dementia and their carers.

About 63,000 people in Scotland have some form of dementia. Most are over 60, but younger people can suffer from dementia too. Dementia is a progressive illness. This means that someone given the diagnosis at an early stage has a chance to plan for the future and make financial and welfare arrangements that best suit his or her needs and those of family and carers.

The Mental Health (Care and Treatment) Act regards dementia as a mental illness. This brings it within the definition of 'mental disorder' in the Act and in the Adults with Incapacity Act. Either or both Acts could apply at certain stages of a person's illness.

The Adults with Incapacity Act contains a range of measures that may be helpful for future planning and for where someone loses ability to manage his or her affairs. The Act contains a hierarchy of measures which can be helpful as the illness progresses. See Part 5 for further discussion.

Use of the Mental Health (Care and Treatment) Act for people with dementia should be rare, but a doctor or mental health officer may consider use of the Act if someone is at risk and is not willing to accept medical help. All the provisions of Part 3 of this book would apply.

MANAGING MONEY

38.02 At first, a person with dementia may become confused about money. A person may fail to remember whether he or she has paid bills or may give money away or lose it. As the illness progresses, the person is likely to become unable to manage finances and someone else may have to take over.

The person with dementia should be helped to set up a system which allows the person to continue to manage his or her own affairs for as long as possible, but provides for someone else gradually to take over.[1] Among the possibilities are granting a power of attorney, opening a joint bank account or setting up a trust.

If a person who can no longer manage his or her own affairs has not made any prior arrangements, there is a range of possibilities. These range from relatively simple and inexpensive procedures, such as Department of Work and Pensions appointeeship and obtaining access to bank accounts, to more expensive options, such as applying for an intervention or guardianship order. Hospitals and authorised care homes may manage funds up to a certain amount.

These options are discussed in more detail in Part 5. This section highlights issues that may be particularly relevant.

[1]   For practical and sympathetic advice, see *Dementia, Money and legal matters: a guide for carers,* free to users and carers from Alzheimer Scotland. For details, call the Dementia Helpline.

Powers of Attorney

38.03 We discuss powers of attorney in detail in chapters 25 and 26. A power of attorney can be either financial (a continuing power) or may deal with welfare matters (a welfare power). The same document can contain welfare and financial powers. A power of attorney may grant wide general powers or may be limited to specific areas where the person foresees problems.

A power of attorney is a relatively cheap[1] and informal procedure. It can be tailored to meet a person's own needs and requirements, provided there is someone the person trusts to act as attorney. It is generally recommended for people with dementia, as the simplest way to forestall future problems. It is not appropriate if a person with dementia is concerned about a potential attorney's trustworthiness or reliability.

A financial power of attorney can come into effect on signing, allowing the attorney gradually to take over as the person becomes unable to manage. It can come into effect at a later stage, when the person is no longer able to manage his or her affairs. The granter can decide which he or she prefers. See 26.15 for drafting issues.

A welfare power of attorney cannot come into effect unless someone is unable to take welfare decisions, but the person must sign it while he or she still has the legal capacity to do so.

Someone may be able to sign a power of attorney even if he or she is beginning to be confused or frail. The test is not whether a person can still manage his or her own affairs but whether he or she is able to decide that he or she wants someone else to manage. See 25.04.

[1]   A solicitor might charge around £150 to £250. The person should ask for an estimate of the cost.

Safeguards

38.04 There have been concerns about confused people being under pressure to sign documents when there are clear doubts about the person's ability to understand the document and make a real choice.

The other major concern is that once someone is unable to manage his or her own affairs, he or she will not be able to monitor the attorney's dealings. No one else will monitor these routinely. The Adults with Incapacity Act deals with some of these concerns.

- A power of attorney must be registered with the Public Guardian. It is a public document and anyone with an interest can view it. The Public Guardian can investigate any concerns.

- A power of attorney cannot be registered unless a lawyer or doctor confirms on the same day that it is signed that the person understands the nature and effect of the document and does not appear to be under any undue pressure to sign. Guidance from the Law Society is clear that a lawyer should not prepare a power of attorney unless he or she is sure the client wants this. See 25.08.

- Someone anxious to ensure that the attorney does not take over while he or she is still able to manage, might impose a requirement that the attorney obtains a medical certificate of incapacity before acting. Another safeguard would be that certain people receive notice and have a chance to object.

- The Scottish Executive is proposing new safeguards.[1] It does not intend to insist that attorneys obtain medical certificates, but will advise that the solicitor should always bring this possibility to the attention of a client. See 25.05.

- If there is concern about the way an attorney is acting, anyone with an interest can ask the court to restrict the attorney's powers. The court can require the attorney to submit accounts and/or accept supervision from the Public Guardian. The sheriff can limit the attorney's powers and can ultimately remove an unsuitable attorney. See Part 5.

[1]   See letter to Scottish Parliament Justice 2 Committee from Deputy Minister for Justice, 6 December 2005. Available on the Adults with Incapacity website.

Establishing a trust

38.05 A person with dementia who is worried about managing his or her financial affairs in the future could set up a trust, transferring his or her property (or part of it), to trustees and requiring them to make appropriate provision for him or her. A 'discretionary trust' should not affect any welfare benefits the person may receive in the future. See 42.26.

A trust may have inheritance tax benefits.[1] If a person sets up a trust for tax reasons or to help manage his or her financial affairs, it could be argued that the purpose of the trust is not to avoid care home fees and the sums should not be regarded as the person's capital.[2]

Professional advice from a solicitor is necessary to ensure that any trust gives the person the security he or she needs for the future.

[1]   For up-to-date advice, see Simon Mackintosh, 'Financial advice and taxation' in *Butterworths Scottish Older Client Law Service* (Tottel Publishing), Div H.
[2]   For further discussion, see David McClements, 'Financial Assessments for residential care' in *Butterworths Scottish Older Client Law Service* (Tottel Publishing), paras D.521–543.

Making a will

38.06 Just because someone has a diagnosis of dementia does not mean he or she cannot make a will. See 34.11 for the tests. The person should make a will while still able to do so.

WELFARE CONCERNS

Planning for the future

38.07 As with financial matters, a person with a diagnosis of dementia should make plans while he or she is still able to do so. This might involve signing a welfare power of attorney, an advance statement under the Mental Health (Care and Treatment) Act and/or appointing a named person. The person may also want to sign an advance directive or living will about what treatment he or she may want at end of life. See chapter 10.

The person might visit care services and should make sure that the relevant people know his or her wishes for care in the future. Anyone who obtains powers under the Adults with Incapacity Act must consider the person's past and present wishes and feelings.[1]

[1]   Adults with Incapacity (Scotland) Act 2000, s 1(4).

Need for guardianship

No one with authority

38.08 If someone with dementia loses the ability to take welfare decisions him or herself, no one (not even a spouse or civil partner) has the legal authority to take such decisions, unless the person has signed a valid welfare power of attorney.

This can cause problems if a significant welfare intervention is necessary, such as a move to residential care. The person cannot sign legal documents or give legal consent to the move.

In some cases financial guardianship may be necessary, if, for example, a house needs to be sold and documents need to be signed. An intervention order may be a less restrictive option, and the court will consider whether this is appropriate.

In other cases, a care service may not require any legal formalities but the local authority may tell the carers that they cannot legally move the person without obtaining welfare guardianship. A guardianship order can be expensive and will take time. This can be a particular problem for carers and we discuss the issues further in chapter 11.

MEDICAL TREATMENT AND AUTONOMY

38.09 So long as the person with dementia can consent to medical treatment, doctors should seek his or her consent and respect any refusals. When someone is not able to consent to treatment, a welfare attorney or guardian may be able to consent on the person's behalf. See 8.21 for what happens if the welfare attorney or welfare guardian refuses consent.

Once a person loses capacity to consent to medical treatment, doctors and health professionals may treat him or her under the general authority in the Adults with Incapacity Act) with the safeguards for special treatments set out in the Act. See chapter 8. Following the *Bournewood* judgement, a hospital could be breaching the person's human rights if it admits a person to a regime amounting to deprivation of liberty and doctors do not comply with the Adults with Incapacity Act rules. See chapter 9.

The Adults with Incapacity Act safeguards for medical treatment largely mirror the Mental Health (Care and Treatment) Act safeguards for people subject to compulsory measures under that Act. The one safeguard missing is a second opinion for long-term drug treatment for mental disorder. This is unfortunate as there is well-documented poor practice in this area.[1] General practitioners' prescribing might improve if community pharmacists were involved.[2]

If someone's refusal of treatment could put him or her or other people at risk, a doctor may consider the use of the Mental Health (Care and Treatment) Act if the person's ability to take treatment decisions is significantly impaired. This authorises treatment for mental conditions (but not for physical conditions). See Part 3.

[1]   In A McGrath, G Jackson's 'Survey of neuroleptic prescribing in residents of nursing homes in Glasgow', 24 % of residents were being given anti-psychotic drugs (powerful drugs with serious side effects), and 88 % of these prescriptions were inappropriate. A South London study revealed similar figures: 24.5% of residents were prescribed anti-psychotic drugs, and 82% of the prescriptions were inappropriate. Paul Burstow, 'Keep Taking the Medicine 2', (2002) 31 Age and Ageing, pp 435–439.

[2]   See A Burns, S Craig, S Scobie, J Cooke, B Faraghe, L Furniss, 'Effects of a pharmacist's medication review in nursing homes', (2000) 176 The British Journal of Psychiatry 563–567.

HELP FOR CARERS

38.10 See chapter 11. A carer may want to ask for a formal assessment of the person's needs and to obtain a carer's assessment under the community care system.

Carers may need help and information, including information about the person with dementia, to help them care. This may sometimes raise difficult issues of confidentiality. See chapters 5 and 11.

Chapter 39

PEOPLE WITH LEARNING DISABILITIES

39.01 This chapter tries to show which parts of this book may be particularly useful for people with learning disabilities. The Mental Health (Care and Treatment) Act, the Adults with Incapacity Act and the Disability Discrimination Act all have things to say about people with learning disabilities.

LEARNING DISABILITY AND THE LAW

39.02 The Millan Committee said that there should be a new committee to decide what laws are right for people with learning disabilities. The Scottish Executive has said it will do this, but it has not happened yet. See 1.02.

The *Same as You* committee looked at services for people with learning disabilities.[1] Some of the people on the *Same as You* committee should meet again with lawyers, independent advocates and people with learning disabilities to think about what the law should say.

---

[1]   *Same as You, A review of services for people with learning disabilities* (Scottish Executive, 2004).

ADULTS WITH INCAPACITY ACT

39.03 If someone is unable to take decisions, the Adults with Incapacity Act may say another person can take the decision in certain circumstances. This could be a medical decision, a decision about a house or day-care, for example, or a decision about money. There is a useful guide to the Adults with Incapacity Act from the Scottish Executive.[1]

Even when a person with a learning disability cannot take a certain decision, people must consider the person's views. If a person disagrees with what a guardian or attorney or doctor is doing, he or she can ask the court to decide. The Mental Welfare Commission can give advice.

People acting under the Adults with Incapacity Act must help the person with the learning disability do things him or herself. They must not do things if the person can do them. See 24.08.

1   *It's your decision,* prepared by Enable for the Scottish Executive (2001).

Guardians

39.04 Some people with learning disabilities have guardians under the Adults with Incapacity Act. Sometimes a family member may be a guardian. Sometimes the social work department may ask for a guardian, perhaps if they think the person is a risk to him or herself or other people.

Anyone wanting a guardian appointed must go to court. This is the sheriff court. Anyone who is unhappy about having a guardian or who needs advice should get a solicitor. If a person cannot appoint a solicitor, the sheriff may appoint a solicitor to investigate. This person is called a curator or a safeguarder. Chapters 25 and 26 deal with guardians.

The Mental Welfare Commission has a useful leaflet about guardians.

MENTAL HEALTH (CARE AND TREATMENT) ACT

39.05 The Mental Health (Care and Treatment) Act is for people with learning disabilities and people with mental health problems. Very few people with learning disabilities have to go to hospital under the Mental Health (Care and Treatment) Act. A learning disability does not mean someone has to go to hospital, and anyway most people agree to go if it is necessary. Chapter 11 has some facts and figures.

If someone has a mental illness as well as a learning disability and needs to go to hospital, doctors may use the Mental Health (Care and Treatment) Act if the person does not want to go. This would only be if the person is a risk to him or herself or to other people and there is treatment that could help. The Scottish Executive has produced an Easy Read guide to the Act.

When someone is not able to agree to medical treatment, a doctor can sign a certificate under the Adults with Incapacity Act to allow some treatments. See chapter 8.

Mental health tribunal

39.06 The tribunal deals with most Mental Health (Care and Treatment) Act cases. If a case comes to the tribunal, the person with learning disabilities must get a solicitor. A mental health officer can help. An independent advocate can also come to the tribunal to help.

When someone cannot appoint a solicitor, the tribunal may appoint a curator *ad litem* to investigate. This is usually an experienced solicitor. He or she visits the person with learning disabilities, talks to doctors and carers and reports to the tribunal.

Just because someone has a learning disability does not mean the person cannot appoint a solicitor. Most people should be able to appoint solicitors. If a person is clear what he or she wants, for example, about being in hospital or taking medicines, he or she should be able to instruct a solicitor. See chapter 22.

People with learning disabilities need an Easy Read guide to the tribunal. At the date of this book, there is no such leaflet.

Unlawful detention

39.07 Sometimes people agree to go to a psychiatric hospital because they feel they have no choice. Other people stay even though they do not want to, because they do not think doctors would let them leave. Some people are kept on locked wards. They are not sectioned but they are not free to come and go. Anyone who feels that he or she is not free to leave hospital can appeal to the tribunal. Chapter 6 of the book talks about this.

State Hospital

39.08 Some people with learning disabilities are patients in the State Hospital. Sometimes a patient stays because there is nowhere else for him or her to go.

From May 2006, a patient in the State Hospital can appeal to the tribunal if he or she does not need the State Hospital. Chapter 17 of the book talks about this.

The Mental Welfare Commission says that some people with learning disabilities who are in the State Hospital do not need to be there. Those people can appeal to the tribunal.

A mental health officer or the Patients Advocacy Service at the State Hospital can give advice. The Mental Welfare Commission can also give advice.

Independent advocacy

39.09 Advocacy can be very helpful for people with learning disabilities. A mental health officer should help the person to find an independent advocate. See chapter 4. If someone needing an advocate cannot find one, the Mental Welfare Commission may be able to give advice. The Scottish Independent Advocacy Alliance has a list of advocacy projects.

The Mental Health (Care and Treatment) Act says everyone with a learning disability is entitled to an independent advocate. This means people in hospital and in the community.

Information

39.10 Staff need to give people information about their rights and make sure that they understand them, as far as possible. See chapter 17.

Services

39.11 The Mental Health (Care and Treatment) Act says local authorities must provide services offering support and help with care. For instance, they should try to help families stay together, provide day care and support and help people have a social life. They should help with training, education, and getting jobs and with transport to training.

People may have to pay for some of these services. These services are for everyone with a learning disability, not just people subject to orders. See chapter 28.

PLANNING FOR THE FUTURE

Named person

39.12 A named person is someone who supports a person under the Adults with Incapacity Act or the Mental Health (Care and Treatment) Act.[1] A person with a learning disability can appoint a named person, if he or she is able to understand in general terms what this means. This means understanding that a named person supports the person with learning disability and that the person can choose who he or she appoints.

Chapter 4 of this book looks at named persons.

1   See *The new Mental Health Act: what's it all about* (Scottish Executive Easy Read guide).

Advance statements

39.13 Most people who can say what medical treatment they want should be able to make an advance statement about treatment in the future. Staff should encourage someone with a learning disability to make an advance statement if the person is concerned about future care or treatment. See chapter 10.

Power of attorney

39.14 A person with a learning disability can sign a power of attorney if he or she is able to understand what an attorney does. An attorney is someone who does things for a person who cannot do them him or herself. It could be things to do with money. It could be deciding about medical treatment or where the person should live.

If the person signing the power of attorney wishes to choose someone to take these decisions, it does not matter that the person cannot take these decisions him or herself. See 25.04.

The person with a learning disability should get advice from a solicitor. The solicitor will check the person wants to sign the papers and understands what the attorney can do. The solicitor should also make sure that the person trusts the attorney and wants the attorney to act. No one should be under pressure to sign a power of attorney. See chapter 25.

DISCRIMINATION

39.15 The Disability Discrimination Act says that people must not be unfair to someone because they have a learning disability.

Chapter 36 looks at discrimination. This could be important if someone has problems in getting a job or with services, such as going to a cinema, pub or club because of their learning disability.

EDUCATION

39.16 Chapter 33 looks at extra help for learning for young people with learning disabilities at school.

MENTAL WELFARE COMMISSION

39.17 The Mental Welfare Commission's job is to try to make sure that people get proper help and support. People working for the Commission visit people in hospitals, training centres, supported accommodation and other places. They will look into things if they think there is a problem. Anyone can ask to see them.

There is now a Mental Welfare Commissioner who uses learning disability services.

The Commission has an Easy Read guide. It also sends out regular news in Easy Read.

ADVICE FOR CARERS

39.18 Chapter 42 looks at carers' legal rights. A carer must consider who will help care in the future, when he or she cannot do it. Enable might be able to give advice.

Enable can also advise about making a will. It is not always helpful to give money to the person with learning disabilities, as it might affect the person's benefits. Sometimes it is best to set up a trust. See chapter 11.

Enable runs a very helpful trustee service for people who cannot manage their money themselves.

Chapter 40

REFUGEES AND ASYLUM SEEKERS

40.01 This chapter highlights some issues concerning refugees' and asylum seekers' access to mental health and community care services. The law is extremely complex and this chapter cannot be comprehensive. For sources of advice, see Appendix 2. See Appendix 1 for further reading.

Most of the people in Scotland currently seeking asylum live in Glasgow under the UK government's dispersal scheme.[1] The health care and other support someone receives will depend on whether he or she is seeking asylum, a late applicant for asylum, a failed asylum seeker or someone who has stayed in the UK after his or her claim has failed.

Poor mental health may strengthen an asylum seeker's claim.[2] The person needs good legal advice.

Under the immigration legislation, help to asylum seekers comes from the National Asylum Support Service (NASS). NASS is an agency of the Home Office, part of the UK government. Scottish local authorities and health boards have limited discretion to act and the Scottish Executive has limited powers. Local authorities in Scotland may receive guidance from the Home Office.

Amid concerns about conditions for refugees and asylum seekers, the Scottish Executive has little power to intervene. In January 2002 it set up the Scottish Refugee Integration Forum to help facilitate the integration of refugees in Scotland.

[1]   For some of the issues, see *Another country: Implementing dispersal under the Immigration and Asylum Act 1999* (Audit Commission, 2000).
[2]   See mental health section in the Caris website, run by Save the Children Fund and Glasgow University Centre for the Child and Family.

HEALTH CARE

People seeking or granted asylum

40.02 A person who has applied for or been granted asylum is entitled to free healthcare in Scotland.[1] This includes GP services and hospital services. The person's spouse and children are also entitled to healthcare.

The British Medical Association has expressed concern that some GP practices agree to register refugees and asylum seekers only as temporary patients or refuse to register people with very poor English.[2] If a health professional refuses to provide an asylum seeker with health care services or provides a lower standard of care, this might be unlawful racial discrimination. (See above.)

A general practitioner can refer a person to hospital and specialist services. There is no charge for such services. There are now some innovative mental health services in Glasgow, such as the COMPASS mental health liaison team.[3]

[1]   National Health Service (Charges to Overseas Visitors) (Scotland) Regulations 1989 (SI 1989/364) (as amended by the National Health Service (Charges to Overseas Visitors) (Scotland) Amendment Regulations 2006 (SSI 2006/141)) ('the NHS charging Regulations.')

[2]   *Access to health care for asylum seekers* (BMA, 2001).

[3]   See *Equal services* (National Resource Centre for Ethnic Minority Health, 2005), Annex 2, pp 66–70.

Failed asylum seekers and overstayers

40.03 If the Home Office rejects someone's claim for asylum, the person is not entitled to free National Health Service support, either from a GP or in hospital. A doctor may treat the person in an emergency and give any necessary treatment.

A person detained in hospital under the Mental Health (Care and Treatment) Act or Criminal Procedure (Scotland) Act, or receiving medical treatment as a condition of probation, is not liable to charges.[1] (See chapter 19 for Scottish Ministers' power to remove the person from Scotland.)

Hospitals may give immediately necessary life-saving treatment and they do not charge for this.[2] The person is expected to return to the country he or she has come from once the emergency is over.

There have been several court challenges to the deportation of people receiving health care, both in the UK and in other countries.

In a case involving a London local authority, the House of Lords said that people subject to expulsion are not entitled to remain in the country for medical, social or other care, other than in exceptional circumstances.[3] This will generally only be if someone with a terminal illness is near death.[4]

1   NHS charging Regulations, as amended by the Mental Health (Care and Treatment) (Scotland) Act 2003 (Modification of Subordinate Legislation) Order 2005 (SSI 2005/445), regs 3(e) and (f).
2   NHS charging Regulations, reg 3(a).
3   *N (FC) v Secretary of State for the Home Department* [2005] UKHL 31.
4   *D v United Kingdom* (1997) 24 EHRR 425. See also *BB v France*, 9 March 1998, RJD 1998-VI, p 2596.

COMMUNITY CARE

Help from NASS

40.04 Asylum seekers are not entitled to cash welfare benefits from the Department of Work and Pensions. They may be entitled to support from the National Asylum Support Service. NASS provides financial and other support for asylum seekers. It contracts with other agencies, including local authorities, to provide support.[1]

The European Commission has issued a directive on the conditions member states must meet.[2] Article 17 of the Reception Conditions Directive says member states must bear in mind the special needs of vulnerable asylum seekers when considering what help to give. Home Office regulations allow the National Asylum Support Service to make special help available to a vulnerable asylum seeker.[3]

NASS support may include accommodation, food and other essential items.[4] To qualify for support, the person must establish he or she is destitute or likely to become so within 14 days. The test is whether the person has enough to meet his or her essential living needs. The courts in England have said that extra needs because of a disability are not relevant in determining this.[5]

NASS cannot give support to failed asylum seekers, people granted refugee status in other countries and people who have not claimed asylum within the appropriate time limits. It may make support available if a failed asylum seeker cannot travel for medical reasons or if support is necessary to avoid a breach of human rights.[6]

1   Immigration and Asylum Act 1999, Pt VI.
2   Council Directive 2003/9/EC. ('The reception conditions Directive.')
3   Asylum Seekers (Reception Conditions) Regulations 2005 (SI 2005/7). NASS has said that it will take account of a community care assessment in considering a person's vulnerability. NASS Policy Bulletin 83, para 4.4.
4   Asylum support regulations 2000 (SI 2000/704), regs 10–14.

⁵   *R (on the application of Ouji) v Secretary of State for the Home Department* [2002] EWHC 1839 (Admin).

⁶   Immigration and Asylum (Provision of Accommodation to Failed Asylum-Seekers) Regulations 2005 (SI 2005/930), art 3. For when failure to provide support may constitute a breach of human rights, see *Secretary of State for the Home Department v Limbuela and others* [2004] EWCA Civ 540.

Help from local authorities

Legal restrictions

40.05 Because such support as asylum seekers receive comes from the National Asylum Support Service, there are statutory restrictions on Scottish local authorities providing help.

The law says that a local authority cannot help an asylum seeker if the person's needs come solely from destitution or from the physical effects, or likely effects, of destitution. These rules stop local authorities providing community care help, residential or nursing home care, or other help under the Social Work (Scotland) Act.¹ There are similar restrictions on providing welfare and other local authority services under the Mental Health (Care and Treatment) Act.²

Local authorities in England and Wales have challenged the scope of similar restrictions. In one case, the Court of Appeal in England said that the rules did not stop a local authority from providing after-care to a mentally ill asylum seeker. Her need arose not from destitution but from physical and mental illness. The court said that if someone's need is in any way more acute for reasons other than lack of accommodation and funds, it does not arise solely because the person is destitute. It authorised the local authority to give the woman community care help.³

In another case, the court authorised a local authority to provide residential accommodation for a destitute asylum seeker with a disability, although his disability would not otherwise have obliged the local authority to provide him with accommodation.⁴

The House of Lords considered another case where the local authority wished to provide support to an asylum seeker suffering from cancer. Again the court held that the need arose not from the woman's destitution but from her illness. It authorised the local authority to help her.⁵

¹   Immigration and Asylum Act 1999, s 120.

²   Mental Health (Care and Treatment) (Scotland) Act 2003 (Consequential Provisions) Order 2005 (SI 2005/2078), art 14.

3   *R v Wandsworth London Borough Council, ex p O* [2000] 1 WLR 2539.
4   *R (on the application of Mani) v London Borough of Lambeth and the Secretary of State for the Home Department* [2003] EWCA Civ 836.
5   *Westminster City Council v National Asylum Support Service* [2002] UKHL 38. See also *R v Leicester City Council, ex p Bhika* [2000] 4 All E R 590.

When help possible

40.06 These court decisions are likely to be persuasive in Scotland. This means that an asylum seeker or failed asylum seeker with mental health or community care needs should seek help from the local authority.

If the local authority is satisfied the person's needs do not arise solely from destitution, they can offer help and/or provide services under the Mental Health (Care and Treatment) Act. The author understands some Scottish local authorities are now providing such help to asylum seekers.

CHILDREN AND YOUNG PEOPLE

Education

40.07 Asylum seekers' children generally go to local schools. The Home Office provides education and health care facilities through NASS, which contracts with Scottish local authorities and health boards.[1]

The Home Office is obliged under international treaty obligations to ensure that children living in detention centres receive appropriate education. There is some debate about whether these children are entitled to ask to go to a local school.[2] This needs to be clarified by the courts.

Children living in accommodation centres do not go to local schools, unless they have special educational needs.[3] At the time of writing, there are no accommodation centres in Scotland.

The child of an asylum seeker may have additional support needs because of trauma or bereavement. The education authority must identify and make adequate and efficient provision for children who require additional support for learning. See chapter 33. Additional support needs are very broad. Some children may require very intensive support for complex needs over a long period. Others may require lower level support over a short period. The child of a refugee or asylum seeker might have language needs, or emotional needs because of bereavement or the disruption he or she has experienced.

1   Nationality, Immigration and Asylum Act 2002, s 29.

2   See the discussion on the Caris website.

3   NIAA 2002, s 36(3).

Childrens services

40.08 As with local authority services for adults, the law says a local authority cannot provide general childrens' services[1] to the child of a destitute asylum seeker.[2]

These restrictions do not affect other provisions of the Children (Scotland) Act, and this means that local authorities have some scope to provide help for children at risk. Local authorities can provide help to any children who are 'children in need'. This includes day-care for pre-school children and after-school care. It may provide day-care services for other children.[3]

A child is in need if he or she is unlikely to achieve a reasonable standard of health or development unless the local authority provides services, or if he or she is disabled[4] or affected adversely by the disability of a family member.[5]

Local authorities can provide help where the child of an asylum seeker is in hospital and has had no parental contact for three months. They must investigate and may need to provide help.[6] They can (and should) provide short-term refuges for young asylum seekers if necessary.[7]

1   Under the Children (Scotland) Act 1995, s 22.

2   Nationality, Immigration and Asylum Act 2002, s 47.

3   C(S)A 1995, s 27.

4   A young person is disabled if he or she is chronically sick or disabled or has a mental illness, learning disability or personality disorder.

5   C(S)A 1995, s 93(3).

6   C(S)A 1995, s 36.

7   C(S)A 1995, s 38.

Children at risk

40.09 If a local authority considers a young person is at risk, it must investigate and may bring the matter before a children's hearing.[1] The children's hearing considers whether there are grounds for making an order.[2]

Any person with an interest may apply to the sheriff for a child protection order if a young person is suffering significant harm because of the treatment he or she is receiving.[3]

Anyone concerned about the welfare of the child of an asylum seeker living in the community or in a detention centre may wish to refer the young person's case to the Children's Reporter. This procedure could be appropriate to question unsuitable conditions in detention centres.

1   Children (Scotland) Act 1995, ss 52–62.
2   The grounds are set out in C(S)A 1995, s 52. They include being beyond the control of any person, being in moral danger, suffering due to lack of parental care and failing to attend school without a reasonable excuse.
3   C(S)A 1995, s 57.

Young unaccompanied asylum seekers

40.10 Unaccompanied young asylum seekers under the age of 18 are not subject to the National Asylum Support Service support system. The local authority should support them in the appropriate way.

Once a young person who has received local authority support reaches 18, he or she should be entitled to local authority support as a care leaver.[1]

1   See *R, ex parte Berhe Kidane Munir and Ncube, v London Borough of Hillingdon and the Secretary of State for Education and Skills* [2003] EWHC 2075 (Admin). A young person who has received accommodation or support is entitled to be treated as a care leaver. (Support in Scotland is provided under the Support and Assistance of Young People Leaving Care (Scotland) Regulations 2003 (SSI 2003/608)).

Chapter 41

CHILDREN AND YOUNG PEOPLE

41.01 This chapter looks at the law relating to children and young people who live with mental health challenges or learning disabilities.

It looks at the rules relating to consent to and refusal of treatment, access to services and patient confidentiality. It also looks at hospital and community care services for children and young people. Chapter 31 looks at other issues relating to children and parents.

CONSENT TO TREATMENT

41.02 Some children and young people may lack the legal capacity to consent to treatment because they are too young to understand what is involved. Their parents (or those with parental responsibilities and rights) may consent (and refuse) on their behalf.

Some young people have the legal capacity to consent to or refuse medical treatment. A doctor should respect their wishes unless the Mental Health (Care and Treatment) Act provisions apply. In some cases the courts may be able to intervene in a young person's best interests.

Young people aged over 16 are free to make medical decisions, without interference from their parents or the courts.

This section looks at these rules in more detail.

Young people unable to consent

41.03 If a child or young person under the age of 16[1] is unable to take decisions about medical treatment, his or her parents (or those with parental responsibilities) can take decisions and consent to (or refuse) treatment on the child's behalf.[2] This includes taking decisions about treatment for mental or physical disorders.

In taking decisions, the child's parents (and anyone with parental responsibility) must act in the child's interests[3] and should take the child's views into account.[4]

The law assumes that a young person aged 12 has the maturity to form a view. See below for good practice where a child or young person resists or objects to treatment for mental disorder.

1   Age of Legal Capacity (Scotland) Act 1991, s 1(1).
2   Children (Scotland) Act 1995, s 2(1)(d).
3   C(S)A 1995, s 1(1)(a).
4   C(S)A 1995, s 6.

Young people able to consent

41.04 When a young person is able to take medical decisions, the law respects this. The test is not the person's age, but his or her ability to understand the treatment or medical procedure proposed.

When a doctor considers a young person can understand the nature and possible consequences of treatment, the doctor can rely on the young person's consent and does not need to seek the consent of the parent or person with parental responsibilities.[1]

Different tests apply for different procedures. A 10-year-old may be able to agree to the use of painkillers, for example, but might be unlikely to be able to weigh up the advantages or disadvantages of using mood-stabilising drugs. A 14-year-old may be able to agree to take anti-depressants, but unable to assess the risks of complex medical or surgical procedures. The decision is a matter of judgement for the doctor and there is no appeal against it.[2]

In assessing capacity, the fact that a decision might appear irrational to the doctor should not, of itself, lead the doctor to consider that the young person is unable to take the decision. A competent adult is entitled to refuse treatment for any reason whatsoever, including a reason a doctor may consider irrational.[3] Of course, irrationality may be a symptom of immaturity or mental disorder and would then be relevant.

While the courts in England and Wales have struggled with this,[4] the Scottish courts appear to have accepted that a young person who can consent to treatment can also refuse it. This also appears to be accepted by professionals. Draft guidance to health professionals in Scotland says that a doctor must respect a young person's competent decision even if the doctor does not agree with it.[5]

1   Age of Legal Capacity (Scotland) Act 1991, s 2(4).
2   See discussion in Scottish Law Commission, *Report on the Legal Capacity and Responsibility of Minors and Pupils,* Scot Law Com No 110, para 3.74.
3   Lord Bridge in *Sidaway v Board of Governors of the Bethlem Royal Hospital and the Maudsley Hospital* [1985] AC 871.
4   See, for example, *Re W* [1992] 4 All ER 627, *Re R (A minor) (Wardship: consent to treatment)* [1992] Fam 11.

5   *Draft good practice guidance on consent for health professionals in NHSScotland,* attached to letter from Chief Medical Officer (6 May 2005). As far as the author is aware, the final version of the guidance has not yet been prepared.

Refusal of treatment for mental disorder

41.05 Significant difficulties can arise if a young person with mental health problems refuses treatment. It can be difficult for a doctor to assess whether the young person is able to consent (even though his or her decision-making may be impaired by mental disorder) or whether the person is too immature to understand the implications of the treatment proposed.

This is not an academic question. If someone with legal capacity refuses treatment, a doctor must respect the patient's decision, unless he or she considers it appropriate to invoke the Mental Health (Care and Treatment) Act. When a young person is unable to consent or refuse, his or her parents (or the person with parental responsibilities) may consent on the young person's behalf.

While in some cases it may be appropriate for doctors to rely on parental consent, there may be others where it would be preferable to accept the child's refusal and consider whether use of the Mental Health (Care and Treatment) Act is appropriate.

The Mental Health (Care and Treatment) Act Code of Practice says that if a child or young person appears to object to, or resist, treatment, those treating him or her should consider whether it would be more appropriate to use the powers contained in the Act.[1] A child or young person has more protections if he or she is subject to a compulsory order, with a right of access to the tribunal and safeguards on medical treatment.[2]

1   Code of Practice, vol 1, para 1.34.
2   For further discussion see, *Medical treatment*, J Blackie and H Patrick in A Cleland and E Sutherland, *Children's rights in Scotland* (2nd edn, W Green/ Sweet & Maxwell, 2001).

Case law

41.06 The Scottish courts have had a chance to consider these matters. In an early case, heard before the Age of Legal Capacity Act, the sheriff refused to accept a 15-year-old girl's refusal of treatment, even though the girl appeared capable of understanding what was involved. The sheriff accepted the parent's consent and refused to make an order under the 1984 Act. She said it was in the best interests of the young woman to protect her from the stigma of compulsory detention.[1]

In a later case, a young man refused treatment. The sheriff said that his refusal was valid under the Age of Legal Capacity (Scotland) Act. However because of the risk, it was appropriate for him to be detained under the 1984 Mental Health Act, with the safeguards and rights of appeals which that Act contained.[2]

This later case shows more respect for the autonomy of the young person. It recognises the validity of his refusal of treatment, but recognises that, as with an adult, the use of Mental Health Act powers may be appropriate. By relying on parental consent, the earlier decision denied the young woman the safeguards of appeal and review available under the Mental Health Act.

1   *V v F*, 1991 SCLR 225 (ShCt).
2   *Re Houston*, 1996 SCLR 943.

The courts and medical treatment

Where child unable to take decisions

41.07 Where a child or young person is unable to take medical decisions, anyone with an interest in the child's welfare (including the child or young person him or herself) may apply to the court for a decision about medical treatment.[1]

A parent is clearly a person with an interest, and a hospital doctor, GP or social worker could also apply to the court. We have seen cases in England where doctors have challenged parents' refusals of medical treatment for their child, on the basis that such refusals are not in the child's best interests.

The court makes its decision in the best interests of the child.[2] It must give the young person a chance to express his or her views and take them into account.[3]

1   Children (Scotland) Act 1995, s 11.
2   C(S)A 1995 s 11(7).
3   C(S)A 1995, s 11(7)(b).

Where child able to take decisions

41.08 It seems unlikely that the courts in Scotland have a role in considering medical treatment for a child or young person who is competent to accept or refuse the treatment under the Age of Legal Capacity Act.[1] A parent cannot exercise his or her parental rights where the young person has legal capacity to take the decision.[2]

A parent has a duty to safeguard and promote the health and welfare of his or her child until he or she reaches the age of 16. It could be argued that a parent (or person with parental responsibilities) should be able to apply to the court if he or she feels a young person's refusal of treatment is not in his or her best interests.

If a doctor could take compulsory measures under the Mental Health (Care and Treatment) Act, court action would not be necessary. But if, for example, a young person is refusing life-saving treatment, a parent may wish to seek to ask the court to look at this in the interests of the child's welfare.

The author is not aware of any cases having come before the courts in Scotland. The courts in England have been prepared to overrule young peoples' competent decisions, in the interests of a young person's welfare.[3]

Clearly, such decisions are an encroachment on the autonomy of a young person and a court should not take a decision to overrule a child's competent decision lightly.

If the sheriff court is not prepared to consider the case, those concerned could apply to the Court of Session. That court has a role to protect the interests of vulnerable people, including children.[4]

---

1   See discussion in Wilkinson and McK Norrie *Parent and child* 2nd Edition (Scottish Universities Law Institute, 1999), para 8.51.

2   Children (Scotland) Act 1995, s 15(5).

3   See *Re M (A Child) (Medical Treatment: Consent)* (2000) 52 BMLR 124. (A heart transplant was authorised for a competent patient aged 15 although she offered good reasons for refusal.)

4   Under what is known as the *parens patriae* (parent of the country) doctrine.

People over 16

41.09 Generally young people over 16 are able to take their own medical decisions.[1] If a young person over 16 has a mental incapacity and is unable to consent to treatment, it may be appropriate to authorise treatment under the Adults with Incapacity Act. See chapter 8.

---

1   Age of Legal Capacity (Scotland) Act 1991, s 1(1)(b).

Special protections

41.10 If a young person aged over 16 and under 18 receives certain treatments under the Adults with Incapacity Act, the doctor giving those treatments must be a child and adolescent psychiatrist or obtain a second opinion from a child and adolescent psychiatrist. This safeguard applies if there is an application to the Court of Session to authorise sterilisation for non-medical reasons or for surgical implantation of hormones to reduce sex drive.

A Mental Welfare Commission appointed doctor must give a second opinion before a child or young person unable to consent to treatment receives drug treatment to reduce sex drive, electro-convulsive therapy (ECT), abortion or any medical treatment likely to lead to sterilisation. The second opinion doctor must be a child and adolescent psychiatrist.[1]

[1] Adults with Incapacity (Specified Medical Treatments) (Scotland) Regulations 2002 (SSI 2002/275), (as amended by the Adults with Incapacity (Specified Medical Treatments) (Scotland) Amendment Regulations 2002 (SSI 2002/302)), reg 6.

PROTECTIONS FOR INFORMAL PATIENTS

41.11 The Mental Health (Care and Treatment) Act mainly deals with compulsory medical treatment. We consider its impact on children and young people below.

Because of concerns about certain rare treatments for children and young people, the Act contains some treatment safeguards for informal patients under the age of 16.[1]

The safeguards apply if the responsible medical officer proposes electro-convulsive therapy (ECT) and other rare treatments for an informal patient aged under 16.[2] The safeguards mirror those available for patients subject to orders under the Mental Health (Care and Treatment) Act.

Doctors are very unlikely to recommend ECT for a young person. Guidelines from the National Institute for Clinical Excellence (endorsed by NHS Quality Improvement Scotland) recommend extra caution in the use of ECT in older people, pregnant women and young people, because of the enhanced risks.[3]

[1] Set out in the Mental Health (Safeguards for Certain Informal Patients) (Scotland) Regulations 2005 (SSI 2005/401) ('The child treatment Regulations'.)

2   The other treatments are transcranial magnetic stimulation and vagus nerve stimulation. Mental Health (Care and Treatment) (Scotland) Act 2003, s 244. Child treatment regulations, reg 6.

3   Guidance on the use of electro-convulsive therapy (NICE, April 2003), para 7.4.3.

Where young person consents

41.12 The doctor treating the young person must confirm in writing that the person is capable of consenting and has consented in writing. The doctor must also confirm the treatment is in the young person's best interests, being likely to alleviate or prevent deterioration in his or her condition.[1]

The doctor should give notice to the Mental Welfare Commission within seven days.[2] A form is on the Scottish Executive's mental health website.

If the young person's doctor is not a child specialist, he or she must obtain a second opinion from a designated medical practitioner who is a child specialist.

Where a young person withdraws consent to the treatment, a new consent and second opinion are necessary.

1   Child treatment Regulations, reg 3.
2   Code of Practice, vol 1, para 10.48.

Young people unable to consent

41.13 If a young person is unable to consent, the parents (or people with parental responsibilities) may give consent. If the doctor treating the person is not a child specialist, he or she must obtain a second opinion from a designated medical practitioner who is a child specialist.[1]

The designated medical practitioner must certify that the young person is incapable of understanding the nature, purpose and likely effects of the medical treatment and that the medical treatment is in his or her best interests, as likely to alleviate, or prevent, deterioration in the young person's condition.

Parental consent must be in writing. A parent may withdraw consent at any time, and a new consent and second opinion will be necessary.

This regulation does not authorise giving of the specified treatments by force.[2] If a doctor considers this necessary, he or she should consider using the Mental Health (Care and Treatment) Act. The Code of Practice says that if a young person appears to resist or object to treatment, a doctor should consider use of the Act.[3]

The doctor should give notice to the Mental Welfare Commission within seven days.[4] A form is on the mental health website.

[1] Child treatment Regulations, reg 4.
[2] Child treatment Regulations, reg 4(2).
[3] Code of Practice, vol 1, para 1.34. See below.
[4] Code of Practice, vol 1, para 10.58.

Urgent treatment

41.14 A doctor can give any of the treatments specified above in an emergency, if the young person is unable to consent, so long as a parent consents and a designated medical practitioner certifies that the treatment is urgently necessary. If the doctor treating the person is not a child specialist, the designated medical practitioner must be.

The certificate authorises treatment even though the young person resists or objects. The certificate does not authorise the use of force for someone who is not in hospital. It authorises the use of force in hospital, but only in an urgent situation.

If the young person is capable of giving consent and refuses it, a doctor cannot give the specified treatments, even in an emergency.[1]

[1] Child treatment Regulations, reg 5.

COMPULSORY MEASURES

41.15 A young person can be subject to the Mental Health (Care and Treatment) Act. Although this is rare, the numbers are growing.[1] This may at least partly be a response to services' growing awareness of the need to ensure proper legal safeguards and less likely to rely on parental consent (see above).

Most young people needing psychiatric help are willing to go to hospital and do not need compulsory measures. Voluntary patients are not subject to the restrictions of the Act, but on the other hand, the Act also contains safeguards, such as the right of appeal and the right to have treatment reviewed.

The Act contains certain provisions specifically for young people, some of which apply to informal patients as well as to patients subject to compulsory measures. These are set out below. They include special safeguards for medical treatments and attempts to ensure that facilities for young people admitted to hospital are appropriate.

[1]   In 2004–5, 83 young people were detained under emergency (72 hours) provisions, 53 under the short-term (28-day) provisions and 27 under the long-term (6-month) provisions of the 1984 Act. Most of the 166 young people so detained were aged 16 to 17. Just 29 were under 16. Annual Report of the Mental Welfare Commission, 2004–5.

Safeguards

Principles of the Act

41.16 The Mental Health (Care and Treatment) Act sets out a special set of principles for children and young people under the age of 18. The fundamental principle is that the welfare of the child should be the primary concern of any intervention under the Act.

Anyone acting under the Mental Health (Care and Treatment) Act should act in what appears to be the best way of promoting the child's welfare.[1] The remaining principles are designed to achieve this aim. In this way, the Mental Health (Care and Treatment) Act complements the Children (Scotland) Act principle that the welfare of the child is paramount.

A doctor considering compulsory measures for a child should consider the effects of detention on the child. The doctor and the mental health officer should ensure that they have fully explored all other options.[2]

The child's responsible medical officer should be a child specialist.[3]

[1]   Mental Health (Care and Treatment) (Scotland) Act 2003, s 2(4).

[2]   Code of Practice, vol 1, para 1.27.

[3]   Code of Practice (above), para 1.28.

Mental Welfare Commission

41.17 The Mental Welfare Commission takes a particular interest in care and treatment for children and young people. It visits young people in hospital and in the community. It has specific functions to inspect facilities in secure accommodation and young offenders' institutions.[1]

Any young person concerned about his or her care or treatment can approach the Mental Welfare Commission for advice.

1   Mental Health (Care and Treatment) (Scotland) Act 2003, s 13(4).

The tribunal

41.18 Neither the Act nor the tribunal rules of procedure contain any specific measures to ensure that the tribunal procedures are appropriate to the needs of any young person appearing before it.

The tribunal procedure can be adapted to the needs of the parties and the tribunal can make efforts to ensure that the proceedings are comprehensible to a young person.[1]

1   See Mental Health Tribunal for Scotland (Practice and Procedure) (No. 2) Rules 2005 (SSI 2005/519), r 52(1).

Medical treatment

Child specialists

41.19 If a patient under the age of 18 is subject to Part 16 the Mental Health (Care and Treatment) Act and the responsible medical officer wishes to treat the patient without consent, the responsible medical officer must obtain a second opinion from a specialist in child and adolescent psychiatry, unless the responsible medical officer is such a specialist.[1]

See chapter 16 for medical treatment rules.

1   Mental Health (Care and Treatment) (Scotland) Act 2003, ss 235(6), 236(6), 283(3) and 241(3).

Advance statements

41.20 A young person can make an advance statement provided he or she can understand what it is intended to achieve.[1] An independent person must certify that the young person has the capacity to make the statement. See chapter 10.

The Scottish Executive's guidance leaflet says a young person can make an advance statement if he or she can understand the 'nature and possible consequences of the procedure or treatment'.[2]

The test in the Mental Health (Care and Treatment) Act is whether the person is able to intend the wishes set out in the statement. An adult can make an advance statement saying he or she does not wish to have ECT, for example, even though he or she does not understand the procedure or its purpose.

1   Mental Health (Care and Treatment) (Scotland) Act 2003, s 275(2).
2   *The New Mental Health Act: A guide to advance statements* (Scottish Executive, 2004), para 5. This links the test of capacity to that in the Age of Legal Capacity Act (see above).

Information and representation

Named persons

41.21 A person under the age of 16 cannot appoint a named person or veto the appointment of a specific named person.[1]

The young person's parent (or the person with parental responsibility) is generally his or her named person. If there is more than one, they can agree between themselves who should act. If there is no such person, the primary carer is named person.[2] If the young person is in hospital, the primary carer is the person who previously provided most of the care and support.

A local authority with parental rights and responsibilities is named person.[3]

Although a young person under the age of 16 cannot appoint a named person, he or she can ask the tribunal to remove an unsuitable named person. In addition, anyone with parental responsibilities can apply to the tribunal for the removal of an unsuitable named person.[4]

1   Mental Health (Care and Treatment) (Scotland) Act 2003 (as amended by the Mental Health (Care and Treatment) (Scotland) Act 2003 (Modification of Enactments) Order 2005 (SSI 2005/465)), ss 250 and 253.
2   MH(CT)(S)A 2003, s 252 (as amended). See chapter 4.
3   MH(CT)(S)A 2003, s 252(3).
4   MH(CT)(S)A 2003, s 256(2).

Information about rights

41.22 A child or young person subject to compulsory measures under the Mental Health (Care and Treatment) Act is entitled to information about his or her rights.[1] See chapter 17. Those responsible for giving information must take all reasonable steps to ensure the young person understands the information. Information designed for adults is not necessarily suitable for young people.

¹ Mental Health (Care and Treatment) (Scotland) Act 2003, s 260.

Advocacy

41.23 Any young person with a mental illness, learning disability or personality disorder is entitled to advocacy services.¹ See chapter 4. Advocacy services can be particularly helpful for young people, who may be very vulnerable.

At the time of writing, specialised advocacy services for young people with mental health needs are not always available, but there are plans to develop some services.

¹ Mental Health (Care and Treatment) (Scotland) Act 2003, s 259.

Criminal procedure

41.24 The measures for transferring someone with a mental disorder from the criminal justice system to the mental health system apply, without modifications, to children and young people. Children and young people can be subject to assessment orders, treatment orders, interim compulsion orders, compulsion orders (with or without restrictions), hospital directions and transfer for treatment directions in the same way as adults. In practice, such orders are likely to be rare.

MEDICAL CONFIDENTIALITY

41.25 Questions of patient confidentiality are particularly difficult where children and young people are involved. Parents have a right and a duty to promote their children's welfare until they are 16, but at the same time, confidentiality is at the heart of the doctor/patient relationship.

A young person seeking help with a mental health problem or drug use may be discouraged from speaking to his or her doctor if he or she knows parents will be informed.

Confidentiality raises mixed issues of law, ethics and professional good practice. The issues are particularly difficult where a young person has a mental disorder. A young person may need protection in the interests of his or her own health and safety or (occasionally) in the interests of others. The person's carers may need information to help them to care.

For more discussion about confidentiality and access to records for children and young people, see chapter 5.

HOSPITAL AND COMMUNITY SERVICES

Hospital facilities

41.26 One of the major concerns of the Millan Committee was the evidence it received that young people with mental health problems were being admitted to adult wards which were unsuitable for their needs.[1]

The Millan Committee recommended the law ensure that young people receive care suitable for their needs.[2] The Scottish Parliament accepted this recommendation.

The Mental Health (Care and Treatment) Act obliges health boards to ensure that where a young person is admitted to a psychiatric hospital, the accommodation and services are suitable for his or her needs.[3] A young person means someone up to the age of 18.[4]

This applies wherever a young person is admitted to hospital, whether as a voluntary patient, or under the Mental Health (Care and Treatment) Act. It applies to all hospitals, including secure and medium secure hospitals.

[1]   *New directions*, chap 18, paras 22–26.
[2]   *New directions*, recommendation 18.5.
[3]   Mental Health (Care and Treatment) (Scotland) Act 2003, s 23.
[4]   MH(CT)(S)A 2003, s 23(2).

Guidance in Code of Practice

41.27 The Code of Practice says that ideally a child should go to a unit specialising in child and adolescent psychiatry. A child should be admitted to an adult ward only in exceptional circumstances.[1] Health boards should notify the Mental Welfare Commission whenever a young person is admitted to an adult psychiatric ward.[2] The form is available on the Mental Welfare Commission website.

[1]   Code of Practice, vol 1, paras 1.48–50.
[2]   Code of Practice, vol 1, para 1.51.

Guidance from Commission

41.28 The Mental Welfare Commission is taking a particular interest in the enforcement of this provision. It regards the admission of young people to adult mental health wards as deeply undesirable and possibly detrimental to the young person. It has issued good practice guidance supplementing that in the Code of Practice.[1]

The Commission says that there may be rare occasions where it is acceptable for a young person aged 16 or 17 to be cared for on an adult ward. This depends on the individual circumstances of the young person, his or her maturity, occupation, and the nature of his or her mental health problems.

A young person on an adult ward must have access to age appropriate specialist care. The hospital should make every effort to provide for the young person's needs. If there is an appropriate young person's unit, the hospital should make every effort to ensure the young person is moved there as soon as possible.

A young person's psychiatrist should always be a child and adolescent specialist. Further requirements as to appropriate services, staff training and facilities are set out in the guidance.

[1]   Available on the Commission's website.

Monitoring

41.29 Whenever the Commission receives notice that a young person has been admitted to an adult ward, it makes further enquiries about the young person's care and treatment.[1]

Anyone concerned that a young person has been admitted to unsuitable accommodation or has not received appropriate services, can contact the Commission for advice. This includes the young person him or herself.

[1]   *Monitoring priorities for 2005–6* (Mental Welfare Commission, October 2005).

Local authority services

41.30 The local authority duties to provide support services and social, cultural and recreational activities extend to people under the age of 16.[1] Local authorities have duties under the Children (Scotland) Act in addition to their Mental Health (Care and Treatment) Act duties.[2]

Local authorities must safeguard and promote the welfare of children in need in their area, by providing a range and level of services appropriate to children's needs.[3] A child in need includes a child with a mental health problem or learning disability.[4]

Local authorities have particular duties to children affected by disability.[5] Disability means chronic sickness, physical disability, mental illness, learning disability and personality disorder.[6]

Services should aim to minimise the effect on the child or young person of his or her disability and give the child the opportunity to lead as normal a life as possible.[7] See chapter 28 for legal effect of these duties.

[1]   Mental Health (Care and Treatment) (Scotland) Act 2003, s 29.
[2]   Children (Scotland) Act 1995, s 22(1).
[3]   C(S)A 1995, s 22.
[4]   C(S)A 1995, ss 93(4) and 23(2).
[5]   C(S)A 1995, ss 23–24A.
[6]   C(S)A 1995, s 23(2).
[7]   C(S)A 1995, s 23(1).

Assessment of need

41.31 A child's parent or guardian can require the local authority to carry out a formal assessment of the child's needs. The local authority must carry out the assessment.[1]

When it assesses the child's needs, the local authority must take into account the views and wishes of the child, and of his or her parent or guardian and carer. (A carer is any person providing a substantial amount of care on a regular basis. This does not include a paid carer or a worker (paid or unpaid) for a voluntary organisation.)[2]

A carer can require the local authority to carry out a formal assessment of the carer's ability to continue to care for the child.[3] The local authority must consider this assessment when it assesses the child or considers how to discharge its duties under the Chronically Sick and Disabled Persons Act.[4]

The local authority must inform the carer of his or her right to an assessment.[5]

[1]   Children (Scotland) Act 1995, s 23(3).
[2]   C(S)A 1995, s 23(4).
[3]   C(S)A 1995, s 24.
[4]   C(S)A 1995, s 24(1A).

5 C(S)A 1995, s 24A. For how this should work in practice, see *Community Care and Health (Scotland) Act: new statutory rights for carers* (Scottish Executive Health Department circular CCD 2/2003).

Transition to adult services

41.32 Child services should continue until a young person reaches 18. When a young person reaches 18, he or she moves from children's services to adult services.[1] The education authority must work with local agencies if the young person has additional support needs. (See chapter 33.)

The local authority should carry out a community care assessment to establish whether the young person needs community care services. See chapter 27.

Either the young person or anyone concerned may ask the local authority to consider whether the young person should receive community care help.

1 Children (Scotland) Act 1995, s 93(2).

Direct payments

41.33 Direct payments allow a person to buy care rather than receive care provided by the local authority. See chapter 27.

Direct payments are available for children's services. When a child or young person is eligible for children's services, the local authority may pay a sum to his or her parents (or to a child aged 16 or over) to enable them to arrange and buy care themselves.

The local authority should be able to provide advice.[1]

1 For more information, see *Social Work (Scotland) Act 1968, sections 12B and 12C Direct Payments: Policy and Practice Guidance* (circular CCD4/2003), paras 38–56.

Relations with family

If young person subject to measures

41.34 If a child or young person is subject to compulsory measures under the Mental Health (Care and Treatment) Act or the Criminal Procedure (Scotland) Act, it may be difficult for the child's parents or other person with parental responsibilities to have contact with him or her.

All those involved in the child's care must do what is practicable and appropriate to help the child keep personal contact with his or her parents and to maintain a relationship with them.[1]

The child's mental health officer has an important role in ensuring this happens.[2]

1   Mental Health (Care and Treatment) (Scotland) Act 2003, s 278.

2   Code of Practice, vol 1, para 1.47.

Where a parent/guardian has mental disorder

41.35 Where a child or young parent has a parent or family member with a mental disorder, has a chronic sickness or other disability, the local authority must do what it can to reduce the effects on the child. The child is a child 'in need' and entitled to children's services.[1] See chapter 31.

The local authority must provide services aimed at helping the child have as normal a life as possible. This applies wherever a child is affected by the disability (including mental disorder) of a member of his or her family.[2]

The child's parent or guardian can require the local authority to assess the child's needs. Unfortunately, the child cannot call for formal assessment of his or her needs. (Although he or she may be able to call for a carer's assessment, see below.)

Despite this, any child needing help should feel free to contact a mental health officer at the local authority. If a child does not get the help he or she needs and his or her parent or guardian is unwilling to ask for an assessment, the child should contact the Mental Welfare Commission for advice.

The Mental Welfare Commission may contact the local authority on the child's behalf.

If a child's parent becomes subject to compulsory measures under the Mental Health (Care and Treatment) Act, those involved in his or her care must do what they can to minimise the disruption of family life and to help the child to maintain contact with his or her parent.[3]

1   Children (Scotland) Act 1995, s 22.

2   C(S)A 1995, s 23(1).

3   Mental Health (Care and Treatment) (Scotland) Act 2003, s 278.

Young carers

41.36 A carer of any age may ask the local authority to assess his or her ability to continue to care. See Part 11. A young carer can contact the local authority for help, even if his or her parent or guardian does not wish this.

Education

41.37 If a young person is under school age, the education authority should meet his or her educational needs.[1] See chapter 33.

The education authority must make such arrangements as are necessary to meet the educational needs of a young person subject to compulsory measures under the Mental Health (Care and Treatment) Act.[2]

[1] Sections 26(2)(b) and (c) of the Mental Health (Care and Treatment) (Scotland) Act 2003 apply only to people over school age.
[2] MH(CT)(S)A 2003, s 277.

VULNERABLE GROUPS

Young people at risk

41.38 The Mental Health Act provisions for people at risk (see chapter 30) do not apply to young people under the age of 16. This is because a children's hearing is the appropriate place to deal with such matters. The Children (Scotland) Act 1995 has measures for dealing with children and young people at risk.[1]

If a child or young person has mental health needs or a learning disability, a children's hearing may require him or her to seek psychiatric help as a condition of a supervision requirement. This could be as an in-patient or outpatient. If a young person (or the young person's parent if the child is unable to consent) does not agree to treatment, compulsory measures under the Mental Health (Care and Treatment) may be appropriate.

In certain circumstances, a community-based compulsory treatment order might be appropriate for a child or young person. Such an order might be a less restrictive option than, for example, a Children (Scotland) Act order that a young person with a mental disorder move into secure accommodation.

Whether this will become an option for children and young people at risk depends on developing practice in both the children's hearing and mental health systems.

1   The procedure is set out in outline in the Code of Practice, vol 1, para 1.39ff. For more information, see K Norrie, *Children's hearings in Scotland* (2nd edn, W Green & Son, 2005).

Looked after children

41.39 Children who are looked after by the local authority may have serious health needs. Many looked-after children have mental health needs.[1]

The local authority must assess the child's health and draw up a health care plan. The local authority must ensure that the young person has access to health services. If a young person with capacity refuses consent to any medical treatment or examination, doctors cannot examine him or her.[2]

If a young person is at risk because of a mental disorder, the local authority may involve a mental health officer to consider whether compulsory measures might be appropriate under the Mental Health (Care and Treatment) Act.

Anyone concerned that a young looked-after person is not receiving the mental health help he or she needs should contact the Mental Welfare Commission.

1   See *The mental health of young people looked after by local authorities in Scotland*, research carried out by the Office for National Statistics for the Scottish Executive. 45% of looked-after children in 2002–3 had mental health problems.
2   Arrangements to Look After Children (Scotland) Regulations 1996 (SI 1996/3262), reg 13(3).

Young people leaving care

41.40 The local authority must offer advice, guidance and assistance to care leavers aged under 19, unless it is satisfied the young person's welfare does not require this.[1] A young person between 19 and 21 may request the local authority for help. The authority should provide this unless satisfied it is not necessary.[2]

The local authority must assess the needs of young people leaving care (including mental health needs).[3] A local authority may provide financial assistance and accommodation.[4]

In considering the young person's accommodation needs, the local authority should bear in mind the young person's needs, including health needs and needs arising from a disability.[5] Disability includes chronic sickness, physical disability, mental illness, learning disability and personality disorder.[6]

A young care leaver with mental health issues who needs additional help should seek a community care assessment. (See chapter 22.) A young care leaver with unrecognised mental health needs can ask for a healthcare assessment. (See chapter 5.)

1   Children (Scotland) Act 1995, s 29(1).
2   C(S)A 1995, s 29(2).
3   C(S)A 1995 (as amended by the Regulation of Care (Scotland) Act 2001), s 29(5).
4   Support and Assistance of Young People Leaving Care (Scotland) Regulations 2003 (SSI 2003/608). ('The leaving care Regulations'.)
5   Leaving care Regulations, reg 14.
6   C(S)A 1995, s 23(2).

THE CHILDREN'S COMMISSIONER

41.41 The UK has signed the United Nation's Convention on the Rights of the Child, passed in 1989. Scotland now has a Children's Commissioner, whose role is to protect the rights of children and young people.[1] Her duties include reviewing the law, policy and practice relating to the rights of children and young people.[2]

The Commissioner can investigate whether a service provider has considered the rights, interests and views of children and young people when making decisions affecting children and young people.[3] She can investigate any cause for concern, unless this is a matter reserved for the Westminster Parliament.

1   Commissioner for Children and Young People (Scotland) Act 2003.
2   CCYP(S)A 2003, s 4.
3   CCYP(S)A 2003, s 7.

PART 11
CARERS

Chapter 42

CARERS

42.01 This chapter highlights some legal issues of special concern to carers.

No one reading this book will be unaware of the crucial role of carers, both paid and unpaid. Since the first edition of this book, there have been some improvements in carers' legal rights, as we will see below. Some of these have come about through the Scottish Executive's *Strategy for carers.*[1]

The Community Care and Health (Scotland) Act 2002 gave carers the right to have a separate assessment of their ability to care. The Act introduced carers' information strategies, obliging health boards to ensure carers get information about their rights.[2]

Alzheimer Scotland, Enable and the Scottish Association for Mental Health are important sources of advice on legal, financial and welfare benefits matters.

[1]   Scottish Executive, November 1999.
[2]   Community Care and Health (Scotland) Act 2002, s 12.

INVOLVING CARERS

42.02 Both the Adults with Incapacity Act and the Mental Health (Care and Treatment) Act stress the importance of ascertaining carers' views. A carer may be the first person to realise a person is becoming ill. Too often carers complain that their concerns are not taken seriously.

The Mental Health (Care and Treatment) Act also recognises that carers may need information to help them care. Whether the Mental Health (Care and Treatment) Act reforms will make a real change to the experience of these carers will be one of the tests of its success.

Carers and Adults with Incapacity Act

42.03 One of the key principles of the Adults with Incapacity Act is that anyone intervening or considering intervening under the Act must consider the views of an adult's nearest relative, named person and primary carer.[1] The primary carer is the person or organisation primarily concerned with caring for an adult.[2] This could be a paid or informal carer.

An intervener is not obliged to consider a carer's views if this is not reasonable or practical, but must consider any information a carer has about the adult's past or present wishes.[3]

1   Adults with Incapacity (Scotland) Act 2000 (as amended by the Mental Health (Care and Treatment) (Scotland) Act 2003), s 1(4)(b).
2   AWI(S)A 2000, s 87(1).
3   AWI(S)A 2000, s 1(4)(a).

Carers and Mental Health (Care and Treatment) Act

42.04 The Millan Committee stressed the importance of the role of carers. It said that carers should receive respect for their role and experience, receive appropriate information and advice and have their views and needs taken into account.[1] The Mental Health (Care and Treatment) Act principles attempt to reflect this concern.

Everyone exercising functions under the Mental Health (Care and Treatment) Act should consider the views of any carer that might be relevant in the circumstances.[2] When making decisions, (other than decisions about medical treatment) the person should consider the needs and circumstances of any carer and what information he or she should give to the carer to enable the carer to care.[3]

A carer falls within these provisions if he or she regularly provides a substantial amount of care or support. These rules apply to individual carers, not to paid carers or people who work on a paid or unpaid basis for voluntary organisations.[4]

When someone is in hospital, the carer is the person who provided care or support before the person went to hospital.

As with the Adults with Incapacity Act, people intervening under the Mental Health (Care and Treatment) Act must give due consideration to information from a carer about a patient's past or present wishes.[5]

1   *New Directions*, recommendation 3.3.
2   Mental Health (Care and Treatment) (Scotland) Act 2003, s 1(3)(b).
3   MH(CT)(S)A 2003, s 1(5).
4   MH(CT)(S)A 2003, s 329.
5   MH(CT)(S)A 2003, s 1(3)(a).

MEDICAL DECISION-MAKING AND CARERS

Access to medical information

42.05 Chapter 5 deals with medical confidentiality. The issues are very complex when a person has a carer providing a substantial amount of care and support. A carer needs sufficient information to be able to care, but on the other hand the person being cared for must be reassured that staff will respect his or her confidentiality. A person may be happy for staff to disclose certain matters, but not others, to carers.

The National Health Service in Scotland recognises the importance of carers. It has said that 'the vital role of carers as major care providers must be recognised at all levels in the NHS and staff must work closely with carers as partners in providing care'.[1] This seems to envisage that NHS staff should be able to discuss matters with carers on a need-to-know basis.

The Royal College of Psychiatrists, working with the Princess Royal Trust for Carers, has produced a useful leaflet.[2] This urges staff to discuss information-sharing with patients at an early stage, when patients are not acutely ill. It encourages the use of advance directives and other means of ensuring that staff know they can discuss a person's care with his or her carer. Even if a patient has restricted the information staff can disclose, staff can give carers general information about medical diagnoses, treatment, side effects and mental health services, without breaching patient confidentiality. Carers should have an opportunity to speak to staff in private, and staff should respect carers' confidentiality.

It may be helpful for local carers' groups to attempt to agree confidentiality protocols with service providers. In Edinburgh, for example, the Carers' Council is discussing an information-sharing protocol with statutory sector and voluntary organisations.

The Mental Welfare Commission has also given practical advice to staff working with carers.[3] It suggests that where a carer does not receive the information he or she needs to enable the carer to care, it may be appropriate to seek an Adults with Incapacity Act order authorising staff to share information. Such an application is appropriate only where the person being cared for lacks the capacity to authorise the sharing of information or is unable to protect his or her own interests.

It is important to stress that a carer has a right to decide whether to continue to provide care and support to someone. A carer who does not receive adequate information may find it impossible to continue to care.

Doctors or mental health officers considering the use of the Adults with Incapacity Act or the Mental Health (Care and Treatment) Act must seek the views of various people, including carers. This does not mean they can ignore confidentiality rules.[4]

1   Scottish Executive White Paper *Partnership for Care* 2003, para 3.7.
2   *Carers and confidentiality in mental health: issues involved in information-sharing* (Partners in Care, 2004). Available from the Royal College of Psychiatrists in London (see Appendix 2) or from www.partnersincare.co.uk.
3   See Annual Report of Mental Welfare Commission 2004–5, para 3.6.
4   See Adults with Incapacity Act Code of Practice for Part 5 of the Act, para 1.8.4. Mental Health (Care and Treatment) Act Code of Practice, vol 1, para 1.05.

Medical decisions

Where person able to take decisions

42.06 The patient decides how much to involve a carer in treatment decisions. Doctors will respect the patient's decision. A patient wishing a carer to be present during consultation with a doctor should ask. A doctor will generally agree, unless there is some reason why this is not appropriate.

Where person unable to take decision

42.07 See chapter 8. The Adults with Incapacity Act gives doctors and other health professionals a general authority to do what is reasonable to promote an adult's mental and physical health, provided the doctor certifies that the adult cannot take medical decisions. Certain health professionals have a similar authority. Certain treatments require either a second opinion or the approval of the court, depending on their seriousness.

Both the Adults with Incapacity Act and (if the person is subject to an order) the Mental Health (Care and Treatment) Act require the doctor to consider the views of carers. The doctor should consider these views, but they cannot be conclusive. The doctor takes a decision based on a clinical judgement of what is best for the patient.

A carer's position is stronger if he or she is a welfare attorney or guardian with powers to consent to medical treatment. See chapter 25.

A carer may have information about the past or present wishes of the person being cared for. The doctor must always consider these wishes.

Compulsory measures

42.08 Under the 1984 Act, nearest relatives (often carers) were formally involved in detention procedures. Doctors could ask for their consent to detention and nearest relatives could apply for long-term orders and formally request discharge from detention.

The Mental Health (Care and Treatment) Act does not give carers or nearest relatives these powers. They often led to friction between people and their relatives or carers.[1]

As a safeguard, the use of compulsory measures requires the consent of a mental health officer, a specially trained social worker who is independent of health services.

1   See *New Directions*, paras 7.2–7.14.

Named person

42.09 The named person receives information and has a formal role in compulsion proceedings under the Mental Health (Care and Treatment) Act. The named person can appeal against compulsory orders and receives information at all stages of the compulsion process.

In many cases, people will be happy for their primary carers to be named person. This is the default position if a person does not appoint anyone. See chapter 4.

Even when someone appoints a person other than a carer, those discussing care and compulsion options must consider the views of carers at all stages.[1]

1   See, for example, Mental Health (Care and Treatment) Act Code of Practice vol 2, paras 2.26, 2.33, 2.34, and 2.43 (involving carers in application for short-term detention certificate). The sections of the Code dealing with compulsory treatment orders contain similar provisions.

The tribunal

42.10 Chapter 23 deals with tribunal procedure. The Mental Health (Care and Treatment) Act and the tribunal rules ensure that the primary carer receives information about any compulsion proceedings. The primary carer can make representations and lead or produce evidence at the hearing.[1]

The primary carer cannot appeal against an order. Only the patient and named person appeal. A carer concerned that an order is not appropriate could contact the Mental Welfare Commission. Although the Commission does not intend to discharge orders, it might investigate and refer the matter to the tribunal.

[1]   See, for example, Mental Health (Care and Treatment) (Scotland) Act 2003, s 64(3).

Healthcare assessment

42.11 A frequently expressed concern of carers is that they sometimes find it difficult to persuade staff that the health of the person they care for is deteriorating, even though the carer can recognise the signs.

A carer can request a healthcare assessment as a way of ensuring that health services formally consider the person's needs. See chapter 5.

WELFARE DECISIONS

Access to social work information

42.12 Carers may need to receive information about the social care proposed for the person they care for.

The Code of Practice dealing with social work records accepts that volunteers and informal carers may need personal information about a client in order to help them care.[1] The local authority should make it clear to the client what kind of information it will disclose.[2] The assumption is that disclosure should be on a 'need to know' basis.

In exceptional circumstances, a social work department can pass on information even if the client does not consent. One of these circumstances would include risk to third parties, including, for example, risk to staff.[3] The department should make a note on the client's file if it decides to disclose confidential information.

When someone is not able to make decisions about access to social work records, a carer may be able to access personal information, if he or she has some legal authority to act, such as being the person's named person, welfare attorney or guardian.[4]

[1]   *Code on confidentiality of social work records* (Scottish Office circular SWSG1/89), paras 4, 12.7.
[2]   Confidentiality code, para 10.3.
[3]   Confidentiality code, para 13.6.
[4]   Confidentiality code, para 19.

Help from local authority

42.13 A carer can seek help for the person being cared for by requesting a community care assessment, and may request a carer's assessment. See chapter 27.

Local authorities carrying out community care assessments must take into account the views of anyone who gives a substantial amount of care on a regular basis.[1] Good practice guidance requires local authorities to consult with both users and carers, separately if there are differences between them. See 27.09.

---

1   Social Work (Scotland) Act 1968, ss 12A and 12AA.

Limits to carers' authority

42.14 When someone is unable to take decisions about welfare matters, such as where to live, or what day care the person needs, the remedies available under the Adults with Incapacity Act are limited.

For financial matters, the Act contains a hierarchy of measures, depending on the sums involved. For welfare matters, if a carer does not have a welfare power of attorney, the only options are an intervention or guardianship order under Part 6 of the Act. These can be expensive and cumbersome options.

Unfortunately, there is some disagreement between legal commentators about when it is appropriate for a carer to seek a Part 6 order relating to welfare decisions on the adult's behalf.

Most commentators agree that a carer does not need Adults with Incapacity Act authority to carry out day-to-day caring, such as helping a person with washing or feeding. At the time of writing, there is still disagreement about whether more significant interventions (such as arranging for the person to move to residential care) always require an Adults with Incapacity Act order.[1]

This question raises complex legal issues. Some lawyers see the Adults with Incapacity Act as an enabling act, introducing new procedures people can access if helpful. Others believe that it is essential to use the Act's procedures wherever there is a legal vacuum in decision-making. They argue this is essential for the protection of the adult's human rights. Even if no one disagrees with the proposed intervention, obtaining a guardianship order ensures the process is fair.

1   See discussion papers written by the author for the Mental Welfare Commission: *Authorising significant interventions for adults who lack capacity* (August 2004) and *Adults with Incapacity (Scotland) Act 2000: When to invoke the Act* (September 2005) and letters from Chief Social Work Officer to heads of local authority social work departments (30 July 2004) and from the Civil Law Division of the Justice Department (29 July 2005). (On the Scottish Executive's Adults with Incapacity website.)

Where order necessary

42.15 There may be a clear need for an intervention or guardianship order. A carer may need to sell a house or sign a contract for care. An adult's finances may need financial management by a guardian. A carer may be exercising such controls over the adult's life that it is appropriate to seek court approval. Carers should consider the principles of the Act when deciding whether an order would benefit the adult.

A local authority may recommend an order if a carer regularly has to restrain an adult or if the care regime could constitute a deprivation of liberty within human rights law.

The *Bournewood* judgment (see 8.04) has complicated the situation. The European Court of Human Rights held that a man with learning disabilities admitted to hospital without his consent was unlawfully deprived of his liberty, even though he did not object to being there and appeared compliant with the regime.

If a person's care arrangements, including restrictions in a person's own home, could constitute a deprivation of liberty, a guardianship or intervention order under the Adults with Incapacity Act may be necessary to comply with human rights requirements.

Borderline cases

42.16 In other cases, a carer may not feel he or she needs an order and will be surprised when the local authority tells him or her that an order is necessary.

The law is clear that, in the absence of a valid power of attorney or an order under Part 6 of the Adults with Incapacity Act, no one has legal authority to take welfare decisions on behalf of another adult, even if the adult lacks capacity. This so even if the people are spouses or civil partners. Any carer needing legal authority to carry out an intervention needs to seek an order.

In some situations, a carer may have to balance the need to obtain legal authority with other needs of the adult. For example, an adult might need to move urgently, because a carer has died or can no longer cope. Remaining carers may have to weigh up the need for urgent action against the time it might take to obtain an order. It could be argued that this balancing of benefits is in accordance with the principles of the Adults with Incapacity Act.

A carer in this situation needs advice. Draft guidance from the Scottish Executive says that, even in emergencies, a carer cannot make a unilateral decision to move an adult to a care home, unless the carer has the appropriate power to do so, as the person's guardian or attorney.

The Scottish Executive suggests that a carer without such legal authority should request a community care assessment under the Social Work (Scotland) Act 1968, or seek advice from the local authority about whether an Adults with Incapacity Act order is necessary.[1] A local authority can give help in an emergency without a community care assessment (see 27.08), and this might be necessary, while an authority discusses what action is appropriate.

When a carer is unwilling or unable to seek an order, the local authority can apply for an order. It must do so if it considers an order is necessary and no one else is applying or likely to apply.[2] The local authority can ask the court to appoint the carer as guardian. A local authority may be able to make arrangements for the person using its powers under the Social Work (Scotland) Act. See 25.36.

[1]   *Adults with Incapacity (Scotland) Act 2000: Draft Guidance for Local Authorities on when to invoke the Act* (Scottish Executive, 18 May 2006).
[2]   Adults with Incapacity (Scotland) Act 2000, s 57(2).

Applying for order

42.17 At the time of writing, legal aid is available for applications for guardianship and intervention orders. The legal aid rules calculate legal aid on the income of the person being cared for. See chapter 24. Without legal aid, these procedures can be costly. The carer should ask for an estimate from the solicitor. From 1 August 2006, legal aid is free for welfare guardianship regardless of the adult's means.

It is not essential to use a solicitor. The Scottish Executive's Adults with Incapacity website has sample forms and explains the procedure.

Powers of attorney

42.18 The solution to many of the problems above is to give a carer a power of attorney with relevant powers. Anyone with the legal capacity to do so can sign a power of attorney.

The fact that a person has a mental disorder does not automatically mean he or she cannot sign. The test is whether he or she understands what the power is for and wants to grant one. A legally or medically qualified person must confirm this. See chapter 25.

YOUNG CARERS

42.19 A carer under the age of 16 can call for an assessment of his or her needs[1] and can request the local authority to carry out a community care assessment.

A young carer of a person with a mental disorder is a child affected by disability under the Children (Scotland) Act. This means he or she can request help from children's services. See 31.23.

If a family member is subject to compulsory measures under the Mental Health (Care and Treatment) Act, a young carer may be entitled to some help to try to keep the family together. See 31.24.

[1]   Social Work (Scotland) Act 1968, s 12AA.

FINANCIAL MATTERS

Adults with Incapacity Act

42.20 A mental disorder may mean a person needs help managing his or her finances. The carer needs to understand the available procedures. Alzheimer Scotland has produced a helpful guide, which has relevance in situations other than dementia. See Appendix 1.

If a person's main income is welfare benefits, a carer may apply to become a Department of Work and Pensions appointee. The Adults with Incapacity Act contains a hierarchy of measures, depending on the amounts involved and the complexity of the person's affairs.

The person may be willing and able to sign a financial power of attorney. See chapter 26.

Financial support

42.21 A carer (or some other person) may wish to give financial support to the person being cared for, either in the granter's lifetime or after his or her death. The position is extremely complex. The granter needs legal and/or welfare rights advice. For more information, see Appendix 1, further reading.

There are many questions to consider. Firstly, there is the effect of a gift, or regular gifts, on a cared-for person's welfare benefits and on any contributions the person makes to care costs. A gift of capital (and certain regular gifts of income) affects most welfare benefits. Increased income or capital may increase a person's contribution to the costs of residential care. Charges for local authority services are generally means-tested, and may increase if someone receives extra income.

Secondly, inheritance and income tax considerations may influence the way a granter should provide any financial support.

A lawyer or welfare rights adviser can give advice based on individual circumstances. What follows is only an outline of the complex rules.

Gifts of capital or income

42.22 A person who has capital in excess of a certain limit (depending on the person's age) is not eligible for income support or pension credit. Smaller amounts of capital may reduce benefits on a sliding scale.

A person with capital in excess of a certain amount (at the time of writing, £20,000) pays the full costs of residential care. Anyone with capital over a certain amount (at the time of writing, £12,250), must contribute towards the cost of residential care.

Any income received by a person who receives means-tested welfare benefits reduces the amount of the benefits by a corresponding amount, unless it complies with the rules set out below.

Regular maintenance payments

42.23 It is possible to give someone money on a regular basis, as long as the money is not intended for items for which welfare benefits are payable, and does not pay for these items.[1] Welfare benefits are intended to cover rent, food, fuel, rates, clothing, water rates and council tax.

This means that it is possible to give someone money to rent a television or a phone, for example, to buy a bus pass, or to pay for entertainment or education. Setting up a separate bank account and standing orders can help ensure the money is used for the right purpose.

Even if the person uses the money to buy items for which benefits are payable, the first £20 a week is disregarded for benefits purposes.

Similar rules apply to money to fund extras for a person living in residential care, unless the person making the payment is under a legal liability to maintain the person in care.[2]

A carer should generally not pay bills such as electricity, fuel, food or clothing for a person receiving welfare benefits. The person's welfare benefits are intended to cover these items. Any sums paid are treated as the person's capital and may take him or her above the capital limits for benefits.

[1]   See, for example, State Pension Credit Regulations 2002 (SI 2002/1792), Sched IV, para 11.
[2]   National Assistance (Assessment of Resources) Regulations 1992 (SI 1992/2977) (as amended), reg 22(7) and Sched 3, para 10(1).

Irregular gifts

42.24 The welfare benefits system treats irregular gifts of money as capital. There is no need to declare them, unless they bring a claimant's capital above the limits. A carer can give money to pay for a holiday or to pay one-off bills.

Wills and/or trusts

42.25 The most important general advice is to make a will. Otherwise money may pass to someone automatically after a carer dies and may simply reduce the person's entitlement to welfare benefits or increase the charges the person she pays for support services.

A lifetime trust may also be helpful. As well as possible tax advantages, other potential givers can be encouraged to leave money to the trust.

Discretionary trusts

42.26 Many advisers recommend setting up a trust, instead of giving money directly to the person being cared for. The granter gives a sum of money to trustees, who decide when and how to hand over any money to the person.

Advisers usually recommend a 'discretionary trust'. This means that the trustees decide when and if to give any money to the person(s) named in the trust. The person named in the trust is not entitled to demand any money at any time.

Money held in a discretionary trust is not normally part of a person's capital for income support, pension credit or for charging for residential care purposes.[1] Sums paid out may, however, be deducted from benefits, unless close attention is paid to the rules above.

[1]   Money is not part of a person's capital if he or she has no right to call on the capital sum. For residential care, see guidance from Scottish Executive Health Department CCD11/2004, Appendix C, para 10.020.

Establishing trust

42.27 A discretionary trust can be set up for just one person.[1] Some advisers suggest that the trust deed should name more than one person. The trust deed must ensure that the person named in the trust has no right to call for the money. The trust deed should make provision for someone else to receive the money if the person named dies before receiving all the money in the trust.

It can be useful to provide that the trust can pay sums to third parties for the benefit of anyone named in the trust. This can be useful if the person named in the trust could not manage a large sum of money.

A person can set up a trust in his or her lifetime or in a will. Trustees can be individuals and/or professionals. Solicitors, accountants and banks offer trustee services, for a fee.

Enable Scotland runs a trustee service for people with learning disabilities. The trustees have both financial expertise and an understanding of people with learning disabilities. See Appendix 2.

[1]   See Simon Mackintosh, 'Financial advice and taxation' in *Butterworths Scottish Older Client Law Service* (Tottel Publishing), para H.333.

Purchasing accommodation

42.28 Buying a house for someone to live in does not affect the person's welfare benefits. The house can be in the person's name or the granter's. A granter can take out a mortgage to fund a purchase.

The local authority can be asked to carry out a community care assessment to see if it can offer help so that the person can live independently. See chapter 25.

Detailed welfare benefits advice is necessary. Ownership Options in Scotland can give information about possible ways of funding a purchase.

If there already is a suitable house, the owner can create what is called a 'life rent', allowing the cared-for person to stay there for life. When the person dies, the house passes as directed by the granter's will. Another alternative is to put the house into a trust. Legal advice is necessary.

PART 12
CRIMINAL JUSTICE AND
MENTAL DISORDER

Chapter 43

CRIMINAL LAW AND MENTAL HEALTH

43.01 This chapter look the legal impact of a mental illness, learning disability or personality disorder on a person's criminal responsibility. The following chapters look at the criminal justice process and the sentencing options if someone is found guilty of a criminal offence.

Mental disorder may be relevant at a criminal trial in a number of ways. It may mean that the person is not fit to stand trial. It may form a defence to the crimes with which the person is charged or may be an important factor when he or she is sentenced. We look at the different ways in which a person's legal representatives may raise these issues at the trial.

MENTAL DISORDER AND CRIMINAL RESPONSIBILITY

43.02 It is a basic principle of the criminal law that a person is not guilty of a criminal offence unless he or she intended to commit it.[1] Guilt is not just a question of the physical act. The person must have a guilty intent as well.

A person will not be found guilty of murder, for example, unless he or she meant to kill the victim or was reckless as to whether or not he or she killed. (The person might have a defence if he or she was acting in self-defence or was provoked beyond what a reasonable person could stand.)

If a court decides mental disorder has so compelled someone to act that what the person did was not of his or her own free will, the law would not regard the person as guilty of the crime. The person may be not guilty altogether on the grounds of 'insanity', or guilty of a lesser crime, depending on the degree of responsibility.

At the other end of the scale, a woman might be charged with shoplifting at a time when she is suffering from postnatal depression. If she is convicted, the court would be likely to regard her as less culpable than a professional shoplifter who steals for profit.[2]

---

[1]   Although there are some offences, generally created by statute law, where there is strict liability regardless of guilty intent.

[2]   See, for example, *Andrews v Lord Advocate*, 1994 SCCR 910. A man with learning disabilities was convicted of indecent assault. The appeal court

724

reduced his sentence from two years to nine months. The appeal court took into account the effects prison would have on him and said that different considerations should apply in his case.

Scottish Law Commission recommendations

43.03 Following a recommendation of the Millan Committee, the Scottish Law Commission has reviewed the law relating to insanity, diminished responsibility and fitness to plead.[1]

Its report suggests clarification and modernisation of the law in light of current psychiatric understanding. The report is crucial reading for anyone wishing a deeper understanding of these issues.

---

[1]   *Report on Insanity and Diminished Responsibility* (SE/2004/92, 2004).

FITNESS TO PLEAD

43.04 If a person accused of a crime is unable to instruct his or her legal representatives, the trial does not go ahead. Once the court is satisfied that someone is unfit to plead, the court holds an 'examination of facts' to attempt to determine whether the person carried out the act in question.

The court may then make various orders, depending on the person's need for further care and treatment and possible risks to the public.

What constitutes fitness to plead

43.05 A person may be unfit to plead because of a mental illness or a learning disability which means he or she is unable to follow the proceedings. This is sometimes called 'insanity in bar of trial'. This is confusing, as the tests are very different from the 'insanity' defence. Fitness to plead relates to a person's ability to take part in the trial and give proper instructions to his or her solicitor.

Fitness to plead means that a person can understand the legal proceedings he or she is facing, follow the trial and give his or her solicitor instructions as the case proceeds.[1] A person may become unfit to plead as the trial progresses, and any person concerned should raise this with the court.

The fact that someone cannot remember the events which are the subject of the charge does not make him or her legally unfit to plead.[2]

The Scottish Law Commission has made suggestions as to how the courts should decide whether someone is fit to plead. It proposes that the test should be whether the person is able to participate effectively in the trial. If a physical or mental condition makes this impossible, the person would be unfit to plead.

Its report suggests consideration of a number of factors. These include whether the person can understand the nature of the charge, what it means to plead guilty or not guilty and what the trial is for. The court should consider whether the person can follow the course of a trial, understand the effect of evidence given against him or her and communicate adequately with, and give instructions to, his or her legal representatives.[3]

1   *HM Advocate v Wilson*, 1942 JC 75.
2   *Russell v HM Advocate*, 1946 JC 37; *Hughes v HM Advocate*, 2002 JC 23.
3   *Report on insanity and diminished responsibility* (above), recommendation 19.

Fitness to participate

43.06 Even though a person may be legally fit to plead, he or she may be unable to participate effectively in the trial because of limited intellectual ability or mental disorder.

The prosecution and court will have to consider whether special arrangements can remedy this, or else the criminal trial may be in breach of the person's human rights. See 44.11.

Establishing unfitness to plead

43.07 The court requires two medical reports. At least one must be from an approved medical practitioner.[1] If the court is satisfied that the trial cannot proceed, it terminates the trial and holds an examination of facts.[2]

It may sometimes be appropriate to incorporate a report from a clinical psychologist into one of the medical reports, but a psychologist cannot give the report.[3] Psychologists are particularly skilled in assessing capacity.

It may not be possible for the accused person to attend court. The case can continue in his or her absence if there are no objections by the accused person or his or her representative.[4]

In summary (less serious) cases, the accused person must give notice that he or she intends to raise the question of fitness to plead before the first prosecution witness is sworn in, although the prosecution or the court can consider the matter at any stage.[5] (The Scottish Law

Commission believes this provision may be in breach of the European Convention on Human Rights and recommends its repeal.)[6]

1.   Criminal Procedure (Scotland) Act 1995 (as amended by Mental Health (Care and Treatment) (Scotland) Act 2003), s 61(1)(a).
2.   CP(S)A 1995, s 54(1). The court generally accepts the medical reports given and the matter rarely goes to a jury.
3.   *McLachlan v Brown*, 1997 JC 222; *Stewart v HM Advocate*, 1997 JC 183.
4.   CP(S)A 1995, s 54(5).
5.   CP(S)A 1995, s 54(7).
6.   *Insanity and Diminished Responsibility* (above), recommendation 31.

Procedure

43.08 If a court decides an accused person is unfit to plead, it remands him or her in custody or on bail.

The court may make a temporary compulsion order committing the person to hospital until the conclusion of the examination of facts.[1] The court must be satisfied that the person has a mental disorder, that there is medical treatment available, that there would be a significant risk to the person's health, safety or welfare or to the safety of others without such treatment and that a suitable hospital is available.

The temporary compulsion order authorises the giving of medical treatment in accordance with Part 16 of the Mental Health (Care and Treatment) Act.[2] The person cannot appeal against the order.

For admission to hospital and the person's rights, see chapter 48. For appeals see below.

1.   Criminal Procedure (Scotland) Act 1995 (as amended by the Mental Health (Care and Treatment) (Scotland) Act 2003), s 54(1).
2.   CP(S)A 1995, s 54(2B).

Examination of facts

43.09 The examination of facts follows as far as possible the order in which the trial would have proceeded.[1] The procedure may take place in the absence of the accused person if there is no objection to this[2] but if the accused person is not legally represented, the court appoints a solicitor for him or her.[3]

The court must decide whether it is satisfied beyond reasonable doubt that the person committed the offence and whether there are any grounds for acquitting him or her (such as self-defence or 'insanity' at the time of the offence). (The standard of proof is the balance of probabilities.)

The court then either makes a finding that the person committed the offence or acquits him or her.[4] See chapter 46 for sentencing options if the court finds the person committed the offence.

1   Criminal Procedure (Scotland) Act 1995, s 55(6).
2   CP(S)A 1995, s 55(5).
3   CP(S)A 1995, s 56(3).
4   CP(S)A 1995, s 55.

ACQUITTAL BECAUSE OF 'INSANITY'

43.10 Someone who was 'insane' at the time he or she committed the offence, is not guilty of the crime.[1] When a person is fit to stand trial, 'insanity' is a matter for the jury. If the person is not fit to stand trial, the examination of facts makes a finding.[2]

'Insanity' is a legal concept, not a medical diagnosis. The 'insanity' defence means that if someone was so mentally disturbed at the time he or she committed the offence, that the person cannot truly be held to be responsible for what he or she did, the person should be acquitted.

A person should be held responsible only if he or she meant to do what he or she did, or was criminally reckless as to the consequences.[3]

Another way of putting the test is to ask what caused the person to act as he or she did. If the answer is a mental illness or other mental disorder, the person should be found not guilty because of 'insanity'.[4]

1   Criminal Procedure (Scotland) Act 1995, s 54(6).
2   See above.
3   For full discussion of the legal and philosophical basis of the concept, see GH Gordon, *The Criminal Law of Scotland* (3rd edn, W Green 7 Son, 2001), chap 10. See also Scottish Law Commission *Report on Insanity and Diminished Responsibility* (above).
4   Gordon (above), para 10.15.

What constitutes 'insanity'

Scottish tests

43.11 One of the great authorities on Scottish criminal law, the writer Hume, spelt out the test over 200 years ago. He said that the person must have been suffering from:

'an absolute alienation of reason … such a disease as deprives the patient of the knowledge of the true aspect and position of things about him,—hinders him from distinguishing friend or foe,—and gives him up to the impulses of his own distempered fancy'.[1]

This description has been quoted in many subsequent cases and (while we might change some of the language) is still relevant today. A later case expanded the definition:

'There must have been some mental defect, to use a broad neutral word … by which his reason was overpowered, and he was thereby rendered incapable of exerting his reason to control his conduct and reactions. If his reason was alienated … he was not responsible … even although otherwise he may have been apparently quite rational.'[2]

There must be a 'total alienation of reason' in relation to the act committed. The accused person may have been suffering from delusions which led him or her to misunderstand the real situation, or he or she may have known that what he or she was doing was against the law, but have been compelled to act because of mental disorder.

[1] David Hume, *Commentaries on the law of (Scotland) respecting Crimes* (1797), i.37.

[2] *H M Advocate v Kidd* ,1960 JC 61, Lord Strachan.

Tests in England/Wales

43.12 In England and Wales, the test for insanity is set out in a series of rules known as the M'Naghten rules.[1] Most commentators agree that the M'Naghten rules do not form part of the law of Scotland, although some decisions seem to rely on them quite heavily.

One of the most frequently stated rules is that a person can be regarded as 'insane' if he or she:

'did not know the nature and quality of his or her acts, or if he or she did, he or she did not know that what he or she was doing was wrong.'

This rule may be relevant in some circumstances, but it has been criticised for linking insanity to defects in the knowledge and understanding of the accused person. The M'Naghten rules fail to cover the situation where someone is able to understand what he or she is doing but is unable, because of emotional disturbance, to use reason or intellect to control his or her acts.

[1] Advice to the House of Lords from the Law Lords, following a controversial murder trial. (1843) 10 Cl & F 200. Also sometimes referred to as the McNaughton rules.

Inability to control actions

43.13 Scots law seems to recognise that a mental illness or learning disability can render a person incapable of controlling his or her actions, if the person can fulfil the 'total alienation of reason' test mentioned above. It is wider than the narrow test in the M'Naghten rules. One of the great legal writers put it clearly:

> 'If, therefore, the accused is in such a situation that, though possessing a sense of the distinction between right and wrong, he cannot apply it correctly in his own case, and labours under an illusion which completely misleads his judgment, as mistaking one person for another, or fastening a dreadful charge, entirely groundless, on a friend, he is entitled to the benefit of the plea of insanity'.[1]

See also Hume, (above). One case concerned a person with a serious depressive illness who killed his children. Although he knew what he was doing and that it was wrong, the court accepted the plea that he was 'insane'. His mental illness rendered him unable to use his reason to control his actions.[2]

In another case, the court refused to accept that the accused person's inability to control his actions (caused by drugs administered to him without his knowledge) should be an excuse. While the drugs had limited his ability to control his actions, he still retained some ability to control what he was doing. The court said unless an accused person could show a 'total loss of control' of his or her actions caused by a mental disorder, the insanity defence could not succeed.[3]

The Scottish Law Commission recommends that the test should be that the person is unable to appreciate the nature or wrongfulness of his or her conduct. This is intended to cover both the person's mental or cognitive functioning and situations where the person's mental disorder in some way distorts his or her reasoning about what is right to do.[4]

1   Alison, *Principles of the Criminal Law of Scotland* (1832), pp 645–646.
2   *H M A v Sharp*, 1927 JC 66.
3   *Cardle v Mulrainey*, 1992 SCCR 658.
4   Recommendation 6.

Pleading 'insanity'

43.14 Because 'insanity' is a complete defence to the crime, the accused person must put forward the defence. It is not up to the prosecution to raise it. Everyone is presumed 'sane' until the contrary is proved.

The accused person's legal representatives will obtain psychiatric reports. The jury decides, based on the medical evidence. The accused person must satisfy the jury that, on the balance of probabilities, he or she was 'insane' at the time of the offence. In summary (less serious) proceedings, the sheriff decides.[1]

1   Criminal Procedure (Scotland) Act 1995, s 54(6).

Limits to defence

43.15 The insanity defence is not available where the person who committed the crime was unable to control his or her actions because he or she was under the influence of drink or drugs,[1] unless someone administered these against the person's will or without his or her knowledge.[2]

However a person with an organic brain disorder caused by alcoholism or drug use may be able to rely on the 'insanity' defence.[3]

1   *Brennan v HM Advocate*, 1977 SLT 151.
2   *Ross v Lord Advocate*, 1991 SLT 564.
3   *H M Adv McDonald* (1890) 2 White 517.

Scottish Law Commission proposals

43.16 The Scottish Law Commission recommends replacing the common law defence of 'insanity' with a defence, set out in statute law, that at the time of the offence the accused person lacked criminal responsibility because of mental disorder.

The test would be that at the time of the crime, the accused person was unable to appreciate the nature or wrongfulness of his or her conduct because of mental disorder.

The test would expressly exclude psychopathic personality disorder, as at present.[1]

1   Scottish Law Commission, above, recommendations 1–8.

Sentencing options

43.17 See 46.02 for the sentencing options available when a person is found unfit to plead and an examination of facts finds he or she has committed the offence, or when the person is acquitted on the grounds of 'insanity'.

Appeals

43.18 An accused person can appeal against a finding that he or she is unfit to plead and against the refusal of the court to find him or her unfit to plead. The person can also appeal against the findings of the examination of facts that he or she committed the offence, and against the failure of the court to acquit on the grounds of insanity.[1] The person can also appeal against any order the court makes.[2]

The prosecution can appeal on a point of law.[3]

[1]   Criminal Procedure (Scotland) Act 1995, ss 106 and 107.
[2]   CP(S)A 1995, s 62.
[3]   CP(S)A 1995, s 63(1).

DIMINISHED RESPONSIBILITY

Background

43.19 To establish the defence of 'insanity', the accused person has to show that he or she was suffering from a mental disorder which totally robbed him or her of reason. Someone with a mental condition which does not totally rob the person of reason cannot rely on the insanity defence.

The law recognises that a mental disorder falling short of 'insanity' should be taken into account when considering the person's responsibility for a serious crime. The concept of diminished responsibility developed at a time when the fixed penalty for murder was capital punishment. The law had to find a way of making allowances for someone who killed unlawfully, but who, because of some form of mental disorder, should not be liable to the full penalties of the law.

Someone who killed another person at a time when his or her responsibility is diminished is convicted, not of murder, but of culpable homicide (in England and Wales, manslaughter). The judge then has the discretion to impose the most appropriate sentence.

Despite the abolition of the death penalty, murder still carries a fixed life sentence. There are still cases, therefore, where it is appropriate to plead diminished responsibility.

Nature of the defence

43.20 The idea that it may not be appropriate to hold a person who suffers from a mental disability legally responsible for a criminal act was first stated 200 years ago.[1] The classic statement of the rule was made by Lord Alness.[2] He said:

> 'It is very difficult to put it in a phrase, but it has been put in this way: that there must be aberration or weakness of mind; that there must be some form of mental unsoundness; that there must be a state of mind which is bordering on, though not amounting to, insanity; that there must be a mind so affected that responsibility is diminished from full responsibility to partial responsibility—in other words, the prisoner in question must be only partially accountable for his actions. And I think one can see running through the cases that there is implied ... that there must be some form of mental disease.'

The important case of *Galbraith v HM Advocate* expanded and clarified this test.[3] The court said that someone can be said to have had diminished responsibility if the person's ability to determine and control his or her acts is substantially impaired because of some abnormality of mind.

> 'The abnormality of mind may take various forms. It may mean that the individual perceives physical acts and matters differently from a normal person. Or else it may affect his ability to form a rational judgment as to whether a particular act is right or wrong or to decide whether to perform it. The abnormality .... may be congenital or derive from an organic condition, from some psychotic illness, such as schizophrenia or severe depression, or from the psychological effects of severe trauma ... While the plea of diminished responsibility will be available only where the accused's abnormality of mind had substantial effects in relation to his act, there is no requirement that his state of mind should have bordered on insanity.'[4]

[1]   In the case of *Alex. Dingwall* (1867) 5 Irv. 466.
[2]   In *H M Advocate v Savage*, 1923 JC 49, at p 50.
[3]   2002 JC1.
[4]   Lord Justice General Rodger in *Galbraith* above.

Limits to defence

43.21 The courts have stressed that they will not extend the defence to people who do not suffer from a recognised abnormality of mind.

A person who was intoxicated at the time of committing the offence cannot plead diminished responsibility.[1] (The courts have always been unsympathetic to people who commit crimes while under the influence of drugs or alcohol.) A mental disorder caused by alcoholism or substance abuse could bring someone within the defence.[2]

A person with a short temper which he or she is unable to control cannot plead diminished responsibility, unless the person shows this is a result of an abnormality of mind.[3]

The Scottish courts have also refused to allow people with personality disorders to plead diminished responsibility.[4] (This should be seen in context. The leading case was heard during a wave of violent crime in Glasgow. The accused person had drunk a great deal of alcohol. The court was not impressed with the medical evidence and was concerned that criminals would escape justice if they could use evidence of a flawed personality as a defence to criminal charges.)

The courts have as yet shown no interest in allowing the defence of diminished responsibility to people suffering from personality disorders. The Scottish Law Commission considers there is no reason in principle why the defence should not be available.[5]

[1]   See *Brennan v HM Advocate*, 1977 JC 38.
[2]   See Scottish Law Commission (above), para 3.37ff.
[3]   *H M Advocate v Braithwaite*, 1945 JC 55.
[4]   *Carraher v HM Advocate*, 1946 JC 108.
[5]   See recommendation 14.

Diminished responsibility and learning disability

43.22 If a person with a learning disability is charged with a crime, he or she may be able to benefit from the diminished responsibility defence. This will depend on the nature and degree of the disorder and its effect on the person's responsibility for his or her actions.

There have been some unfortunate cases. In one case, the court refused to say that a person who was 'emotionally immature and vulnerable' had diminished responsibility.[1]

In another case, medical reports indicated that the person had 'gross emotional immaturity' and 'severe personality disorder' which could have made him liable to detention under the Mental Health (Scotland) Act 1984. The court held that he should be held fully legally responsible for the crimes with which he was charged.[2]

These decisions now have to be reconsidered in the light of the decision in *Galbraith*. That court criticised them as 'unduly restrictive'.

1   *Connelly v HM Advocate*, 1990 SCCR 504.

2   *Williamson v HM Advocate*, 1994 JC 149.

Pleading diminished responsibility

43.23 Although diminished responsibility is a mitigating factor affecting sentence rather than a defence to the crimes alleged, the accused person must establish diminished responsibility on the balance of probabilities test.[1] The person must obtain psychiatric reports (and possibly psychological reports) and the prosecution will seek reports.

The courts are unwilling to allow psychiatrists to give opinions as to whether the accused person has diminished responsibility. They have stressed that the role of the psychiatrist is to provide the medical evidence of mental illness or disorder.[2]

If the defence appears to have made a case to answer, the judge puts the question of diminished responsibility to the jury. If the accused person's own psychiatrists do not confirm that the person has a mental disorder of some kind, the judge is free to withhold the case from the jury.[3]

Diminished responsibility is usually only raised in cases of murder, to avoid the fixed life sentence, but it has been used to reduce a charge of attempted murder to one of assault.[4]

1   *HM Advocate v Kidd*, 1960 JC 61. The defence in *Lindsay v HM Advocate*, 1997 JC 19 challenged this rule, but the court said it was for Parliament to change the rules, not the courts.

2   See, for example, *Carraher* (above) and *HM Advocate v Martindale*, 1992 SCCR 400, where the psychiatrist gave evidence that the accused person had diminished responsibility even though he had no mental illness or disorder. He was on the 'borderline of mental disease'. The court said this was not enough and it was not for the psychiatrist to direct the court on whether the accused person had diminished responsibility. The duty of the psychiatrist is to give evidence as to the person's mental state, *Galbraith v HM Advocate* (above).

3   See *Connelly* (above).

4   *HM Advocate v Blake*, 1986 SLT 661.

PROVOCATION

43.24 We have seen that the law does not allow a person to plead lack of self-control in mitigation of a crime committed. The law recognises that in certain circumstances a person may lose self-control because of the acts of others. The law calls this provocation, and this section looks at how the rules apply to people living with mental health challenges and learning disabilities.

If a person can prove that he or she lost self-control because another person provoked him, he or she will be found guilty not of murder, but of culpable homicide.[1] Provocation may consist of physical assaults, sexual betrayal, but probably not abusive words.

The test of what kind of action might constitute provocation is what would cause a 'reasonable person' to lose self-control. The court does not take into account any additional difficulties a person might suffer because of a mental disability. Action or abuse which might be particularly difficult for a person to bear because of a disability, would not attract any special legal treatment, although it might, of course, be taken into account on sentence.

Provocation may make someone mentally ill. One person killed a workmate after continual taunting. The judge held that the long course of provocation had so affected his mind as to render his responsibility diminished. He was convicted of culpable homicide.[2]

Similar cases may arise where spouses kill their partners after a long course of abuse. The person may be able to plead provocation or diminished responsibility.[3]

---

[1]   For a full discussion, see Gordon (above), chap 25.

[2]   *HM Advocate v Robert Smith*, 1893 1 Adam 34.

[3]   See *Galbraith* (above).

AUTOMATISM

43.25 It can be a defence to a crime that the accused person was unconscious at the time of the offence. This could be due to the effect of, for example, an epileptic fit. The law calls this 'automatism'. The test is very similar to the 'alienation of reason leading to complete lack of control' that is used in 'insanity' cases.

If automatism is the result of a mental disorder, the person will be found not guilty because of 'insanity'. If it was from some other external factor, the person can plead automatism, provided the factor was not self-induced or foreseeable.[1]

A person cannot claim the defence if he or she has voluntarily used drink or drugs and become unconscious.[2]

[1] See *Ross v HM Advocate*, 1991 JC 210. *Sorley v HM Advocate*, 1992 SLT 867.
[2] *Finegan v Heywood*, The Times, May 10, 2000.

MENTAL DISORDER AS MITIGATION

43.26 Although a person's mental disorder may not amount to 'insanity' or diminished responsibility, it is clearly something the court should know about when it passes sentence. The person should always tell his or her legal representative about any mental condition he or she may have.

The legal representative will want to get as much information as possible. He or she might want to contact the person's named person, carer or advocate, as well as the GP and the social work department, to see if they can offer any help. A solicitor may try to persuade the prosecution to drop the case if the offence is not serious and the person is able to get the help he or she needs.

A solicitor may seek psychiatric or psychological reports to establish the person's condition at the time of the crime and to ask for recommendations as to what help the person might need.

SUICIDE

43.27 Whilst it is generally agreed that it is not a crime to kill oneself, unfortunately some people who have unsuccessfully attempted suicide have been prosecuted for committing a breach of the peace. The standard textbook on criminal law says such cases are rare,[1] but the national press reported two such cases, in a six month period between November 1997 and April 1998.[2]

In 1998 the then Lord Advocate (the person in charge of criminal prosecutions in Scotland) confirmed that:

> 'It is not normally in the public interests to prosecute mentally ill people on charges of breach of the peace relating to suicide attempts. It has been the long standing policy of the Procurator Fiscal Service to avoid prosecution in such cases and to endeavour to have persons in respect of whom such allegations are made dealt with, where appropriate, by the Mental Health Services. Police are under instruction to deal with cases of attempted suicide by means other than arrest and to attempt to invoke the procedures under Mental Health legislation wherever possible'.[3]

The author understands that guidance has been given to Procurators Fiscal to re-emphasise this policy. The guidance reminds Procurators Fiscal that the police faced with a suicidal person may be able to use the powers given to them to take the person to a place of safety (see 30.20).

1   GH Gordon, *Criminal Law of Scotland*, (3rd edn, W Green & Son, 2001), para 23.01.
2   'Man in court over new suicide threat', *Edinburgh Evening News*, 13 November 1997; 'Suicide bid woman sent to Cornton Vale', *The Scotsman*, 1 April 1998.
3   Letter to the author, 2 June 1998.

Suicide pacts

43.28 A person who survives a suicide pact after killing a partner may be charged with homicide even if the other consented, as the victim's consent is no defence. However, unlike England and Wales, Scotland does not have a specific criminal offence of assisting another to commit suicide.

Chapter 44

SPECIAL MEASURES FOR SUSPECTS AND WITNESSES

44.01 This chapter looks at what happens if a mentally vulnerable person comes into contact with the police because he or she has been involved with a crime as a suspect or witness. (See 30.20 for police powers when someone may be at risk in a public place.)

If a case comes to court, the court can implement special measures to protect vulnerable witnesses. These may be appropriate whether someone is accused of a crime, or is a witness or victim. They may also be appropriate in civil (non-criminal) cases. Chapter 35 considers these issues.

APPROPRIATE ADULT SCHEME

44.02 Anyone interviewed by the police as a possible suspect will feel very vulnerable. Some people are perhaps particularly vulnerable. They may be at risk of being misunderstood, of making incriminating statements or of not understanding their rights.

The police may ask a person to go to a police station to help the police with their enquiries. The person should understand that he or she has a right to refuse to go. It may be difficult for someone in a confused state to understand this.

Where the police take someone to a police station because they suspect the person of having committed a crime, they may detain the person for up to six hours. Even when the police charge someone, the person cannot insist on seeing a solicitor. The only right is to see a solicitor before the person appears in court.[1] These rules could seriously compromise someone who is vulnerable.

---

[1]   Criminal Procedure (Scotland) Act 1995, ss 14 and 15.

Use of appropriate adult

44.03 Unlike England and Wales, which have a statutory Code under the Police and Criminal Evidence Act 1984, Scotland has no statutory protection for vulnerable people during police interviews. In Scotland, the rules are in guidance from the Scottish Executive. This requires that an 'appropriate adult' is involved in such cases.[1]

An appropriate adult should be present whenever the police interview someone who may have a mental disorder. This includes people with mental illness, learning disability, acquired brain damage and dementia.

If the police interview someone who appears to be mentally disordered, they should arrange for a psychiatrist or the police surgeon to examine him or her. If the doctor confirms the person has a mental disorder, they should suspend the interview until an appropriate adult can be present.

The appropriate adult should also be present if the police charge someone or if prosecution or defence lawyers wish to take statements from the person. The appropriate adult can also support the person in court. See below.

[1]   *Interviewing people who are mentally disordered: Appropriate Adult schemes* (Scottish Office, June 1998). ('The appropriate adult guidance'.)

Identifying appropriate adult

44.04 The appropriate adult should be someone who has received special training, who understands the mental disability from which the person suffers and who will help him or her understand the police interview process.

A close friend, relative or carer should not generally act as appropriate adult, even though he or she may be the person most able to communicate with the person. A friend, relative or carer may attend alongside the appropriate adult, provided this does not prejudice the police's ability to conduct the interview.[1]

[1]   Appropriate adult guidance, para 2.2.

Appropriate adult's duties

44.05 The appropriate adult has clearly defined and limited duties. The role of the appropriate adult is to provide 'support and reassurance' to the person, assist communication and make sure the person understands police questions. The appropriate adult should ensure that a person under suspicion understands his or her rights.

The appropriate adult must not advise the person how or whether to answer questions. He or she cannot object to any questions or tell the police if he or she thinks any questioning is unfair.

An appropriate adult could find it extremely difficult to 'reassure' someone suspected of a crime if the appropriate adult is unhappy about the way a line of questioning is going, yet unable to do anything to stop it. The appropriate adult can advise the police officer if he or she considers the interviewee is becoming distressed and can request the police officer to suspend or stop the interview. The final decision rests with the police officer conducting the interview.

Limitations of system

44.06 There have been very few court cases concerning the use of an appropriate adult in Scotland.

In one case the court refused to allow the prosecution to rely on a confession by the accused person, even though an appropriate adult had been present at the police interview. The appropriate adult reported that the person understood his right to remain silent, but the sheriff was not satisfied.

The sheriff said it was essential that appropriate adult have 'at least a basic knowledge' of suspects' rights and can advise suspects of their rights in simple terms.

The sheriff said it might have been preferable if a solicitor had acted as appropriate adult. The questioning of the suspect had been unduly 'robust' for a vulnerable person. The court would have refused to hear the confession on those grounds.

The Scottish Office guidance does not envisage solicitors being appropriate adults, but does not rule it out.

The appropriate adult was not in court to explain her report and the sheriff criticised this.[1] An appropriate adult should generally be prepared to attend court and answer questions on the conduct, but not the content, of the interview.

[1]   *HM Advocate v Milligan* (2003) Sheriff Stewart, 19 March 2003.

Impact of scheme

44.07 Most of Scotland now has access to appropriate adult schemes.[1] Research carried out on behalf of the Scottish Executive shows that the scheme has not been widely used. The research suggests that appropriate adults were not available for everyone who required them.[2]

It is also a matter of concern that solicitors and advocates were generally unfamiliar with the scheme. A legal representative could challenge police action as unfair if an appropriate adult was not present when the police interviewed a person with a mental disorder.

Forensic medical advisers, (who are supposed to ensure that an appropriate adult is present at any examination of the mentally disordered person) were also unfamiliar with the scheme.

For all these reasons, the researchers recommended that Scottish Ministers put the scheme on a statutory basis. At the time of writing, the Scottish Executive is reviewing this.

[1] See Dr Lindsay Thomson, Viki Galt, Dr Rajan Darje, *An Evaluation of Appropriate Adult Schemes in Scotland* e (Scottish Executive Social Research 78/2004). 86% of the population are covered.
[2] In 2002, such records as were available (not all areas kept records) showed the police used appropriate adults on 827 occasions; but 1,557 people appearing to have a diagnosis of schizophrenia, learning disability or dementia faced criminal charges in court. Thomson, Galt and Darjee (above). The researchers (two psychiatrists and a psychologist) observed proceedings in one police station. They saw high levels of mental disorder but no use of appropriate adults.

Failure to use appropriate adult

44.08 The absence of an appropriate adult in a police interview does not necessarily render evidence the police obtain at the interview inadmissible. It is for the court to decide whether the evidence was obtained fairly and for the prosecution to prove this.[1] The court can admit the evidence if it does not think the absence of an appropriate adult means the interview was unfair.

What is fair depends on all the circumstances of the case. The person must make the statement freely and voluntarily. The police must not extract a statement by unfair and improper means.[2] The court will take into account the vulnerability of the accused person, and whether the person understood the situation and appreciated his or her right to silence.[3]

[1] *Thompson v Crowe*, 2000 JC 173 at p 1043.
[2] Lord Justice General Rodger in *Thomson v Crowe* (above), at paras 191H–192A.

3   Lord McCluskey in *LB v HM Advocate*, Appeal Court, High Court of
      Justiciary, 11 April 2003.

Where confession not allowed

44.09 In England and Wales, where the scheme is on a statutory basis, the
courts have disallowed confessions obtained where an appropriate adult
was not present.[1]

In one case, the police did not provide an appropriate adult for a
person with a diagnosis of schizophrenia, because at the time he seemed
lucid and fit to be interviewed. The Court of Appeal said the judge had
failed to consider the reasons for having an appropriate adult present at
the interview and the safeguards it could provide. It set aside the
conviction.[2]

As appropriate adult schemes become better established in Scotland,
it may be difficult to prove that police have obtained information fairly if
they fail to secure the presence of an appropriate adult.

1   See *R v Lamont* [1989] Crim LR 813, *R v Kenny* [1994] Crim LR 284.
2   *R v Aspinall* [1999] 2 Cr App R 115.

PROTECTIONS FOR PERSON ON TRIAL

44.10 If someone with a mental illness or learning disability faces a
criminal trial, the judge is responsible for ensuring that the trial is fair
and that the person is able to participate effectively. The judge should
bear in mind any special needs of the person, such as youth or
vulnerability.[1]

The judge may agree to the use of special measures if he or she
decides the accused person is a vulnerable witness. Chapter 35 deals with
special measures for vulnerable witnesses, including the accused person.

1   See *SC v UK* [2004] ECtHR 263 (below).

Ensuring effective participation

44.11 Article 6 of the European Convention on Human Rights says that
everyone facing criminal charges is entitled to a fair hearing. The person
has a right to hear the charges promptly, in a language he or she
understands, and to have an interpreter if he or she does not understand
or speak the language used in court.

The United Kingdom has failed to meet these standards on several occasions. In one case the court failed to provide an interpreter for a person whose first language was not English.[1] In another high-profile case, an English court was criticised for failing to make proper arrangements for young people facing serious criminal charges.[2]

[1]   *Cuscani v UK* [2002] ECtHR 630.
[2]   *T v UK* [2002] ECtHR 630, *V v UK* [1999] ECtHR 171.

Effective participation in trial

44.12 In a case of particular relevance, the UK was found to have breached human rights at the trial in England of a young man of limited intellectual abilities. The court did not make adequate arrangements for him to participate fully in his trial.[1]

A doctor reported that the young man understood that what he had done was wrong and he was fit to plead. The human rights court said this did not mean that he was able to participate properly in his trial. He did not appear to understand the role of the jury (and the importance of making a good impression on them) or that he risked a custodial sentence.

Effective participation means that the accused person has a broad understanding of the nature of the trial process and of what is at stake, including the significance of any penalty the court may impose.

The person should be able to understand the general thrust of what is said in court, if necessary with the assistance of an interpreter, lawyer, social worker or friend. He or she should be able to follow what prosecution witnesses say. An accused person who has legal representation should be able to explain to the lawyer his or her version of events, point out any statements with which he or she disagrees and tell the lawyer any facts which may be relevant to the defence.[2]

When a child or young person is not able to participate fully because of his or her age or maturity, the court should adapt the trial procedure to his or her needs.[3]

Although the court did not say so, it is likely that similar considerations will apply wherever someone with special needs, including communication needs, faces trial on criminal charges.

[1]   *SC v UK* [2004] ECtHR 263.
[2]   *SC v UK* (above) at para 29.
[3]   *SC v UK* (above) at para 35.

Special measures

44.13 The court may decide that an accused person is a vulnerable witness. Criminal procedure is being reformed to allow special measures for vulnerable and intimidated witnesses. See chapter 35.

If the accused person is a vulnerable witness, the court will consider whether it is appropriate to use special measures. It will consider whether the person will have legal representation at the trial and, if not, whether he or she is entitled to it. It will also consider any alleged intimidation of the accused person by any co-accused or his or her family.[1]

Any of the special measures may be appropriate, except that an accused person cannot give evidence from behind a screen.[2]

[1]   Criminal Procedure (Scotland) Act 1995, s 271F.
[2]   CP(S)A 1995, s 271F(8).

WITNESSES AND VICTIMS OF CRIME

44.14 Most commentators accept that people with mental health needs are more likely to harm themselves than pose a risk to other people.[1] They are also more likely to be the victims of certain crimes.[2]

There has been substantial reform. The appropriate adult scheme can help witnesses and victims. There have been reforms to court procedures following the Vulnerable Witnesses (Scotland) Act 2004. See chapter 35.

[1]   See, for example, comments by Mental Welfare Commission in its Report of the Enquiry into the care and treatment of Philip McFadden, 1995, p 24.
[2]   *An exploration of harassment of people with mental health problems living in Scottish communities* (Nuffield Centre for Community Care Studies, Glasgow University with the National Schizophrenia Fellowship (Scotland) and the former Scottish Users' Network, 1991). See also KM Berzins, A Petch and J M Atkinson 'Prevalence and experience of harassment of people with mental health problems living in the community' (2003) 183 British Journal of Psychiatry 526–533.

Appropriate adults at police interviews

44.15 An appropriate adult (see above) should be present when the police interview a person with a mental disorder as a witness to or victim of a crime.[1]

The appropriate adult can help the person tell his or her story adequately. If a witness or victim can give evidence to the best of his or her ability, there is more chance of a successful prosecution.

¹   Interviewing people who are mentally disordered: 'Appropriate Adult' schemes (Scottish Office, June 1998).

Witness statements

44.16 Before a trial, witnesses may have to make witness statements for the prosecution and/or the defence. The people who take these statements are not necessarily qualified lawyers, and they may have little experience in working with people with special needs.

The appropriate adult guidance says it may be advisable for an appropriate adult to be present when people make witness statements.¹ These interviews can be extremely stressful.

The Law Society has a Code of Conduct for criminal work.² Solicitors must take account of any special needs of the witness and ensure that the person taking witness statements is aware of these needs.

The solicitor is responsible for any distress or inconvenience caused to the witness by any failure to comply with this responsibility.³ Unfortunately, while the Code suggests that a witness may have a friend or supporter with them during the taking of statements, it does not mention the use of appropriate adults. The Law Society is currently updating the Code and considering this matter.⁴

¹   See para 4.4.
²   See Law Society of Scotland website.
³   Code of conduct, para 13.
⁴   Correspondence with the author.

Chapter 45

THE CRIMINAL COURT PROCESS: FROM ARREST TO SENTENCE

45.01 This chapter looks at the legal process, from the decision to prosecute to the end of the trial. Chapter 46 deals with sentencing options.

People with varying kinds of mental disorders may come before the criminal courts. The courts may need psychiatric reports to see if the person is fit to stand trial, or the person should be acquitted on the grounds of 'insanity'. See chapter 43.

A person charged with an offence may need psychiatric help while awaiting trial. If the person is convicted, the court may need psychiatric reports to help it decide the appropriate sentence.

The rules are in both mental health legislation and in the criminal procedure legislation.[1] They are very complex. The Mental Health (Care and Treatment) Act has simplified and rationalised them somewhat, by modifying some provisions of the Criminal Procedure (Scotland) Act 1995. Anyone working or interested in these matters needs an up-to-date copy of the Criminal Procedure Act, taking in all the relevant amendments.

This chapter outlines the procedures. Anyone transferred to hospital under the criminal procedure receives a Scottish Executive booklet explaining the rules.[2] Volume 3 of the Mental Health (Care and Treatment) Act Code of Practice contains detailed information about the rules.

---

[1]   In Parts 8 to 13 of the Mental Health (Care and Treatment) (Scotland) Act 2003 and Part VI of the Criminal Procedure (Scotland) Act 1995. The Criminal Justice (Scotland) Act 2003 has made further amendments.

[2]   *The New Mental Health Act: A guide for people involved in criminal justice proceedings*, available from the Scottish Executive Health Department. On the Scottish Executive's mental health law website.

Grounds for criminal justice orders

45.02 A criminal court makes a mental health order only if someone needs care and treatment for his or her mental disorder.

So far as possible, the Mental Health (Care and Treatment) Act provisions are the same, whether the person comes from a 'civil' (non-criminal) order or from the criminal justice system. Differences arise when someone is subject to special restrictions because of concern about public safety.

The grounds for making an order are also broadly similar. The person must suffer from a mental disorder. Treatment must be available to alleviate or prevent deterioration in the person's condition. The treatment must be necessary because of a risk to the health, safety or welfare of the person or the safety of other people.

Unlike civil orders, the criminal court is not concerned whether the person has a significant impairment of his or her medical decision-making. This is because a criminal court is considering an order as an alternative to punishment, such as a prison sentence. Whether or not the accused person can make treatment decisions is not relevant to the court's decision.

Impact of principles

45.03 The principles of the Mental Health (Care and Treatment) Act apply to everyone subject to compulsory measures under that Act, including those who have come through the criminal justice system.

The only difference is that the Mental Health (Care and Treatment) Act principles do not bind the criminal courts, which make the original orders, as the court makes these orders under the Criminal Procedure Act and not the Mental Health (Care and Treatment) Act.

If a person subject to compulsory measures has a named person, he or she has an important role if the court makes a mental health order. Doctors and mental health officers should be in contact with the person's named person and aware of his or her views throughout the criminal justice process.[1]

---

[1]   Code of Practice, vol 3, para 2.52.

PROSECUTION TO COMMITTAL

Decision to prosecute

45.04 When a crime is committed, the Procurator Fiscal or the Crown Office (depending on the seriousness of the crime) decides whether to prosecute. They decide whether a prosecution is in the public interest,[1] bearing in mind the interests of the victim, of the accused person and of the wider community.[2]

Anyone who believes it is not in the public interest to prosecute someone with a mental disorder can contact the Crown Office or Procurator Fiscal. A solicitor can do this on the person's behalf.

1 For more information about how decisions are made, see *Who is responsible for the investigation and prosecution of crime?*, information provided by the Crown Office and the Procurator Fiscal service at www.crownoffice.gov.uk.
2 See Crown Office Prosecution Code (available on Crown Office website), pp 8–10. The health of the suspect is a factor the prosecution take into account.

Diversion from prosecution

45.05 There may be situations where someone with a mental disorder commits a crime but it would not be in the public interest to prosecute the person. A diversion scheme may be able to help prevent the person from offending again.

A number of such schemes are now in operation. They may involve referring the person to a social worker, psychiatrist, or psychologist, or to a scheme run by a local authority or voluntary organisation.

People living with mental health challenges or learning disabilities are one of the priority target groups for diversion schemes.[1] Diversion may be appropriate where the prosecution is satisfied that there is a case for prosecution and the crime is not serious.[2]

A person offered a place in a diversion scheme is entitled to decline the offer. The prosecution then decides whether to continue with the case.

1 See the Scottish Executive's criminal justice website.
2 See Code of Practice, vol 3, paras 2.16, 2.19.

Instructing a solicitor

45.06 A person charged with a criminal offence should instruct a solicitor as soon as possible. Legal aid may be available to help towards the cost.

The solicitor can advise. The Public Defence Solicitor's Office can offer help to clients eligible for legal aid in Edinburgh, Glasgow and Inverness.

The client may be unable to give the solicitor a clear account of what happened or proper instructions on how to proceed. The trial cannot go ahead unless the solicitor can properly represent the client's point of view. This is called 'insanity in bar of trial'. See 43.04.

A friend, carer or advocate can attend the meeting with the solicitor. He or she may be able to help the solicitor get clear instructions or advise when would be a better time to visit.

The solicitor may need to obtain a psychiatrist's report. It is essential that he or she gives the psychiatrist clear instructions and ensures that the psychiatric report addresses the questions the court may have.

Duties of prosecution

45.07 The Crown Office or Procurator Fiscal Service must give the court any evidence they have about an accused person's mental state.[1]

Anyone with an interest can advise the court at any time that the accused person may have a mental disorder. This includes the procurator fiscal, the police, the defence solicitor, the accused person him or herself and a relative or carer.

The prosecution can make enquiries and may arrange for psychiatric reports. Local psychiatric services may be able to assess the person and give the court information about the person's mental health and fitness to stand trial.

When considering whether to prosecute, the prosecution considers the way in which the police interviewed the accused person and in particular whether an appropriate adult was present at the police interviews. See chapter 44. Statements made by an accused person without the use of an appropriate adult might not be admissible in court.

[1]   Criminal Procedure (Scotland) Act 1995, s 52(1).

Psychiatric reports

45.08 The psychiatric reports should establish whether the accused person is able to instruct legal representatives and stand trial, whether the person needs further assessment or treatment and the person's current needs for care and treatment.[1]

The psychiatric reports should not attempt to uncover evidence about the facts of the crime or to help the prosecution establish their case.[2] Any such information is generally not admissible at the trial.

[1]   For guidance on good practice, see Mental Health Act Code of Practice, vol 3, paras 2.02–26 and 6.77–102.Useful advice to doctors is in Prof J McManus and Dr L Thomson, *Mental health and Scots law in practice* (W Green & Son, 2005), chap 8.

[2]   See *Sloan v Crowe*, 1996 SCCR 200 and *MacDonald v Munro*, 1996 SCCR 595.

TRANSFER FROM DISTRICT COURT

45.09 When a person with a mental disorder faces charges punishable by imprisonment in the district court, the court should transfer the case to the sheriff court.[1] The sheriff has powers not available to the district court.

[1]   Criminal Procedure (Scotland) Act 1995 (as amended by Mental Health (Care and Treatment) (Scotland) Act 2003), s 52A.

COMMITTAL FOR TRIAL

45.10 When a person first comes before a court charged with an offence, the court may send the person to prison or a young offenders' institution to await trial. (This is called being 'remanded in custody').

The court may release the person on bail. The court decides whether to grant bail. A person requesting bail has to show that he or she can comply with the bail conditions, perhaps with the help of a carer.

A number of courts operate bail supervision schemes. These can be an alternative to remand in custody. Such a scheme may be appropriate if a person with a mental disorder is charged with an offence.[1] The criminal justice section of the local authority social work department may be able to provide care, if the court is satisfied it can supervise the person properly.

Alternatively, the court may make an order sending the person to hospital for assessment and/or treatment. It can make an assessment or treatment order at any stage during the criminal justice process. This could be before the trial, during the trial, or before sentence. Assessment and treatment orders allow doctors to prepare reports for the courts and ensure that the person receives medical help.

An assessment order requires one medical report, not necessarily from a psychiatrist. It authorises the person's detention in hospital and treatment for up to 28 days.

A treatment order authorises the person's detention in hospital until the end of the trial. It can stay in force until the court acquits or sentences the person. If the person no longer needs psychiatric care, the court can discharge the order.

Prescribed forms for reports in connection with assessment and treatment orders are on the Scottish Executive's mental health law website. Although not statutory forms, most professionals use them, as they contain all the necessary information the court requires.

1   See guidance from the Scottish Office, *Health, Social Work and Related Services for Mentally Disordered Offenders in Scotland* (1999), para 3.4.

ASSESSMENT ORDER

Application for order

45.11 The prosecution or Scottish Ministers may apply to the court for an assessment order.[1] Scottish Ministers should apply for an order if a person remanded in custody needs medical treatment in hospital or assessment by a doctor before the trial or sentence.[2]

If a person remanded in custody becomes ill, the prison or young offenders' institution should arrange for a psychiatrist and mental health officer to visit. The prison authorities can then ask Scottish Ministers to apply for an order.[3] In an emergency, the prison doctor can report to the governor and Scottish Ministers can apply for an assessment order.[4]

The court can make an order on its own initiative.[5] It will commission a medical report before reaching a decision.

The court notifies the accused person and his or her solicitor of the application.[6] The accused person should generally attend court, but if the court is satisfied this is inappropriate or impractical, it may make an order in a person's absence. The person's lawyer must be present and given a chance to speak.[7]

One medical report is necessary. The doctor need not be a psychiatrist. The court may require the doctor to attend or may rely on a written report. A form for the report is available on the mental health law website.

1   Criminal Procedure (Scotland) Act 1995, (as amended by Mental Health (Care and Treatment) (Scotland) Act 2003), ss 52B and 52C.

2   MH(CT)(S)A Code of Practice, vol 3, para 2.65.

3   Code of Practice, vol 3, para 2.26.

4   Code of Practice, vol 3, para 2.72.

5   CP(S)A 1995, as above, s 52E.

6   CP(S)A 1995, ss 52B(2) and 52C(2).

7   CP(S)A 1995, s 52G(8).

Grounds for order

45.12 The court can make an assessment order if it is satisfied that the grounds exist for making an order and that an order is appropriate, bearing in mind all the circumstances of the case.[1] The grounds are that it is likely that:

- The accused person has a mental disorder;
- The person needs to be detained to assess whether there are grounds for making a treatment order (see below); and
- The order is necessary to prevent a significant risk to the health, safety or welfare of the accused person or a significant risk to the safety of other people.[2]

The court must be satisfied that the hospital is suitable for assessing the person's needs,[3] that the hospital can admit the person within seven days of the order and that doctors cannot assess the person without an order.[4]

1   Criminal Procedure (Scotland) Act 1995, s 52D(2).

2   CP(S)A 1995, s 52D(3).

3   The hospital could include the State Hospital.

4   CP(S)A 1995, ss 52D(3)(b)–(d).

Impact of order

45.13 The order authorises the detention of the person in hospital for 28 days. The person can receive medical treatment under Part 16 of the Mental Health (Care and Treatment) Act.[1] The court notifies the parties and the Mental Welfare Commission of the making of the order.[2]

There is no right to appeal against the making of an assessment order.

1   Criminal Procedure (Scotland) Act 1995, s 52D(6).

2   CP(S)A 1995, s 52D(10).

Transfer to hospital

45.14 The court may issue directions for moving the person to hospital and detaining the person in a place of safety before this.[1]

The most appropriate place of safety is a hospital. The law allows keeping the person in the detention area at the court, a police station, a prison or a young offenders' institution,[2] but the Code of Practice says this should be only in exceptional circumstances[3] and the person should move to hospital as soon as possible after the order.[4]

Scottish Ministers or the court may change the name of the hospital specified in the order if necessary in an emergency or in other special circumstances.[5] The responsible medical officer should seek the consent of Scottish Ministers before recommending a change of hospital.[6]

[1]   Criminal Procedure (Scotland) Act 1995, s 52D(9).
[2]   CP(S)A 1995, s 307.
[3]   Code of Practice, vol 3, para 2.82.
[4]   Code of Practice, vol 3, para 2.83.
[5]   CP(S)A 1995, s 52F.
[6]   Code of Practice, vol 3, para 2.69.

Care in hospital

45.15 A person subject to an assessment order is subject to the general provisions of the Mental Health (Care and Treatment) Act and, in particular, the medical treatment provisions in Part 16 of the Act. (Special rules apply, see 16.13.)

A person subject to an assessment order is a restricted patient. Any suspension of the order requires the consent of Scottish Ministers.[1]

[1]   Mental Health (Care and Treatment) (Scotland) Act 2003, s 221.

Duties of authorities

45.16 The hospital managers must allocate a responsible medical officer for the person and must notify the local authority within two working days of the person's admission to hospital.[1]

The local authority should appoint a mental health officer within two business days of receiving this notification.[2] The mental health officer should prepare a social circumstances report, unless there is no practical benefit. See 14.35. The mental health officer should specifically consider whether the person might need a treatment order.[3]

The hospital should give the person information about his or her rights and consider any special communication needs the person may have. For more information, see chapter 17.

[1]   Code of Practice, vol 3, para 2.81.
[2]   Code of Practice, as above.
[3]   Code of Practice, as above, para 6.106.

Report to court

45.17 Within the period of the assessment order, the responsible medical officer reports to the prosecutor or court, as requested by them. The report covers such matters as whether the person is fit to stand trial and whether he or she was 'insane' at the time of the offence.

Before the end of the order, the responsible medical officer must report to the court whether there are grounds for making the person subject to a treatment order.[1] The responsible medical officer should consult with the mental health officer and the care team.[2] A form for the report is available on the mental health law website. If the mental health officer considers a treatment order is necessary, a second medical report will be obtained. See below.

If the responsible medical officer believes the court should consider making a compulsion order or hospital direction at this stage, he or she must discuss this with the mental health officer, who must also report to the court.[3]

On receiving the responsible medical officer's report, the court revokes the assessment order and either makes a treatment order (if a second report also recommends this) or makes such other order as it thinks appropriate, such as remand to custody or remand on bail.[4]

The court can extend the assessment order for up to seven days after the receipt of the report if this is necessary, but the accused person or his or her lawyer must have a chance to be heard.[5] The Code of Practice gives guidance on when it is appropriate to extend an order.[6]

[1]   Criminal Procedure (Scotland) Act 1995, s 52G(1).
[2]   Code of Practice, vol 3, para 2.102.
[3]   See *Mental health officer reports for the court under s57C and 59B of the Criminal Procedure (Scotland) Act* (Scottish Executive Health Department letter HDL, 2006). On mental health law website.

4   CP(S)A 1995, s 52G(3).
5   CP(S)A 1995, s 52G(4).
6   Code of Practice, vol 3, para 2.114.

Variation of order

45.18 If the condition of the person changes, the responsible medical officer may ask the court to vary the order.[1] The responsible medical officer should consult a mental health officer and seek the consent of Scottish Ministers.[2]

The responsible medical officer may wish to vary an order if the level of security in the hospital is not appropriate for the person. If the person no longer needs to be in hospital, the responsible medical officer may ask the court to cancel the order. The person then goes to prison or such other institution as the court thinks appropriate.[3]

1   Criminal Procedure (Scotland) Act 1995, s 52G(9).
2   Code of Practice, vol 3, paras 2.98–99.
3   CP(S)A 1995, s 52G(10).

Termination of order

45.19 The order ends on:

- The expiry of the period of the order;
- The making of a treatment order in respect of the person; or
- The sentencing (or deferred sentencing) of the person.[1]

It may end before this, if the court cancels the order, perhaps because of a change in an accused person's mental condition.

1   Criminal Procedure (Scotland) Act 1995, s 52H.

TREATMENT ORDER

Application for order

45.20 As with the assessment order, the prosecution or Scottish Ministers may apply for a treatment order, or the court may make an order on its own initiative.[1]

The court must consider evidence from two doctors. One doctor must be an approved medical practitioner.[2] One must work in the hospital where the person will go if the court makes an order.[3] The court may require the doctors to submit a written report or give oral evidence. A form for the reports is available on the mental health law website.

The court notifies the accused person and his or her solicitor and they have the right to address the court.[4]

1   Criminal Procedure (Scotland) Act 1995, ss 52K, 52L and 52N.
2   CP(S)A 1995, s 52M(3).
3   CP(S)A 1995 (as amended by Mental Health (Care and Treatment) (Scotland) Act 2003), s 61(1A).
4   CP(S)A 1995, ss 52K(2), 52L(2) and 52M(7).

Grounds for order

45.21 The court can make a treatment order if it is satisfied that the grounds exist for making the order and that an order is appropriate, bearing in mind all the circumstances of the case.[1]

The grounds for making the order are that:

- The accused person has a mental disorder.
- Medical treatment is available which is likely to prevent the mental disorder worsening or alleviate any of its symptoms or effects, and
- If the person does not receive such treatment there would be a significant risk to his or her health, safety or welfare or to the safety of any other person.[2]

The court cannot make an order unless it is satisfied that that the hospital proposed is suitable for the person's needs[3] and that the person can be admitted within seven days of the making of the order.[4]

1   Criminal Procedure (Scotland) Act 1995, s 52M(2).
2   CP(S)A 1995, s 52M(3)(a).
3   This could include the State Hospital or a medium secure unit such as the Orchard Clinic in Edinburgh if the court is satisfied that the person needs special security.
4   CP(S)A 1995, s 52M(3)(b)(c).

Impact of order

45.22 The order authorises the detention of the person in the hospital specified in the order and the giving of medical treatment under Part 16 of the Mental Health (Care and Treatment) Act.[1] The order lasts until the court acquits or sentences the person or defers sentence.[2] The court may discharge the order if the person no longer needs hospital care. (See *Review of order*, below.)

The person should be moved to hospital as quickly as possible.[3] The court may issue any special directions about the removal of the person[4] and either Scottish Ministers or the court may change the name of the hospital specified in the order.[5] The rules are as for assessment orders.[6] See above.

The court notifies the parties and the Mental Welfare Commission of the making of the order.[7]

There is no right to appeal against the making of a treatment order.

1	Criminal Procedure (Scotland) Act 1995, s 52M(6).
2	CP(S)A 1995, s 52E(3).
3	Code of Practice, vol 3, para 2.133.
4	CP(S)A 1995, s 52M(8).
5	CP(S)A 1995, s 52P.
6	CP(S)A 1995, s 52M(8).
7	CP(S)A 1995, s 52M(9).

Care in hospital

45.23 As with an assessment order, the person is a restricted patient.[1] The person must have a responsible medical officer and mental health officer and receive information about his or her rights. The mental health officer must prepare a social circumstances report.[2] See 14.35. The Code of Practice contains good practice guidance for reports during treatment orders.[3]

The rules for suspending orders are as for other restricted patients.[4] See chapter 48.

The treatment order authorises the person's treatment in hospital in accordance with the provisions of Part 16 of the Mental Health (Care and Treatment) Act. The person's responsible medical officer uses the period of the order to consider such matters as whether the person is fit to stand trial, whether he or she may have been 'insane' at the time of the offence or what might be the appropriate sentence or order if the person is convicted. The prosecution or court will ask the responsible medical officer for a report.

If the responsible medical officer asks the court to consider making a compulsion order or hospital direction, he or she must discuss this with the mental health officer, who must also report to the court.[5]

[1]   Criminal Procedure (Scotland) Act 1995, s 52M(6).

[2]   Mental Health (Care and Treatment) (Scotland) Act 2003, ss 229–232 and ss 260–261.

[3]   Code of Practice, vol 3, para 106.

[4]   MH(CT)(S)A 2003, s 224.

[5]   See Scottish Executive Health Department letter HDL (2006), referred to at 45.17 above.

Review of order

45.24 The responsible medical officer should keep the person's condition under review. If any of the grounds for making the order no longer apply or circumstances have changed so that the order is no longer appropriate, the responsible medical officer should report this to the court.[1] The review should involve all members of the care team[2] and the responsible medical officer should obtain the approval of Scottish Ministers before proposing any change of hospital.[3]

The court may discharge or vary the order. If it discharges the order, the court may remand the accused person to custody or deal with the person as it thinks appropriate.[4]

[1]   Criminal Procedure (Scotland) Act 1995, s 52Q.

[2]   Code of Practice, vol 3, para 2.137.

[3]   Code of Practice, vol 3, para 2.152.

[4]   CP(S)A 1995, s 52Q(2).

BEFORE SENTENCING

45.25 When someone with a mental disorder is convicted of an offence or found not guilty because of 'insanity', the court has various sentencing options. It may require a psychiatric assessment of the person before it decides. There are various procedures available to the court.

Assessment or treatment order

45.26 The court can make an assessment or treatment order at any time before passing sentence or deferring sentence. When someone needs to be in hospital for assessment, this is the preferred option.

Remand for enquiries

45.27 If someone is convicted of an offence that could carry a prison sentence, the courts may remand the person for an enquiry into his or her physical or mental health.[1]

The person may be remanded to prison (or a young offenders' institution) or on bail. A doctor should not recommend remand in custody.[2] The court can remand a person to hospital, but should generally make an assessment or treatment order instead.

A person remanded for enquiries is not subject to the compulsory treatment rules of the Mental Health (Care and Treatment) Act, even in an emergency. The Code of Practice recommends that a doctor needing to give medical treatment to someone without consent should follow the procedure for an assessment order.[3]

1   Criminal Procedure (Scotland) Act 1995, s 200.
2   Code of Practice, vol 3, para 2.39.
3   Code of Practice, vol 3, para 6.73.

Remand on bail

45.28 The court may remand the person on bail for up to two medical reports. The person must agree to attend for examination.

Bail conditions may require the person to live in a place specified in the order, such as a bail hostel or some form of supported accommodation.[1]

1   Criminal Procedure (Scotland) Act 1995, s 200(6).

Remand to hospital

45.29 The court can remand someone to hospital if it is satisfied by evidence from a doctor (who need not be a psychiatrist) that the person appears to be suffering from a mental disorder and that a suitable hospital can admit him or her.[1]

If the hospital cannot complete its assessment within three weeks, the court can extend the remand for up to three weeks.[2] The person need not come back to court for this, unless he or she objects to the extension. If at any time during the remand, the doctors consider the person no longer needs to be in hospital, they may ask the court to change the order.[3]

A person remanded to hospital is not subject to compulsory measures under the Mental Health (Care and Treatment) Act. He or she also lacks the safeguards available to people detained under that Act. For this reason the Code of Practice says that remand to hospital for psychiatric reports is appropriate only in exceptional circumstances.[4]

¹ Criminal Procedure (Scotland) Act 1995, s 200(2)(b). A suitable hospital could include the State Hospital or a medium secure unit.

² CP(S)A 1995, s 200(3). In non-jury cases, the person should not be held in custody for more than 40 days in total, or the case cannot come to trial. CP(S)A 1995, s 147.

³ CP(S)A 1995, s 200(5).

⁴ Code of Practice, vol 3, para 4.08.

Appeals

45.30 A person can appeal to the High Court against any bail conditions or against the refusal of bail. The person must submit the appeal within 24 hours of the making of the order.[1] A person remanded to hospital may appeal at any time while the remand is in effect.[2]

¹ Criminal Procedure (Scotland) Act 1995 (as amended by Mental Health (Care and Treatment) (Scotland) Act 2003), s 200(9).

² CP(S)A 1995, s 200(9), as amended.

Interim compulsion order

45.31 Where a person with a mental disorder has committed a serious offence or been acquitted on the basis of 'insanity' or where there are serious concerns about public safety, the court may wish to make a compulsion order with restrictions or a hospital direction. See chapter 46.

A person subject to a compulsion order with restrictions is a hospital patient but Scottish Ministers take decisions about his or her leave of absence into the community and hospital transfer. A hospital direction is a prison sentence linked to a hospital-based compulsion order.

Before making either order, the court needs to be satisfied that it is appropriate. An interim compulsion order authorises the person's detention in hospital for up to 12 months (with renewals), allowing a lengthy assessment of the person's needs and of any risk the person may pose.

Whenever the court is considering a compulsion order with restrictions or a hospital direction, it should make an interim compulsion order, unless there are good reasons for not doing so.[1]

1   Code of Practice, vol 3, paras 4.07 and 5.86.

When interim compulsion order available

45.32 The court can make an interim compulsion order if a person is convicted in the High Court or sheriff court of a crime punishable by imprisonment and when someone is sent from the sheriff court for sentencing in the High Court.

An interim compulsion order is not available following conviction for murder, where the sentence is fixed by law.

The court may make an interim compulsion order when someone is founds not guilty of an offence because of 'insanity', and when someone is unfit to plead and the examination of facts finds that the person committed the offence.[1]

The convicted person should generally attend court but if this is impracticable or inappropriate, the person's legal representative should attend and have a chance to make representations.[2]

1   Criminal Procedure (Scotland) Act 1995 (as amended by the Mental Health (Care and Treatment) (Scotland) Act 2003), ss 53 and 57. See chapter 43 for 'insanity' and unfitness to plead.
2   CP(S)A 1995, s 53(9).

Grounds for order

45.33 The court can make an order if it is considering making a compulsion order with restrictions or a hospital direction.[1] The court must be satisfied that it is appropriate to make the order, bearing in mind all the circumstances (including the nature of the offence) and any alternative options available.[2]

The court requires two medical reports confirming that it is likely that:

- The person has a mental disorder.
- There is medical treatment available for the person which could prevent deterioration or alleviate any symptoms or effects of the disorder.

- If such medical treatment is not provided there will be a significant risk to the person's health, safety or welfare or to the safety of any other person; and
- The making of an interim compulsion order is necessary.[3]

The court must be satisfied that the person can be admitted to hospital within seven days and that it is not practicable to assess the person's needs without an interim compulsion order.[4]

If the court is satisfied that the person needs special security which only the State Hospital can provide, the order may specify the State Hospital.[5]

[1] Criminal Procedure (Scotland) Act 1995, s 53(2).
[2] Mental Health (Care and Treatment) (Scotland) Act 2003, s 53(4). Where someone is convicted of a serious violent or sexual offence, section 1 of the Criminal Justice (Scotland) Act 2003 will require the court to make an interim compulsion order if the grounds for making an order apply and the medical reports indicate that the person poses a serious risk to public safety. This will not be necessary if the person is already subject to an order for lifetime restriction). These provisions are expected to come into effect in mid-2006.
[3] CP(S)A 1995, s 53(5).
[4] CP(S)A 1995, s 53(3).
[5] CP(S)A 1995, s 53(7).

Effect of order

45.34 The order authorises the detention of the person in the specified hospital for up to 12 weeks and the giving of medical treatment in accordance with Part 16 of the Mental Health (Care and Treatment) Act.[1]

The court or Scottish Ministers may direct that the person goes to a different hospital from that specified in the order within seven days of the making of the order, if necessary.[2] Thereafter it is not possible to change the hospital.[3] If this becomes necessary, the matter will have to return to court.

Following reports from the responsible medical officer, the court may extend the order for periods of up to 12 weeks at a time. The maximum length of the order is 12 months.[4] If at any time the responsible medical officer considers the order is no longer necessary, the court may revoke the order and consider sentencing options.[5]

In the final report to the court, the responsible medical officer must confirm whether he or she considers a compulsion order (with or without restrictions) or a hospital direction is appropriate.[6] This assessment should reflect the input of the care team.[7] The mental health officer must also submit a report.[8] The person and his or her legal representative receive copies of the responsible medical officer's reports.[9]

The rules about care of the person in hospital, information to the person and duties of the authorities are as for assessment orders. See above.

A person subject to an interim compulsion order is a restricted patient. Only Scottish Ministers can authorise the suspension of the conditions of the order.

The person has a responsible medical officer and mental health officer, receives information about his or her rights, and any necessary help with communication needs. The mental health officer should prepare a social circumstances report. Among the issues the mental health officer should consider is whether to recommend the court consider a restriction order or a hospital direction for the person.[10]

---

1   Criminal Procedure (Scotland) Act 1995, s 53(8).
2   CP(S)A 1995, s 53A(1).
3   See Code of Practice, vol 3, para 4.41.
4   CP(S)A 1995, s 53B(5).
5   CP(S)A 1995, s 53B(8).
6   CP(S)A 1995, ss 57A(2) and 59A(2).
7   Code of Practice, vol 3, para 4.32.
8   See Scottish Executive Health Department letter referred to at 45.17.
9   CP(S)A 1995, s 53B(3).
10   Code of Practice, vol 3, para 6.106.

Chapter 46

THE CRIMINAL COURT PROCESS: SENTENCING

46.01 The court has a range of sentencing options when a person with a mental disorder is convicted of a criminal offence or is found unfit to plead or not guilty because of 'insanity'. The court bears in mind the seriousness of the person's disorder, the degree of punishment that is appropriate and any public safety issues.

The law recognises that a mental disorder may limit a person's responsibility for a crime, and can tailor the sentence accordingly. Where a court considers mental disorder contributed to the crime, it can impose measures aimed at preventing the same thing from happening again. These can range from keeping the person in a secure hospital to requiring him or her to accept psychiatric help as a condition of probation.

Generally the court has a discretion about what sentence to pass. If someone is convicted of murder, the court must impose a life sentence. If a person is acquitted because of 'insanity' or found unfit to plead, the court's options are limited. In all other cases, the court has a range of options. These are:

- A compulsion order, an order similar to a compulsory treatment order, either detaining the person in hospital or making him or her subject to community-based controls.

- A compulsion order with restrictions, authorising detention in hospital for an indefinite period.

- A hospital direction, a fixed prison term linked to detention in hospital.

- An order for lifelong restriction.

- Guardianship or an intervention order.

- Probation.

- A supervision and treatment order (in 'insanity' cases only).

- A deferred sentence.

This chapter looks at these options.

OPTIONS IN 'INSANITY' CASES

46.02 The court has a range of options when someone is acquitted because of 'insanity' (or was not fit to plead and an examination of facts decides the person committed the offence).

The court may make:

- A compulsion order authorising detention in hospital (with or without restrictions).
- An interim compulsion order.
- Welfare guardianship or a welfare intervention order under the Adults with Incapacity Act.
- A supervision and treatment order; or
- No order.[1]

If the court makes a compulsion order, it must add a restriction order when the medical reports indicate there will be a high risk to the public if the person remains at liberty.[2]

In 'insanity' cases the court has discretion even where the charge was murder, depending on the facts of the case and the risk the person poses. Because the person has not been found guilty of the offence, the life sentence for murder is not appropriate.

[1]   Criminal Procedure (Scotland) Act 1995, s 57, as amended by Mental Health (Care and Treatment) (Scotland) Act 2003 and Criminal Justice (Scotland) Act 2003.
[2]   CP(S)A 1995, s 57(3) (as amended by Criminal Justice (Scotland) Act 2003, s 2(b)).

COMPULSION ORDER

46.03 The court may decide that it is appropriate for the mental health system rather than the criminal justice system to deal with a person with a mental disorder who has been found guilty of a criminal offence.

When someone is convicted of an offence (other than murder) which is punishable by imprisonment, the court may make a compulsion order if satisfied this is the most appropriate way of dealing with the case.[1] A compulsion order is the criminal justice equivalent of the compulsory treatment order.

Both the sheriff court and the High Court may make compulsion orders. If someone with a mental disorder is charged in a district court with an imprisonable offence, the case goes to the sheriff court, and the sheriff can impose a compulsion order if appropriate.[2]

Compulsion orders are also available in 'insanity' cases. See above.

1   Criminal Procedure (Scotland) Act 1995 (as amended by the Mental Health (Care and Treatment) (Scotland) Act 2003), s 57A(2).
2   CP(S)A 1995, s 52A.

Reports to the court

Medical reports

46.04 The court requires reports from two doctors, confirming that the grounds for an order apply to the person. At least one of the medical reports must come from an approved medical practitioner and one must come from a doctor working in the hospital to be specified in the order.[1]

Each doctor must give details of any financial interest he or she has in the hospital to which the person may be admitted.[2]

The Mental Health (Care and Treatment) Act Code of Practice gives advice on completing the reports.[3] The doctors should recommend the least restrictive option necessary in the circumstances and should consider whether community-based solutions may be appropriate.

If the medical reports recommend detention in hospital, they should explain why compulsory powers in the community are not appropriate.[4] If the doctors recommend hospital, the level of security should be proportionate to the risk.[5]

1   Criminal Procedure (Scotland) Act 1995, s 61(1A).
2   CP(S)A 1995, s 61(2).
3   Code of Practice, vol 3, para 5.12.
4   Code of Practice, vol 3, para 5.29.
5   Code of Practice, vol 3, para 5.30.

Mental health officer report

46.05 The court requires a mental health officer to interview the person and prepare a report.[1] Good practice guidance is in the Code of Practice.[2] A form for the mental health officer's report is on the Scottish Executive's mental health law website.

The court must consider the mental health officer's report when deciding whether to make an order.[3] It may require a report from a criminal justice social worker as well as or instead of this report.[4]

1   Criminal Procedure (Scotland) Act 1995, s 57C. See Scottish Executive health department letter HDL (2006)1 referred to at 45.17.

²   Code of Practice, vol 3, paras 5.32–34.
³   CP(S)A 1995, s 57A(4).
⁴   CP(S)A 1995, s 294(2A)(a).

Grounds for order

46.06 The grounds for making a compulsion order are that:

- The person has a mental disorder.
- There is medical treatment available for the person which is likely to prevent the disorder worsening or alleviate any of the symptoms or effects of the disorder.
- If the person does not receive such medical treatment there will be a significant risk to his or her health, safety or welfare or to the safety of any other person; and
- The making of the order is necessary.[1]

Unlike civil orders, the court does not need to consider whether the person's ability to take medical decisions is significantly impaired. See 45.02.

¹   Criminal Procedure (Scotland) Act 1995, s 57A(3).

Orders available

46.07 The court may make a hospital or community-based order. It may make a hospital-based order only if it is satisfied that the person needs to be detained in hospital to receive medical treatment and that a suitable hospital will be available within seven days.[1]

A community-based order may require the person to live in a certain place.[2] If the place is a care home service, such as a hostel or supported accommodation, the court must satisfy itself that the service is willing to receive the person.[3] It will require the responsible medical officer to confirm this.[4]

If the court believes the person should be a restricted patient, (see below) it must make a hospital-based order.

The person may be detained in the State Hospital if the court is satisfied that he or she needs special security that only the State Hospital can provide.[5]

Where a court makes a compulsion order, it cannot impose a sentence of imprisonment or a fine, a probation order, or a community service order, but it may make other orders, such as a compensation order or a driving disqualification.[6]

1 Criminal Procedure (Scotland) Act 1995, s 57A(5).
2 A community-based order to ensure that a person in prison receives compulsory medication is not appropriate. Code of Practice, vol 3, para 5.14.
3 CP(S)A 1995, s 57A(8).
4 Code of Practice, vol 3, para 5.31.
5 CP(S)A 1995, s 57A(6).
6 CP(S)A 1995, s 57A(15).

Effect of order

46.08 The order authorises the person's removal to and detention in the specified hospital or that he or she comply with community-based measures.[1] The order usually makes the person subject to the medical treatment rules in Part 16 of the Mental Health (Care and Treatment) Act.

The court or Scottish Ministers may change the hospital from that specified in the order within seven days of the making of the order.[2] This should happen only in exceptional circumstances.[3]

The court may give instructions for the person's transfer to hospital (or to the place where the person is to live on a community-based order) and for keeping the person in a place of safety until then.[4] This place should generally be a hospital.[5] For issues concerning transfer to hospital, see 14.25.

If the court imposes a restriction order, the compulsion order continues without any time limit.[6] The patient and his or her named person have rights of appeal. All those involved have a duty to keep the order under review.[7]

For care of the person in hospital, see chapter 48.

1 Criminal Procedure (Scotland) Act 1995, ss 57A(8) and 57B.
2 CP(S)A 1995, s 57D.
3 Code of Practice, vol 3, para 5.49.
4 CP(S)A 1995, s 57A(14)(b).
5 Code of Practice, vol 3, para 5.45.
6 CP(S)A 1995, s 57A(7).
7 See chapter 48.

Appeal against compulsion order

46.09 The person can appeal against the making of a compulsion order in the same way as against an appeal against sentence.[1]

1   Criminal Procedure (Scotland) Act 1995, s 60.

COMPULSION ORDER WITH RESTRICTIONS

46.10 Where the court makes a compulsion order, it may also impose special restrictions on the person, in the interests of public safety. These might be because of the nature of the crime committed or because of medical evidence about the risk the person might pose in the future.

The court can make a restriction order if it believes this is necessary to protect the public from serious harm. The court considers the nature of the offence of which the person has been convicted, the person's past history, and future risk.[1]

(The Mental Health (Care and Treatment) Act Code of Practice advises that a compulsion order with restrictions is appropriate if there is a significant link between a person's mental disorder and the offence, and/or between the disorder and the risk the person may pose in the future. If there is no such link, a hospital direction (see below) is more appropriate.[2])

Before the court reaches a decision, it must hear oral evidence from an approved medical practitioner.[3] It also hears from a mental health officer. Good practice guidance on reports is in the Code of Practice.[4] All members of the person's care team should contribute to the assessment.

In most cases, the court should not make a compulsion order with restrictions without first making an interim compulsion order, to allow the doctors properly to consider the case. If there has been no prior interim compulsion order, the court should make a restriction order only if it is satisfied that it is not appropriate to make an interim compulsion order.[5]

1   Criminal Procedure (Scotland) Act 1995, s 59(1).
2   Code of Practice, vol 3, para 5.59.
3   CP(S)A 1995, s 59(2).
4   Vol 3, paras 5.64–72; paras 5.89–92 deal with the mental health officer report.
5   CP(S)A 1995, s 59(2A), inserted by Mental Health (Care and Treatment) (Scotland) Act 2003, Sched 4.

Effect of restriction order

46.11 Where a person is subject to a restriction order, Scottish Ministers must give their consent to any suspension of the order to allow leave of absence and to any transfer of the person to another hospital.[1] The Scottish Executive Health Department advises Scottish Ministers, based on information they receive from the responsible medical officer.

A restriction order has no time limits. It can apply for as long as the person is subject to the compulsion order. The tribunal may remove the restriction order if it is no longer appropriate.

Neither Scottish Ministers, the responsible medical officer nor the Mental Welfare Commission can discharge the person from hospital. Scottish Ministers and the Mental Welfare Commission may refer a patient to the tribunal for discharge. The patient and his or her named person can appeal to the tribunal for discharge at regular intervals.

For restricted patients' rights in hospital, see chapter 48.

[1]   Mental Health (Care and Treatment) (Scotland) Act 2003, ss 224 and 218.

Appeal against restriction order

46.12 A person may appeal against the making of a restriction order in the same way as an appeal against sentence.[1]

[1]   Criminal Procedure (Scotland) Act 1995, s 60.

HOSPITAL DIRECTION

46.13 When a court considers that the link between an offence and a person's mental disorder is not clear, or that medical treatment is unlikely significantly to reduce the risk a person poses to the public,[1] the court may make a hospital direction.[2]

A hospital direction combines a prison sentence with a hospital-based compulsion order. When the person no longer needs to be in hospital, he or she returns to prison to complete the sentence.

This order was originally recommended for people with anti-social personality disorder,[3] but it is currently available for anyone with a mental disorder facing a sentence of imprisonment.[4]

[1]   Code of Practice, vol 3, para 5.103.
[2]   Criminal Procedure (Scotland) Act 1995, s 59A.

3 *Review of health and social services for mentally disordered offenders and others requiring similar services* (Department of Health, Home Office, 1993). (Known as the 'Reed Committee report'.)

4 CP(S)A 1995, s 59A(1).

Grounds for direction

46.14 The procedure is as for the compulsion order.[1] The court requires two medical reports and a mental health officer report, confirming that the grounds for making a hospital direction apply to the person. The Mental Health (Care and Treatment) Act Code of Practice contains guidance on the content of these reports.[2] The person will usually have been subject to an interim compulsion order before the court makes the direction.[3]

The grounds for making a compulsion order must apply to the person.[4]

A hospital direction authorises detention in hospital, not a community-based order.[5] The hospital may be the State Hospital.[6] The court must be satisfied that a suitable hospital has a place available within seven days of the order.[7]

1 See above.

2 Code of Practice, vol 3, paras 5.109–115 for medical reports, paras 5.116–121 for mental health officer reports.

3 Code of Practice, vol 3, para 5.102.

4 Criminal Procedure (Scotland) Act 1995, s59A(3).

5 CP(S)A 1995, s 59A(7).

6 CP(S)A 1995, s 59A(6).

7 CP(S)A 1995, s 59A(4).

Effect of direction

46.15 A person subject to a hospital direction is a restricted patient as long as he or she is in hospital. Scottish Ministers take all decisions about leave of absence and transfer. Questions of discharge are for the Parole Board.

The person can make regular appeals to the tribunal. If an appeal is successful, the person serves the remainder of the sentence in prison (or a young offenders' institution).[1] For more details about the person's rights in hospital, see chapter 48.

[1] Mental Health (Care and Treatment) (Scotland) Act 2003, s 216.

Appeal

46.16 There is a right of appeal against the making of the hospital direction, as with any sentence.[1]

[1] Criminal Procedure (Scotland) Act 1995, s 60.

PRISON SENTENCE

46.17 The court may impose a prison sentence if it thinks this appropriate, even when the person convicted has a mental disorder.

This does not necessarily mean that the person will spend all his or her time in prison. People in prison can be moved to hospital if their mental health requires this. See chapter 47.

ORDER FOR LIFELONG RESTRICTION

46.18 Where a person is convicted in the High Court of a serious sexual, violent or life threatening crime, the court may make an order for lifelong restriction. An order for lifelong restriction means that the person is subject to a period of detention or imprisonment of indefinite duration. Discharge or release depends on the assessment of risk. A new body, the Risk Management Authority, will help in the assessment of risk.[1]

Before making an order for lifelong restriction, the court will order a risk assessment, or may make an interim compulsion order to assess the risk. If, following such an assessment, the court decides that the person could pose a serious threat to the safety of the public, it will make an order for lifelong restriction.[2]

The court might make an order for lifelong restriction if a person with a mental disorder is convicted of murder. The court cannot make a compulsion order if the person is convicted, although it can if a person is unfit to plead or acquitted because of 'insanity'. If the mental health grounds apply, the court can add a hospital direction to the order for lifelong restriction.

In cases other than murder, the court can make either a mental health disposal or an order for lifelong restriction.

If the court makes a mental health disposal, such as a compulsion order, in respect of someone acquitted of an offence because of 'insanity', and the medical and other reports it receives indicate the person is a risk as above, the court must impose special restrictions on the order.[3]

The order for lifelong restriction is likely to come into effect in the autumn of 2006.

1   Criminal Procedure (Scotland) Act 1995 (as amended by the Criminal Justice (Scotland) Act 2003), ss 210B–210BH.
2   CP(S)A 1995, s 210F.
3   CP(S)A 1995, s 57(3).

GUARDIANSHIP OR INTERVENTION ORDER

46.19 Instead of a Mental Health (Care and Treatment) Act based order, the court can make an order for guardianship under the Adults with Incapacity Act. The court can appoint a guardian with full or partial welfare powers.[1] The court cannot give a guardian financial powers.

The court can make a welfare intervention order if it thinks this would be an appropriate alternative to guardianship.[2]

The court requires two medical reports and a report from a mental health officer. It must be satisfied that the person is incapable of protecting his or her own welfare and that no other means are available for protecting the person's welfare.[3]

The mental health officer must interview the person within 30 days of the hearing. The report should confirm that that guardianship is in the person's interests, that the proposed guardian is suitable and willing to act and that no other guardianship order is in force in respect of the person.[4]

The court may appoint the local authority, or some person named by it, as guardian.[5] The guardianship may last for three years, some other period specified by the court, or indefinitely.[6] For how these orders work in practice, see chapter 24.

1   Criminal Procedure (Scotland) Act 1995 (as amended by the Adults with Incapacity (Scotland) Act 2000), s 58A.
2   CP(S)A 1995, s 60A.
3   CP(S)A 1995, s 58(1A).
4   CP(S)A 1995, s 58(1A)(6).
5   CP(S)A 1995, s 58(1A).
6   CP(S)A 1995, ss 58(1) and 58(5).

PROBATION

46.20 The court may put a convicted person on probation to seek psychiatric or psychological treatment. The court must receive evidence from the person who is to provide the treatment that the treatment is appropriate and the person can provide it.[1]

A probation order can contain such conditions as the court considers appropriate. It can require the person on probation to live in a certain place. The person may be required to receive in-patient or outpatient treatment from a psychiatrist or a chartered psychologist.[2]

If the treatment specified in the order is not appropriate, the person treating the patient and the patient can agree to change it. They should notify the court.[3]

A person on a probation order is not subject to compulsory treatment under the Mental Health (Care and Treatment) Act and cannot receive medical treatment against his or her will.[4]

If a person on probation does not comply with the regime proposed, he or she may be in breach of the probation order and brought back to court. The court then considers whether the refusal of treatment was reasonable.[5]

A probation order can last for up to three years.

[1]   Criminal Procedure (Scotland) Act 1995, s 230(3).
[2]   CP(S)A 1995 (as amended by the Mental Health (Care and Treatment) (Scotland) Act 2003), ss 228 and 230.
[3]   CP(S)A 1995, s 58(1A) and ss 230(4)–(7).
[4]   CP(S)A 1995, s 230(9).
[5]   CP(S)A 1995, s 232(5).

SUPERVISION AND TREATMENT ORDER

46.21 When someone is acquitted of an offence on the grounds of 'insanity' or is found unfit to plead and an examination of facts decides the person committed the offence, the court may make a supervision and treatment order.[1] This order is not available for mental disorders falling short of 'insanity'.

The order requires the person to accept supervision from a social worker and to submit to medical treatment,[2] but if the person does not comply with the order there are no sanctions. For this reason it is rarely used.[3]

It is a less restrictive alternative than a compulsion order, and in terms of Mental Health (Care and Treatment) Act principles, should be the first option. Whether a supervision and treatment order is appropriate or feasible depends on the likely risk to the person or others and/or the likelihood and consequences of non-compliance.[4]

1   Criminal Procedure (Scotland) Act 1995, s 57(2)(d).
2   CP(S)A 1995, Sched 4, para 1.
3   See *Mentally disordered offenders and criminal proceedings. The Operation of Part VI of the Criminal Procedure (Scotland) Act 1995* (Scottish Office Central Research Unit, 1999). In 22 cases where the person was found unfit to plead between 1996 and 1998, the courts made 16 hospital orders, one guardianship order, four supervision and treatment orders and in one case made no order. In 10 cases where the person was acquitted because of 'insanity', the courts made seven hospital orders, one supervision and treatment order and no order in two cases. The court made hospital orders in all three cases where the person was found unfit to plead and not guilty by virtue of 'insanity'.
4   Mental Health (Care and Treatment) Act Code of Practice, vol 3, para 3.77.

DEFERRED SENTENCE

46.22 The court may decide to defer sentence, subject to certain conditions.[1] This might be appropriate where someone can satisfy the court that he or she will get help to reduce the likelihood of re-offending.

1   Criminal Procedure (Scotland) Act 1995, s 202(1).

POWER TO DETAIN FOLLOWING ACQUITTAL

Grounds for order

46.23 A person with a serious mental disorder may be acquitted of a crime. The doctors' reports to the court may have indicated urgent concerns about the person's mental health. The Millan Committee was concerned that the person or others could be at risk if the person was allowed to leave the court following acquittal.[1]

The court can now make an order detaining the person for a medical examination when there is no doctor immediately available to examine the person. The court must be satisfied, having received two medical reports, that the person has a mental disorder, that there is appropriate treatment available and that if the person does not receive such treatment there will be a significant risk to the person or others.[2]

1   *New directions*, Recommendation 25.8.

2   Criminal Procedure (Scotland) Act 1995, s 60C(3).

Effect of order

46.24 The order authorises the person's detention for up to six hours to enable a doctor to examine him or her.[1] The person can be taken to a place of safety and kept there for up to six hours. The place of safety should be a hospital if possible. The court holding cells should be used only in exceptional circumstances.[2] The court will specify that either a police officer or someone authorised by the court should take the person to the place of safety and may return the person there if he or she absconds.

The order lapses if a doctor signs a short-term or emergency detention certificate.[3]

The court must report the detention to the Mental Welfare Commission within 14 days. The notification should set out the name and address of the person removed, the date and time of the removal, where the person was removed to and if this was a police station, the reasons.[4] There is no form prescribed for this report.

This procedure is not available where a person is acquitted because of 'insanity'.[5]

1   Criminal Procedure (Scotland) Act 1995 (as amended by the Mental Health (Care and Treatment) (Scotland) Act 2003), s 60C.

2   Code of Practice, vol 3, para 6.14.

3   CP(S)A 1995, s 60C(6).

4   CP(S)A 1995, s 60D(3).

5   CP(S)A 1995, s 60C(7).

Medical treatment

46.25 A person detained under these provisions cannot receive compulsory treatment under the Mental Health (Care and Treatment) Act. If someone requires treatment urgently, a doctor must use common law powers until he or she can consider whether to sign a certificate under the Mental Health (Care and Treatment) Act.

Chapter 47

PRISONERS AND THE MENTAL HEALTH SYSTEM

47.01 Many people in prison and young offenders' institutions (both on remand and after sentence) have mental illnesses, learning disabilities and personality disorders.[1] This chapter looks at care in prison and the duties of the prison authorities to provide adequate services.

A small percentage of people in prison have severe mental illnesses and clearly need to be in hospital. There are procedures to allow the transfer of prisoners to hospital in such circumstances.

The Mental Welfare Commission reports that these arrangements appear generally to work well,[2] but it is also important to ensure that the large number of people with mental illnesses, personality disorders and learning disabilities get the help they need in prison.

[1]   J Gunn, A Maden, M Swinton, 'Treatment needs of prisoners with psychiatric disorders' (1991) 303 British Medical Journal 338–341. M Davidson, MS Humphreys, EC Johnstone, DG Owens, 'Prevalence of psychiatric disorders among remand prisoners in Scotland' (1995) 167 British Journal of Psychiatry 545–548.

[2]   See Annual Report of Mental Welfare Commission 2004–5, p 15, but see the case of Mr M at pp 15–17.

HEALTHCARE IN PRISON

47.02 The National Health Service does not supply health services in prisons. The Scottish Prisons Service provides health care, and delegates responsibility for managing it to prison governors. Prison governors are responsible for developing strategies and liaising with the National Health Service as appropriate.

An assessment carried out by the Scottish Prison Service[1] found that the rate of psychological disturbance and personality disorder in prisoners was twice as high as in the general population. Suicide rates are generally higher in prisons than in the community.

Despite this, the report revealed that not all prisons have dedicated mental health teams within the prison. Access to hospital and specialist services was limited and there was limited evidence of joint working with the National Health Service.

The Department of Health in England has transferred prison health services back to primary care trusts, but the Scottish Prison Service report claimed there was little enthusiasm for this in Scotland.

Further discussion may be necessary. The Mental Welfare Commission believes that the English solution might have advantages in Scotland.[2]

1   *Nursing Services Review* (Scottish Prison Service, 2003).
2   See its Annual Report 2004–5, p 17.

Legal framework for healthcare

47.03 It is the duty of Scottish Ministers, through the Scottish Prison Service, to provide an 'appropriate' health service for prisons in Scotland.[1] This should include cover for routine and emergency health care and the provision of information to the prison governor about the treatment and health of prisoners.

As health services are run directly by the Scottish Prison Service, policies of the National Health Service in Scotland, such as making mental health a priority, are not necessarily part of the prison heath service.

1   Prisons (Scotland) Act 1989 (as amended by the Crime and Punishment (Scotland) Act 1997), s 3A.

Complaints about healthcare

47.04 This does not mean that prisoners have no remedy if health services, particularly mental health services, are inadequate.

Prisoners may make a complaint under the prison complaints system.[1] Complaints about medical services are made first to the prison health service and then to Scottish Ministers.

If a prisoner remains dissatisfied, he or she can approach the Prisons Complaints Commission. This is a type of ombudsman, created in 1994 by the Scottish Executive. Unlike most ombudsman services,[2] it lacks a statutory basis. This may reduce its effectiveness and remit.[3]

Unfortunately the Prisons Complaints Commission cannot investigate medical matters involving clinical judgment decisions.

The author would argue that a general complaint about the inadequacy of services is not a complaint about clinical judgement.

1   See 'prisons' on Scottish Executive Justice Department website.
2   See chapter 50.
3   See its Annual Report 2003–4, p 8.

Role of Mental Welfare Commission

47.05 The Mental Health (Care and Treatment) Act has brought prisons within the investigatory remit of the Mental Welfare Commission for Scotland.[1] The Mental Welfare Commission can visit prisons and young offenders' institutions and can meet with prisoners and staff and inspect facilities.[2] It can also carry out formal investigations into inadequacies in care or treatment.[3]

It takes a great interest in issues relating to prisoners' mental health and can highlight concerns. Anyone believing that services in prison are not adequate for a prisoner's mental health needs may wish to contact the Commission. (For general information about the Commission, see chapter 3.)

1   Mental Health (Care and Treatment) (Scotland) Act 2003, s 8.
2   MH(CT)(S)A 2003, s 13(4).
3   MH(CT)(S)A 2003, s 11.

PRISON STANDARDS AND LEGAL REMEDIES

Negligence

47.06 If the Scottish Prison Service fails in its duty of care to a prisoner and the person suffers loss or damage as a result, the prisoner, or next of kin, may be able to take legal action under the law of negligence. See chapter 51.

Historically, the common law has been of limited help. The courts in England and Wales have held that that the same standard of care should not be applied to prison as to psychiatric hospitals. The primary function of prison is to detain prisoners. A prison is required to care for physically and mentally ill prisoners, but the courts have said that it cannot be expected to provide the same degree of care as the National Health Service.[1]

The situation is different where the prison is aware that a prisoner may be at special risk. The House of Lords held that the police owe a duty of care to a person in custody they know to be suicidal and should take special steps to protect him or her.[2]

These cases should now be read alongside human rights law, which has strengthened people's rights.

1   *Knight v Home Office* [1990] 3 All ER 237 But see *Brooks v Home Office*, The Times, 18 February 1999, where the High Court held that ante-natal care for a pregnant prisoner should be the same as she would have received in hospital, subject to any security constraints.

2   *Reeves v Commissioner of Police for the Metropolis* [1999] 3 All ER 897.

Human rights law

47.07 For obvious reasons, human rights law has been particularly interested in protecting the interests of people in prison. There have been several cases where people have challenged prisons' failure to provide adequate services. Either Articles 2, 3, 5 or 8 might be relevant.

Right to life

47.08 Article 2 of the European Convention of Human Rights is the right to life. The Human Rights Court has said that this Article imposes a duty on public authorities to protect people whose lives may be at risk, including risk to themselves.[1]

A prison failing to protect a mentally ill person at risk of suicide could be liable for breaching the prisoner's human rights.

1   *Osman v UK* [1999] 1 FLR 193.

Inhumane treatment

47.09 Failure to provide adequate medical care or support may also be inhumane or degrading treatment within Article 3 of the European Convention on Human Rights.

The European Court of Human Rights has held that the authorities are under an obligation to provide appropriate medical care (including psychiatric care) for people deprived of their liberty.[1]

Lack of appropriate medical care may amount to treatment contrary to Article 3.[2] When assessing whether the treatment or punishment of a mentally ill person is in breach of Article 3, the court will take into consideration the person's additional vulnerability.[3]

The Human Rights Court held that the United Kingdom had breached Articles 3 and 13 following the death of a mentally ill prisoner in England.[4] The court criticised the doctors for lack of record keeping and for allowing the prison hospital doctor to treat him, with no reference to a psychiatrist. These represented 'significant defects in the medical care provided to a mentally ill person known to be a suicide risk'.

The prison subjected the person to disciplinary procedures which were inappropriate for someone with his degree of vulnerability. They may have led to his suicide. The court said this was inhumane and degrading punishment within Article 3.

1   *Hurtado v Switzerland*, judgment of 28 January 1994, (Series A No. 280-A), opinion of the Commission, pp 15–16, para 79.
2   *Ihan v Turkey* (22277/93), para 87. See also *McGlinchey v the United Kingdom* [2003] ECtHR 211 (Failure to provide proper treatment for heroin addict in prison was breach of Article 3.)
3   *Herczegfalvy v Austria* ((1992) A 244) para 82.
4   *Keenan v UK* [2001] 33 EHRR 913.

Unauthorised detention

47.10 Failure to provide appropriate care for a prisoner who is mentally ill may also be a breach of the person's Article 5 rights. In a case in Belgium, a man who had been acquitted because of mental illness was kept in the prison psychiatric wing instead of being transferred to hospital. The court held that the psychiatric wing was not appropriate for his detention, as it could not provide regular medical attention or a therapeutic environment. It held the man had been unlawfully detained in breach of his Article 5 rights.[1]

1   *Aerts v Belgium* [1998] ECtHR 64.

INDEPENDENT ADVOCACY

47.11 A prisoner with a mental illness, personality disorder or learning disability is entitled to access independent advocacy services. See chapter 4. As far as the author is aware, there are not currently any mental health advocacy services specifically for people in prisons in Scotland, but general advocacy services may be able to offer help on request.

TRANSFER TO HOSPITAL

47.12 If a sentenced prisoner needs to go to a psychiatric hospital because of a mental illness, personality disorder or learning disability, Scottish Ministers may make a 'transfer for treatment direction', authorising the person's transfer to hospital.

A transfer for treatment direction can be made for people in prison (or young offenders' institutions), including people convicted of crimes and people in prison because of failure to pay a fine.[1] They can also be used for people detained under the Immigration Act 1971 and the Nationality, Immigration and Asylum Act 2002.[2]

[1]   Mental Health (Care and Treatment) (Scotland) Act 2003, s 136(9).
[2]   Mental Health (Care and Treatment) (Scotland) Act 2003 (Consequential Provisions) Order 2005 (SSI 2005/2078), art 13.

Remand prisoners

47.13 For people on remand awaiting trial or sentence, the appropriate order is an assessment or treatment order. See chapter 45.

Application for transfer for treatment direction

47.14 The prison healthcare staff should contact the appropriate hospital and ask for an assessment. If the hospital agrees the person should be in hospital, the prison governor can apply for the transfer. The governor must submit two medical reports, including one from an approved medical practitioner, to Scottish Ministers.[1] The other report is usually from the prison doctor.

If possible, the approved medical practitioner should be from the hospital or unit to which the prisoner would go. Where possible, the two medical practitioners should examine the prisoner within five days of each other.[2] The form of their reports is on the Scottish Executive's mental health law website.

Scottish Ministers normally require a report from a mental health officer. The Code of Practice sets out good practice guidance.[3]

[1]   Mental Health (Care and Treatment) (Scotland) Act 2003, s 136(2).
[2]   Code of Practice, vol 3, pt 2, para 5.08.
[3]   Code of Practice, vol 3, pt 2, paras 5.18–19.

Grounds for direction

47.15 Scottish Ministers consider whether the grounds for making an order apply. The grounds are similar to other orders in the criminal justice system. Scottish Ministers must be satisfied that the person has a mental disorder,[1] that treatment which could prevent it worsening or alleviate its symptoms/affects is available, that failure to provide such treatment could lead to significant risks to the person or others and that it is necessary to make an order.[2]

The hospital must be suitable for the patient's needs and available within seven days of the order.[3] The level of security of the hospital should be the least restrictive setting, taking into account possible risk and the person's clinical needs.[4]

The person should go to the State Hospital only if the medical reports show that the person needs to be detained in under conditions of special security which only a State Hospital can provide.[5]

[1]   Mental Health (Care and Treatment) (Scotland) Act 2003, s 136(7). (The medical reports must show agreement on at least one form of mental disorder.)
[2]   MH(CT)(S)A 2003, s 136(4). The Code of Practice envisages that an order will be necessary even where someone consents to go to hospital for treatment. See vol 3, pt 2, para 5.14.
[3]   MH(CT)(S)A 2003, s 136(3).
[4]   Code of Practice, vol 3, pt 2, para 5.12.
[5]   MH(CT)(S)A 2003, s 136(5). See 17.15.

Effect of direction

47.16 If Scottish Ministers sign the direction, the Scottish Prison Service should transfer the person to hospital within seven days of the transfer for treatment direction.[1]

A transfer for treatment direction has much the same effect as a compulsion order with a restriction order attached. See chapter 46. The person is detained in hospital and subject to the compulsory treatment provisions of Part 16 of the Act.[2]

A person transferred from prison to hospital is a restricted patient. This means that Scottish Ministers make all decisions about transfer between hospitals and suspension of the order, subject to the person's rights to appeal to the tribunal.[3] If the person's health improves, he or she may go back to prison to complete the sentence.

1   Mental Health (Care and Treatment) (Scotland) Act 2003, s 136(6). Code of
     Practice, vol 3, pt 2, para 5.04.
2   MH(CT)(S)A 2003, s 136(6).
3   MH(CT)(S)A 2003, ss 207–213, 218 and 224.

Patients' rights

47.17 The hospital authorities must give the person information about his
or her rights, help with communication needs (if appropriate), and
appoint a responsible medical officer and mental health officer, as for
people subject to compulsion orders. See chapter 48.

The mental health officer must prepare a social circumstances report
and submit a copy to Scottish Ministers, unless he or she sees no practical
benefit in this. For more detail about the mental health officer's duties,
see the Code of Practice.[1]

The responsible medical officer and mental health officer will need to
ensure they understand the effect of the person's sentence, rights of early
release, etc.[2]

The patient has rights to advocacy and to appoint a named person (if
able to do so). See chapter 4. If a patient has made an advance statement,
doctors must consider its terms. See chapter 10.

Chapter 48 considers the rights of restricted patients.

1   Code of Practice, vol 3, pt 2, paras 6.23–26.
2   A brief outline is in the Code of Practice, vol 3, pt 2, paras 6.28–36.

Appeal

47.18 Within 12 weeks of the date of the making of the transfer for
treatment direction, the patient and his or her named person may appeal
to the tribunal against the direction.[1]

No further appeals are possible until six months have elapsed from
the date of the direction. Thereafter appeals can be at 12-monthly
intervals. If the appeal is successful, the person returns to prison or
wherever Scottish Ministers consider appropriate.[2]

The Mental Health (Care and Treatment) Act does not provide an
appeal against Scottish Ministers' failure to authorise a transfer. The Act
does not oblige Scottish Ministers to make a transfer for treatment
direction, even if they receive the appropriate reports, but gives them
discretion. Such a failure would be very unlikely if the medical reports

recommend a transfer, and could be challenged on human rights grounds.

For more details on basis of appeals and procedures, see chapter 48.

1   Mental Health (Care and Treatment) (Scotland) Act 2003, s 214(5).
2   MH(CT)(S)A 2003, s 216.

Chapter 48

IMPACT OF ORDERS AND PATIENTS' RIGHTS

48.01 This chapter looks at the impact of orders under the criminal justice system, and the rights of and restrictions on patients. These are in addition to the rights and restrictions in Part 3 of this book, above which apply to everyone who is subject to a compulsory order.

In the criminal justice system, there are two groups of patients. People subject to compulsion orders without restrictions are generally in a similar position to people subject to civil compulsory treatment orders. See Part 3. This chapter highlights the differences only.

Restricted patients are people subject to compulsion orders with restriction orders, people subject to hospital directions and people transferred to hospital from prison under transfer for treatment directions. People transferred temporarily to hospital during the course of a trial, such as people subject to interim compulsion orders and assessment and treatment orders, are also restricted patients.

The Scottish Executive has circulated detailed guidance for people involved with the management and care of restricted patients.[1] This supplements the guidance in the Code of Practice.[2]

---

[1] *Memorandum of procedure on restricted patients* (Scottish Executive Health Department, October 2005). Available on the Scottish Executive's mental health law website. The memorandum is currently being updated.

[2] Volume 3 deals entirely with people subject to orders under criminal procedure.

DUTIES OF AUTHORITIES

48.02 Following the making of an order, the relevant hospital managers must appoint a responsible medical officer for the person[1] and the local authority should appoint a mental health officer.[2] The mental health officer should prepare a social circumstances report.[3] These duties are the same as those in the civil system and are not covered in detail here.

When someone is subject to a compulsion order with restrictions, the hospital should notify Scottish Ministers and the Mental Welfare Commission of the person's admission as soon as possible.[4]

The person subject to the order should receive information about his or her rights and, if someone's first language is not English or he or she has communication difficulties, the person should receive information at certain stages of the procedure in language or a medium he or she understands.[5]

These rules apply to people subject to assessment orders, treatment orders, interim compulsion orders, compulsion orders, hospital directions and transfer for treatment directions.

[1]	Mental Health (Care and Treatment) (Scotland) Act 2003, s 230.

[2]	MH(CT)(S)A 2003, s 229.

[3]	MH(CT)(S)A 2003, s 231.

[4]	Code of Practice, vol 3, pt 2, para 2.14.

[5]	MH(CT)(S)A 2003, ss 260 and 261.

Advocacy

48.03 Everyone with a mental disorder has a right of access to independent advocacy services.[1] A person coming to mental health services through the criminal justice system may have particular needs. Specialist advocacy services are the ideal. For example, the Patients Advocacy Service at the State Hospital has special expertise in the issues facing people subject to criminal procedure, as well as those for people who come to the State Hospital following a civil admission.

Where a former State Hospital patient lives in the community because a compulsory treatment order or compulsion order has been suspended, or while on conditional discharge, he or she may face particular issues. The person remains entitled to an independent advocate and may need advocacy while in the community.

The State Hospital must collaborate with the local authority and health board for the area where the person is living to ensure the person receives advocacy services.[2]

[1]	Mental Health (Care and Treatment) (Scotland) Act 2003, s 259.

[2]	MH(CT)(S)A 2003, ss 259(8)–(10). See Code of Practice, vol 1, para 6.91.

Children and young people

48.04 The criminal procedure rules apply to children and young people. A child or young person can be made subject to any of the available orders, if appropriate. This includes orders transferring him or her from prison or a young offenders' institution.

The special principles of the Act relating to children and young people apply to such patients, and the hospital must provide services appropriate for the age of the child or young person. See chapter 41. The young person's responsible medical officer should be a specialist in child and adolescent psychiatry.[1]

1   Code of Practice, vol 3, para 1.21.

COMPULSION ORDERS

Similarities to compulsory treatment order

48.05 The effects of a compulsion order without restrictions order largely mirror those of compulsory treatment orders. For reasons of space, they are not set out in detail here.

People subject to compulsion orders have similar rights of review and appeal to those of people subject to compulsory treatment orders. The responsible medical officer must keep the person's condition under review at all times and must cancel ('revoke') the order if the grounds for an order no longer apply or if it is no longer necessary.[1]

As with compulsory treatment orders, there are provisions for the variation and extension of orders, suspension of orders to allow rehabilitation in the community and for patients and their named persons to apply to the tribunal for discharge.[2]

Responsible medical officers can transfer patients to different hospitals (including the State Hospital) and patients can appeal against any transfer.

Patients have rights to advocacy, to appoint a named person and to have any advance statements taken into account.

The Mental Welfare Commission can cancel compulsion orders but has said it will not use this power. See 12.19. The remedies for breach of a compulsion order are as for breach of compulsory treatment orders.[3]

1   Mental Health (Care and Treatment) (Scotland) Act 2003, ss 141 and 142.

²   MH(CT)(S)A 2003, Pt 9, Chap 2.
³   MH(CT)(S)A 2003, ss 176–179.

Differences from compulsory treatment order

48.06 There are some differences from the civil procedure.

Grounds for renewal

48.07 The grounds for continuing or extending the order are different, as were the grounds for the original order. See above. The doctor does not have to consider whether the person has significantly impaired medical decision-making ability.[1]

(This is because the order is an alternative to a prison sentence or other punishment. The person's ability to take treatment decisions is not as relevant as in the civil procedure.)

[1]   See, for example, Mental Health (Care and Treatment) (Scotland) Act 2003, s 139(4).

First renewal

48.08 The responsible medical officer must apply to the tribunal if he or she wishes to extend the order on the first occasion after it was made.[1] See below.

Thereafter renewals do not require the authority of the tribunal and the process is the same as for compulsory treatment orders.

[1]   Mental Health (Care and Treatment) (Scotland) Act 2003, s 148. The tribunal is not involved in the renewal of civil orders, unless the person or named person appeals. MH(CT)(S)A 2003, s 86.

Recorded matters and reports to tribunal

48.09 A compulsion order does not contain recorded matters, as the court imposing the order does not consider a proposed care plan for the person. The Code of Practice recommends that the responsible medical officer list any matters he or she regards as essential to the person's care as 'recorded matters' in the care plan he or she draws up.[1] (See below.)

The documents the responsible medical officer must deliver to the tribunal vary from those used in civil cases. There are separate regulations.[2] See below.

1   Code of Practice, vol 3, pt 2, para 1.06.
2   Mental Health (Compulsion orders—documents and reports to be submitted to the tribunal) (Scotland) Regulations 2005 (SSI 2005/365). ('The compulsion orders documents Regulations'.)

Absconding

48.10 Regulations deal with unauthorised absences of people subject to criminal justice orders. See below. These rules apply to people on compulsion orders.

Care plan

48.11 The responsible medical officer should draw up a statutory care plan for the person and keep this with the person's records.[1]

Unlike the compulsory treatment order, the criminal procedure does not require the preparation of a proposed care plan for the court, but the Code of Practice envisages that the care team should have assessed the person's needs at this stage.[2] If not, there should be a multi-disciplinary review as soon as possible after the compulsion order comes into effect.[3]

The contents of the care plan are set out in regulations.[4] It must show the medical treatment plans for the person and the treatment he or she is currently receiving. It should include details of any community care or other services the person is to receive, details of the person's offence and any requirement to register under the Sexual Offences Act 2003.

The regulations detail the occasions on which the responsible medical officer must amend the care plan.

1   Mental Health (Care and Treatment) (Scotland) Act 2003, s 137.
2   Code of Practice, vol 3, pt 2, para 1.18.
3   Code of Practice, vol 3, pt 2, para 1.21.
4   The Mental Health (Content and amendment of Part 9 care plans) (Scotland) Regulations 2005 (SSI 2005/312).

First renewal of order

48.12 The responsible medical officer must apply to the tribunal if he or she wishes to renew a compulsion order on the first occasion after it was made.[1] The form of application is on the mental health law website.

Regulations set out the documents which must accompany the application. The responsible medical officer must send the tribunal a copy of the person's care plan and any amendments to it and a copy of any medical and mental health officer reports submitted to the court which made the order.[2]

The regulations also list the documents the responsible medical officer must deliver at different stages of the process.

1   Mental Health (Care and Treatment) (Scotland) Act 2003, s 148.
2   Compulsion orders documents Regulations, reg 2.

COMPULSION ORDER WITH RESTRICTIONS

48.13 Someone subject to a compulsion order with a restriction order is under extra restrictions not experienced by people under compulsion orders or civil orders. These reflect the involvement of Scottish Ministers and the fact that public safety grounds are taken into account when the person's discharge is being considered.

The differences affect the procedure for reviews and appeals, the basis on which appeals are considered, the transfer of the person to another hospital and suspension of the order.

Otherwise, people's rights, such as the right to advocacy, to appoint a named person and to have any advance statement taken into account, are as for people on compulsion orders.

Duties of responsible medical officer

48.14 The responsible medical officer should prepare a care plan for the person as for a compulsion order[1] and send a copy to the patient, the named person, Scottish Ministers, the mental health officer and other relevant members of the person's care team.[2]

The responsible medical officer should update the care plan as appropriate and notify the relevant parties.[3]

The responsible medical officer reports to Scottish Ministers within three months of the person's admission to hospital and then annually.[4] Scottish Ministers may require further information from time to time.[5]

1   Code of Practice, vol 3, pt 2, para 2.17.
2   Code of Practice, as above, para 2.18.
3   Code of Practice, as above, paras 2.19–21.
4   Code of Practice, as above, para 2.22.
5   Mental Health (Care and Treatment) (Scotland) Act 2003, s 287.

Duties of mental health officer

48.15 The mental health officer should prepare a social circumstances report (unless he or she thinks one is not necessary) and send a copy to Scottish Ministers.[1]

1   Code of Practice, vol 3, pt 2, para 2.23.

Reviews and appeals

48.16 Orders are reviewed annually[1] and from time to time as necessary.[2]

1   Mental Health (Care and Treatment) (Scotland) Act 2003, s 182(5).
2   MH(CT)(S)A 2003, s 184.

Review by responsible medical officer

48.17 As with a compulsory treatment order, the responsible medical officer must keep the person's condition under regular review.[1] Following such a review the responsible medical officer might recommend to Scottish Ministers that the person is discharged from hospital or that the restriction order is removed.

The responsible medical officer must examine the person (or arrange for another doctor to examine him or her) and should consult the mental health officer.[2]

The responsible medical officer considers whether the person still has a mental disorder, whether the grounds for the order apply and whether a compulsion or restriction order remains necessary.[3]

He or she must also consider whether the person needs to continue to be detained in hospital on grounds of risk of serious harm. The risk of serious harm grounds apply whether or not the person is to receive medical treatment for the mental disorder.[4]

The responsible medical officer should consult the mental health officer before reaching a decision.[5] The responsible medical officer reports to Scottish Ministers and makes recommendations accordingly.[6]

1   Mental Health (Care and Treatment) (Scotland) Act 2003, s 184.
2   MH(CT)(S)A 2003, s 182(3).
3   MH(CT)(S)A 2003, s 182(3).
4   MH(CT)(S)A 2003, s 182(3)(b).
5   MH(CT)(S)A 2003, s 182(3)(c).
6   MH(CT)(S)A 2003, s 183(2).

Review by mental health officer

48.18 The Code of Practice gives good practice guidance to the mental health officer.[1] He or she should consult all relevant people, including the care team, the named person and relatives, carers and significant others.[2]

A form for the responsible medical officer's report is on the mental health law website. More guidance on the content of the report is in the Code of Practice.[3]

[1]   Code of Practice, vol 3, pt 2, paras 3.22–27.
[2]   Code of Practice, vol 3, pt 2, para 3.09.
[3]   As above, paras 3.12–21.

Tests for responsible medical officer review

48.19 There are various tests. The rules are very complex. The responsible medical officer has to review all the grounds for the order, as follows:

- **Mental disorder** Does the person have a mental disorder? ('The mental disorder test').

  A person may have a mental disorder even though he or she is not experiencing any symptoms at the time of the hearing. In a case in England, the court said that the fact that someone was showing neither positive nor negative symptoms of the disorder with which he was diagnosed did not mean that it was not appropriate for him to remain liable to detention because of his mental disorder.[1] The human rights court has confirmed this approach.[2]

- **Medical treatment** Is medical treatment available for the person which is likely to prevent the mental disorder worsening, or alleviate any of its symptoms or effects? ('The treatability test').

  'Medical treatment' is widely defined. It includes medical treatment, care, nursing, psychological interventions, rehabilitation and help with daily living skills.[3] If any of these can help the person or prevent his or her condition from getting worse, the person is treatable. This does not include mere containment but does include, for example, anger management in a structured setting.[4]

- **Risk to others** If the person does not have such medical treatment, would there be a significant risk to his or her health, safety or welfare or to the safety of any other person? ('The risk to others test').

794

- **Risk of serious harm** Because of the person's mental disorder, is it necessary for him or her to be detained in hospital, whether or not for medical treatment, to protect any other person from serious harm? ('The risk of serious harm test').

  (This extends to the safety of people in the prison or institution where the person might be living, not just the wider public.[5])

- **Need for compulsion order** Does the person need to be subject to the compulsion order? ('The compulsion order test')

- **Need for restriction order** Does the person need to be subject to the restriction order? ('The restriction order test').

1   *R v Mental Health Review Tribunal for South Thames Region, ex parte Smith*, The Times, 9 December 1998.
2   *Johnson v UK* [1997] ECtHR 88, at para 61.
3   Mental Health (Care and Treatment) (Scotland) Act 2003, s 329.
4   *Reid v Secretary of State for Scotland*, 1999 SC (HL) 17.
5   *Anderson, Doherty and Reid v Scottish Ministers*, 2001 SLT 1331, Lord Clyde.

Recommendations by responsible medical officer

48.20 Having reviewed the person in accordance with the various tests, the responsible medical officer may make various recommendations.

- **Absolute discharge** The responsible medical officer may recommend the cancellation of the compulsion order and restriction order and that the person receives an absolute discharge. The responsible medical officer should do this if he or she is not satisfied that the person has a mental disorder.[1]

  The responsible medical officer may recommend an absolute discharge if he or she is satisfied that the person has a mental disorder but not satisfied that the person meets the treatability test or the risk to others test, *unless* the responsible medical officer is satisfied there is a risk of serious harm.[2]

  (If the responsible medical officer is satisfied the person has a mental disorder and there is a risk of serious harm, he or she cannot recommend discharge of the compulsion order or the restriction order, even if not satisfied that the treatability test is met.)

- **Cancellation of restriction order** The responsible medical officer can recommend that the restriction order (but not the compulsion order) is cancelled.

The grounds are that he or she is satisfied that the person has a mental disorder, that the treatability test and the risk to others test apply and that a compulsion order continues to be necessary but not satisfied that a restriction order continues to be necessary and that the person needs to be detained in hospital because of the risk of serious harm.[3]

If the responsible medical officer recommends discharging the restriction order, he or she may also request the tribunal to vary the compulsion order.[4]

- **Conditional discharge** The responsible medical officer may recommend a conditional discharge.

The grounds are that he or she is satisfied the person has a mental disorder, that the treatability and risk to others tests apply and that the person needs to be subject to a compulsion order with restrictions, but he or she is not satisfied that the person needs to be detained in hospital on grounds of the risk of serious harm.[5]

[1]   Mental Health (Care and Treatment) (Scotland) Act 2003, s 184(3).
[2]   MH(CT)(S)A 2003, s 184(4).
[3]   MH(CT)(S)A 2003, s 184(5).
[4]   MH(CT)(S)A 2003, s 183(7). The Code of Practice says that the responsible medical officer should not recommend discharging the restriction order unless all members of the care team agree, (Code of Practice, vol 3, pt 2, para 3.29) but there may be occasions where the responsible medical officer is unable to reach agreement with a member of the team. The author suggests that the responsible medical officer's recommendations to Scottish Ministers must finally be a question of his or her professional judgement.
[5]   MH(CT)(S)A 2003, s 183(6).

Duties of Scottish Ministers

48.21 Scottish Ministers must keep the person's condition under review and apply to the tribunal for any appropriate changes to the order.[1] If Scottish Ministers receive a responsible medical officer's report recommending discharge or a variation of the order, they must refer the case to the tribunal.[2]

Scottish Ministers must ensure that the tribunal reviews every restricted patient's case at least once every two years, and must refer the case to the tribunal if this has not happened.[3]

[1]   Mental Health (Care and Treatment) (Scotland) Act 2003, s 188.

2   MH(CT)(S)A 2003, s 185.

3   MH(CT)(S)A 2003, s 189.

Role of the Mental Welfare Commission

48.22 The Mental Welfare Commission may ask the Scottish Ministers to refer a case to the tribunal[1] and Scottish Ministers must comply with this request.[2] The Mental Welfare Commission should consider whether to make a referral by reference to the statutory tests the responsible medical officer uses.[3]

1   Mental Health (Care and Treatment) (Scotland) Act 2003, s 186.

2   MH(CT)(S)A 2003, s 187(2).

3   Code of Practice, vol 3, pt 2, para 3.47.

Appeal to tribunal

48.23 The patient and his or her named person can apply to the tribunal for conditional discharge, the cancellation of the restriction order and/or the compulsion order and the variation of the order.[1]

No appeal is possible within six months of the making of the order or three months of a tribunal decision. Only one appeal is possible in each 12-month period from the anniversary of the making of the order.[2]

Where the named person makes an application to the tribunal, he or she must notify the patient.[3] The responsible medical officer and mental health officer should ensure that the patient and named person have access to advocacy services and legal services to assist them make an application.[4]

1   Mental Health (Care and Treatment) (Scotland) Act 2003, s 192.

2   MH(CT)(S)A 2003, s 192(2). (But see *Kolanis v UK* [2005] ECtHR 411. The mental health act rules for England and Wales prevented a person from referring her case back to the Mental Health Review tribunal for 12 months. This was held to be in breach of Art 5(4) (right to speedy review). The rules did not allow sufficiently speedy access where there is a significant change in person's health or needs.)

3   MH(CT)(S)A 2003, s 192(6).

4   Code of Practice, vol 3, pt 2, para 3.53.

Constitution of tribunal

48.24 In cases relating to restricted patients, the President of the Mental Health Tribunal or a sheriff or sheriff principal chairs the tribunal.[1] The tribunal must give all parties a chance to be heard and to produce evidence and must always hold a hearing.[2]

For procedure at the tribunal, see chapter 43.

[1]   Mental Health (Care and Treatment) (Scotland) Act 2003, Sched 2, para 7(4).
[2]   MH(CT)(S)A 2003, s 193(8).

Tribunal decision

48.25 The tribunal considers the facts of the case and decides whether an order should stand or the tribunal should vary it. If an order is to stand, the doctors and mental health officer must satisfy the tribunal that it is still necessary. The law does not require the patient to prove the order is no longer necessary[1] (although in practice, it may still appear like that).

The determinations the tribunal may make are as follows. (See above for the tests.)

- **Absolute discharge** The Tribunal may cancel the compulsion and restriction order and grant the person an absolute discharge. It will do so if it is not satisfied the person has a mental disorder.[2]

  It will also grant an absolute discharge if it is satisfied that the person has a mental disorder but not satisfied as to his or her treatability or risk to others, *provided* there is no risk of serious harm to public safety.[3]

- **Refuse application** The Tribunal may refuse the application. It will do so if it is satisfied that the person has a mental disorder and, as a result, needs to be detained in hospital to protect the public (or any person) from serious harm.[4] The risk of serious harm test applies whether or not doctors consider the person treatable.

  (The equivalent provision in the 1984 Act[5] was challenged in the courts. The applicants argued that it was a breach of their human rights to detain them in hospital if they could not benefit from medical treatment.

  The Privy Council said that the European Convention on Human Rights did not say a person could only be detained if effective treatment is available. If a person's disorder means he or she is a threat to public safety, it may be appropriate for the person to be

detained in hospital. The legislation was a proportionate response
by the Scottish Executive to the risks posed.[6])

- **Discharge restriction order** The tribunal may discharge the
restriction order. The grounds are that the tribunal is satisfied that
the person has a mental disorder and about his or her treatability,
the risk to others and the need for a compulsion order, and not
satisfied that the person needs to be detained in hospital because of
risk of serious harm.[7]

- **Conditional discharge** The Tribunal may grant a conditional
discharge. The grounds are that it is satisfied that the person has a
mental disorder, about his or her treatability and/or risk to others
and that it is still necessary for the person to be subject to a
compulsion order with restrictions, but that it is not satisfied that
the person needs to be detained in hospital because of the risk of
serious harm.[8]

The tribunal may impose such conditions on a conditional
discharge as it thinks fit. The Code of Practice gives examples.[9]
Conditions could cover where the person should live, what day
care and other services he or she must attend, allowing access to
certain people, taking of medication,[10] restrictions on the use of
drugs and/or alcohol and screening for their use, and restrictions
on places the person may visit.

The tribunal may defer conditional discharge until the appropriate
arrangements are in place.[11] If Scottish Ministers recommend the
discharge, the arrangements should be in place. See below.

The courts in England have said that it is not possible to grant
conditional discharge if the effect of the restrictions imposed would
be to continue to deprive the patient of his or her liberty in the
community. This would be a variation of the conditions of the
person's detention. The tribunal does not have this power and the
variation would be beyond its powers.[12] It is different if the main
purpose of the conditions is to protect the interests of the person.[13]

- **Variation of measures** The tribunal may vary the measures in an
order as requested by the responsible medical officer, the patient or
his or her named person.[14] The scope of this power has yet to be
tested by the tribunal services. The power could include moving
someone to a unit providing a lower level of security (if such a
hospital is available and willing to accept the patient) or

discharging a restriction order and replacing detention in hospital with a community-based compulsory treatment order.

For more detail about conditional and absolute discharge, see below.

¹   See *R (H) v MHRT North & East London Region* (2001) EWCA Civ 415, *L v Scottish Ministers*, Inner House, Court of Session, 17 January 2002, *Hutchison Reid v UK* [2003] ECtHR 94.
²   Mental Health (Care and Treatment) (Scotland) Act 2003, s 193(3).
³   MH(CT)(S)A 2003, s 193(4).
⁴   MH(CT)(S)A 2003, s 193(2).
⁵   (Introduced by the Mental Health (Public Safety and Appeals) (Scotland) Act 1999.)
⁶   *Anderson v Scottish Ministers*, 2002 SC (PC) 63.
⁷   MH(CT)(S)A 2003, s 193(5).
⁸   MH(CT)(S)A 2003, s 193(7).
⁹   Vol 3, pt 2, para 4.05.
¹⁰ The person cannot be subject to compulsory medical treatment in the community, but failure to take medication is generally a breach of the order. See chapter 20.
¹¹ MH(CT)(S)A 2003, s 195. For human rights concerns, see 48.30 below.
¹² *R (G) v Mental Health Review Tribunal* [2004] EWHC 2193.
¹³ *R (Secretary of State for the Home Department) v Mental Health Review Tribunal* [2002] EWCA Civ 1868.
¹⁴ MH(CT)(S)A 2003, s 193(6).

Notifications by tribunal

48.26 If a restricted patient discharged from of the discharge hospital is on the register of sex offenders, the police must be informed of the discharge.[1] The Scottish Executive says there may be other cases when it is appropriate for the tribunal to breach confidentiality in the interests of public safety.[2] The tribunal should first try to seek the person's consent.

It is not easy to imagine situations where the tribunal will discharge from hospital a person whose mental disorder means he or she poses a risk to others, so such cases are likely to be rare.

¹   At the time of writing, this is the responsibility of the person on the register. The UK government intends to make regulations under s 96 of the Sexual Offences Act 2003 requiring hospital managers to notify them if a person on the register is discharged from hospital.
²   *Memorandum on restricted patients* (above), para 14.15.

Appeal by Scottish Ministers and others

48.27 Scottish Ministers may appeal to the Court of Session on a point of law against the tribunal's cancellation or variation of an order and against the granting of conditional discharge.[1]

Scottish Ministers may request the Court of Session to continue the order until the outcome of the appeal.[2] Such an order authorises the person's continued detention until any appeal to the House of Lords is determined or the time limit for making an appeal has expired.[3]

The person's mental health officer and his or her responsible medical officer may also appeal against the tribunal's decision.[4]

1   Mental Health (Care and Treatment) (Scotland) Act 2003, s 322.
2   MH(CT)(S)A 2003, s 323.
3   MH(CT)(S)A 2003, s 323(2).
4   MH(CT)(S)A 2003, s 322(3).

Appeal to Court of Session

48.28 The patient may appeal to the Court of Session against a tribunal's refusal to discharge or vary the order or to grant conditional discharge.[1]

The person must submit the appeal within 21 days of the date on which he or she received notice of the tribunal's decision or received a note of the tribunal's reasons for the decision.[2] The named person, welfare attorney or guardian may also appeal.[3]

Appeal to the Court of Session is possible only where the person allege an error of law or procedure, unreasonable exercise of discretion by the tribunal or that the tribunal's decision was not supported by the facts established at the tribunal.[4]

1   Mental Health (Care and Treatment) (Scotland) Act 2003, s 322.
2   Mental Health (Period for Appeal) (Scotland) (No. 2) Regulations 2005 (SSI 2005/441).
3   MH(CT)(S)A 2003, s 322(3).
4   MH(CT)(S)A 2003, s 324(2).

Conditional discharge

48.29 The tribunal may conditionally discharge a restricted patient if it believes he or she does not need to be detained in hospital on grounds of risk of serious harm. See above. The tribunal may grant a conditional discharge on the recommendation of Scottish Ministers, or following an application by the patient or named person.

Before Scottish Ministers recommend conditional discharge, the person has usually spent some time in the community on a suspended order and has been in contact with the services he or she will receive if conditionally discharged.[1]

A person on conditional discharge is subject to formal social work and medical supervision in the community. Those planning conditional discharge should work with local services and with Scottish Ministers to provide a package of care acceptable to the person and to Scottish Ministers.[2] The person is usually on the care programme approach.[3] See 6.12.

When the patient is required to register with the police on discharge, for example, under the Sexual Offences Act, the police may be involved in planning his or her discharge. Whenever anyone is acquitted of a crime of violence on the grounds of 'insanity' or if a compulsion order with restrictions is made following a crime of violence, the police, local authorities, health board and Scottish Ministers must establish joint arrangements for the assessment and management of any risks the person may pose.[4]

Scottish Ministers require regular reporting from medical and social work supervisors. They may also request reports from the person's community psychiatric nurse.[5] For the first year of conditional discharge, Scottish Ministers require monthly reports, and thereafter they may consider extending the interval to three months.

1   Code of Practice, vol 3, pt 2, para 4.04.
2   Code of Practice, as above, para 4.02–3.
3   Scottish Executive *Memorandum of procedure on restricted patients* (above) para 11.13.
4   Management of Offenders etc (Scotland) Act 2005, s 10.
5   *Memorandum of procedure on restricted patients*, para 11.20.

Delayed discharge

48.30 It may be necessary to delay discharging a person from hospital until the appropriate conditional discharge arrangements are in place. The Mental Health (Care and Treatment) Act allows this,[1] but the delay must not be excessive.

While there is no time limit for making such arrangements, human rights law does not allow unreasonable delays. A person detained in a special hospital in England remained there for three years after a tribunal had ordered his conditional discharge. The court held this was a breach of his human rights.[2]

If someone needs appropriate care in the interests of her own health and safety, the authorities do not have an absolute duty to provide after-care. The European Court of Human Rights held that it was lawful to continue to detain a person when it proved impossible to fulfil the conditions necessary for her discharge.[3]

1   Mental Health (Care and Treatment) (Scotland) Act 2003, s 195.
2   *Johnson v UK* [1997] ECtHR 88.
3   *Kolanis v UK* [2005] ECtHR 411. (She might have had remedies under English law if she could establish that the local authority did not use its best efforts to make the necessary arrangements or if psychiatrists were in breach of their duty to accept her as a patient.)

Deferred discharge

48.31 Where a tribunal has deferred discharge and there is a material change of circumstances before the discharge, the tribunal may need to reconsider its decision to direct a conditional discharge.

The Mental Health (Care and Treatment) Act does not contain provisions for the case to be brought back to the tribunal, but the House of Lords has said (on similar provisions in the Mental Health Act 1983) that a tribunal should treat its original decision as a provisional decision, and should monitor progress towards implementing it.

It could do this by considering deferring for a further period, by varying or removing the proposed conditions to reduce the difficulties in meeting them or by deciding that the person should remain detained in hospital for treatment.[1] This guidance is in line with human rights law[2] and could be relevant in Scotland.

In another case in England, the Court of Appeal held that the tribunal should grant a stay of the conditional discharge if new facts come to light which mean the tribunal needs to reconsider the decision to grant the conditional discharge. In this case, the tribunal had not received evidence concerning the need for a consultant psychiatrist to supervise the person.[3]

1   *R (IH) v Secretary of State for the Home Department and Another* [2002] EWCA Civ 646. Lord Phillips at para 70. Guidance from the Court of Appeal on interpreting equivalent provisions in the 1983 Act in light of human rights requirements was endorsed by House of Lords. Lord Bingham at para 27.)

2   See *Johnson v UK* (above).
3   *R (on the application of C) v Secretary of State for the Home Department* [2002] EWCA Civ 647. The Secretary of State had tried to refer the matter to a new tribunal, but should have brought the case back to the original tribunal.

Varying conditions of discharge

48.32 Scottish Ministers may vary any of the conditions attached to a conditional discharge if they think this necessary.[1] Scottish Ministers must give written notice to the patient, his or her named person, the responsible medical officer and the mental health officer.

Either the patient or named person may appeal to the tribunal against any variation of the conditions. The person must submit the appeal within 28 days of receiving the written notice of variation.[2]

The procedure is as if the person has applied for an order for conditional discharge.[3] The tribunal must be satisfied that conditional discharge remains appropriate and reconsiders what conditions should attach to the order.

1   Mental Health (Care and Treatment) (Scotland) Act 2003, s 200.
2   MH(CT)(S)A 2003, s 201(1).
3   MH(CT)(S)A 2003, s 201(3).

Reviews and appeals

48.33 A person on conditional discharge retains all his or her rights under the Mental Health (Care and Treatment) Act. The responsible medical officer and Scottish Ministers continue to be responsible for keeping the person's condition under regular review, with a view to absolute discharge.

The patient and his or her named person continue to have the right to appeal to the tribunal, the Mental Welfare Commission remains involved and Scottish Ministers must refer the case to the tribunal if it has not otherwise come before the tribunal within two years. The person remains entitled to advocacy support and should enquire of the hospital discharging him or her where he or she can access appropriate support.

The hospital managers must ensure the patient and his or her named person are aware of their rights.[1]

1   Mental Health (Care and Treatment) (Scotland) Act 2003, s 260. The Mental Health (Provision of Information to Patients) (Prescribed Times) (Scotland) Regulations 2005 (SSI 2005/206) reg 2(r).

Recall

48.34 If the responsible medical officer considers the health of a person on conditional discharge gives cause for concern, he or she should discuss this with the mental health officer and may recommend that Scottish Ministers recall the person to hospital.

Scottish Ministers may recall a person on conditional discharge if they consider he or she needs to be detained in hospital.[1] The recall is by warrant signed by Scottish Ministers and may be to a hospital other than that named in the compulsion order.[2]

Scottish Ministers may consider recalling a person if there are concerns that his or her mental state has deteriorated, that there is an increased risk to others, or that the person has breached any of the conditions of the order.[3]

The principles of the Mental Health (Care and Treatment) Act require that Scottish Ministers' action should be the least restrictive alternative in all the circumstances of the case. It may be the person can receive effective help in the community.

A recall not linked to health or risk issues is likely to be a breach of human rights. The Secretary of State in England recalled a person on a restriction order to hospital when there was no evidence he was mentally ill. The European Court of Human Rights held this was a breach of the person's human rights.[4]

The patient and his or her named person may appeal to the tribunal within 28 days of returning to hospital.[5] The procedure is as for an application for conditional discharge. The tribunal considers whether conditional discharge is appropriate and whether the conditions of the discharge are appropriate.[6]

[1]   Mental Health (Care and Treatment) (Scotland) Act 2003, s 202.
[2]   MH(CT)(S)A 2003, s 203.
[3]   Code of Practice, Vol 3, pt 2, para 4.08.
[4]   *K v United Kingdom* (1998) 40 BMLR 20. His unsuccessful application to the English courts was reported as *R v Secretary of State for the Home Department, ex parte K*, Times Law Report, 6 July 1990, CA.
[5]   MH(CT)(S)A 2003, s 204.
[6]   MH(CT)(S)Λ, s 204(3).

Where person becomes ill/commits offence

48.35 If a person on conditional discharge becomes ill while in the community, he or she may be admitted to hospital as a voluntary patient, provided doctors are satisfied the person can consent and is giving voluntary consent. If a long-term admission is likely, Scottish Ministers should recall the person to hospital.[1]

In an emergency, a doctor may use compulsory measures under the civil procedure, such as short-term or emergency detention. The courts in England have held that it is acceptable to invoke the relevant parts of the Mental Health Act independently of each other in this way.[2]

The Code of Practice give guidance on what Scottish Ministers may do if someone commits an offence while on conditional discharge.[3]

[1] Code of Practice, vol 3, pt 2, para 4.10.

[2] *R v North West London Mental Health NHS Trust ex parte Stewart*, Times Law Report, 27 August 1997.

[3] Vol 3, pt 2, paras 4.19–21.

Absolute discharge

48.36 The tribunal may discharge a restricted patient following an application by the patient or the named person, or a reference by Scottish Ministers. Scottish Ministers normally recommend absolute discharge only after a period of conditional discharge in the community.

There should be full consultation between the responsible medical officer, the mental health officer and other members of the care team before the responsible medical officer recommends absolute discharge to Scottish Ministers.

The responsible medical officer should ensure that there are suitable aftercare arrangements in the community before he or she makes the recommendation. The person is generally expected to continue to have contact with services on a voluntary basis.

If the responsible medical officer considers the tribunal may grant an absolute discharge against the recommendations of Scottish Ministers, he or she should ensure that there are appropriate contingency aftercare arrangements, or that arrangements are put in place as quickly as possible.[1]

Unlike conditional discharge, Scottish Ministers cannot defer absolute discharge until appropriate arrangements are in place.

[1] Code of Practice, vol 3, pt 2, paras 4.22–24.

Hospital Directions/transfer for treatment directions

48.37 For the making of hospital directions see chapter 46. For the making of transfer for treatment directions, see chapter 47. Generally people subject to such directions are subject to the same rules as other restricted patients, on such matters as care in hospital, access to information, etc. See above.

Reviews and appeals

48.38 The rules for reviews and appeals are broadly the same as for people subject to compulsion orders with restrictions. Good practice guidance to professionals is similar and, for the sake of space, is not repeated here.

There are certain differences in procedures, reflecting the different backgrounds to the orders. Scottish Ministers may discharge a hospital direction or transfer for treatment direction without referring the matter to a tribunal.[1]

The recommendations the responsible medical officer can make to Scottish Ministers are more limited than under a compulsion order with restrictions. There is no possibility of conditional discharge or of the person being discharged on a community-based order.

The outcomes if the tribunal discharges a hospital direction or transfer for treatment direction are different. If the person no longer meets the mental health grounds for being in hospital, he or she goes to prison or a young offenders' institution to finish his or her sentence. If the person is a life sentence prisoner, the Parole Board may grant parole.

[1] See Pt 11 of the Act.

Review by the responsible medical officer

48.39 The responsible medical officer must formally review the person's condition at 12-month intervals, consulting with the mental health officer and such other people as he or she considers appropriate,[1] and reports to Scottish Ministers. The form of the report is on the Scottish Executive's mental health law website.

The responsible medical officer must regularly consider whether the direction remains necessary and must report if he or she considers there should be a change in the order or it should be cancelled.[2] For the tests he or she uses, see 48.19 above.

The responsible medical officer must recommend that Scottish Ministers cancel the direction where he or she is not satisfied that the person has a mental disorder.[3] The responsible medical officer must also recommend cancellation where he or she is satisfied that the person has a mental disorder but does not believe that because of the disorder the person needs to be detained in hospital on grounds of risk of serious harm and is not satisfied that the treatability and risk to others tests apply.[4]

If the responsible medical officer is satisfied that the person has a mental disorder and that there is a risk of serious harm, the responsible medical officer cannot recommend discharge of the direction. This applies even if the doctor does not believe that medical treatment could help the person, as required by the treatability test.

[1] Mental Health (Care and Treatment) (Scotland) Act 2003, s 206. Guidance to mental health officers is in the Code of Practice, vol 3, pt 2, paras 7.24–26.
[2] MH(CT)(S)A 2003, s 208.
[3] MH(CT)(S)A 2003, s 208(3).
[4] MH(CT)(S)A 2003, s 208(4).

Duties of Scottish Minsters

48.40 Scottish Ministers must keep the person's case under regular review. They must cancel the direction if they are satisfied it is no longer necessary, as above.[1] They do not need to apply to the tribunal for cancellation of the order. This differs from the procedure for compulsion orders. See above.

If the responsible medical officer recommends cancelling the direction and Scottish Ministers do not agree, they must refer the case to the tribunal.[2]

As with compulsion orders, Scottish Ministers must ensure that the tribunal reviews the person's case at least every two years, where there is no other reference to the tribunal.[3]

[1] Mental Health (Care and Treatment) (Scotland) Act 2003, s 212.
[2] MH(CT)(S)A 2003, s 210(3).
[3] MH(CT)(S)A 2003, s 213.

Role of Mental Welfare Commission

48.41 The Mental Welfare Commission may require Scottish Ministers to refer a case to the tribunal.[1] Scottish Ministers must refer the case to the tribunal as soon as possible after they receive notice from the Mental Welfare Commission.[2]

A patient, named person or anyone with an interest may ask the Mental Welfare Commission to review a patient's case. Even if the Mental Welfare Commission does not recommend discharging the order, it may suggest changes, such as a different hospital or different treatment.

1   Mental Health (Care and Treatment) (Scotland) Act 2003, s 209.
2   MH(CT)(S)A 2003, s 211.

Appeal to tribunal

48.42 The person and his or her named person also can apply to the tribunal for the cancellation ('revocation') of the direction.[1]

They cannot make an application in the first six months after the making of a hospital direction.[2] A person may appeal against the making of a transfer for treatment direction within 12 weeks of the making of the direction, but may then not make another appeal until six months have elapsed from the making of the direction.[3]

Thereafter appeals can be on an annual basis.[4]

1   Mental Health (Care and Treatment) (Scotland) Act 2003, s 214.
2   MH(CT)(S)A 2003, s 214(4).
3   MH(CT)(S)A 2003, s 214(5).
4   MH(CT)(S)A 2003, s 214(6).

Role of the tribunal

48.43 As with applications for the discharge of compulsion and restriction orders, a sheriff, sheriff principal or the President of the tribunal service chairs the tribunal.[1]

The options available to the tribunal are limited.

- The tribunal should direct Scottish Ministers to cancel the direction if it is not satisfied the person has a mental disorder.[2]
- It should also direct Scottish Ministers to discharge the direction if it is satisfied that the person has a mental disorder but not satisfied that both the treatability and risk to others tests are met, *unless* it is satisfied that the direction is necessary on grounds of risk of serious harm.[3]
- The tribunal does not have to require Scottish Ministers to cancel the direction if it is satisfied that the person has a mental disorder

and needs to be detained in hospital on grounds of risk of serious harm, whether or not for medical treatment.[4]

If a tribunal directs Scottish Ministers to cancel a direction, Scottish Ministers will send the person to prison, a young offenders' institution or such other institution as they consider appropriate.[5] The person usually returns to the institution from which he or she was transferred to hospital.

1   Mental Health (Care and Treatment) (Scotland) Act 2003, (as amended by the Mental Health (Care and Treatment) (Scotland) Act 2003 (Modification of Enactments) Order 2005 (SSI 2005/465)), Sched 2 para 7(4).
2   MH(CT)(S)A 2003, s 215(3).
3   MH(CT)(S)A 2003, s 215(4).
4   MH(CT)(S)A 2003, s 215(2).
5   MH(CT)(S)A 2003, s 216.

Appeal to the Court of Session

48.44 A person can appeal against a decision of the tribunal to the Court of Session on grounds of error of law.[1] (See above.)

1   Mental Health (Care and Treatment) (Scotland) Act 2003, s 322.

Termination of direction

48.45 A hospital direction and transfer direction last only so long as the original sentence of imprisonment. If the person is discharged under the early release scheme,[1] the direction ends.[2] This means the person may be discharged from hospital. For more information, see the Code of Practice.[3]

If the person continues to have mental health needs, a mental health officer may apply for a compulsory treatment order under the civil procedure. The Mental Health (Care and Treatment) Act specifically provides for applications in respect of people subject to hospital directions and transfer for treatment directions.[4]

The mental health officer may make the application to the tribunal at any time within 28 days before the end of the direction.[5] If the tribunal makes an order, the measures come into effect on the termination of the direction.[6]

A compulsory treatment order may authorise the person's detention in hospital or a community-based order. An application is possible where a patient has been released on licence.[7]

It would rarely be appropriate to use short-term or emergency certificates in respect of someone being discharged from a hospital direction or transfer for treatment direction, but staff can use these in genuine emergencies.[8]

[1]   Under the Prisoners and Criminal Proceedings (Scotland) Act 1993, Pt 1.
[2]   Mental Health (Care and Treatment) (Scotland) Act 2003, s 217(2).
[3]   Vol 3, pt 2, paras 6.28–36.
[4]   MH(CT)(S)A 2003, s 71 and Sched 3.
[5]   MH(CT)(S)A 2003, Sched 3, para 2(1)(a).
[6]   MH(CT)(S)A 2003, Sched 3, para 2(1)(b).
[7]   Code of Practice, vol 3, pt 2, paras 6.10–12.
[8]   Code of Practice, vol 3, pt 2, paras 6.08–9.

RESTRICTED PATIENTS: HOSPITAL TRANSFER

48.46 The responsible medical officer must seek the consent of Scottish Ministers before transferring a restricted patient to another hospital.[1] This is the case even when a responsible medical officer wishes to transfer someone in an emergency.[2]

The Code of Practice envisages that the responsible medical officer will consult the mental health officer before recommending a transfer, or notify the mental health officer of any urgent transfers.[3] The mental health officer should interview the patient and, with his or her consent, the primary carer, named person and others in the care team.

If the responsible medical officer wishes to move the person to a more secure hospital, the level of security should be the least restrictive setting necessary to meet any risk to others and the clinical needs of the person.[4]

When a patient needs treatment for physical illness, Scottish Ministers usually suspend the detention condition of the order. See below. When someone is likely to be in hospital for more than three months, Scottish Ministers sign hospital transfer forms.[5]

The patient and named person can appeal against transfer, as with appeals in the civil procedure.[6] A patient may also appeal against transfer to the State Hospital,[7] as under civil procedure.

The transfer does not proceed until the outcome is known, but Scottish Ministers may request the tribunal to authorise the transfer in advance of the hearing.[8]

1   Mental Health (Care and Treatment) (Scotland) Act 2003, s 218.
2   For good practice guidance, see Code of Practice, vol 3, pt 2, paras 21–26.
3   Code of Practice, vol 3, pt 2, para 9.15.
4   Code of Practice, vol 3, pt 2, para 9.14.
5   Code of Practice, vol 3, pt 2, para 9.19.
6   MH(CT)(S)A 2003, s 219. (See chapter 19 for civil procedure.)
7   MH(CT)(S)A 2003, s 220.
8   MH(CT)(S)A 2003, s 220(4)(b).

RESTRICTED PATIENTS: AUTHORISED ABSENCES

48.47 The responsible medical officer may suspend the conditions of orders, either for a short period, such as a home visit, or for a longer period as part of a patient's rehabilitation. The responsible medical officer must obtain Scottish Ministers' consent. This applies to patients subject to assessment orders, treatment orders, interim compulsion orders, compulsion orders with restrictions, hospital directions and transfer for treatment directions.[1]

A suspension certificate may last for up to three months,[2] with total absences not exceeding nine months in any one year.[3] As with civil orders, the responsible medical officer may attach conditions to the order and may cancel the suspension in the interests of the person or third party safety.[4] The suspension certificate form and recall forms are on the mental health law website.

The responsible medical officer must discuss any proposed suspension with the person's care team and with the patient, named person and anyone who may be providing care for the person in the community. If the patient is unwilling to allow consultation with carers, Scottish Ministers are unlikely to allow a suspension.[5] The Memorandum of Procedures on Restricted Patients contains further detailed requirements.[6]

Scottish Ministers may cancel ('revoke') the suspension if they are satisfied this is necessary in the patient's interests or for third party safety reasons.[7]

1   Mental Health (Care and Treatment) (Scotland) Act 2003, ss 221 and 224.
2   MH(CT)(S)A 2003, s 224(2).
3   MH(CT)(S)A 2003, s 224(4).
4   MH(CT)(S)A 2003, ss 222 and 225.
5   Code of Practice, vol 3, para 6.37.
6   See chapter 5.
7   MH(CT)(S)A 2003, ss 223 and 226.

ABSENCE WITHOUT LEAVE

48.48 Regulations under the Mental Health (Care and Treatment) Act deal with unauthorised absences of people subject to orders under the criminal justice system.[1] The rules apply to people subject to compulsion orders, interim compulsion orders, assessment and treatment orders, temporary compulsion orders and to all restricted patients.

The rules are broadly similar to those for people who abscond under the civil procedure (see chapter 20) and are covered in outline here.

[1]   Mental Health (Absconding by mentally disordered offenders) (Scotland) Regulations 2005 (SSI 2005/463). ('The absconding Regulations'.)

Notification

48.49 The main difference is in the notification procedures. If someone absconds while criminal justice proceedings are continuing, the responsible medical officer must advise Scottish Ministers, the court which imposed the order and the Mental Welfare Commission. The prosecutor should be informed if the person is subject to a temporary compulsion order or an assessment or treatment order made before conviction.[1]

When someone who absconds is subject to a compulsion order, the responsible medical officer should notify the Mental Welfare Commission.[2] If a person subject to a compulsion order with restrictions, a hospital direction or a transfer for treatment direction absconds, the responsible medical officer should notify the Commission and Scottish Ministers.[3]

Where the responsible medical officer has to advise Scottish Ministers, he or she should do so immediately, and should also advise the local police and the mental health officer.[4]

[1]   Absconding Regulations, reg 6.

[2]   Absconding Regulations, reg 7.

[3]   Absconding Regulations, reg 8. (The current guidance in the Code of Practice, vol 3, para 6.54, incorrectly summarises the Regulations.)

[4]   Code of Practice, vol 3, para 6.54.

Impact of rules

48.50 The rules list the situations from which a person may abscond and to where he or she may be returned when he or she is retaken. These are broadly similar to the rules for absconding from civil orders. Various people may re-take the person and if a police officer is involved, he or she may use reasonable force, if necessary and as a last resort.[1]

[1]   Absconding Regulations, reg 5. Code of Practice, vol 3, para 6.59.

Effect on detention

48.51 The effect of absconding from a compulsion order without restrictions is as for a compulsory treatment order. See chapter 20.

   If someone subject to an assessment order or an interim compulsion order absconds, the order continues. Any days the person is absent without leave are ignored in calculating the duration of the order.[1]

   Orders of indefinite duration, such as treatment orders, temporary compulsion orders and compulsion orders with restrictions, continue once the person has returned to the hospital or place where he or she is to live.

   If someone subject to a hospital direction or transfer for treatment direction absconds, any unauthorised absence does not affect his or her sentence of imprisonment.[2]

[1]   Absconding Regulations, reg 9(4).
[2]   Absconding Regulations, reg 9(5).

Review

48.52 The review of compulsion orders following return to hospital is as for compulsory treatment orders.[1] See 20.12.

   When a person is subject to a compulsion order with restrictions, a hospital direction or a transfer for treatment direction returns to hospital, the responsible medical officer must generally review the order within 14 days of his or her return.[2] If the responsible medical officer considers that the patient should move to a hospital providing a higher level of security, he or she should recommend this to Scottish Ministers.[3]

   When someone subject to an assessment or treatment order, an interim compulsion order or a temporary compulsion order returns, the responsible medical officer should review the order.[4] He or she may request the court to vary the order, perhaps by increasing the level of security.[5]

If the person who absconded was living in the community on a suspended order, the responsible medical officer may cancel the suspension.[6]

1   Absconding Regulations, reg 10.
2   Absconding Regulations, reg 11. (Unless the absence was for less than 28 days and took place during a review or near the expiry of the direction.)
3   Code of Practice, vol 3, para 6.69.
4   Absconding Regulations, reg 12.
5   Absconding Regulations, reg 12(2).
6   Absconding Regulations , reg 13.

PART 13
CARE STANDARDS

Chapter 49

REGULATION OF CARE

49.01 This chapter looks at some of the bodies which monitor and enforce standards in health and social care in Scotland. These bodies may provide useful information about standards and may be able to help when things go wrong.

SOCIAL CARE STANDARDS

Scottish Executive

49.02 Local authorities are independent of the Scottish Executive, but are obliged to perform their social work duties under the 'general guidance' of Scottish Ministers.[1]

As we have seen, the Scottish Executive has issued extensive guidance to local authorities on community care, the Adults with Incapacity Act and the Mental Health (Care and Treatment) Act. There may be grounds for legal action if local authorities do not follow this official guidance, particularly when guidance is clearly and unequivocally stated. See 51.02.

The Scottish Executive can also issue formal directions to local authorities.[2] These directions have the force of law.[3]

Scottish Ministers have wide powers to inspect local authority social work services and services provided by voluntary and independent bodies.[4] This work is generally carried out by the Care Commission (see below), but the independent Social Work Inspection Agency inspects local authority services on behalf of the Scottish Executive.

The Scottish Executive may hold enquiries into the carrying out of social work functions by local authorities. Enquiries can be held either in public or in private.[5] If an enquiry finds a local authority has breached the law, Scottish Ministers can give the authority a legal directions requiring it to fulfill its duties.[6]

This power has been used only infrequently. It was used in 1987 to compel local authorities in Dundee and Stirling to comply with legal requirements on the sale of council houses to tenants.

Someone with a complaint about local authority services would normally complain to the local authority rather than the Scottish Executive, but in exceptional circumstances a person could approach the Scottish Executive if the person considers he or she is not making progress with the local authority.

1   Social Work (Scotland) Act 1968, s 5.
2   SW(S)A 1968, s 51A.
3   See, for example the Social Work (Scotland) Act 1968 (Choice of Accommodation) Directions 1993 (contained in Social Work Services Group circular SWSG5/93).
4   SW(S)A 1968, s 6.
5   SW(S)A 1968, s 6A.
6   Under powers contained in the Local Government (Scotland) Act 1973, s 211.

Care Commission

49.03 The Care Commission is the independent body responsible for inspecting and monitoring a wide range of health and social care services for vulnerable people, including care home services, housing support services, respite care services, support services, some children's services, home care services, independent hospitals and nursing agencies.

Inspection of services

49.04 All local authority care services and all other services offering personal care and/or support are registered with the Care Commission).[1] A person employing a carer him or herself (not through an agency), does not need to register with the Care Commission.

Inspectors can enter and inspect premises used for a care service at any time.[2] The inspectors can inspect records and interview staff and users of the care service, provided the service user agrees to be interviewed. Family members, carers and advocates can also be questioned.

When a service does not meet care standards, the Care Commission can serve an improvement notice.[3] It can follow this with an enforcement notice and may then cancel the service's registration.[4] There is a complex appeals procedure.

In an emergency the Care Commission can apply to a sheriff for the immediate cancellation of registration.[5] The sheriff can cancel the registration if he or she believes there is a serious risk to any person's life, health or well-being. The sheriff may impose immediate conditions on the service,[6] such as that no new clients are admitted, or that a member of staff is replaced.

[1]   Regulation of Care (Scotland) Act 2001, s 2.
[2]   ROC(S)A 2001, s 25.
[3]   ROC(S)A 2001, s 10.
[4]   ROC(S)A 2001, s 12.
[5]   ROC(S)A 2001, s 18.
[6]   ROC(S)A 2001, s 20(2).

Care standards

49.05 The Care Commission inspects facilities against national care standards.[1] Additional standards are incorporated in regulations from the Scottish Executive.[2] These deal with (among other things) the welfare of service users, the use of restraint, records to be kept and complaints procedures.

[1]   Regulation of Care (Scotland) Act 2001, s 5.
[2]   The Regulation of Care (Requirements as to Care Services) (Scotland) Regulations 2002 (SSI 2002/114). (As amended. For up-to-date list of standards, see the Care Commission's website.)

Care Commission and complaints

49.06 For the Care Commission's role in hearing complaints, see chapter 50.

Local government monitoring officer

49.07 Every local authority must appoint a monitoring officer, whose duty is to ensure that the authority complies with the law.[1] Generally the Chief Executive or the head of legal services acts as monitoring officer. The monitoring officer must report to the council if he or she believes the council is acting illegally or that there may be questions of bad management.

It might be appropriate to contact the monitoring officer prior to taking legal action or making a complaint to an ombudsman. The monitoring officer might be able to resolve the matter without the need for further action.

1   Local Government and Housing Act 1989, s 5.

HEALTHCARE STANDARDS

Scottish Executive

49.08 The National Health Service in Scotland is the responsibility of Scottish Ministers. The Scottish Executive Health Department manages the National Health Service in Scotland and is responsible for developing health and community care policy. Health boards report to the chief executive of the National Health Service in Scotland, who reports to Ministers.

Health boards now run hospital services, with the abolition in 2004 of National Health Service Trusts.[1] Health boards are setting up community health partnerships, to plan services for their localities.[2] The public should be involved in these partnerships.

Scottish Ministers are ultimately responsible for the quality of healthcare in Scotland and it is, therefore, appropriate to contact them (or an MSP) if services are not adequate.

1   National Health Service Reform (Scotland) Act 2004, s 1.
2   Under the National Health Service (Scotland) Act 1978, s 4A, as amended by National Health Service Reform (Scotland) Act 2004.

NHS Quality Improvement Scotland

49.09 NHS Quality Improvement Scotland (NHS QIS) is a Special Health Board set up by the Scottish Executive in 2003. It aims to improve the quality of healthcare, by setting standards in clinical and non-clinical matters, monitoring performance and providing advice, guidance and support to the National Health Service in Scotland.

NHS QIS's Strategic Work Programme states its intention to improve the quality of mental health services in Scotland.[1] It is currently auditing services for children and for mothers with postnatal depression.

1   October 2005.

Scottish Health Council

49.10 The Scottish Health Council is part of NHS QIS. Its role is to involve the public in assessing and evaluating health services. It is independent of health boards and aims to help patients feed back their experience to the boards. Local Advisory Councils will monitor how health boards involve the public in their decision making.

Scottish Intercollegiate Guidelines Network

49.11 The Scottish Intercollegiate Guidelines Network, (SIGN) is part of NHS QIS. It produces national clinical guidelines for the National Health Service in Scotland. There are several guidelines in mental health, dealing with schizophrenia, bipolar affective disorder, attention deficit disorder and head injury.

These guidelines, which are based on evidence of what works, make interesting reading. For example, the guideline on the management of schizophrenia mentions the importance of involving family and carers and highlights the importance of cognitive behavioural therapy for resistant symptoms of psychosis.

A person receiving treatment that does not reflect SIGN guidelines may want to raise this with the health professional(s) concerned. A complaint or even legal action may be appropriate. There have been cases in England where health boards which failed to consider the recommendations of similar bodies have been criticised by the courts.[1]

---

[1]   See, for example, *R v North Derbyshire Health Authority, ex parte Fisher*, The Times, 2 September 1997. F suffered from multiple sclerosis, but his local health authority refused to allow doctors to prescribe the drug, beta interferon. A National Health Service circular had asked health authorities to facilitate the introduction of beta interferon, but the Derbyshire heath authority refused to do so unless this was part of a national trial. The court held that although the advice in the government circular was not mandatory, the authority had failed to give it 'serious consideration'. It had imposed a blanket policy of refusing to use the drug. The court required the local authority to reconsider its decision.

PROFESSIONAL STANDARDS

49.12 Various professional bodies set standards for their professions and deal with complaints of misconduct and poor performance.

There are differences in the type of conduct which they can investigate and their powers to deal with poor performance. Further information can be obtained from the relevant organisation.

General Medical Council

49.13 The General Medical Council sets standards for the medical profession and regulates all doctors licensed to practice in the UK. It investigates complaints about serious professional misconduct or incompetence.

It has a range of remedies, from striking a doctor off the register, to issuing a warning. A complaint to the General Medical Council can be in addition to, or as an alternative to, the NHS complaints system.

The General Medical Council is concerned only if there has been a serious breach of professional standards which might threaten the doctor's registration. It would not, for example, consider a complaint about a doctor's rudeness, although this could be the subject of an NHS complaint.

People give evidence to General Medical Council hearings on oath and witnesses are cross-examined. The witness should generally have a solicitor present. Although legal aid is not available, the General Medical Council normally pays the cost of legal representation for the complainant.

The General Medical Council's Manchester office deals with matters of doctors' fitness to practice.

The General Medical Council also produces many interesting leaflets about doctors' duties, covering matters such as patient confidentiality, conflict of interest etc. The main guidance is contained in a series of booklets called *Good Medical Practice*.

Nursing and Midwifery Council

49.14 The Nursing and Midwifery Council[1] maintains a register of all nurses (including mental health and learning disability nurses and community psychiatric nurses), midwives and health visitors licensed to work in the UK. It sets standards for nurses' education, practice and conduct and considers allegations of misconduct and unfitness to practice.

As with complaints to the General Medical Council, the conduct complained of must be sufficiently serious to justify potential removal of the nurse's registration. The Nursing and Midwifery Council may suspend a nurse from the register before the outcome of the disciplinary hearing if there is a clear and unacceptably high level of risk to patients.

As with the General Medical Council, the procedure is similar to a court hearing. The Nursing and Midwifery Council acts only if any allegations are proved beyond reasonable doubt. There is no legal aid if the complainant wishes to have a solicitor present.

1   Set up under the Nursing and Midwifery Order 2001 (SI 2002/253).

Health Professions Council

49.15 This council regulates the professions allied to medicine, including occupational therapy, physiotherapy, radiography, speech and language therapy, art therapy, etc.

It deals with allegations of unfitness to practice, which must be made in writing. The procedure is broadly similar to the procedures of the General Medical Council and Nursing and Midwifery Council.

Scottish Social Services Council

49.16 The Scottish Social Services Council is the body responsible for the registration, education and training of social service staff.

Everyone working in social services, (such as social workers, child care workers and staff in care homes), will eventually be registered with the Scottish Social Services Council. The registration of social workers began in 2003 and most other staff should be registered by 2007.

The Scottish Social Services Council has produced codes of practice for social service workers and for their employers. Failure to comply with the Code or other misconduct could lead to a social service worker being removed from the register.

PART 14
WHEN THINGS GO WRONG

Chapter 50

COMPLAINTS

50.01 This part of the book looks at remedies if people do not receive the services they need. This chapter deals with making complaints. The following chapter deals with taking legal action.

Generally, if a complaint will achieve the desired result, this is preferable to taking legal action. It costs less money and is generally less stressful. Taking legal action may harden people's attitudes and make it less likely that any changes in practice will result.

A person should decide what outcome he or she desires when considering what type of action to take. For example, a person wanting financial compensation may consider legal action. Someone wanting to bring about changes in practice should make a complaint or a suggestion. The person should discuss the options with an adviser.

MAKING COMPLAINTS

50.02 Complaints procedures often comprise various tiers, beginning with an initial complaint to the person on the ground, moving to the more formal complaints procedure, and finally, if necessary, going to an ombudsman.

In this section we look at complaints in the health service, in social work and for voluntary and independent providers.

Complaint in the health service

50.03 The National Health Service complaints system applies to all areas of the National Health Service in Scotland, including hospitals, clinics and GP services. Each service has its own complaints procedure, but there are common features for the handling of complaints.[1] Complaints can cover the management of services and clinical judgement.

Every service should have information about how to make complaints, and there should be advice about support and advice available to help with complaints. Conciliation services may be helpful if both parties agree.

Someone remaining dissatisfied with the response from the National Health Service may refer the matter to the Scottish Public Services Ombudsman, who is independent of both the NHS and government. See below.

Health boards must set up bodies to help patients make complaints,[2] but these bodies are not independent of the NHS. A complainant might prefer to receive help from an independent advocacy service, Citizens Advice Bureau or other independent advice service.

For more information about NHS complaints, see *Making a complaint about the National Health Service* by Health Rights Information Scotland.

[1]   Guidance to the National Health Service is contained in *Can I help you? Learning from comments, Concerns and Complaints* (National Health Service in Scotland, 2005). This circular contains Directions from Scottish Ministers to health boards, which came into effect on 5 April 2005.

[2]   See draft corporate plan of Scottish Health Council, October 2004, p 5.

Social work complaints

50.04 The Scottish Executive requires all local authorities to establish procedures for dealing with complaints about their social work functions.[1] Different authorities have slightly different complaints procedures, but all must comply with the legal requirements in the directions.

The local authority must make information about its complaints procedures available to the public.[2] The local authority should be able to offer help to people who have difficulty in formulating a complaint.

There are strict time limits for dealing with complaints.[3] These cannot be extended unless a complainant agrees.

A complainant who is not satisfied with the local authority's response can ask for the matter to be referred to a complaints review committee, which includes lay members. The committee may make recommendations to the local authority.

There will be occasions when it is not appropriate to use the complaints procedure. For example, if an employee has committed a criminal offence, the local authority must notify the police. A local authority will not continue to deal with a complaint where a complainant starts legal action.

The Scottish Executive is currently reviewing local authority complaints procedures.

[1]   Social Work (Representation Procedure) (Scotland) Directions 1996. ('The complaints procedure directions') Set out in Scottish Office Guidance circular SWSG 5/1996.

[2]   Complaints procedure directions, paras 6 and 8.

Complaints against voluntary and independent providers

50.05 Most care providers have their own complaints procedures. Local authorities can deal with complaints about services provided under contract to the local authority, but generally local authorities delegate complaints to individual service providers.

Independent or voluntary providers should give the local authority details of any complaints and of their response.[1]

A person can make a complaint to the Care Commission about any service registered with it. (See below).

[1]   Complaints procedure directions, para 10.

Complaints to Care Commission

50.06 The Care Commission (see chapter 49) deals with complaints about any care service registered with it. A person may make a complaint to the Care Commission even if he or she has not complained to the service itself.[1]

A person using a service or anyone acting on his or her behalf can make a complaint. More information is available on the Care Commission's website.

[1]   Complaints procedure directions (See SWSG 5/1996 above) para 12.

MENTAL WELFARE COMMISSION

50.07 The Commission no longer hears complaints about mental health services (see below) but it can investigate concerns about deficiencies in care and it must investigate certain complaints about welfare interventions under the Adults with Incapacity Act where the local authority's investigations have not satisfied the complainant. See chapter 3.

It is also possible to make a complaint about the Commission's own action or failure to act. Further information is available from the Commission.

OMBUDSMEN

50.08 An ombudsman is an independent, non-governmental official, who investigates poor management by public authorities. An ombudsman does not provide a right of appeal. If an authority has acted properly, an ombudsman does not set aside its decision, even though he or she might have made a different decision.

The advantage of using an ombudsman, as opposed to taking legal action, is that the ombudsman's investigation does not cost any money. Nor does it involve any ongoing effort from the complainant, once he or she has submitted the initial complaint.

Ombudsmen generally expect people to use a local complaints procedure first. There are strict time limits for applications, although these can be extended if the person can show good cause.[1]

Ombudsmen can recommend compensation if there has been poor management, but the amounts involved is not large.

Ombudsmen's enquiries can take some time to complete. The ombudsman is not the best option for a complainant requiring a speedy response.

[1]   Regulation of Care (Scotland) Act 2001, s 6(2).

The Scottish Public Services Ombudsman

50.09 The Scottish public services ombudsman is responsible for dealing with complaints about Scottish government departments, the Scottish Parliament, local authorities, housing associations, and the National Health Service in Scotland.[1]

The Scottish public services ombudsman can also look into the actions of certain other public bodies (including the Care Commission, the Mental Welfare Commission, the Scottish Social Services Council, and the administrative functions of the Mental Health Tribunal for Scotland).[2]

The public services ombudsman can look into poor service, failure to provide a service and administrative failures. She can also deal with complaints about the National Health Service, including complaints about hospital staff, GPs, nurses and other health professionals.[3] These include complaints about clinical judgments made by staff, poor care or treatment, failure to provide services, delay, use of incorrect procedures, discourtesy and failure to explain decisions.

The Scottish public services ombudsman has taken over complaints about mental health services from the Mental Welfare Commission. (For example, in June 2006 the ombudsman reported her findings into a complaint that Lothian Health Board had failed to provide adequate care to a young woman with *anorexia nervosa*. The ombudsman concluded that there was a lack of adequate in-patient facilities to treat this condition within the National Health Service in Scotland.)[5]

There is inevitably some overlap between the roles of the ombudsman and the Mental Welfare Commission. In September 2002 the Commission and the public services ombudsman signed a memorandum of agreement clarifying their respective responsibilities.

1   In *R v Commissioner for Local Administration ex parte Bradford City Council* (1979) QBD 287, Lord Denning said that the courts should not rigidly enforce time bars against a complainant where justice required that the time be extended and the person's complaint heard.

2   See the Scottish Public Services Ombudsman Act 2002, Scheds 2 and 3 for a full list.

3   SPSOA 2002, (as amended by the Mental Health (Care and Treatment) (Scotland) Act 2003), s 4A.

4   SPSOA 2002, s 5.

5   Report no 200400447, 27 June 2006.

Matters ombudsman cannot investigate

50.10 The public services ombudsman does not generally investigate if a matter could be the subject of legal action or an appeal to Scottish Ministers.[1] She may look into such a case if it would not be reasonable for the complainant to take such action. This might be the case if a complainant is vulnerable because of mental disorder.

The Scottish public services ombudsman does not look into a complaint when a complainant has begun legal action. She cannot look into complaints about services in non-National Health Service hospitals or nursing homes, unless the NHS pays for these services.[2] Neither can she investigate complaints about private medical care.

The Scottish public services ombudsman cannot investigate the Mental Welfare Commission's use of its power to revoke short-term detention certificates, compulsory treatment orders or compulsion orders under the Mental Health (Care and Treatment) Act.[3]

1   See *R v Commissioner for Administration ex parte H*, The Times, 8 January 1999. *R v Commissioner for Local Administration ex parte Bradford City Council* (1979) QB 287; and *R v Commissioner for Local Administration ex parte Croydon LBC* (1989) 11 ER 103.

2   Scottish Public Services Ombudsman Act 2002, Sched 4, para 7(2).
3   SPSOA 2002, (as amended by the Mental Health (Care and Treatment) (Scotland) Act 2003 (Modification of Enactments) Order 2005 (SSI 2005/465)), Sched 4, para 11.

Making a complaint to the Scottish public services ombudsman

50.11 A complaint should be submitted within 12 months of the incident. The ombudsman can waive this time limit if this would be reasonable. A complaint may be made by a user of services him or herself or by someone given written authority by him or her.[1]

The ombudsman's office may be able to help a person who has difficulty making a complaint or in authorising another person to act.

1   Scottish Public Services Ombudsman Act 2002, s 9.

Powers of Scottish public services ombudsman

50.12 The ombudsman may be able to resolve a complaint informally or may carry out a formal investigation. This can take several months. The complainant receives a copy of the ombudsman's report at the end of the investigation, with a copy of the ombudsman's recommendations.

As well as considering whether there has been poor decision-making, the ombudsman must consider whether the complainant has suffered injustice or hardship. This could include being denied a benefit or service, direct financial loss, emotional distress, and wasted time and trouble.

At the end of an investigation, the ombudsman discusses the findings with the relevant body and, if there was poor decision-making, asks what remedial action the body intends to take. The majority of cases are resolved in this way.

If the ombudsman is dissatisfied with the response and considers that the relevant body has not remedied any injustice, she may issue a special report to the Scottish Parliament.[1]

Reports of the ombudsman's inquiries are available. The majority dealt with health matters (including three about removal from GP's lists).[2] There were no reports of any complaints about social work or children's services. This means either that there is no cause for concern or that the recipients of such services are not aware of their right to contact the ombudsman.

1   Scottish Public Services Ombudsman Act 2002, s 16.

[2]   27 out of 37 reports as at 1 December 2005.

The Parliamentary Ombudsman

50.13 The UK Parliamentary Ombudsman[1] deals with complaints about UK government departments, such as the Inland Revenue and the Department for Work and Pensions.

The parliamentary ombudsman's remit and way of working is very like that of the Scottish public services ombudsman, but a major difference is that a complainant cannot contact the parliamentary ombudsman directly. The person must take his or her complaint to a Member of the UK Parliament, who will contact the ombudsman.

A person should normally approach his or her own MP, but can contact another one if necessary.

[1]   Established by the Parliamentary Commissioner Act 1967.

Chapter 51

LEGAL REMEDIES

51.01 This chapter outlines of some of the legal remedies available to a person who suffers harm because of poor services.

In some cases, there may be no remedy. All public authorities are constrained by their budgets. The courts recognise this. They have been reluctant to question how public authorities make decisions about their priorities for spending.

There may be circumstances where the authority has not complied with its legal duties in reaching a decision. A legal challenge by way of judicial review may be appropriate. Legal action may be appropriate if an authority has been negligent and someone has suffered loss or damage. We look at these issues in outline below.

JUDICIAL REVIEW

Nature of remedy

51.02 If a public body acts unlawfully in carrying out its statutory duties, judicial review might be appropriate.[1] The case goes to the Court of Session in Edinburgh.

If an authority has acted unlawfully, the court can make various orders, including setting aside a decision, requiring the authority to reconsider the matter, an award of damages and requiring the authority to perform its legal duties.

Generally, if a decision is flawed, the court does not substitute its own decision but requires the authority to reconsider the matter. Judicial review does not allow an appeal against action which has been properly taken.

Proceedings for judicial reviewed can consider:

- Unreasonable delay in carrying out statutory duties.[2]
- Failure to consider relevant information when making decisions.[3]
- Failure to give the complainant a chance to make his or her case.[4]
- Failure of a public body to carry out its statutory duties. (The courts must be satisfied that it was the intention of the legislators that the

statute should give rights to individuals as well as public law remedies.)[5]

- Making decisions which no reasonable authority would have made.[6]

- Failure to follow official guidance.[7]

- Imposing blanket policies which remove the authority's discretion in particular cases.[8]

- Failure to comply with stated policies, for example in a patients' charter or explanatory leaflet.[9]

These examples all come from England and Wales. There have been fewer cases in Scotland.

1 See Lords Clyde and Edwards, *Judicial Review* (W Green & Son, 2000).

2 See *R v Gloucestershire County Council ex parte P* [1993] COD. (Alleged delay by a local authority in providing a statement of special educational needs—not proved on the facts.)

3 *R v Avon County Council ex parte M* [1994] 2 FCR 259. (A local authority arranging residential care for a man with learning disabilities had failed to consider his wishes and had not sufficiently considered the findings of the independent complaints review.)

4 *R v Devon County Council ex parte Baker*, The Times, 21 January 1993. (Closure of a local authority home without proper consultation with residents and carers.)

5 See *Cutler v. Wandsworth Stadium Ltd* [1949] AC 398 (If a statute contains no remedy for breach, a person injured by the breach should be able to take legal action.) Taken further in *Lonrho Ltd v Shell Petroleum Company Ltd (No 2)* [1982] AC 173 (Even where a statute includes a remedy for breach, other remedies might be available to a person for whose benefit the obligation was imposed.)

6 The legal test is in *Associated Provincial Picture Houses Ltd v Wednesbury Corporation* [1948] KB 22.

7 See *R v North Yorkshire County Council ex parte Hargreaves*, The Times, 9 November 1994 (The local authority failed to assess a disabled woman's needs for respite care in accordance with government guidelines.) See also *R v Islington London Borough Council, ex parte Rixon*, The Times, 17 April 1996, and *R v North Derbyshire Health Authority ex parte Fisher*, The Times, 2 September 1997.

8 See *R v Hampshire County Council ex parte W* [1994] ELR 460 (The local authority refused a request to consider whether a child had special educational needs.)

9 Under the doctrine of 'legitimate expectation'.

When not available

51.03 Judicial review is not available to appeal against a decision lawfully taken. It is not available if a statute provides another way of appealing or reviewing a decision.[1] It is only appropriate for public law actions, not for example, for breach of contract or negligence.

---

[1] See *Walker v Strathclyde Regional Council (No 1)*, 1986 SLT 523. (The fact that the Secretary of State could intervene to decide whether a local authority was carrying out obligations under the Education Acts was not a reason to bar judicial review.)

ORDER TO CARRY OUT STATUTORY DUTY

51.04 A person affected by the failure of a public body to comply with its statutory duties can apply to the Court of Session for a declaration that the body is in breach of its duties. The applicant can seek an order requiring performance of the duty.[1]

This action uses the judicial review procedure, but there are differences. The procedure has not been widely used[2] but it may be of use where an authority is under a clear legal duty to act and fails to do so.

An attempt to use these provisions to compel Scottish Ministers to improve facilities in Scottish prisons failed, despite the fact that the conditions in the prison breached prisoners' human rights. The court did say, however, that it was possible to envisage using this procedure where Scottish Ministers were alleged to be in breach of clear specific legal duties.[3] (An example might be where a health board fails to provide alternative accommodation for a person held in conditions of excessive security. See chapter 17.)

---

[1] Under the Court of Session Act 1988, s 45.

[2] It was used in *T Docherty v Burgh of Monifieth*, 1970 SC 200, (Where a local authority was ordered to construct sewers); *Strathclyde Regional Council v City of Glasgow District Council*, 1989 SLT 235 (The authority was ordered to provide suitable prison cells for people brought before the district courts); and *Tayside RC v British Railways Board*, The Times, 30 December 1993 (The railway board was ordered to maintain gates at a level crossing). See also *Magnohard Ltd v UKAEA* (The court made a declaration that UKAEA had failed in statutory duties to avoid escapes of radioactive material.)

[3] *McKenzie v Scottish Ministers*, 2004 SLT 1236.

NEGLIGENCE

Duty of care

51.05 A health or social care professional generally owes a duty of care to a person to whom he or she provides services or care. A professional who fails to do what a reasonable person in his or her position would do may be liable in negligence if someone is injured or suffers loss as a result. As well as physical damage, the person injured may recover compensation for psychological damage.

Medical negligence is the best-known example,[1] but a person could suffer damage because of the negligence of any other person or body which has a duty to take care of him or her.[2]

A professional sometimes owes a duty to third parties. When a hospital in England was negligent in discharging a person from hospital and he assaulted a member of the public, the person injured successfully sued for damages.[3]

In another case a man recently discharged from hospital killed a young girl. The girl's mother sued the hospital for negligence. The court said that the hospital did not owe a duty of care to anyone the former patient might injure, but the situation might have been different if there had been threats to a specific person.[4]

Because of space restrictions, this book cannot cover these rules in detail. Any person in this situation should consult a solicitor. There are strict time limits for bringing such cases.

[1]   See *G's Curator Bonis v Grampian Health Board* (OH) 1995 SLT 652 (A health board was held liable for failing to take proper care of a person at risk of suicide.)
[2]   See, for example, *Reeves v Commissioner of Police for the Metropolis* [1999] 3 All ER. (Police owe a duty to a person they know to be suicidal.)
[3]   *Holgate v Lancashire Mental Hospitals Board* [1937] 4 All ER 19.
[4]   *Palmer v Tees Health Authority* [1998] 45 BMLR 88, QBD.

Liability of public authorities

51.06 A public body could be negligent if, in carrying out its statutory duties, it fails to provide a satisfactory standard of care for a client. The courts have had to consider whether to find an authority responsible for the consequences of a less than adequate standard of care.

Most of the cases (from England and Wales) have involved children and young people receiving care from local authorities, but there are striking parallels with the kind of situations in which some people living with mental health challenges might find themselves.

Scope for claims

51.07 The courts have been reluctant to interfere with the way public authorities carry out their duties. Even when a local authority has apparently failed to act reasonably, the courts have not let the case proceed.

In one particularly distressing case, the House of Lords said that it would be contrary to public policy to allow children to sue a local authority in Bedfordshire which had allegedly failed to protect them against abuse.[1] Other cases have taken a similar line.[2]

Two decisions of the European Court of Human Rights have compelled the courts to revise their views. These cases looked at the scope of public authorities' duties to members of the public.

In the first case, the court said that the Court of Appeal in England was wrong to say that it could not consider a case where the police were allegedly negligent in protecting a family against attacks from a known individual who was threatening them.[3]

The Court of Human Rights also struck down the House of Lords' ruling in the Bedfordshire case.[4] It said that a local authority has an obligation to take effective and practical steps to safeguard children in its care.[5]

Following this case, a local authority was found liable for negligent advice given by an educational psychologist it employed.[6] The courts have said that a local authority could be liable where staff were negligent in arranging foster care.[7] In a Scottish case taken to Strasbourg, the court held that a local authority has a positive duty to ensure proper protection for children at risk of abuse or neglect.[8]

The importance of these cases cannot be overemphasised. Local authorities, health authorities and others may be liable for the actions of their staff in administering their statutory duties under mental health and community care legislation.[9] The author is not aware on any cases coming before the Scottish courts, but in one case, the Court of Session refused to hold a public authority landlord liable for failing to take steps to protect a tenant against a violent neighbour.[10]

[1]   *X v Bedfordshire County Council* [1995] CLY 3452.

2   See *H v Norfolk County Council* [1997] 1 FLR 384 (A person who had been abused by foster parents was held to have no remedy against a local authority which allegedly failed to supervise the placement.) Also *T (a minor) v Surrey County Council* [1994] 4 AllER 577 (No common law duty of care was imposed on a local authority carrying out its statutory duties to advise parents about childminders.)

3   *Osman v the UK* [2000] 29 EHRR 245.

4   See footnote 1.

5   *Z and others v. the United Kingdom* [2001] ECHR 333.

6   *Phelps v Hillingdon LBC; Anderton v Clwyd County Council; Re G (a minor); Jarvis v Hampshire County Council* [2000] 4 All ER 504 (HL).

7   *W1-6 v Essex County Council* [2000] 2 WLR 601. (Social workers had placed a child with foster parents without warning of his history of sexual assault.)

8   *E v UK* (2003) 36 EHRR 31.

9   *DS v Gloucestershire County Council, RL v Gloucestershire County Council and L v Tower Hamlets LBC* [2000] 3 AllER 346.

10   *Mitchell v Glasgow City Council*, 2005 SLT 1100. The claimant had failed to establish that the landlord knew or ought to have known of the existence of a real and immediate risk.

Chapter 52

OFFICIAL ENQUIRIES

52.01 Most causes for concern in the mental health system can be dealt with by complaints or using one of the methods discussed in chapter 50. Sometimes an event is so serious (such as a death or serious injury) that there is a call for an enquiry into what has happened.

The Mental Welfare Commission may decide to hold an enquiry, or Scottish Ministers may request it to make inquiries. If an incident involves an unexpected death, there may be a fatal accident inquiry, but these are not the norm.[1] Scottish Ministers may hold an enquiry themselves, although they usually ask the Commission to investigate.

Public enquiries into deaths of psychiatric patients are rare in Scotland, unlike England and Wales, where the government recommends an independent enquiry in certain circumstances, in light of human rights requirements.[2]

---

[1] In 2004–5, the Crown Office received details of a total of 13,825 sudden or suspicious deaths in Scotland. There were just 68 fatal accident inquiries. (Crown Office and Procurator Fiscal Service Review 2004–05.) The statistics do not show how many of these people were in contact with mental health services.

[2] See Department of Health guidance, *Independent investigation of adverse events in mental health services* (June 2005), which replaces guidance in DoH circular HSG (94) 27. The Zito Trust (see Appendix 2) keeps details of published reports of enquiries.

CRITICAL INCIDENT REVIEWS

52.02 Following a serious incident, such as a suicide or other death, health services should hold a critical incident review.[1] Any patients and carers affected by the incident should be involved in the review. Independent advocacy workers may support people, if necessary.[2]

The Mental Welfare Commission reports that most health boards now have policies for such reviews, but there are still inconsistencies in practice.[3] The Commission continues to report failures to hold criticial incident reviews in some cases where in-patients have died in hospital.[4] In the year 2005–6, the Commission intends to give some attention to critical incident reviews, both monitoring progress and promoting good practice.

1   See *Risk Management* (Mental Health Reference Group, 2000), para 111ff. A protocol for such a review is set out at Appendix D of the report.
2   Reference Group protocol (above), para 3.4.
3   Annual Report 2004–5, p 22.
4   See Annual Report 2002–3, para 2.6.

MENTAL WELFARE COMMISSION ENQUIRIES

52.03 This section looks at the role of the Mental Welfare Commission in monitoring suicides, accidents and incidents. It does not deal with the other issues surrounding suicide. A very useful booklet is available.[1]

The suicide or sudden death of a patient known to health services, as well as any other serious accident or incident, should be reported to the Mental Welfare Commission. Health services should contact the Commission, whether or not the person was in contact with services at the time of his or her death.[2] A form for the report is available from the Commission.

Local authorities and voluntary and independent providers are also urged to report such incidents.[3]

The Mental Welfare Commission makes such further enquiries as it considers necessary. It liaises with the appropriate procurator fiscal's department to find out if a fatal accident inquiry is appropriate. The Commission considers whether there may have been a failure in care and also uses the reports to draw attention to trends and to suggest good practice for the future.

1   Sandra McDougall, *After a suicide* (Scottish Association for Mental Health, 2004).
2   Scottish Office Home and Health Department Circulars, NHS 1977 (GEN) 4 and 13, and Annual Report of the Mental Welfare Commission, 1992–3, pp 7–10.
3   See Annual Report 2003–4, p 17.

FATAL ACCIDENT INQUIRIES

52.04 A fatal accident inquiry may be held when a person dies suddenly or unexpectedly. A sheriff, sitting without a jury, holds the inquiry.

The procurator fiscal must be informed of (among others) any violent, sudden or unexplained death, any death following an accident, the death of a homeless person if not in a house, and any death where medical negligence may be a factor.[1] The procurator fiscal makes enquiries and reports to the Lord Advocate, the chief law officer in Scotland.

The decision to hold an inquiry depends on the circumstances of the death. There must be an inquiry when someone dies in the course of his or her employment. There must also be an inquiry if a person dies in 'legal custody'.[2] This includes people in prison, people held in police cells and people subject to detention, such as prisoners being transferred to prison.

In these circumstances, the Lord Advocate decides whether it is in the public interest to hold an inquiry. This could be because the death was sudden, suspicious, or unexplained or if it occurred in circumstances giving rise to serious public concern.[3]

There is no appeal against the refusal of the Lord Advocate to hold a fatal accident inquiry. Judicial review might be available.

[1]   Fatal Accidents and Sudden Death Inquiry (Scotland) Act 1976, s 1.
[2]   FASDI(S)A 1976, s 1(1)(a).
[3]   FASDI(S)A 1976, s 1(1)(b).

Need for inquiries

52.05 The Fatal Accidents Inquiry Act does not oblige the Lord Advocate to hold a fatal accident inquiry where a detained patient dies, although if a prisoner dies in custody, there must be an inquiry. Fatal accident inquiries involving psychiatric patients are rare.[1]

The Lord Advocate is a public official and must act in accordance with human rights law. Failure to properly protect a detained patient or to account for his or her death or injury could be open to challenge under Articles 2 or 3 of the European Convention on Human Rights.

Human rights case law requires the state to investigate and account for any injury to or death of a person in custody.[2] Where someone dies because of the use of force, there should be some form of effective official investigation.[3] This should generally involve public scrutiny, not simply an official enquiry.[4]

Even though the human rights cases refer to prisoners, it is suggested that the deaths of detained patients are in the same category. They are effectively 'in custody'. The state should be required to investigate and account for any such deaths. The Mental Welfare Commission's statistics detail the deaths of patients from, among other causes, the use of restraint.[5] There should be an automatic public enquiry into such deaths.

The standard textbook on fatal accident inquiries argues that where a person who dies was in hospital because of an order under the Criminal Procedure (Scotland) Act, he or she should be regarded as having been in legal custody for the purpose of a fatal accident inquiry.[6] Similarly a fatal accident inquiry is appropriate where the person who died is detained under the Mental Health (Care and Treatment) Act.[7]

The author agrees. An independent enquiry into such deaths may be necessary to comply with the United Kingdom's obligations under the European Convention on Human Rights. It is interesting to note that, in England and Wales, all deaths of detained patients must be reported to the Coroner.

[1]   Of the 80 fatal accident inquiries reported on the Scottish Courts database since 1999, not one deals with the death of a psychiatric in-patient or outpatient. (The Scottish Courts Service concedes that its database is not complete, so there may be some inquiries not reported.) Each year the Mental Welfare Commission receives reports concerning the deaths of people receiving mental health services. For example in 2003–4, it was told of 126 suicides, 24 probable suicides and 21 possible suicides of in-patients and outpatients. It also received reports of 30 deaths which either followed an accident or incident or were otherwise sudden and unexpected. It is not clear whether a fatal accident inquiry was held into any of these deaths.

[2]   See *Selmouni v France* [1999] ECHR 66, para 87 (injury) *Salman v Turkey* [2000] ECHR 357, para 99 (death in custody), *Keenan v UK*, [2001] ECHR 242, para 91 (suicide of prisoner).

[3]   *Edwards v UK* (2002) 35 EHRR 487 at para 69.

[4]   *R (on the application of Amin) v Home Secretary* [2003] UKHL 51.

[5]   See Annual Report of Mental Welfare Commission, 2001–2, p 28. Unfortunately, the Mental Welfare Commission's statistics do not state whether the person who died was a detained patient.

[6]   Ian H B Carmichael, *Sudden deaths and fatal accident inquiries* (3rd edn, W Green & Son, 2005), para 2.19.

[7]   Carmichael (above) para 2.21.

Relatives and carers

52.06 If a family believe there should be a fatal accident inquiry, they might want to obtain letters of support from other individuals or organisations who believe there is a public interest issue. This should be done at as early a stage as possible.

The procurator fiscal meets the next of kin soon after the death to explain the procedure and to establish whether the next of kin desires a fatal accident inquiry. The procurator fiscal reports to Crown Counsel, who recommend to the Lord Advocate whether there should be a fatal accident inquiry.

Although it is not possible to rely on the findings of the sheriff in any subsequent civil or criminal proceedings,[1] a fatal accident inquiry is sometimes seen as a forerunner to taking out legal action for negligence.[2] This is not necessarily the appropriate use of the inquiry. There must be some matter of public interest. The Lord Advocate is less likely to agree to a fatal accident inquiry where it is alleged, for example, that one doctor made a mistake than where the alleged mistake could indicate a failure of systems, structures or resources.

There is no need for relatives to obtain legal representation at a fatal accident inquiry, but many do. This is because the procurator fiscal, who speaks at the inquiry, represents the interests of the public rather than the family. Legal aid could be available.

In a complex case, legal aid should be available even where the person's means would otherwise exclude it. The European Convention on Human Rights requires full effective representation of, and participation by, next-of-kin in the enquiry process.[3]

[1]   Fatal Accidents and Sudden Death Inquiry (Scotland) Act 1976, s 6(3).
[2]   See Anderson, Leitch and Warner, *Public Interest and Private Grief: a study of fatal accident inquiries in Scotland*. (Scottish Office Central Research Unit, 1995), p 28.
[3]   See *R (on the application of Mohammed Farooq Khan) v Secretary of State for Health* [2004] 1WLR 971. The person seeking an enquiry had income and capital slightly above legal aid limits. The Court of Appeal in England held that strict financial limits in such a complex case were not necessarily appropriate.

Findings of sheriff

52.07 The sheriff may make purely a formal finding about the cause, place and date of death. The sheriff may also make a finding as to whether any reasonable precautions would have avoided the death, whether there are any defects in a system of working which contributed to the death and any other relevant circumstances.[1]

The Lord Advocate receives a copy of the findings and the transcripts of the fatal accident inquiry. The sheriff may also request that a Scottish Minster, government department or the Health and Safety Executive receive a copy.[2]

The Scottish Executive says that the responsibility for effecting any recommendations made by the sheriff lies with those who have responsibility for managing the systems in question.[3] If a fatal accident inquiry reveals a general failure in systems, the relevant Scottish Executive department could give advice to the relevant bodies, such as health boards or local authorities. Anyone affected by the issues could ask the Scottish Executive to consider giving such advice.

[1]   Fatal Accidents and Sudden Death Inquiry (Scotland) Act 1976, s 6(1).
[2]   FASDISA 1976, s 6(4).
[3]   Adam Ingram MSP, Scottish Parliament Written Answers, 24 July 2003 (S2W-1236).

ENQUIRIES BY THE SCOTTISH EXECUTIVE

52.08 The Scottish Executive can hold an enquiry into the way a local authority carries out its functions under the Social Work (Scotland) Act.[1] It can also refer matters to the Mental Welfare Commission for investigation.[2] It generally asks the Commission to investigate and report to it.

[1]   Social Work (Scotland) Act 1968, s 6A.
[2]   Mental Health (Care and Treatment) (Scotland) Act 2003, s 9. For example in 2003–4, the Commission investigated services in the Scottish Borders for people with learning disabilities, jointly with the Scottish Executive's Social Work Inspection Agency.

APPENDICES

Appendix 1

FURTHER READING

Suggestions for further reading are also found at the relevant chapters of this book.

Some of the best information is to be found on the internet: on the Scottish Executive's websites relating to adults with incapacity, mental health law, vulnerable witnesses and criminal justice.

Similarly helpful information and good practice guidance is available from the Mental Welfare Commission and the Public Guardian. There is much valuable information from the important voluntary agencies in Scotland and, in particular, Alzheimer Scotland, Enable, NSF Scotland and SAMH, the Scottish Association for Mental Health. For reasons of space we cannot list all the relevant publications here.

Some of the internet information is available in leaflet form: ask the relevant information service.

ADVOCACY

Jan Killeen, *Advocacy and Dementia* (Alzheimer Scotland, 1996)

CRIMINAL LAW

Gerald Gordon, *Criminal Law* (3rd edn, W Green & Son, 2001). The classic text, although there are simpler texts.

Robert Wemyss Renton and Henry Hilton Brown, *Criminal Procedure According to the Law of Scotland* (6th edn, W Green & Son). (Looseleaf service and regularly updated). A detailed guide to procedural matters.

The New Mental Health Act—A guide for people involved in criminal justice proceedings (Scottish Executive, 2005)

COMMUNITY CARE

Colin McKay and Hilary Patrick, *The Care Maze* (Enable and Scottish Association for Mental Health, 1998). Now out of print and largely our of date, but available in libraries.

Community care circulars:

(For circulars since 1999) www.show.scot.nhs.uk/sehd/ccd.asp
(For circulars prior to 1999) www.scotland.gov.uk/library/swsg/index-ls/indexb-f.htm

EMPLOYMENT

Norman Selwyn, *Law of Employment* (13th edn, LexisNexis, 2004). A readable and authoritative guide, accessible to non-lawyers.

DIVERSITY

Working with an interpreter— a toolkit for people who need to use interpreters in mental health and learning disability settings. (Mental Welfare Commission, 2006)

HUMAN RIGHTS

Lord Reed and Jim Murdoch, *A Guide to Human Rights* (Butterworths, 2001)

Simon Collins, 'Mental Health' in *Scottish Human Rights Service* (W Green & Son). (Looseleaf service and regularly updated)

FAMILY LAW

Professor Joe Thomson, *Family Law* (Tottel Publishing, 2006). A guide by senior academic, it manages to be both comprehensive and accessible to non-lawyers.

Kenneth McK. Norrie, *Children's Hearings in Scotland* (2nd edn, W Green & Son, 2005). A clearly written guide to the procedures for children at risk.

Who'll look after the children? A guide to financial and legal matters for parents with serious illness (Waverley Care and Barnardos). Available from Waverley Care.

MEDICAL LAW AND ETHICS

Carers and confidentiality—good practice guidance (Mental Welfare Commission, 2006)

Consent to treatment: A guide for mental health practitioners (Mental Welfare Commission, expected autumn 2006)

Margaret Brazier, *Medicine, Patients and the Law* (3rd edn, Penguin Books). A readable guide, based on the law in England and Wales.

Graeme Laurie, *Mason McCall Smith's Law and Medical Ethics* (7th edn, Oxford University Press, 2006)

Ian Kennedy and Andrew Grubb, *Medical Law* (Butterworths, 2000). Comprehensive materials casebook for the enthusiast.

Good Medical Practice (General Medical Council, 2001)

Medical Ethics Today (British Medical Association, 2001)

MENTAL HEALTH LAW

New directions: Report on the review of the Mental Health (Scotland) Act 1984 (Scottish Executive, 2001)

Renewing Mental Health Law (Scottish Executive, 2001)

Dr Sandra Grant, *Towards implementation of the Mental Health (Care and Treatment) Act 2003: The National Mental Health Services Assessment* (Scottish Executive, 2004)

Jill Peay Ashgate, *Seminal Issues in Mental Health Law* (Ashgate Publishing, 2005). A collection of learned essays and papers tracing the development of reform of the law. Primarily focused on England and Wales.

The Institute of Mental Health Practitioners' website at www.markwalton.net/is a fascinating source of information. For full value, a paid subscription is needed.

MONEY AND FINANCES

Dementia, money and legal matters Alzheimer Scotland. (Regularly updated.) Although aimed at carers of people with dementia, it is relevant to anyone who requires information about helping a person needing help with financial and property matters.

Butterworths Scottish Older Client Law Service (Tottel Publishing). Helpful information on paying for care, taxation, wills and trusts

Financial futures: wills and trusts (NSF Scotland). A guide to making financial provision for a family member

Trusts: Information for families and carers Enable booklet aimed at family members of a person with a learning disability.

Wills: Information for families and carers (Enable).

Welfare benefits

Housing benefit and council tax benefit legislation 2006/7 (19th edn, Child Poverty Action Group, 2006). (Updated regularly)

Welfare benefits and tax credits handbook 2006/7 (8th edn, Child Poverty Action Group, 2006). (Updated annually)

Paying for care (5th edn, Child Poverty Action Group, 2005). (Updated regularly)

Disability Rights Handbook 2006–7 (31st edition Disability Alliance, 2006) (Updated annually).

SAMH self-help series: *Unable to work due to illness or disability?/ Community Care Grants from the Social Fund/Incapable of Work? The personal capability assessment/Crisis Loans from the Social Fund/Claiming Disability Living Allowance*

INCAPACITY LAW

Adrian Ward, *Scots Law and the Mentally Handicapped* (Enable, 1984)

Adrian Ward, *The Power* (Enable, 1990)

Mentally disabled adults: Legal arrangements for managing their welfare and finances (Scottish Law Commission Discussion Paper 94, 1991)

Report on Incapable Adults (Scottish Law Commission (1995) SLC 151)

Adrian Ward, *Adult Incapacity* (W Green & Sons, 2003)

Jan Killen, Fiona Myers and others *The Adults with Incapacity (Scotland) Act 2000: Learning from Experience* (Scottish Executive, 2004)

REFUGEES AND ASYLUM SEEKERS

Immigration, Nationality & Refugee Law Handbook (Joint Council for the Welfare of Immigrants, 2006 Edition). (Regularly updated.)

Information for families and children, the Caris website (Run by Save the Children and Glasgow University Centre for the Child and Family) www.savethechildren.org.uk/caris

VULNERABLE ADULTS

Report on Vulnerable Adults Scottish Law Commission Scot Law Com No 158, (1997)

Sex, laws and red tape: Scots Law, Personal Relationships and People with Learning Difficulties Colin McKay (Enable, 1991).

JOURNALS

SCOLAG Journal. A long established and well respected journal dealing with issues of law and social welfare, human rights etc. in Scotland.

Journal of Mental Health Law Published by Northumbria University Law School, this mainly deals with the law in England and Wales, but contains some stimulating and challenging articles.

EASY READ GUIDES

It's your decision An easy read guide to the Adults with Incapacity Act (Enable for the Scottish Executive.)

The New Mental Health Act—What's it all about?: An easy read guide (Scottish Executive).

The Mental Welfare Commission also produces information in easy read format.

Appendix 2

CONTACT DETAILS

KEY BODIES

Mental Health Tribunal for Scotland
First Floor
Bothwell House
Hamilton Business Park
Caird Park
Hamilton ML3 0QA

Tel: (For service users/carers) Freephone 0800 345 70 60.
(For health care professionals) 01698 390 000

Email: mhts@scotland.gsi.gov.uk
Website: www.mhtscot.org.uk

Mental Welfare Commission for Scotland
Floor K
Argyle House
3 Lady Lawson Street
Edinburgh EH3 9SH

Tel: 0131 222 6111
User and carer advice line: Freephone 0800 389 6809

Email: enquiries@mwcscot.org.uk
Website: www.mwcscot.org.uk

Office of the Public Guardian
Hadrian House
Callendar Business Park
Callendar Road
Falkirk FK1 1XR

Tel: 01324 678 300
Fax: 01324 678 301

Email: opg@scotcourts.gov.uk
Website: www.publicguardian-scotland.gov.uk

INFORMATION AND FORMS

Adults with Incapacity website
www.scotland.gov.uk/Topics/Justice/Civil/16360/4927

Mental health law website
www.scotland.gov.uk/Topics/Health/health/MentalHealth/mhlaw/home

(Paper copies of forms available from the Scottish Executive's stationery supplier, Banner Business Supplies 01506 448 417.)

Office of Public Sector Information
(For Acts of Parliament, statutory instruments and explanatory notes) www.opsi.gov.uk

INFORMATION, ADVICE AND ASSISTANCE

Advocacy

Scottish Independent Advocacy Alliance
138 Slateford Road
Edinburgh EH14 1LR

Tel: 0131 455 8183

Email: enquiry@siaa.org.uk
Website: www.siaa.org.uk

Carers

Carers Scotland
(For information and details of local groups)
91 Mitchell Street
Glasgow G1 3LN

Tel: (CarersLine): 0808 808 7777
 (Office) 0141 221 9141
Fax: 0141 221 9140

Website: www.carerscotland.org

Children and young people

Children in Scotland
Princes House
5 Shandwick Place
Edinburgh EH2 4RG

Tel: 0131 228 8484
Fax: 0131 228 8585

Email: info@childreninscotland.org.uk
Website: www.childreninscotland.org.uk

Scotland's Commissioner for Children and Young People
85 Holyrood Road
Edinburgh EH8 8AU.

Tel: 0131 558 3733
Fax : 0131 556 3378

Email info@sccyp.org.uk
Website: www.sccyp.org.uk

Dementia

Alzheimer Scotland

(Provides information and support for people with dementia and their carers, through its national office and information centre, the national dementia helpline and local services. Has an important campaigning role and was one of the key bodies pressing for an Adults with Incapacity Act.)

(Head Office)
22 Drumsheugh Gardens
Edinburgh EH3 7RN

Tel: 0131 243 1453
Fax: 0131 243 1450

E-mail: alzheimer@alzscot.org
Website: www.alzscot.org

Direct payments

Direct Payments Scotland
27 Beaverhall Road
Edinburgh EH7 4JE

Tel: 0131 558 5200
Fax: 0131 558 5201
Minicom: 0131 558 5200

Email: info@dpscotland.org.uk
Website: www.dpscotland.org.uk

National Centre for Independent Living

(For details of local centres)

4th Floor, Hampton House
20 Albert Embankment
London SE1 7TJ

Tel: 0207 587 1663
Fax: 0207 582 2469
Text: 0207 587 1177

E-mail: info@ncil.org.ukliving centres

Discrimination and equal opportunities

Commission for Racial Equality Scotland
The Tun
12 Jacksons Entry
Holyrood Road
Edinburgh EH8 8PJ

Tel: 0131 524 2000
Fax: 0131 524 2001
Textphone: 0131 524 2018

Email: scotland@cre.gov.uk
Website: www.cre.gov.uk

Disability Rights Commission in Scotland
DRC Helpline
FREEPOST MID02164
Stratford upon Avon CV37 9BR

Helpline: 08457 622 633
Textphone: 08457 622 644
Fax 08457 778 878

Email: enquiry@drc-gb.org
Website: www.drc-gb.org

Equal Opportunities Commission
St Stephens House
279 Bath Street,
Glasgow G2 4JL

Tel: 0845 601 5901
Fax: 0141 248 5834

Email: scotland@eoc.org.uk
Website: www.eoc.org.uk

Employment and volunteering

Social Firms Scotland
54 Manor Place
Edinburgh EH3 7EH

Tel: 0131 225 4178
Fax: 0131 225 9985

Email: sfs@socialfirms.org.uk
Website: www.socialfirms.org.uk

Volunteer Scotland
(For details of local volunteer centres)
Website: www.volunteerscotland.info/index.php

Healthcare

Health Rights Information Scotland
Scottish Consumer Council
Royal Exchange House
100 Queen Street
Glasgow G1 3DN

Tel: 0141 226 5261

Email: hris@scotconsumerorg.uk
Website: www.scotconsumer.org.uk/hris/contact.htm

MedicAlert
1 Bridge Wharf
156 Caledonian Road
London N1 9UU

Tel: Freephone: 0800 581420
Fax: 020 7278 0647

Email: info@medicalert.org.uk
Website: www.medicalert.org.uk

Royal College of Psychiatrists
External Affairs Department
17 Belgrave Square
London SW1X 8PG

Tel: 0207 235 2351

Website: www.rcpsych.ac.uk

(Scottish Division)
12 Queen Street
Edinburgh EH2 1JE

Tel: 0131 220 2910
Fax: 0131 220 2915

Email: kaddie@scotdiv.rcpsych.ac.uk
Website: www.rcpsych.ac.uk/college/division/scot.asp

Scottish Health Council
Delta House
50 West Nile Street
Glasgow G1 2NP

Tel: 0141 241 6308
Text Phone: 0141 241 6316

Website: www.scottishhealthcouncil.org

Housing

Ownership Options Scotland

(Advice and information about homebuying for disabled people and their carers)

The John Cotton Centre,
10 Sunnyside
Edinburgh
EH7 5RA

Tel: 0131 661 3400

Website: www.oois.org.uk

Shelter Scotland
Scotiabank House
Edinburgh EH2 4AW

Tel: Housing Advice Line 0808 800 4444

Website:
http://scotland.shelter.org.uk/home/index.cfm/

(For details of local Shelter Housing Aid Centres, see website.)

Learning disability

ENABLE Scotland

(Campaigns for better services for people with learning disabilities and their families and provides advice, support and information, both through its Information Centre and its website. Runs local services and will be able to provide information about other services.)

(Head Office)
6th Floor
7 Buchanan Street
Glasgow G1 3HL

Tel: 0141 226 4541
Fax: 0141 204 4398

Email: enable@enable.org.uk
Website: www.enable.org.uk

People First Scotland

(Self-advocacy movement of people with learning difficulties)

Macdonald Business Centre
107 Macdonald Road
Edinburgh EH7 4NW

Tel: 0131 478 7708

Scottish Consortium for Learning Disability
(Set up to help people make the changes in *The same as you?* review. See
39.02)

The Adelphi Centre, Room 16
12 Commercial Road
Glasgow G5 0PQ

Tel: 0141 418 5420
Fax: 0141 429 1142

Email: administrator@scld.co.uk

Legal assistance

(Enable and SAMH (above) both have legal departments which may be
able to offer help and advice. The Information Service at Alzheimer
Scotland may also be able to offer advice on a range of legal matters.)

Law Society of Scotland

(Operates scheme for accrediting solicitors experienced in mental health
and/or incapacity. Its Mental Health and Disability Committee considers
matters of public law policy. Contact: Committee Secretary.)

26 Drumsheugh Gardens
Edinburgh EH3 7YR

Tel: 0131 226 7411
Textphone: 0131 476 8359
Fax: 0131 225 2934

Email: lawscot@lawscot.org.uk
Website: www.lawscot.org.uk

Office of the Public Defence solicitor

(For criminal law cases)

37 York Place
Edinburgh EH1 3HP

Tel: 0131 557 1222

Email: postbox@pdso.org.uk
Website: www.pdso.org.uk.

 Also offices at:

24A Bernard Street
Leith Edinburgh EH6 6PP

Tel: 0131 555 1030

17 Queensgate
Inverness IV1 1DF

Tel: 01463 709680

120–124 Saltmarket
Glasgow G1 5LB

Tel: 0141 553 0794

Scottish Association of Law Centres

(Law centres deal with matters such as housing, disability, welfare benefits and community care. Most are in Glasgow and the West of Scotland, including Castlemilk, Drumchapel, East End, Govan and Paisley. There is also a specialised Ethnic Minorities Law Centre with offices in Glasgow and Edinburgh.

The Legal Services Agency, in Glasgow and Edinburgh, has specialised mental health projects offering information, advice and representation. The Fife Rights Forum Project offers legal advice and representation to mental health clients in Fife.)

For addresses, see SALC website: www.govanlc.com/salc

Scottish Legal Aid Board
44 Drumsheugh Gardens
Edinburgh EH3 7SW

Tel: 0131 226 7061.
Calls by BT Text Direct are welcome.

Email: general@slab.org.uk
Website: www.slab.org.uk

Mental health

Bipolar Scotland

(Provides information, support and advice for people affected by bipolar disorder and all who care.) (Formerly the Manic Depression Fellowship Scotland)

Studio 1016
Mile End Mill
Abbeymill Business Centre
Seedhill Road
Paisley PA1 1TJ

Tel: 0141 560 2050
Fax: 0141 560 2170

Website: www.bipolarscotland.org.uk

Depression Alliance Scotland

(Information, advice and support for people with depression and carers.)

3 Grosvenor Gardens
Edinburgh EH12 5JU

Tel: 0131 467 3050 (10am–2pm Mon, Tues, Thurs and Fri)

Email: info@dascot.org
Website: www.depressionalliancescotland.org

National Schizophrenia Fellowship Scotland (NSF Scotland)

(As well as running services, it provides comprehensive advice and information for users of services and carers)

Claremont House
130 East Claremont Street
Edinburgh EH7 4LB

Tel: 0131 557 8969
Fax: 0131 557 8968

Email: info@nsfscot.org.uk

Website: www.nsfscot.org.uk

National Resource Centre for Ethnic Minority Health

NHS Health Scotland
Clifton House
Clifton Place
Glasgow G3 7LS

Tel: O141 300 1057

Email: nrcemh@health.scot.nhs.uk

Website: www.nrcemh.nhsscotland.com

Scottish Association for Mental Health (SAMH)

(Runs services throughout Scotland and provides a comprehensive information and advice service, as well as campaigning for better services. Can give details of local services, including local Associations of Mental Health)

(Head Office)
Cumbrae House
15 Carlton Court
Glasgow G5 9JP

Tel: 0141 568 7000

Email: enquire@samh.org.uk
Website: www.samh.org.uk

Scottish Recovery Network
Europa Building
450 Argyle Street
Glasgow G2 8LG

Tel: 0141 240 7790
Fax: 0141 221 7947

Email: info@scottishrecovery.net

Stresswatch Scotland

(Help for people affected by stress, anxiety, phobias, panic attacks and obsessive compulsive disorders)

Tel: Office 01563 570886
Helpline 01563 574144

Email: info@StresswatchScotland.org
Website: www.stresswatchscotland.org

Prisons

Prison Reform Trust

(Although its work covers England and Wales, it may be able to give advice to people in Scotland.)

15 Northburgh Street
London EC1V 0JR

Tel: 020 7251 5070
Fax: 020 7251 5076

Email: prt@prisonreformtrust.org.uk
Website: www.prisonreformtrust.org.uk

Refugees and asylum seekers

Caris website

(Information for young refugees and asylum seekers in Scotland) www.savethechildren.org.uk/caris/

Scottish Refugee Council

(Its website gives details of local sources of advice and assistance)

(Head Office)
5 Cadogan Square
(170 Blythswood Court)
Glasgow G2 7PH

Tel: 0141 248 9799
Freephone (For newly arrived and dispersed asylum seekers) 0800 085 6087
Fax: 0141 243 2499

Website: www.scottishrefugeecouncil.org

Respite care

(Enable, Alzheimers Scotland, SAMH (see above) or the community care department of the local authority may have details of local respite care schemes.)

Penumbra

(For people with mental health conditions)

Cairdeas House
5 Coates Gardens
Edinburgh EH12 5LG

Tel: 0131 313 5081
Fax: 0131 313 4580

Email: cairdeashouse@yahoo.co.uk
Website: www.penumbra.org.uk/nat_respite_home.htm

Service users' groups

Contact the Information Service at SAMH, Alzheimer Scotland or Enable for advice about groups in your area.

Stigma

See me (anti-stigma campaign)

9–13 Maritime Street
Edinburgh
EH6 6SB

Tel: 0131 624 8945
Fax: 0131 624 8901

Email: info@seemescotland.org
Website: www.seemescotland.org.uk

Welfare rights

(Most local authorities in Scotland will be able to offer welfare rights advice. A law centre or Citizens Advice Bureau can also offer advice. Both Alzheimer Scotland and SAMH offer specialist advice, and some local associations for mental health, such as Glasgow (GAMH) have specialist workers.)

Alzheimer Scotland
Contact their welfare rights service on 0141 418 3936

Child Poverty Action Group

(Produces a range of authoritative welfare benefits manuals and offers training courses. Unable to give individual advice.)

94 White Lion Street
London N1 9PF

Tel: 020 7837 7979
Fax: 020 7837 6414

Email: staff@cpag.org.uk
Website: www.cpag.org.uk

CPAG in Scotland
Unit 9, Ladywell
94 Duke Street
Glasgow G4 0UW

Tel: 0141 552 3303
Fax: 0141 552 4404

Email: staff@cpagscotland.org.uk

Disability Alliance

(Publishers of the highly respected Disability Rights Handbook)

Universal House
88–94 Wentworth Street
London E1 7SA

Telephone (Voice and Minicom): 020 7247 8776
Fax: 020 7247 8765

Email: office.da@dial.pipex.com
Website: www.disabilityalliance.org

SAMH welfare rights

Contact their Benefits Adviser:

By telephone, Monday to Friday, on 0141 568 7000
By e-mail: benefits @samh.org.uk

STANDARDS AND REGULATION

The Care Commission
Compass House
11 Riverside Drive
Dundee DD1 4NY

Tel: 01382 207100
Lo call: 0845 603 0890

Website: www.carecommission.com

Disclosure Scotland
PO Box 250
Glasgow G51 1YU

Tel: 0870 609 6006

Email: info@disclosurescotland.co.uk
Website: www.disclosurescotland.co.uk

Financial Services Ombudsman
South Quay Plaza
183 Marsh Wall
London E14 9SR

Tel: 0845 080 1800

Email: complaint.info@financial-ombudsman.org.uk
Website: www.financial-ombudsman.org.uk

General Medical Council
(For fitness to practice issues)
St James's Buildings
79 Oxford Street
Manchester, M1 6FQ

Tel (Lo call) 0845 357 0022

Email: gmc@gmc-uk.org
Website: www.gmc-uk.org.

Health Professions Council
Park House
184 Kennington Park Road
London SE11 4BU

Tel: 020 7840 9814

Email: ftp@hpc-uk.org
Website: www.hpc-uk.org.

NHS Quality Improvement Scotland
Elliott House
8–10 Hillside Crescent
Edinburgh
EH7 5EA

Tel: 0131 623 4300
Textphone 0131 623 4383

Website: www.nhshealthquality.org

Nursing and Midwifery Council
23 Portland Place
London W1B 1PZ

Tel: 020 7637 7181

Email: fitness.to.practise@nmc-uk.org
Website: www.nmc-uk.org

Parliamentary Ombudsman
Millbank Tower
Millbank
London SW1P 4QP

Tel (Lo call): 0845 015 4033

Email: phso.enquiries@ombudsman.org.uk
Website: www.ombudsman.org.uk

Risk Management Authority
St James House
25 St James Street
Paisley PA3 2HQ

Tel: 0141 567 3112

Fax: 0141 567 3111

Email: info@rmascotland.gsi.gov.uk
Website: www.rmascotland.gov.uk

Scottish Prison Complaints Commissioner

(All prisoners and young offenders have the right of confidential access to the Commission. Prisoners should mark any letter 'Confidential Access')

Government Buildings
Broomhouse Drive
Edinburgh EH11 3XD

Tel: 0131 244 8423 Fax: 0131 244 8430

Email: spcc@scotland.gsi.gov.uk
Website: www.scotland.gov.uk/Topics/Justice/Prisons/18780/14980

Scottish Public Services Ombudsman
4 Melville Street
Edinburgh EH3 7NS

(Freepost EH641
Edinburgh EH3 0BR)

Tel: 0870 011 5378
Text: 0790 049 4372

Email: enquiries@scottishombudsman.org.uk
Website: www.scottishombudsman.org.uk

Scottish Social Services Council
Compass House
11 Riverside Drive
Dundee DD1 4NY

Tel: 01382 207101
Lo call: 0845 60 30 891

Email: enquiries@sssc.uk.com
Website: www.sssc.uk.com

Appendix 3

SUGGESTED FORMS

1A APPLICATION FOR DISCHARGE FROM SHORT-TERM DETENTION (PATIENT)

(Under Mental Health (Care and Treatment) (Scotland) Act 2003, s 50)

Important note: This form is a suggestion only. It is no substitute for legal advice. Patients, named persons and carers are strongly advised to get legal advice and assistance when making appeals and applications to the Tribunal.

To: The Mental Health Tribunal for Scotland
First Floor
Bothwell House
Hamilton Business Park
Caird Park
Hamilton ML3 0QA

Name of patient .... *(please print)*

Address..

On .... *(date)* a doctor made me subject to a short certificate.

I am detained in ....*(name of hospital).*

The hospital's address is ....

My named person is .... *(name)*

His/her address is ....

....

I apply to the Tribunal to cancel the certificate.

My reasons are: *(briefly state why you think the tribunal should cancel the certificate)*

....

....

....

....

....

....

.... **Signed**

.... **Date**

1B APPLICATION FOR DISCHARGE FROM SHORT-TERM DETENTION (NAMED PERSON)

(Under Mental Health (Care and Treatment) (Scotland) Act 2003, s50)

Important note: This form is a suggestion only. It is no substitute for legal advice. Patients, named persons and carers are strongly advised to get legal advice and assistance when making appeals and applications to the Tribunal.

To: The Mental Health Tribunal for Scotland
First Floor
Bothwell House
Hamilton Business Park
Caird Park
Hamilton ML3 0QA

Name of patient .... *(please print)*

Address ....

....

Named person .... *(please print name)*

Address ....

....

....

On .... *(date)* a doctor made the patient subject to a short certificate.

The patient is detained in ....*(name of hospital).*

The hospital's address is ....

....

I am the patient's named person and I apply to the Tribunal to cancel the certificate.

My reasons are: *(briefly state why you think the tribunal should cancel the certificate)*

....

....

....

....

....

....

.... **Signed**

.... **Date**

2A APPLICATION FOR DISCHARGE FROM EXTENSION CERTIFICATE (PATIENT)

(Mental Health (Care and Treatment) (Scotland) Act 2003, s 50)

Important note: This form is a suggestion only. It is no substitute for legal advice. Patients, named persons and carers are strongly advised to get legal advice and assistance when making appeals and applications to the Tribunal.

To: The Mental Health Tribunal for Scotland
First Floor
Bothwell House
Hamilton Business Park
Caird Park
Hamilton ML3 0QA

Name of patient .... *(please print)*

Address *(please print)* ....

....

My named person is .... *(name of named person)*

His/her address is ....

....

On .... *(date)* a doctor issued an extension of a short certificate.

I am detained in ....*(name of hospital).*

The hospital's address is ....

....

I apply to the Tribunal to revoke the extension certificate.

My reasons are: *(briefly state why you think the tribunal should cancel the extension certificate)*

....

....

.... **Signed**

.... **Date**

2B APPLICATION FOR DISCHARGE FROM EXTENSION CERTIFICATE (NAMED PERSON)

(Mental Health (Care and Treatment) (Scotland) Act 2003, s 50)

Important note: This form is a suggestion only. It is no substitute for legal advice. Patients, named persons and carers are strongly advised to get legal advice and assistance when making appeals and applications to the Tribunal.

To: The Mental Health Tribunal for Scotland
First Floor
Bothwell House
Hamilton Business Park
Caird Park
Hamilton ML3 0QA

Name of patient .... *(please print)*

Address *(please print)* ....

....

Named person .... *(print name)*

Address..

....

On .... *(date)* a doctor issued an extension of a short certificate.

The patient is detained in..*(name of hospital)*.

The hospital's address is ....

....

I am the patient's named person and I apply to the Tribunal to revoke the extension certificate.

My reasons are: *(briefly state why you think the tribunal should cancel the extension certificate)*

....

....

....

....

.... **Signed**

.... **Date**

3A APPLICATION FOR ORDER AGAINST UNLAWFUL DETENTION
(PATIENT)

(Under Mental Health (Care and Treatment) (Scotland) Act 2003, s291)

Important note: This form is not for anyone who is detained in hospital the Mental Health Act or the Criminal Procedure Act. If you are not sure whether this applies to you, ask ward staff or an independent advocate.

To: The Mental Health Tribunal for Scotland
First Floor
Bothwell House
Hamilton Business Park
Caird Park
Hamilton ML3 0QA

Name of patient .... *(please print)*

Address *(please print)* ....

....

....

I am being treated for mental disorder in...
hospital *(name of hospital).*

The address of the hospital is ....

....

I apply for an order that I am unlawfully detained in hospital.

My reasons are: *(briefly state why you think you are illegally detained in hospital)*

....

....

....

....

.... **Signed**

.... **Date**

Important note: This form is a suggestion only. It is no substitute for legal advice. Patients, named persons and carers are strongly advised to get legal advice and assistance when making appeals and applications to the Tribunal.

3B APPLICATION FOR ORDER AGAINST UNLAWFUL DETENTION (APPLICANT OTHER THAN PATIENT)

(Under Mental Health (Care and Treatment) (Scotland) Act 2003, s 291)

Important note: This form is not for anyone who is detained in hospital the Mental Health Act or the Criminal Procedure Act. If you are not sure whether this applies to the patient, ask ward staff or an independent advocate.

To: The Mental Health Tribunal for Scotland
First Floor
Bothwell House
Hamilton Business Park
Caird Park
Hamilton ML3 0QA

Name of patient ....

Address of patient *(please print)*..

....

Name of applicant.. *(please print)*

Address *(please print)* ....

....

Relationship to patient *(delete as appropriate)* named person/person with parental responsibilities/mental health officer/welfare guardian/welfare attorney/ Mental Welfare Commission/other person with interest in patient's welfare

The patient is being treated for mental disorder in ....
hospital *(name of hospital)*.

The address of the hospital is ....

....

I apply for an order that the patient is unlawfully detained in hospital.

My reasons are: *(briefly state why you think the person is illegally detained in hospital)*

....

....

....

....

.... **Signed**

.... **Date**

Important note: This form is a suggestion only. It is no substitute for legal advice. Patients, named persons and carers are strongly advised to get legal advice and assistance when making appeals and applications to the Tribunal.

4A APPEAL AGAINST HOSPITAL TRANSFER (PATIENT)

(Under Mental Health (Care and Treatment)
(Scotland) Act 2003, s 125/126)

Important note: This form is a suggestion only. It is no substitute for legal advice. Patients, named persons and carers are strongly advised to get legal advice and assistance when making appeals and applications to the Tribunal.

To: The Mental Health Tribunal for Scotland
First Floor
Bothwell House
Hamilton Business Park
Caird Park
Hamilton ML3 0QA

Name of patient *(please print)*...

Address of patient ....

....

I am detained in ....*(name of hospital)*

The hospital's address is ....

....

My named person is .... *(name of named person)*

His/her address is ....

....

*On... *(date)* **the hospital gave me notice that they**

were going to transfer me to.................................... **hospital** *(name of new hospital)*
OR

*On .... **I was transferred to this hospital from**

.... **hospital** *(name of hospital you came from)*

(** Delete which is inappropriate*)

I wish to appeal against this transfer.

My reasons are: *(briefly state why you think the tribunal should set aside the transfer)*

....

....

....

....

.... **Signed**

.... **Date**

4B APPEAL AGAINST HOSPITAL TRANSFER (NAMED PERSON)

(Under Mental Health (Care and Treatment)
(Scotland) Act 2003, s 125/126)

Important note: This form is a suggestion only. It is no substitute for legal advice. Patients, named persons and carers are strongly advised to get legal advice and assistance when making appeals and applications to the Tribunal.

To: The Mental Health Tribunal for Scotland
First Floor
Bothwell House
Hamilton Business Park
Caird Park
Hamilton ML3 0QA

Name of patient .... *(please print)*

Address ....

....

The patient is detained in .... *(name of hospital)*

The hospital's address is ....

....

Named person .... *(name of named person)*

Address ....

....

On..(date)* **the hospital gave notice that they** were going to transfer the patient to ....

.... hospital
(name of new hospital)

OR

*On .... the patient was transferred to this hospital from

.... **hospital** *(name of hospital patient came from)*
(* Delete which is inappropriate)

I am the patient's named person and I wish to appeal against this transfer.

My reasons are: *(briefly state why you think the tribunal should set aside the transfer)*

....

....

....

....

.... **Signed**

.... **Date**

5A APPEAL AGAINST EXCESSIVE SECURITY (PATIENT IN STATE HOSPITAL)

(Under Mental Health (Care and Treatment) (Scotland) Act 2003, s 264)

Important note: This form is a suggestion only. It is no substitute for legal advice. Patients, named persons and carers are strongly advised to get legal advice and assistance when making appeals and applications to the Tribunal.

To: The Mental Health Tribunal for Scotland
First Floor
Bothwell House
Hamilton Business Park
Caird Park
Hamilton ML3 0QA

Name of patient .... *(please print)*

Address ....

....

I am detained/liable to detention** in the State Hospital. The hospital's address is Carstairs Junction Motherwell ML11 8RP.

I am detained under a compulsory treatment order/compulsion order/hospital direction/transfer for treatment direction** *(delete as appropriate)*

The order/direction was made on... *(date)*

I am/am not** a restricted patient

The order is/is not** suspended and I am currently living at ....

....

(hospital or address in community as appropriate)

**(Delete as appropriate)*

My named person is... *(name)*

His/her address is ....

....

I believe I do not need to be detained in the State Hospital and I apply to the Tribunal to declare that I am being held in conditions of excessive security.

My reasons are: *(briefly state why you think you do not need the special security of the State Hospital)*

....

....

....

....

.... **Signed**

.... **Date**

5B APPEAL AGAINST EXCESSIVE SECURITY (OTHER APPLICANT: PATIENT IN STATE HOSPITAL)

(Under Mental Health (Care and Treatment) (Scotland) Act 2003, s 264)

Important note: This form is a suggestion only. It is no substitute for legal advice. Patients, named persons and carers are strongly advised to get legal advice and assistance when making appeals and applications to the Tribunal.

To: The Mental Health Tribunal for Scotland
First Floor
Bothwell House
Hamilton Business Park
Caird Park
Hamilton ML3 0QA

Name of patient .... *(please print)*

Address ....

....

The patient is detained/liable to detention** in the State Hospital. The hospital's address is Carstairs, Motherwell ML11 8RP.

The patient is detained under a compulsory treatment order/compulsion order/ hospital direction/transfer for treatment direction** *(delete as appropriate)*

The order/direction was made on.. *(date)*

The patient is/is not** a restricted patient

The order is/is not** suspended and the patient is currently living at ....

....

(hospital or address in community as appropriate)

***(Delete as appropriate)*

The patient's named person is .... *(name)*

His/her address is ....

....

Name of applicant .... *(please print)*

Address *(please print)* ....

....

Relationship to patient *(delete as appropriate)* named person/welfare guardian/ welfare attorney/Mental Welfare Commission/

I believe the patient does not need to be detained in the State Hospital and I apply to the Tribunal to declare that the patient is being held in conditions of excessive security.

My reasons are: *(briefly state why you think patient does not need the special security of the State Hospital)*

....

....

....

.... **Signed**

.... **Date**

5C APPEAL AGAINST EXCESSIVE SECURITY (PATIENT IN MEDIUM SECURE UNIT)

(Under Mental Health (Care and Treatment) (Scotland) Act 2003, s2 68)

Important note: This form is a suggestion only. It is no substitute for legal advice. Patients, named persons and carers are strongly advised to get legal advice and assistance when making appeals and applications to the Tribunal.

To: The Mental Health Tribunal for Scotland
First Floor
Bothwell House
Hamilton Business Park
Caird Park
Hamilton ML3 0QA

Name of patient .... *(please print)*

Address ....

....

I am detained/liable to detention** in ....*(name of hospital)*

The hospital's address is ....

....

I am detained under a compulsory treatment order/compulsion order/hospital direction/transfer for treatment direction**

The order/direction was made on.. *(date)*

I am/am not** a restricted patient

The order is/is not** suspended and I am currently living at....................................

....

(hospital or address in community as appropriate)

**(Delete as appropriate)*

888

My named person is.. *(name)*

His/her address is ....

....

I believe I am being held in conditions of excessive security and I apply to the Tribunal to declare that the level of security in the hospital is excessive in my case.

My reasons are: *(briefly state why you think you do not need to be subject to the level of security in the hospital)*

....

....

....

....

.... **Signed**

.... **Date**

5D APPEAL AGAINST EXCESSIVE SECURITY (OTHER APPLICANT: PATIENT IN MEDIUM SECURE UNIT)

(Under Mental Health (Care and Treatment) (Scotland) Act 2003, s 268)

Important note: This form is a suggestion only. It is no substitute for legal advice. Patients, named persons and carers are strongly advised to get legal advice and assistance when making appeals and applications to the Tribunal.

To: The Mental Health Tribunal for Scotland
First Floor
Bothwell House
Hamilton Business Park
Caird Park
Hamilton ML3 0QA

Name of patient .... *(please print)*

Address ....

....

The patient is detained/liable to detention** in

.... Hospital. *(name of hospital)*

The hospital's address is ....

....

The patient is detained under a compulsory treatment order/compulsion order/ hospital direction/transfer for treatment direction**

The order/direction was made on.. *(date)*

The patient is/is not** a restricted patient

The order is/is not** suspended and the patient is currently living at.....................

....

(hospital or address in community as appropriate)
 **(Delete as appropriate)*

890

The patient's named person is .... *(name)*

His/her address is ....

....

Name of applicant .... *(please print)*

Address *(please print)* ....

....

Relationship to patient *(delete as appropriate)* named person/welfare guardian/ welfare attorney/Mental Welfare Commission/

I believe the patient is being held in conditions of excessive security and I apply to the Tribunal to declare that the level of security in the hospital is excessive in the patient's case.

My reasons are: *(briefly state why you think the patient does not need to be subject to the level of security in the hospital)*

....

....

....

....

.... **Signed**

.... **Date**

6A APPLICATION FOR HEATHCARE ASSESSMENT (PATIENT)

(Under Mental Health (Care and Treatment) (Scotland) Act 2003, s 228)

To... (name of health board)

Address...

....

Name of patient .... *(please print)*

Address..

....

I hereby apply for an assessment of my needs for services for mental disorder under the above Act.

The mental disorder I have is mental illness/learning disability/personality disorder (*delete as appropriate*)

Reasons for applying for assessment (*optional*)

....

....

....

....

.... **Signed**

.... **Date**

6B APPLICATION FOR HEATHCARE ASSESSMENT

(Named person or primary carer)

(Under Mental Health (Care and Treatment) (Scotland) Act 2003, s 228)

To: ....*(name of health board)*

Address ....

....

Name of patient .... *(please print)*

Address...

....

Name of applicant.. *(please print)*

Address *(please print)* ....

....

Relationship to patient *(delete as appropriate)* named person/primary carer

I hereby apply for an assessment of the patient's needs for services for mental disorder under the above Act.

The mental disorder the patient has is mental illness/learning disability/ personality disorder *(delete as appropriate)*

Reasons for applying for assessment (*optional*)

....

....

....

.... **Signed**

.... **Date**

7A APPLICATION FOR DISCHARGE FROM DETENTION (PATIENT DETAINED FOLLOWING ALLEGED BREACH OF COMPULSORY TREATMENT ORDER OR INTERIM COMPULSORY TREATMENT ORDER)

(Application under Mental Health (Care and Treatment) (Scotland) Act 2003, s 120)

Important note: This form is a suggestion only. It is no substitute for legal advice. Patients, named persons and carers are strongly advised to get legal advice and assistance when making appeals and applications to the Tribunal.

To: The Mental Health Tribunal for Scotland
First Floor
Bothwell House
Hamilton Business Park
Caird Park
Hamilton ML3 0QA

Name of patient .... *(please print)*

Address ....

....

I am detained in ....*(name of hospital)*

The hospital's address is ....

....

I am subject to a compulsory treatment order/interim compulsory treatment order* *(delete as appropriate)*

The order was made on .... *(date)*

On .... *(date)*
the responsible medical officer granted a certificate under s114/115 of the Mental Health (Care and Treatment) (Scotland) (Scotland) Act detaining me in hospital for 28 days.

My named person is.. *(name)*

His/her address is ....

....

I apply to the Tribunal to cancel the certificate.

My reasons are: *(briefly state why you think the tribunal should cancel the certificate. The tribunal will consider whether detention in hospital is necessary to avoid serious harm to your mental health)*

....

....

....

....

.... **Signed**

.... **Date**

7B APPLICATION FOR DISCHARGE FROM DETENTION (NAMED PERSON OF PATIENT DETAINED FOLLOWING ALLEGED BREACH OF COMPULSORY TREATMENT ORDER/INTERIM COMPULSORY TREATMENT ORDER)

(Application under Mental Health (Care and Treatment)
(Scotland) Act 2003, s 120)

Important note: This form is a suggestion only. It is no substitute for legal advice. Patients, named persons and carers are strongly advised to get legal advice and assistance when making appeals and applications to the Tribunal.

To: The Mental Health Tribunal for Scotland
First Floor
Bothwell House
Hamilton Business Park
Caird Park
Hamilton ML3 0QA

Name of patient .... *(please print)*

Address...

....

The patient is detained in ....*(name of hospital)*

The hospital's address is ....

....

The patient is subject to a compulsory treatment order/interim compulsory treatment order* *(delete as appropriate)*

The order was made on .... *(date)*

On .... *(date)*
the responsible medical officer granted a certificate under s 114/115 of the Mental Health (Care and Treatment) (Scotland) Act detaining the patient in hospital for 28 days.

Name of named person ....

Address...

....

I am the patient's named person, and I apply to the Tribunal to cancel the certificate.

My reasons are: *(briefly state why you think the tribunal should cancel the certificate. The tribunal will consider whether detention in hospital is necessary to avoid serious harm to the patient's mental health)*

....

....

....

....

.... **Signed**

.... **Date**

8A APPLICATION AGAINST COMPULSORY TREATMENT ORDER OR EXTENSION OF COMPULSORY TREATMENT ORDER (PATIENT)

(Under Mental Health (Care and Treatment)
(Scotland) Act 2003, ss 99/100)

Important note: This form is a suggestion only. It is no substitute for legal advice. Patients, named persons and carers are strongly advised to get legal advice and assistance when making appeals and applications to the Tribunal.

To: The Mental Health Tribunal for Scotland
First Floor
Bothwell House
Hamilton Business Park
Caird Park
Hamilton ML3 0QA

Name of patient .... *(please print)*

Address...

....

....

I am detained/liable to detention** in ....*(name of hospital)*

The hospital's address is ....

....

I am detained under a compulsory treatment order .

The order was made on.. *(date)*

[On .... *(date)*
the responsible medical officer made an order extending the detention.] (*delete if not appropriate*)

My named person is.. *(name)*

His/her address is ....

....

I apply to the Tribunal to cancel the compulsory treatment order/extention of the order* (delete as appropriate)

My reasons are: *(briefly state why you think the tribunal should cancel the order)*

....

....

....

....

.... **Signed**

.... **Date**

8B APPLICATION AGAINST COMPULSORY TREATMENT ORDER OR EXTENSION OF COMPULSORY TREATMENT ORDER (NAMED PERSON)

(Under Mental Health (Care and Treatment)
(Scotland) Act 2003, ss99/100)

Important note: This form is a suggestion only. It is no substitute for legal advice. Patients, named persons and carers are strongly advised to get legal advice and assistance when making appeals and applications to the Tribunal.

To: The Mental Health Tribunal for Scotland
First Floor
Bothwell House
Hamilton Business Park
Caird Park
Hamilton ML3 0QA

Name of patient .... *(please print)*

Address...

....

The patient is detained/liable to detention** in ....

....*(name of hospital)*

The hospital's address is ....

....

The patient is detained under a compulsory treatment order.The order was made on .... *(date)*

[On .... *(date)* the responsible medical officer made an order extending the detention.]*(delete if not appropriate)*

Named person .... *(please print name)*

Address ....

....

I am the patient's named person and I apply to the Tribunal to cancel the compulsory treatment order/extention of the order* (delete as appropriate)

My reasons are: *(briefly state why you think the tribunal should cancel the order.)*

....

....

....

....

.... **Signed**

.... **Date**

INDEX

Guardians—*contd*
recall—*contd*
local authority, by 25.51
Mental Welfare
Commission, by 25.51
sheriff, by 25.52
removal 25.48
replacement 25.48
resignation 25.49
restraint, and 9.19
Guardianship orders
applications 25.37
appropriate situations
MWC guidance 25.35
Scottish Executive
guidance 25.36
carers, and 42.14–42.18
criminal orders
generally 46.19
'insanity' cases, in 46.02
dementia, and 38.08
effect
enforcement powers 25.43
generally 25.40
powers of guardian
25.41–25.42
enforcement powers 25.43
financial management, and
applications 26.52
changes 26.63
death of adult 26.64
discharge of guardian
26.65
duties of guardians
26.58–26.59
effect 26.55
generally 26.51

Guardianship orders—*contd*
financial management,
and—*contd*
gifts 26.51
interim orders 26.53
introduction 26.43
powers of guardians 26.57
sale and purchase of home
26.60
sheriff's role 26.54
supervision 26.62
third party protection
26.56
generally 25.34
grounds 25.39
guardian's duties 25.44–25.45
guardian's powers
generally 25.41
limits 25.42
'insanity' cases, in 46.02
interim orders 25.38
joint welfare guardian's
duties 25.45
local authority's duties 25.46
Mental Welfare Commission
guidance 25.35
role 25.47
overview 25.24
recall of guardian
human rights, and 25.53
introduction 25.50
local authority, by 25.51
Mental Welfare
Commission, by 25.51
sheriff, by 25.52
removal of guardian 25.48
replacement of guardian
25.48

Parental responsibilities
adjustment by court
31.25–31.27
children at risk 31.28–31.29
children in proceedings 31.31
generally 31.21
local authority help 31.23
parent subject to compulsory
measures 31.24
parental responsibilities
orders 31.26–31.27
parties to proceedings 31.30
private care arrangements
31.22

Parliamentary Ombudsman
complaints, and 50.13

Participation
compulsory measures
principles, and 11.04
generally 2.408
Millan principles, and 2.26

Parties
tribunal procedure, and
23.02–23.03

Partnerships
consumer rights, and 34.09

Patient information
adequacy 7.16
breach of duty 7.16
children, and 41.22
compulsion, and
generally 17.02
interpretation assistance
17.05
legal rights, as to 17.03
prescribed times 17.04

Patient information—*contd*
compulsory measures, and
11.30
compulsory treatment orders,
and 14.32
emergency detention, and
13.13
guidance 7.19
hospital transfers, and 19.05
interpretation assistance, and
17.05
introduction 7.16
legal rights, and 17.03
patient's in criminal
proceedings, and 48.02
persons with learning
disabilities, and 39.10
professional guidance 7.19
'reasonable doctor' test 7.17
'reasonable patient' test 7.18
short-term detention, and
12.14
side effects 7.20
transfer for treatment
directions, and 47.17
withholding 7.21

Patient representation
statutory overview 2.23

Patient's rights
complementary therapies,
and 5.13
compulsion, and
and see PATIENT'S RIGHTS
(COMPULSION)
adequate services, to 17.10
appeal against excessive
security, to 17.11–17.21

51